THE
PERFECT
FASCIST

THE
PERFECT
FASCIST

A Story of Love, Power, and Morality
in Mussolini's Italy

VICTORIA DE GRAZIA

THE BELKNAP PRESS OF
HARVARD UNIVERSITY PRESS
Cambridge, Massachusetts and London, England
2020

Library of Congress Cataloging-in-Publication Data

Names: De Grazia, Victoria, author.
Title: The perfect fascist : a story of love, power, and morality
in Mussolini's Italy / Victoria de Grazia.
Description: Cambridge, Massachusetts : The Belknap Press of
Harvard University Press, 2020. | Includes bibliographical references and index.
Identifiers: LCCN 2019054630 | ISBN 9780674986398 (hardcover)
Subjects: LCSH: Teruzzi, Attilio, 1882-1950. | Mussolini, Benito, 1883-1945. |
Fascists—Italy—Biography. | Politicians—Italy—Biography. |
Italy—Armed Forces—Officers—Biography. | Italy—History—1922-1945.
Classification: LCC DG575.T38 D4 2020 | DDC 945.091092 [B]—dc23
LC record available at https://lccn.loc.gov/2019054630

For my beloved brothers, who died on the home front.
For my dearest father, who was always at war.

CONTENTS

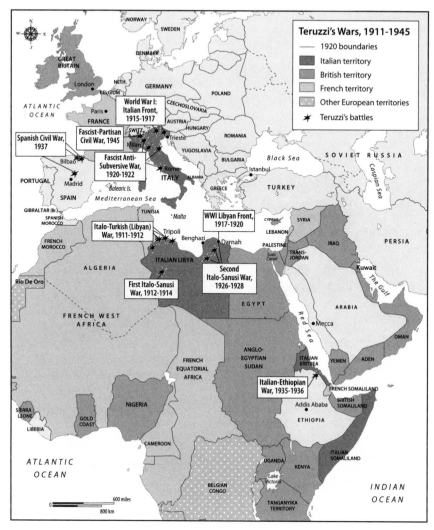

Teruzzi's Wars, 1911-1945

— 1920 boundaries
- Italian territory
- British territory
- French territory
- Other European territories
★ Teruzzi's battles

Spanish Civil War, 1937

Fascist-Partisan Civil War, 1945

World War I: Italian Front, 1915-1917

Fascist Anti-Subversive War, 1920-1922

WWI Libyan Front, 1917-1920

Italo-Turkish (Libyan) War, 1911-1912

First Italo-Sanusi War, 1912-1914

Second Italo-Sanusi War, 1926-1928

Italian-Ethiopian War, 1935-1936

0 — 600 miles
0 — 800 km

© Victoria de Grazia

"Attilio sent me this snap photo of himself, Foxy and Liù after he had them shaved for the summer. Aren't they too sweet?" Benghazi, summer 1927

Lilliana Weinman Teruzzi Estate

PROLOGUE

When Benito Mussolini welcomed Attilio Teruzzi into his office at Palazzo Venezia on March 17, 1926, hugged him, teased him about his upcoming marriage, and flirted with his attractive American fiancée, it was a private moment with a public purpose. This was the first time that Mussolini, in his double capacity as president of the Council of Ministers and duce of fascism, had been asked to bless a marriage. He was touched. "I am happy that you are marrying an American," he told Teruzzi. "English women are ugly, French women perverse, Spanish women bring us bad luck, and we get along with America. There are also a few dollars there, which doesn't hurt."[1] In sum, he heartily approved.

At the time, Teruzzi, a one-time career military officer, was undersecretary at the Interior Ministry and a rising star in the fascist establishment. His fiancée, Lilliana Weinman, a rising opera diva known by her stage name Lilliana Lorma, had left her calling to marry. The couple was in love, idealistic, and eager to promote Teruzzi's political career.

When they made their engagement official, word quickly spread. One of the most visible and vigorous New Men of the Fascist Revolution was marrying a powerful specimen of America's New Woman. But as the late June wedding date approached, Teruzzi and Lilliana were faced with a predicament. They wanted their union to express Mussolini's latest dictum: "All within the state, nothing outside of the state, nothing against the state." But there was no protocol for a fascist wedding. With Lilliana's notions of staging and celebrity, and Teruzzi's instinct for ritual and rank, they decided they would have to fashion the event themselves.

No expense would be spared. The dollar was strong, and the bride's father's elastic-webbing factory on Manhattan's Lower East Side was booming. He would pay for everything, settle a rich allowance on his daughter, and even outfit the groom's family—all good and humble people. The wedding would be a true affair of state, with cabinet ministers and the whole Fascist Grand Council in attendance. The groom had asked Mussolini to act as his witness at the civil ceremony, together with his own immediate superior, the minister of the interior. The bride would have as her witnesses the American ambassador and her mentor, Tullio Serafin, formerly of La Scala and now the Metropolitan Opera's lead conductor.

The prenuptial reception, for four or maybe five hundred guests at the Hotel Palace on Via Veneto, would be exquisitely bon ton, with a string quintet, cocktails, and masses of flowers. The couple would invite only the crème of the emerging fascist elite: the quadrumvirs (who had led the March on Rome), Milanese businessmen, illustrious prefects, and wheeler-dealer lawyers. There would be representatives of the arts and the doyennes of the regime's new salon life, journalists and foreign correspondents, aristocrats, a sprinkling of the international smart set, and the bride's proud party of fifty relatives and friends, who would come from New York City, Vienna, and Rzeszów, the onetime "Little Jerusalem" of Austrian Galicia, her family's homeland.

In a nod to Mussolini's recent rapprochement with the Vatican, the couple decided they would hold a church wedding as well as the civil ceremony. For that, they would need the pope's dispensation, as the bride, being of the Jewish faith, was an infidel in the eyes of the Catholic Church. The civil ceremony would come first, to show that the Italian state was the paramount authority. It would be officiated by the governor of Rome at the Campidoglio, with the groom in plain black shirt with war decorations and the bride in lavender silk georgette. Since the Catholic Church held that it was a sin for a couple to consummate the union before sanctifying their marital vows, the religious rites would take place that same afternoon at the Basilica of Saint Mary of the Angels, with the groom in tuxedo and black tie and the bride in white lace, with a long train.

June of Year IV of the Fascist Era could not have offered more propitious timing for this event. It had been close to four years now since Mussolini had threatened to occupy Rome with his army of 20,000 Blackshirts, and King Victor Emmanuel III had capitulated to this show of force by inviting him to form a new governing coalition. But it was only over the previous year, 1925, that Mussolini—struggling to recover from the political crisis caused by the kidnapping and killing of the socialist Giacomo Mat-

The bridal party, from left to right, Isaac Weinman, Maestro Tullio Serafin, Rose Weinman, Benito Mussolini, Ambassador Henry Prather Fletcher, Lilliana Weinman, Attilio Teruzzi, Amelia Teruzzi, and Celestina Teruzzi

Alinari Archives/Getty Images

teotti, chief of the parliamentary opposition—had pushed full throttle to turn his government into a dictatorship of unlimited power and duration.

With the first unruly years behind him, normalization was now the byword. Instead of unleashing bands of *squadristi* to break the opposition, Mussolini used the law to muzzle the press, issued emergency legislation to establish a one-party state, took steps to turn the Fascist Militia into a national guard, and set up special military tribunals with provisions for capital punishment to silence dangerous political opponents.

Normalization meant that Italy would return to the international capital markets by settling on a schedule for paying its war debts to the United States, outlawing opposition unions, imposing budget austerity, and slashing workers' wages. It also meant that Mussolini hoped to gain the respect of bourgeois society by embracing good values like Church marriage, licensing brothels to get prostitutes off the street, and imposing a bachelor tax on celibate men so that they would do their duty to the nation, marry, and have children. The fact that Attilio Teruzzi, the notorious rowdy, was settling down with a bride of such uncommon talent was a wholly positive sign, from the perspective of the many women who had welcomed fascism and so far gotten nothing for it.

And so their nuptials became, as the *New York Times* put it, "a fascist wedding." Instead of the usual monogrammed white card, the wedding invitation was engraved with cherubs tying a love knot between the American stars and stripes and the fascist ax and lictors. Instead of a military honor guard with raised daggers, a troop of fascist boy scouts was stationed at the church exit to shout, "Hip hip hurrah!" and sing "Giovinezza." Between the music by Maestro Antonelli's string quintet and the elegant silver party favors from Chiappe, the Milanese jeweler, Teruzzi and Lilliana's wedding showcased the refinement of Italian culture and craftsmanship. Ostentatious gifts piled up in the salon of the hotel (their value, somebody leaked to the press, was estimated at upward of $100,000), and cash-stuffed envelopes were pressed into the groom's pockets and hands.

Puccini's *Turandot* had debuted two months earlier, and the opera held a special significance for the couple. Teruzzi was Prince Calaf, Lilliana had joked, the impetuous stranger who had braved the Ice Princess's murderous tricks to win her hand. As they sped north in the railroad carriage of the head of state, which Mussolini had given them for their two-week honeymoon to Mitteleuropa, they consummated their marriage. As dawn rose over the Po valley, Teruzzi hugged Lilliana and sang Calaf's song, "I will triumph." He couldn't believe his good fortune.

Three years later, in March 1929, just after Mussolini had named him national commander of the Blackshirts, Attilio Teruzzi renounced his wife peremptorily and publicly. He said she had betrayed him and brought him dishonor, and he refused to be swayed by her cries of innocence. Since Italy had no divorce law, the only way he could end the marriage was if he proved before the Church courts that the marriage had never been valid in the first place. That process put both Teruzzi and Lilliana in thrall to celibate priest-judges, who conducted a tortuous judicial inquisition to determine whether their original vows had been taken in good faith. For the next eighteen years, Teruzzi battled to dissolve the marriage, and Lilliana resisted mightily.

Later, when Mussolini was rampaging about demoting childless hierarchs, and Teruzzi tried once again to find love and settle down, he ended up with another attractive, tall, exuberant outsider. She, too, was Jewish. They had a love child, and a kind of family life ensued. Then the Fascist Race Laws kicked in, and Teruzzi, who had risen to become the minister of Mussolini's African empire, was faced with the dilemma of having two Jewish wives: one he couldn't divorce, the other he couldn't marry. The status of this second wife would become more and more of an issue as Fascist Italy's Nazi allies complained to the Duce that his inner circle was tepid about implementing the Final Solution.

Marriage, in every society, is a foundational act, whether based on a civil contract or religious vows. It is about sex and children and acquiring property and status; about family and reproducing one's lineage, class, or race; about love and friendships and where to put one's primary loyalties. It lies at the heart of how we think about what is truly valuable in life.

The Perfect Fascist takes the marriage of Attilio Teruzzi as a springboard to explore moral life under fascist rule. It explores Mussolini's purpose in conceiving of his movement as a "spiritual" and "ethical" revolution, a "politics of the heart," in contrast to what he denounced as liberal society's sterile "politics of the brain." It explores how Mussolini instrumentalized a new moral order celebrating a racially wholesome hypermasculinity to consolidate his power, and reveals the degree to which this new moral order hinged on making war abroad and at home. It considers the nature of fascism's New Man and reveals the ultimate insufficiency of Mussolini's ambition to create a twentieth-century reincarnation of the Roman Empire.

Mussolini's aim was nothing less than the sweeping away of the status quo—the Catholic Church, the king, the old military establishment, the bourgeoisie, the "lamblike" nature of the Italian people—and the overthrow of Anglo-Saxon hegemony in the Mediterranean world. He wanted, like many charismatic and reactionary leaders, to blow up the old order. How to rebuild, aside from aggrandizing his own power, by warmongering, and more destruction, was another matter.

My hope is that this book will offer a new understanding of the social and affective nature of the men who are the principal players to a greater or lesser degree in all totalitarian political systems. We will consider what the story of Attilio Teruzzi, the "perfect fascist," can tell us about the ever-messier line drawn between the personal and political under totalitarian rule: between the diktats of one's leader and the demands of one's heart.

Hannah Arendt, in *The Origins of Totalitarianism* (1951), wrote that the "iron band of total terror leaves no space for private life." She believed that totalitarian states exploited the "loneliness" of the masses atomized by capitalist modernity.[2] Once in power, totalitarians turned to ideology and terror to subsume ever more isolated individuals into the "Oneness" of the leader; they destroyed every capacity for the free expression of moral sentiments. In effect, in her view, they created a heartless political system.

I make a different argument here by taking us behind the facade of fascist totalitarianism and into the private life and moral compromises of one of its most exemplary foot soldiers. I show that social, affective, and moral needs and choices continued to exist under fascist rule. We find all of the usual good sentiments and values—family devotion, motherhood, faith, fidelity to the cause, duty to the nation, even love. Fascist Italy was horrible, but full of heart.

Yet these values and beliefs acquired a peculiar political and emotional valence under fascist rule. Conflicts under liberal democracy could be expected to sort themselves out more or less openly through freely elected political bodies, open debates, and by drawing a line between secular and religious and between personal and public affairs. However, once these methods and institutions were banned, censored, or renegotiated, the temptation was to dump these conflicts into all of the wrong places. The social arena expanded grotesquely, taking on a febrile quality, characterized by all-or-nothing thinking, sensational rumors and slander fed by letters of denunciation, spies and informers, by a misplaced religious afflatus, by the jealousies fomented by elites jostling for position, and by Mussolini himself, who stood at the center of this national melodrama. The social arena saw politics intrude increasingly into religious life, and saw religion seek affirmation in the political order. Society seethed with class animosities, patronage fights, and status sleights, because fascist rule never delivered its promised and ever-touted revolution. Italian society saw intimate and personal life, discombobulated by great swerves in the collective moral compass, confuse family with political interests, affairs of the heart with affairs of state, and love for a mother or father, for a spouse or child, with love for the Duce. In sum, civil society persisted, but it became illiberal.

Understanding the relentlessly contradictory way in which Mussolini conceived of fascism's New Man is one key to understanding how Attilio Teruzzi was shaped by, and exemplified the moral order of civil society under fascist rule. Mussolini's only real intellectual anchor for his notion of the New Man, was his disdain for its Enlightenment progenitor, the keenly rational, secular homo economicus envisaged by the eighteenth century reformers, who, even if he was only acting out of his self-interest and sense of being a social being, would change the world for the better. Mussolini's conception was by contrast a patchwork of all of the disillusioning commonplaces of the time. There was the crass social Darwinism that made Mussolini see life as a struggle, and resource-poor Italy as locked in a fight for survival amidst declining global riches. This vision convinced him Italy would always be at war, and the Italians had to be shaped up physically and racially to fight on its behalf. There was the perennial favorite, Machiavelli, the political realist. Mussolini saw himself as the Modern Prince. Like the Florentine's idealized pure politician, he was the centaur, who being half-beast and half-man, purely instinctual yet keenly intelligent, had no inhibitions about grasping for power. There was the readily plagiarized Friedrich Nietzsche, from whom Mussolini, like untold other men of his generation (and subsequent ones), filched the idea of the super-man. Mussolini's hierarchs would partake of the charisma of their God-leader and be utterly loyal to him. Like the warlords of antiquity, they would be devoid of the petty yearnings of ordinary mortals for happiness. They would eschew the venality of conventional clientele politics. At the same time, they would cultivate fascism's version of noblesse oblige by fostering the conviviality and comradely behavior necessary to cement the new elite's group identity. The code word was "pure."

Teruzzi promised to be exemplary in this sense. He was a much-decorated career army officer with ramrod posture. He was violent, but Mussolini always distinguished between "a violence that is moral, and a violence that is stupid and immoral."[3] Teruzzi had the vigor and discipline of a military man, though off duty he was a cad and a rascal and loved a good time. He had a "beautiful fascist face," as Mussolini's son-in-law Galeazzo Ciano wrote. Teruzzi was "mediocre but loyal," Ciano added—"but *very* loyal."[4] No matter how much he was put to the test, he craved to be a perfect fascist.

To be a perfect fascist, however, was always a struggle. To start with, the perfect fascist had to find a way to navigate and accommodate himself to

7

the exclusive world of the Italian bourgeoisie, the same one he wanted to overthrow. Having welcomed the fascists into office and celebrated the defeat of the Left, Italy's traditional elites now wanted nothing more than to wish the fascists away and reinstate Italy's old status barriers and boundaries. The perfect fascist had to accommodate himself to the monarchy, and to all of the trapping of the King and Crown, though he had no love for the House of Savoy. Beyond this, the perfect fascist had to make peace with the Catholic Church, a formidable political and moral power in Italy.

The perfect fascist would also have to confront the frustrations of everyday Italians. Unable to hold men of power accountable for their misdoings through conventional legal or political channels, Italians found outlets for their anger in gossip, blackmail, and scandalmongering. Though it was practically impossible for men of power to be prosecuted, libertine behavior and accusations of corruption invited official investigation and risked Mussolini's personal reproach.

Then there was the unfathomable world of women, vulgarly reduced to either angels or whores. Their complicated needs for love, solace, family, and status were often incompatible with the virtues Mussolini imagined for his warrior furies. And of course, his script gave all of the best parts to men.

Finally, the perfect fascist would have to confront his own demons. Whether jealousy or anger, ambition or vanity, a foible could become a terrible flaw, turning a rigid little potentate into a raging tyrant. Was fascist despotism any different from other forms of despotism throughout time and place? I will argue that, yes, it was—that fascism's overwhelming preoccupation with virility engendered a distinctive set of problems.

The story behind this history was brought to me by relatives of Teruzzi's wife, Lilliana Weinman, who wanted to know why their cousin, a worldly and self-assured woman from a good Jewish family, would ever have married an old and bearded fascist. Why did such a talented girl give up her career? One look at the photograph of the Duce, standing with the bridal couple, and I wanted to make sense of why this man who was so unassuming behind his chestful of decorations and dark beard would have chosen to marry such a determined and talented woman.

What could her papers tell? I had written about fascism in the past, about workers and about women, the victims and subjects of fascist rule. I was intrigued by the possibility that I might be able, through this story, to write a history of fascism that would have some resonance today, when issues of ultra-nationalism, white-male supremacy, and racial conflict have taken on a new yet familiar urgency, and the whole framework in which we have been used to thinking about progress and reaction, good and bad, has been shaken out of joint.

Fascists are made, not born. That Attilio Teruzzi became in some sense the archetypal virtuous warrior of the imperial West invites us to consider how individuals, in their lusts and longing, in their dreams and prejudices and petty quarrels, are swept up and reshaped by the course of history. In that sense, it is not a biography. It is a social history of a man who, as he makes his way in the complexity of his political and human relations, often captured from the vantage point of his women, shows us how Italian fascism really worked.

Everybody's relations with everybody would change as fascism's moral compass swerved, as the fascist movement identified new enemies: the "cowardly," "draft-deserting," "defeatist" socialists, to start with; then the unfeeling, geriatric liberal elite; followed by hypocritical Catholics and pederast priests. Later, the regime targeted conniving Arab rebels, sexual perverts, out-of-control women, Zionist Jews, the sob-sister bourgeoisie, and arrogant British imperialists. By the end, it would execrate the mentally enslaved males of a Europe fast being overwhelmed by Judeo-Bolshevik forces that only the Duce, in alliance with the Führer, could defeat.

Fascism's moral compass also shifted as the dictatorship, after seeking bourgeois respectability in the 1920s, with its salons and constellation of fascinating women, turned to consolidate its all-male apparatus of power in the 1930s. Embracing a racially pure, warrior ideal of masculine virility, fascism sought the grandeur of a global empire within the framework of a Nazi-Fascist New Order.

Finally, the compass shifted again as Mussolini charged ahead, conscious of his own vulnerability, of the passage of time and the resistance of society. Still, he summoned up the nation's forces—physically, morally, and militarily—to restore the greatness of Italy. When this fevered dream gave way to frustration, he targeted his own elite, making the old guard and onetime poster boys of his movement his whipping boys.

But that would happen over time, in the twenty-five years that Attilio Teruzzi was embarked on his long march through fascism. In the two decades before 1920, when our story begins, he was an officer in the Army of the Kingdom of Italy and, by all accounts, a decent man and fine soldier.

I

STRIVE

1

THE SOLDIER

Come, sing the immense joy of living,
of being strong, of being young,
of biting the fruits of the earth
with sound, white, voracious teeth,
of laying bold and covetous hands
on every sweet living thing,
of drawing one's bow at each new prey desire targets.

—GABRIELE D'ANNUNZIO, *Canto novo*, 1882

The first time Attilio Teruzzi appeared in the news, he was attending a wake. It was March 13, 1912, and he was a colonial infantry officer. The preceding September, the Kingdom of Italy had invaded Libya in a bid to wrest the territory from the long rule of the Ottoman Empire. On February 11, Teruzzi's unit, the Fifth Eritrean Battalion out of Massawa, had landed at Tripoli. After a skirmish with Turkish forces at Bir El-Turki on March 4, they were burying their first casualty, a sweet-tempered lad, tall and skinny with big, tender eyes. Cirum Ciahai had been Lieutenant Viola's orderly. Wounded in the abdomen, he had fought on for another hour only to die a week later at the field hospital. The men of his company were bereft.[1]

The story Teruzzi appeared in was a novelty for readers of the Italian press. The correspondents, mostly from Milan, who had crossed the Mediterranean to cover the fighting, had no prior experience of a "Great War," as Italians called the Libyan conflict. Many were excited at the sight of the magnificent but fearsome troops recruited in Italian Eritrea. This was the first time the Royal Italian Colonial Army was deploying its Askari—African mercenaries serving European armies—outside the Horn of Africa.[2]

Press and propaganda had led the home public to believe that the Arabs would welcome the Italian forces as liberators. So the correspondents had to work hard to repair the news from the stunning events of October

23–24, 1911. A force of Ottoman army troops and Arab armed resisters had massacred five hundred Italian soldiers stationed at Shara al-Schatt, a village on the outskirts of the Tripoli area, leaving piles of crucified, eviscerated, castrated corpses. Italian forces then went berserk, killing 4,000 civilians, maybe more. Wanting to be informative yet reassuring, the correspondents reminded their readers of Italy's civilizing mission, of the soldiers' "profound sentiment" of humanity in the face of battle, and of the upstanding character of Italy's loyal Eritrean hirelings, in contrast to the ferocious Turks and treacherous Arabs.

The account of Cirum Ciahai's funeral in the *Corriere della Sera* let everyone back home know that in Libya there were "black faces crumpled by weeping." Though they were Muslim, they too mumbled their prayers, and the service had taken place in the consoling presence of two Catholic military chaplains. Lieutenant Teruzzi was the senior officer at the graveside when the wooden casket was lowered into the earth. The honor guard stood at attention while Teruzzi spoke of his comrade as a "humble hero who had fallen for the glory of his second country, for his country of election."[3] As the orangey earth was shoveled into the grave, Teruzzi made the delicate gesture of strewing it with a bunch of the wild poppies and daisies growing in the oasis.

At that moment, Teruzzi was being forged as a new type, the humane soldier-hero of the young Kingdom of Italy's brave new imperial saga. Indeed, the whole of the military was being cast in a bright new light. Before the Libyan invasion, the Italian armed forces had not particularly enjoyed the attention of the press. One of their few glorious moments came when mounted *carabinieri* with swords and high, plumed hats had accompanied the king and queen from the Quirinale to Montecitorio to open the proceedings of Parliament. More ordinarily, the military was newsworthy when it was rushing to sandbag the overflowing Po or Tiber Rivers or ordered to the site of some catastrophic earthquake in Abruzzi or Sicily, to help claw people from the wreckage, or being excoriated in the radical press for deploying its conscripts to scatter peasant protesters, break up taxpayer rebellions, or protect scab labor brought in to replace striking workers. For the press and the public, the military's most visible moments had unfortunately been its most inglorious ones. When an Italian expeditionary force of 500 was wiped out by Ras Alula at Dogali in 1887, and the army of 18,000 men at the command of General Oreste Baratieri was annihilated at Adwa on March 1, 1896, by Ethiopian Emperor Menelik II's army, leaving 7,000 dead and hundreds taken prisoner, the disasters were covered in almost pornographic detail.

The Libyan War was Italy's first major foreign conflict since the country's unification and the public's enthusiasm seemed unquenchable. The barracks were unlocked, their doors thrown open, and civilians fraternized with the soldiers. The press was filled with pages of multicolor lithographs of the troops on the attack and glossy stills of handsomely uniformed officers. Assuming Teruzzi's family was keeping one eye out for news of him, they could have seen him after the Battle of Zanzur on June 7, 1912, in *Illustrazione Italiana*, Italy's most prestigious illustrated weekly. He was on the third page of the June 23 issue, to be exact, the last soldier to the left on the second row: the cocky-looking bearded fellow with the dark glasses, smirking at the photographer. Another image from around the same time, this one a close-up, showed him standing at ease, dapper and dutiful, with two brother officers.[4]

By the time he returned to Milan on a four-month furlough in December 1912, Teruzzi had been awarded a bronze medal for demonstrating "great initiative and courage in successive battles." In his bright blue uniform, with his straight-backed posture and decorations, he could count on being looked at as he strolled through the Galleria, the giant arcade of iron and glass that connected the La Scala opera house and Palazzo Marino to the Cathedral Square with its fabulous white-spiked Duomo advertising the sublime omnipotence of the Holy Catholic Church. It was here, in the Galleria, that the Milanese fought their political battles, mounted their social protests and victory parades, massed for funeral processions, strolled, sat, and argued in the cafés and bars, shopped with the zealousness of Parisians, and courted one another in memorable displays of chivalry, coquetry, rudeness, and passion.

This was the age of Italietta, as the Milanese called their nation. They could joke fondly about its provincialism. After all, most Milanese believed they lived in Italy's "moral" capital—"the electric power plant of the energies and optimism of Italy," as the futurist poet Filippo Marinetti called it in his "Ode to the Great Milan."[5] Rome, by contrast, was an excrescence on the body politic, with the Church of Rome a giant parasite and culture practically nonexistent—no opera, no modern craft, and zero artistic experimentation. Milan grew muscle from the war, with its industrious people, booming factories, and hyped-up mass media, while Rome claimed all of the glory.

Marinetti's futurist co-conspirator Emilio Settimelli remembered the "intense, affable lieutenant" from around that time.[6] Everybody passed by the Galleria's favorite cafés: Savini's, Fiaschetteria Toscana, La Grande Italia, Biffi's. Opera stars, politicians, writers, merchants, fixers, and facto-tums could all be seen there, joined on Sunday afternoons by bourgeois families and their children. At the sight of the handsome soldier, one of the regular patrons would surely have waved him over for an aperitif and a good conversation.

On one of those lazy days, Teruzzi put on his dress uniform and, sword clanking at his side, made a visit to the studio that Emilio Sommariva had just opened on Via San Paolo, five minutes from the Galleria. Soon to be Italy's most famous portrait photographer, the thirty-two-year-old Som-mariva was already well known to Milan's rising classes for his romantic portraiture. His images revealed certain qualities of being that his sitters might not have recognized in themselves—the shrewd glances and clenched fists of insecure parvenus. In Teruzzi, Sommariva captured the mismatch between a poetic gaze and a certain flame of ambition, as the lieutenant's outsized hands idly fingered his dress sword.[7]

Attilio Teruzzi had the distinction of being the first professional military man in his family, on his street, and conceivably from his whole bustling neighborhood of Porta Genova. To understand what that meant for a man of his background, we will need to travel briefly back to 1882, the year of his birth. The Kingdom of Italy had scarcely been unified two decades, and the nation was on the cusp of giant shifts in its political and cultural outlook, which would profoundly shape Teruzzi's youth and world view.

On May 12, 1882, Italy signed a defense treaty with Hapsburg Austria and imperial Germany known as the Triple Alliance, which it would renew periodically until 1915. By shifting away from France and Great Britain, with which the country had aligned itself in order to win independence and after which it had modeled its founding institutions, Italy tacitly aban-doned its claims to the Italian-speaking lands along the northwestern border of the Austrian empire. The decision underscored the fact that King Victor Emmanuel II of Piedmont-Savoy had more in common with the conser-vative monarchies of Austria-Hungary and Prussia than with British or French parliamentary liberalism.

The young Kingdom of Italy was intent on embracing the state-led "Prus-sian model" of economic development, hoping to spur German investment

Lieutenant Teruzzi, 1913. Photographed by Emilio Sommariva.

in heavy industry and construction. Italy formally joined the international gold standard that year, kicking off lopsided growth. Its leading northern cities exploded in size, with Milan in the lead, propelled by real estate speculation, a manufacturing boom in textiles and small machinery, and a population surge driven by peasants escaping the impoverished country-side. It was not by chance that, with inequality on the rise, the elections of 1882 established the progressive Left as the biggest bloc in Parliament. That year saw the founding of the Italian Workers Party in Romagna, Italy's first anarcho-syndicalist political party.[8]

It was also in 1882 that Gabriele D'Annunzio, then only nineteen years old, published the second of the eventual forty-nine volumes that, by the turn of the century, would cement his place as the most famous writer in Italy. In the *Canto Novo*, he wrote of young pagans—of their "immense joy of living" powered by "voracious teeth" and "bold and covetous hands" that made "every sweet living thing" theirs.[9] In reality, the world of the young would soon be one of barriers and boundaries, so ferociously com-petitive that instead of "drawing one's bow at each new prey" and rising above the limitations of their parents, the youth of Italy would have to settle, in most instances, for much less.

Teruzzi's family was in its own modest way synchronized with the times. Both of his parents had been born in the Lombard countryside: his mother, Celestina Rossi, in Solbiate Comasco, a village of four hundred on the well-traveled road from Varese to Como; and his father, Cristofaro Fermo Teruzzi, in Barlassina, a village in the rolling hills of the lower Brianza. As the daughter of the estate manager, or *fattore*, for the local potentate, Count Rasini, Celestina was a social cut above her husband. The one photograph we have of her in her youth shows a tall, self-possessed young lady with a crown of thick blonde plaits.[10] As a girl she may have milked the cows, cleaned their stalls, and taken them out to pasture. But as she moved into adulthood, with her big bustle and silk capelet, she let the world know that as a child she had been the Contessina Rasini's playmate.

Many Teruzzis (or Terruzzi, as it was also spelled) emigrated from the Brianza to Milan or went abroad, where they found work as stonemasons, coal mongers, carpenters, laundresses, servants, shoemakers, grocers, and waiters. A number of them later became socialists, but not Cristofaro Fermo, who trafficked in wine and spirits. The only portrait we have of Attilio's father shows him with an honest gaze, droopy mustache, and

18

handkerchief necktie, the classic image of a mid-nineteenth-century salt-of-the-earth northern Lombard countryman. He must have had a calm, if not good, character for the praetor of his village to have matched him up with the Rossi girl, who was staunchly Catholic, physically imposing, and eight years his junior.[11]

When Cristofaro Fermo and Celeste made their big move from Barlassina to Milan's southwestern edge, the couple had two children—Amelia, born in 1877, and Guido, in 1880. Two others had died in infancy. Cristofaro Fermo set up his wine shop at Corso Genova 13, on the ground floor of a handsome new five-story building. The neighborhood of Porta Genova was a good choice for a wine merchant. With the completion of the new terminus for the Milan-Mortara railroad, the neighborhood had become an important transportation hub. With the traffic from the central docking area for the system of canals that connected Milan to the Po and Ticino Rivers and to Switzerland, the neighborhood pivoting around Porta Genova looked like a little Amsterdam.

Attilio was born in their upper-floor apartment on May 5, 1882. He was baptized two days later at what was then the neighborhood's parish church, the nine-hundred-year-old Basilica of Saint Ambrose. The proud parents invited two minor capitalists, the building's owner and a contractor, to be his godparents.[12] Attilio was a Christian name, but unconventional. He was their first Milanese-born child, and because Celestina's subsequent child, also a boy, died in infancy, he was fated to remain the baby of the family and his mother's favorite.[13]

Physically, he more closely resembled his father, with his small figure, wavy and dark chestnut hair, wide brow, and pale skin. But he had his mother's watchful blue eyes and double chin—an unfortunate feature that he would later conceal with a beard. He was a devoted mama's boy, sensitive to his mother's terrible anxieties. His older sister, Amelia, a schoolteacher and good judge of character, described him as scrappy and ingenuous but noted that his vanity sometimes prevented him from distinguishing legitimate self-interest from amour propre.

Henry James, that master observer of repressed characters, elegantly captured Milan's hypocrisy. Milan, he wrote, was both "the last of the prose cities of Europe's north" and "the first of the poetic cities of the South."[14] The prose was manifest in the killjoy Catholicism of Milan's founder, the early medieval sourpuss Saint Ambrose. It showed in the punitive work ethic of emerging industrial titans who, if they operated in the textile sector, drove their workers with the merciless discipline of the Manchester cotton barons; if they operated in iron and machinery, they did so with the heavy fist of the Prussian capitalists of the Ruhr. The prose was in the energetic do-gooding of the fascinating, high-minded feminists on behalf of fallen women. And it deeply permeated Milan's venerable socialist leaders in their efforts to civilize the city's rebellious underclasses with the virtues of humdrum reformism.

If Milan's puritan establishment was the prose, Porta Genova was the poetry. By the time Attilio reached adolescence, the city had grown from 355,000 to 450,000 inhabitants, and Porta Genova was its liveliest neighborhood. The newly inaugurated tram line drew people from all over the city to Porta Genova's covered market, pawnbrokers, outdoor fairs, and festivals. The photography studio of Italo Pacchioni, the inventor of Italy's first moviola, was catty-corner to the family wine shop, and the Stabilini Theater, Italy's first variety entertainment show with cinema, opened nearby on what is now Piazza Cantore.

Puccini had set *La Bohème* in Paris, but the inspiration came from the cafés and garrets of his student days around St. Ambrose Square. Attilio grew up with the real-life Mimìs and Musettes, insolent, flirtatious shop girls or textile hands, who were as sexually complaisant as the Parisians but more democratic in their favors, especially when their suitors were from the neighborhood.[15] Attilio had something of the handsome Rodolfo about him, living for his male friends, confiding in them about the objects of his passion and the pleasures of his conquests.

Schooling was the only way to make a social leap, and that called for a family strategy. Attilio's fiercely disciplined older sister went as far as a woman of her background could in turn-of-the-century Italy by graduating from a state teacher's college and finding a position in the expanding elementary school system. The men needed a bigger boost. Attilio's maternal uncle's entire family had moved from Solbiate Comasco to Pavia so that their oldest son, Attilio's first cousin, Ottorino, could test into the Collegio Ghislieri. Ottorino graduated from medical school with highest honors, setting him on a path to becoming a renowned psychiatric neurologist, Italy's foremost expert on war trauma. Assuming Attilio's family strategy had him pursue the course of study normal to his lower-middle class status, he would have continued beyond the third grade, when most workers' children left school, and also past the sixth grade, when most artisans' boys finished the trade school track, until he was sixteen, when he would have earned a diploma in accounting or commerce, with the prospect of becoming a bookkeeper, salesman, or perhaps a tradesman himself.

Fate had it that around the time Attilio turned thirteen, Cristofaro Fermo was stricken with one of the wasting diseases of the time—tuberculosis, cirrhosis of the liver, maybe a heart condition. He died sometime before 1896, leaving La Bella Celestina, as customers called the scarcely forty-year-old widow, struggling to keep the business open, pay the rent, and send her teenage boys out into the world. Celestina had no pension, so Amelia would have to look after her. As for Attilio's older brother, Guido, all we can glean is that he lived abroad for seventeen years, caught tubercular syphilis at some point, and died from it at Milan's Sant'Anna's hospice in 1930, the costs of his medical care having been borne uncomplainingly by his younger brother.[16]

In the best of times, Milan was a model of commerce and a showcase for reformist politics. But when the going got tough, it became bitterly divided, a hotbed for all of the isms of the moment. In the mid-1890s, as the tariff war with France set back the textile industry, the stock market plunged, investment dried up, and the building boom collapsed. This crisis fed radical republicanism, socialism, and anarchism. Ten years later Milan would be swept by futurism and feminism, and later it would become the birthplace of fascism.

In 1898, the year Attilio turned sixteen, and would have obtained his diploma, Milan was in the throes of its greatest tumult in five decades. The city fathers had planned to commemorate the fiftieth anniversary of the Milanese people's "Five Days" of insurrection, March 18–23, 1848, to free themselves from Austrian rule. It was going to be a big event, but the plan was aborted twelve days before the anniversary, after a right-wing politician killed Milan's favorite son, the Radical Party leader Felice Cavallotti, in a duel. The funeral was a public occasion, and the immense cortège clashed with the police. Demonstrations against the authorities followed. Soon after, the price of bread spiked, deepening tensions. The left declared a general strike on May Day. On May 6, city authorities lost control of the crowds; the government imposed martial law to suppress the emerging riots. The commander of the local military garrison, General Fiorenzo Bava Beccaris, advanced into the center of town through Porta Genova, stationing cannons along the route. When the crowds taunted the troops and threw rocks, Bava Beccaris ordered his soldiers to fire point-blank to disperse them.

By the time the cannonades and gun fusillades ceased three days later, eighty-one "innocents," as the post-massacre inquiry called them, lay dead—mostly adolescent boys. Scores had been wounded. In the days that followed, the authorities made hundreds of arrests, broke up public meetings, shut down workers' circles, and barred people from circulating on their bicycles. When the cloddy King Umberto I rewarded the general with the kingdom's highest medal for service to the crown, many young Milanese gave up on Italy: that year eighty thousand or so left Lombardy, mostly for France, to work as waiters, in construction, or in the coal mines.[17]

Attilio chose instead to enlist in the army. He wasn't going to be able to get a university deferment as many bourgeois boys did. Nor could he buy his way out. And he had decided not to emigrate to avoid military service, like his brother and many other poor boys, including Mussolini who was just his age. Some godparent or uncle may have advised Attilio that if he enlisted, he could retire as a sergeant after twelve years of service at the age of thirty and enjoy a lifetime sinecure in the state railroad or postal service. In Milan, that hardly seemed like an ambitious choice, but not everybody had the right kind of motivation to make it in business.

That Teruzzi's desire to live differently came to be expressed in the disciplined violence of war making rather than the cut and thrust of commerce is important for this story. At the time, the Kingdom of Italy was under heavy pressure to expand its military to keep pace with Great Britain, France, and imperial Germany. Italy's professional classes were providing more and more officers to the Italian Royal Army, though half of the officers were still of aristocratic origin. By the turn of the century, however, they much preferred positions in law or industry to submitting themselves to the slow pace of promotion, low pay, scant prestige, and delayed marriages that were the career military officers' fate.[18]

Lacking the right diploma or family wealth to apply to the elite officers' training schools, Teruzzi would have had to volunteer, trust that a superior officer would take a shine to him, and hope that he would be nominated to take the special entry examinations. And so it happened. A year after enlisting in the infantry, on December 21, 1899, he requested a two-year tour of duty in the Royal Corps of Colonial Troops. In August 1903, he was posted to Eritrea, Italy's recently established colony on the Red Sea. At Adi Keyh, a lively little market town on the Eritrean high plain, his superiors evidently saw that he had street smarts and knew his numbers.[19]

Within a matter of months, he was promoted to quartermaster, the senior noncommissioned officer of the unit.

In Italy, the *furiere* is a function and also a character type. He is the man in charge of food and supplies, who hands out ammunition and delivers the mail. He is indispensable but also infuriating. He sits there snug and cozy in the safety of the garrison storerooms, and everybody has to curry his favor. Everything in the colonial army is overstocked. But he keeps the books and has a hawk eye for pilferers. You want him to be your friend, for he's especially useful if you need a wool blanket, canned goods, tin spoons, or useful currency to barter on market day or when wooing the local women. But by becoming your friend, he learns everything about you and the whole unit—the hope is that he will be discreet.

Teruzzi must have been a good quartermaster. After being transferred to Massawa, a step up in itself, the military governor Michele Salazar promoted him to marshal in charge of the garrison's mail. Colonel Salazar must also have been the superior who recommended him for officer training school. Teruzzi took the examination and placed high enough to win one of the ten or so supplementary places. In November 1904, he reported to Modena for the two-year course.

The military academy at Modena was Italy's West Point. What a leap in status to pass through the gateway into the Ducal Palace and look up at great escutcheon over the arches that read "One Force," and "Here the New Heroes of Italy Are Forged!"[20] Teruzzi soon acquired all the skills and habits appropriate to an officer and gentleman. He quickly internalized the military code of honor. First, officers must fight for traditional glory. They were expected to behave with decorum, as officers could be tried for scandalous behavior and, if convicted, dismissed from the service. Fealty to one's military commander was personal, and officers were members of a brotherhood—with all attendant solidarity.

Teruzzi learned to embrace traditional conceptions of culture and to despise socialistic ideas. No other occupation, except for diplomacy, was as concerned with courtesy, protocol, and ceremonial obligations. Like military men everywhere, he was an energetic socializer. He was trained as a horseman, fenced, and played tennis. He learned French, taught himself how to waltz, acquired a taste for gorgeous dress uniforms, and began to groom his facial hair into the fanciful mustaches, sideburns, and beards favored by the European officer corps at the turn of the century.[21]

Though officers had prestige, especially if they were stationed in small towns, their careers were slow, pay was low, and daily life took place under the watchful eyes of the garrison commander. Unhappy wives were the bane of garrison life. Permission to marry thus had to be granted by one's superior officer, in the name of the king, and military wives were expected to come with a dowry and to know the elaborate rules of protocol and etiquette that ruled military social life. Given that she could speak with anybody, including his superiors, while he could not, the good wife of a young officer could make his career.[22] If, however, she was a troublemaker, she could ruin it.

At the very end of 1909, after four years of infantry service, including a year in Parma, Teruzzi was promoted to first lieutenant and asked to return to Eritrea. There was no fighting going on. The sun-parched towns of the Eritrean high plain were sleepy little places. Had he been ambitious, he might have learned Tigrinya, the local language, the Amharic of the nearby Abyssinian tribes, or Arabic, the language of traders. He could have collected flora, embalmed fauna, and made contact with the explorers, scholars, and entrepreneurs who regularly convened in Asmara. That is what Lt. Rodolfo Graziani, Teruzzi's exact contemporary and a future marshal of Italy, did while he was stationed at nearby Adi Ugri.[23]

Or he could have sped up his advancement by contracting under army auspices with King Leopold II of Belgium, who, after officially annexing the Congo, employed Italian officers to turn the killer gangs he had used to terrorize and enslave the native population into a disciplined colonial army. Ottorino Mezzetti, Teruzzi's future commander in the field in Libya, had leaped at this opportunity. Mezzetti later remembered the cold ferocity he had been forced to show not to be massacred by the disorderly troops on first arrival, and the implacable training he had conducted to subdue these men and retain their loyalty.[24]

That the conduct of the Libyan War turned the perfectly competent if somewhat lackluster Lieutenant Teruzzi into a war hero speaks less to his professional qualities than to the extravaganza that the media made of Italy's liberal elite's terrible decision. The normally restrained prime minister, Giovanni Giolitti, obliged the press by portraying the kingdom's endeavor to act like a colonial great power and grab this last chunk of the crumbling Ottoman Empire as an act of "historical fate."[25]

Italy's chattering classes had in only two years created a culture of war that was mesmerizing in its lyricism and misogyny. "The Italian Nation"—or

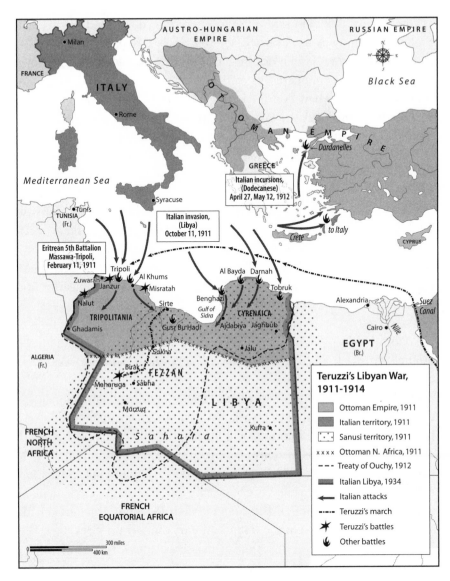

FRANCE

ITALY
Milan
Rome

AUSTRO-HUNGARIAN
EMPIRE

RUSSIAN EMPIRE

Black Sea

Mediterranean Sea

OTTOMAN EMPIRE

GREECE

Dardanelles

Syracuse

TUNISIA
(Fr.)
Tunis

Crete
to Italy
CYPRUS

**Italian incursions,
(Dodecanese)
April 27, May 12, 1912**

**Italian invasion,
(Libya)
October 11, 1911**

**Eritrean 5th Battalion
Massawa-Tripoli,
February 11, 1911**

Zuwarah
Tripoli
Al Khums
Janzur
Misratah
Nalut
Sirte
TRIPOLITANIA
Ghadamis

Al Bayda   Darnah
Tobruk
Benghazi
*Gulf of
Sidra*
Gusr Bu Hadi
CYRENAICA
Ajdabiya   Jaghbūb
Jālū

Alexandria
Suez
Canal
Cairo
EGYPT
(Br.)
Nile

ALGERIA
(Fr.)

Sakha
Birak
Maharuga   Sābha
FEZZAN
Mūrzuq

LIBYA

**FRENCH
NORTH
AFRICA**

S a h a r a

Kufra

**Teruzzi's Libyan War,
1911–1914**

Ottoman Empire, 1911
Italian territory, 1911
Sanusi territory, 1911
x x x x Ottoman N. Africa, 1911
– – – Treaty of Ouchy, 1912
Italian Libya, 1934
◄—— Italian attacks
·—·—· Teruzzi's march
✷ Teruzzi's battles
💥 Other battles

**FRENCH
EQUATORIAL AFRICA**

300 miles
400 km

© Victoria de Grazia

as Giovanni Pascoli, Italy's unofficial poet laureate, declaimed—the "Great Proletarian, had bestirred herself," so that a world that had taken Italian emigrants for granted could "no longer dismiss them as Lads, Gringos, Wops, Dagos." Italy had conquered its own El Dorado, where the rural dispossessed could find a new home. Making war killed off "the Italian spirit of passé ideas," the futurist Marinetti chimed in: "notably, sentimentality, morbid compassion, love of the blind and crippled."[26]

Teruzzi's birth as a war hero was contemporaneous with this early bronze age of Italian war culture. Guelfo Civinini, one of the *Corriere*'s war correspondents and a sometime librettist, who in 1910 had co-authored Puccini's *Girl of the Golden West*, saw in Teruzzi (after their first meeting at Misurata, after which they became fast friends) something of Giacomo Puccini's histrionic tenors. He was "thin and agile as a deer, strong as a leopard," Civinini wrote, "his full beard stuck out, like a banner of youth and courage." He saw in Teruzzi the soldier who "still saw war-making as a game, and life as a throw of the dice, so spend it now in its fullness, with the pay you just pocketed, to lay what might be your last girl, your hands smelling of the one you'd just left."[27] Teruzzi, who had developed an appetite for the brothels of Milan and Eritrea and every stopover in between, was rarely without a woman.

On December 25, 1913, Teruzzi was at the command of Colonel Antonio Miani, on the eighteenth week of the campaign to occupy the Libyan backlands, when the column was ambushed at Maharuga. His captain was killed. Though his own arm had been shattered by a bullet, Teruzzi rallied his half company and won a silver medal for "his prompt and fearless reactions by advancing under fire to save a gun post from encirclement."

True, he was smirking at the camera when the Arab chieftains made their acts of submission to the Italian military authority a week later. Perhaps he shared, by then, the cynical belief that these acts of obeisance lasted only as long as Italian troops were in the area. In January, he was repatriated to nurse his wounds.[28] He was thus at home in Milan on August 4, 1914, when World War I started.

2

THE GREAT WAR

The Isonzo scoured
Me like
One of its stones.

—GIUSEPPE UNGARETTI, *Rivers*, August 1916

At the outbreak of the war, the Kingdom of Italy was still part of the Triple Alliance. Even though most people wanted Italy to stay out of the fighting, public opinion strongly favored the Triple Entente, the coalition binding France, Great Britain, and Russia—Russian participation notwithstanding—especially after the German imperial army invaded Belgium to attack France. Once that happened, the government of Italy declared neutrality on the grounds that its treaty with the alliance had been defensive, not offensive, and Italy had not been consulted before the attack. The reality was that nobody responsible thought the country could sustain the war effort.

As the war dragged on, Parliament closed down, and Italy's archconservative cabinet was wooed by the Entente nations to pull off a coup by secretly signing the London Pact. This obliged Italy to renounce its neutrality and intervene against Austria-Hungary with the promise of substantial territorial rewards from the defeated belligerents. By then, Gabriele D'Annunzio had returned from Paris and joined up with Benito Mussolini and mobs of nationalist and radical interventionists to clamor for war, inspired by the fervent hope that over the course of the conflict the old Italy would die in one way or another and a new Italy would be born.

On May 23, 1915, King Victor Emmanuel III signed a formal declaration of war against Austria-Hungary; in the next year, the Kingdom of Italy would declare war against the German and Ottoman empires as well. When the conflict ended three and a half years later, Italy's 35 million people would

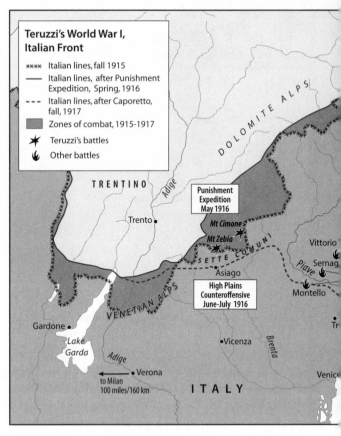

Teruzzi's World War I,
Italian Front

✗✗✗✗ Italian lines, fall 1915
——— Italian lines, after Punishment
       Expedition, Spring, 1916
- - - Italian lines, after Caporetto,
       fall, 1917
       Zones of combat, 1915-1917
✱   Teruzzi's battles
🔥   Other battles

DOLOMITE ALPS

TRENTINO

Adige

Punishment
Expedition
May 1916

Trento

Mt Cimone
Mt Zebio

SETTE COMUNI

Vittorio
Sernag
Piave

Asiago

High Plains
Counteroffensive
June-July 1916

Montello

Gardone

VENETIAN ALPS

Lake
Garda

Adige

Vicenza

Brenta

Tr

Verona

to Milan
100 miles/160 km

ITALY

Venic

© Victoria de Grazia

be left with 689,000 men dead and 947,000 wounded. With its economy overtaxed and the political system unhinged, its people would be deeply split over how worthwhile the war had been.

Upon his mobilization on January 3, 1915, Attilio Teruzzi was promoted to captain and assigned to the 137th regiment of the Barletta Brigade, which, with its companion 138th regiment, was divided into three battalions with three companies, each of about 250 men. Teruzzi was now responsible for his lieutenants (mostly noncommissioned officers), their sub-officers, and their troops: artisans and semiliterate peasant conscripts who regarded the conflict as a "war of signori." Above him was his battalion colonel, who reported to the brigadier general, who in turn reported to the division commander, who reported to the commander of the Third Army. That was Emanuel Philibert, Duke of Aosta, the king's cousin, a

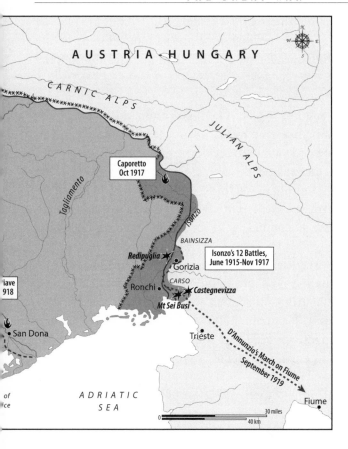

tall, imposing, melancholy figure who drew solace from D'Annunzio's wartime poetry, snippets of which were worked into the carefully embroidered speeches he made to raise the morale of the men.

Teruzzi was thus a tiny cog in an immense, creaky military machine, slowly mobilizing its twelve-army corps of 23,000 officers, 850,000 troops, and 9,000 civilian employees. Luigi Cadorna, chief of the general staff, was the commander in the field. The son of and later father to distinguished generals, the Piedmontese Cadorna himself was the relic of an old school of warfare that made a religion of being on the offensive. He was obdurate on this question; and he learned nothing from the Western Front, which had shown—with its immense casualty rates and stalemated battles since September 1914—that this doctrine had become obsolete in the face of formidable defensive firepower. Before Cadorna's command ended in October 1917, after the rout of the Italian army at Caporetto, he had become infamous for the "judicial savagery" he brought to executing Italian troops for stalling at orders to go over the top, disbanding under fire, or mutinying.[1]

In principle, Italy's grand strategy was simple, given that its army far outweighed the Austrian empire's in size. The high command envisaged the frontier between the two forces as a vast crescent extending from the Austrian Tyrol above Lake Garda and curving down through the Carnic Alps toward the Adriatic at Trieste. The idea was first to cross the Carso Plateau along the Isonzo River and slip down through the sixty kilometers of Alpine foothills to take Trieste. Then, with Trieste secured, a second offensive would pass over the Dolomites, with the combined forces reaching Vienna by Christmas 1915.

Over the next two years, the Barletta Brigade would serve on the front lines for sixteen months and nine days and be present at practically every failed effort to implement that strategy. It fought on the Carso, Asiago, and Bainsizza Plateaus in five major battles, taking some of the highest casualty rates of any infantry brigade, and earned two silver medals for the regimental flags and an encomium for its valor from General Cadorna before it was demobilized in 1919.[2]

Three of Teruzzi's wartime experiences bear telling. They may not account for his anger at the war's end, much less for his decision to become a fascist, nor his personal furies. But they do help explain why he wept easily, spoke often of the men sacrificed, and paid his respects to the war dead at every occasion set up to commemorate them; and why he showed a visceral loyalty not only to his command but also to fellow veterans, even if in civilian life they turned out to be incompetent, deadbeat, or worse.

First, there was the sheer carnage. On June 1, 1915, just as the supreme command launched the first battle on the Isonzo River, his regiment reached the front lines on the Carso Plateau. In its first two days of fighting around Mount Sei Busi and Redipuglia, his regiment lost 83 officers and 869 troops, fully a third of its men. In North Africa, he had commanded Askari, who were eager to engage the enemy, never retreated, and were loyal to the death to their commanding officers. Here, he commanded "those poor devils," Italian conscripts who were citizens of his same country, yet had to ask what they were fighting for; they had no confidence in the commands as they were driven to wriggle like tailless lizards across a no-man's-land of crevices, rocks, and shrubs to slip their way through tangles of barbed wire under barrages of shells; and they screamed for their mothers more or less intelligibly in some variant of Italian as they lay wounded and dying.

Then there were the orders to shoot your own troops. In June 1916, the brigade was moved to the high plateau of Asiago after the Austro-Hungarians unleashed their surprise "Punishment Expedition," moving up over the Tridentine Alps to threaten the whole plain all the way from Vicenza and Verona to Venice. The brigade's duty was to push back from the mountain crests and ridges the Bosnian and Hungarian gunners, who, hunkered down in the caves, tunnels, and crevices above, were equipped with imperial Germany's most deadly weaponry to fire away at any advance through the barbed-wire entanglements.

Captain Teruzzi kept the regimental diary for the 137th, recording the orders for the assault on Mount Zebio, via the crest of Mount Cimone. It started with Supreme Commander Cadorna's order to employ "rapid, violent" action, as "nothing discouraged the enemy more." The order was subsequently operationalized by the divisional commander, Lieutenant General Carlo Carignani, who instructed his officers that "coercive methods" were to be employed in the assault, adding, "there was no excuse for physical or moral depression." The brigade commander, Lieutenant Colonel Antonio Barco, was emphatic that "no hesitation whatsoever be tolerated": "officers were to use their weapons, so that [the troops] understand that if they go forward they may risk being wounded. If they halt or retreat, they have the certainty of being executed." Upon the "totally urgent" requests for reinforcements from the regimental commander, Colonel Gaspare Leone, who reported "grave losses" especially among the officers and the men trapped in the entanglements, "as enemy fire is blowing up the hands reaching out to cut the wires," the order was reaffirmed: "take the crest, relaunch offensive on Mount Zebio."[3]

That was the day, June 20, 1916, when Teruzzi won his first silver medal of the war. The citation tells us that "at a critical moment he intervened efficaciously to back up the Regimental Commander to reestablish order in the troops, shaken and under the adversary's intense fire, helping to reposition the line and regroup dispersed soldiers."[4] The war diaries of the 137th and 138th Regiments don't really help us to reconstruct the tumult and slaughter. Oral testimony tells us that units of the 138th rebelled and were shot. Whatever Teruzzi did—screaming, kicking, shoving, threatening murder, perhaps even shooting his men himself—his regiment, the

137th, escaped the executions for desertion in the line of battle known to have been inflicted that week on the slopes adjacent to his against the mutinous men of the Ravenna Brigade.

To Teruzzi's good fortune, and the Barletta Brigade's as well, July brought a change of command. Colonel Giuseppe Vaccari had insisted on being reassigned to frontline duty from Libya, where, after being chief of staff, he had become Italy's top political affairs officer. He, too, was a graduate of the Modena Academy, but he was born and bred to be a high officer, from a patriotic Vicenza family and a widower "married to his mission." He was universally described as a "noble figure, of keen intelligence," unflinchingly brave and "super-strict," who believed, as Seneca had admonished, that one should "always act as if you were in the presence of witnesses."[5]

Vaccari saw the future of Italy in the new officers corps being shaped in the trenches. When the war was over, they would contribute to remaking

Aides-de-camp Teruzzi and Raffaele Mattioli with General Giuseppe Vaccari, Castagnevizza, spring 1917

Archivio Storico Intesa Sanpaolo

the nation in a thoroughly tough-minded but more modern and more generous way. This corps would make room for the self-made, seasoned colonial officers; it would blend them in with the NCOs, who volunteered out of the universities, ready to sacrifice on behalf of the nation with no notion of a military career. Vaccari appointed his two aides-de-camp accordingly. His senior man was the churlish, chain-smoking, heavy-drinking thirty-eight-year-old Teruzzi, a seasoned captain who connected Vaccari to the rank and file. His junior man was the tall, cerebral, abstemious twenty-two-year-old Lieutenant Raffaele Mattioli. A delightful conversationalist, Mattioli was the son of wealthy Abruzzi-landed gentry, a future economist and banker, patron of the arts and letters, and friend of John Maynard Keynes; some likened Mattioli in wealth and taste to the British Rothschilds. He handled Vaccari's relations to the command.[6]

Mattioli was hit by a bomb fragment on April 4, 1917, while inspecting fortifications at Castegnevizza. Having left the front for treatment of his injuries, he missed the ceremonies early the following month when the whole brigade won an encomium from Cadorna. The Duke of Aosta, in front of the entire regiment, commended the pointy-bearded Captain

General Vaccari's inscription reads: The Duke decorates Captain Teruzzi, aide-de-camp of General G. Vaccari, Commander of the Barletta Brigade

Fondo Giuseppe Vaccari / Museo del Risorgimento e della Grande Guerra, Vicenza

Teruzzi, who in the meantime had garnered another silver medal as "a constant example of energy and ardor also in the most critical moments, the most difficult moments of combat." It was a morale-boosting exercise for the whole brigade on the eve of the Tenth Battle of the Isonzo, which would take off from practically the same rubble-pocked positions the troops had held at their arrival at the front on June 1915, two years earlier."[7]

In July, General Vaccari was named chief of staff to the Duke of Aosta. On July 8, 1917, before taking leave of his command, he had Teruzzi promoted to the rank of major. He also had him reassigned to Libya. The army chief of staff expected that with the entry of the United States into the European war, in April 1917, the worldwide conflict would soon end. Since 1914, Arab forces, led by the warriors of the Sanusi Empire and armed by the Turks and Germans, had taken back most of Tripolitania and Cyrenaica, other than a few redoubts on the coastline. The final setback had been the Battle of Gasr bu Hadi, on April 28–29, 1915, when Teruzzi's onetime commander Miani suffered Italy's worst colonial defeat since Adwa.[8] If the Italians wished to have their conquest recognized under international law at the peace-making conference, they would need seasoned colonial officers to re-secure control over the whole territory. Cadorna launched the Eleventh Battle of the Isonzo on July 19. On July 27, the Third Army finally made a dent in the Austrian lines.

Just two days before that, Teruzzi had left the war zone to ship out to Benghazi and take command of the garrison at Darnah. His Great War was over.

3

MUTILATED VICTORY

Blood is still, outside of human veins. If it could scream, if the
living could hear it scream, Italy would never again sleep.

—GABRIELE D'ANNUNZIO, *Il sudore di sangue*, June 1919

D arnah was known as the "pearl of the Eastern Mediterranean" in the
early twentieth century. The small town sat amid a forest of palm
trees on the coast midway betweeen Tripoli and Alexandria, cooled by
sea breezes and copiously watered by the wadi that coursed through its
center, carrying the rainfall of the Jebel Akhdar to the sea. In 1917,
Darnah had maybe five thousand inhabitants, mostly Arabs and Berbers, a thriving Sephardic Jewish community, and very few Italians, all
jumbled together in the flower-trellised back streets behind the souk and
Great Mosque.

When Teruzzi took command of the garrison, with its hundred Italian
officers, four hundred men and a Libyan regiment of nine hundred, it was
a relatively peaceful time. The war had come to a close in the region after
the British naval blockade, imposed to prevent the Turks and Germans
from arming the Arab resistance, disrupted local trade and caused widespread starvation, bringing the Sanusi leaders to seek an accommodation.
On that basis, in 1916, the Italians were able to bring the First Italian-
Sanusi war to a conclusion. The truce they signed with the Sanusi leaders
at Zuwaytina in 1916, and another truce concluded at Akrama a year later,
established an uneasy coexistence. As the Italians asserted their authority
on the coastline, and the Sanusi over the highlands and in the oases, Teruzzi established friendly relations with the elders of the nearby Obeidat
tribe, the biggest and wealthiest in Cyrenaica. He also met his first love, a
Jewish girl (he later told Lilliana), likely the daughter of a local merchant
or café owner.[1]

From Darnah, Teruzzi followed the war. Military protocol called for him to assemble the garrison to read out the war bulletin from the commander-in-chief for October 29, 1917. General Cadorna spoke of the rout of the Second Army at Caporetto during the twelfth battle on the Isonzo and shamelessly blamed the troops. Teruzzi must have been relieved to learn that the Third Army had held; that his own general, Vaccari, had conducted an orderly retreat; and that Cadorna had been replaced with General Diaz, who in quick order promised "a reverse Caporetto." The following October, during the counteroffensive concluding at the Battle of Montello, Vaccari would win a gold medal, and on November 3, 1918, after the Italian forces occupied the town of Vittorio Veneto, the enemy finally capitulated. Upon hearing the news of the armistice on November 4, Teruzzi and his men celebrated. Italy had won the war. Now what would happen?

Teruzzi was a distant witness to the passage from the highly imperfect myth of victory as the "purest glory" to the downright pernicious notion, propagated by the ever-mesmerizing D'Annunzio, that if Italians didn't press all of their demands at the peace conference, Italy would suffer a "mutilated victory," "its knees broken, its wings clipped."[2] That would have proved a tall order even if president Woodrow Wilson, the so-called mutilator, had not used his bully pulpit at Versailles to castigate Italy's designs on the city of Fiume on the Dalmatian coast. Given the circumstances, the triumphant peace Italian nationalists hoped for was highly unlikely. In any case, the Kingdom of Italy would still have to face the many old problems left unsolved by war—like the extremes of social inequality, lopsided growth, and the impasse in Parliament that had caused it to be closed down over the entire course of the war. And this was to say nothing of the many new problems that had arisen from the war itself: how to demobilize a force of two million, compensate the war casualties, rebuild the nation's economy and infrastructure, and widen the base of democracy, as had been promised repeatedly.

Only by a stroke of political genius could the nation regain its confidence. Where that would come from was hard to say. Even before the war, the monarchy seemed hopelessly outdated, the old liberals' popularity had been fading, and new mass political parties were on the rise. All of this added to the political turmoil.

The war spirit that nationalists had been whipping up ever since the Libyan War, insisting that Italy enter into World War I whatever it cost, now fastened onto the public debate to urge that Italy get not only what it had bargained for, from the secret Pact of London, but more. It was as if relief from the inner problems of the nation could be found only in the gratification of Italy's international ambitions, and any party that had not actively backed the war was ipso facto defeatist and, now that there was peace, as inimical to the nation as its former foes. This included the socialists, who had been doggedly antiwar, and the pacifistic new Catholic party as well.

Teruzzi was halfway through a 100-day furlough on September 12, 1919, when, at the Paris Peace Conference, the final decision was made not to give Fiume to Italy. The unanimous feeling among Italian nationalists was that this former Hapsburg town on the Adriatic Sea had always been Italian and that the nation's victory in the war had finally secured it for Italy. Yet the Pact of London had only stipulated that Italy would get Dalmatia. President Wilson wanted the new state of Yugoslavia, which was being shaped out of the Balkan lands, to have its own port. With a company of Arditi, the wartime special assault troops, and two battalions of soldiers, D'Annunzio occupied Fiume and announced its annexation in the name of the Italian people.

It was a violation of international law and a coup against the government of Francesco Saverio Nitti, which had signed the peace treaty. It was also mutinous from the point of view of the army command and a criminal aggression against the town of 49,000, a large minority of whom were non-Italians who, having been liberated from the Hapsburg Empire, now found themselves occupied by Italian freebooters. Not least, it gave a preview of Mussolini's March on Rome three years later, with its goal of overthrowing the decrepit liberal elite.

For most of his brilliant, creative life, D'Annunzio had been mainly interested in giving his own egomania and eroticism an aesthetic solution. But at Fiume—under the world's watchful eye—the poet-prophet took a giant step further to give political as well as cultural expression to the "voracity" that had made it possible for a man like Teruzzi to wave his men over the top, to see them die, to believe that there was some higher good that had made their sacrifices worthwhile. D'Annunzio made the Free State of Fiume his transgressive personal dictatorship, where he could legislate against the "doctrines of renunciation—feminism, socialism, evangelism" by promoting free love and divorce, by publicly funding music and art, and by creating an anarcho-syndicalist trade union and an anti-League of Nations to reach out to the oppressed peoples around the world.[3]

Later, D'Annunzio spoke of Teruzzi as his "beloved comrade in arms," as if he had been a legionnaire at Fiume. Whether Teruzzi was more than an enthusiastic bystander is unlikely.[4] When his leave was over in November, Teruzzi had to return to his command.

We can only speculate that upon his return to Darnah, Teruzzi must have been of two minds. The place had a legendary allure: soldiers returning to the continent named their firstborn "Derno" or "Derna" and forever spoke of their "Mal d'Africa," or "Homesickness for Africa."[5] But what mark could you make in Darnah? It helped that when his sister visited on her holidays, she became hysterical at the thought that her brother wanted to marry his Jewish Libyan girl. Even before the orders came to repatriate, in August 1920, Teruzzi was reconciled to returning home.

By 1920, when our story properly begins, the Milan that Attilio Teruzzi knew as a young soldier had practically ceased to exist. The population was now close to a million; Porta Genova, the onetime neighborhood of the respectable poor and strivers, had become both more working class, with the growth of war manufactures on the nearby city periphery, and less neighborly, having become a busy thoroughfare for traffic to and from the city's center. Most of his own relatives were now socialists who condemned the military-industrial-monarchist clique for having caused the war, having profited richly from it, and for now wanting to crush protests for change.

Even if they didn't say it out loud, they thought he was the dupe of that clique. In his neighborhood in December, after socialist workers and officers had gotten into a fistfight, Second Lieutenant Agnelli had been thrown into the canal and half drowned. On another occasion, a lieutenant of the Alpine troops was beaten bloody on Via Ugo Foscolo. The military police had to be brought in to break up a scuffle between anarchists and military officers in the Galleria but only after the free-for-all with gunshots and stones smashed out the windows at the Biffi, Savini, and Campari cafés. Even his mother was telling him to change into civilian clothes when he went to the Galleria, for fear that he, too, would be accosted.

At some level he was being treated no differently from the 1.2 million other shabbily treated men in the process of being demobilized. The economy was in such turmoil and prospects for work so dim that the folks at home showed the soldiers little other than contempt, as if the privations and uselessness of the war had been their fault.[6] At the same time, Teruzzi was now close to forty, he had served his country for his entire adult life, and he had been wounded and decorated with a bronze and three silver medals. What would the government do for men like him, men for whom the military had been both a profession and a vocation to which they had devoted their entire adult lives?

The war had promoted too many men too quickly, so there were too many men in the higher ranks. The current plan was to set up a reserve corps, called the PAS (Posto Ausiliario di Servizio), to reduce the number of higher officers on active duty, in the hope of keeping the most seasoned of them available in the event of a new call-up.[7] It would provide a pension, but with the galloping inflation, a month's income hardly covered a new set of civilian clothes, much less the gabardine suits, silk neck scarves, shirt cuffs and collars, two-tone shoes, and bowlers appropriate to the dress of a Milanese gentleman.

What occupation then? With so many job seekers, the onetime certainty that Teruzzi would find a sinecure in the railroads or state bureaucracy was gone. He had skills as an accountant. He talked to his cousins, the Sozzi, who had a booming haberdashery store downtown, and it may have been through them that he lined up a job as a traveling salesman. He spoke with other veterans, old friends, and acquaintances who were in the same position. One thought was to organize a cooperative, to distribute wine or produce. But that called for all kinds of permissions, and with the soaring inflation, nobody could obtain credit or stock. Teruzzi was a Freemason, like many colonial officers, and a loyalist of its more democratic wing, the Grand Lodge, based at Piazza Gesù in Rome. But Milan's government was socialist, so the "Brothers" wouldn't have been of much help.

With no obvious prospects, Major Teruzzi took life one day at a time: living at home with his mother in his old neighborhood, he got up, hung around, ate his mother's cooking, put on his uniform to show that he was still an officer under arms, and took the tram to the Duomo. Chances are that in the nearby Galleria he would find friends and old acquaintances. And that was where his friend Guelfo Civinini captured him one late September afternoon, a scene that Civinini rendered, in his librettist style when he wrote it up years later, as a tenor role. There were the usual raggedly attired young war veterans—standing around, sullen-faced and silent, as if awaiting orders, when suddenly a figure pushed out from the shadows to open act 1, scene 1, of Italy's national redemption.

"Strong and handsome," Civinini recalled, "pacing back and forth, with a fearsome leather kurbash gripped in one hand and nervously tugging at his beard." As the two men embraced, Teruzzi pulled back: Repatriated! And this was the Italy he had found on his return! His buddies told him to wear civilian clothes, to leave his uniform at home, not to "show off" his decorations. "What the hell have they done to our country?" Teruzzi implored, his voice choking back a sob, "[t]o hear us told we shouldn't provoke these bastards with our war medals." He brought down his kurbash with a great crack. "so we've come down to this! How revolting." Jolted by the ferocity of the whip snapping, the passersby who had stopped to gawk quickly scattered.[8]

If you were a benevolent observer rather than the butt of his anger, you might have felt some sympathy at the sight of his big hands clenched, his arms flailing around, as he hopped, right foot then left, shouting and cursing. After all, the poor guy had some good reasons to protest. Even buttoned-up bourgeois men sympathized, once they realized he was an officer of the king and a Milanese, not a derelict or some histrionic Neapolitan. Women easily succumbed at the vulnerability of a man who so openly bared his emotions.

September must have been the month that Teruzzi first saw Lilliana Weinman. She had been in Milan since the previous June, lodged at the nearby Hotel Continental with her mother, and she cut through the Galleria several times a day. She could have been walking by while he was making this scene and been one of the passersby who picked up their pace to hurry away. It would have been hard to miss her. She was nearly twenty-one, five-feet-eight-inches tall, robust and blue-eyed, with a big pouf of ash-brown hair. Usually she was seen arm in arm with the Signora, a comely, big-bosomed woman, her mother Rose, née Reisla Ohlbaum, whom local people often mistook for her older sister.

4

ENTER THE DIVA

I feel I will become a great prima donna, and a great prima
donna's prerogative is to take, not give.

—LILLIANA WEINMAN, 1920

On May 14, 1920, two women arrived in Milan. Lilliana Weinman's
purpose, her father had written on her passport application, was "to
complete her operatic studies and make her debut"; her mother's was to
"chaperone her daughter."[1] The young New Yorker came with a letter of
introduction from Maestro Moranzoni at the Metropolitan Opera addressed to Carlo Clausetti, the manager of Ricordi, Italy's leading music
publisher. The conductor said he had followed her training and felt she
was "endowed with a very beautiful voice and uncommon culture," ready
for "a career full of difficulties, displeasures, and struggles."[2]

At their arrival, they stayed at the Hotel Continental on the corner of
Via Manzoni and Via Romagnosi, before moving to the Hotel Regina-
Rebecchino, two streets beyond La Scala on Via Santa Margherita, which
was cheaper and well known for housing visiting artists. In short time, it
was obvious they weren't mere tourists who had overstayed the two or
three days that Cook's Tours allotted for a visit to the Duomo, an evening
at La Scala, and a turn around the Sforza Castle before catching a glimpse
of Leonardo's *Last Supper*.

They were busy all day and at dinner, when they could invariably be
found at the Café-Restaurant Cova; the maître d'hôtel made a show of
seating the two women under the immense chandelier in the front room;
there, the Signora could be observed chitchatting with the waiter about
the day's menu, while her daughter tilted her handsome heart-shaped face
to show off her droopy eyes, finely arched nose, and long neck. Within a
few months, they were familiar to the degree that if they were absent for a

few days, waiters and shopkeepers asked where they had been. Some went so far as to gossip with one another about how rich they really were and what had really brought them to Milan.

Lilliana entered this world greatly advantaged by her credentials. But if she stood out, it was in large measure because she knew what she wanted and was confident of what she could attain, which was everything. From the very start of her stay in Italy, she ordered her father to keep a record of her weekly letters, "in the order which you receive them, as I may want them in the future. And under lock and key."[3]

By the time the war in Europe started, her parents had been living in the United States for fourteen years. Both of them had been born in villages near Rzeszów, the "Little Jerusalem" of Austrian Galicia, a city of 15,000 that was about half Jewish and urban to the core—with an elegant central square, majestic synagogues, wealthy merchants, many schools, and even its own orchestra.[4] After marrying in 1896, when he was twenty-three and she just eighteen, Lilliana's father, Izak Weinman, and her mother, Reisla Ohlbaum, moved to Rzeszów, where their daughter was born in 1899. Reisla and the baby would stay with her father, while Izak would go on ahead with his brother-in-law, Adolf, to the Lower East Side of New York City and set up in the Garment District. There, they would identify a specialization—which turned out to be elastic webbing—and innovate, which Izak did by patenting a design for elastic trouser belts. The daughter who was born just as Izak was about to leave turned out to be her parents' only child. She was also her doting grandfather's first grandchild, and his favorite, her imperious character taking much from his.

Once mother and daughter joined Izak in New York, the couple was hypervigilant about the strides to take thereafter. First they changed their names: Leonora became Lilliana, nicknamed Lily and also called Babele or Bubula; Reisla became Rose; and Izak was Isaac, Ick, Ike, or, at his most self-important, I. Walker Weinman. Their housing went upscale as they moved from West 117th Street to 67 West 75th Street, before settling at 885 West End Avenue. Isaac gave up pinochle for poker under pressure from his daughter, but he refused to play bridge, resisted taking up golf on the Westchester greens, and cut back only a little on betting at the Belmont Park racetracks. Having been Orthodox Jews in Galicia, they soon assimilated to the more progressive local Jewish identity: they no longer kept kosher, they celebrated ever more elaborate bar mitzvahs, and they began to attend Sabbath services at Temple Emanu-el.[5]

The most important way forward was to invest in their child. Lilliana started the piano at age four and a half or maybe six. In May 1914, at the Class Day recital to celebrate her graduation from the Bettelheim School for Girls, founded by the prominent social and educational reformer Rebekah Kohut, Lilliana triumphed with her solo voice performance. She attended Hunter College High School for Girls and Camp Tripp in Maine, one of the country's first sleepaway camps for girls, soon to be known as "the Harvard of summer camps" after its main clientele, the daughters of striving East Coast Jewish families. She swam, dove, and played mediocre tennis. By the time she was a teenager, she could tell a Chandler from a Packard and knew how to flirt with young men and get along with adults. Thanks to Mrs. Kohut, she was imbued with a firm belief that reformed Judaism was at once "beautiful and stimulating to the imagination."[6] She had the strong ego formation that Freud attributed to firstborn males, a distinct narcissistic streak, and a distractibility that made it impossible for her to keep a diary for more than a couple of weeks at a time. At fifteen, she had embraced her calling as an opera singer. About that time, she confided to her diary that she had no intention of tolerating anybody who put a damper on her "effervescent personality."[7]

Lilliana's precocious sense of her own vocation coincided with two moments in New York City's ambition to become the world's cultural capital. The first took place in 1908, when Jewish-American wealth and influence joined forces with Italian artistic circles at the Metropolitan Opera, and the financier Otto Kahn, its chairman, hired Giulio Gatti-Casazza away from La Scala to become the Met's artistic director for thirty-five years. He, in turn, brought leading Italian *maestri*—including Toscanini and Tullio Serafin—to conduct and commission new hybrids, like Puccini's long-running *Girl of the Golden West*. Gatti's commitment to opera as a business and to recognizing opera divos and divas such as Enrico Caruso, Ezio Pinza, Maria Jeritza, Geraldine Farrar, and Sophie Braslau as celebrities as well as artists enabled them to command the salaries that Hollywood offered its stars.[8]

The second moment, accelerated at the outbreak of the European war, was to fulfill what the American soprano Geraldine Farrar called "the ideals of a National Music."[9] By the time the United States declared war against Germany in 1917, the cultural home front had mobilized against all aspects of German culture. The Met, which had typically put on forty or fifty German operas each season, eventually banned all German directors, German repertoires, and German singers until the war was over. That move, plus the disruption of transatlantic traffic, created a real famine for American prima donnas of European caliber.

Lilliana joined the war effort shortly after May 7, 1915, when German submarines torpedoed the RMS *Lusitania*, killing more than 120 US citizens. Americans were outraged, and, like many other people, Lilliana threw herself into organizing charity benefits for the survivors. She was at one such undertaking on the following Thursday when, in the interlude between the third and fourth acts of *Carmen*, the Irish-American politician W. Bourke Cockran came out onstage. After making a "most powerful speech," he brought out Geraldine Farrar, the star singer that evening. Farrar was dressed as the "Goddess of Liberty" and stood on a pyramid of five or six steps, and Sophie Braslau and Leonora Sparkes flanked him in Red Cross nurse uniforms. The whole audience arose as Farrar launched into the "Star-Spangled Banner": she sang it "marvelously well going up to B at the end." Lilliana thought, "It was the most effective scene ever produced on that stage."[10]

By that time, Lilliana was getting solid preparation in *bel canto* traditions from the well-known Russian baritone and vocal teacher Lazar Samoiloff, who, out of his small studio in Carnegie Hall, started her with simple vocal exercises and singing "Caro Mio Ben" over and over again, accompanied by the patient Emil J. Polak. At her debut at the "grand concert" Samoiloff held on March 1, 1916, at Delmonico's to send off his students, her repertoire of Italian, French, and Russian arias showed "beauty of voice," "beauty of presence," and "abundant temperament."[11] Buzzi-Peccia worked with her as well—not the famous Buzzi, conductor at La Scala and later director of the Moscow Conservatory, but rather his son, Arturo, a classmate and good friend of Puccini, Mascagni, and Toscanini from their student days at Milan, who taught voice to earn a living while trying to compose commercially successful popular songs. The fact that he introduced her to Toscanini's successors at the Metropolitan, Vincenzo Bellezza and Roberto Moranzoni, speaks to Lilliana's talent and discipline.[12] They, in turn, strongly recommended that she go to Milan to perfect her Italian diction and have an opportunity to do grueling stage work. Sophie Braslau, the reigning queen of opera contraltos, made the same recommendation in her best-selling self-help book for aspiring prima donnas. She had also studied with Buzzi-Peccia. Lilliana took her advice.[13]

Gatti-Casazza worried that though the American singers have "beautiful natural voices," were "extremely intelligent," and had "unusual talents," they would not have the grit to succeed; they were overly susceptible to celebrity culture, to the lure of money and fame, and "demand action and are often so impatient that they ruin their opportunities by failing to work hard enough."[14] "Shoals of young women" failed, the self-help books warned, at great cost to their self-esteem, and disappointing patrons and parents.[15] But Lilliana was also a European; her cultural exposure wasn't that of the ordinary, striving American opera star—her European Jewish background supplied her with a degree of grit and cosmopolitanism that would be to her advantage in Milan. And her family would come with her: Isaac intended to pivot his business interests around Vienna so that his pursuits might overlap with hers. The family made a contract, as Lilliana called it. Her parents would support her for five years, at the end of which, upon her return to New York, she would make her debut as prima donna at the Met.

It was to Lilliana's advantage that the Italian opera world was rushing to take advantage of Italy's victory in the war. With the German and Austrian economies in ruins, the fabulous opera houses of Vienna and Budapest, Salzburg, Dresden, and Munich were facing hard times. Milan was making its bid to become the new European leader, and La Scala, the world's most perfectly-managed opera house under Arturo Toscanini, who saw to it that the finances were bolstered, its sound system and stage machinery completely updated, and its musical repertoire audaciously revised to combine the best of the German and Italian operatic traditions.[16]

Lilliana came armed with the introductions and the means to leapfrog into Milan's most talented artistic milieu. She began voice lessons with Giuseppe Fatuo, a highly esteemed musician known for arranging Mascagni and other contemporary opera composers for chamber orchestras. He was a harsh disciplinarian: she had "a fine natural voice, pure and well trained that, perforce, required corrections of various sorts," he told her. He explained that his task was "to remind her of each note's value and let nothing slip by."[17] She took acting lessons with Mario Malatesta, professor at the Italian Academy of Bel Canto, and rehearsed her parts with his

Lilliana flanked by her parents, Rose and Isaac Weinman, San Marco, Venice, 1921

Lilliana Weinman Teruzzi Estate

former student, the lyric soprano Rosina Storchio, the original Cio-Cio San in *Madame Butterfly*, also famous for her renditions of *Tosca* and *La Traviata*, whose voice was now giving out.

Nothing was too good for Isaac Weinman's "Great Kid." Anxious that they knew nothing about their new environment, which was true, the family hired the services of one Mr. Ferulli, who presented himself as a well-connected fixer. In truth, Giuseppe Umberto, or Umberto, as they soon called him, was more at home in New York City than Milan. He had emigrated to the United States from the dead-end town of Grumo Appula, in the flatland behind Bari, around the turn of the century, worked for several years as a Wall Street shipping agent, and successfully exploited his melodramatic sensibility, southern Italian charm, and good looks to marry Irma Mayer, a Jewish woman two years his senior who had enough inherited wealth to enable the two of them and their daughter, Ida (who was Lilliana's age), to buy an apartment in a new building on West End Avenue at 73rd Street, leaving Ferulli to move along in life with no manifest profession of his own.[18]

When Lilliana met Ferulli in New York, he was attached to the court of Enrico Caruso, the world's most famous opera singer, whose fabulous earnings sustained a gaggle of retainers with orgies of pasta eating, interminable talk, and music. Since Ferulli hadn't returned to Italy to fight in the war, unlike tens of thousands of his compatriots in the United States, he was considered a deserter and hadn't dared to make a visit to Italy until after the amnesty.

If you were coming from America, it was a good time to be in Italy. Inflation was terrible, and the dollar was strong. Leaving his family who periodically came to visit, Ferulli relocated to Milan, where he lived on the stipend Isaac gave him for handling Lilliana's career and a cut on any textile business he could drum up for him. It was Ferulli who arranged for Lilliana's piano to be sent from New York and who tapped the music publisher Sonzogno's best piano tuner to tune it. He made travel arrangements, grubbed free tickets, and acted as his budding diva's full-time manager. By the end of the year they had front row seats at La Scala to all three of the season's Toscanini concerts, box seats anytime they wanted to go to the Carcano Theater, and free tickets to the Dal Verme Theater of Emma Carelli. Once Lilliana began to perform, Ferulli had her introduced to the chief costume designer of La Scala, Caramba, the diminutive, goateed one-man assembly line. Once a well-known political cartoonist,

47

he now whipped out costume sketches, hundreds of them every year, attaching swatches of cloth, buttons, and decorations to each, before sending them to the seamstresses.

Lilliana often expressed the need for rigorous self-discipline to make it on her own. "What I have chosen is no easy task, and you must be able to read people to make any kind of a success," she wrote to her father. The fact that she had not "chosen to become a house-wife" meant she had "to acquire all wisdom in human psychology."[19] Her critical ear and a sharp tongue helped her to manage the people around her. She had just seen the "worst *Rigoletto* ever," she confided, but the tenor was "very, very good." She had also heard him in Florence singing Puccini's *Gianni Schicchi*. It was Giacomo Lauri-Volpi, who could be "one of the tenors" of the future, she opined—"if he studies."[20] She commanded the life of the family: to her father, who attended every important Met performance to size up the competition and pluck the sleeve of this or that critic or conductor, her advice to him was to step back. "I feel I will be a great prima donna and a great prima donna's prerogative is to *take*, not *give*."[21]

Later, when Teruzzi was courting Lilliana, he confessed that on occasion he had done more than follow her with his eyes. He had followed her as she and her mother headed to one or another of her maestros for music lessons, loitered nearby while they window-shopped on Via Manzoni, and watched them while they dined at the Café-Restaurant Cova.[22] With what intentions? He didn't have the money or guts to court her. He was lonely, vindictive, territorial, and predatory—a stalker.

During the war, Teruzzi had acted as if he owned the Galleria. Like all of the other officers on leave, including the British, Americans, and Canadians, he would congregate at the cafés with the expectation of seducing and being seduced by "patriotic courtesans," local girls eager for contact with military men.[23] But now that the war was over, the whole ecosystem had changed, giving way to a new species of human female: typists, telephone operators, tourists, shoppers, wives and girlfriends of men newly rich from war profits: they were younger, hard-eyed, quicker, and thinner. The Galleria had become a sexual minefield. If, by chance, he caught their eyes, they looked past him or met his gaze only to look away, as if to say, "The war is over, get a life!" And the men, anachronistic figures in their outmoded uniforms, reciprocated with misogynist insults and vile gestures.

Practically every week since the Weinmans had arrived, the Galleria had been the scene of clashes between demonstrators and police, spilling out of the nearby piazzas, as pedestrians were forced off of the sidewalks, and café chairs and tables were knocked over, causing merchants to shutter their store windows. Rose was frightened by the violence. It brought to mind the wave of anti-Semitism relatives had been experiencing as Galicia was incorporated into the new Republic of Poland after the breakup of the Austro-Hungarian empire. This had culminated in the pogrom on Polish Constitution Day, May 3, 1919, with attacks on worshippers at the Great Kloiz synagogue, pillage, theft, and many injuries. Though Liliana did not share her mother's fear, she had developed a gut aversion to the left. "Election day meant riots and demonstrations on every corner of the Piazza della Scala and Piazza del Duomo," Lilliana wrote her father, after the November 1920 municipal elections, the first since the war. The Socialists had "swept themselves to victory," but only after the Nationalist bloc appeared to have won.

> That meant a holiday and an anarchistic parade, with many red flags and every socialist wearing a red sweater, a tie or muffler or a flower. We saw the whole parade from our windows . . . hideous. When these people passed any well-dressed by-standers they poked their fists in their faces.

They themselves had braved

> a great mob running from the Scala down Via Manzoni. We became frightened and flew into the first available open door. Fortunately it happened to be our furrier. We stayed quite some time there, all locked up and when the coast was clear again, scooted quickly home. It was very thrilling![24]

If Attilio Teruzzi's desire to live differently arose from the conflict between the chivalric codes of the colonial officer-gentleman, the disciplined violence of war-making, and the collapse of his hard-won status, Lilliana Weinman's was more a reflection of the rising hegemon, the United States' cultural voracity and of the immigrant's ardor for success.

What could ever bring their life paths to cross is at this point hard to imagine.

5

IN MUSSOLINI'S CAMP

Coup d'oeil: The notion or faculty of rapidly taking a general view of a position and estimating its advantages and disadvantages.

Coup de main: A sudden and vigorous attack.

Coup d'état: A sudden and great change in the government carried out violently or illegally.

Coup de foudre: A sudden unforeseen event, in particular an instance of love at first sight.

—*Oxford English Dictionary*

In 1920, the seat of the *Popolo d'Italia*, Mussolini's newspaper and most formidable political weapon, was located in a ratty three-story building on Via Paolo da Cannobio, a bleak commercial street just beyond the Duomo. That was where Guelfo Civinini was headed on that fateful September evening when he ran into Attilio Teruzzi in the Galleria. It was a five- or six-minute walk, and, hoping to cheer up his old friend, Civinini decided to bring him along.

Mussolini was at his desk when they arrived. Civinini captured his customary scowl as he looked up, "as if bearing the whole weight of all of Italy's woes on his shoulders." When he saw the "valorous officer" standing at attention, his whole face relaxed. Giving Teruzzi's hand a hard shake, he said, "I am pleased to meet you, Major. If you stay in Italy, come by and see me some time. We are going to need men like you."[1]

The major fiddled with his beard as they left and then burst out: "What an amazing man!" And a second later: "What an amazing effect he had on me, an old soldier used to pulling rank in the colonies; even if he was in civvies, his stare made me feel like some pathetic grunt."

Civinini's anecdote, told with his usual melodramatic flair, highlights the human sympathy sparked when this impetuous and self-interested professional soldier was first introduced to this cleverest of political operators. But to the best we can reconstruct, that encounter took place in September 1920. And at that time, Mussolini's most significant political invention, the party-militia established in November 1921, was barely a glimmer in his eye. If we are to understand what fascism meant then, and how Attilio Teruzzi joined his fate to the nascent movement, we need to delve further. When did he actually decide to move from the military into Mussolini's camp? How did he transfer his skills at waging war against enemies abroad to waging the fascists' war against the "reds" and "subversives" at home? What, finally, did he contribute, in his small way, to the fascist coup d'état against the liberal order that culminated, in late October 1922, with the March on Rome?

From the start, as Civinini clearly captured, Teruzzi recognized Mussolini's qualities as a leader. It didn't matter to him that Mussolini had no general's stars or chevrons or that he looked like the caricature of an anarchist, with his dark, protruding eyes and stubble; his shabby black suit, string tie, and soiled collar. More than a specific political project, Teruzzi saw the power that arose from the force of Mussolini's personality. In a second, Mussolini had grasped Teruzzi's rank, understood what it meant to the major himself, and recognized what it could mean for the fascist movement, which elsewhere in Italy had been recruiting veteran officers but rarely professional soldiers and, so far, none higher than the rank of captain. He had sensed Teruzzi's eagerness to do his duty and guessed at the experience and skills he could bring to the task. Only a natural leader could have captured all of this in an instant from behind his desk in the grubby cubicle that was his command post.

Still, Teruzzi had his interests, and he had to make his calculations. Even if he hadn't yet become an avid reader of the *Popolo d'Italia*, which over the previous year had dedicated more and more space to Italy's humiliation, the disgraceful treatment of its veterans, and the "Bolshevik" outrages in Russia and elsewhere, he had to have begun to rethink the role of the military in the life of the nation, and in his own life, too. His two decades of service had allowed him to live unconventionally: as an outlaw with respect to the pusillanimity of bourgeois manners and mores yet with a rank that made him a stalwart of the very same class. Beyond that, he had sworn an oath to uphold the king and the Constitution. This meant that he could be court-martialed if he joined an avowedly revolutionary armed movement.

Teruzzi's service records give November 30, 1920, as the date he went into the PAS, or officer reserve corps.[2] The fascists always brandished the moment of joining the movement as a sign of steely resolve, but before the National Fascist Party was formally established in November 1921, they didn't keep good records. Even afterward, there was always lots of back-dating, bluster, and forgetfulness. Twenty years later, Teruzzi would say he had joined the party in 1919. My best guess is that he joined the fascist movement the first week of December 1920, at the exact midpoint of fascism's three-year rise to power.

It had been twenty months since March 23, 1919, the founding date of the first Fasci Italiani di Combattimento. That was when Mussolini established his new antiparty social movement at the assembly hall at Piazza San Sepolcro. *Fascio*, literally meaning "bundle" but more generally taken to mean union, had long had a radical-populist resonance in Italian political life: in the 1890s, peasant protesters in Sicily had leagued together with socialist townsmen to form the Fasci Siciliani. In late 1914, Mussolini's first action after his expulsion from the Italian Socialist Party for supporting Italy's entry into the war was to cobble together the Fasci d'Azione Rivoluzionaria, or Revolutionary Action Leagues, to rabble-rouse on behalf of intervening in World War I. Resuming the political fight at the war's end, he intended for the Italian Combat Leagues, to confront the inevitable. The war had rendered the old political party system obsolete. Domestic "class wars" had to give way to mobilizing the people as "producers and combatants" on behalf of nationalist-imperial struggles to make Italy a great power. The right hated everything, Mussolini insisted; the left was purely destructive. His own movement of *combattenti* would be deliberately opportunistic and disruptive in order to subvert and cannibalize the prevailing party system. Fascism had no scruples against appealing across class and party lines to "aristocrats and democrats, conservatives and progressives, reactionaries and revolutionaries, the law-abiding and the disobedient— according to the circumstances, timing, place and action."[3] And it had no scruples against using violence.

Accordingly, the Fasci's initial program was a patchwork of the radical, republican, and anticlerical ideas of the day: universal suffrage, the eight-hour day, minimum wage for workers, taxes on war profits, the sale of

Church property to pay the national debt, and a peace-oriented foreign policy, secured by the nationalization of the military-industrial complex and the creation of a national militia intended for home-defense only. The earliest joiners, mostly from around Milan, were all heretics of one movement or another: anarcho-syndicalists and ex-socialists, a handful of futurists, and nine women, all feminists after their own fashion, several with significant intimacy with Mussolini. The movement attracted the genius conductor Arturo Toscanini (to suggest the outsize male egos angling their way onto the political podium) and one especially violent, self-described poet, Ferruccio Vecchi, a veteran of the wartime volunteer assault brigades, who in April 1919 took it upon himself to mount Milan's first *squadrista* raid on the Socialist Party's paper, *Avanti!*

Teruzzi could never have been one of the "San Sepolcristi," or "fascists of the first hour," with their crypto-radicalism, cultishness, and half-cocked violence. He would never have voted for the party when, in November 1919, Mussolini ran for the first time for deputy to parliament on the *fasci* list, hoping to snatch votes from the left—not that Teruzzi was likely to have voted at all, since he was still under arms and at Darnah. The socialist left did well at the polls, as did the recently founded Catholic Popular Party and a newly founded veterans' party, but Mussolini's list did poorly. He was punished, his political enemies said, for his arrogance. His political career looked dead.[4]

Yet scarcely three years later, Mussolini commanded a national political party with 350,000 members. After cowing the opposition and ingratiating himself with the Italian establishment, he would threaten to occupy Rome with 20,000 black-shirted militia, compelling the king to summon him to lead the government. By that time, the onetime perfect soldier, Teruzzi, had become vice president of the National Fascist Party, chief liaison between the party and the fascist squads, and one of ten or so key leaders of the coup. By any reckoning, he qualified as a member of the "fascist old guard."

The historian wants to fly high here, to pose Olympian questions of the little man. How could this professional soldier—who had idolized General Vaccari, the strictest, ablest, and most honorable of army commanders—have shifted his loyalties to a onetime socialist rabble-rouser, a journalist whose only military experience was as an infantry corporal invalided out of the war by a misfired mortar launcher? How could he, imbued as he had been with the military's firm notions of hierarchy and honor, have

53

embraced this chaotic, ideologically factious political movement? Why would an Italian military man, accustomed to battling enemies mostly on foreign soil according to the laws of war, target his fellow citizens and seek to annihilate them through a "civil war"—as the fascists called it in an effort to dignify their assault on the left and on Catholics, conducted by means of "punitive expeditions" against mostly unarmed foes?

Judging by his actions, Teruzzi's calculations appear to have been both patriotic and self-interested. In effect, he was responding to two morally modest propositions: If the king's military no longer embodied the nation under arms, if it no longer safeguarded the social order and had ceased to offer him a career, why should he stay loyal to it? And if fascism promised to carry out the military's glorious mission, could it ensure him a future if he enlisted?

From the vantage point of the army man eager for the armed forces to save Italy from international humiliation and domestic disorder, the fall of 1920 was the nadir. Gone were the days of valiant and decisive action in the early summer of 1919, when the Duke of Aosta and his senior staff—with the sympathy if not outright complicity of the upright General Vaccari, his onetime chief of staff—had schemed to set up a breakaway Kingdom of the Three Venices in defiance of the Versailles accords' decision to give Fiume and Dalmatia to the Yugoslavs.[5]

Unfortunately, Prime Minister Nitti, a liberal-democrat, had caught them out. Thereafter, successive postwar governments had sought, often clumsily, to return the high command to civilian authority, slashing back military expenditure and drastically shrinking the officer corps. It was a measure of their success that Nitti's government had relieved the duke of his command and disbanded the Third Army and that the head of the joint chiefs of staff, Armando Diaz, the architect of Italy's victory, had dispatched his cadgey Piedmontese protégé, General Pietro Badoglio, to Trieste to brace for the fallout from D'Annunzio's occupation of Fiume. In November 1920, once Badoglio had replaced General Diaz as head of the joint chiefs of staff, he had brought Vaccari to Rome as his deputy chief of staff.

Perhaps the most telling signal that the military establishment had turned from saber rattling against the Versailles peace settlement to preparing for the future within its framework—and embraced the postwar opportunity to build a leaner, more technologically modern and diplomatically sophisticated military establishment—would come in February 1921. That was when General Vaccari, who had by then succeeded Badoglio as head of the joint chiefs of staff, had as his first mission to represent the Italian military as part of Italy's all-star delegation to Washington, D.C., in a Naval Conference. Presuming—as it turned out, wrongly—that the United States would rule the West with a Pax Americana, the delegation was eager to earn its favor. Italy was still treated as a second-rate power, but it left the conference with America's blessing to build as many cruisers, destroyers, and submarines as the French fleet and thus to challenge, presumably peacefully, French and British domination of the Mediterranean.[6]

None of that meant anything to the half of the 120,000 officers who were about to be pensioned off in the fall of 1920. The problem was not so much the ingratitude of civilians for their service or the disrespect for their uniforms. Nor was it the government amnesty of tens of thousands of deserters and soldiers convicted of military infractions. Nor was it even the repeated postponement of nationwide Armistice Day commemorations on the grounds of public safety. It was the perception that the days when the king's army not only defended the glory of the nation abroad but also upheld the sacrosanct principles of hierarchy and order at home were over.

With the disbanding of their units, many officers and enlisted men saw the hard-won solidarity of the wartime nation disintegrate. They saw the rank and file, whom they had led by means of harsh discipline, fatherly affection, and soldierly camaraderie, being abandoned to their destiny. For lack of the employment bureaus, pensions, job training, physical rehabilitation centers, and all of the other services they had been promised as they went back to civilian life, they risked returning to being the half-literate, exploited, impoverished, land-scarce peasants and miserably paid employees they had mostly been before the war. No wonder they fell prey to the demagoguery of agitators and deserters.

At the same time, the military was frustrated at being prevented from pitching in to uphold public order, as Italy was swept by a wave of strikes, protests, and insubordination. Major General Emilio De Bono—who would later become one of the four commanders of the March on Rome—perfectly captured this anguish and frustration when, after having been reassigned to garrison duty in Verona in March 1920, he was prevented from intervening against striking peasants in nearby Polesine, and promptly resigned his command. A "warrior," "born soldier," and "man of arms," what was he to do? In January he had confided in his diary that he felt a "sense of disorientation at being demonized, separated from fellow combatants, at the strikes, the uncertainty about the future . . . our work devalued,

the army neglected even more than before the war."[7] The needy old senti-
mentalist suffered especially from the loss of his men's affection. "So very
much tenderness of heart sprang from the war," he wrote. How would he
ever replenish that loss? After considering the question for a few days, he
answered it himself: "Long live war, by God," he wrote, "war always and
forever."[8]

From De Bono's perspective, Nitti's decision to set up a new national
police corps, the King's Guard Unit, at the command of the Interior Ministry,
was not an effort to modernize public security but a left-wing usurpation
of the army's sacred duty to protect the nation. The military was horrified
at the Bolshevik Revolution: nothing was more frightful than rebellious
troops slaughtering their officers. Italy seemed to be headed in that direction in June 1920 as the government stood haplessly by as infantry marksmen
and Arditi troops embarking for service in Albania mutinied and joined
forces with local anarchists to sack the city.[9]

We can only imagine Teruzzi's view of all this and of events closer to
home in September 1920, when thousands of metallurgical workers occupied the factories of Milan to protest their employers' attempt to lock
them out of strike negotiations. When Nitti's successor, Giovanni Giolitti,
Italy's most seasoned statesman, refused the industrialists' request to declare martial law and call on the military to dislodge them, it seemed like
a capitulation to the forces of subversion and also an invitation to the industrialists to mobilize their own vigilante troops.[10]

As Teruzzi awaited news of the terms of his pension, he would have taken
notice of numerous circulars coming from, or rumored to have come from,
the War Ministry. A staff circular of September 20, 1920, spoke of the Fasci
di Combattimento as "virtuous forces that might eventually be deployed
against subversive and anti-national elements."[11] That same month a rumor
circulated that the War Ministry had secretly ordered that the 60,000 officers who were being phased out were to be paid four-fifths of their current
salary if they reported for drill duty at local fascist headquarters. A War
Ministry report, attributed to a certain Colonel A. R., a self-styled "military expert in civil war," advocated for a "militia of idealists," capable of
conducting "local punitive expeditions."[12] The logic was self-evident. The
military command still believed that the officers' God-sworn duty was to
uphold the nation against subversion. And some had to believe that the
fascist movement stood exactly for that.

We don't know the specifics of Teruzzi's decision, but we do know that it coincided with the moment historians have identified as the great change-over in fascism, when a movement that had arisen first and foremost to exploit the crisis of the left and undertake a national-socialist revolution to overthrow the old and reactionary in capitalist Italy was transformed into a movement to crush the left and activate the forces of reaction. In other words, Teruzzi joined the movement just as the belief that the fascist movement could uphold the nation and protect it from subversion became the commonsense view of the establishment in Italy. And that was right in the wake of the November 1920 national administrative elections.

Starting on October 24, Italian voters had been invited to go to the polls for the first time since 1914 to elect town councilors for the kingdom's 8,092 municipalities and provincial representatives of its eighty provincial governments. When the results were announced on November 4, the socialists had swept to victory in about a fifth of all administrative locations. That was five times the scarce 4% they had won in 1914. More than size of the victory, it was the quality that counted: the left had won almost all of the medium and small towns of the Po Valley and plains, Italy's richest agricultural lands, from Lower Piedmont through Lombardy to Emilia-Romagna. They had triumphed in Bologna and reconfirmed their hold over Milan. They had picked up big and small towns across the central regions of Tuscany and Umbria and made significant inroads into the heel of the Italian boot, in Apulia.[13]

True, Italy had a highly centralized state. Local governments kept vital records, tended to public health, sanitation, zoning, and local transportation, and they oversaw traffic police and fire stations But they had no taxing power of their own, and they could not collect revenues except for fees for garbage, water, and the like. Moreover, if they incurred debts, say, by overspending or floating bonds, or were demonstrably corrupt, or worse, proved incapable of handling public security, they were subject to having their executive, the mayor, removed. The government, working through the all-powerful Interior Ministry, would authorize the prefect of the province to replace him with a special prefectorial commissioner to manage town affairs until new elections were held.

For the left, then, the electoral victory seemed like the culmination of everything the people had been struggling for. Local political control would give more voice to the tight-knit communities of workers, artisans,

and peasants that in small towns and working-class neighborhoods piv-
oted around the often magnificent Chambers of Labor with their party
headquarters, trade union seat, employment office, people's library, people's
theater, and food cooperative. From the perspective of the time, it seemed
like the true Italy—the Italy of the people—had finally spoken.[14]

The provincial bourgeoisie, in turn, was terrified. Their class privileges
under assault, and their arrogance reinforced, they looked on in alarm as
the newly inaugurated socialist town councils insolently hoisted the red flag
over the Town Hall. They overheard with disgust the vulgarities of schoolteachers, barkeepers, and ignorant peasants standing around on market
day, stirred up by socialist demagogues invoking the "new era of peace
and justice" and outlining plans, in the midst of crippling postwar inflation, for walk-in medical clinics, free books and lunches for poor children,
and municipalizing water or electricity.

This was class warfare, not revolution. At the time, Mussolini saw that
as well as anybody. In reality, the glass was half empty: the socialists had only
won one-fifth of the towns in Italy: four-fifths of them were in the hands
of other parties. Since the occupation of the factories in September 1920,
the left's power had crested. The strike waves and protests were petering
out as the economy went into a deep recession. The splits about how to
proceed divided the left further, causing the venerable Italian Socialist Party
to break into three: a social democratic faction opposed to revolution; a
large group called the Maximalists, in support of it but unsure of how to
sustain the momentum; and a new communist vanguard that fiercely embraced the Soviet model only to recognize that for the foreseeable future
Italy had no "Winter Palaces" to storm, and the Italian working class had
to gird itself for a long march. The fascists, by contrast, were evolving a
focused project by claiming that they were carrying out the unification
promised by nineteenth-century Italian nationalists by subjecting a divided people to the authority of the Italian state. If Italy's ruling class entrusted its future to an all-powerful central government, it could finally
harness the forces of capital and labor in the nation's interest.

The massacre in Bologna on November 21, 1920, after fascist squads attacked the crowd celebrating the inauguration of the new socialist administration at Palazzo d'Accursio, signaled the turning point. The fascists
became nationally popular not because of the foresight of their political
program but as paladins of counterrevolution. Guns went off and hand

grenades were thrown, some by red guards defending the Town Hall. Ten people died in the melee, and at least sixty were wounded. On the grounds that the democratically elected socialist administration could not keep the peace, the prefect disbanded it and appointed a special commissioner. The press, meanwhile, played its part by picking up and amplifying fascist propaganda: since the left had caused the mayhem, the government in Rome was right to step in to protect the public. If the government didn't rise to the occasion elsewhere, the forces of order would have to mobilize to neutralize the subversion of the antinational parties. In the next few weeks, *fascisti* organizations were founded wherever the left had won, their composition mostly middle class, with squads of enforcers attached to them, often with military officers at their command.[15]

Mussolini was not yet positioned to take command of the movement. Until the fall of 1920, he was best known as editor in chief of the *Popolo d'Italia*, a task that sucked up most of his organizational energies. The newspaper produced an avid, mostly urban following for his mix of antileft political invective, lively cultural polemics, and mud-slinging quarrels over what the Fascist Revolution would do once it had seized power—interspersed with spine-chilling accounts of the Soviets' westward advance. But Mussolini had notable rivals. Gabriele D'Annunzio was still ensconced in Fiume, and he still had significant political clout. In the provinces, half a dozen local leaders aspired to national, or at least regional, influence, notably Roberto Farinacci, whose base extended from nearby Cremona to Milan; Cesare Forni in Pavia; Italo Balbo in Ferrara; Dino Grandi and Leandro Arpinati in Bologna; Dino Perrone Compagni in Florence; and Giuseppe Caradonna in Apulia. All of these men had gained political momentum over the previous year, less because of their platform than their reputation for running a tight, military-style organization and for putting their armed squadrons at the service of local potentates eager to break strikes, disperse protests, and run union activists out of town.

Most of these provincial political bosses still looked to D'Annunzio and his inspired if desultory plot to march on Rome in order to close down Parliament and expunge Italy's decrepit ruling class. But Mussolini calculated that D'Annunzio's cause was politically doomed once Prime Minister Giolitti signed the Treaty of Rapallo with the Yugoslav Federation in November, recognizing Fiume as a free city. D'Annunzio's self-styled

Regency of Carnaro had reacted by issuing a declaration of war on Italy. Rome was fed up with D'Annunzio's antics, which meant that he would be ousted sooner or later.

As it happened, the king's army did its duty. Over Christmas 1920, at Giolitti's orders, and after a cannonade from the Royal Navy and D'Annunzio's proclamation that he would resist to the death, ground forces headed by General Caviglia occupied Fiume. Fifty-six deaths and many wounded later, D'Annunzio surrendered. The government then paid him a huge bribe to retire from politics, and he retreated—head high, with twenty-two truckloads of loot—to his self-imposed exile at a giant estate overlooking Lake Garda.

Mussolini would prove the beneficiary. In November 1920 he had begun to ramp up the organization of the Milan *Fascio*, making it the base of his national political operation. In that context, he weighed the successes the provincial bosses had achieved from leading paramilitary squads.[16]

Up until that point, Mussolini had not incorporated military competence in any systematic way into the fascist movement—not that his movement wasn't explicitly violent, and he a violent man. He was the true son of Red Romagna and of his father, Alessandro, the anarchist blacksmith who named his firstborn after the Mexican revolutionary Benito Juarez (and his second, Arnaldo, after the medieval heretic-martyr from Brescia). From his youth, Benito was a brawler, an enthusiast of hard sex and lovers' quarrels. In the socialist movement, he had become a pugnacious sectarian, master of the ad hominem attack, and provocateur of duels and fisticuffs among his own comrades—and against the opposition as well. Ever at the ready to harass the police, he had been arrested, beaten, and jailed on more than one occasion.

Once he was conscripted, this violent man turned into a vehement militarist. Mussolini had been called up to serve with his class in August 1915. Promoted to corporal, he had embraced army discipline in full, identifying with the officers rather than the troops. Making a great show of his pseudo-knowledge of guns and the caliber of the shells whistling overhead, he endorsed all of the clichés about the necessity of death to the human struggle for life, the élan of battle, and the courage and resilience of long-suffering troops.[17]

But militarists rarely know how military discipline actually works. This was plainly Mussolini's case. The Milan *Fascio* had its official headquarters on Via Monte di Pietà, where it handled routine matters like helping veterans, war widows, and orphans get soldiers' benefits, connecting with patriotic associations, and communicating with the thirty or so *fasci* elsewhere around the country. The offices on Via Paolo da Cannobio where Mussolini ran his newspaper were defended by a praetorian guard of toughs, who hung around the courtyard making a ruckus by day and slept in the fetid cellar at night.

According to Cesare Rossi, also an ex-socialist revolutionary who was then Mussolini's closest collaborator, the fascists who collected around Mussolini were "hopeless when it came to military discipline." Their military preparedness was so slight, he recalled, that in late April 1919, after the fascist commando team led by the reckless Ferruccio Vecchi raided *Avanti!* to destroy its new type presses, the riffraff band at the seat of the *Popolo d'Italia* proved unable to put forward even a "simulacrum of a defense." Fortunately, the socialists had decided not to mount a reprisal. Later, Mussolini would muse about "how in the hell Trotsky had managed to organize the Red Army. We tried for a week and couldn't even muster a single squadron."[18]

6

ON THE MARCH

Tell me who your enemy is, and I will tell you who you are.

—CARL SCHMITT, *Glossarium*, Book II. 1949

It is unlikely that Mussolini asked Teruzzi to set up and operate a paramilitary force. More likely, Teruzzi saw what was needed and came up with his own plan. In principle, the squads were all-volunteer operations. In smaller towns, where they were the only going operations, it was easy to attract recruits, pick up donations, and amass the trucks, service revolvers, clubs, and hand grenades that were their stock and trade. In Milan, they had competition. Big industries had their own company goon squads to handle union militants. Blue-shirted nationalists and other patriotic associations recruited their own bands. And they all had to operate under the radar, as carrying firearms was illegal. Milan's bourgeoisie still had confidence in the police and a horror at armed gangs. It was to Teruzzi's credit that he was a local boy, a major still in uniform, with a comrade officer in Captain Cesare Forni, a great landowner of the Polesine, his superior in social status but subordinate in rank and a ferocious disciplinarian. No riff-raff conduct would ruin their reputation.

For the moment, they recruited from the local fascist sections of the city, turning to veterans, of course, but also students from good families too young to have fought in the war. It was enough to outfit them with some semblance of a uniform: army pants and a dark shirt, with war decorations if they had them; if not, they could be borrowed from fathers or brothers or purchased for a few lire at the flea markets. The black shirts and tasseled fezzes popularized by the squads under the command of Italo Balbo would come a year later. Teruzzi struggled to teach his recruits basic drill commands and parade routines. "Fresh from the colonies, with his blond beard and chest amply covered with medals," Cesarino Rossi recalled, Major Teruzzi "sweated blood to persuade the comrades that when he gave a command, it had to be obeyed; it wasn't meant as an insult."[1]

It was four months before Mussolini would see significant results from this endeavor. The first moment came on March 28, 1921, which happened to be Easter Monday, when an immense public funeral was being held for the victims of the terrorist attack at the Diana Theater. Five days earlier, local anarchists seeking to avenge the jailing of their legendary comrade Errico Malatesta had planted 160 sticks of nitroglycerine at the front entrance of the hotel where Milan's police commissioner, Giovanni Gasti, lived. This was right by the Diana's rear stage door. Had the curtain not been delayed while management negotiated the end of the orchestra union's walkout, the theater might have been empty. Instead, the bomb exploded near the end of the final performance of Franz Lehar's *Blue Mazurka*. Blasting across the stage, ripping through the orchestra pit, between stagehands, musicians, and front-row spectators, it killed twenty-one and mutilated scores of others.[2]

Milan had by this point seen several months of armed assaults, shootouts, and bomb throwing, along with protests and strikes. Everybody knew a victim, relative, or friend who had been hit, especially in the theater and music world. The city looked "like a morgue," Lilliana Weinman wrote home the next day; "tragically," her drama coach's sister, Bianca Malatesta, a harmonium player, was among the dead.[3]

As the right blamed left-wing terrorists and the left blamed right-wing provocateurs, the Socialist City Council hesitated to step in to organize a public funeral out of fear of provoking more unrest. The government prefect, Alfredo Lusignuoli, took charge of the funeral, in cooperation with Milan's so-called patriotic associations, who issued the call for the whole city to shut down all activities on the day of the funeral so that "the entire population [could] accompan[y] the dead, united in grief and condemnation."[4]

Mussolini excoriated the recently established Communist Party of Italy as morally, if not materially, responsible for the deed. The bombing, he alleged, was a "Moscow Plot." The communists had shown "solidarity with the assassins" with their cynicism, by calling the bombing "a fatality of the capitalist system which, by its exploitation of everybody, inexorably reduces everything to violence."[5] All fascists had "to stand up for family, religion, Fatherland," he insisted, by attending the funeral.[6] The March 27 edition of the *Popolo d'Italia* gave the exact place and time for them to muster.

By this time, Attilio Teruzzi was no stranger to the concept of the funeral as a staged event. The prefect's plan had the cortège moving out from the Monumental Cemetery at 9:30 A.M., with the wreath-covered funeral caissons in the lead. Over the next three hours, the procession would wend its way south through the center of the city, with a pause at the Duomo for the archbishop to bless the dead, before heading back to the cemetery to return the bodies to their families for burial.

The fascists turned the funeral into their own moment of glory. Thousands had assembled at the Volta Gate to watch the procession as it crossed from Via Ceresio. The caissons rolled by, followed by horse-mounted *carabinieri*, a troop of war mutilees, then more *carabinieri* on foot, various other military units, and 150 musicians, orchestra directors, and professors of music, when, suddenly, the fascist column with Major Teruzzi at its head swung out of Via Borgonuovo, cutting in front of the left-wing Confederation of Labor. Teruzzi had mobilized five companies of 400 men each, thirty-six abreast, representing thirty-seven fasci from across north-central Italy. It took twenty minutes for them to file past, their movements perfectly synchronized, "silent, martial, and grave-looking." Mussolini, who took his place after the first platoon, dressed in black with his central committee surrounding him, walked at a dirge-like pace, his eyes flickering around to catch the people in the crowd who recognized him.[7]

By the time the cortège had reached the Duomo and turned back—as church bells pealed, a plane buzzed overhead, and spectators from upper-floor windows showered the crowds below with flowers—the fascist contingent, followed by the wreath-bearing fascist women's groups, Arditi troops, and blue-shirted nationalists, had grown to 5,000 or 6,000 strong. In the next day's coverage, the *Corriere della Sera* and the *Popolo d'Italia* concurred: the good people of Milan, who had previously regarded the *fascisti* as one more type of assassins, now saw them as men of order and good faith. "Bei giovani," the old ladies were quoted as saying: "What handsome young men!"[8]

The next time Teruzzi made the news only six weeks later, it seemed like another era. It was the eve of the May 15, 1921, general elections. Italy's most powerful politician, Giovanni Giolitti, had invited Mussolini's Fasci di Combattimento to be part of his electoral coalition, and Mussolini was now running for Parliament under the auspices of Giolitti's newly constituted liberal-authoritarian National Bloc. The past master of Italian machine politics, the seventy-eight-year-old Giolitti was in his fifth term as premier. With only a narrow party base of his own in the outdated Liberal Party, having failed to bring the centrist Catholics into a stable coalition upon his return to the premiership the previous June, he was now reaching out to the right, including the far right, meaning the fascists. If his National Bloc did well, cutting into the Catholic and Socialist vote, Giolitti intended to refashion a center-right majority with assorted nationalists, conservatives, and right-wing social democrats, along with a new junior partner, Mussolini.

This was Mussolini's first bid to enter electoral politics since his devastating November 1919 defeat. The Milan *Fascio* was running a lurid and violent political campaign against the left. Blood-red flyers showed bourgeois women being blown to bits under the slogan "The Diana Theater, Never Forget." "For the love and salvation of the Nation, vote for *the* Fasci di Combattimento's List," read another.[9] On May 4, 40,000 people showed up at Piazza Belgioioso to hear fascist and nationalist speakers kick off the election campaign, promising to lead what Gaetano Polverelli, another one of Mussolini's ex-socialist comrades, called "the healthy majority of the nation." By this, he meant "the great swath of medium-size producers, veterans, the moral-intellectual, and technical elite," as distinct from "the coalition of plutocrats and deserters backed by Anarcho-Bolshevik gangsterism."[10] Mussolini brought the crowd to a screaming pitch when he urged the *fascisti*, as they embarked on "the work of rebuilding," "to be both revolutionary and implacably reactionary," as fascism had been "when the people, invaded by the Russian madness, marched toward the abyss."[11]

From newspaper accounts we can see that Major Teruzzi still had his old knack for attracting coverage. On May 6, he reportedly instigated a shoot-out after being heckled at a campaign rally in Seregno, an industrial town of 15,000 people twenty miles north of Milan. From what we can piece together from accounts of the incident in *Corriere della Sera*, *Avanti!*, and the *Popolo d'Italia*, he had escorted three National Bloc candidates to the gathering at the town center. It was late afternoon; nobody had organized the conventional rebuttal time because the socialists had boycotted the rally, and the central square was filled mainly with women, kids, and a few pensioners. The speakers went on for two hours, interrupted by hecklers, and at one point some prankster paraded a dwarf in front of a window above the balcony where the speakers were standing, to the hilarity of the crowd.

When Teruzzi turned to speak, at the end, the clamor rose. Here the accounts diverge: *Avanti!* reported that Teruzzi shouted, "Stop the obstructionism, or you will all be exterminated," and when the kids hooted, he pulled out his gun, yelled "To us [*A noi*]!," and fired a shot, at which point two truckloads of fascists pitched into the crowd, leaving a fifty-six-year-old carpenter dead and several people, including a policeman, wounded. The *Corriere* said that the melee had been caused when the crowd broke out singing "Bandiera Rossa" and the fascists had stepped in to restore order.

Teruzzi was just getting his sea legs. Maybe he was embarrassed by the coverage. In any event, he gave his own version in a letter to the *Corriere*: he had been trying to explain the "concept" that the communists were "incapable of anything but noisy obstructionism" and "merited nothing but contempt." Since he was speaking from the balcony at the time, he could not have fired the shot. In any case, "as a fascist," he "never went about armed."[12]

On May 11, he was once again in the news. This time, also under the cover of protecting the fascists' right to electioneer, he had conducted a joint operation with the Milan police and *carabinieri* to clean out a "subversive" stronghold in Vigentino, just outside the city walls to the southeast. The incident had started in early evening, when a truckload of fascists heading to a campaign rally at Locate Triulzi (population 2,800) had stopped in Vigentino to force the local mayor to hoist the tricolor in place of the red flag. Alerted that the fascists would be ambushed on their way back, Teruzzi had called for two truckloads of reinforcements, one from the Milan *Fascio* and one from the *Questura*, or city police commissioner's office. After exchanging shots with unknown assailants, the police pursued them to a nearby farmhouse with the fascists in tow, rammed open the front door with the police truck on the pretext of looking for weapons, and arrested four socialists, all unarmed. It was toward midnight that the fascists, now with the police in tow, raided the town's socialist headquarters, before moving on to ransack the town's labor cooperative and carry off a portrait of Lenin, two red banners, and one captive, a twenty-one-year-old blacksmith who had been found armed with a stick and carrying several rocks in his pocket. The toll, according to the police docket, was several fascists lightly wounded, only one of whom required medical treatment, and two dead, including the blacksmith, who after being hospitalized with a bashed-up head was found to have been shot in the back, and another worker whose body had been left at the labor cooperative with a gunshot in the head, whose death the police promised to investigate.[13]

The election was four short days away.

If past experience was anything to go by, the master politician Giolitti had hoped to solidify the nation's broken-down institutions by harnessing Mussolini's nationalist thunder, doling out political favors and instituting minor reforms to weather the storm.[14] In principle, the plan had worked: Mussolini, having conducted a brilliant campaign as a man of both order and disorder, won thirty-six deputies in the May 15, 1921, election, after drawing votes away from Giolitti's party, and the fascist movement entered Parliament for the first time.

But in reality, Mussolini's agenda had nothing to do with Giolitti's. His goal now was to gain political leverage by forming tactical alliances with other parties and to destroy the liberal parliamentary order as soon as it was politically opportune. Mussolini's victory wiped out the ignominy of his earlier electoral defeat. It earned him the name of the duce, or leader, of fascism. He celebrated this new status with his first oceanic rallies in the provinces. Two months later, on July 4, 1921, Giolitti resigned. He had failed to form a solid coalition with either the left or the right. With no other competent liberal politicians available to negotiate a new majority, one short-lived cabinet succeeded another for another year.

At first, Mussolini conducted himself as if true to his anti-establishment origins, using his parliamentary perch to find common ground with the socialists and radical republicans on social justice issues. He even embraced Catholic democrats, much as he despised the Church. By midsummer 1921, the fascist parliamentary delegation had worked out the Pact of Pacification with the socialist leadership as the basis for future collaboration. This called for both sides to cease "intimidation, reprisals, vendettas, punishments, personal violence, etc." against one another. It also called for them to "respect one another's banners, emblems, etc." and "disavow and deplore any violations."[15]

But the powerful fascist bosses in the provinces refused to go along. Contemporaries called them the ras, though not to their faces. The Amharic term for tribal chief or viceroy captured their picturesque masculinity— their fanciful uniforms, giant steeds, and retinue of warriors—not to mention their bizarre and terrifying conduct.[16] The ras are best understood as latter-day equivalents of the *condottieri* hired to settle scores back in the days when the Italian peninsula was fought over by emperors, popes, and powerful city-states. They thrived as the liberal state lost its grip, becoming local power brokers, lending their squadrons to employers to fight the unions, protect scab labor, and right wrongs as they saw fit. They, not Mussolini, were the best judges of how to manage local affairs, and the most reliable way to demonstrate to him how much power they really had was to intensify their local battles. From this perspective, the story of fascism can be seen as a chapter in the ongoing conflict between oligarchy and tyranny; between the local fascist notables, the ras, on the one hand, and the Duce (and eventual head of government) on the other.[17]

To address this dilemma, Mussolini had to convince the *fascisti*, who now numbered 220,000, of the need for a national political party and a common strategy. That was the purpose of the upcoming Third Congress, set to open at the Augusteo's lyric concert auditorium in Rome on November 7, 1921. At the outset, the positions of the two groups seemed irreconcilable. Mussolini, with the support of his Milanese cadres, wanted a centralized party apparatus, responsive to his double-dealing. The provincial party bosses wanted a democratic structure, to preserve their local power and also to enable them to recruit and arm more and more *squadristi* to mount an armed national insurrection. So-called revisionists, including Massimo Rocca, Dino Grandi, and Giuseppe Bottai, though they believed in employing both legal and illegal means, also wanted the party to be open and far-sighted enough to attract the technical and intellectual expertise they would need once they were in power.

The Augusteo could hold up to 1,500 people, but 10,000 fascists descended on Rome. Most had no interest in politics. They wanted to seize power directly and were soon launching expeditions against Roman workers, who, to retaliate, planned a general transportation strike that would strand their enemies in Rome. After two days, short on reasoned debate and faced with the growing tumult outside the convention hall, the assembly cut a deal that suited Mussolini.

Coming out of the Third Congress, the far-flung *fascisti* movement would become the National Fascist Party (PNF), with a central directory, an executive staff, and headquarters in Milan and Rome. It would build a full-fledged electoral machine with membership cards, youth groups, women's sections, and trade union affiliates, with the aim of winning seats in Parliament. It would also operate as a paramilitary force, by attaching bands of militia to the local party *fasci*. In sum, this was not a party in the old sense. It was a "party-militia," to use the historian Emilio Gentile's term. This was Mussolini's greatest political invention: it endorsed both law and order and disorder; it was at home both in Parliament and in the piazza; it intended to undermine the state to establish a more authoritarian one; and it would use all means—both legal and illegal—to seize power. Short of a program, this grotesque creation was unified by "love." That was the gist of Mussolini's closing words: like St. Francis who "married himself to poverty and loved it every day more and more," fascism vowed to embrace "its adored mother Italy and to love her every day more and more."[18]

The first task of the party's new directory, when it met in Milan on November 19, was to appoint the PNF's executive committee. These would include so-called democrats and decentralizers, like Dino Grandi and Massimo Rocca, but the party secretariat, which would always be in operation, would consist of the zealous Michele Bianchi, Mussolini's longest-standing collaborator, and the party administrator, Giovanni Marinelli, an ex-socialist and Mussolini's longtime accountant and hatchet man. Operations would be handled by three executive vice presidents: the thirty-three-year-old Achille Starace, a war-crazed former infantry captain from Apulia, would take charge of the new national headquarters in Rome; twenty-one-year-old Giuseppe Bastianini, an agronomy student at the University of Perugia who had demonstrated his precocious grasp of Mussolini's need for a party by leading 4,600 Umbrians to his support at the November congress, was named vice president for coordination at large; and the thirty-nine-year-old Attilio Teruzzi would liaise between national headquarters and the far-flung and ever more fractious local *fasci* springing up all over Italy.

Massimo Rocca, a loud-mouthed fascist dissident but also an acute observer of men, called them the "oligarchy," and in his memoir he recalled the moment of their installation as the point of no return.[19] He characterized Bianchi as a ferocious, small-minded fascist Robespierre and Marinelli as pusillanimous, sly, and conservative. He had no brief with the young Bastianini, who would go on to establish the *fasci all'estero*, to promote the movement abroad. But he felt that Starace had no interest whatsoever in politics or thinking about means, ends, and people. He only understood what to his mind was military rigor, which meant regulating the party as if it were a giant army barracks and party recruits like military draftees.

Rocca, the onetime typographer, prided himself on being an intellectual. He wanted the new National Fascist Party to be a sounding board for great ideas. That meant idealism, factions, and fierce polemics. Teruzzi knew none of that: he was an "ex-colonial officer," Rocca underscored, as if that could account for Teruzzi being "unprincipled and pleasure-loving" and "politically a blank sheet." Teruzzi, to his mind, was a sectarian, obstreperous, and he could be counted on to side with the so-called intransigents. That wasn't because he understood their principles; it was because the party was his "way to make his fortune and the enemy anybody who undercut [the party's] cohesiveness."[20]

Within six months of the National Fascist Party's founding, its headquarters in Milan reportedly had the efficient, busy look of an English political party, complete with a blonde-haired secretary-receptionist. To demonstrate that fascism was also on the side of the workers, the party had established its own national trade union confederation. The *Popolo d'Italia* was now flanked by a new monthly, *Gerarchia*, directed by a leading fascist intellectual, Margherita Sarfatti, Mussolini's mentor and lover. In the provinces, the "violence started up again," Italo Balbo wrote in his memoir. But now it had become "an 'intelligent,' surgical violence," coordinated from the top by Mussolini in "strict relationship to the political strategy of the Party."[21]

Teruzzi undertook two different kinds of missions to make the PNF's violence "intelligent." One was to act as a "peace-maker," as he described one mission, "to curb all disputes among individuals and factions."[22] No job was more important to the cohesiveness of the movement, given the unending equivocation about whether fascism, in Mussolini's words, was "revolutionary" or "implacably reactionary." Was joining the movement, now that it had become a party on the way to power, an act of selfless idealism or nihilism, selflessness or naked opportunism? Teruzzi's other job was to "keep regional initiatives in proper perspective."[23] This meant curbing the excesses of the ras or, if worse came to worse, to cover them up with stupendous lies.

On the first front, Major Teruzzi was invariably courteous as he responded to his comrades' requests for speakers to inaugurate their new *fascio*, congratulated newcomers as they filed the paperwork to join the party, and offered advice on how, say, to prevent teenage fascists from jumping on and off the sideboards of trucks and getting themselves killed. He sought to salve the honor of men who, wounded in sectarian disputes, threatened suicide or self-exile or to repair their lost pride with a duel. His natural reserve seemed to serve him well: his silence was understood as sympathy, a comforting reassurance that on the word of a soldier, the wrongs would be righted, and the matter at hand brought to the attention of the Duce and the party. In short, a solution would be found. It was his style, if not his nature, to suffer at seeing personal conflicts undermine the esprit de corps. He took pleasure when he could report back that he had brought "relative tranquility" to a bad situation, and he was genuinely pained when "every attempt at conciliation failed."[24] That often meant that the party section in question would have to be dissolved and the old leadership replaced. Almost invariably it meant bringing in young men from the establishment: lawyers, doctors, or businessmen who had no prior history with the movement and could be counted on to be men of order, solid in their fealty to the party hierarchy.

The second job was more wearing. In effect, he was not given "full powers" to adjudicate such-and-such a situation. Unlike a Soviet Red Commissar operating in the Ukraine on behalf the Bolshevik Party, or a Nazi Gauleiter, who could call on S.A. troops, Teruzzi had no means to enforce the party's decisions. What could an enforcer do? Mussolini was always operating tactically, so the boundary between what he condemned and what he condoned was unpredictably thin.

Nobody understood this as keenly as Italo Balbo. A quick-witted, loquacious, handsome man with his musketeer mustache and goatee, flamboyant uniforms, and ever-present cigarette, Balbo was the disquiet son of patriotic schoolteachers, and had been volunteering for combat duty in one form or another since he was fourteen. At twenty-five, after a medal-studded stint as captain of assault brigades in the First World War and a brief fling with D'Annunzio, he had emerged as the only brilliant military mind native to the fascist movement. Historians have always gone easy on him, because he was likeable, philo-Semitic, and often critical of the Duce in his disarmingly impertinent way.[25] Balbo never minced his words. If "the objective of our battle" is the "current regime," and "if we want to destroy it with all of its venerable institutions," he wrote, we need "a regime of permanent illegality."[26] Bravado was better than honor. Political action was more effective than a political agenda. Outright lies and tricks were good to fool and humiliate the enemy, mendacity a virtue, bourgeois hypocrisy a vice. In sum, "the more scandal we generate, the more we should be satisfied."[27]

Neither the parliamentary delegation nor the Fascist Party Directory had bought into that logic in December 1920, when, for the first time, on party orders, Teruzzi was sent to Cremona to investigate the murder by fascists of an opposition leader, thirty-three-year-old Achille Boldori, a so-cialist provincial councilor and father of three. Cremona was the home territory of Roberto Farinacci, Lombardy's most powerful fascist boss, second in notoriety only to Italo Balbo. The facts provided by the police were clear: a truckload of fascisti from Cremona, who had gone to Crema to inaugurate the town's new *fascio* and were under the escort of the city police commissioner and twenty King's Guardsmen to prevent trouble, had thrown off the escort on their return by taking a country road. It was chance that they come across Boldori, who, with two companions, had stopped to fix their stalled car. Once the *fascisti* recognized who they were, and the men fled, they gave chase. Pursuing them into a nearby farmyard, they un-covered Boldori hiding in an animal stall, and clubbed him to the ground, shattering his skull. The police had immediately arrested the thirteen men responsible, including a sixteen-year-old, who had confessed, "I'm the one, Giorgio Passanti, student, age sixteen."[28]

The murder had taken place at the very moment Mussolini was working out his Pact of Pacification with the socialists. To placate his fellow depu-ties, and public opinion more broadly, Giacomo Acerbo, head of the fas-cist parliamentary delegation, announced that the party directory would un-dertake "a rigorous political inquiry to determine the guilty parties, together with the eventual instigators, and subject both to public execration."[29]

That meant trespassing on Farinacci's political fiefdom, and he was un-touchable. The poorly educated, obstreperous son of an often-transferred police commissioner from Isernia, the earthquake capital of Italy's center-south, Farinacci had eventually settled with his family in Cremona, where, at a very young age, he had found employment as a railroad clerk. This position let him pass himself off as a genuine working man, and he quickly advanced as the protégé of Leonida Bissolati, the best-known reformist socialist of prewar times. Being a railroad employee also gave him a draft deferral for most of the war, which, like Mussolini, he had supported en-thusiastically. A fascist of the first hour, Farinacci had used his bragga-docio, charm, and keen organizational sense, together with his armed gangs, to flip to his side (or destroy) the socialist organizations of the province, one of Italy's richest. How could so personally generous a man be politi-cally so vile? Massimo Rocca, his onetime political comrade, wondered.[30] Teruzzi, like many others, was captivated.

By the time Teruzzi arrived in Cremona, Farinacci had taken matters in hand. He had denounced Boldori as the organizer of the local red guards,

ON THE MARCH

"ultra-infamous, for his hate propaganda and violence." Boldori, by Farinacci's account, was armed and had accosted the unarmed fascists first; the
whacks he had been given were only enough to lay him up for ten days, so
no felony had been committed. He suffered from "cranial insufficiency."
That had made his head bones weak. It was fate, an accident, and his own
fault that he died. Finally, the local newspaper was the sole source of all of
the wicked lies about the incident. To remedy this situation, Farinacci had
challenged its director to a duel for defamation of character.[31]

Adolf Hitler would later reflect on the use of the noble lie as a key element of the art of statecraft. Magnitude was key. The masses, he said, lied
about little things: they were incapable of the Big Lie and incapable of
disbelief.[32] Teruzzi, the little man, took his cues from Farinacci. The events
had been "enormously exaggerated," he reported, their "savagery" a "pure
invention." To claim that Cremona's citizens were "unanimously indig-
nant" about the events was simply "partisan bad faith." The student had
confessed and then gone off to a dance afterward because "his conscience
was at rest." He lacked the intent to murder. In any case, Teruzzi added,
the communists did worse. He had personally met with a fascist from nearby
Gussola who had been kidnapped, "brutalized all night," and dumped in
the river to drown if he hadn't been rescued by passing fishermen. (The
Corriere's version was that he had only been shoved and punched in the
face after he imprudently went into a communist cooperative.)[33]

The Corriere della Sera published Teruzzi's account with no comment,
as if he were their correspondent, and his report provided the last word on
the matter. The Fascist Party Directory's first "official inquiry" into the
murder of an opponent turned out to be its last. Mussolini's Pact of Pacification with the socialists was dead before the New Year.

By midsummer of 1922, Mussolini was faced with the threat of a coup de
main. It was Balbo this time who decided to rehearse the squadristi at his
command to occupy the quadrilateral formed by his hometown of Ferrara, Parma, Bologna, and Ravenna in Emilia-Romagna. Balbo did so, as
he professed in his memoirs, out of his "utter allegiance to the only leader
[Mussolini], who offered the youth of the times a program of radical negation of the present." The mobilization would face the nation "with the
paradox that the provinces were fascist, yet the central government was
still anti-fascist."[34] His goal was to force the hand of the political establishment to appoint Mussolini as prime minister and call elections, with the

certainty that the number of fascist deputies, now only thirty-two, would increase commensurate with the Party's 300,000 members and with the 700,000 workers enrolled in the fascist trade unions.

This coup de main would be the culmination of the nine-month campaign Balbo had started on September 12, 1921, when he marched on Ravenna at the head of two columns of 1,500 men each. Ostensibly, he had organized this feat to commemorate the 600th anniversary of Dante's death in exile at Ravenna. In reality, he was looking for a showdown with the Republican Party, an anticlerical competitor to the fascists, at the place of its greatest strength. The main effect of that first show of force had been to push Mussolini to turn the out-of-control fascist movement into a hierarchically organized party. Balbo had made his second show of force on May 12, 1922, in Ferrara, this time with fascist party approval, mobilizing 60,000 unemployed workers to force the government to release to the newly established fascist trade unions the funds for unemployment benefits that had been traditionally channeled through the socialist unions. In June 1922, Balbo had ordered the occupation of Bologna by 60,000 *squadristi* cyclists to demand the removal of one of the only prefects, Cesare Mori, to resist the fascists, only to send them home at Mussolini's command before the police intervened. That feat, too, had party approval.

But Balbo's final coup, the decision to occupy Ravenna once more in late July, envisaged as the grand rehearsal for a "general insurrection," was a step too far. At that very moment yet another liberal government coalition had collapsed, and Mussolini was maneuvering to get the Republican Party's support to form a government. He had sent Teruzzi, backed up by Dino Grandi, to negotiate, only to see Balbo, who had reached Ravenna in command of thousands of "super-intransigent" troops, use a ruse to distract the public authorities from defending the magnificent *Casa del Popolo* at the center of town and then occupy and burn it to the ground. Balbo had then extorted trucks from the city police commissioner with the intention of carrying out a twenty-four-hour "reprisal" throughout the province to end forever the "red terror." July 29 was "a terrible night," in Balbo's words; his route to Rimini was "signaled by giant columns of flames and smoke."[35] In the wake, according to the historian Angelo Tasca, lay "smoldering ruins, tortured bodies, and broken minds."[36] Teruzzi and Grandi went along.

Teruzzi was back in Milan on July 31 when he learned that Balbo's feat had paid off, after a fashion. Liberal and moderate politicians' hopes that

Teruzzi's Anti-Subversive War
1920-1922

—— 1920 boundaries
▨ Zones of Squadristi Action
—— Marches
······· Railway
☆ Coups
✳ Teruzzi's battles

© Victoria de Grazia

they could form a new coalition to stop the violence were dashed. To call on the state to do its duty and restore order, the Labor Alliance, a loose coalition of party and trade union leaders, called for a nationwide "legalitarian" strike starting on midnight July 31, 1922, with no end date. But this only showed the Alliance's credulity, their misguided faith that the liberal state existed to protect their rights, and their tactical haplessness, for another service stoppage could only infuriate the public, not garner its sympathy.

The strike did the Fascist Party the favor of enabling it to send an ultimatum to the government that if the strike didn't end within forty-eight hours, it would take the law into its own hands and stop it with its own forces. The fascists intended to exploit the strike to take a big step closer to seizing power. The party secretary, Michele Bianchi, sent secret orders to *fascisti* across the capitals of the provinces, saying that if the strike hadn't ended in forty-eight hours, they should occupy their town halls. The orders appeared in print in the *Popolo d'Italia* on August 1.

By the evening of July 31, Milan's leading fascists had formed a "war committee." At 5:45 A.M. on August 1, fascists, nationalists, and military veterans, dressed in their blue, black, or khaki shirts with decorations, reported to volunteer with non-strikers to drive the street cars, collect garbage, sweep the streets, and furnish other public services. Taking advantage of the absence of the socialist mayor, who was in Germany, the prefect, under pressure from the fascists, appointed a temporary commissioner, Dr. Lalli, who upon his arrival at the office at 7:30 A.M. on August 2, took over the mayor's office. On August 3, upon hearing the news that the strike was ending at 3:30 P.M., the fascists made a show of celebrating in Piazza Duomo, while completing their plans to occupy Palazzo Marino, Milan's city hall.[37]

Raffaele Mattioli, Colonel Vaccari's other aide-de-camp, captured the scene. In the five years since he had last seen the then captain, Teruzzi, Mattioli had become the embodiment of the temperate, responsible new elite that Vaccari had wanted for Italy once the war ended. Demobilized in June 1920, after a fling as press spokesman for D'Annunzio, who regarded him as too serious-minded, he had married his Triestine fiancée, finished his degree, worked for a banker, and, after taking the civil service exam and winning the top place, at twenty-seven years old was about to become general secretary of Milan's Chamber of Commerce. On the afternoon of August 3, Mattioli had been heading toward his favorite café, La Grande Italia, with his best friend, the economist Piero Sraffa, only to see the sign "closed for restoration" tacked on the gated windows.[38] He saw horse-mounted police and royal guards prancing like an "Aida's March" at the barricades in front of City Hall. They were pressing back a crowd of men who became ever more unruly as they caught sight of the tricolor and fascist banners that had been sneaked onto the palace's balcony. Suddenly, a large truck pushed through the police cordon, followed by several cars, and smashed open the giant front doors. The men leapt out. In just a few seconds, Mattioli saw Teruzzi at the balcony with the others, to the cheers of the onlookers.[39]

Mattioli was a sober-minded liberal democrat. He never believed that the fascists he saw in action at Palazzo Marino could mount a national coup. Still, "it was like falling into the abyss," he wrote, to see that people hardly blinked at the sight of the gangs of men marching around the center. It made him feel a "tremendous solitude" as he was "tortured by conscience, revulsion at his complicity, a disgust at living." "The only comfort in that solitude," he confided in his memoir, was "to keep working with eyes wide open and mind awake."[40]

Over the next twenty-four hours, the fascist command, after escorting the socialist administrators to safety, set up guards and barricades at every entrance and sent an envoy to the prefect to say that they would restore the "legal order" but only if the government respected the will of the citizenry by installing a special commissioner in place of the mayor. They added, for good measure, that they were ready to die for their cause. They then glorified their action by bringing Gabriele D'Annunzio to Palazzo Marino to speak. He was still the great poet, the Vate, though he had been pretty much cloistered away at his villa since his ouster from Fiume and only happened to be in Milan to see his publisher. It was perhaps at the urging of Interior Minister Paolino Taddei, who hoped that he would deter the leading conspirators from mounting a full-fledged coup, that D'Annunzio met with Aldo Finzi (who had been his adjutant in Fiume), Cesare Rossi, Teruzzi, and Cesare Forni in his room at the Hotel Cavour on the night of August 2. Whoever took the initiative, the meeting, the *Popolo d'Italia* reported the next morning, lasted well past midnight and was "cordialissimo."[41]

D'Annunzio had no intention of sanctioning the coup. It was only after huge crowds had gathered at 7 P.M. expecting him to appear that Finzi and Teruzzi had rushed to his hotel to plead with him to come. They told him that "it was the people, not the fascists, who wanted him," and the old narcissist, seduced by the bright light of his comrades' idealism, acquiesced. He was speaking from a balcony for the first time since Fiume, he told the assembled crowd as he opened his speech at 11:30 P.M. It was fitting that this be in Milan, "the brain trust of the nation, restored to Italy and the Nation." He insisted on national reconciliation, however, by telling a parable. He said he had overheard a peasant cursing the war, who, after he had reasoned with him about how the soil had to be nurtured with sacrifices if it was to give fruit, threw himself into his arms and wept. He didn't mention fascism—not that it mattered: nobody in the crowd could hear his words.[42]

At three o'clock the following afternoon, August 3, upon the arrival of the prefect's new commissioner, the fascists turned over the city administration. They did so bowing, as their spokesman Forni put it, to "the majesty of the law," which "at times had to be disrespected in form to be respected in practice."[43] Teruzzi and Captain Forni, both with swagger sticks in hand, were photographed welcoming the acting commissioner. We see Teruzzi with a long beard, his face flaccid with the fatigue of sleepless nights, his black shirt sweat-sodden.

The operation completed, the fascists set off in a triumphant procession with the intention, after wending their way through Corso Vittorio Emanuele and Corso Venezia, to parade under D'Annunzio's window at the Hotel Cavour. Teruzzi had evidently had had time to clean up by that time. He was photographed freshly shaven and wearing a clean uniform as he and his comrades stood out on the hotel balcony, preening as D'Annunzio, a pale homunculus in a bespoke suit, gave the Roman salute to the squads in the street below.[44]

Teruzzi had one last appointment for that day. At 4:00 P.M., an hour before the 5:00 P.M. ultimatum the authorities gave to the squads to disperse, he led a raid against *Avanti!*, which, after surviving two devastating attacks since April 1919, had built a brand new office on Via Settala at the city center. The plan called for an airplane to bombard the building. It didn't materialize. But there was no need. In no time, the squads overwhelmed the meager police lines and the few workers on guard duty. After taking a casualty or two surmounting the electrified fence around the premises, and several more in the subsequent shoot-out, they ransacked the premises. The stores of paper were set on fire, and the whole building burned to the ground.[45]

As the government in Rome communicated with the prefecture about returning the city to order, local authorities reported that the Milan "War Committee" was so exhilarated by its success that it was floating the idea of a national coup to overthrow the current government and install a full-fledged directory in Rome with Gabriele D'Annunzio as its head and

Teruzzi with Cesare Forni, left, and, at left behind Forni, Roberto Farinacci, during the Milan coup, August 3, 1922. Photographed by Argo di Strazza.

Civico Archivio Fotografico, Milano

Mussolini and major industrialists like Giovanni Agnelli, the founder of Fiat Motor Cars, in key positions.[46]

Mussolini, who had long wavered on the timing, now felt that the moment had come to act decisively. It was only a matter of time before the king would recall Giolitti to form a cabinet. And Giolitti, who had had no qualms about giving the order to bombard D'Annunzio at Fiume, would likely face down Mussolini's threats. Just as the left had lost momentum after the red offensive of 1919–1920, splitting apart, the fascists were now at risk of frittering away theirs by squabbling over whether to take power legally or illegally. The risk was that any hesitation would allow liberals to retake the initiative and proceed with a liberal-nationalist reconstruction, as had happened elsewhere in western Europe. Planning started in mid-August, and firmed up in Rome on September 29, 1922, when Attilio Teruzzi and nine others agreed with Mussolini to launch an armed insurrection to seize power.

Back in Milan on October 16, Teruzzi joined Mussolini, two other party men, and three generals to appoint four leaders—or "quadrumvirs"—to organize and lead the coup d'état. It fell to Balbo, as commander-in-chief, to select his co-commanders. Together with Cesare Maria De Vecchi, the perfect Piedmontese fascist—a Catholic monarchist, pro-business, a captain in the war with many medals for his bravery—Balbo thought of Teruzzi in consideration of his "great and noble military experience,"[47] but concluded that Teruzzi was more useful in his current position as liaison between the squads and the party. Besides, the fascists needed at least one real general in the command. That could not be the third man, Bianchi, Mussolini's liegeman, a Jacobin-style terrorist and the party's secretary. By chance, they fell on the perfect fourth, the white-bearded General De Bono, who, over the previous months, while consorting with the young *squadristi*, had developed a childlike enthusiasm for the fascist movement, and had some credibility with the army establishment.

By mid-October, a single national Fascist Militia, formed out of the hundreds of local *squadristi* units, had been provided with its own sixty-two-point governing regulations. It is worth remarking on the puerility of the document De Bono and De Vecchi drew up in the tiny Piedmontese mountain town of Torre Pellice on September 17, 1922, for it sounds like a throwback to the Christian medieval vision of the crusading warrior-knight. The Fascist Militia, they wrote, "at the service of God and the Italian nation," would swear by solemn oath "to serve God and Italy, in the name of all who had fallen for the greatness of Italy." Additionally, "they would serve to impart a new masculine virility to Italy, to establish the base for formidable hierarchies, serve Italy with a purity of spirit permeated by profound mysticism, upheld by unwavering faith."[48]

"The fascist militiaman has his own moral compass," the document further clarified, "which partakes not of conventional family, political, or social morality. For him, honor is like for the knights of old, a law that is held up, but can never be attained, of limitless perfection, susceptible perhaps to being excessive, ferocious, harsh, absolute justice, outside of, and always above formal and written law."[49]

On October 25, 1922, the night before the party congress was slated to open in Naples, Teruzzi closeted himself with Mussolini and other top leaders to plan and execute the coup. From a military perspective, the strategy was as amateurish as could be expected. It assumed that the king would not declare a national emergency, and that the army would not be called upon to stop them. If it was, they would be willing to die for the cause. Fortunately for them, Mussolini would be working the legal path to convince the establishment of his bona fides, and persuade it that he represented no threat personally, and offered Italy its best chance of returning to its former greatness.

As they settled the matter in Naples, Italy would be divided into twelve zones of command, each with its own commander. Each zone would be mobilized secretly on Friday, October 27, to exploit the weekend. They had orders to seize and occupy prefectures, police headquarters, train stations, newspaper offices, radio stations, antifascist party seats, and socialist chambers of labor—and, at their discretion, to destroy them. They set their headquarters in Perugia to have rapid rail access to the capitol. Three columns would move out from Santa Marinella, Monterotondo, and Tivoli with a "simultaneous leap" toward Rome, avoiding contact with the military as much as possible. The ecstatic send-off from the 40,000 *fascisti* pressed into Piazza del Plebiscite with shouts of "To Rome, to Rome!" made the threat of the coup anything but secret. As they dispersed, the commanders each received 25,000 lire for their expenses, hugged one another, and saluted, saying, "Arriverderci a Roma!"[50]

On October 27, in his capacity as commander for Emilia-Romagna, Teruzzi gave orders for the occupation of Bologna. The following day, after shooting their way past the military police, the two legions—one captained by Arcnovaldo Bonaccorsi and the other by Gino Baronicini— occupied City Hall; broke open the jail; took over the post office, train station, and courthouse; and ransacked the opposition's headquarters, only to be repulsed at the well-defended military airfield. Heading out into the surrounding countryside, they ravaged the socialist stronghold of Molinella and sacked the surrounding villages, driving all known socialists out of the province. By that evening, the king had still not extended his invitation to Mussolini to form the government. The military commanders who had wanted him to declare a state of siege (Badoglio later insisted that if he had, the fascists would have scattered) were still debating with one another whether to invite Mussolini to form a government. In the early evening hours of October 29, Teruzzi would have been just north of Rome inspecting the lines, when the word spread that the king had asked Mussolini to form a government. "A thrill of joy courses through the fascist squads. Radiant faces, fezzes flying, songs of triumph," Balbo recalled.[51]

Mussolini with Teruzzi behind him, left, and, from left to right, Quadrumvirs
Bianchi, De Bono, De Vecchi, and Balbo, Piazza del Popolo, Rome, October
31, 1922. Photographed by Adolfo Porry Pastorel.
Archivio VEDO/Archivi Farabola

The following day, speeding ahead of the 17,000 or so other fascists
clumping through the narrow streets toward Rome, Teruzzi reached Mussolini's headquarters at the Hotel Savoia. On October 31, he strutted at the
forefront of the impromptu victory parade out of Piazza del Popolo, stop-
ping to pose for Adolfo Porry Pastorel, Italy's most celebrated photojour-
nalist. It was a group portrait with the Duce. We see Mussolini with his
quadrumvirs: Bianchi and De Bono, were to his right, De Vecchi and
Balbo to his left. Teruzzi was the fifth man. The dashing Balbo may have
been the handsomest, but the newly minted Lieutenant General of the
Militia, perfectly positioned to profile his manicured beard and show off
the glint of his war decorations, promised to be the most photogenic.

7

LITTLE MAN, WHAT NOW?

Was the Revolution carried out for you alone, or for all of us?

—Italo Balbo to Mussolini, 1923

The first anniversary of the March on Rome saw Attilio Teruzzi in Cremona, together with three of the quadrumvirs, Costanzo Ciano, a wartime naval hero who was now Mussolini's undersecretary for the navy, and Achille Starace, a vice president of the party and member of its national directory. This was Roberto Farinacci's home territory, and he did the honors, dressed preposterously in top hat and tuxedo. It was the first time they had been on parade together since the March on Rome.

Mussolini's top men had not found equal satisfaction from the seizure of power. De Bono, the most senior and most establishment figure, had his hands overly full, having been appointed both chief of police and chief of staff of the Fascist Militia. De Vecchi, who had been a captain in the war and aspired to become the minister of war, was the most disappointed. Mussolini had the good sense to give the portfolio to General Diaz instead, who denied De Vecchi the gold medal he had hoped for in recognition of his wartime feats on Mount Grappa. (De Vecchi made his disappointment clear upon his return to Turin by condoning the local squads' murderous assaults on opponents of fascism.) Costanzo Ciano had hoped to be the minister rather than just undersecretary of the navy. Once more, Mussolini had shown his political acumen by giving the position to a nobleman, Admiral Thaon de Revel. Starace was satisfied enough, as his life's ambition was to be in the midst of battle. On leave from his position as PNF vice president, he was given command of the vicious fascist militia squads in Trieste, a still-troubled nationalist hotspot.

Farinacci had made the best overall use of his time. After making up for his educational lacunae with a catch-up course for veterans, he got a

First-anniversary celebration of the March on Rome at Cremona, with, left to right, Quadrumvirs Balbo, De Bono, and De Vecchi; Farinacci; Teruzzi; and Undersecretary of the Navy Costanzo Ciano, October 28, 1923. Photographed by Adolfo Porry Pastorel.

Archivio Istituto Luce

quickie Lyceum diploma before enrolling for a degree in law from the University of Modena. On the first try, he would bait his professors with the thesis: "The administration of castor oil to subversives on the part of fascists should not be regarded as violence against an individual, but simply as an insult . . . " They failed him. His second thesis he plagiarized, but they resignedly passed him.[1] He was on the cusp of establishing a new law firm in Milan as a stepping-stone to operating a Lombardy-wide political machine. His *Cremona Nuova* was the most widely read fascist newspaper after Mussolini's *Popolo d'Italia*. By the time he hosted the anniversary celebration of the March on Rome, he could showcase Cremona as a prototype of the totalitarian structure the fascist dictatorship would eventually establish nationwide.

Balbo, too, had flourished. After setting a date to marry his wartime fiancée, the wealthy, pretty Countess Florio from Friuli, he had once again taken up flying, started his own local newspaper, and created his own little duchy in Ferrara, as if he were the Fascist Duke of Este with his own court Jews and his own artist-jesters from among the so-called "Selvaggi" painters of the Val d'Elsa. In his realm, Balbo quipped, "nobody knew who Mussolini had appointed to his cabinet and nobody cared."[2]

For Teruzzi, the year had been a mixed bag. He sat on the Grand Council, Mussolini's shadow cabinet. He was still vice president of the PNF and a member of its directory. In December, Mussolini's government had passed the Oviglio Law, to amnesty all crimes committed in the previous two years "for the sake of the national good." Teruzzi, who had been charged with criminal trespassing for occupying Palazzo Marino and with who knows what else, was given a clear slate, alongside many thousands of other *fascisti*. In February, the king signed the law Teruzzi had helped draft reorganizing the *squadristi* legions as the Voluntary Militia for National Security (MVSN). Since the militia took its oath of allegiance first to Mussolini and only secondarily to the king, its establishment is rightly considered to be Mussolini's first step toward setting up a personal dictatorship.

But there were innumerable dissatisfactions. Teruzzi had no true political base of his own. In Milan, to have any real hope of success, you had to be a suave operator who paid lip service to efficiency and reform, like the current mayor, Luigi Mangiagalli, a preeminent gynecologist and university professor, or a gangster-folk hero from the lower depths, like Mario Giampaoli, the new fascist *federale*. True, he had a prospective base in the province of Como, given his family originated from there. To that end, he had helped a local veteran, Alessandro Tarabini, to get a political start, not that the latter had been especially effective so far. Local Catholics and socialists were still putting up a strong resistance. The socialist town council at Solbiate Comasco, Teruzzi's mother's home village, resisted up until May 16, 1923, when, on the "good advice" of local fascists, it resigned its office and was physically removed from the premises.[3]

Short of a command to relaunch the Fascist Revolution, Teruzzi was now a glorified sergeant major who felt he had been left behind. "My whole soul has been dedicated to the party, coherent with my past as a soldier," he wrote a wartime comrade just after the March on Rome.[4] At PNF headquarters in Rome, they worked ecstatically, day in, day out. However, in the year since, he had made innumerable trips to godforsaken towns to salve the feelings of idealist "fascists of the first hour," brutalized, they claimed, by opportunistic newcomers. He wrote long, judicious reports to resolve local disputes that the party directory barely consulted. He had full powers at the party level. But Mussolini was pushing for the party to subordinate itself to the government prefects and local police to restore law and order. Teruzzi was the most senior member of the militia, a lieutenant general. That made him equal in rank to a two-star army general so far as the militia was concerned. But who would salute whom first, if he, an army major in the reserve, ran into his onetime superior, an army colonel?

General Diaz wasn't interested in playing games with these upstarts. He wouldn't salute Teruzzi, even if they happened to pass one another on a state occasion. The gadfly paparazzo Porry-Pastorel captured Teruzzi's embarrassment on November 4, 1923, the day of commemoration of the Armistice—when the king was hosting the king and queen of Spain. As he stood watch outside the Quirinale alongside the regular *carabinieri*, Diaz rushed past, his hands stuffed in his pockets, giving no sign of recognizing his fellow officer.[5]

Teruzzi, like many fascists, had fallen for the fantasy that fascism was a political revolution, that it would get rid of the old ruling class and make way for them. He was not alone. That Mussolini had sold out to the bourgeoisie, the Church, or the monarchy was routine talk. The Duce repeatedly insisted it wasn't so. "The March on Rome wasn't taken to carry out routine administration," he said.[6] But an alternative political program was foreclosed. All the self-proclaimed true fascists could really boast of was a posture of intransigence. This involved making minute calculations about the forces of your enemy and then pushing back intractably, on the grounds that your own motives were pure and the others' were morally reprehensible. Even if your specific goal wasn't gained, the sheer pigheadedness of the position would turn the tide in your direction. Intransigence had proven invaluable whenever Mussolini had wavered, weighing the ras's violence against the need to conciliate the establishment.

Rome was expensive, housing scarce, and the Romans treated him with the same indifference they treated everybody of little obvious consequence, all of the *buzzurri*, the hicks, who arrived with every change of government.

Teruzzi had always wanted a family, though he had hardly given it much thought since leaving Darnah. In principle, his prospects of finding a mate were excellent, given the superabundance of women as a result of the war. But marriageability is never a simple demographic calculus. Men of his social background traditionally married late, say at thirty, to make sure they could afford a family. Military men sometimes had to postpone marriage for reasons of duty; still, he was pushing forty.

The New Men of Fascism had seemed like attractive mates at the high moment of the Fascist Revolution, when women of good family—of the "Milano Bene"—had helped the neighborhood fascists to furnish their newly opened headquarters with proper furniture, curtains, and wall decorations. The most established and senior matrons had even stood as *madrine*, or godmothers, at the inauguration of their banners. There had been good times after the Milan coup, when mothers had invited young fascists to their afternoon salons, hosted them for weekends at their country villas, and approved when their daughters smiled at them on the streets.

But just as all such fads pass, once the Bolshevik menace was over, the good bourgeoisie of Milan changed its mind about these beautiful fascist brutes. A year after the March on Rome, fascist uniforms looked badly outdated. It became passé to read the *Popolo d'Italia*, sing "Giovinezza," and receive fascist commanders at home. "What goes into a fascist deep fry?" went a joke from the time. "Lots of gall, little heart, and no brains." Then again, the Milanese were no different from social snobs elsewhere. All else being equal, the New Men of Fascism were *instrumenti regni*. They had done their job. They had put the house in order. But they shouldn't pretend to own it.

Better to stay with one's own kind, Attilio's gentle cousin Bimby Teruzzi used to admonish him. She had fallen deeply in love with him upon his return from Cyrenaica, and he had real affection for her. They became lovers, and she kept it a secret. But the relationship had no future if his mother and sister were to have a say. And they often did.[7]

When had his eye settled on Lilliana Weinman? She had debuted at La Fenice on October 27, 1921, under her stage name Lilliana Lorma, singing Michaela in *Carmen*. After a brilliant performance at the Carlo Felice at

Genoa a few months later, Tullio Serafin, Arturo Toscanini's successor at La Scala, had started to mentor her. Toscanini had always regarded the prima donna as just one more instrument in the orchestra, only as good as the whole ensemble. But Serafin placed her front and center. Lilliana's voice teacher, Maestro Fatuo, urged Lilliana to embrace the fact that she had the voice and figure to become a Wagnerian soprano. Serafin saw this too, and after a grueling two weeks of rehearsal in July 1922 he had her sing Elsa in *Lohengrin* at the Arena of Verona before a crowd of 20,000. It was the first time Serafin—really anybody—had conducted Wagner since the war. Lilliana was substituting for Mercedes Llopart, the seasoned Spanish soprano. Ezio Pinza sang Enrico, and Aureliano Pertile was Lohengrin.

Lilliana finally understood what it meant to rehearse as part of an ensemble. She gloried in her first triumph: ovations, curtain calls at the end of every act, bouquets flung wildly at the stage even after the curtain fell, the compliments of the Count of Turin, the king's cousin, who at the intermission told her she was *"primissima* among prime donne." Serafin thrilled her when he said it wouldn't be three years before she debuted at the Met.[8]

For Lilliana the high point of the year came exactly on the eve of the first anniversary of the March on Rome. On October 28, 1923, she was at the Teatro Verdi in Trieste. The opera was Verdi's *Otello*, and she sang Desdemona. "I wasn't nervous and gave much more voice and *scena* and after the last act people stood and cheered for six curtain-calls and then finally I went out alone, and stood there throwing kisses, and half hysterical," she wrote home to her father. From her manager Ferulli she had received "a tree of flowers like pizzas, but three times as big, of white Chrysanthemums and red carnations, as yesterday was my second anniversary of my debut." "[B]elieve me," she added, "the performance was the best present I could have hoped for."[9] The critics paid her the highest compliment of all: she "was one of the very few Americans who has understood perfectly how to Italianize herself, by taking inspiration from the indisputable superiority of our school of lyrics."[10]

Perhaps it is no wonder, then, that on December 19, 1923, as he started on his third bone-jarring trip to Sicily since the March on Rome, Teruzzi was put in good humor at the sight of Lilliana Lorma on the station platform. She would have been hard to miss with her outsize fur stoles and all of the fuss being made over her by her entourage—a lady's maid with her

Lilliana at the monument to Giuseppe Verdi, Busseto, 1922

traveling case, the dandified Italian gentleman passing her the large bouquet as she boarded, and her mother, who mounted the train with her.

Other men were gossiping about her, and one boasted he knew her. As the train pulled out, while her mother settled into their compartment and she stood in the corridor, Lilliana turned to find herself face-to-face with a certain Mr. Ciulla. At first, she didn't recognize him. Then he reminded her that he was the dry goods dealer she'd often met at the Hotel Regina when he'd come by to deliver purchases to her friend, the opera star Rosa Raisa. After some verbal bowing and scraping, Ciulla confided that there was a "big boss of the Milan *Fascio*" on board who wanted to make her acquaintance. Lilliana's mother later recalled that she had ducked in to say she was going to the next carriage for a moment. And she had replied, "Why not? There is no harm in that." Ciulla accompanied her the ten steps to the rendezvous, then made himself scarce.[11]

Teruzzi was the perfect gentleman. He said that he had seen her around Milan with her mother, knew she was a singer, and had long wanted to meet her. He learned that she was heading to Cairo, embarking from Naples, just as he had so many times en route to East Africa. They chit-chatted about the opera, her current repertoire—*Otello, La Bohème, Pagliacci, Compagnacci*—and about the port of Alexandria, the Royal Opera House, Shepheard's (her hotel)—the best in Cairo—and her intention to visit the pyramids. After a half hour or so, because it was late and the corridor by the sleeping compartments was dimly lit, stuffy, and becoming uncomfortably intimate, and because her mother was probably still awake waiting for her, she withdrew, leaving the general satisfied that he had now learned a great deal about her.

The woman Teruzzi knew as Lilliana Lorma turned out to be younger, fresher, and more refined up close. She was not at all a "Milanese singer," the sniggering term his café companions used when they spoke about women in the theater, which is to say, a high-class—and for them, unattainable—cocotte. Nothing suggested that the Italian man she had been seen chiding and hugging at the Milan train station was her fiancée. That would have been Mr. Ferulli. In sum, she was a charming lady, who was dressed splendidly and smelled delightful.

This reaction can be deduced from his gallant behavior upon their arrival in Rome. The train arrived late. The women would have missed their connection to Naples had the general not turned up as they were descending from their car. Seeing that they were in difficulty with their bags and five trunks, he urged them to run ahead to the connecting train. He would deal with the porters.[12] The women, we imagine, would have exchanged glances and giggled: "now, that's an efficient man for you!" And attractive, too, with his tasseled black fez and sweeping gray-green military cape. At the track, after more brusque commands, the luggage was loaded, the porters paid, and they said their good-byes: "A presto," "buon viaggio," "arrivederci." To the interested male ear, their accented pleasantries may have sounded like promises.

Sometime after leaving the station to go to party headquarters, Teruzzi recalibrated his plans. He was heading to Sicily for a tour of inspection. Now he moved up his departure time from Rome, so he could stop over in Naples to catch the women before they embarked. Too late: when he reached the docks, their ship, the SS *Brazil,* was just a fleck in the great blue gulf below Vesuvius.

From Agrigento, he sent a note addressed to the Shepheard's Hotel, expressing his regret at having just missed them.[13]At further stopovers around the island as he carried out his mission of political pacification— which meant cajoling factious loyalists into line and informing the politically intractable "demo-liberals" that they should emigrate to some place in the Americas—he sent off another postcard or two. They would have been couched in the usual conventions: "Many cordial regards," "Sincere best wishes from Syracuse," in his meticulously looped hand.

If Lilliana answered, it was a "thanks for the thought" scribbled on one of her engraved calling cards. From the moment she left Rome, other concerns had grabbed her attention. In Naples, she met Mr. and Mrs. Laganà and other opera people for tea at the Gambrinus Café, made a quick visit to the San Carlo opera house where she had sung Desdemona the previous season, and cabled her doting, anxious "Popsie" in New York City to update him on her doings. Once they had disembarked in Alexandria, and gone on to Cairo, they had all sorts of new people to meet.[14] All the excitement, reinforced by the doting company of Mr. Ferulli, her long-time manager, who joined them from Milan a month later, and of her father, who joined the family a few weeks further on, encouraged the young prima donna's natural inclination to concentrate on herself.

Puccini's *Fanciulla del West,* in Civinini's libretto, was taken from David Belasco's *Girl of the Golden West.* In his first meeting with "the Girl," the heroine, Minnie, the "Mexican bandit" Ramirez's "thoughts tumble out as he is struck with pleasure at her free-and-easy reception of him." She's an American, "a new and unique type," and "no [Italian] lady would have received the advances of a stranger in like fashion."[15] Civinini would have recognized Teruzzi as the Ramirez of Belasco's script. Lilliana Lorma: so open, so amiable, such a civilized person. Our hero had experienced a coup de foudre.

II

GRASP

8

EROS AND THANATOS

Love that doesn't kill isn't love at all.

—ASTERIA, Act 1, Boito's *Nerone*

Italy wants peace, tranquility and calm industriousness, with
love, if possible, and with force, if necessary. . . . I am driven
neither by personal caprice, nor by love of power, nor by ignoble passion, but solely by strong and boundless love for the
fatherland.

—MUSSOLINI, Speech, January 3, 1925

Attilio Teruzzi was at the Cova on April 10, 1924, when he saw Lilliana
sitting down with her parents to dine. She had just come back from
Egypt. He dropped by their table to say hello. More than three months had
passed since they had met on the train to Rome, and as he stood there,
passersby wished him well, called him "Your Excellency," squeezed his hand,
and patted him on the back. Her admirer was no longer just a "big boss of
the Milan *Fascio*." He was an elected deputy to the national parliament.

The previous Sunday, Italy had conducted its first national vote since
Mussolini had come to power. Lilliana and her parents would have observed the turnout at the polls that Sunday to decide the new occupants of
all 535 seats for the Chamber of Deputies, the Italian Parliament's lower
house, as well as the rowdy celebrations that followed. The fascists' "Big
List" (or *Listone*) of candidates, drawn up by the party to run in the elections district by district nationwide, had won overwhelmingly practically
everywhere.

The elections for the 27th Legislature were the first to take place under
the Acerbo Law, after its sponsor, the fascist deputy Giacomo Acerbo. Under
its terms, the electoral ticket receiving the largest number of votes (provided

it got at least 25 percent of the total cast) would automatically obtain two-thirds of all of the seats in the chamber. The remainder would be apportioned among the minority parties. The purpose of the reform was ostensibly to give the government a strong majority to pass legislation, something that had been missing under the liberal regime. The antifascist opposition understandably referred to it as the "Trickster Law," as it effectively sidelined competing parties. If Mussolini's list were to win, he would not only control the chamber but the whole legislature as well; the senate, an appointed body of establishment figures, had effectively been rubber-stamping every piece of legislation he proposed anyway.[1]

As it turned out, the April 6, 1924 elections sounded the death knell of Italian liberal democracy. They were the last free vote until 1946. Before then, the fascists had held only thirty-seven seats of their own, plus the twenty from the Nationalists, whose party had merged with the PNF in 1923. Once the ballots were counted, the 200 fascists elected to Montecitorio, as the Chamber of Deputies is known, were still well shy of the majority. But they comprised the biggest party group in the chamber. Most of them had never run for office before. Many had expressed nothing but contempt for the parliamentary system.

One wonders then why Teruzzi—a member of the PNF Directory and party mainstay—would even have wanted to be a deputy. The answer is probably quite simple. Notwithstanding the fascist coup of 1922, parliament was still as important to Italian political life as it had been before the coup, maybe even more so. Mussolini himself had inadvertently made becoming a parliamentarian desirable for party men as well, when he had appointed an ad hoc group of five advisors, his "Pentarchy," to draw up a single list of candidates to run in every one of the nation's electoral districts. His goal was to coopt far and wide, to pick and choose whomever would locally strengthen his national list—and lend themselves to cooption. Ostensibly he would stand above the fray while the Pentarchy culled the perfect candidates. War mutilees and recipients of gold medals for valor would be ideal. Staunchly conservative Catholics, trustworthy big-city machine politicians, and the old-time great estate owners of the Mezzogiorno all had their place, as did the leading men of arts and letters, and a handful of titans of industry and finance, but only the most indispensable local fascist party bosses. Suddenly, all the party heavyweights wanted to be on the list.

Mussolini quickly backtracked. Trying to make it a point of political principle, he insisted that being a top party functionary was incompatible with other political offices. What use was it for a Teruzzi or a Starace, with their chests covered with medals, to be in the chamber anyway, he asked Cesare Rossi, one of his Pentarchs?[2] Going forward, the Fascist Revolution intended to do away with the petty cronyism and status seeking of the liberal-democratic parliamentary system. In its place it would establish a national chamber of corporations. Instead of the archaic and inequitable method of giving one man one vote—which never addressed the national interest and only perpetuated the grip of traditional notables over their atomized voters—fascism's system of representation would give clear voice to the people's collective interests. In its most democratic formulation, the people would be organized according to whether they were producers of labor, profit, or various categories of expertise, select their delegates, and in the national chamber they would debate their specific interests, reconcile them with their antagonists in the national interest, and legislate.

One or two fascist idealists might have been convinced by Mussolini's argument. But Teruzzi was no idealist, not on that score. The Pentarchy had initially put him on the *Listone*. And his keen quartermaster's nose had already sniffed out all of the goodies of rank and status that were in store: from the honorific "Your Excellency" and discounts on practically everything to never having to pay the bar tab. No, he wasn't going be denied his chance at the spoils. When Mussolini's order arrived that members of the party directory could not run, Teruzzi happened to be in Naples on party business. By a "strange chance," he could not be reached until the deadline had passed, and it was too late to replace him.[3]

Teruzzi turned out to be a perfectly good candidate for Mussolini's purposes. Short of a coherent electoral agenda, the Duce professed his nakedly dictatorial ambitions. Of his two foremost goals, the first was to force the legal-constitutional parties—the old liberals, right-wing Catholics, and other conservative groups—to figure out how to subordinate themselves to the regime (or face being outlawed). His second goal was to annihilate once and for all the so-called subversive parties—the socialists, communists, and republicans who had demonstrated that they wouldn't cooperate with the regime. At the March 24, 1924, rally for the mayors of five thousand Italian municipalities in Rome's Costanzi Theater, Mussolini brought down the house with the slogan he had snitched from the resolutely intransigent Farinacci: "Whoever is not with us is against us."[4]

The electoral campaign finally gave Teruzzi what, with some propaganda work, he could call his home constituency. This quick learner kicked off his campaign on March 10 by hyping his Lombard roots, though he was careful never to specify the name of his mother's village, a backwater, or her origins, rumor had it, as a milkmaid. He presented himself in a dark suit and stiff collar, setting aside his military uniform with its chestful of decorations, grooming his facial hair like a country squire: the beard pompously full, the mustaches twirled up and waxed into devilish points. He would connect with the textile industrialists, rural gentry, and wealthy Milanese vacationing in Como and Lecco and tell them what the regime could bring them in the way of modernity and efficiency. This included pliant trade unions and Italy's first highway project, the Milan–Como toll road, the first stretch of which would be inaugurated in September 1924.

Teruzzi could count on the PNF's radio propaganda (this was the first time radio had been used in Italy for political campaigning) and on the party press—not just the *Popolo d'Italia* but also the local newspaper, *Il Gagliardetto*. And he could count on Alessandro Tarabini, his eager political protégé, to intimidate the opposition candidates, block voters from going to the polls, and destroy ballot boxes. Even then, Como country folks proved to be an obstinate lot. While the fascists won big in most of Lombardy thanks to Farinacci's political machine, in the Como-Lecco electoral district, the turnout was low and the Listone won only 30 percent of the vote, with the socialists and Catholics dividing most of the remainder.[5]

No matter. The ex-*squadrista* had become a deputy, and the deputy practically immediately became a local notable, feted like the previous "Your Excellencies" at the time-honored banquet. Margherita Sarfatti, the only prominent woman of the new regime, had a country home in nearby Soldo, and she, along with another glamorous local woman, hosted the affair. Teruzzi's star had risen.

For Lilliana Weinman, the Honorable Teruzzi was surely a more intriguing figure than General Teruzzi. From local scuttlebutt and from the *Corriere della Sera*, she learned that he was something of a celebrity. When they chanced to meet again a fortnight later, this time on her own turf, he soared in her estimation.

It was the evening of May 1, 1924, at La Scala, and Toscanini was conducting the world premiere of Arrigo Boito's *Nerone*. What an event! Boito was renowned locally as Verdi's librettist and heir. Opera people had been waiting for the work for two decades. The curtain lifted at 9:00 P.M., and with countless ovations and several intermissions came down at two o'clock in the morning, when the last act culminated with horse-drawn chariots dashing out from the scene of the conflagration of Rome, as if they would leap over the orchestra pit. The whole audience gasped in fright. It was an opera for the times, set in the interregnum between paganism and Christianity. Nero, the Roman emperor, was a modern man: an autocrat with a dual compulsion to create and destroy, made vulnerable by his guilt over the murder of his mother and his sexual possessiveness. His love object was a Christian, Asteria, a wild woman and a hero-worshipper. "Vo' seguirlo," she sings in her Act 1 aria: "I yearn to follow him . . . Horror attracts me like a lover/my ecstasy in violent dreams, drunken tears." In her mysticism, carnality, and cruel ambitions, she was a novelty, a far cry from the love-besotted self-sacrificing female protagonists of nineteenth-century opera.[6]

Lilliana relished every moment. She had been to the dress rehearsals and knew the lead singers: Rosa Raisa, in the role of Asteria, was a mentor and friend, and Miguel Fleta, Nerone, had been Don Jose when she had played Micaela at La Fenice. Lilliana missed nothing: each act, she wrote her father, was "followed by a crescendo of enthusiasm, the performers called out again and again to take bows with Maestro. . . . Yes, the scenery was stupendous, and Toscanini superhuman. The music in places excellent. The rest, junk???"[7]

"Still," she added, she "had a marvelous time and Mother and I looked, if not the best last night, certainly as well as the best." In a cryptic last sentence, she added, "I would not have missed it for many reasons."[8]

Teruzzi was no doubt one of them. During one of the several intermissions, he had presented himself in the manner of a real Milanese gentleman: with a sharp click of his heels and a peck on her hand. The next day, he sent Lilliana a large bouquet with a request to visit. And after she had telephoned to thank him and invited him to tea with her mother, he had left the hotel with a photograph of Lilliana Lorma as Elsa in *Lohengrin*—the best that Viennese celebrity portraiture could produce, her bejeweled figure elongated like a Klimt portrait, her expression chaste, her face, neck, and hands aglow. Over the next few weeks, Teruzzi visited several more times. They met in the hotel sitting rooms. He always addressed her as

Lilliana as Elsa in *Lohengrin*, July 1923. Photographed by Franz Löwy.

"Signorina Lorma" and with the formal "Lei." Her mother was invariably present.

Lilliana was surely flattered by these visits, but she was totally focused on her career. When she left for Cairo in mid-December 1923, she was on her way to "great things," to use her family's phrase, with offers coming in from Montevideo, Oporto, Barcelona, and Madrid. But the season turned into a total debacle. The tenor had fallen ill and, unable to find a strong male voice for the lead parts, management had replaced *La Bohème* and *Manon Lescaut* with *Aida, Andrea Chénier*, and *Norma*. Lilliana, who had never performed any of them before, decided they were "too heavy" for her voice. To take something "too heavy just to be able to sing doesn't pay," her mother explained to her father.[9] She could still sing *Otello*. But another soprano had also been contracted to sing Desdemona, and though, as Lilliana indelicately put it, she had only "a tenth of my talent," she wasn't "going to yield one single performance to her younger, better competitor."[10]

Except for a command performance at the Royal Palace at the outset of her stay, where the king had introduced her to the entire court and paid her high compliments, she had left Egypt not having performed at all. Still, she professed herself undaunted: "They can all go to hell as long, thank God, as my voice is good. . . . We look fine and feel great despite the heartless Camorra."[11]

Upon returning to Milan, she had to face the consequences of having invested so much in that one engagement. Serafin, who was about to leave to take up a position at the Met, offered reassurance. "Maestro, do you think two or three years, will be enough for me here?" Lilliana had asked him. To which he had replied: "Three years!!!! *Sei pazza!* Work hard and it won't be very long."[12]

This had given her the courage to break the ice by arranging a heart-to-heart conversation with Italy's leading impresario, Giuseppe Lusardi. She was told that she had it all, Rose wrote to Isaac, "a beautiful voice, intelligence, gorgeous costumes, and you present yourself very well." Her only drawback was her "apparent wealth." Every impresario Lusardi had tried to "sell" her to "didn't want a rich American unless she put up some money." They all said, "let's take a poor girl with a little less merit."[13] Lilliana had often professed her scorn for the "American girls," whose fathers rented La Fenice or San Carlo for their debut, hired the orchestra, paid for the advertising, bought off reviewers, and in Naples even bribed the Camorra, the local Mafia, to make sure there was no

Lilliana at the Great Pyramids, January 1924

Lilliana Weinman Teruzzi Estate

enemy claque in the auditorium, only to see them whistled off the stage
with shouts of "out with the barbarians."

When Lusardi told her that it would cost her family 20,000–25,000 lire
to front the costs at Bergamo, she stood her ground. Her family was far
from rich, she insisted. Moreover, she had a vocation: "something higher,
nobler" such that "I need it more than the others that need it for bread."[14]

In sum, if she had to, she would front the costs with her own hard-earned money, but she would give it to Lusardi outright, not to some middleman. Lusardi liked how she played her hand. They struck a deal for her to open the season at Bergamo in the new production of Rossini's *William Tell*.

Bergamo inaugurated the opera season in Lombardy, and the Milanese public invariably came. The audience would surely warm to the story of the patriotic struggle of the Swiss against the Habsburgs, the music promised to be divine, and the performance would be covered by all the Milanese media. For Lilliana, this engagement marked a "Napoleonic moment." She had won the contract, she proclaimed, "on my own merit and with everything and everybody against me."[15]

Having committed herself to the performances, Lilliana would now have to practice for the better part of the awfully hot month of August. She and her mother would pass the holidays at the Excelsior Grand Hotel at Varese, one of a cluster of magnificent hotels that had won this small lakeside town its renown as the Versailles of Milan. They invited Maestro Fatuo and his wife to help her rehearse. The Lusardis would be coming through as well, and they were keen to court them. The expenditure for the whole undertaking promised to be high. She wouldn't tell her father how high: "It [is] a very crucial point in my career where we must sacrifice much, but, I pray God, only for a short time."[16]

Teruzzi had his own dragons to slay. When the 27th legislature opened on May 24, 1924, and the parliament convened at Montecitorio, the new deputies got their first glimpse of the political establishment the fascist intransigents were so intent on destroying. Upon entering the immense palace, they must have felt some awkwardness on seeing the Fascist Militia's honor guard flanking the entrance, dwarfed by the rows of colossally tall *carabinieri*. Then they were forced to defer to that incongruous royal couple, the minute Victor Emmanuel III and his Montenegrin giant of a queen, seated as per tradition under the high baldachin at the center of the theater, flanked by the princes of the blood.

From that point, extending outward and up into the galleries, one could find the representatives of the nation, with the senators, distinguished by their blue sashes, on red leather chairs. All of them, senators and deputies, were dressed in black tails and white gloves, except for Cesare Forni, who wore a black shirt and boots and would later pay for his impertinent radicalism by being beaten within an inch of his life by his comrades. The king asked the whole assembly to swear to uphold the Constitution, impressing upon its members that this, the opening day, May 24, was the ninth anniversary of Italy's entrance into the Great War. Italy's parliamentarians would have to redouble their efforts to safeguard the nation's sacrifices. He then processioned out with his entourage, in keeping with the Statues of 1848, leaving the work of governing the nation to the president of the Council of Ministers, Mussolini.

Mussolini began to exercise his lock on parliamentary procedure the very next day. Upon entering the assembly hall, the fascist deputies could measure by the vast expanse of seats they occupied on the right of the chamber how greatly they outnumbered the opposition. Even so, parliamentary protocol operated to protect this miserable minority's right to speak and vote: everybody had to register with the president of the chamber to intervene; the best orators could hold the rostrum and make their points stick, even if they were being hooted down.

One of only twenty military men to have been elected to parliament, Teruzzi was dutiful in his new position. Once again we see him playing a double role: as the stickler for rules, he was assigned to the electoral commission to verify the vote district by district, to check for fraud and other illegalities, and to send the final tally to the chamber for debate and ratification. And as the enforcer, with three equally pugnacious new deputies—Bernardo Amidei-Barbiellini, Ulisse Igliori, and Starace, notorious ex-*squadristi* every one of them—he formed an "advanced patrol" whose mission was to prevent opposition deputies from hiding behind parliamentary privilege and decorum.[17]

The esteemed assembly was buttressed by decades of protocol, civilities, and precedence required to make the law. The fascists' aim was to undermine and disrupt these enshrined conventions. Accordingly, they hovered behind the aisles on the left, stalked the members of the opposition in the corridors, stole their papers, whooped and shouted while they held the rostrum, and threw punches or shoved them as they passed to and from it.

Six days after Parliament opened, on May 30, amid these growing disruptions, Giacomo Matteotti, the thirty-nine-year-old socialist deputy from Polesine, took the rostrum. The chamber's president, a Nationalist Party dignitary turned fascist, the esteemed jurist Alfredo Rocco, had unexpectedly brought the electoral commission's report to certify the April 1924 election results to the floor for the final vote without entertaining the usual debate. The opposition was completely caught off guard. Matteotti didn't like to extemporize. Yet he saw no alternative but to hold the floor. Otherwise, there would be no debate at all.[18]

The fascists now had before them a figure their leadership had known and loathed for years. They knew him from the First World War, when, as a young deputy who had known Mussolini as a fellow socialist, he had been unreservedly neutral. Though exempted from military duty because of illness, he had been called up as a form of punishment and spent almost the entire war period quarantined in a Sicilian military labor camp. They knew him from Polesine, which, like most of the neighboring agricultural provinces, had been overrun by fascist militia. In March 1921, they had captured and tortured him, which he had braved, forcing the fascists to recognize his temper and back off. Since then, he had lived in exile from his hometown. They also knew him as the head of the newly formed Socialist Unitary Party, the abhorred "PUS;" as heir to the esteemed socialist Filippo Turati, and understood that with his strident voice, whiplash rhetoric, agile command of parliamentary procedure, and prestige as an opinion-maker in the anglophone world, he was a far more dangerous antagonist than his aristocratically mannered Milanese mentor. Finally, they knew Matteotti as an incorruptible family man, married to the Roman poet-intellectual Velia Titta, who, along with their three young children, had been sacrificed to his political career and had themselves been threatened.

Matteotti was about to go public with an exposé of old-fashioned political corruption that would accuse leading Milanese fascists, perhaps even Mussolini's brother, Arnaldo, of having accepted American oil company bribes to access the Italian market. Beyond that, Matteotti intended to warn off the socialist trade unions from having anything to do with Mussolini's promises that his regime would create a pro-labor, anti-capitalist front under fascist leadership.[19] Matteotti held the rostrum for the next two hours over shouts and threats. After denouncing the illegalities accompanying the election, saying that Italy had become like Mexico—only then to apologize to the Mexicans—he persevered.

A government whose parliamentary majority had been contrived by fraud and intimidation had no right to govern, no matter what the electoral results showed, he said. The militia was an illegal private army. The Fascist Grand Council was unconstitutional. "You are hurling the country backwards, into absolutism."[20]

Nothing infuriated the fascists more than denying the legitimacy of their electoral victory. Mussolini fumed, his arms crossed and his face set like stone, but his deputies ran riot. "We're in power and we are staying there"—that was only the first shout from the chamber. "We'll teach you to respect us with rifle butts in your backs, you cowardly scum! Long live the Militia! Hireling! Traitor! Demagogue!" Teruzzi was heard yelling two or three times: "Enough." By cutting off the "Gold-Medal" war-hero deputy Count Suardo from speaking, Matteotti had, according to Teruzzi, insulted the officer corps. Showing his usual impetuousness in the face of the enemy, as the exhausted Matteotti came off the podium, Teruzzi rushed at him, only to be pulled back by his comrades.[21] Matteotti, meanwhile, turned to his colleagues and said words to the effect of: "Now you can sign my death warrant," or "Now you can work on commemorating me."

Eleven days later, on June 10, 1924, a Lancia pulled up alongside Matteotti as he walked along the Tiber on the way to his office. Two men, followed by a third, jumped out and pummeled him. The back door flew open, and another yanked him into the back seat. When he continued to resist as they picked up speed to leave Rome, they stabbed and punched him onto the car floor, fracturing his skull and killing him.

Matteotti's disappearance was quickly noticed, and a nationwide search was launched: police, hunters, private investigators, psychics, the man in the street—everybody pitched in. The consternation was global and visceral. It was not that the fascists hadn't killed before. "Cemeteries could be filled with the people killed in the last two or three years," wrote Paolo Valera, known as the Emile Zola of Milan, a popular author and fascist dissident who was promptly expelled from the party for writing this screed: "There had been deputies beaten up, thrown out of windows, dosed with castor oil, attacked with scissors to hack off their beards, knifed, assassinated."[22]

But Matteotti's murder was different. He had just emerged as the public voice of the opposition, and people were horrified at the idea that Italy was in the hands of a terrorist Cheka—like the Bolshevik secret police—that could not only kill with impunity but also cause bodies to disappear. Long before Matteotti's putrefied remains were found in the woods near Quartarella on Rome's then-rural outskirts in mid-August, everybody assumed he was dead. And everybody asked whether Mussolini had ordered his murder. Awakened from its torpor, the opposition began to regroup.

Whether Mussolini explicitly ordered this assault has never been answered conclusively. Ultimately, he admitted to having created the moral and political conditions for the violence and took responsibility for doing so, only to push back, saying that the opposition could do nothing about it. Attilio Teruzzi was also implicated. He had been recorded shouting him down, and he had roughed up Matteotti as he had come down from the rostrum. Enough people knew of the plan to kidnap and beat Matteotti that it is hard to imagine he would not have known of the intention, if not to kill Matteotti, at least to kidnap and beat him close to his last breath. The assassins had passed through the Milan *Fascio* and he knew them all, both from their old hangouts in Milan and their new hangouts in Rome.

Teruzzi could, of course, be counted on for his implacable reserve and for that delicate complicity that made him the ideal confidante. In future years, he would be trusted with settling with Matteotti's widow, Velia, so that she would withdraw her civil suit, not flee abroad, and show her confidence in the fascist state by sending her children through the public school system. Later, he oversaw the payoffs to the killers who, once convicted and released after practically no time in prison, had to be provided for, for years, to keep their silence. And much later Arcnovaldo Bonaccorsi, a fascist militia general and erstwhile friend, alleged that Teruzzi was known to have been involved in Matteotti's murder and may even have arranged it—which explained why Mussolini had not only promoted him but covered up faults that would otherwise have caused his ouster.[23] Whatever the truth, Mussolini found Teruzzi's silence absolute and invaluable.

Teruzzi suffered from being implicated in Matteotti's murder, if for no other reason than that his boss suffered hugely, emotionally as well as politically. The momentum garnered from his overwhelming electoral victory had been lost. Mussolini's best-laid plans to normalize his rule by giving space to the opposition had been upset. The opposition press, far from being co-opted, was once again stirring up national and international opinion to denounce the fascist government's brutality, claiming that it was about to collapse.

Mussolini could only reclaim his authority by kowtowing to the king and the establishment. This meant that he had to remove his head of police, General De Bono, and send him into semi-exile as governor of Tripolitania; he had to fire his two most capable and trusted men, Aldo Finzi, undersecretary at the Interior Ministry, and Cesarino Rossi, his press and propaganda secretary. Finally, he suffered because he had to turn his most important cabinet portfolio, the interior, over to Luigi Federzoni, his colonial minister, an arrogant nationalist beholden to the king. The provincial party bosses were back to their saber rattling, all to the benefit of Roberto Farinacci who, in Parliament and back in Lombardy, agitated to relaunch the revolution, with the fascist militia taking the lead. The corridors around Mussolini's office at Palazzo Chigi were emptied of the usual political sycophants and postulants, leaving the Duce to feel that everyone had abandoned him.[24]

In fact, Mussolini could still count on the strong nerves and warm shoulder of his muse, advisor, and longtime lover, Margherita Sarfatti. His own family, meaning his wife, Rachel, and their three children, had not yet moved to Rome, and on his advice they now left Milan for their summer residence, where they would be more protected should his government come under attack. In any event, Sarfatti's husband, Cesare, had died the previous January, so she was more available than previously. With her refined, affectionate, and helpful sycophancy, Margherita Sarfatti could bolster Mussolini's self-confidence. Whether it was thanks to her good advice or the threats from his own stalwarts or both, he decided not to throw in the towel, which he had been on the verge of doing around June 15. Instead, he staggered on at considerable cost to his health. For the whole month of July, he disappeared from view.[25]

Teruzzi had no lover to console or advise him. With Mussolini out of view, he lacked clear marching orders. Yet it was another turning point. In June, the militia began to mobilize in the provinces, six legions of them. They had no strategy, but their leaders managed to convince the army to give them a slew of weapons to defend the nation from anarchy. Meanwhile, Farinacci and Balbo repaired to their redoubts, swearing that if Mussolini capitulated to the opposition, they would lead a new march on Rome. They organized huge demonstrations, first in Bologna and then in Milan, bringing out tens of thousands. Teruzzi had to be everywhere, traveling back and forth between Milan and Rome, consulting with the Duce, meeting with party bosses and militia leaders, until the PNF Directory after a final meeting in Rome broke up in mid-August in the hope of rest and recuperation with their families.[26] By the time Teruzzi returned to Milan, it was sweltering hot. The mood in the Galleria was hostile. Nobody was wearing fascist insignia. Everybody who was anybody had left the heat of the city for the Riviera, the Alps, or the lake districts, and he intended to follow suit as soon as he could figure out his plans.

Varese is only fifty miles from Milan. Electric trains made the hour-long trip, leaving every hour or so. Lilliana had been at the Excelsior for a week with her mother, practicing in the green silk-papered music room with Maestro Fatuo. Imagine her surprise when Attilio Teruzzi showed up without warning. Whether bravado or abjection had brought him there is hard to say. His impetuousness always smacked of both. Over the following four days, he approached Lilliana at tea time, he talked to her over dessert and coffee, on the terrace, in the gardens. He had fallen in love. She had all the qualities he desired in a mate. Did she feel the same? Could she think of giving up the theater to marry him?[27]

Lilliana was kindly toward this awkward figure, a notorious fascist, but he was the last person any respectable singer would want to be involved with. The Milan opera world had been particularly stricken by Matteotti's murder as the world-famous baritone Titta Ruffo, Matteotti's wife Velia's older brother, was one of their own. When Ruffo received news of his brother-in-law's disappearance, he had rushed back from Buenos Aires to help his sister prepare for the worst.

Lilliana didn't want to offend. She was a guest in a foreign country. All the same, she needed to rehearse for Bergamo. Finally, she told Teruzzi: "Please, I think of you as a friend." He left right away, very angry.[28] We only have her mother's account of what transpired between them, but provincial men were known to conduct imperious, lovelorn courtships like that, and young women to cool their ardor with common good sense.

Lilliana finished her rehearsals for *William Tell* against this unfolding national and personal drama. On August 15, the Feast of the Ascension, Matteotti's body was found close to Rome. Once it was positively identified, Velia prepared the funeral. When she learned that Mussolini wanted to turn the event into a state funeral, she insisted with the interior minister that the family only wanted one thing: to be left in peace to bury their husband, father, brother, and son. She wanted no government ceremonial, no fascist militia escort, and no Blackshirts saluting the bier on the voyage home. She wanted to mourn

as a normal citizen, who fulfills her duties in order to demand her rights; therefore, no special train cars, no reserved seats, no discounts or privileges, no change of course from what is publicly available. If for reasons of public order, there is a need for additional security, then only use Italy's soldiers.[29]

Velia Matteotti did not intend to make a brave political statement to prevent Mussolini's totalitarian urge to expropriate the family's mourning for his political purposes. She had to resist him, for, in his shame, or rather to expiate it, he would continue to assault her and her family's privacy with payouts, admonitions, and offers of protection for the next twenty years.

Lilliana's first performance of *William Tell*, on September 6, 1924, was a triumph. Over the previous half year, her voice had grown beautifully: she was a commanding and tender Mathilde, the Austrian princess who renounces her birthright to embrace her Swiss lover Arnold's cause, steeled by William Tell's unflappable courage, to free Switzerland from the Austrian tyrant Gessler. "All Milan was in the theater, and they were all enthusiastic," Rose wrote to Isaac. There were the usual bouquets of gorgeous, wonderful flowers, telegrams from all her opera friends, and the Milanese papers carried excellent reviews.[30]

None of this had turned Lilliana's head, Rose wanted her lonely husband to know; she was still "daddy's little girl." "She took your picture to the dressing room and showed it to everybody, her Papa, and kissed it before each [time she went] out on the stage."[31]

At the news of Lilliana's success, Teruzzi stopped by her hotel to congratulate her. She was kind and polite. Her career was launched. More than that, she had found her voice. What greater praise could there be in the opera world than that La Lorma could cover the biggest dramatic tenor with the strongest voice or, after she sang Elsa in *Lohengrin* in Genoa at the end of the year, that her voice was a true Wagnerian coloratura, maybe even a spinto, so powerfully did it "shoot" through the orchestra and the auditorium, so "at ease in its upper register."[32]

As Teruzzi nursed his rejection, fascism's tides turned once again. Going into the fall, it still looked as if Mussolini's regime could be toppled. The parliamentary opposition, to impress upon the king that the fascists were violating the constitution, had in June begun a boycott of parliamentary politics. Everyone spoke of it as the Aventine secession, after the protest of the Roman plebs, who, to resist the Patriciate in 464 BCE, withdrew to the Aventine Hill. But their self-imposed exile provoked no nationwide consternation, as the deputies had hoped, much less did it cause the king to use his constitutional right to end Mussolini's mandate and call on another political figure to form a new cabinet. The king had never liked "sordid (political) parties," and he wasn't going to risk his kingship by disturbing the status quo. One after another, the institutional pillars of the Italian state—the Vatican, the military establishment, the worried business elites—took their cues from the king and quietly stepped up to express their support for the prime minister, out of fear of what might happen if he fell.

When the new parliamentary season opened on January 3, Mussolini rallied. The militia leaders who had shown up at his office on the last day of 1924 to accuse him of the "terrible crime" of failing the revolution had jolted him into reestablishing his regime as a full-fledged dictatorship. As the Chamber of Deputies reopened for work and the fascists paraded in singing "Giovinezza," the advanced patrol was ready to tackle the only opposition left in the halls: the seven communist deputies who had not followed the others. They pummeled and kicked them and heaved them out of the building. Teruzzi's constituents at Como headlined their newspaper's coverage of the day's events "Bravo, Teruzzi," and congratulated him for not standing around "with his hands in his pockets."[33]

From the moment Mussolini took the rostrum "to assume full political, moral, historical responsibility for everything that has happened," and to dedicate "all my power and to the exclusion of all else" to destroying the enemies of fascism, he laid out the basis of fascism's totalitarian rule. Might had created right! "If fascism has been simply castor oil and cudgels, and not the magnificent passion of the very flower of Italian youth, the fault is mine! If fascism has been a criminal association, I am the head of that criminal association!" he exclaimed. "Italy wants peace, tranquility and calm industriousness, with love, if possible, and with force, if necessary." He then came to this conclusion: "You can be certain that in forty hours . . . the situation on every front will be clarified." Nobody could doubt that this was the start of something new for Italy. "This is not a personal caprice, a lust to govern, or an ignoble passion," he declared, "only a boundless and mighty love for the nation."[34]

That was January. Four months later, on May 15, 1925, Mussolini—who earlier had not wanted Teruzzi, with his "chestful of medals," to run for deputy to Parliament—appointed him undersecretary of state at the Interior Ministry. The interior minister had always been the Kingdom of Italy's most powerful cabinet position. Italy's conservative founding elite had intended it that way so that, from its control center at Palazzo Braschi in Rome, the same building that housed the offices of the President of the Council of Ministers at the time, Italy's highly centralized state could administer the seventy or so provincial prefects, as well as the national police. From that position, the head of government, whatever his political persuasion, could fiddle in local elections, spy on the opposition, and crack down on public disorder.[35] In 1925, the ministry had recently completed its move into the gigantic Palazzo Viminale, a sign of its growing might and significance.

Mussolini had held the portfolio of interior minister himself until the Matteotti crisis, when he had been forced to step down and name a figure in whom the king had full confidence. That was Luigi Federzoni. A conservative nationalist, Federzoni was already serving in Mussolini's cabinet as minister of the colonies. A war hero and blue-shirted legionnaire at the command of D'Annunzio, he had been willing to join the Fascist Party only, he maintained, out of his belief in Mussolini's political genius, Mr. Tuberose, his friends called him—intoxicating scent but quick to wilt. He was the son of an esteemed Dante scholar, highly cultivated but no intellect himself, at once affable and condescending and always wearing a three-piece suit. As far as Federzoni was concerned, all fascists except for Mussolini were riffraff, incapable of grasping the ethical imperatives underlying Italy's civilizing mission, much less the international struggle Italy would have to undertake to return to its ancient grandeur.[36]

Up until January, Mussolini had kept a foothold in the ministry by appointing Dino Grandi, the ex-*squadrista* from Bologna, a trained lawyer and skilled negotiator who was congenial to Federzoni, as the undersecretary. But Mussolini had also responded to pressure from the intransigents pressing for the "second wave of fascism" by appointing Roberto Farinacci as national secretary of the Fascist Party. Federzoni pushed back: Italy's establishment wanted peace and quiet. He made it clear that the ministry had every intention, going forward, of distinguishing between "responsible elements" and "irresponsible ones" and beginning a massive crackdown on the latter. Farinacci, to make a show of his power, wanted his own man, not the diplomatic Dino Grandi, to police the minister. Mussolini capitulated. In May, he moved Grandi to foreign affairs and, in what passed as a routine move, appointed Teruzzi to replace him as undersecretary at the Interior Ministry.[37]

Because this was a cabinet position, it was subject to the king's approval. On May 19, 1925, according to the release of the state news agency, "His Excellency, the Honorable Cabinet Minister" Attilio Teruzzi had a "cordial meeting" with his "Highness the King" at the Quirinale Palace. There "they recalled intently the African campaigns and episodes of the Italian-Austrian War to which the new Undersecretary, decorated four times with medals of valor, made a significant contribution."[38]

The intransigents were elated. Farinacci's *Cremona Nuova* welcomed the move as the "start of the revolution." The *Corriere* worried on its front page that Teruzzi represented the "extremist wing" of the Fascist Party, maybe even more than Farinacci himself. Teruzzi's Como claque acclaimed him as fascism's "First Assault Minister."[39]

Did the appointment of this "unhinged and criminal creature" signal the rebirth of *squadrismo?* Filippo Turati, Matteotti's mentor and now the leader of the antifascist opposition, was asking his companion Anna Kuliscioff, who was politically the more astute of the two. He and the others should stop "dramatizing," she responded. Once in office, "even the most violent and intransigent" become more "moderate, more reasonable and more prudent."[40] Her point was that Teruzzi was a cog in the wheel, no better or worse than his predecessor, Dino Grandi, who, everybody forgot, had once led Bologna's squads.

Federzoni was unperturbed when his informers told him that Teruzzi had been overheard at the café by Palazzo di Gesù, favored by his Freemasonic brothers, saying, "We have an enemy at the Viminale." He would not have been surprised, or overly concerned if they had overheard him repeating Farinacci's gang's puerile chant: "Farinacci to the Interno (Ministry), Federzoni to Inferno." A man of such "comical officiousness," Federzoni noted in his diary, will only be "a minor nuisance."[41] Sternness and small favors would suffice to bring him around.

Fascist Milan was at once surprised and elated by the appointment, due to take effect in late June. Teruzzi's friends called for a "gastronomic-political" send-off to beat all, that they might "show their love and affection." Planning was adjusted so that at the banquet on June 25, guests would stream into the ground-floor rooms of the Cova on the early side, around 7:30 P.M. That way all the city councilors, as well as the mayor, could come and still make their late-evening meeting at Palazzo Marino. Four hundred people attended, including the whole leadership of the Milan Fascio, the City Council, the Prefect, notables from Como and Lecco, capitalists of various ilk, militia generals, consuls, centurions, and his salt-of-the-earth mother and Professor Amelia, as well as "numerous elegant *signore.*"[42]

The crowd toasted the Duce, the nation, and the Fascist Revolution; it chanted "hip hip hooray"; sang several verses of "Giovinezza"; and dipped black banners and the tricolor to remember the war dead and martyrs. Teruzzi's friend Eugenio Castracane, the organizer, then read the telegram he had solicited from the Duce "to express his affection and love." Mussolini himself never attended banquets, as a matter, he said, of "moral and political rigor." He was in Rome attending to the affairs of the nation. His appreciation was perfectly calibrated: he toasted Teruzzi as "a soldier and fascist, valorous in the great war and loyal in every moment of the fascist revolution, a man like the men I want and am making."[43]

He was a perfect fascist, valorous and loyal, but the jury was still out on whether he had the stuff of a statesman.

9

CONQUERING THE ICE PRINCESS

She loved me for the dangers I had pass'd,
And I loved her that she did pity them.
This only is the witchcraft I have used.

—SHAKESPEARE's *Othello*, Act 1, Scene 3

The first evidence that Teruzzi and Lilliana had resumed contact sur-
faced around the time of his promotion. "I wonder if you know that
Teruzzi became Secretary of State, if you please," Lilliana let drop on
May 19, 1925, at the end of a letter home. He had told her about his promotion two days before the nomination became official, she boasted, and
"he was very sweet to me."[1] Teruzzi had clearly learned from his rejection
at Varese and had turned his courtship into the more tempered, admiring
friendship she seemed to welcome. Since she lived right by the Galleria,
there was no lack of opportunities to run into one another. Her mother
had been in New York for several weeks, and Lilliana was out all the time.
Maybe her mother's absence emboldened him to share the news. A couple
of weeks later, she coyly added, "Can you imagine that Teruzzi is in one
of the most important positions in Italy today?"[2] And who knows, perhaps
she was one of the "numerous elegant ladies" the press described as having
adorned his going-away party at the Cova Restaurant.

Their courtship can be dated to the late summer of 1925. Lilliana had
told him she would vacation at the Hotel Casino, by the seaside at Rapallo,
and he arrived for a stay in the company of his cabinet secretary, Macciotta, and an aide. Unlike the previous August, when he had shown up
unannounced, this time he found a cordial welcome. He was just coming
off an intense first three months as undersecretary and had met with Mussolini one-on-one four times in the last week alone. Lilliana's parents were
both with her—her father was visiting from New York—and all three of

them enjoyed his uncensored talk. Not only that, at the holiday's end, she took the same train as Teruzzi back to Milan, with only his Calabrian aide, Ferdinando Solimena, as their chaperone. In September, Teruzzi came by the Hotel Regina-Rebecchino for lunch or dinner whenever he was in Milan. One afternoon, before heading out on maneuvers with the king, he popped in to show off his fancy general's regalia. He telephoned daily, sometimes three or four times. And once or twice, when she missed his calls or he hadn't told her he was coming to Milan and she wasn't available, he made a jealous scene. Time and again, he pressed her to marry him.[3]

Teruzzi evidently had developed a significant degree of trust in Lilliana's judgments, if by the fall of 1925 he was divulging his political worries to her. And his position in Rome was worrying, indeed. He found himself in the uncomfortable situation of being in service to three commanders, all three of whom were working at cross-purposes. There was Farinacci, the Fascist Party secretary, who wanted to keep the revolution going by stirring up political trouble in the provinces and relied on Teruzzi as his spy in Rome. There was Federzoni, his arrogant, all-knowing superior at the Interior Ministry, who wanted to reestablish law and order by bolstering the power of the central government's prefects to crack down on the local party bosses; he wanted Teruzzi to understand the sense of his directives, as well as apply them to the letter. And there was his willful and implacable Duce, who, at this moment, intended to consolidate his dictatorship over both the party and the state by allying himself with Federzoni; he expected Teruzzi to act like his factotum but also with the dignity of a junior statesman in his cabinet. At the same time, Teruzzi was at the beck and call of an emotional life that became ever more turbulent as he became more and more politically visible, with his sexual escapades making him increasingly vulnerable to blackmail.

He could not have divulged his first infraction to Lilliana. Just after he took up his cabinet position, he was informed by Amalia F., a twenty-one-year-old cashier at a Roman haberdasher, that she was pregnant and he was responsible. When her employer learned of her situation, he fired her. Teruzzi behaved as honorably as the times and his position recommended, and used his new influence to find her a position in the State Telephone Company. Unfortunately, by the time the job became available, her pregnancy showed. The telephone company didn't hire pregnant women, and she was turned away. Meanwhile, her family had disowned her, and she was out on the street. Whether or not this was in fact true, her relatives acted as if it were so and were harassing him to provide for her.[4]

Fortunately, Federzoni himself took an interest in the matter, being keen to avoid a public scandal—and perhaps out of pity for Teruzzi for having fallen prey to this *sciagurata*, this poor wretch of a woman. His was hardly an uncommon male predicament. A solution was found by consulting with his wife. Signora Federzoni—or Gina, as everybody knew her—whom he had met during the war while she was serving as a Red Cross nurse, and who, like other high-born patriotic Italian women, continued to be involved in philanthropic causes. Italian family law was a disgrace on many counts, and especially backward insofar as it did not oblige men to recognize their illegitimate offspring, much less pay for their support. Like other women close to power, she had been pressing Mussolini's new government to update the laws. Meanwhile, she made the welfare of abandoned women and illegitimate children her main philanthropic cause.[5] Gina quietly saw to it that Amalia F. was placed in a shelter for wayward women until she gave birth and the infant was weaned.

These missteps were being managed when Mussolini seized on Teruzzi's sexual indiscretions in the company of Roberto Farinacci and threatened to dismiss him. Once Mussolini appointed Teruzzi as undersecretary, the Fascist Party secretary had expected to deal a further blow to the central government's effort to rein in the Fascist Party at the local level. When Farinacci made a show of his power as head of the PNF by instigating local *squadristi* to attack the opposition, Federzoni, knowing that the conservative establishment was with him, had held firm, and Mussolini had done nothing to interfere. To make certain that Teruzzi toed the line, from the moment he arrived at the Viminale, Federzoni sent one circular after another to the local prefectures instructing the police to use every measure they could, including search warrants, preventive arrests, and jail time, to stop the illegal activities.[6]

From Mussolini's perspective, once Teruzzi became undersecretary, he had to stop being a "Farinaccean." Yet he and Farinacci still regarded one another as "best friends," in Lilliana's words, and saw each other frequently. The easiest, as well as the most pleasurable, occasions were in Rome after hours, when their stays overlapped and they could prowl around the city together.

One of the more innocuous of these outings had brought the two men to the home of Vittoria Lepanto. By 1910, after starring in stage and film productions of *Otello, The Lady of the Camellias, Carmen, Salomé, Lucrezia Borgia,* and the many other melodramatic vehicles created for the leading divas of the time, Lepanto had become Italy's most celebrated silent screen and theater actress. She was in some measure a creation of Gabriele D'Annunzio, who had her star in several of his plays—or, better, her highfalutin stage name belonged to him. His sense of aesthetics was said to have been violated when he was introduced to the one-time painter's model from grubby little Saracinesco in the back hills of Rome. A woman of such stunning beauty had to be liberated from the vulgar birth name Vittorina Clementina Proietti. As the Pygmalion in him flitted from Vittorina to Victory, it settled on Lepanto, the great naval battle of 1571, where the Christian West, united behind the Venetian fleet, had crushed the Turks. The name stuck.

By the time Teruzzi met Vittoria Lepanto, Hollywood imports had destroyed the native film industry, and her notoriety as a *pasionaria*—born of her adulterous attachment to the great love of her life, the brilliant Neapolitan writer and publisher Edoardo Scarfoglio—was largely behind her. Yet, Lepanto was only thirty-one, and her allure was intact. Though she was affianced to Romeo Cametti, the ultra-wealthy builder of Rome's public transport system, she held court on her own, in her three-story art nouveau shrine of a villa on Via Piemonte in the aristo-chic Sallustian District, under the gaze of dozens of portraits of herself. Teruzzi, if not Farinacci, was easy game for D'Annunzian women. The exact favors she, and her circle of friends, offered them—hospitality, sexual liaisons, real estate deals, dishing out dirt about fellow politicos—are hard to know.

When Mussolini called him out for frequenting Vittoria Lepanto, Teruzzi had been undersecretary for six months. He was thunderstruck. The Duce's fantasy that Vittoria Lepanto's bibelot-stuffed home was a bordello and her soirees occasions for orgies was just that, a fantasy. In its misogyny, the police security apparatus saw female debauchery at every turn, and Mussolini was kept well supplied with lurid insinuations. But why focus on this? Had he truly wanted to berate Teruzzi with information provided by informers, he had other, better material. What of the report about the exchanges of favors that had allowed Teruzzi, on a deputy's salary, to move into the large pied-à-terre on Via di Villa Ruffo? And there was the matter of the spacious upper floor apartment in the handsome art nouveau building at Via Emiliani number 1 in Milan—a favor, perhaps, for help on a zoning permit. In sum, Mussolini was in possession of a constantly updated archive of information on his men, though it is not always evident how he used it.

His real interest appears to have been to reveal the extent of Teruzzi's current relationship to Farinacci and make him grovel. Teruzzi fell right into the trap and blamed Farinacci for having brought him to Lepanto's. At that, Mussolini glowered, cut him off, and shouted: "Farinacci is not a member of my cabinet. You'd better learn the ropes."[7]

To hear the details from Lilliana, to whom Teruzzi confided all of this, he had left Mussolini's office with the best of intentions, only to run into Farinacci, who had then convinced him that the whole incident was Federzoni's doing.[8] By the end of their train ride back to Milan, Farinacci had persuaded him that he was being used as a pawn. If they stood together and called Mussolini's bluff by threatening to resign en bloc, his hand would be forced—he would remove Federzoni, take back control of the Interior Ministry, and perhaps solve the impasse by promoting Farinacci himself to that position. The government crisis would thereby advance the cause of the Fascist Revolution.

Farinacci's ultimate goal, as he explained it at another moment, was "to insert the Fascist Revolution in the state," by legalizing "fascist illegality."[9] That had been Teruzzi's position, too, albeit one he had never thought through in any rigorous way. His appointment to the cabinet had made him a part of the governing establishment. But he was still the little guy from Porta Genova, the rough-mannered colonial soldier, an angry apparatchik who still hadn't grasped that his means of advancement no longer lay in the so-called revolution.

It shows just how naïve Teruzzi was that when he arrived home, he drafted a letter of resignation to Mussolini and had his factotum, Luigi Licci, an up-and-coming officer in the *carabinieri*, deliver it to Farinacci in Cremona. And Farinacci, who was using Teruzzi for his own purposes, sent it straight off to Mussolini to demonstrate that Teruzzi's loyalties lay with the Fascist Party instransigents.

When Teruzzi told Lilliana about all of this, she consoled him. He had to be true to himself and the president would forgive him, she said. Mussolini was "only acting like a good father when he ordered him to mend his ways."[10] Otherwise, he would simply have dismissed him outright. As for the letter of resignation he had written at Farinacci's request, she told him he should destroy it immediately. Upon learning that the letter was already in Mussolini's hands, Lilliana urged him to go straight to the president and to confess that he had been misled by Farinacci. And that is what he did.

Mussolini was apparently pacified at seeing Teruzzi squirm like a prodigal son and then pull himself up straight like a generalissimo's aide-de-camp to reaffirm his loyalty. Just as Lilliana had predicted, he forgave his gullible, faithful, and useful lieutenant. And as in any rupture healed by a reavowal of faith and commitment, the bonds of complicity and affection between the two men tightened.

In late October, on the third anniversary of the March on Rome, Teruzzi took his courtship public. It was the biggest celebration of the regime yet, and the Duce was brought back to his political hometown for several days of festivities. The kickoff on October 28 was an early morning review of 35,000 fascist militia men at Sempione Park, and the festivities culminated that evening at Duomo Square with trumpets and drum fanfares, a band concert of patriotic music, and toward midnight, the fly-over of an air squadron exploding red, white, and green fireworks over the cathedral spires.

The event of real long-term significance took place at La Scala that afternoon. Mussolini couldn't bluff when he took the stage to speak. The Milanese bourgeoisie wanted an accounting, facts, a clear plan. He wouldn't bluster: the way forward, he explained, was soberingly difficult. The ruling party had carried out its duty to reimpose a military-like discipline on Italian society, he said. But the larger war—understood as the competition among nations in the world arena—continued. And that called for the state, not the party, to become "the central idea of our movement."

Fascism now meant, "All in the state, nothing outside the state, nothing against the state." Toward that end, in only three years Mussolini's government had issued 3,000 directives. There were so many problems still afoot—the economic recession was only one of them—for his regime to endure: every day was hard work, every day another step. The public at La Scala greeted the speech with rapture, exclaiming, "Duce! Duce!," and the cheers and applause lasted until everybody was exhausted.[11]

Mussolini's visit to Milan also produced the first propaganda news short for nationwide theater release. This came on the heels of the recent re-branding and reorganization of the Italian Cultural and Educational Cinema Institute (LUCE) as the official state propaganda office. We find Teruzzi as co-star, first prancing on horseback alongside Mussolini and then in a cameo shot that revealed "His Excellency Teruzzi" as a personable B-movie actor cavorting with female and male celebrants.[12] Paparazzi captured the Duce in profile, beaming from his open car as he is introduced to Lilliana, in her fox-trimmed coat and clasping a bouquet of long-stemmed roses, who looked for everything like a member of the royal family. Rose's matronly figure found its way into the camera's eye, too, as she watched the Duce address the crowd from her place on the dais beside Mayor Mangiagalli of Milan, her face lit up by an ecstatic smile.[13]

The Weinman women, mother and daughter, had been swept away. "Darlingest Popsie," Rose wrote her husband on October 31, 1925. "Now you must excuse me for not writing this week, I know I did wrong, but I could not help it, it just happened that way . . . Teruzzi was here all week, and was in and out, all the time." Lilliana added: "We had such a thrilling week that we neglected you, you poor darling. We saw Teruzzi on an average of four times a day, and when he wasn't here he was telephoning."[14]

In Rose's account, the visit had its comical moments. Teruzzi wore several different hats—party old guard, militia commander, deputy to Parliament, and undersecretary of state—so he was a principal at all the official banquets being hosted at the Cova Restaurant. Whenever he could, while rushing back and forth between tables, he would snatch a moment to visit with Lilliana, leaving his dinner companions in the lurch and a file of people lined up to see him.

His impetuousness disquieted them. Early that week, when "Teruzzi asked that he wants to marry Babele, I got so flustered that I could not answer," Rose wrote. "What do you say, Popsie?" "The Kid is all gone," she added. On the last day, as Lilliana and her mother swept in for lunch, he "told all his friends, 'You see this young lady, I am going to get engaged to her.' They all congratulated him on his good taste and told him to hurry up as they wanted to give him a nice present."[15]

Lilliana, still guarded about her feelings, as if she hadn't the words to confess to her father that she had fallen head over heels in love, pressed him instead. "By the way, every time Teruzzi comes he proposes and wants to know what you think and how you advise . . . so please, Papa Darlingest, write me a nice, long letter on receipt of this and tell me just what you feel in your heart."[16]

Isaac Weinman had been so stunned in mid-September when his daughter had first sought his advice about the proposal that he was at a loss to answer. He hoped that Tullio Serafin would be able to advise him. He was the Maestro; he would know. Serafin had an only daughter, Vittoria, who was only nine but similarly gifted. What could today's modern father say? "If she loves him, let her go ahead," Serafin advised Isaac. Lilliana would always remain "an artist," he added, for "it is in her blood. She loves her work and either she won't marry him or in a year she will be back on the stage."[17] The latter observation set Isaac's merchant mind to wheeling and dealing: if only Serafin could arrange for her Met debut to take place sooner rather than later.

Isaac agonized until Lilliana's birthday, on November 16, when he delivered a soliloquy as hapless and heart wrenching as the hunchbacked father Rigoletto's, on discovering that the Duke of Modena had seduced his sweet Gilda. "Volumes of books I could dictate to a writer for either way," Isaac opened his birthday letter, then: "My Child, My Heart, do what your heart dictates to you."[18]

Teruzzi happened to be in Milan the Sunday after Isaac's letter arrived, having jumped at the opportunity to impress Lilliana by "representing the government" at the inauguration of La Scala's memorial to Puccini on the first anniversary of his death. At midnight, after attending *Madama Butterfly* with Toscanini conducting—Teruzzi seated in the government box, Lilliana with her mother viewing the opera from the orchestra—he had come by the Regina-Rebecchino expressly to hear Lilliana translate every word of her father's anxiously awaited response. Isaac wrote this:

> What weighs on my heart mostly is this! You are to give up this country, to give up your career, to give up practically everything! But again comes the question! All giving up means *nulla* if my Babele could be happy and which way can anyone say will my Babele be happier! If I only could know one iota that he will be good to you, that you will be happy, how easy I could say: Yes, go and be happy. But God forbid you should not be treated right—then being as good as dead would mean zero to me.[19]

It was two o'clock in the morning when Teruzzi left Lilliana. His eyes had welled with tears as they reread and discussed Isaac's messages. Over lunch with his friends at the Cova the following day, he had shared his recollection of Isaac's words, and then, too he had misted up with emotion. Lilliana was lucky to have such a loving father, they said, and Teruzzi, who had a chance to marry this woman, was a fortunate man. They also bemoaned the impending loss of their man to marriage. His perpetual bachelordom had been their last link to the good old days: to the "first hour" of the revolution when, from the crack of dawn, they were on the march, braving rain-sodden sorties and the Red's ambushes, men alone, living only for one another and for their magnificent love of the motherland.

Why would Teruzzi have risked such a public courtship when so much was at stake both sentimentally and politically? Material circumstances may explain his ardor up to a point. Lilliana lived in the public eye, and it didn't take much cunning to understand that she was susceptible to the *convenienze* due a prima donna—gorgeous bouquets, grand entrances, box seats, and special courtesies. But when it came to choosing his life companion and future mother of his children, perhaps he wished to exhibit the same sense of high purpose and devotion to the cause he had displayed when he had attached himself to Mussolini, and before that to General Vaccari, and before that to the idea of the motherland, and before that to the large, domineering Celestina Rossi. Lilliana was smart, opinionated, and forbidding. When Teruzzi later spoke of Lilliana as his soul mate, his "pure Lily," he regarded her as partaking of the same ideals that undergirded his own intransigence as a fascist. She was what he wanted to be.

He could see that Lilliana believed in family. The daily living proof was her chaperone and mother, the handsome Rose, only two years Teruzzi's senior and a little in love with him herself; she was a thoroughly unassuming woman, wholly dedicated to her family's well-being. And there was her absent but omnipresent father, whose approval Teruzzi anxiously sought, and whom he too would call "Papa" once Isaac had finally succumbed. From the moment Lilliana accepted his courtship, he belonged to a rock-solid foursome, a far cry from his own family life, wracked by his father's sickness and his widowed mother's poverty.

Lilliana believed in her art, hard work, and the success arising from both. Unlike the Italian woman of aristo-bourgeois wealth, she had no family estates, no stash of ancestral porcelain and silver plate, baroque paintings, or antique furniture. She was the pure product of America's grand experiment in meritocracy, entirely self-made, deservedly successful and thus a demonstrably superior person. This was equally true of her hardworking father. It made their wealth perfect for Teruzzi's purposes. Like most fascists, he distinguished the productive wealth of the creative capitalist from the parasitical gains of the speculator or rentier. Beyond that, there was much confusion about how wealthy the Weinmans really were, even in Lilliana's mind. She had the habits of rich expatriates—living in hotels and eating out in fashionable places. But *en famille*, they were always talking about bargains, exchange rates, overspending, and contracts. Isaac was always on tenterhooks when it came to money, never sure what it meant to be rich with so many new fortunes arising out of the speculative bubbles of the 1920s.

As Teruzzi pursued his courtship, he had his informers at the Interior Ministry investigate the real size of Lilliana's family wealth and was satisfied at their conclusion that Isaac was, indeed, a "wealthy American industrialist."[20] He himself loved the good things in life and was more concerned with decorations and the perquisites of service—bespoke suits, a silver cigarette case, a platinum watch, one or two gold rings set with precious stones, and a decorous place to live—than with the accumulation of vast wealth. It was his associates who, upon hearing that I. Walker Weinman Jr. was a famously rich American industrialist, fantasized that the father of his fiancée was as rich as a Croesus, a Rockefeller, or Carnegie, and personally connected to the men of Wall Street.

But beyond her wealth, status, and public desirability, Lilliana had shown that she understood his worries. She was levelheaded and as intuitive as the Duce himself in judging the merits of people. She could also be just as harsh. Upon hearing of Farinacci's deviousness, she had given him a good scolding. He was "about the worst anti-fascist in Italy for going around preaching about the need to *credere, obbedire, combattere*," only to "incite her fiancé to revolt against Mussolini." Mussolini "could change the members of his cabinet every month and in alphabetical order and the people would still follow him blindly; it has evidently escaped your keen political eye," she told Farinacci, "that the Italians are not *fascisti* but Mussolinian." And finally: "You will be expelled from the Party if you criticize [him] like this in six months' time."[21] As she told all this to his face, she appears not to have feared his or any of Attilio's other friends' disapproval. But she had to step in: her fiancé's passions could get the better of him, and he had to do the right thing for himself, his country, and the people who loved him. Lilliana steeled him, so that he could confront Farinacci himself, on his own terms, to tell him, that he had to back off; Farinacci was downright mistaken to think that Federzoni was plotting against him; they all wanted the same great good for Italy, and he, Teruzzi, gave him his word on that, as "a fascist, a friend, and a soldier."[22]

In the quiet of her hotel suite, in the shadow of this big woman and her doting mother, Attilio Teruzzi appears to have found great calm.

Teruzzi had to be impressed by how much Lilliana loved her homeland, the United States, though she hadn't been back home in five years. Yet she also shared his love for Italy and believed in its renewed greatness thanks to fascism and Mussolini. She admired Teruzzi's deeds and the honors being showered on him for his service. And she promised to open the door to American money. Ever since 1924, the US government had, at the behest of its business leaders, been eager to renegotiate the huge debts European states had contracted to fight the war. Teruzzi told Dino Grandi, now undersecretary of foreign affairs, that Isaac would take him to the Ritz and introduce him to Wall Street circles when he passed through New York on his way to Washington, D.C., for the negotiations.[23]

As it happened, the debt question was settled in November 1925. Italy's payments would stretch out over sixty-two years at a rate of interest of less than 1 percent. Within four days, the Morgan Bank lent the Italian government $100 million. And, practically overnight, America went from being caricatured as Uncle Sam, the Shylock, stroking his hands as he squeezed the life-blood out of Lady Italy, to being embraced for its blockbuster films and as home to everything modern. That, of course, included its energetic and rich New Women, who, if they found the right man in the old world, would, shake up stodgy social circles, replenish depleted fortunes, and bring personal bliss to a few lucky men.

Teruzzi was surely familiar with that expression—the "New Woman"—for it was controversial and frequently used in Italy at the time. The women he kept company with—his sister, his friends' wives, and the young women coming of age—were all New Women after an Italian fashion. He had seen this new desire for autonomy and self-fulfillment in his older sister, Amelia, now forty-five and never married, who had become a school teacher and moved to Genoa against their mother's wishes. After post–World War I reforms gave women the right to go into public administration, she had returned to the university to complete her degree, to accredit herself to become a lower-school administrator. Indeed, he could admire those qualities in many women of his generation and background. But they had been forced to choose between family and work, and in many instances, to settle for second-order jobs. Not infrequently, he made their acquaintance when they came to him to ask for favors for their fathers and brothers. Lilliana had their seriousness of purpose, but she was young, with none of their inhibitions. And she was judicious. There was nothing about her of the American flapper or the French *garçonne*.

Above all, Mussolini approved of the match. He had been introduced to Lilliana in Milan and had behaved as a true gallant, with a smooch on the hand and a jaw-splitting smile. The whole thrust now of Mussolini's politics was normalization, and that meant men and women making peace with their private lives, with family, and with religion. He himself—who as a young man had not believed in marriage, and who had married civilly in 1915 only to guarantee his common-law wife, Rachele, and their firstborn, Edda, war benefits if he was killed—was to be remarried to her in a private Catholic ceremony that very December.

This did not mean that Mussolini didn't make a show of his cynicism. He had a gift for acting as if every one of the numerous women in his life was slotted into serving some different, implacably urgent need. The message he delivered to Teruzzi upon being informed of his decision to marry was nothing if not original: "I am happy that you are marrying an American. English women are ugly, French women perverse, Spanish women bring us bad luck, and we get along with America. There are also a few dollars there which doesn't hurt."[24] Teruzzi thought these words were simply brilliant and repeated them to Lilliana. She, who thrived on invidious comparisons if they played to her advantage, took them as wholehearted approbation.

So visible a courtship created its own problems. A few months before, he had been one of the scores of men who at one time or another had speculated about the love life of this substantial and self-regarding young woman. She was a mystery in her relations with men, especially with the omnipresent "Commendatore Ferulli," whom she treated like a kept man. She could be high-handed and disdainful. She was wealthy yet had a reputation for being an erratic tipper and driving a hard bargain. And, even though she had lost ten kilograms from the "butterflies in her stomach," she was a forbidding Valkyrie in a city where most women were slight of build.

How was Teruzzi to establish his possession over this unwieldy figure? Lilliana's appearance of untouchability helped: there was her mother the chaperone, Ferulli the guard dog, and her father as her oft-invoked ideal. As late as the spring of 1925, Lilliana's notion of her life's vocation resonated with that of the Scottish-American prima donna Mary Garden, who in her autobiography spoke of her need for "fierce, stubborn self-assertion," and found the company of men "poor substitutes for the endless fascination of work."[25] Until that fall, intuitively, explicitly, and with fierce rigor, she had embraced an American style of professionalism that her monied family permitted—and had no inclination to exploit her sexuality as a bargaining device.

To the degree that she thought about a marriage partner, she thought in terms of the close-knit coupledom of her parents or of her brilliant friend Rosa Raisa's loving bond with her husband, the handsome Italian baritone Giacomo Rimini or the soprano Edith Mason, married to the conductor Giorgio Polacco, or Serafin and his wife, the Polish soprano Elena Rakowska, who had continued her career as a Wagnerian, only less intensely. Lilliana often spoke scornfully of women who abandoned their careers for marital bliss, to wed wealthy businessmen or aristocrats as a way to cover up the real truth of their careers having reached a dead end.

What logic, then, permitted Lilliana to open herself up to Teruzzi's courtship? The same, it appears, that she brought to her career. She held him to her same high standards and compelled him to conduct his courtship with a deference and respect he had never shown in his previous amorous undertakings. The notion that she would consummate their relationship in any conventional way before they were married was out of the question. She had dated Moe and Lou, at sixteen, and made out with them, but here in Italy it was different. Maybe it was the age difference or the gaping gulf between his sexual experience and hers or some ideal that swept them both up, that they wanted their bond to be pure. Or maybe it was simply the proximity of her mother and Lilliana's perception that in Italy, chastity at marriage had some overweening cultural value. Anyway, once, when he started to follow her into the bedroom, she gave him a good scolding, and he didn't try that again.[26]

Teruzzi was left to manage the sexual enigma posed by this chaste American diva. And it was not simple: his erotic escapades had always been central to the cock-of-the-walk conviviality of the Galleria. Not being able to satisfy his friends' inquisitiveness on that score, he left himself open to their taunts. At his response that Lilliana was "pure" in the sense that fascists were "pure," we can imagine them responding with the tedious refrain: all women are angels or whores, not even the Virgin Mary was a virgin.

10

A FASCIST WEDDING

I want the triumph!
I want love!

—THE UNKNOWN PRINCE, Puccini's *Turandot*, Act 1

Throughout Attilio Teruzzi's dogged courtship, Lilliana managed her career as if it were her sole life passion. In the fall of 1925, she could boast of having made two major breakthroughs. The first occurred in September, when Emma Carelli, the director of the venerable Costanzi Theater, signed her to open the winter season at Rome's premier opera house, singing *Bohème*, *Otello*, and *La cena delle beffe*. She was especially proud of having negotiated the second contract herself, which scheduled her to perform at the Royal Theater of Madrid in early December.

Isaac was still withholding his permission. He needed more time to study the man closely, he said, and planned to do so when he came to Italy in January for he had misgivings: "If I would know that he will treat you like an American husband I would say quickly yes, yes. . . . [Will] he be to you what we call a companion, or will he be his Excellency and you simply a wife?"[1]

Lilliana didn't register the wisdom of her father's questions; she responded flippantly: "you should be able to face everybody joyously when I have the contracts of two of the most important theaters in Europe in my pocket." Gatti-Casazza continued to say "complimentary things" about her; Serafin was enthusiastic for her future. In short, she admonished him, "You ought to laugh and sing the whole time live-long day like Mother and I do. Thank God a million times I never felt happier about my future."[2] Still, they left it that the matter would be decided in the new year, once he arrived in Italy.

When the Madrid engagement was called off and the whole season canceled because the construction of the new subway system had caused giant cracks in the opera house's foundations, Isaac took it as a bad omen.[3] Timing was everything. Lusardi, the Milanese impresario who had given her such good advice, had died suddenly the previous spring, and his son-in-law and heir was an incompetent. Serafin was more and more occupied with his newest protégée Rosa Ponselle, an Italian-American prodigy. Gatti-Casazza had sent her to him in 1924, and he was coaxing her to sing *La Norma*, assuming she overcame her paralyzing stage fright. Nonetheless, Gatti-Casazza was still "desperate to get American singers." This was Lilliana's moment, then. She needed to make "a big hit in Rome." Get "a professional press agent," her father urged her. "Have SET [*Sua Eminenza Teruzzi*] get some great celebrities at the performances." They should emphasize that she was the first American to sing in the capital since the Italian war debt had been negotiated. "Write the American ambassador, use all means to do it . . . it will make a good story for here."[4]

At another moment Ferulli would have handled everything. But he was nowhere to be found. When Lilliana had told him about Teruzzi in September, it was a "great shock" to him, and he had called it "all nonsense." He wrote her father that it was a "great calamity," fumed about having wasted five years of his life, and demanded compensation, if for that reason she intended to break her contract with him.[5] Maybe it was in October that he had been overheard at a café in the Galleria grousing that "Lilliana Lorma didn't need Teruzzi; she was bigger than he would ever be." A couple of hours later, a friend had tipped him off that Teruzzi was out to get him, and he had slipped away and boarded the first train to Paris.[6]

Though Lilliana had no clue about these events at the time, she had already settled in her mind that "in the future we will arrange things differently with Ferulli." Rome was not a problem, she reassured her father: "Teruzzi will help me there."[7] The date for her debut at the Costanzi had been pushed up a few days, so it was mere coincidence that on December 16, two years to the day from when she first met Teruzzi, she left Milan on the night train to Rome. Once there, she waited ten days to tell her father the baldest lie of her life:

Upon my arrival in the sleeper the 17th of December with all the precautions of this world, as mother will corroborate me,

I caught a most dreadful cold, and in my very good fortune, as
the *Bohème* was such a fiasco that not even a Melba in her prime
could have made it a success. I begged Carelli for one day to
stay in bed, which she refused me, as she hoped that Teruzzi
would come and beg for me. He did nothing of the kind, and
she wired for somebody to come from Milano who came and in
good condition was one hundred times worse than I with influenza
and a very heavy bronchial cough.[8]

Not only did she not sing *La Bohème*, she didn't sing the scheduled
Otello either. Maybe she had the sniffles when she arrived, but it is clear
that she exaggerated her illness. Thereafter, she refused, on the professionally inexcusable grounds that the production was not good enough for
her, under the influence of fascist gossip about the current vicissitudes of
the Roman opera world.

It turned out that Emma Carelli had signed Lilliana Lorma up for the
Costanzi Theater knowing full well of her relationship with Teruzzi. Her
hope was that with his patronage, she would obtain the big government
subsidy she desperately needed to turn around the financially ailing theater. It was the talk of the town that Mussolini himself was invested in
giving Rome an opera with the world-class status of La Scala, and the
"two-legged lioness," as D'Annunzio dubbed the redoubtable ex-opera
diva Carelli, intended to direct it. But others were conniving against her,
and Lilliana had been led to fear that they would organize claques to boo
the performances. Whether true or not, the upshot, Rose wrote Isaac, was
that "the season was going to hell. Carelli was losing her shirt." "We were
at the second performance of *Otello*. [Teruzzi] took us in the government
box! And the house was empty. We will talk everything over when you come
here."[9] Lilliana added a final epistolary flourish: "Here in Rome, we have
been having a really glorious time. We have been entertained at dinner
by some very lovely people. . . . We have been a number of times to the
Chamber of Deputies to hear Mussolini speak. We have a gorgeous apartment at the very nicest hotel and not paying much as T got it for us."[10]

Isaac arrived in late January, only to be faced with a fait accompli. Teruzzi showed up at the hotel at midnight in full dress uniform, brought gifts
for the whole family, and stayed to talk until four o'clock in the morning.
Isaac wanted to get to know Teruzzi better and offered to stay in Italy for a
few more months. That would not do: Lilliana had promised Teruzzi an

answer in January. So she orchestrated things such that old man Ohl-baum, her mother's father, who was sick with cancer and undergoing treatment in Vienna, who had never said no to his first and favorite grand-child, should play the part of the family patriarch and give his blessing to the marriage. And Isaac, who had always been at his manipulative old father-in-law's beck and call, capitulated.[11]

Teruzzi was a stickler for all the formalities of rank. Had he still been in the military, his commanding officer would have signed off on the nup-tials. As a cabinet officer, it was the king's role. But the Duce was his true commander. Mussolini hadn't officially met her yet, but to signal his ap-proval, he sent Lilliana via Teruzzi the signed autograph he gave to every-body who visited his office. Lilliana wrote a thank-you note in her big hand running on three pages, expressing her gratitude for the "preziosa dedica," for his kindness and goodness, and also to convey her hope that she could "prove herself worthy of his expectations, at the side of his most faithful of collaborators, from whom, each day, she learned more about the country in which she was guest."[12] On March 17, the couple finalized their engagement with a visit to his office.

On March 19, New Yorkers who read the tabloids could learn that "girl singer leaves stage to wed hero" and that Lilliana Lorma had "cancelled her opera contracts and retired from the stage" to marry General Attilio Teruzzi, "one of Premier Mussolini's most intimate friends," and so on.[13] Renouncing her career had always been a condition for the betrothal, though why he made it so and why she accepted, is not self-evident. True, few women had professions at the time, and the wives of government no-tables, if they were women of talent, used their gifts to adorn society by doing charitable work, by painting or writing, or simply by being present on social occasions. But there was no law there, and one might have ex-pected fascism with its own New Women, who welcomed "the very intel-ligent" fiancée of the undersecretary of state as a breath of fresh air, to be less conventional. One suspects that Teruzzi's insistence reflected his old-fashioned sense of honor. The garrison commander's wife had to be un-impeachable and always present. His insistence also had something of the melodramatic fantasy: when a man of power had won the showgirl's hand, he demonstrated his conquest by removing her from the stage.

What Lilliana thought she was doing is harder to know. She had found negotiating her own contracts the previous fall emotionally exhausting. She would still sing and still intended to take lessons and practice, but it would be a relief to be freed of the burden of performing professionally. Or maybe, she just intended to put her career on hold. For now, her duty was to fulfill their conjoined ideals. Her passionate idealism had a new cause, akin to her vocation as an artist. All of her life she had been training for the stage, and here was her chance to shine on the world stage.

"Friends talk about how wonderful Lily Weinman is—how much richer it is to have your 'ideals' not like New York flappers or Jazz boys," Isaac wrote her on his return to New York. In the end, Isaac had embraced both his future son-in-law and his cause. "You can tell Attilio that I haven't as yet stopped talking here about Mussolini," he wrote, "and believe me people listen with both ears what a great Man he is and by God how quickly they get converted to love him and idolize him."[14]

In 1923, the fascists had established April 21, the Birth of Rome (753 BCE), as a national holiday in place of socialist May Day, the workers' holiday, which they banned. In April 1926, in preparation for the third celebration of that date, Lilliana Weinman traded her ideal of making a grand entrance into the world of opera for the thrill of mounting the celebrity train as the fiancée of Mussolini's undersecretary of the interior. Teruzzi was to officiate the commemorative events in Como, and he begged her to come along. Lilliana and her mother had never heard him speak before. They would stop over in Milan on the way to his home district. Lilliana, as usual, shared all of the details with her father. As she boarded the train, "I carried dozens and dozens of long red roses which Attilio's friends sent me and looked much more the prima donna now than before." For the first time, she saw the whole political force of the regime turned out for her future husband, and was overwhelmed, in her telling, by "one of the greatest emotions of my life."[15]

At Milan, they were met at the station like royalty and conducted to their first appointment. It was the Duchess of Aosta who told them that her husband, Teruzzi's commander in World War I, remembered him as one of the most responsible of his officers. Teruzzi, the duke had said, "was like a cousin to me." They went to the Lyrical Theater to hear Farinacci, and thousands of people shout, "Viva Mussolini," "Viva Farinacci," "Viva Teruzzi." Afterward, thousands of people gathered at Farinacci's hotel and, seeing Teruzzi on the balcony with him, yelled for him to speak, only to hear him tell the crowd: "I am sorry to disappoint you, but I cannot keep my fiancée waiting. I am going to lunch with her." When he came down from the balcony, the two of them were "'bombarded' with flowers."[16]

While at Milan, Lilliana had also gone on her own to lunch at Margherita Sarfatti's and returned the invitation by taking her to the Cova, where, she wrote her father, "they created a great stir." At Como, 20,000 people bearing "baskets and bouquets of flowers in countless numbers" stood under torrential rain to hear Teruzzi speak. Lilliana and her mother stood beside him "like royalty." He was "a really magnificent orator" and kept the people for more than an hour. They left for nearby Gallarate, a "notoriously red town before Attilio took it over," Lilliana commented, where he visited "all of the charitable institutions." And well he might have, for the once booming textile town was now deeply economically depressed, the socialist trade unions had been outlawed, worker wages had been slashed, and the fascists were making a bid to come across as the working people's protectors by setting up their own class-collaborationist unions.

"Teruzzi made another wonderful speech about 'Capital and Labor,'" Lilliana crowed. "Dozens of bouquets were given me." Enrico Stucchi, the owner of the local silk textile mill, Italy's largest, held a banquet in Teruzzi's honor, entertaining them "on a scale that I have never seen before."[17] Lilliana had scarcely given up her career, and she seemed to be playing the star role on a new and far larger stage.

The courtship had been conducted so impetuously that the couple wavered about how soon to set the wedding date. Lilliana wanted it later, given her father's schedule, to savor the pleasure of being affianced with no other obligations but to plan the wedding. And why not? She suggested it take place in the fall, around November 16, to coincide with her twenty-seventh birthday.

But Teruzzi pressed for it to happen as quickly as possible. Life experience had turned him into a *putschist*. Timing was everything: the Duce had been the target of two assassination attempts in the last year alone, and he felt he had no time to lose. The most recent and frightful attempt had taken place on April 7 when a crazy English woman had barely missed killing him. He had escaped death only by turning his face at the right moment so that the bullet had grazed his nose instead of lodging in his head. With debts piling up and a couple of ongoing love affairs he would have to end, Teruzzi felt the sooner he settled the marriage matter, the better. The couple compromised and set the date for June 24.

Both agreed that their wedding would be an affair of state. They would abide by all the legal and political protocols, of course, and send all the

The betrothed, spring 1926

right political and social signals. It had to be expensive—her family would bear the full costs—impressive, and tasteful, as well as entertaining. The regime's expanding elite would be invited by the hundreds, but so would family and friends. The couple wanted their nuptials to be amply publicized by the press. By that time, they had a good sense of how to script their story: Lilliana wished to signal that the rising star Lilliana Lorma had left the stage to marry a key member of Mussolini's cabinet, and Teruzzi that he had made a brilliant conquest for himself and for his government with this marriage to a wealthy and attractive American woman. The wedding invitation, with a humorous sketch drawn by one of Teruzzi's Milanese artist friends, showed clunky cherubs unfurling a banner that bound together the stars and stripes with the Roman axe and lictors, joining American optimism and fascist idealism, a prima donna and a war hero, love and politics.[18]

It was a given, since Mussolini had just married in the Church and the regime had recently become very interested in demonstrating its Catholic face, that the couple would have two wedding ceremonies. The civil ceremony would be held at the Campidoglio and officiated by Filippo Cremonesi, the governor of Rome. The Church wedding was a more complicated operation. Lilliana had been forewarned of this prospect and had dismissed it. At worst, if she had to become a Catholic, it would be pro forma. It could even be good for her career, she flippantly told her father: look at how much being Catholic had helped John McCormack, the renowned Irish tenor's career.[19]

In any case, the mixed marriage didn't appear to be an obvious problem. Marriages between Catholics and Jews had become more common in Italy since the war. In fact, because people saw Lilliana first and foremost as an American, and because her family didn't go to synagogue or celebrate the Jewish holidays in a public way, they might not even have registered that she was Jewish. In any case, nobody would have expected her to convert. Most of Teruzzi's party comrades were anticlerical in one measure or another and had married in civil ceremonies. For Teruzzi, the fact that the brilliant, wealthy, and worldly Margherita Sarfatti, Mussolini's helpmate and lover, was Jewish and nobody seemed to care had to have weighed in his decision to be indifferent. Perhaps he considered Lilliana's lightly worn Jewishness a plus: he could believe she was his Sarfatti. As far as Mussolini was concerned, there was no issue, not at the time. To him, too, Lilliana was an American.

For the purposes of a Church marriage, however, Lilliana was an infidel, meaning she was of another faith, and she would need a dispensation from the papacy, through the Vicariate, the office of the Archdiocese of Rome, to marry in church. For that, she had to learn her catechism and take an oath to baptize her children and uphold her husband's religious inclinations. She had several meetings with the archdiocesan registrar, Monsignor Giuseppe Candidori, who was touched by her religious sensibility and family feelings and certified the dispensation.[20]

None of that was public, of course. However, their decision to wed at the Basilica of Santa Maria degli Angeli made a clear statement about the fascist social world's slide toward Catholicism and the monarchy. The royal family had used the basilica for their family baptisms, marriages, and funerals since 1896, when the Prince of Naples and heir to the throne, Victor Emmanuel, had wed Princess Elena. Since the Armistice, it had become a kind of church of state, as the government had decided to honor its fallen generals by burying them in the basilica's hallowed crypts. Teruzzi would be the first fascist statesman to use the basilica to marry. They would not stand before the high altar, of course, so sumptuous and immense, nor celebrate their nuptials with a High Mass. The elegant little chapel of the Epiphany just off the central nave, with a more restrained religious service, would be perfect for their purposes. The custom, following Victor Emmanuel's example, was for the civil marriage to be given precedence over the religious rites. But the Church considered it a sin for the couple to consummate their union before it had blessed it, so the civil and religious rites had to take place on the same day. Two weddings, then, with two ceremonies, two sets of witnesses, two wardrobes, and several trips back and forth between the Hotel Plaza on Via Veneto, the Campidoglio and the basilica. It made for a long wedding day.

They must have discussed the choice of witnesses at length. Once they had secured Mussolini for the civil wedding—a real coup since he professed to despise ceremonies—they carefully selected their superiors in rank as the other witnesses. Teruzzi chose Federzoni, and when at the last minute Federzoni was indisposed, he was replaced by Giacomo Suardo, the undersecretary of Mussolini's cabinet. Lilliana's witnesses were the American ambassador, Henry Prather Fletcher, and Teruzzi's friend and fellow cabinet minister Giovanni Giuriati. For the Church wedding, the groom's witnesses were the Fascist Party Secretary Augusto Turati and the Militia General Ettore Varini, and the bride's were her mentor Tullio Serafin and General Vaccari, who was now commander of the Army Corps of Rome. Vaccari had recently married the young Veronese countess Irene de Bernini and, as of March 1926, had become a Fascist Party member.

Isaac finessed the question of the financial arrangements for his daughter. Dowries had become passé, even in the military. His aim in any case was to make sure Lilliana had complete economic autonomy in the marriage. And so he settled a rich sum on her—10,000 lire a month would be deposited in her bank account in Rome, which at the time was perhaps twice Teruzzi's monthly salary.

On the day of the wedding, the *Popolo d'Italia* ran its first-ever society news item to announce that "our brave colleague and friend, Attilio Teruzzi—Undersecretary of State of the Interior—was united today in marriage in Rome with Miss Lilliana Weinman, daughter of the great American industrialist I. Walker Weinman." The *Carnet Mondaine*, the Roman copycat of the Parisian magazine, covered the marriage as the "social-political" event of the season. There were six hundred guests at the reception, including sixty friends and relatives of the bride from New York and illustrious personages from outside Rome, notably Gino Olivetti and Antonio Stefano Benni, Milanese men who represented the apex of Italian capitalism.[21]

It was the custom to give and display lavish gifts at the wedding, with cards from their donors attached. The most remarked upon was the antique silver jewelry box studded with the Italian tricolor in rubies, emeralds, and crystals given to the couple by Mussolini, and the most conspicuous, the "artistic silver dinner service for twelve from the PNF Directory." Lilliana overheard someone valuing the total at "$100,000, if the estimate takes into account the weight of their metal ore and carets." That wasn't counting fifty gifts that had had no name on them; two hundred floral arrangements presented in silver, porcelain, and crystal vases; and the envelopes stuffed with banknotes that several of the groom's comrades slipped into his pocket.[22]

The *New York Times* society page, to signal the novelty of this particular match, called it a "Fascist Wedding in Rome."[23] The civil ceremony started at 8:45 A.M. sharp in the Red Room of the Campidoglio. Lilliana, twenty pounds lighter than in her opera days, wore rose pink georgette crepe with a sheer silk capelet. She looked majestic beside Teruzzi, who made a show of wearing a plain black shirt decorated with only his silver and bronze medals, dress pants, brightly shined shoes, and the fascist fez. The central figure was of course the Duce himself, in top hat and morning suit, whose constant twitching made him a blurry figure in the photographs.

At noon, the bridal party made its way to Santa Maria degli Angeli. Teruzzi had his mother-in-law by his side now and pulled out the wedding bands, asking her to "kiss these rings, bless them." Then he added, "I've arranged this marriage so that God alone can dissolve it."[24] The chapel was decorated discreetly, with velvet drapery and magnificent flower arrangements to distract from the tormented Christ on the cross. Maestro Antonelli instructed the piano and string quintet to play Mendelssohn's "Wedding March" as the bride entered, accompanied by her father. The young children of Federzoni and Count Gasparini, the current governor to Eritrea, were the pages, holding up her long train. Monsignor Giovannelli, the parish priest, blessed the rings to the music of Thomé's *andante*. As Maestro Antonelli's quintet picked up again with Mendelssohn's *finale*, the bride and groom exited the church.

Teruzzi looked exhausted. Once outside, they were met with the "hip hip hoorays" of the Vangardisti, the boys' auxiliary of the Railroad Militiamen's unit of Rome, named in honor of Enrico Toti, the heroic civilian amputee who, as he fell to shellfire on the Carso, with his last breath, threw his crutch at the enemy. That was Teruzzi's touch. The war was never far from his mind.

Back in his home constituency of Como, Teruzzi's political protégé Tarabini practically wept as he editorialized about losing his patron to marriage. Yet it was right, Tarabini concluded, "to find personal happiness after the war and revolution." Teruzzi should know that his local comrades were still "as close to him on this day of joy as during the days of struggle."[25]

At ten o'clock that evening, after their families had accompanied the newlyweds to the train station and waved them off on their honeymoon, Lilliana and Teruzzi were finally alone. They settled into the presidential train car, offered them by Mussolini, and talked for hours about the events of the day. Lilliana went into the bedroom suite and put on her beautiful nightgown, and Teruzzi joined her. When they had consummated the marriage, they stood at the window, and he gathered her in his arms.

Everybody had been singing arias from *Turandot* that spring, after it premiered at La Scala on April 25, with Toscanini conducting—and Teruzzi and Lilliana in the government box. It had become their little joke that she was the Ice Princess who, in order to reject her many suitors, subjects them to riddles and executes them when they fail, only to meet her match in the Unknown Prince, the impetuous Prince Calaf. As the train click-clacked through the Apennines toward dawn, he sang Calaf's aria: "the stars atremble with love and hope." He pressed his "name on her lips with a passionate kiss." "Vanish, o night! Set, stars! Set, stars! At dawn, I will triumph! I will triumph! I will triumph!"[26]

The next morning, unbeknownst to Lilliana, her husband, doting, grateful, and incredulous at his good fortune, wrote to his mother-in-law to thank her for "the precious gift of this flower of a child."[27]

Mitteleuropa was the fashionable travel destination of the moment. The Locarno Pact of 1925, which Mussolini helped broker, allied Italy with France and Great Britain to bring Germany into the League of Nations and thereby signal the true beginning of the postwar era. The couple's ten-day honeymoon would take them to Venice and Trieste and then on to Vienna, Budapest, Prague, and Berlin. Beyond fighting them during World War I, Teruzzi had never had any contact with the German-speaking people before. On the way, Lilliana had her first concrete glimpse of his war experience. At their stopover in Trieste, they drove out to the giant skull-filled ossuary at Castagnevizza and then on to the acre upon acre of cemetery at Redipuglia, where 30,000 of his war comrades lay buried under the flinty shards of the battlefield. Who knows what Lilliana made of it? After touring the final resting places, bizarrely decorated with crucifixes, silk and straw flowers, barbed wire sculptures, spent shells, and glass-encased photographs of the dead, Teruzzi telegrammed General Vaccari to "pay moving tribute love (to the) unforgettable dead, to Barletta's everlasting glory and to his General's."[28]

Now he tried to put the war behind him. The newlyweds were passionately in love. For the next ten days, between her father, his business contacts, and the Italian diplomatic service, the couple was treated like royalty.

When they returned to Rome, hard work awaited. Mussolini had ousted Farinacci in April 1926, and Augusto Turati, the new party secretary, ran a tighter ship. Under Teruzzi, the Interior Ministry often had equivocated when carrying out Federzoni's orders to crack down on the ongoing illegalities of local *squadristi*, but Turati's regime brought in a new level of oversight. It wasn't just a question of obedience. None of the local party bosses would admit that the squads still existed or, if they did, that they made any trouble, and Mussolini still worked his own extra-ministerial channels to wheel and deal locally. True, Teruzzi still saw Farinacci as a good friend, more than he admitted to Mussolini, who had practically exiled him from the capital. But he no longer acted the part of the intransigent: he had become unequivocally loyal to Mussolini, to his office, and, by extension, to his minister and soon-to-be family friend, Federzoni.

Time moved fast now as the couple settled down. Lilliana, who set the pace for their social life, turned every event they attended into an opportunity to signal their status as fascism's new notables. She made the most of the Horseshow at Stresa, for members of the international smart set, where the foreign press reported they sat with Crown Prince Umberto in the royal box and attended the grand ball in the company of the Countesses Calvi di Bergolo and Sant'Elia. In humble Lecco, her husband's home constituency, she conspicuously donated 3,000 lire, her father's "dowry gift," to the poor.[29] Fall saw a well-publicized visit to D'Annunzio, who, in return for Teruzzi's satisfying his latest whim—to obtain a fascist membership card from Pescara, his hometown, backdated to the time of the revolution—worked his magic on the press by hailing the couple as leading patrons of the modern arts.[30]

Rome, not Milan, had become the cultural and social citadel of fascism. And between the all-male Vatican, the high state functionaries with their important wives, the papal aristocracy, the court nobility around the house of Savoy, and a growing number of commoners ennobled for their endeavors, what constituted "good society" was not at all self-evident.

Lilliana quickly acquired a keen sense of the people to know, places to live, and the *convenienze* of her new status—whether it was the discounted train ticket for the public official and his family, sourcing brocade to cover the divans, or the little gift, birthday telegram, postcard, or publicity gained from cultivating foreign correspondents. Above all, she grasped the need to connect with the high-placed women who were angling through their salons, journals, and charitable undertakings to find a new voice for women—and for the children and indigent on whose behalf they spoke—in the quickly consolidating regime. The young American was an attractive figure. Aside from having demonstrated that with the right muse even the most lubricious old wolf could be tamed, she was a rare talent and a promising recruit for their good works.

She could not avoid attaching herself to Margherita Sarfatti, who made a habit of cultivating Mussolini's favorites and had become well acquainted with Teruzzi by then. Sarfatti's thoughts on Italian colonialism had ripened since her visit to Tunisia in 1924. Fascism was once again looking for a core concept to guide it, and she had put forward her view as to why Italian settlers had proved such inept imperialists in the small book she had written on the subject, *Tunisaica* (for which Mussolini, under the alias Latinus, had written a preface). Fascist imperialism was the answer.[31] Listening to Teruzzi, it was clear he knew far more about colonial problems than his simple soldier demeanor let on. Over the course of the past year, Sarfatti felt her interest in him had been validated. Not only had he become a statesman, he had married a cultivated American woman. Sarfatti's daughter, Fiammetta, liked Lilliana, too. She was a precocious twenty-year-old, and Lilliana, at twenty-seven, offered an appealing model of a talented, self-confident, and cosmopolitan young woman who was both genuinely in love with and doted upon by her powerful husband. Both Teruzzis were welcome guests at Margherita's salon whenever they could get there.[32]

But Lilliana was more genuinely attached to Gina Federzoni, a kinder person, whose marriage, Lilliana thought, resembled hers in a number of ways. Gina was sixteen years her husband's junior, and they were true soul mates. Gina was descended on her mother's side from the Austrian Jewish physician Taussig, ennobled by the Grand Duke of Tuscany in 1834, and given the name de Bodonia. Gina's father, the well-known engineer and artist Raffaele Ferri-Melotti, a gentile, when he redid his estate house at Crespellano in Bologna after his marriage, had added over the entryway the Taussig de Bodonia's Star of David to the Ferri's iron armor and the Melotti's apples.[33] The fact that Gina's branch of the family had converted to Catholicism and Gina and her husband were devout Catholics didn't lessen Lilliana's sense of affinity. Gina's cousin, Leopoldo Taussig, was the director of the Roman branch of the Banca d'America e d'Italia, Lilliana's banker, and she was friends with the flirtatious Senator Teodoro Mayer, Mussolini's financial advisor—and soon to be Lilliana's.

Lilliana was right to think that these women's opinions mattered. Fascist Rome was a gossipy place, and it was a commonplace, fed by both the women and the men, that Mussolini had a particular sympathy for Teruzzi. When the onetime futurist Settimelli wrote a fanciful exposé of the half dozen men he despised in public life and the half dozen he adored, he included as an example of the latter the "likeable, passionate, simple, cheerful, balanced" officer whom he had met long ago at the Savini Café. "The fascists love Teruzzi," he wrote. "They love the brave solder who spilled real blood for the Fatherland on Italian soil and in distant colonies; they love his spark and steely temperament. Not a drop of pedantry, intellectual arrogance, professorial nitpicking. He is our Duce's enthusiast. He has all of Mussolini's esteem."[34]

Mussolini's esteem, or better yet, his reliance on Teruzzi, had only grown over the summer and fall of 1926. On September 16, there had been another assassination attempt, the third since August 1924, this time at the hands of an anarchist whose bomb had landed just wide of his limousine, wounding several passersby. Then, on October 28 in Bologna, Mussolini had barely escaped a fourth assassination attempt. The Bolognese fascists in his escort had immediately massacred the unlikely perpetrator, Anteo Zamboni, a local anarchist's pudgy sixteen-year-old son. There were rumors that it was an inside job, but nothing could be proven. The minister of the interior was responsible for security, so it was logical that the party intransigents should exploit this latest deed to oust Federzoni.[35] By now, Mussolini wanted to take back the ministerial portfolio; he had begun to collect cabinet positions, as much from a mania for control as to show off his competence in all walks of government. No portfolio was more important to extending his grip over day-to-day policing than that of the Interior Ministry. It was not in his interest this time to rebuff the intransigents' demands to put a true fascist in charge.

Teruzzi turned out to be a stalwart. Upon hearing that Federzoni was in trouble, he had rushed back to Rome from northern Italy to "defend" him. As Lilliana wrote her father: "When things looked very black for him, Attilio gave him proof of esteem, friendship and support which he appreciated beyond bounds."[36] Mussolini postponed replacing Federzoni, not needing to offend an invaluable ally. On November 6, when he did finally assume Federzoni's position, he moved him back to the position he had held in the Colonial Ministry from 1922 to 1924. Italy's imperial mission had been badly neglected since the Matteotti crisis; the nation was once more at war with the Sanusi, and nobody was better suited to take the crisis in hand.

Teruzzi was rewarded for his loyalty. "Attilio and I go to Cyrenaica to govern there as Vice Roy and Vice Reine," Lilliana wrote her father on November 6, 1926, "the youngest couple for that position in the History of

Italy and perhaps any other Nation." Her enthusiasm was palpable: "Attilio's position is strengthened politically one thousand percent." Giuseppe Volpi (now the finance minister and one of Italy's wealthiest men) had "the same position," but in neighboring Tripolitania, he was "made Senator and then Count, and that is the future that everybody predicts for Attilio."

Mussolini had suggested as much when he had embraced him, Lilliana wrote: "Teruzzi," he had said, "Don't worry, you will be taken care of well, very, very well." They would have a palace "inferior to no Royal Palace," a "court just like a reigning monarch, with our own stables, garage full of cars, our troops, our own torpedo boat, hydroplanes etc., etc."[37]

Six years had passed since the new plenipotentiary to Italy's largest colony was garrison major at Darnah. His salary was tripled as he returned to active duty, and he was promoted from major in the reserves to lieutenant colonel. Their send-off was a two-day-long social event. Attilio was received by the king, Mussolini, and Federzoni, and Lilliana was invited to call upon the queen herself. Queen Elena was "wonderful," Rose gushed. She kept them for fifty minutes and complimented Lilliana: "she told her she looked exactly like a cousin of hers (from Montenegro), that she didn't look like an American."[38] At the farewell at the train station, there were "Ministers, Generals, society people, and people of all walks of life," Rose reported. Lilliana added, "many Senators and Deputies." "Many many" (*moltissimi*) friends, and *Il Messaggero* noted, an "elect crowd of women bearing bouquets of gorgeous flowers for his wife."[39]

This was Lilliana's moment, too. Gina Federzoni, who had confided to her that she had "very little real friends," asked Lilliana to call her by her first name and confessed she was sorry she was leaving. But it was "for the good of the country," she said: "in very high circles they discussed Attilio as a wonderful man for Governor" but also Lilliana as "governess."[40]

As Lilliana rushed about to prepare for the trip and make their farewells, she told her father:

> When I got engaged, you were worried that nobody would look
> at you in New York because of the religious differences. Can
> you show me any other Jewish girl who married as I did, kept
> her religion in the face of all Catholicism and religious preju-
> dices, imposed myself so much that they send Attilio and me to
> govern their most important colony?[41]

Back in New York City, her father fed the local tabloids. This was rewarded with the headline "New York Girl Is Vice-Queen of Cyrenaica: Elevation of Her Husband to Italian Governorship Follows Real Life Romance." Subtitle: "American Bride, at only 26, the youngest governor's wife ever." Informers sent the piece to Rome. The Duce read the translation. With his blue pencil, he underlined the exaggerations: that Teruzzi "had more medals for valor than any other officer in the Italian army," and "they took their honeymoon in the King's own car at the personal request of Mussolini."[42] In the margin, he jotted a big question mark.

Self-promotion was one quality he couldn't abide.

11

MISSION TO BENGHAZI

The laurel with the lotus bound
The victors' brows enwreathing,
Let flowers, sweet perfume breathing,
Veil their grim arms from sight.

—VERDI'S *Aida*, Act 2, Scene 2

On December 3, 1926, when the SS *Garibaldi* dropped anchor a mile off the coast of Benghazi, Lilliana Teruzzi learned that Italy's fabled gateway to the African continent had no port. The hot winds from the storm blowing off the desert had created giant swells. Often when that happened, the ship's captain would turn back to Syracuse. But the newly appointed governor and his wife were on board, and they had to disembark. They did so the usual way, "Singapore style"—meaning that they were trussed into rope slings and lowered like bales of hemp into the outstretched arms of Arab boatmen.

The governor's wife would later recall this landing as the grand overture to her African idyll: Arab sheiks in billowing white caftans piloting the official launch through the roiled water to the dock, amid face-pricking gusts of wet yellow sand, her stomach churning.

Then the sun broke through the storm clouds. As they were greeted by the crowd of colonial authorities and city notables, the garrison band struck up the "Royal March" and "Giovinezza," troops presented arms, and party men gave the Roman salute. Fascist boy scouts piped out their "hip hip hoorays" to shouts of "Long live Italy!" and "Long live Fascism!," after which the couple were chauffeured in a limousine all of two grit-swept blocks to the governor's mansion. Libyan guardsmen rode on either side, and two Sicilian marching bands brought up the rear. A festive crowd of a few thousand representing "all Benghazi" fell in behind them. At the residence, before disappearing through the grandiose Moresque portico, the two were photographed, the governor looking solemn, his young consort resolutely gracious as if still stunned by the rough landing.[1]

As the clamor of the crowd grew louder and louder, Attilio Teruzzi reappeared alone on the second-floor balcony, where he shouted out his first speech. Its essence was: "All the good and willing will find in me a careful guardian of their just rights and honest aspirations; all the bad, the troublemakers, and dishonest, will find in my government the rigorous, severe, and implacable executor of the law of Rome."[2] Benghazi was a charmingly ramshackle, mostly Arab town of around 30,000.

"The day was a personal triumph for each of us," Lilliana wrote that evening to her parents, "especially Attilio, as they adore him here." "Believe me, when he addressed the populace, he made me shake too, and his voice thundered so."[3] Every step they took now was in some way their own invention. By the end of the next day, they had telegraphed Mussolini, the king, and the colonial minister, together with a dozen other top people in the regime, to inform them of the enthusiastic welcome. Two mornings later, when "all Benghazi" opened *Cirenaica Nuova*, the first local fascist newspaper—launched providentially the day before the governor's arrival—the front page offered a flood of congratulations from Rome.

The Duce thanked Teruzzi "for his welcome greeting" and wrote that "the fascist homeland is following its strong colony with eager interest in its growing prosperity." The king, too, "vividly" responded with "thanks, too, for the greetings from the people of Cyrenaica." The colonial minister sent "hopeful good wishes for the arduous and worthy mission undertaken with the purest fascist faith and sustained passion."[4] The first week was hardly out, and "all Benghazi" had been informed not only of their new governor's tough expectations of them but that the king, the Duce, and the minister stood right at his shoulder.

When Teruzzi arrived in Benghazi, the Kingdom of Italy held two smallish colonies it had occupied in the Horn of Africa since the late nineteenth century, Eritrea and Italian Somalia. Neither of these promised much by way of prestige or riches; nor did the miniscule concession at the Chinese port city of Tianjin, a sop to the Italians after the Western powers divvied up control over China in the wake of the Boxer Rebellion. With the defeat of the Ottomans during the 1911–1912 Libyan war, Italy had also acquired a handful of islands in the Dodecanese, off the west coast of Turkey, which one day might have strategic value for Italy's naval

Teruzzi, governor of Cyrenaica, with Lilliana, her parents, and escort, Benghazi, spring 1927

Lilliana Weinman Teruzzi Estate

ambitions in the Eastern Mediterranean. As the far outposts of the Venetian Empire at its sixteenth-century pinnacle, these islands could showcase the legacy of Italian civilization in that part of the world, but only to the extent that the Italian government was willing to pour money into port facilities and town infrastructure and finance archeological digs to excavate Venetian and Roman ruins.[5]

Italy's only immediate hopes of enhancing its prestige as a colonial power came down to its two Libyan provinces, Tripolitania and Cyrenaica. The Ottomans had ruled them as separate administrative units, and under Italian occupation, once the caravan trade across the Sirtic Desert fell off, the vastness of the sun-cracked salt marshes, dense scrub, and chalky cliffs made the two even more separate. Cyrenaica had thus turned to Egypt and the Mashriq, while Tripolitania had oriented itself more toward Tunisia and the Maghreb. Not having a grip on either region, except for a few towns along the coastline, the minister of colonies had continued to administer them separately, favoring Tripolitania, with its capital of Tripoli, as by far the more promising of the two.[6]

When Mussolini made his first visit to North Africa in April 1926, Tripoli, a fine-sized city of 70,000, was far and away Italy's leading colonial town. It was a day by ship from Sicily and lay adjacent to French Tunisia, which had many Italian settlers. It also had a decent natural harbor that, when fortified by a breakwater, permitted unloading right at the piers. Italians had invested heavily in the town under the Venetian entrepreneur Giuseppe Volpi's governorship. The shoreline boulevards made Tripoli look like Via Reggio or some other prosperous Italian seaside resort. The town had clean, comfortable hotels; an array of showy, bright white state buildings in a pastiche of colonial styles; numerous fine cafés and cinemas; a tidily circumscribed native quarter; a half-built cathedral; and plans afoot for a regular opera season. From afar, Benghazi, less than half Tripoli's size and with no port to speak of, was Tripoli's mousy cousin.

That very year, however, Cyrenaica had soared in fascism's phantasmagorical geopolitical imagination. Now that Federzoni was back at the Colonial Ministry, Mussolini pushed his imperial agenda full throttle. Currently, Europe was ruled by the "Spirit of Locarno," a reference to the European powers' well-meaning pact to end war in Europe forever. And Fascist Italy, its back secured, could reembrace its colonial ambitions. Italy needed an empire. It was a poor nation whose people were its riches, and these people needed to cultivate new lands and to settle new colonies abroad. Federzoni's role was to develop the larger geopolitical vision that, sooner or later, would make fascism's newborn empire the heir to Augustan Rome.

Hegemony over "Mare nostrum," Our Sea, as the Romans had called the Mediterranean, was only the start. From the outset, Mussolini envisaged what would later be called "Eur-Africa." Italy's true rival was not to be found in the Turks, who had been defeated; nor in the Arab nationalists, whom he expected to become allies in a shared struggle against plutocratic imperialism; nor in France, which had occupied Algeria in 1840 and snatched away Tunisia in 1882, just as Italian settlers were getting a foothold there. Instead, the historic enemy the fascists saw themselves in competition with was imperial Great Britain.

In Federzoni's telling, England had overreached its power when it had allowed itself to be drawn into the Mediterranean Sea to defeat Napoleon Bonaparte. The British Empire, after seizing the Mediterranean's gateways at Gibraltar and Port Said, had gone on to occupy the ports at Malta, Cyprus, and Alexandria and to colonize the Levant. But England was an island in the Atlantic Ocean. It had no true ethical, historical, or cultural investment in the Mediterranean—the glorious frontline of Greco-Roman civilization—and was interested only in crass material: the region served as its commercial pipeline through the Suez Canal to India.[7]

Mussolini's ambition to outdo Britain and become a new Rome once more set colonial civil servants, population experts, journalists, and travel writers to chattering about empire. The touchstone of Italy's new imperial geography was a more or less literal reading of D'Annunzio's incandescent phrase that "the Italy of three seas" had been transformed by the 1912 conquest of Libya into "the great fatherland of four shores."[8] Cyrenaica boasted of the longest border on the Mediterranean's southern coast; it sat right at the midpoint between east and west and just a day's sail, or 160 nautical miles, from Apollonia to Cape Krios in western Crete—which is why ancient Rome combined Crete and Libya into a single province. As Fascist Italy built up its merchant marine and naval fleet, it would put the squeeze on the British forces at Malta. Pushing down from its outposts in the Dodecanese to extend a friendly hand to the oppressed Arab peoples of the Levant, it promised to rival British and French influence in the region. For a start, the British would have to concede to Italy vastly improved terms on the fees its ships paid to pass through the Suez Canal to reach East Africa. But more demands would be made, and further concessions granted, in due time.

Fascist Italy's fanciful new imperial geometry had also started to make its moral and political claims on the African continent. One wedge extended from the Italian peninsula through Libya to the Sudan. The other jutted up from the Red Sea and the Indian Ocean at the Gulf of Aden, cutting through Eritrea and Somalia. The two connected across Ethiopia and the Sudan at Khartoum, more or less. Consider the prowess of Italy's new superliners, the SS *Duilio, Giulio Cesare, Saturnia* and *Vulcania*, which promised to speed passengers from Trieste to Durban, South Africa, in six days via the Suez Canal. Then add to this logistical feats attained by the small-gauge railroad, the best engineered anywhere, that would make it possible to reach Addis Ababa via British Khartoum or overland from French Djibouti. Meanwhile Italo Balbo was planning new air routes from his position as undersecretary of the Italian Royal Air Force. There were practically no limits to the fascist geopolitical imagination.[9]

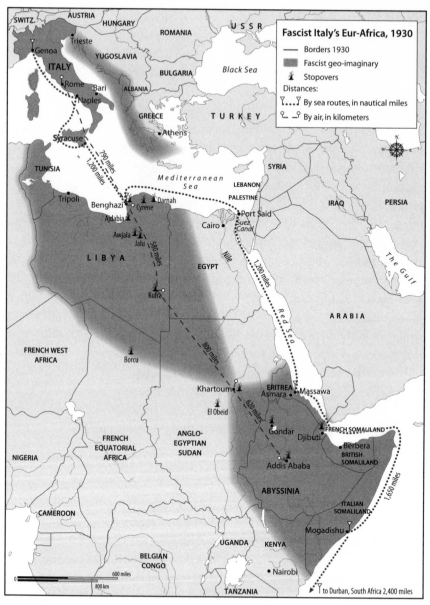

Fascist Italy's Eur-Africa, 1930

- Borders 1930
- Fascist geo-imaginary
- Stopovers

Distances:
- ⚲···⚲ By sea routes, in nautical miles
- ⚲—⚲ By air, in kilometers

© Victoria de Grazia

The imperial chattering class imagined untold riches coming from Cyrenaica. Whereas in Tripoli, the desert started practically at the city gates, and the coastal settlements of Homs and Misrata had little vegetation around them, Cyrenaica was renowned since ancient times for its fertile ribbon of coastal lowlands, watered by springs and seasonal cascades through the wadies from the heavily forested Jebal Akdar. Beyond that, parched steppes and seas of sand, punctuated by an occasional oasis, extended as far south as modern-day Chad and Sudan.

All eyes focused on the coast, and first and foremost on Cyrene, 282 kilometers by mostly impassable roads from Benghazi, 13 from its ancient port at Apollonia. Immense ruins of temples the size of the Acropolis, public baths, a colossal stadium, aqueducts, marble tombs, and kilometers of paved roads dominated the grassy landscape, undisturbed except by nomads grazing their flocks. Only fifty generations earlier, according to Fascist Italy's accelerated clockwork, Cyrene had produced harvests of wheat, barley, millet, salt, and fish so bountiful that it had fed its own population of upward of 100,000 as well as ten times that number in the Rome of the Caesars. In no time, once Cyrenaica was settled, Mussolini's New Roman Empire would restore the untold riches depleted by centuries of barbarian depredations.

Unlike Tripolitania, Cyrenaica had not been pacified militarily, and the chief obstacle to this future abundance was the resistance of some 120,000 Arabs and Berbers belonging to ten major tribes living in small agricultural settlements and towns along the coast. Another 60,000 or so lived more nomadically, moving according to the seasons with their families and herds up through the coastal highlands or from oasis to oasis along the crescent that cut southward through the Sirtic Desert to the twenty-ninth parallel and then eastward, before curving north to meet the sea near Bardia on the Egyptian border.

The Bedouins' resistance to outside encroachments had long been fed by their attachment to the Sanusi brotherhood, founded in 1836, when the Algerian-born philosopher-cleric Muhammad ibn Ali al-Sanusi established his religious confraternity at Mecca. Like the Wahhabis in Arabia or the Mahdis in Sudan, the Grand Sanusi, as his followers called him, alarmed at the incursions of Christian imperialists, denounced the Ottoman caliphate for having weakened Islam's resistance to the Western infidels. By the late nineteenth century, the Sanusi brotherhood had become an "empire," though not in the bureaucratic-militarist sense of late nineteenth-century European imperialism. Its 150 or so *zawiyas*, or monastic waystations, established across Africa and Arabia, with the capital at the oasis of Al Kufrah, still operated within the interstices of the Ottoman Empire.

These stations provided religious succor, market days, and protection for pilgrims and camel trains on the trans-Saharan routes and from the Sudan to the North African coasts. But with the hardening of resistance in the wake of the Italian invasion of Libya in 1911, the Sanusi elite— sometimes in agreement with, sometimes overriding the interests of local tribal leaders—formed a de facto transregional state, administered by their brotherhood of sheikhs. As they were pushed back by French and British colonizers from Algeria and Egypt and then by the Italians from Tripolitania, Cyrenaica became their most important redoubt. The piety and good works of the Sanusi preachers had endeared them to the austere tribes of the region. The unmapped coastal highlands offered well-watered land and refuge. The border with Egypt was nearby, and they had reached a modus vivendi with the British, so they could always move to safety on the other side of the frontier.[10]

By the 1920s, Cyrenaica had the largest concentration of *zawiyas* in the entire region, forty or more by the most accurate account. By garnering tribute and gifts from grateful Arab and Berber tribes for their services, the priest-brotherhood had acquired control over tens of hundreds of hectares of the most fertile land. The Bedouins, or "nomads" of Cyrenaica—as they are misleadingly called—thus unwittingly became the protagonists of the last of the post–World War I pan-Arab insurgencies suppressed by Western European colonialism. And the Italians, with their delusions of imperial grandeur, became their brutally determined exterminators.

Teruzzi arrived as governor just as the fascist regime was coming to its ruthless conclusions about how to deal with an Islamic power that was faith-based. If the Italians were confronting a conniving, fanatically anti-Christian sect, it would have to be eradicated. If, on the other hand, the Sanusi were regarded as a legitimate local elite with their own rational interests, the Italians could pursue what they called the *politica dei capi*, or "chieftain politics," wheeling and dealing to cut power-sharing deals with the local notables. Politically, this would not have worked too differently from the *trasformismo* used by the political elites in liberal Italy to get provincial notables of the most varied ideological persuasions to submit to their political agendas with payoffs and favors. Mussolini despised such deals, but he did them anyway, and Teruzzi had often acted as his emissary.

Then again, if the real enemy was not the Sanusi at all but opportunistic tribal leaders or rebellious, conniving tribesmen whom neither the Sanusi nor the tribal elders could rein in, more decisive action was imperative. In other words, racially and religiously, Arab notables, unlike southern Italian notables, the targets of *trasformismo* at home, were simply inferior: they could not be rational actors. The most drastic conclusion was that the Bedouins, or nomads, by the very nature of their uncivilized, anarchic existence, were refractory to any rule. That view would point to their elimination, however conceived. That mind-set was in the making, but it was one Teruzzi did not share: he still had the stuff of the seasoned Italian colonial officer for whom, all else being equal, the philosophy was live and let live.

Mussolini could hardly wait to denounce the sham truces negotiated by his predecessors. Practically from the moment that the Treaty of Lausanne between the Allies and Turkey was signed on July 23, 1923, recognizing once and for all Italy's right to Libya, he put the military on the offensive. The Sanusi once again became Italy's sworn enemy. This marked the unofficial start of what would be called the Second Italian-Sanusi War. The notables of Tripoli tried to resist by asking the Sanusi emir, Idris, who was based in Cyrenaica, to become their emir as well, so as to unite the two provinces' defenses. But the Italian forces, under the command of the ferocious General Graziani and bolstered by out-of-work bands of fascist militia, were relentless. By 1924, they had secured Tripolitania, but not Cyrenaica, and Idris had wisely exiled himself to British Egypt.

In his absence, the leadership of the insurgency fell to Sheikh Umar al-Mukhtar. The onetime Koranic scholar educated at the Sanusi college at Jaghbub, then close to seventy, had long fought the Western powers. Before the Italians, it had been the French and English. When Teruzzi arrived as governor of Cyrenaica, Sheikh Umar was rebuilding the resistance by drawing in young men from the tribes along the coast. He could call on 1,500 or so men under arms at any given time, not all of whom had mounts. They had few weapons other than German Mausers from World War I, captured Italian arms and munitions, and military matériel trafficked from Egypt, but they were classic guerilla insurgents with all of the advantages of what the American anthropologist James C. Scott aptly calls the "resistance of the weak." Sheikh Umar's soldiers knew their homeland step by step and were good at disrupting Italian lines of communication the moment they were left unguarded. They harassed the clans who had submitted to the Italians, and they ambushed Italian troops if they pushed too far from their garrisons. Whenever they were counterattacked, they retreated into the unmapped highlands, regrouped, and bided their time.[11]

For Federzoni, Italian Cyrenaica was an insulting "terra nullius, abandoned to the anarchy of barbarian tribes." Nobody really owned it; the Italians claimed it but could not establish their right of settlement. What was needed was "total reconquest," Federzoni emphasized, like Rome's conquest of Carthage or Western Christendom's crusades against Islam.[12] By that he meant no more catch-as-catch-can settler colonialism. In the past, impoverished Italian migrants had set off one by one or in small bands to the Americas, Tunis, Tripoli—or Benghazi, for that matter—bringing with them the intense conviviality of their club life, cafés, cuisine, clientele-oriented politics, and churchgoing but no sense of "La Grande Italia." Now that the whole nation was invested in the colonial project, and the date of Italy's entry into World War I had even been set aside to commemorate Colonial Day, every Italian settler had to stake his or her labor and savings toward the "rebirth of a colonial mindset."[13] And so Cyrenaica would have to be developed economically for Fascist Italy to properly assert its claim to challenge the British Empire's grip over the Mediterranean.

But Fascist Italy had neither the means nor the political capital to fight a prolonged war. If Arab victims of Italian repression were to stir up the pan-Islamic press in Egypt, international creditors would grow uneasy. The ever-envious British and French stood at the ready to exploit any bad press, eager to condemn fascist colonialism as especially brutal. The League of Nations could be counted on to show its usual hypocrisy, pretending to defend the rights of colonial subjects by denouncing Italy when everybody knew that the British and French were the worst offenders. If this happened, Italians at home would pick up on the tales of woe and insist on a retreat. Like the fascist coup d'états of 1922 and 1925, timing was everything. Teruzzi was under orders to act quickly, decisively, and conclusively.

"Pray God that Attilio will do great things," Lilliana would write to her family.[14] From the morning of his arrival, Teruzzi set out to achieve just that. By the end of his first week, Governor Teruzzi had harangued the Fascist Party into action, received all of the town's dignitaries, and met with religious leaders, including the Catholic vicar, the chief rabbi Fargian, and the cadi, whom his predecessor had kept at arm's length. To size up the military situation and eager to save time (and the embarrassment of not being able to cross wide swathes of rebel-controlled territory) he flew on a nine-day junket, two thousand kilometers, to Tobruk and then Jaghbub with stopovers on his return at Scegga, Bardia, Darnah, and Cyrene. Wherever he stopped, he heard "well-founded complaints" but also "lots of nuisance talk."[15]

Meanwhile, Lilliana bustled around, setting up the household, organizing their domestic staff of twenty ("practically an impossible task"), and adding her opinions to her husband's. She "had never worked so hard in her life," she wrote her parents, "and never loved work so much." Teruzzi, too, worked "three times as hard as in Rome (but with ten times the satisfaction)."[16] Within a month, the governor concluded that the colony was not mismanaged so much as unmanaged.

In principle, the total overhaul of the colonial administration that had been carried out in Rome just after he took office made Governor Teruzzi "infallible as to anything he sanctions."[17] He had no local parliament to constrain him, no government prefect, and no mayor—only a city commissioner whom he appointed. He was de facto minister of justice, and he was empowered as commander in chief of the military to declare and enforce martial law. He appointed himself Fascist Party *federale* after retiring the self-appointed current figure, a bumbling sycophant. The one power he did not have was the power of the purse, at least not for the half of the budget coming from Rome.

With so much power, Teruzzi became "interesting" in the sense that Friedrich Nietzsche uses the term when he speaks of the travails of conscience faced by dutiful men as they shake themselves free of conventional moral constraints. Hitherto, he had been a duty-minded subordinate who had twisted and turned to oblige one superior or another. Now he alone willed his actions. He made the choices for which he would be held responsible, and, assuming he was a man of good faith, he had to hold himself responsible for their effects. What's more, he had a wife he had chosen to reinforce these moral sentiments at his side. This, then, was the Fascist New Man at his most liberated, trying to be truest to himself.

And so the pragmatic, detail-minded Teruzzi, who had always struggled to see the forest for the trees, evolved into the so-called good face of fascist imperial conquest. Under this guise, fascism's civilizing mission promised to bring all the civilities of Italian life to out-of-the-way places. It professed itself as philo-Arab, tolerant of Islam, sensitive to the aesthetics of the locality, and eager to invest hugely using Italy's resources in money, knowledge, labor, and blood. This conviction sustained Teruzzi in the belief that fascist colonialism was superior to the imperialism of Britain or France, and it encouraged him to disbelieve any notion, however factually informed, that it could be just as ruthless, if not more so.

Governor Teruzzi wanted a wise administration for Benghazi. At hardly a square kilometer, the town was no larger than City Hall, the Galleria, and the Piazza Duomo combined—a space Teruzzi had once patrolled as chief of the *squadristi* of the Milan *Fascio*. He imagined himself now as a city founder in the Roman or Renaissance style rather than a capitalist city manager with an eye to profitable development. He envisaged the whole "Roman package," the bundle of buildings and services one could find in Greco-Roman Cyrene or its nearby port of Appolonia. That meant military barracks and fortifications, places of worship, stadiums, theaters, and public baths. He wanted the people to fear him but also to love him. But the true driving force for his visions lay in his own "nature." Happily married, in his own bailiwick, he saw in himself as "a soldier" and "also a bit of a poet"; his "optimism" made him impetuous; he was full of projects, "eager to gallop into the realm of fantasy."[18]

His prominence and pliant nature attracted a retinue of acolytes. Or better, friends, good friends, for Teruzzi was too earnest and eager to please to be worshipped. There were the fifteen or so men of the so-called Milan circle, old friends and acquaintances, all eager for business deals. Others, like dear old Civinini, who arrived in Cyrenaica unannounced with his daughter Giulia, hoped to reconnect with him in this moment of high adventure. Tom Antongini, D'Annunzio's long-time secretary-manager, decided to exercise his skills on a less madcap personality in a more exotic milieu, arrived with his family to become Teruzzi's cabinet secretary. Federzoni's protégé, Ferdinando Nobili Massuero, became his city commissioner, and the owlish General Ottorino Mezzetti, a longtime Libyan hand, a like-minded commander of the troops. Then there was the prickly know-it-all representative of the Colonial Ministry, Antonio Anceschi, who Teruzzi couldn't abide, and his successor, a rising star, the self-effacing, methodical Ottone Gabelli, whom he quite liked. Finally, there was the vigorous new Bishop Bernardino Bigi, a onetime Franciscan missionary, who, after heroic if ineffectual efforts to convert the Bedouins of Tripolitania, had arrived in Benghazi to take command of the newly established archdiocese.[19]

Nobody doubted that Lilliana held pride of place on this new stage. But short of the long letters they exchanged, which were lost, it is hard to know exactly how her views mattered to Attilio. His wife was "a great help to him," he would tell the Duce.[20] Had he been tasked to detail how, he would not have said that he told her everything, for that helped him to clarify his thoughts, though that seems to have been the case. He might have spoken of her taste and elegance, her energy, adventurousness, and open way with the people. Or he may have touted her sharpness at sizing up situations and individuals, as well as her eagerness to synthesize, pass judgment, and keep him on course. She insisted he have only the best people to help him, spurred him to do better, and steeled him against wavering. If only she didn't make such invidious comparisons and wasn't so dismissive of people who were not useful but not harmful either—women especially—he would have had an easier time of things.

Lilliana was reportedly a gracious hostess. In early spring 1927, when Sir Samuel Hoare, Viscount Templewood, and the Secretary of State for Air stopped over with Lady Maud on their way to Delhi to inaugurate the British Empire's new air route to India, Lilliana had overwhelmed them with her fashion sense—as if straight from Paris, the menu, and the many speeches, so much so that Sir Samuel had left wondering "how they had managed such a splendid reception in such a remote spot."[21] The more important takeaway for the British Foreign Office was that the Italians had huge ambitions for that spot. The couple had outdone one another to welcome Teruzzi's old comrade Italo Balbo, with "highest honors." Balbo was also on an air junket, though his route only took him 3,300 miles on a loop around the Eastern Mediterranean to inspect potential Aegean and Libyan air bases and showcase Italian aviation manufacture to potential foreign buyers. At the "state dinner" attended by all of the local notability, served by twelve Askari dressed in red brocade to match the table setting, the tipsy Balbo had proposed a toast to "their ménage as worthier of an emperor than a governor." Balbo was also a big gossip. On return to Rome, he spoke of Teruzzi as a "natural born governor" and Lilliana as a brilliant diplomat-hostess.[22]

Yet Benghazi would be nothing without a proper port, and from the start that had been Teruzzi's foremost priority. It was an "infuriating and absurd situation," he would later write, that since 1911—when the Italian naval squadron, after bombarding the town from a kilometer off shore, hadn't been able to occupy Benghazi until it had mobilized a flotilla of fishing boats and rafts—the government had done nothing. The lack of docking facilities made the cost of living 25–35 percent higher than in Tripoli. Milan and Rome were getting huge loans from the Morgan Bank; Teruzzi, on Lilliana's advice, insisted that he needed 300 million lira for five years if he was to succeed. Promptly turned down, he had to work piecemeal and focus on other projects.[23]

Short of a five-year plan, Governor Teruzzi issued orders with a rapidity that was "more American than colonial."[24] Over the protests of Benghazi old-timers distraught at the loss of their landmarks, Milanese contractors cleared away the debris of the Ottoman castle, completed the Roman architect Marcello Piacentini's new theater, and squared off the jagged edges of the piazza around the Grand Mosque to set off its dignity as a place of worship. They widened Corso Italia, Via Statuto, and Via Roma to open up the city to waterfront views to the west that would soon be beautified with fountains and palm plants, oleander, and hibiscus. As to the northern waterfront: once the cadi had agreed to move the dead from the Sidi Sciabbi cemetery to Ain Selmani on the city's outskirts near Berka, the three layers of tombs spread over the 15,000 square meters took another year to disinter; meanwhile, contractors put the finishing touches on the two-story officers' club, with its attached tennis courts and housing for government functionaries.

The Army Corps of Engineers, working with conscript labor, helped the mother superior of the Sisters of the Immaculate Conception to complete the dormitories for the hundred girls she boarded at her school. The burned-out souk, redesigned by architects from Rome to be more hygienic and graceful, reopened. Once the bridge was built over the laguna to the palm-fringed beaches at Point Giuliana, concessionaries provided the seaside amenities—a restaurant and wooden cabanas, umbrellas, a diving board, raft, and pedal boats. To those who criticized this beach resort as a luxury for the rich, Teruzzi answered that there were countless metropolitans who liked to swim and sun themselves and that it was disturbing for the natives to have to see men and women together in various states of undress.[25] All the biggest streets were renamed: Piazza

Tobruk became Piazza 28 October, Via Suez became Via Trieste, and its
continuation, Via Trento. Donkeys and camels were steered away from
the city center. Still, this urban once-over couldn't address the habitual
"ever-so flagrant promiscuity" with which poor Italians lived side by side
with the indigenous people, sometimes even in the same "hybrid and
filthy" houses.[26] The city never cobbled the fetid tangle of back alleys of
the native quarters. But uniformed garbage men gave them a good sweep
more or less daily.

By 1928, Teruzzi's impulse to make the town attractive gave way to a more
ambitious aesthetic urge, namely, to draw up Fascist Italy's first urban plan
for a model capital city. This ambition started with a vanity project, the governor's own residence, the Palazzina. At first Lilliana had started helter-
skelter to refurbish the four salons and nine bedrooms of the mansion
with gestures to the rococo salon style of her Roman friends and Billy
Baldwin's Newport Beach luxe via *Good Housekeeping Magazine*. For the
kitchen, she ordered a Delco refrigerator, the largest in Africa ("Thank
Goodness, the government pays for the electricity," she told her parents).
Then they brought down Alfredo Del Corno, bourgeois Milan's leading
interior decorator, to give the whole place a makeover, as the existing
layout did not lend itself to elegant living—or how they imagined it once
they saw photographs of the gorgeous governors' residences in Tripoli and
Mogadishu. People with more educated taste let on that their blocky three-
floor building fronted in the Alhambra style by the eight-arched pseudo-
Moresque veranda was pure colonial kitsch, having been built—and here
one can imagine Teruzzi spluttering the words disdainfully—"in different
periods and with no criteria whatsoever, neither artistic, nor simply as décor."
The rough soldier was revealed to have the design instincts of a true Milanese. Governor Teruzzi's bottom line was that "beauty" had to be the
"norm in all of the city's urban undertakings." The goal had to be "a
worthy statehouse for the colony, but also a city of a beauty that is at once
picturesque and artistic."[27]

That ambition wouldn't be satisfied until Teruzzi commissioned the
Milan-based architect Guido Ferrazza, the founder of Italy's first urban
planning group and a favorite of Margherita Sarfatti's Novecento movement, to rebuild the governor's mansion. When the result pleased everybody, Teruzzi commissioned an urban renewal plan for Benghazi from
Ferrazza, which was delivered in 1930 and set for completion by 1935, by
which time his tenure as governor was long over.

This was Milanese modernism at its finest, combining sober classical lines with the local vernacular. The new fascist-European Benghazi would be set against the "characteristic panorama of old Benghazi with its simple squared masses of terraced roofs profiled against the sea and sky" and against "the suggestive beauty" of the mosques, *zawiyas*, and dilapidated cemeteries.[28]

Rather than destroy the old neighborhoods, as development projects were doing elsewhere, the city would preserve them, thereby saving money by not having to create any new services for those quarters. It would also keep indigenous workers close at hand. The better off among the Arabs might wish to move into the new neighborhoods, "assuming they wanted to conform to our way of life," but most wouldn't want to abandon the "spontaneous simplicity" of their old neighborhoods.[29]

This idea of treating the native way of life as an aesthetic prop was totally congenial to the well-disposed fascist imperialist: admire the natives in their spontaneity, for their glossy darkness and sinuous shapes, but only at a safely voyeuristic remove. In 1929, Tripoli would ask Ferrazza to draw up a similar project, and once the fascists had conquered Ethiopia in 1936, Ferrazza headed to Asmara, Harrar, and Addis Ababa to draw up plans at the request of Teruzzi, who had by this point, 1938, become undersecretary for Italian Africa. By then, the relations with the "colored races" had deteriorated, and urban planners were rigorously tasked with preventing racial mixing.[30]

Teruzzi's vision of the new fascist city was the perfect backdrop for his notion of governing the people of Benghazi. The small well-to-do metropolitan community, especially the wives of the original elite and the 200 functionaries brought to Benghazi in 1915, were, of course, enchanted by the bon ton this seemingly perfectly matched, fun-loving couple brought to Benghazi society, such as it existed.

The governor tapped into his inner populism well before Mussolini started to "reach out to the people" in 1930. With Lilliana, he joined the Trapanese fishermen the night they prepared their boats for the start of the season's tuna hunt. The wind from the Levant whipped up the waves, so it took five attempts to launch the boats. They finally set out at one o'clock in the morning under the crescent moon and cast their nets two and a half hours later. Inshallah! On their return ten days later, they slaughtered 400 tons of fish, the record for the entire Mediterranean that year. Surely, the governor and his enchanting wife had brought them luck.[31]

Teruzzi's greatest satisfaction as governor came at the end of his first month, when an Arab merchant told him he felt safe for the first time when crossing through the European quarter. From the Arab notables of the city, Teruzzi had learned how "ill-used" they had felt by the "purely instrumental relations" of the past. Whenever the government had a truce with the Sanusi, they would be treated with an "excess of forbearance and condescension." When events turned, however, the Arab notables felt "absolute and preconceived intransigence" as if they were all "Sanusi sympathizers," or worse yet, "Sanusis in flesh and blood," "the enemy himself to be eliminated."[32]

Benghazi's Arab notables were still shaken by the reversal of their fortunes. In 1920, they had been seated as guests of honor alongside Governor De Martino at the daylong banquet hosted by Omar Pasha el Kekhia—Cyrenaica's wealthiest man, now in exile in Sicily—to celebrate Idris as emir and take their place in their own parliament. By 1923, Idris had fled abroad, the parliament had been put under lock and key, and they themselves had been ostracized in favor of the parvenus the Italians found to do their bidding. It was no wonder, Teruzzi concluded, that these men, "whose spirit of chivalry was no different from that of Europe's feudal aristocrats, reacted the way Muslims generally did: [with] an obstinate, invincible silence—as secretive as the most powerful Mafia vow."[33]

Teruzzi wouldn't concede them any real power, of course. But prestige and respect he would do. To miscreants committing violent acts in the name of fascism, he laid down the law: there would be zero tolerance for "bullying by individuals or collectively," and doing so risked instant expulsion from the colony.[34] He and Lilliana made a show of welcoming the Arab notables—tall, princely figures in gold-filigreed red robes—to all state receptions. They always added color and a sense of occasion. He restarted the celebration of Eid as an official holiday. The end of Ramadan and the most important festivity of the year became the occasion for a big reception at the municipal building, with speeches by him and the cadi. He operated the court system according to new laws that had the cadi swear in Muslim jurors for cases falling under Islamic law and the chief rabbi do the same with Jewish jurors for cases under Jewish law.

At the same time, he brought the 1926 Fascist Special Laws to the colony. These empowered military tribunals to try outlaws and impose capital punishment, outlawed opposition political parties (not that there were any), and imposed stiff penalties for "lifestyle" crimes—public drunk-

enness, price gouging, gambling, street prostitution, and brothels. Benghazi, so small and somnolent, had generally been a peaceful place down
to then. With the crackdown, it was noticed that lost keys were returned,
and angry camels no longer snarled traffic; the few Arabs who drank and
got into fights were rightly jailed, an Italian whose dog bit an Arab boy was
remanded to justice, and the few metropolitan grocers who watered down
the milk and gouged on the price of mortadella were fined, but nobody
was killed or seriously wounded.[35]

The strong consensus, both in Benghazi and in Rome, a year into
Teruzzi's tenure was that the new governor had brought good government
to Benghazi. The British consul, Stanhope Palmer, who had been following Mussolini's intention to make Benghazi a major Mediterranean
seaport, reported to the Foreign Office that the city had "changed out
of all knowledge even since this spring and nearly every week shows
further progress."[36]

12

INSURGENCY AND BETRAYAL

Wet your gullet!
Drink, swallow it down,
Before the song and the glass
Disappear!

—IAGO, Act 1, Verdi's *Otello*

Oh Governor of the Colony, you with your sacred charge. . . .
If you, in your position, don't keep your promise, then promises are worth nothing.

—Sheik Abdellaziz el-Isaui to Attilio Teruzzi,
March 3, 1928/10 Ramadan 1346

Benghazi had 7,000 "metropolitans," as the Italians called themselves, and from the size of the crowd on one late November evening in 1927, most of them were out along the sea front. As Mario Bassi, *La Stampa's* war correspondent, sat jacketless in the tepid air, he captured the sense of well-being. People strolled in family groups and filled the sidewalk cafes. Children ran around. The waves lapping the promenade flickered from the light of the buoys at Point Giuliana and the turbines at the tuna cannery at El Mongar, which this year, under new ownership, had processed a record catch. The sound of a jazz group came from the nearby Albergo Italia, and later, the garrison band would play Verdi in Piazza del Re. As Bassi caught the echoes of some family celebration from the native quarters in back, trumpet squeals, a tambourine's thump-thump, a raggedy snatch of song, and the *zagarlia*, as the local Italians called the lacerating ululations of the women, he mused about the important markers of Benghazi's recent great transformation. The celebration of the fifth anniversary of the March on Rome on October 28, 1927, had brought a huge mixed crowd into Piazza del Re, and the recently inaugurated stretch of railroad on the Benghazi–Darnah line extended the line all the way to Barca. All this, he concluded, was "due to His Excellency Attilio Teruzzi, an optimal governor, wise administrator, and fatherly ruler."[1]

The only obstacle Bassi saw to Teruzzi's "inspired projects, passionate zeal, and will to do good" was that "despicable, implacable tyranny, the budget."[2] Budgetary constraints had been Teruzzi's constant bitter complaint. He was forever the regimental bookkeeper. His own household accounts looked like those of the proverbial Italian bourgeois housewife of the time, who punctiliously totted up everything, including her infant's intake and excretions. His income was now paid monthly, and everything was budgeted: on the credit side, his monthly salary; on the debit side, 1,300 lire for rent and utilities in Rome, between 1,500 and 1,900 lire for his brother Guido's hospital care, and 400 lire for savings.[3] It pained him to have to trick the government's books to make the budget balance, to delay payday for the troops, to plead for new funds, to postpone the port or stint on military preparation. "It can't be avoided; no escaping it; with its unassailable figures, it regulates every step forward for the colony, and, oh so often so very stingily."[4] That, again, was the colonial expert Bassi.

Lilliana brought to the issues her own seemingly capricious New York view: that the money had to be somewhere. If you had it, you could always find more. If you could buy it, you could always sell it again at a profit or a discount. Her monthly allowance from her father was equal to Attilio's salary. She set it up as a joint account and kept back-of-the-hand calculations about their expenditures—really hers—assuming the account would cover them, which it always did. She believed in lines of credit, like the one her father had extended to finance her opera career, which is why they had to press Federzoni for a big government loan, which, exceptionally, he eventually granted. But why not a bigger one from Wall Street—perhaps even from the Harriman Bank itself?[5] As her ambitions for the budget suggested, Lilliana still lived in a world of *convenienze*: the government paid all the help, except for her lady's maid, Lina. It paid for redecorating repeated times, the electricity bill, the myriad telegrams to her parents, and her trips to and from the continent. That she actually spent any of her family money on the colony is unlikely. But she did make flippant remarks about doing so, especially when she heard of the fabulous sums other colonial governors purportedly received for their expenses.

The budget was not the problem, in reality. The problem was the whole political economy of fascist colonialism. For Cyrenaica to prosper—instead of clinging to the city and living off state subsidies, military expenditures, and enterprises like car dealerships, grocery stores, or cafés that all depended on imports—the Italians would have to develop their export economy. Tuna and sea sponges alone could hardly be expected to make a dent in the import-export deficit.

But farming was a lonely, fearsome, and altogether risky proposition, no matter how many incentives the government offered in the way of land concessions, tax rebates, and loans for tractors, equipment, and seed. Who would actually work the land was a problem as well, Italian laborers didn't emigrate to slave away on other people's land. That's why they escaped from Italy in the first place. Some thought Aldo Jung, the Jewish entrepreneur from Palermo, could figure it out. He was Federzoni's good friend, and while Teruzzi was governor, Jung was granted a giant allotment of the best-watered highland terrain, the biggest yet. He did so after his fashion, by press-ganging farm labor from his own estates in Sicily.[6]

Milan's Fascist Federation, which was allotted the second biggest terrain to establish a settler consortium, placed its faith in another plan, sending down some of the city's thousands of unemployed. Back in the day, the Romans had used slaves. As for the Arab-Berber peoples, if they ranked high enough, they too used slaves trafficked from the Sudan. The Bedouins had no interest in abandoning their nomadic existence for sharecropping or wages. They were content, so long as they were masters of their own fates.

None of this had really been thought through as the colony appeared to leap and bound into the fascist future, reborn to its original grandeur two millennia after the decline of Rome.

While Benghazi was in the spotlight, the Arab insurgency had begun to flare up again. The main terrain under dispute from the spring of 1927 was between Cyrene and Darnah, around the mouth of Wadi Cuf, the gorge leading up into the valleys and ravines of the Green Mountain, where the rebels pastured their animals over the summer months. Teruzzi knew as well as anybody their motives and their modus operandi, but perhaps he didn't understand that something else was afoot. The old sheiks made a show of their religious piety. Faith in Allah was "simplicity itself: the body must be strengthened by a healthy and abstemious life, so that it becomes a worthy dwelling for the soul," and "you must be a slave of nothing save God, that is, you must be the master of circumstances." Those were the words of Idris. "The civilization which the Italians want to introduce into Cyrenaica makes us the slaves of circumstances," he said, "therefore, we must fight against it."[7]

Religiosity was not what attracted younger men to the rebels. They saw no future once their tribal elders had submitted to the Italians, disarmed, and been forced to set up their encampments and graze their herds in the miserable pasturelands adjacent to the Italian garrisons. They would have to pay taxes to the Italian government, and they would not be allowed to move through the districts where those Bedouins who had not yet submitted lived. When they fell short of grazing land for the sheep, they would have to sell their livestock to buy fodder for the remainder. Whenever there were disturbances, the military closed the markets. "It must be the will of Allah," the elders would say, while the younger men saw otherwise: "We are getting more and more ignorant, more and more poor, more and more like the animals they call us."[8]

The elders of the Obeidats of Darnah, who had been Teruzzi's closest friends among the tribal chiefs, were telling him they could no longer afford to play by the Italians' rules. They had always made payoffs to the insurgents, if only to keep them at bay. That worked until poorer tribes, who were unable to pay tribute and were raided or had their animals rustled complained to the district commissioner. Put on notice, the Obeidats had given tokens of their good faith by intercepting a band of Sanusi warriors and turning them over to the Italians, who executed them. But then the Italian military had done nothing to protect them so that the Sanusi, in reprisal, had burned down an entire encampment.[9]

In January 1927, when Badoglio, now a marshal, the military's highest rank and the chief of staff of the king's army, resolved to mount a major offensive in the coming year, with colonial minister Federzoni's backing, Teruzzi was caught off guard. The battle plan called for one column under Teruzzi's orders, with General Mezzetti as the commander in the field, to march dead south from Benghazi to the oases on the twenty-ninth parallel. There it would join up with the column marching south from Tripolitania at the orders of Governor De Bono, who, under the command of General Graziani, would occupy an advance point in the desert of the Fezzan. Teruzzi had barely started his governorship at the time. His budget was terribly tight, even for military spending. He was afraid of falling behind on the military payroll at a moment when his soldiers were complaining that with no declaration of war, they weren't even receiving combat pay.

Since he was familiar with tribal politics, at least enough to know the tribal chiefs with whom he could negotiate, Teruzzi wanted time to arrange truces. At the very least, he needed peace and quiet to the rear as the men under his command marched south. Ideally, he would persuade the chieftans on the Italian line of march not to resist, and he would use their acquiescence to persuade the tribes around the oases to submit without a fight.[10]

Imagine his shock then, on March 28, 1927, when he learned that the Seventh Libyan battalion, while out on patrol in the valley at El Raheiba, close to the Gebel, had been ambushed by Umar al-Mukhtar's band. It was a massacre. The insurgents had killed the commander, Captain Bassi, three other officers, and 300 Libyan soldiers. They had captured two Italian officers and ran off with a large amount of weaponry and munitions. Teruzzi was playing an after-lunch hand of scopa with Lilliana and friends when his ashen-faced adjutant pulled him out of the room. At the news, he "shriveled like an old man."[11] All Italian soldiers had felt the mortification of the routs at Adwa and Caporetto in some measure, and in Libya there had been Shar al-Shatt and Gasr Bu Hadi, but this disaster was *on his command.*

Colonial Minister Federzoni first heard of the massacre through army channels. When he received Teruzzi's forty-one line telegram on April 3, it was so inchoate about what happened, so confused about whether or not to go on the counteroffensive, and so perplexed at the contradictory advice the two generals assigned to his command were giving him that Federzoni shook his head: It was enough to "sink him." Teruzzi's letter of explanation after fifteen days of dead silence, was "an inane effort" to blame Ramadan fasting for making the Libyan troops listless, blame General Cei for being absent, and blame the colony's general secretary for failing to coordinate civilian and military affairs. The promising Teruzzi, so "cordial, happy, and self-confident," whom Federzoni had seen only a month earlier reporting to him in Rome, had proved hapless and ineffectual after all. What could he do but to upbraid him and carry on?[12]

What nobody mentioned was that the ambush had been organized as retribution for the execution at Cyrene on March 20 of "three traitors": two prominent tribal sheikhs, for collaboration, and a leading Sanusi cleric-warrior, for spying. The execution had taken place as in earlier times, with

the gallows set up in the public square, the condemned men's kinfolk
rousted out to watch, the native troops standing at attention and then dismissed, and the bodies left to dangle for days. In short, Italian justice had
meted out "exemplary punishment" to have "the widest, most effective
resonance."[13]

The governor gave orders that "all mention be suppressed under pain of
instant arbitrary arrest and expulsion from the colony."[14] But everybody
knew about El Raheiba from one source or another. The Military Circle
buzzed with the news that the governor had secretly flown to Cyrene to
gather information and that the two young wives of the officers who had
been captured, realizing that their husbands would be tortured to death,
had gone insane and would have to be repatriated.[15] Federzoni, in turn,
having realized that the massacre was a far bigger setback than he had
originally understood it to be, took Teruzzi's too-candid dispatch for the
government news agency, rewrote it more "euphemistically," and submitted it to the Duce, who "pruned it some more of any untoward points,"
declaring, "a fact that's unknown is a fact that doesn't exist."[16]

The point now was payback. Ottorino Mezzetti, the new commander
of the troops, would surely make a success of that. He was an old Libya
hand, having been redeployed to Tripolitania from the Austrian front in
1917, just when Teruzzi was sent to Darnah. The strategy was twofold: in
the July heat, he would march his columns of Italian officers and Askari
from their fortresses on the Marj plain through the Wadi Cuf into the
hitherto impenetrable ravines of the Green Mountain to catch the rebel
units by surprise while they summered in the highland pastures, chase
them down, and annihilate them.

Meanwhile, Teruzzi would reinforce the Italians' truce with the Obeidats, whose lands lay around the mouth of the Cuf. In July, when Lilliana
would be back from a visit to Rome, he would meet with them not as "a
Governor, but as a fellow citizen, not just with the customary frankness
but with the warmth of friendship."[17] To that end, Teruzzi mustered a
convoy of twelve armored cars and 100 soldiers for the five-hour trek to
Cyrene. From there they would proceed the eighty-seven kilometers to
Darnah, where, after a rousing visit with the local population, he would
proceed to Gubba to meet with 125 tribal elders.

To show his good faith, Teruzzi would bring a small entourage comprised of his wife, a translator, his secretary Solimena, and a small escort.
In describing the first leg of the trip, which at moments passed scarcely

four kilometers from the front lines, Lilliana wrote home that she would have "preferred taking a walk down Fifth Avenue." At Darnah, "The people were ecstatic . . . for their battalion commander [had returned], as he promised; no prime minister could have had a superior welcome."[18] At Gubba, we have blurry Kodak snapshots of the group huddling beneath ancient fig trees, Teruzzi at the center, making what Lilliana described as a "marvelous speech." Teruzzi told the tribal elders: "Those of you who have contact with the rebels, because we know that you do, you must let these men know that under my governorship they have only two prospects: either alive under the shade of the tricolor flag or dead."[19] After drinking to peace from a shared chalice, with Lilliana by his side in her solid gold wrist cuffs—gifts from the elders she would show off for the rest of her life—the governor and his party left with the sense of a mission well accomplished.

Teruzzi's grand diplomatic gesture may have had an illusory effect, but the impact of the military blow was real. By August, General Mezzetti was getting the results he hoped for. Having hemmed the rebels, their

Visit to the Obeidats, July 1927

families and belongings on all sides, he proceeded to bomb and machine-gun them from above with renewed tenacity and ferocity until they dissolved and dispersed into a swarm of terrified fugitives, the warriors abandoning their old people, women, children, clothing, foodstuffs, and even their livestock and weapons. By the end of the campaign, the army had killed 1,226 rebels, captured 269 rifles, killed 2,844 camels and captured 842, captured 18,070 goats and sheep and killed another 5,050, seized 172 cows and 26 horses, and confiscated almost the entirety of the rebels' tents and household effects. The army had also "saved" 232 women and children "ignobly abandoned by the rebels."[20]

Lilliana had gone back to Rome for the first time just as the spring campaign in the Jebel was opening and found that people made an "enormous fuss" over her.[21] May 1927 was a brilliant moment to be an American in Rome and the wife of a leading fascist. Mussolini had decided to hike the value of the lira on international financial exchanges, at great cost to consumers and workers, and Wall Street now saw wonderful investment opportunities in Italy. American banks had just made their first big loan to the city of Rome; another to Milan would follow. Charles Lindbergh had recently landed at Paris-Le Bourget, and everybody said his next adventure would bring him to airplane-crazed Italy.

"We [Americans] are usually considered nothing," Lilliana wrote her father. "The people here in Rome now look at Americans with renewed respect and admiration as they realize that we are a people noted for more things than 'dollars' and 'Prohibition.'"[22] She felt very proud.

Cyrenaica, too, was in the news. Lilliana had so many demands on her time in May and June from people she hardly knew that she intended, she told her father, to meet "only with people who could benefit Attilio politically" and keep him "informed over the very important and very secret things I get to know here." When they had an "adequate house" in Rome, she planned to organize a salon and to have on her "visiting list only the finest in Rome." Often, she stayed up half the night to write "extremely long letters" to her husband, making sure to phrase them "just right." Attilio reciprocated, covering pages and pages in his smallest hand, like "small books." She was his publicist and spy in Rome; she was also his proud wife, confidante, and great love.[23]

At Margherita Sarfatti's soiree, she cultivated the new journalists of the anglophone press: Cyrenaica now had the attention not only of the pro-fascist Cortesi father and son from the *New York Times* and *Herald Tribune*, but also the anti-fascist Cyril Sprigge from the *Guardian*. On her second trip to Rome, in early fall, she was the center of attention at the Federzoni's home, where Luigi joked at her self-aggrandizing account of their August mission to the Obeidat tribe, saying she deserved the Cordon of the Star of Italy for Colonial Service for sipping from the cup of tea the Obeidat chief had spat in to bring them all good fortune.[24] In Milan, she went out with Teruzzi's friends Varenna and Farinacci, and had a lesson with Maestro Fatuo, who said her voice was like a "beautiful bell and four times as big as it was."[25]

Attilio missed her, and that made her happy. Sometimes she wasn't sure if he understood how much his fellow fascists envied him such a wife. Late at night, after a long day, staying up to write him long letters in her American-inflected Italian about what she had seen and heard—"quando tutto tace," she quoted from their favorite, *Turandot*—she spoke eloquently of her deep love for him, but especially for what he stood for: "Let me now kiss you ardently on your mouth, my joy joining with yours at the incessant blows dealt the rebels and their acts of capitulation, all of that procuring me immense joy, knowing as I do, all too well, how skeptically your plans were regarded, how much you were inspired by your enthusiastic, marvelous 'sacred fire' of true sincere love for country and not 'love for personal self-striving.'" And, "I am happy and proud, and nobody can give me a more beautiful gift than to speak to me of your deeds and your rule."[26]

Nothing escaped Mussolini. Having learned from police reports that Lilliana was in Rome on her own, he asked Teruzzi later in August, when he finally returned to Rome, why she had come ahead of him. Teruzzi said that he had been detained by the war effort, adding, "She is a great help to me."

"I know," Mussolini said, "give her my regards."[27]

Teruzzi was over the moon. Mussolini asked whether he wanted to become a senator or a deputy. The Senate was "best for him," both Attilio and Lilliana agreed. That was the appropriate sinecure for military men who had served their country with distinction. Federzoni, usually so begrudging, complimented him on his good work. They went to a dinner party, Lilliana sang, and the whole company was touched beyond words. It was a sign of Mussolini's esteem that, when they returned to Benghazi in early September, the head of state's train car had been put at their disposal once more, this time to take them to Syracuse, from whence they would embark for Benghazi. There was a big send-off at the train station this time too, and Margherita Sarfatti and her daughter Fiammetta were conspicuously in attendance.[28]

In Benghazi itself the fall passed uneventfully. With Christmas approaching, Teruzzi commented playfully to his in-laws about the family division of labor between the war front and the home front: "Dear Mommy and Popsie," he wrote, his gist: "I am throwing all of my forces into the military campaign, and Lilliana into the campaign for the Christmas tree."[29]

The campaign to conquer the Fezzan that had been agreed upon in Rome in October was planned for the first of January. The thrust seemed altogether clear. Moving from Cyrenaica at the command of Mezzetti, and from Tripolitania under General Graziani, the forces would meet at the 29th parallel, occupy the Fezzan, and then go on to conquer Kufra, the last bastion of the Sanusi Empire, which lay six hundred miles southeast of Benghazi. With that, the Roman province of Libya would be reunified, and the fascist government could think of combining Cyrenaica and Tripolitania under a single administration.

The strategic concept for the whole operation belonged to Marshal Badoglio, who had in General Rodolfo Graziani, the commander of the troops in Tripolitania, a peerless executor of orders.[30] In October 1927, Graziani was going into his sixth year of duty in the colony. By 1923, when he was promoted to brigadier general after crushing the local insurgency, he had assumed the *physique du rôle* of the desert warrior: tall, lean, and chisel-faced like a sheik, riding a camel or on horseback at the head of his troops. He spoke Arabic well enough to recruit onetime enemy warriors to staff his command and captain his fearsome bands of irregular forces. He was fiercely competitive with other generals, also with the British and French, and thus was always pressing to combine radio reconnaissance, fast-moving mounted troops with armored cars, and air force strikes to put Italy at the leading edge of desert warfare.

The more his ambitions grew, the more he publicized himself by embedding journalists in his command and writing his own hyperbolic accounts of his military feats under the nom de plume Gebelicus. Fascist censorship didn't dare touch him. He had arrived in Libya when the truce system was dead. There was no need, to his mind, for the consent of the *capi*, much less of the civilian population. It was imperative to control the entire territory. The more success he had, the more he denounced the negotiations of the old-time colonial army as obsolete. The more he spoke of the need to control the territory, cutting off all contact between rebels and people, the more the elimination of the uncivilized nomads sounded like a public good. So it was increasingly and fatally accepted that cleansing the Fezzan, then the Sanusi capital at the oasis of Kufra, and after that the Gebel of Cyrenaica of the last dribble of insurgency was the only solution.[31]

Teruzzi, meanwhile, felt more and more torn between his new civilian self and his old-colonial soldier self. The more the pace of life in Benghazi quickened, the more its residents worried about war—which would hurt commerce, damage relations with the Arabs, and never accomplish anything permanent. The more contact he had with the town's Arab notables, the more he learned that Idris's brother, al-Rida, who had now formally become his deputy in Cyrenaica, would be prepared to submit to the Italians if they opened channels. And with al-Rida's support, the Mogarba, Sciammac, and Auaghir tribes on the path of the Italian column's march southward would do likewise. If he could strike this deal, the whole of Libya would be a big step closer to pacification. He would demonstrate his own astute command of colonial affairs and silence the naysayers.

Timing was critical. It was almost October and al-Rida was at Jalu. Sharif el-Ghariani, the Benghazi notable, had contacted the famously intelligent Abd el Aziz el-Isaui ez Zintani, de facto foreign minister to the Mahdi, Idris's and al-Rida's father. He would be the go-between. Once al-Rida was convinced to come to the capital, el-Ghariani would host him, in keeping with his high rank, at his villa outside of Benghazi while they negotiated the final truce. By late October, the aged Ichaun had arrived with a letter from al-Rida. After consulting with Federzoni, Teruzzi sent el-Isaui back bearing another letter, which left auspiciously on November 16, Lilliana's twenty-eighth birthday. At el-Isaui's return on December 22, the government's prestige was at an all-time high. Al-Rida called Teruzzi's letter "sublime" and professed his "absolute faith in [his] loyal word and the Government's arrangement for assuring our honor."[32] By that time, he was already on the move, camel mount, due any day at Ajdabiya.

From Federzoni's vantage point, the Arab revolt was Mediterranean-wide. Weapons flowed in from Egypt. The Sanusi had shifted their base from the Gebel to Kufra. From Egypt, the exiled Emir Idris was fomenting anti-Italian sentiment across the Arab world, denouncing Italy's brutality and ineptitude. He mused about the need for a "furrow of blood" between insurgents and civilians: "Delenda Carthego!"[33] At the same time, Badoglio was stepping outside of his role as a military man, as if he, not Mussolini, were the foreign minister, by insisting that Italy's colonial pretentions would never be taken seriously by the Great Powers by means of treaties alone. Italy had to secure its territory militarily.

Teruzzi's view was more local. He listened to his own counsel, his people in Benghazi, and to Lilliana, his chief booster. When the *Popolo d'Italia* interviewed him in late October in Rome, he opined: "The secret for winning over the Muslim populations and especially the nomads lies concretely in the wise reconciling of the use of force with the use of persuasion."[34] His policy may have been politically right, and his uncharacteristically sophisticated words picked up from the cosmopolitan crowd he met at Margherita Sarfatti's salon. In that moment, other colonial powers had decided to pursue such a conciliatory policy, after having been similarly harsh. It might well have worked. But it was not current Italian policy. Late on New Year's Day, Teruzzi was jubilant. Al-Rida had arrived at Ajdabiya to clinch the truce. He telegraphed Mussolini a fourteen-line telegram, its essence: "leader Sanusi rebellion four years submitted."

The next day, Federzoni telegrammed him. He was to place al-Rida under arrest.[35] Teruzzi argued against it but to no avail. One week later, shackled together with the aged el-Isaui, al-Rida was embarked for Sicily and exile on the island of Ustica. To his host, el-Ghariani, he confided his jeweled dagger, the symbol of his command.[36]

All of Benghazi was outraged at the government's breach of trust. Teruzzi was forced to grovel. He had on his conscience not just al-Rida but also the exile of Ikuan el-Isaui, who on March 3–10, 1928 —Ramadan, 1346— wrote him, pleading for Teruzzi to free him before he died of cold, reminding him that he had traveled back and forth across the desert for six months at "orders on high," "with pure hands and sincere heart," wanting "only his praise, not compensation."[37]

At the official celebration of Eid, the end of Ramadan, two weeks later, Teruzzi claimed that he had actually helped al-Rida by having him sent to Sicily, where he could not be suspected of conniving with Umar al-Mukhtar. Later, he would argue that the ultimate order was right but that "his concept" was right too. That was to keep al-Rida in Benghazi for two or three months "to maximize the resonance" of his act of submission. By that time, nobody in metropolitan Italy cared. Anybody who followed the story would likely have nodded at the official version, namely, that exile in Sicily was a pleasurable holiday compared to the punishment the pseudo-Emir richly deserved for his years of treachery.[38]

In the meantime, Teruzzi had flown to the 29th parallel to be present at the head of the troops as they entered the oases of Jalu and be photographed on his horse as the sheiks swore to submit to Italian rule. In late July 1928, Federzoni alerted Teruzzi that the current military operations were not "contributing to a decisive resolution to the pacification of the country."[39] He then ordered that the campaign be completed as quickly as possible and by every means authorized. Following the example of the army in Tripolitania, Teruzzi had already started down that path. The Italian government had only recently signed the international covenant outlawing the use of poison gas in warfare. Marshal Badoglio recommended its use, and Mussolini signed off on that decision. In his daily report on February 16, 1928, Teruzzi noted that a squadron of eighteen Caproni fighter planes had gas-bombed and strafed with machine-gun fire

Commander-in-Chief Teruzzi, on horseback, officiates the oath of submission for Arab leaders at Jalu, Cyrenaica, February 1928. Photographed by Manlio Lega.

Lilliana Weinman Teruzzi Estate

encampments in the vicinity of Wadi Engar. They had destroyed forty tents, including twenty belonging to large family units, and killed hundreds of animals.[40]

By the late spring of 1928, according to contemporary military opinion and later Italian military histories of the war, all the inhabited territory of Cyrenaica had been secured. All that remained were some mopping-up operations. But that was not Graziani's view, as he pressed into the Fezzan, nor Mussolini's, who was smitten by the general's outsize personality, audacity, and mercilessness. A latter-day Scipio Africanus, Graziani prided himself on having been a fascist general before Mussolini himself knew what a true fascist general should be.

By the spring of 1928, the glow of being the vicereine of Cyrenaica had worn off for Lilliana. Life at the Palazzina had been so much fun that first year. Even when they had no house guests, they always had eight or ten people for lunch and dinner. Lilliana had enjoyed the adulation. The "populace" loved her, as far as she knew. The newspaper celebrated her birthday and their wedding anniversaries. The fishermen named the alleyway by the boat ramps in her honor. A town clerk baptized his firstborn Lilliana.

Later, Lilliana blamed the arrival of her mother-in-law, Celestina, for the change of mood. When the couple was engaged, Lilliana had rarely had occasion to see her mother-in-law and no reason to think that the old lady would ever live with them. But Celestina was now seventy-three, pensionless, and had no other close family in Milan. She had chronic asthma and couldn't take the city's sweltering summer heat. On July 27, 1927, a large and enthusiastic crowd welcomed "the elect lady" at the Marine Terminal, "in full flower and indescribably happy at her son's embrace."[41]

With her broad, deeply lined Lombard face, white hair in a bun, Mother Hubbard dresses, and dainty purse on a chain, Celestina turned out to be a more sympathetic personage than her American daughter-in-law. Within a few days "La Mamma" could be found at home hovering around the kitchen, positioned prominently at the dining room table, or at her seat in the parlor, where she followed the conversation, knitting a sweater sleeve or vest and commenting at a pause in the conversation with one of her endearing Lombard aphorisms. After a few months, she had become a public fixture: on the dais behind her daughter-in-law, out taking her afternoon constitutional, or on a mission of charity, making her way through the Arab quarter on a mission of charity to deliver food or clothing to indigent Italians.

Whenever the wife of the governor was back on the continent, which happened on at least two occasions over the next year, Celestina did the honors at the Palazzina. She also began to bring in her own friends. Teruzzi's second cousin on his mother's side Enrico Carissimo arrived with a commission from Como textile manufacturers to lobby the governor to set up a monopoly for the cotton burnooses and headscarves worn by the locals. Attilio had to weigh his Arab subjects' restiveness against his mother's hurt feelings. Later, he made up for his refusal by appointing his cousin as his personal secretary, then promoting him to the rank of consul in the Fascist Militia.

Then there was the Catholic bishop, Monsignor Bigi. Since he was without a family or entourage of his own, he often ate at the Palazzina. In Celestina, he found a living exemplar of the simple faith of nineteenth-century Lombard Catholics. Their table conversations made Teruzzi reflect hard on the little esteem that he had hitherto shown toward the Catholic faith, as compared to the genuflections of respect toward the rabbi and the Jewish community and the cadi and the Muslims. His mother tugged on him to please the new archbishop, a hearty and handsome man, the scion of an important Orvieto family, who was eager to convert Teruzzi to his plan to make Benghazi the seat of the biggest cathedral in all of Africa.

If Lilliana is to be believed, her mother-in-law encouraged Teruzzi's worst habits. She waited on him hand and foot. She hovered around his sickbed when he came down with a high fever, as if he were about to expire. Lilliana suspected Teruzzi of having sexual adventures, which he was. His mother covered up for him when she made jealous scenes. "What did she expect?" Celestina said in effect: "he was a forty-five-year-old man; he had never pretended to be a virgin; he would settle down as soon as she had given him a child."[42]

Nobody in Italy expected daughters-in-law not to resent the way their besotted mothers-in-law idolized their sons or the mothers not to resent their daughters-in-law. But Lilliana's own pumped-up notion of Teruzzi's power and their shared mission made it hard for her to accept her husband's peccadillos. She had been covering up for them practically since they had returned from their honeymoon. She had been hurt to discover that he still had at least one girlfriend, the irrepressible Pupy Torelli,

Teruzzi, with Lilliana, his mother, Celestina, and friends at Giuliana Beach, Benghazi, 1928

daughter of a fascist official from Piacenza and Alassio, whom he'd not yet broken off with. She was devastated to learn that he had very significant debts, and she was worried about what her father would say if he knew that she had drawn out her entire first allowance to pay them off. In Cyrenaica, debts were no longer the problem, but sex was. Lilliana tried to be high-minded when they went to the theater and her husband would scan the audience to see if there were any new female faces.

What wife would not have been tempted, when her husband left for the battlefield, knowing he had cheated on her, to break into his safe and read the packet of letters he had kept from old girlfriends? Doing so led to the discovery of yet another woman whom he had taken up with when they were just married. You can well imagine her horror on reading the letter from Maria whom he knew from Sondrio. "Dear Atti," she wrote, disclosing that she had aborted their infant to free him "from the tiny hands that could obstruct your path."[43]

The governor had dismissed his trusted secretary, Ferdinando Solimena, in late 1927 after some scandal with a woman and cocaine and replaced him with Antonio Zamboni, "that p. and p.," she wrote prudishly—pederast and pimp—one of the war-damaged flotsam and jetsam of Milan who had found comfort in Teruzzi's tolerant company and had gone to Benghazi to run away from who-knows-what legal problems. And from his wife as well, according to Lilliana. She would have had to be megalomaniacally self-possessed to believe that their love was of a higher order, after Zamboni and others physically blocked her from going into her husband's office while he was in there with a woman. Whatever she suffered was not the point: his behavior was unworthy of their shared ideals, of Teruzzi's good reputation and his duty to set a good example for others.[44]

Time and again, there are references to Teruzzi's double face, his "austerity" and "hedonism," his gravity and his excess. Lilliana anchored the former; Zamboni procured for the latter, which in the colonies meant drugs and sex. That was the colonial soldier's prerogative, even if this particular colonial soldier was now governor and commander-in-chief. There were the Italian young women, increasingly arriving on their own to seek their fortunes, who came around to the governor's offices for information and for work. There was the so-called Black Fonduk, or Sudanese quarter, infamous for its open-air love dances. The officers in the nearby garrisons were always holding wild parties, entertaining white and black women with equal prodigality but strictly separately.

And then there were the Arab boys. As Benghazi became more and more Italianized, in the words of one interested observer, the "audacious early settlers with their helmets and keen boots, spurs and whips, gave way to . . . a new generation with a predilection for noble frippery and eccentric frivolities."[45] They, in turn, were charmed by "the mobs of children, with none of the dignity and distance of" the Bedouin tribesmen:

bright little devils, precocious, disquiet[ing] and smiling, Arab boys, thin, nervy, petulant, bold . . . always ready to play tricks, wriggle their little tummies in belly dances, and parody soldiers' movements, insolent mouths, intrusive, curious, enterprising. . . . They hang about the hotels, the campsites, the barracks, on the lookout for bread or for a few lira. . . . ragamuffins all, to be kissed and castigated.

If Lilliana made jealous scenes about the women (the boys didn't show up in purloined letters or around the Palazzina), Teruzzi must have told himself he had to be less clumsy, not, he insisted, that his behavior bore any relationship to the love and respect he bore her. When she raged to her mother-in-law, the old lady was unsympathetic: "he would change when she had a child" was the familiar refrain. Exasperated, Lilliana hissed what must have sounded like blasphemy to the old Lombard Catholic crone: "If your son isn't careful, I should divorce him."[46]

Motherhood didn't seem at all urgent at the time, though both would have been happy if she had conceived. When it seemed she might be pregnant in August 1927, Attilio gave her a portrait of himself as governor in his admiral's hat with the inscription: "To my dear Lilli, with my heart overflowing with tenderness and the same hope."[47] But she miscarried. When she had herself checked by Dr. Artom, her gynecologist in Rome, and he found nothing wrong, he joked that they should bring her back by hydrofoil when their heir was due.

Nothing was lacking in the public honor Teruzzi paid to his wife: the sirens and the fascist salutes as they with their escort made their way to the beach, the mail boat delayed by 24 hours when the weather was bad, so she wouldn't suffer from seasickness. Telegrams to the continent alerted the prefects to treat her as if she were a dignitary as she landed in Syracuse, boarded the train to Naples, and in Naples changed for Rome, with a crowd of well-wishers and flower bouquets.

Teruzzi had become so convinced that his wife was indispensable to him that in October 1928, on her latest return to Rome, he entrusted her with a special mission that mixed friendship and politics in a way that he himself had not yet learned to carry off. Elections for the chamber of deputies were coming up in the spring, and Francesco Malgeri, his ambitious journalist friend from Messina, wanted his help to get on the ballot. Imagine his wife huddling with Federzoni, the quadrumvir Michele

Bianchi, and a couple of other party notables to convince them, and their pleasure at stymying her (such an inappropriate messenger if he really considered it such an important mission) by asking why "dear Teruzzi" would propose "such a perfidious and incompetent person."[48] Malgeri would not forget that fumble. The other misstep was to use a government car to chauffeur her to appointments just when the new party secretary was cracking down on those abuses. When the usual informers alerted the Duce, he had his personal secretary alert Teruzzi "to tell Lady Lilliana to desist."[49]

Well before then, in May 1928, Lilliana had marked the eighth anniversary of her arrival in Italy. She had been away for a long time and had developed several reasons to return home. The most urgent of these, she told herself, was to renew her soon-to-expire US passport. America had been a godsend to her family. Besides that, she was heir to her father's business, so he didn't want her to lose her American citizenship. She also wanted to let people at home know she was still proudly Jewish and showed that whenever she could, however surreptitiously. In Darnah, for example, when they had visited the synagogue and the congregants had seen that she had told Teruzzi to take off his hat and the chief rabbi, who spoke Portuguese, Arab, and Hebrew, was encouraged to show them the 500-year-old Sefer Torah, they had looked at her like she was "a rare jewel of intelligence and wisdom."[50]

Her thoughts had also turned to their next act. Nothing was quite right anymore in Benghazi. If only she could take charge, she mused in notes to herself, but in what language? Governing in Italian involved so much specialized terminology.[51] They both heard rumors that Mussolini, unhappy at the impasse in Libya, was about to replace both governors with his army chief of staff, Marshal Pietro Badoglio. Isaac, who sensed from afar that his son-in-law's self-confidence seemed shaken, proposed an American solution: the two of them should go on a trip around the world.[52]

Then again, this was a propitious time to visit the United States. Italo Balbo was leaving in late November for the meetings of the International Civil Aeronautical Conference in Washington, D.C., and would stay through early January to tour US aviation facilities. The United States was everywhere in the news as the stock market soared. American public opinion was more enthusiastic than ever about Fascist Italy.

Their plan to set off together for New York on December 16 was disrupted by rumors that at any moment Mussolini would announce a changing of the guard. Marshal Badoglio would become governor of both colonies. Another rumor had it that Teruzzi would be named chief of staff of the Fascist Militia. Nothing could be known until the Duce, following his own counsel, decided.

Lilliana would go ahead to the States as planned but in the company of her mother, who joined her from Amsterdam where her father was on business. Attilio would follow once he had wound up their affairs in Benghazi. On her departure from Naples, Attilio wept inconsolably. She was his rock.

He would soon join her in New York City, she comforted him. The welcome he would get in America would make him soar in Mussolini's eyes.

13

A MATTER OF HONOR

Poor fool! You believed / Her to be pure as a lily! / Instead, dishonor falls / on your greying head.

—VERDI'S *Ernani*, Act 1, Scene 2

Look outside and you will see your husband's power.

—TERUZZI'S FRIENDS, April 1929

On December 18, 1928, five days after Lilliana embarked for America, the Stefani News Agency announced Teruzzi's appointment as chief of staff of the Fascist Militia. By the time the SS *Augustus* was on the open sea, Teruzzi had handed in his resignation as governor. On December 22, just as the ship berthed in New York City, Mussolini confirmed in person his new assignment. It was a daunting prospect. The 350,000-man Fascist Militia reported directly to the Duce, and the position, alongside that of the PNF secretary, was the highest in the fascist political hierarchy. For the first time, Teruzzi had the Duce himself as his commander-in-chief.

Teruzzi was stricken at the news of his appointment. Racked by chills and a fever, all he could think about was having to abandon Cyrenaica: "this land I loved," he wrote to his "dearest Lilli," "the country I thought of as mine and is no longer." It pained him to have started this work, "my labors, the fruit of my faith and will, only to see somebody else bring them to completion."[1] Mussolini expected him to start in the New Year. This meant that before he left for New York City, he would have to return to Benghazi, accompanied by his sister, to wrap up his affairs and pack up the household. He was still running such a high fever on their arrival in Syracuse on Christmas Eve that the ship's departure was delayed twenty-four hours for him to recover enough to travel.

Upon his arrival in Benghazi, his bleak mood had given way to "resignation." Whether the stay would be a "joy" because he was back or a "torture" because he had to leave, he couldn't say. In its grayness, even the normally terse winter sky seemed to protest "at the departure of a governor who loved Cyrenaica as maybe nobody had ever loved her before."[2] All the auguries were depressing, starting with the death of his friend Nobili Massuero, his city commissioner, from the frightful burns he had received on Christmas Day when the bathroom heater in his home had exploded. At the funeral, rumors floated about that he had been cursed by the evil eye; everybody responsible for desecrating the Muslim cemetery at Sidi Sciabbi seemed to be cursed. Lilliana's *tenerissimo* telegram helped relieve the "immense squalor at leaving this land I so loved and still love." Even so, the Palazzina was "cold and empty" and "the packing up much harder than I had foreseen."[3]

The final whirlwind of activity only deepened his melancholy. He inaugurated the train line to Barca (present-day Al-Marj); attended the first meeting of the National Fascist Federation of Schoolteachers, which pleased his sister to no end; had Zamboni replace him as head of the Fascist Federation—a terrible choice; and laid the cornerstone for the high altar of the bulbous Venetian Baroque Cathedral, Africa's largest church and Guido Ferrazza's capstone project. The outpouring "of affection and sympathy" during the final forty-eight hours of banquets, receptions, and public ceremonies both gratified and overwhelmed him.

Teruzzi's last official act was to share these very feelings with "all Benghazi," meaning the several thousand metropolitans, Arabs, Jews, and Levantines who gathered at the Palazzina for the final send-off. He spoke so intimately about wanting to be "remembered as a good father whose heart would always be with them" that many were near tears. He wanted to thank all of them, "from the highest to the humblest," for having "understood and been close" to him with their "work, discipline, enthusiasm." He wanted "the indigenous people to understand that I had followed the orders, customs and laws of Rome, and I never failed to be generous with the good, and inflexible with the bad." He confessed his disappointment that the "payout" for all he wanted to accomplish "was less than projected." Still, he could signal to the beautiful new streets the pride the people of Benghazi felt at the renovation of the governor's mansion and the new woodlands he had planted across the lagoon, where they could find respite from the heat. Above all, the port was no longer "a mirage, a lost and lonely dike in the sea." The financing had been arranged, the contracts were underway.[4]

His closing words to the people of Benghazi were the battered war survivor's rhetoric. "If they were truly strong and worthy" when they thought of him, they should also think of "those who gave more than we could because as they fell, their last thoughts were for their faraway homeland. Sublime heroes immolated by the fire of passion and tenacious will for life [. . .] Let those heroes guide us, renew your faith [. . .] in the august name of Benito Mussolini, Duce. [. . .] Victorious and invincible let's shout out together, 'Long live Italy.'"

At two o'clock exactly, with cannons firing salvos, boat sirens screaming, and the crowd at the floating dock yelling, Teruzzi boarded the launch to the ship, resigned to take up his new assignment in Rome.

From New York, Lilliana only picked up the happy ending. After a few dispirited notes on leaving Benghazi—"as if he were leaving his mother, it broke his heart"—her husband, once he had returned home, was his usual self.[5] His two scores of cables and several letters brought hugs, infinite big kisses, "his affection huge and immutable," "infinite tenderness," and news about mutual friends, about Foxy and Liù, their fox terriers, and his sister, mother, and brother.

He wrote of his joy at being reappointed to the Fascist Grand Council, his elation, on February 11, 1929, at the "immense success of Mussolini," the "glory of fascism" at the signing of the Lateran Accords with the Vatican to end the six-decades-long war between the Church and the Kingdom of Italy, and the excitement at the forthcoming elections for the Chamber of Deputies. He didn't blame her, but he did note that his own satisfaction at being on the ballot had been tempered by his good friend Malgeri's grief at being excluded. She, in turn, wrote him of all her "doings." He replied that hearing about them "brought him joy and comfort."[6]

Lilliana was making her social debut in a city that had changed immeasurably since she had left eight years earlier. No place on earth was wealthier than New York City in the winter of 1929. The stock market was soaring to higher and higher peaks, and her own family's wealth had grown by leaps and bounds, as had that of thousands of other Jewish families. The Weinmans now lived in a fine apartment on West End Avenue. But what was that compared to the Palazzina, where she had lived as if they had an "income of $500,000 a year"? With the expectation that upon

Teruzzi's arrival they would have at least as many social obligations as they'd had in Rome, and since her father was still in Europe, she and her mother had settled into a suite at the Savoy Plaza on Fifth Avenue at 59th Street.

The gala opera performance on January 6, which she attended as General Director Gatti-Casazza's guest, presented the first occasion for her to introduce herself into the public eye. The Metropolitan Opera had of course changed hugely, along with everything else. Another hungry, gifted immigrant's daughter, Rosa Ponselle (born Ponzillo), now occupied center stage. On November 16, 1927 (Lilliana's twenty-eighth birthday), Rosa had overcome her stage fright at Maestro Serafin's coaxing to deliver a Norma in her effortless, perfectly intonated voice. Serafin called it a "triumph" that revealed Bellini's utter genius. Henceforth, Ponselle was America's "Caruso in petticoats."[7]

To read the Hearst tabloid *New York American*'s coverage of Lilliana's presence at the Met on January 6, 1929, two melodramas unfolded. One was on the stage; the other took place during intermission, when "people caught sight of the elegant young matron in Gatti-Casazza's box and speculated about who she might be." They had seen her "listen[ing] to the opera with such intensity, every once and a while brushing a glistening tear from her cheeks. Word spread among the spectators that she was Donna Lilliana Teruzzi, wife of the head of Mussolini's Fascist Militia."[8]

The full story, concocted with Lilliana's or her father's or both of their unsubtle knack for self-publicity, which ran under the title "East Side Girl, Now Retired Opera Star, Visits Scenes of Childhood," contained only one substantial truth. "Fate," she was quoted as saying, "had brought her back in a very different role from that she had imagined from her hard work and her parents' sacrifice." Italian tradition, "dictated by the prerogative of royalty," said that fulfilling her official duties was incompatible with being a great opera singer. "Lilliana Lorma had to become Lady Teruzzi, the wife of his Excellency."[9] And so she had broken her contract in order to marry him. She certainly didn't regret it, but there "is just a wistful sort of feeling about what might have been," as if "there were two of me—the one who had been in Italy for nine years and the other who belonged here." She could have told her parents, who had decided to sacrifice everything: "Here it is, all back! A contract for a thousand dollars a night." Between the lines, one could understand that by nullifying that contract, she had given up an important part of herself.[10]

With the start of the post-holiday season, everybody—the Italian consul in New York, the ambassador in Washington, the whole Italian community—was asking when her husband would arrive. The luncheon she gave in honor of the ambassador was a great success. "Everybody regrets your absence," she wrote. "Mapa hugs you dearly, also Amelia, I send all my affection." She sent "dearest greetings" through Balbo, who had been feted at the Biltmore Hotel with a dinner dance. Lilliana promised Attilio his welcome would be at least as enthusiastic.

Around eight weeks into her stay, when Teruzzi had to postpone once more, she began to fret. Her father had to return to Antwerp for business. If he couldn't come to New York, she wrote her husband, she would head straight back. In late February, he cabled, asking her to be patient: "You have the certainty my love is unchanged," he wrote. Then again, four days later, he wrote that he would leave on March 15. And once that date drew close, he wrote he would leave on March 23. "On orders from above," he had one last mission, but he would stay through April. If he couldn't, she cabled, she would board the SS *Augustus* and return right away. "Don't," he cabled back, as he was just about to board the SS *Vulcania*. If she did, they would pass one another on the high seas.[11]

Nothing in her whole life had prepared Lilliana for the telegram she received on March 23, 1929. It was the 150th or so communication since they had been apart. She had anticipated that this one would let her know when exactly he would finally arrive. Instead, his telegram read:

> I haven't left, and I won't leave. Stop. I didn't want to end your illusions about that because I wanted you to wait there for a letter to arrive on March 25. Stop. In it you'll find everything that concerns you. Stop. Regards: Attilio.[12]

Since a rapid rereading of his confiding, tender correspondence over the previous ten weeks convinced her that nothing had changed in his relationship with her, she could only conclude that something horrible must have happened. She was certain of it. The government was cracking down on the Milan *Fascio*, her husband had confided to her a few days before. Since the Fascist Party federal secretary Mario Giampaoli, his longstanding comrade, was being purged and Farinacci was involved, Teruzzi must be in trouble. Her duty was to be at his side.

She cabled that she was returning right away and then waited twenty-four hours. When she heard nothing, she bought a ticket on the first boat to Europe, packed her bags, and the next evening boarded a German liner bound for Cherbourg, where her father would meet her, coming from London. The crossing took nine days. She had never traveled alone before, and sitting at the captain's table was no comfort.

By the time Lilliana's ship docked on April 2, the letter announced in Teruzzi's telegram had reached New York. Her mother, who had stayed behind to close up the suite, read it and telephoned Isaac in London. The contents were shocking and not at all what any of them had expected. Their son-in-law's issues weren't political at all. They were personal. "Ferulli's lover cannot be Attilio Teruzzi's wife," were his utterly bizarre words. "Therefore, you will never again appear before my eyes." The marriage was *over*.

"Stay in America," Teruzzi admonished, "subsequently we can quietly get a legal separation, or if you want to use the possibility that the law of your country gives to ask for a divorce, I will have no objection[. . .]. I will be bound by Italian law, but I don't care since this atrocious delusion will prevent me from ever again tying my life to another woman." His final words were blasted out as if he were on a dais, his fist pumping into the air: "these decisions are irrevocable and nothing and nobody in the world could influence my decision."[13]

The moment Rose arrived in Paris, the three of them huddled in their suite at the Hotel Lutetia to pore over the letter. The first several pages, composed in small orderly cursive, as if Attilio had copied it over, presented a whiny litany of minor faults, as if he were the garrison commander and she his termagant wife. Lilliana had treated his mother badly. She had acted like a snob and a hypocrite toward the decent young women congregating around the governor's offices in Benghazi. She stole things. She boasted to everybody that she used money from her own pockets to maintain the Italian colony of Cyrenaica. She made jealous scenes and slandered him to anybody who would listen, including his own sister, the maids, even the Askari. The last two pages, scribbled out in a more and more agitated hand, concluded with her most outrageous offense: it was not just that Lilliana had betrayed him with her manager, worse, she had tricked him. She hadn't been a virgin at the time of their marriage.

About this preposterous accusation, that Lilliana had been Ferulli's lover—Umberto Ferulli, her opera agent, whom she hadn't spoken to since 1925, when she became engaged and left the stage—Teruzzi gave no details. Knowing him like the back of her hand, Lilliana concluded that somebody had influenced him to take a decision she couldn't fathom. It was a political plot. Or maybe he had been seized by a mad passion for another woman. It was all a mix-up. If she could just go back to Rome, she could talk him back to his senses.

What had brought Teruzzi to act so bizarrely? We can only guess. The start of the rift surely lies in the moment Mussolini named Teruzzi his chief of staff for the Voluntary Militia for National Security (MVSN). That appointment entrusted him with what was becoming the most important mission of the regime, namely to transform the armed guard of the revolution, the Blackshirts, his movement's ex-*squadristi*, into a formidable fighting force. They had been brought to new levels of discipline, equipment, and training. But they were still a restive force at the effective command of the Duce rather than the king, and they were still susceptible to the intransigent spirit of the fascist old guard. If Mussolini had his way, the Blackshirts would be the force to break Italy out of the restraints imposed on her under the terms of the Treaty of Versailles.

This goal—and his choice of Teruzzi as the tool to achieve it—could only just be glimpsed on December 19, 1928, when Mussolini's press office gave notice of Teruzzi's appointment in the context of "a vast movement of the top hierarchies of the state and the regime."[14] With this latest changing of the guard, Mussolini was, in effect, making the most significant move since the March on Rome to show how he intended fascism to wield its double power: to unleash its violence and to rein in the establishment. At that time, he had counted on the fascist *squadristi* to bring him to power and had expected the established military's complicity. Six years later, he had both the power and the experience to reset the relationship between the militia and the army so that both would work together to pursue fascism's imperialist designs. First, he retired Federzoni and took over the Colonial Ministry himself, with the quadrumvir, General De Bono, as his undersecretary. With that move, he signaled more strongly than ever fascism's heightened colonial ambitions. Then, he ceded his own cabinet portfolio as war minister to a well-regarded Piedmontese military professional, General Pietro Gazzera, presumably to modernize the woefully out-of-date military establishment.

He also named Marshal Badoglio to the governorship of Libya, with the goal of uniting Cyrenaica and Tripolitania. Since May 4, 1925, Badoglio, in addition to being army chief of staff, had been chief of the defense staff, in charge of war preparation advising Mussolini on strategy, and coordinating the armed forces. It was a post he would hold until 1940. Mussolini was sending Badoglio to Libya with two purposes. First, with General Graziani as Badoglio's vice governor, he hoped to annihilate the Libyan rebels. And, second, he wanted to ensure Badoglio's fealty. To that end, Badoglio would be paid a salary several times that of Teruzzi and De Bono combined, 500,000 lire a year; he would acquire the noble title of Marquis of Sabotino, and all the emoluments that went with it, including his son's right to inherit it; and he would be given a free hand in Libya, which he would govern until 1934.

Finally, he upgraded the Fascist Militia by appointing Teruzzi—a highly visible stalwart of the fascist Old Guard, whose esteem had grown greatly in Mussolini's eyes thanks to his governorship of Cyrenaica—as his chief of staff. Teruzzi would take the place of army Brigadier General Enrico Bazan, who since 1924 had quietly done his best to shape up the ranks by purging incompetents and thugs. Like Federzoni, Bazan was retired to a red-velvet sinecure in the Senate, the very same august position that Teruzzi had naïvely hoped for once his service as governor was over.

If we were only to read the press communiqué, we could be forgiven for believing that Teruzzi, as a soldier and fascist of the first hour, was "technically" and "politically" the "perfect choice." But spy reports, anonymous letters to the Duce, and phone wiretaps culled at the time reveal that many people had reservations. A wiretap of a telephone call between General De Bono and Balbo suggests that both were concerned and confused by the appointment: "Unbelievable, that man [Mussolini] is really incomprehensible when it comes to certain things. He always manages to dredge up ugly types," General De Bono offered. To which Balbo, who always professed to be Teruzzi's friend and promoter, replied: "Right, an ignoramus, a clown as well as a lush and a pervert." "He's a familiar face in every disreputable spot in the capital." Their drastic judgment: Teruzzi is "the sort who causes wrack and ruin, then tries to remedy it by bowing and scraping."[15]

For the comrade from the old guard who wrote anonymously to Mussolini, Teruzzi was a "little corporal"—*un corporaletto*—at best, whereas the position needed a true *condottiere*, a leader who was at once "strict, honest, upright, rigorous, who knows always and everywhere how to hold his place fascistically." It must have been a relief for Teruzzi to see the press orchestrate reports that news of his appointment was welcomed with "great satisfaction."[16]

Let's now imagine Attilio Teruzzi in his role as husband to Lilliana, suddenly freighted with the jealousy of his friends and comrades at his latest turn of fortune. He was saddled with the day-to-day duties of chief of staff, which were all under review as he took charge, and bombarded with a plethora of pieties about the qualities attendant upon the position: not only "faith and will-power," but also purity, duty, honor. Let's recall that he had long internalized the now anachronistic idea that the wife-consort of an officer had to be an asset to the garrison. No soldier was a free agent. He had secured the permission of both of his commanders, Mussolini and the king, to marry. His *generale*, Vaccari, had acted as their witness at the Church wedding. He would be dishonored if Lilliana ever shamed him in public.

Instead of going to New York, Teruzzi had been obliged to return to Cyrenaica on December 27. From there, after more than two weeks of psychic pain at failing his mission, he had returned to the continent on January 14, reaching Rome on January 15. On January 17, the Duce inducted him into his new position at the Viminale, where the fascist command still had its seat.

From then on, he was in the maelstrom. His first meeting was with the war minister, General Gazzera. It was his first exposure to this pure product of the Military Academy of Turin, Piedmontese and diffident, a logistics man, humorless, brusque, a nitpicker, all work and family. They worked out a plan to sponsor joint maneuvers for the late spring. Teruzzi then visited his needy, inept clique at Lecco-Como. The province's fascist federation was roiled by kickback scandals, and he had to use all of his influence with the party, the prefecture, and Mussolini to cover up for his protégé Tarabini's misdoings. Coming and going through Milan, where he saw Farinacci and Varenna, he tried to steer clear of the political scandals involving bankruptcies, kickbacks, and bribes, which Farinacci—who had now crowned himself the Cato of the Fascist Revolution—was exploiting to purge the local party head, his onetime comrade Giampaoli.

In Rome on February 1, Teruzzi conducted the first meeting with the MVSN's newly reorganized territorial command. The next day, the whole Fascist Militia was on parade for the king to display its loyalty to the Crown. Mussolini was on horseback wearing his uniform as "First Corporal" of the nation for the first time, and Teruzzi rode alongside him. On February 11, with millions of others, he had experienced a tsunami of emotion as the

Lateran Accords were announced: the Vatican reconciled with the Kingdom of Italy: Mussolini and fascism had completed the nation's unification! The following week in Rome, he had reviewed the 112th Infantry Legion and been a judge at the militia's national fencing team competition.

On February 27 Teruzzi presided over the inauguration of the first exposition of the Fascist Militia's history, with Farinacci, De Bono, General Vaccari, and other notables attending. Five days later, together with the top military, he attended the funeral mass of Marshal Diaz at the Basilica of Santa Maria degli Angeli. On March 7, he was back north in the Piedmontese Alps to judge the militia ski jump contest, with Mussolini's chubby adolescent sons, Bruno and Vittorio, in tow. Three days later, he was sat at the center of the party hierarchs' meeting to prepare for the upcoming parliamentary elections. The whole next day he attended the Fascist Grand Council to draw up the candidates for deputy, himself included, who would be elected by a national referendum on March 24. On March 12, he made the ten-hour train trip to Apulia, where, after reviewing military maneuvers at Barletta, the home base of his Great War brigade, he visited Bari to kick off the electoral rally.

Though he missed his wife, and he had telegraphed her practically every day, he had no lack of company. Andalù, his Eritrean adjutant whom he had brought from Benghazi, went everywhere with him, even to the top of the ski slopes at Limone in Piedmont, a striking presence in his colonial uniform, tall, dark-skinned, and unflappable, with only his orange-striped regimental scarf to fend off the Alpine cold.[17] Returning to Rome, with nobody at home, Teruzzi always ate out with friends. How was his wife? Everybody would ask. Really, where is she? And why away for so long? Sensing that His Excellency missed her just when he needed her most, Alberta, the maid, was especially solicitous. Wives, by her definition, were never away.[18]

The truth is that Lilliana Teruzzi had not a clue as to what it meant for her husband to have been promoted to chief of staff of the Fascist Militia as she settled into her suite at the Savoy Plaza and began to unfold her grand plan to win them a permanent place within the Duce's inner circle. Her letters to Attilio were destroyed together with all of his correspondence related to the marriage that was not in her possession, so we have no idea how she had recalibrated her perception of their future together.

It is altogether possible that no significant ill would have come from Lilliana's long absence had Teruzzi not read the packet of letters he was given—thirteen of them, to be exact, twenty or so pages in total, written on her stationary in her inimitably bold, rushed hand. The letters had been written between April and October 1925, when Umberto Ferulli was coming and going between Paris and Milan, Lilliana's career was at the acme of intensity, and Teruzzi had just begun to press his courtship.

Vincenzo, Ferulli's younger brother, had found them at the family home in Grumo Appula. Everybody was looking for an entrée or a job or a party card or who-knows-what favor or another. Up until then, Vincenzo Ferulli's life chances had been pretty dim: he had a diploma in commercial studies, was working as an accountant, and had married a local woman who, if Lilliana is to be believed, had sworn to shoot him if he didn't make good on his vow to marry her after taking her virginity.[19] Suddenly he had seen Teruzzi all over the news. Maybe it was when Teruzzi visited Bari in early March that his entourage got wind of the existence of the letters. Maybe it was the resourceful Malgeri at *Il Messaggero* who acted as Teruzzi's publicist who turned them up or his friends Farinacci and Varenna, who had long decided that Lilliana was a loose cannon and were on the lookout for something to compromise her. A wife-consort was not useful to him in his new position, they may have decided, especially not a domineering, intrusive, foreign, dare one say, Jewish woman.

The letters certainly sounded compromising. Once they had been translated, badly, into Italian, Lilliana emerged as a hen-house cackle of endearments, non sequiturs, commands, and oddball and obscene Italian vernacular. She started each letter much as she did when she wrote to her parents, "Carissimo—Beloved," and signed off "Tutto mio amore—all my love," "your loving," "Now good night darling, all my love and God bless you. I love you more than ever before," and once, "la tua mogliettina" (your little wife).

She told him she looked forward to their rendezvous in Barcelona. She wrote that her "mother non sa niente di quel memorabilissimo viaggio— mother knows nothing of that most memorable trip" they had taken together to Florence. "I am very well, thank God, and la mia felicità sarebbe completa se tu fosti qui con noi—my happiness would be complete if you were here with us." And, "Here I am without your news; how can you be so cruel?" "Tesoro caro, stai bene, amoruccio mio, mi manchi assai, assai. Che felicità con te qui, eh?—Dear treasure, stay well, my little love, I miss you terribly, terribly," she ventured in another. "What happiness it would be with you here, don't you think?" "Dormo malissimo, I have been sleeping terribly as I have become so accustomed to stretching out my hand and finding my Umbertucciolo." "Non ho fatto cambiare ancora il lenzuolo perché odorano di te, amore—I've not had the sheets changed because they smell of you, love."[20]

In Italian, some of the phrases sounded like prostitute talk: "Il marchese domani, capisci, amore mio?—My period tomorrow, do you understand, my love?" "Million kisses and niente seghe"—no messing around, literally, "no jerking off."

Intimacy is always ambiguous out of context. And who would really understand the campy salacity of "Diva talk" outside of the opera circuit? The Lilliana Lorma on tour with her manager, half-naked as he helped her change costumes, sighing as she closed the hotel door to go to bed, was a sexual tease because she was the Prima Donna; her every physical pang—her period, a throat ache, a sniffle—was an issue because her whole divine body was her instrument. The Queen Bee, who treated everybody around her like drones, was not the forbidding woman Teruzzi had courted. She was not the "pure lily" she had made herself out to be when she had thrown her jealous scenes in Benghazi. For anybody not in the opera world or who didn't get what a prude she was, from the maladroit translations, she certainly sounded as if she had been Ferulli's lover.

Had Teruzzi's character been more stalwart, had he not been feeling vulnerable anyway, faced on his return with the roil of plots, investigations, informers, and political gossip; had he not been the new commander of the Fascist Militia; had he not tried to make sense of the letters with his many confidantes, including his men friends, his sister, and the maids, conceivably he would have brushed them aside, or if he was jealous, furious, and flabbergasted, perhaps he would have waited to confront his wife at her return.

But everybody wanted a piece of him. Nobody could be trusted, and informers were everywhere. Everybody was engaged in some plot or another, and his only solace, short of confiding everything in her, was groupthink. When his retinue was pressed to make sense of the letters, it turned out they did not like her very much—and, in fact, had never really liked her at all. Her habits, in retrospect, appeared more and more bizarre. Alberta was especially observant, as only a lady's maid can be, noticing idiosyncrasies she might never have divulged had she not been urged to speak up. It turned out that in Benghazi, Alberta had often discussed with Lina, the lady's maid recommended by Serafin, who had stayed on in Benghazi to take care of Celestina, how Lilliana was such a fake. She would burst into tears over anything, only to laugh a moment after. She made outrageous comments about her husband, only to lavish him with kisses, hugs, and proclamations of undying devotion the moment he came into the room. Any excuse was enough to squabble with Mamma Celestina. She was a snob, and she said terrible things about people. She was utterly self-centered. She was a miser. Once she tried to sell a ticket she had gotten for free. She was brazen about her nudity and always shaving her arms and legs.[21]

Teruzzi believed his retinue. "If you had made yourself more sympathetic to people I would have never learned what I know now," he wrote her in that explosive letter. But, "You never felt one iota of sympathy for these honest folks, raised like me through the hard work of the honest poor and highly esteemed by everybody around them!"[22]

Within a very few days, his Lilli—his willful, exuberant, self-important, talented, loyal, adorable Lilli—had been transformed into a scheming, smut-talking whore. As he wrote the letter to end the marriage, he remembered the first night of their honeymoon, that "I was Calaf," he wrote, and he thought he had conquered the Ice Princess. "Instead," he concluded, "you were the one to triumph."[23]

As Attilio sought to understand the exact nature of Lilliana's treachery, every feature that had previously been appealing became repugnant. She was a rich American just as the wolves of Wall Street were being accused of gobbling up Europe's capital and public opinion was turning anti-American; she was Jewish just as Italy had begun to turn into a Catholic nation under the influence of the Concordat, and non-Catholics were becoming suspect. She was an intrusive female, always trying to beguile and connect people, just as the fascist regime was poised to relaunch its mostly male political machinery and its prominent *salonnières*, from Vittoria Lepanto and Countess Bice Brusati to Margherita Sarfatti, were being relegated to the backstage.

To confirm the truthfulness of the letters, Teruzzi spoke with Umberto Ferulli. And Ferulli, hearing what he was being asked in a purely private conversation, between two men about a woman, who was herself absent and with whom he had not been in contact for four years, confessed to having been her lover. His motivations here, though ugly, were understandable. He had played the slave to Lilliana's divadom: she was the next Caruso, his greatest passion. The amateur impresario and the ingenuous debutante had pledged fifteen years of fidelity to one another in the silly contract they had signed in May 1921. Intoxicated by that prospect, by his pivotal role in the heady success she was sure to achieve, and, above all, by the beauty of late spring, he had come on to her. She had pushed him away, and he was embarrassed. They had both made amends, but not in a carnal way, when his greatest love, the divine Caruso, died suddenly that summer. She was in Milan, he at Grumo Appula. He wanted to expire from grief. Her letters were his only comfort. He renewed his vows of love for her, but chastely. She resumed her sexual teasing, her only real ardor being for the opera, which he understood as meaning she would give herself to no one else.

Ferulli could not tell Teruzzi that by marrying him Lilliana had betrayed his dreams and that he was still angry at her and her father for having turned their backs on him after all he had done.[24] Here, then, was his chance for revenge. The upshot was that his onetime nemesis came away convinced he had a new friend, a true gentleman, and Ferulli that he had acquired an important acquaintance, one who could do him an immediate favor by getting him a party card for *fascisti* living abroad.[25]

What now? That lapidary sentence at the end of Attilio's final letter to Lilliana said it all: "Ferulli's lover cannot be Attilio Teruzzi's wife." He had told her that she should stay in the United States and follow the customs of her land, namely, divorce. Having composed his indictment, advised by his friends Marigo, Malgeri, and Azzoni, he read the letter to his sister, sealed it, and gave it to his cousin Enrico Carissimo, now his personal secretary, telling him to post it by express mail to Naples, so it would make the next boat for New York City. The next day he had cabled his wife: "I am not leaving; I won't leave—*non parto, non partirò*." "Wait for the letter, which concerns you."

From her own reading of the situation, Lilliana was certain that if only she could speak with her husband, they would clear up any misunderstanding. On April 6, she left Paris for Rome. In the morning, when the train reached Turin, she telegraphed ahead that she and her parents were arriving at 7:55 that evening. He should meet her. She told friends as well. She expected that the welcome would be the usual: everybody there, bouquets of flowers, the dogs leaping about, hugs, squeals of excitement. But only two people were on the platform when she arrived, her best girlfriend, Bice Pio di Savoia, her sweet-looking face crumpled with distress, and Prince Alberto, her stalwart and ineffectual spouse.

They went to the apartment: nobody was home, not Alberta, the maid, nor Andalù—only the dogs, who could be heard yelping inside. Not finding her own keys, Lilliana had the concierge break down the door. Everything was a mess: drawers and cabinets had been flung open, the telephone yanked out of the jack; the dogs were starving and had defecated everywhere. The next morning, when she called around to friends from a neighbor's phone, her husband was nowhere to be found. Servants answered: nobody was available, and nobody returned her calls.[26]

Around nine, a familiar face showed up. It was Federico Azzoni, the patents lawyer-inventor, her husband's old friend from Milan. During his long stays with his son at their home in Benghazi, the one they had always joked with at dinner about buying stock in his new-fangled sponge-diving bell, he had become as much her friend as he was Teruzzi's. Right away he made clear that he was there in his capacity as her husband's lawyer, to obtain her consent to a separation. She was alternately incredulous and furious. Did they think they could dismiss her as if she were some servant girl or an office typist? "I only want to speak with my husband before I do anything," Lilliana kept insisting. Her mother recalled the words: "I will certainly not sign anything before I see my husband."[27]

Azzoni persisted: it was "useless to put up any resistance," given her husband's "eminent political position," and "no lawyer in Italy would dare to take up her defense." If she resisted, the general would deport her parents and have her exiled. He said: "look outside and you will see your husband's power."[28]

She looked out and saw four plain clothes policemen. If she was sensible, she would just sign and take a long trip abroad.

That evening, Teruzzi had a letter delivered to the "Weinman Family," saying that the parents had "illegally installed themselves" in his home: if they didn't leave in two hours, he would have them removed by force. After Mr. Weinman rushed over to Azzoni's, Teruzzi relented, but only on condition the family find a lawyer by the following day.[29] That evening, at ten, they went to the American Embassy. Ambassador Fletcher met them as soon as he could the following morning and urged them to go to Vittorio Scialoja.

III

OVERREACH

14

TO KILL A MARRIAGE

My hands already
grasp the threads;
now, Iago,
to weave the web!

—IAGO, Act 2, Verdi's *Otello*

Seventy-three-year-old senator Vittorio Scialoja was Italy's best-known jurist. A Turin-born Neapolitan, the Risorgimento statesman Antonio's first child, who had been schooled in Florence and Rome; a former minister of justice and of foreign affairs, Scialoja was currently Italy's ambassador to the League of Nations, whose covenant he had helped write. If he didn't stand up to the fascists on the big political issues so much now, he still took his stand on the majesty of the law. "Everything within the law, nothing against the law, nothing outside of the law," he said, to contradict the fascists' slogan: "Everything within the state, nothing outside of the state, nothing against the state."[1]

Male vanity reinforced his belief that his generation, the sons and heirs of the Kingdom of Italy's founding fathers, represented the nation's true ruling class. In all ways they were better than Mussolini's fascists—their untutored, uncultured successors—except, alas, in age.

Lilliana had never met a member of Italy's now decapitated liberal ruling class. At their introduction at his office behind the Palace of Justice, she saw a fussily dressed, dark-eyed little man practically levitating with energy. And Scialoja, seeing that his new client was an attractive young woman, leaped into action. It helped that Mussolini regarded him as his mentor. A revered professor at the University of Sapienza, Rome's leading university, he had tasked himself with educating the president of the Council of Ministers, who had no previous experience of public office. "Distinctly intelligent" he had said of his pupil; he "doesn't always get it, but when he does, he really does." The problem, Scialoja quipped, to underscore who was the venerable teacher and who the neophyte pupil, was that Mussolini was "wanting in three senses—a sense of the economy, of politics, and of justice."[2]

For the old man, justice for Lilliana, or anybody else for that matter, meant applying the law. He believed in taking cases against the regime that were winnable—not the usual moral foot stamping about fascist brutality. He had just turned away Paolo Treves, the brother of the exiled Socialist Party founder, Claudio Treves, who had come with his sister-in-law for advice on how the family could shake the police detail that stalked them night and day. Scialoja had told them there was nothing to be done. The only thing they could do was to follow Treves into exile, and the "ignoramuses, the police" would follow them until they "realize they had overstepped their bounds." He refused to accept anything for this advice, of course: he only dealt with "rights," he quipped; Treves's case was about "wrongs."[3]

Lilliana's case, as Scialoja saw it, was about a woman wronged before the law. For the gentleman Scialoja—son of the Risorgimento economist-statesman Antonio and his emancipated French wife, Giulia Achard; the father of three daughters himself—liberal society was first and foremost about the good order of the relationship of public and private. True progress called for "making women freer" by reforming Italy's antiquated laws on dowries, divorce, unwed mothers, and out-of-wedlock children.[4]

Glancing through the sheaf of cables and letters, Scialoja saw in Lilliana an exemplary victim of despotic government. Not only was her dowry-grabbing husband an Italian, and she a vulnerable young foreign lady, he was also a leading fascist.

"*Mascalzone* (rascal)," "*mantenuto* (freeloader)," he concluded, slapping down the evidence in disgust.[5]

Scialoja agreed to take the case. First things first: he urged Lilliana to check her bank account. She did, confirming his surmise that the cad, after renouncing her, had drawn out the remainder of the last payment her father had made into their joint account. This information was perfect for Scialoja's purposes. He threatened Teruzzi with arrest as a thief, and the money was returned. He turned away another of Teruzzi's self-styled lawyers, the same Francesco Malgeri who had been wounded by Lilliana's clumsy political interference in 1928 and who, out of some combination of motives—true affection for Teruzzi, intense dislike for the wife, and pandering for support as he strove to become *Il Messaggero*'s editor-in-chief, which finally happened in 1930—kept interfering on Teruzzi's behalf.

Scialoja said he would take her case pro bono after Malgeri insinuated that he should milk the rich American family for all it was worth. He stood his ground against Mussolini, who was inclined to step in to mediate a separation between Teruzzi and his wife after Malgeri tattled that Scialoja was heaping ridicule on fascism's leading men. When Mussolini quoted his words back to him, he didn't deny that he had compared the Italy of today to the good old times, "when the men in government had clean motives. When the honesty of political leaders was proverbial, when serving one's country was routine, not something to be flaunted." The story goes that Mussolini dismissed him, and since he was disenchanted with the League of Nations anyway, he never saw Scialoja again.[6]

Lilliana's self-assurance rebounded with Scialoja's support, and she continued to refuse to sign the separation agreement. Certainly, she thought, if she could speak to Attilio they would reconcile. So she persisted in trying to see him. He, meanwhile, in the hope of driving her from the country, kept her and her parents under constant surveillance. When her mother—who was on the verge of a nervous collapse—bought a train ticket to Paris, where she intended to see her husband for a few days, his spies let him know.

As the night train pulled to a stop at the Italian frontier at Bardonecchia around four o'clock in the morning, a secret police agent banged on the train compartment door. He told Rose to get dressed and, when she balked, had two *carabinieri* hustled her to the station house, where a woman guard strip-searched her. She was then ordered to swear that she would not try to return. When she refused, she was frog-marched to a nearby hotel. There the police drew up a form and forced her to sign it (adding words they could not make out—"I want to stay in Italy") before rushing her across the border to Modane with no luggage or travel documents.

In Rome, before dawn, Lilliana was awakened by the knock of the building's custodian who said that a police commissioner had a message from her mother. When she opened the door, five plain clothes men pushed into her apartment, demanding her passport. When she said she didn't have it, they ransacked the place, found her US passport, and confiscated it. Her father, trying to get in touch, learned that none of his telegrams had arrived. They had mistakenly been delivered to the command of the

Fascist Militia, he learned from the note attached them on their return, which closed with "Saluti Fascisti."[7]

The American Embassy made it its business to protect United States citizens abroad, and Lilliana, despite its confiscation, still carried an American passport. Lilliana and her father, who'd rushed to Rome when he couldn't reach them, alerted the ambassador. He contacted Dino Grandi, Mussolini's undersecretary at the Foreign Ministry, who, wanting to avoid a diplomatic incident, pressed the chief of the political police "very urgently" for "clarification." The chief, Arturo Bocchini, minimized. He said that Rose Weinman had been found in a state of "agitation"; her misadventure was an unfortunate case of mistaken identity; she and her husband were free to come and go. No report was filed on the apartment incident. They had taken Lilliana's expired American passport, but her Italian passport was safe and sound, locked up, on her lawyer's advice, in his office strongbox.

After three weeks, Lilliana capitulated. If she signed, she reasoned, her husband would stop his harassment. They might become friends again, even reconcile. That is what his friends advised: "just to sign, if that's what he wanted;" "in Italy it means nothing. It is just a caprice. You will see in no time that you will make up again. You don't know Italian men," they said. Meanwhile, she was being inundated with anonymous threats.[8]

Since Teruzzi was about to go abroad on a mission, the lawyers set the court day for June 2, 1929. Scialoja wanted to stipulate that there had been "wrongful action" on the part of the husband. But Teruzzi's lawyers insisted that the couple was separating by mutual consent on the grounds of "incompatibility of character."[9] Lilliana still treasured the hope that she would have the opportunity for a private face-to-face conversation with her husband. The law insisted on this, in the hope that couples would reconcile at the last moment. But Teruzzi's lawyers prevented it, telling her they would arrange the meeting of the two after his return. Lilliana was so browbeaten by then that she just wanted to sign the separation agreement. She picked out a few items of sentimental value among the wedding gifts, though under Italian law she had a right to half of the whole lot, and sent him her elephant pin to keep him safe on the journey, with the notion that she looked forward to recovering it in person on his return. It was just a jeweled trifle on a gold chain, a present from her father. She always wore it when she traveled, and she had often lent it to him in Cyrenaica.

In his note of reply, he thanked her for the "kind and delicate thought," which he took "to want to convey that no rancor hovers in your heart." For his part, "even with the bitterness of painful disillusionment, I nurse neither hatred nor rancor, but my heart is not and cannot be the same as the day I departed to Darnah carrying with me the same memento which will now keep me company in the Orient."[10] Lilliana rightly deciphered his contortedly gracious words to mean that the memento she had blandished as a "loan," hoping for it to be returned in person so she would have the opportunity to see him, had been taken as a "gift," really a "theft." She never lost hope of retrieving it.

Though Lilliana had hoped to hush up what was happening, the break-up soon became the talk of the town. Even before her return, Teruzzi had been heard unburdening himself about his wife's infidelity. Margherita Sarfatti's guest book shows that on March 11, two days before he wrote to Lilliana, he had gone by her house alone.[11] Sarfatti would have heard him out, however doubtful she may have been that the high-minded young American she knew could be as culpable as Teruzzi claimed. And of what? All an affair with her manager really showed was that she had poor taste in men. Teruzzi's story must have sounded distastefully hysterical. At Lilliana's return, she would hear her side of the story.

Otherwise, people were divided. One crowd suggested that Teruzzi's wife was lucky to be rid of him. A real man would never have been cuckolded. If he had been, he'd keep quiet rather than maligning his wife. Others, his friends, saw a sentimental man whose vanity had led him to overreach. Better for him to find a wiser, more seasoned Italian woman whom he could depend on. As for his American wife, a pompous moneybags, had she possessed one iota of common sense, she never would have married him, much less have left him to his own devices for so long.

Teruzzi let everybody know that from now on his friends were to be her enemies. And now that he was chief of the Fascist Militia, his circle of friends was wider than ever. A rare few, like the current Fascist Party secretary Giovanni Giuriati, who had been a witness for the bride at the Church wedding, conducted themselves graciously, even kindly. He was "deeply sorrowful not to receive her," he said. But as "Teruzzi's longtime friend" he had "reason to believe it would cause him to suffer."[12] The Hotel Palace, their home away from home for the previous six years, was ruled off limits. They "must understand his embarrassment," the general manager wrote.[13]

But they could not. They only understood, to their mortification, that they had been turned away on Teruzzi's orders.

Only one or two of the illustrious women from her old Roman circle kept in touch. Bice Brusati made a point of having Lilliana and Rose around for tea and hoped she would stay involved in their charity work on behalf of abandoned mothers and children. A kindly person, Contessa Bice also had the freedom to be kind. No fascist, especially not the head of the Fascist Militia, who had every interest in ingratiating himself with the army general staff, would have dared to lift a finger against General Pedotti's daughter, the wife of General Brusati, commander of the Rome Presidium.[14]

Beatrice Pio di Savoia never wavered in her friendship, either. But she now had a newborn to occupy her, and the day after she had gone by Lilliana's to comfort her about the separation, her husband, Alberto, a *carabinieri* lieutenant, had been transferred from Rome to Codogno, a garrison town outside of Milan. Teruzzi was behind it.[15]

Margherita Sarfatti received her former protégée, as she promised herself she would, but only once. Nobody could really fault her. Teruzzi had stopped being interesting soiree material once he had become head of the Fascist Militia. And his separated American wife only wanted to talk about her wounds. Fiammetta, Sarfatti's daughter, whom Lilliana had regarded as a good friend, was overheard telling people, "she should just go away."[16] That hurt. But Lilliana was a proud woman. She never complained, but her change of station took a physical toll. Now unendingly susceptible to influenzas, bronchitis, and migraines, she thinned down by several sizes.

For all her past posturing about true romance, Lilliana was an implacable realist. At the Met in 1929, as she had mused about her life choices, she had been certain she had made the more audacious choice. She was quite certain she was superior to her husband—more cultivated, more capable, more farsighted, physically stronger, and emotionally more complete than he, with his tears, indecisiveness, and need for firm advice. In her magnificent self-love, he was still a projection of her own willfulness. She didn't know that he had seen her letters to Ferulli. She was certain someone had conspired to influence him against her. One man had told another who had told her: "Teruzzi, when he was with his well-off wife, who was trying to keep him straight and honest, wasn't as manageable as Teruzzi on his own and subject to the procurers of pleasure."[17]

Where now could she invest her huge ambition? Her parents hoped she would resume her career—not that she could now take the Met by storm, repair their broken dreams, or console Isaac for having let his misconceived family interest corrupt his basic common sense. She had not given a performance since Barcelona, five years earlier. Whether she sang or not, if she stayed in Europe, she could live well from her allowance, and she would not have to explain to her snooping extended family a turn of fortune that she hadn't yet figured out for herself.

At first, she batted around Milan, living in the hotels that were familiar from earlier times. It was good to get away from Rome and to take lessons once again with her old *maestri*. As time passed, she was more and more unsure if her hope to restart her career was realistic. Even if her instrument still worked and she had the discipline, nobody in Italy could give her a hand.

Serafin had returned from the United States, at Mussolini's personal insistence, to take in hand the Teatro Reale dell'Opera. That was the very same theater, now completely rebuilt, where Lilliana, coming to Rome for her debut in December 1925, had refused to sing. In a dirty operation, the Costanzi had been snatched from Emma Carelli, and she had killed herself in the crash of the fancy car she had bought with the settlement. After a few twists and turns, the theater had ended up in Serafin's hands. He could not have delivered what by this point she no longer wanted: a stage career. But he was in good odor with the fascist regime, and he could afford to laugh at Teruzzi's petulant threats that he stop seeing Lilliana, delivered through Lina, his onetime maid. Lilliana would always remain a good family friend.

The Milanese painter Giuseppe Amisani, famous for his portraits of D'Annunzio's muses, cinema divas, and British society women, captured the pathos of her situation when she sat for him in 1931 for his usual 10,000 lire fee. He envisaged her eight heads tall, luminously draped with a silver fox, majestic yet unsensual, her gaze on the world at once intensely wide-eyed and vexed.

Lilliana's own image of herself was registered in the society pages with a finality that, with some small variations, would endure until she died. When she was mentioned at some stopover or another of American expatriate society at the Crillon, Villa d'Este, or Bagnoles-de-l'Orne, she was invariably "Madame Lilliana Teruzzi, daughter of Mr. and Mrs. I. Walker Weinman of New York and London, the opera singer who performed

Portrait of Lilliana Teruzzi by Giuseppe Amisani, Milan, 1931

Lilliana Weinman Teruzzi Estate

under the name of Lilliana Lorma at La Scala, Barcelona, Cairo, and so on, and retired from the stage to marry Mussolini's one-time undersecretary of state, now commander in chief of the Fascist Militia, from whom she separated in 1929."

The couple's separation had left Teruzzi with the same problem that any number of other Italians faced when their marriages failed. They lived in a modern nation with the scandalously unmodern situation of having laws to marry people, but no legal provisions for them to divorce. Short of getting a divorce abroad, the only way to overcome the tyranny of an unwanted marriage was to have it dissolved by a Church trial. For anticlericals like Teruzzi, that was tantamount to submitting to the tyranny of Catholic theocracy.[18]

The fascist dictatorship had added new complications to the marriage contract in 1929, when, as a condition for concluding its treaty with the Vatican, it had acceded to the Holy See's one nonnegotiable demand, aside from the restitution of Church territories: that was for the Italian state to hand over the sole power to invalidate marriages, both secular and religious, to the Catholic Church. From the start of the negotiations between the dictatorship and the Vatican that led to the Lateran Accords, Mussolini had rejected the idea out of hand. The legislation would open the door to turning Italy into a theocracy. It would encourage the Church to meddle in yet other domains of public and private life.

But the prestige to be had nationally and internationally was so immense if a reconciliation could be achieved that Mussolini eventually conceded on everything. He capitulated without even consulting his Fascist Grand Council, knowing that the anticlerical old guard had always been in favor of divorce. When the matter of Article 34 of the Concordat finally came up for a vote on June 11, 1929, to speak, much less vote, against it was presented as jeopardizing the whole accord with the Church. Everybody was on tenterhooks, in the expectation that Vittorio Scialoja would use his still immense prestige to argue it down. But he just threw up his hands, using his time to say that Italy's founding fathers, with their Law of Guarantees for the Church had been wiser lawmakers, and he voted with the majority. Only a brave handful of anticlerical liberals voted no.[19]

Teruzzi likely shared the belief, widely held at the time, that "Catholic divorces," as anti-Catholics called them, could be purchased with money and influence. This belief had the pope himself machinating at the

Church's highest court, the Sacra Rota, and the Church tribunals, willing to cite some technicality or another, like the lack of a proper birth certificate or the failure of the priest to register the marriage, to fill church coffers and allow desperate souls with the means to secure their freedom an opportunity to escape.[20]

With this understanding, in late 1929, Teruzzi consulted Giuseppe Buonocore, a professor of Church Law at the University of Naples with frustrated political ambitions. Buonocore would later become Naples's first post-fascist mayor, but at the time, he was just emerging from a bad spell. His political career had begun precociously in 1919 when he was elected to Parliament a Bourbon-populist, then again in 1921 as a Masonic-Catholic, only to find himself excluded from the Fascists' *Listone* in the 1924 elections on the grounds that he was an opportunist. For several years he had been angling for a comeback. Article 34 of the Concordat—by recognizing Italian marriage as a Catholic affair and opening up a whole new field of litigation for Catholic lawyers—offered him an opportunity. His 450-page volume, *The Sacrament of Matrimony in Canon Law: Doctrine and Legislation,* came out with the Vatican's stamp of approval in the summer of 1929. In time, Buonocore would be one of those clerical-fascists who propagandized that Saint Thomas Aquinas was a progenitor of fascism for his belief in the well-ordered society. He seized the moment to demonstrate his fascist bona fides by stepping up as Teruzzi's annulment counselor.[21]

To start, Buonocore had to demonstrate that there had been some defect of procedure in contracting the marriage. To establish that, he interviewed Father Giovanelli, the officiant at the Basilica of Santa Maria degli Angeli, only to hear that everything had been done correctly: the papal dispensation for the disparity of cult had arrived, the bride appeared sincere in her pledge to encourage her husband's religious vocation and to raise their children as Catholics, and the couple's vows had been properly registered at the marriage registry of the Vicariate of Rome. When he called on Monsignor Candidori, he saw a couple of possibilities: Candidori wanted to make certain that his predecessor, Father Sinibaldi, had the authority, which properly belonged to the pope himself, to grant the dispensation for a mixed marriage.

It turned out that he did. Also, Lilliana had never filed her birth certificate. But Father Candidori had to disappoint him on that as well. Since there was a letter from Rzeszów attesting that the bride's parents lived there at the time of her birth, "the lack (of the birth certificate)," Candidori told him, "did not represent grounds" for invalidating the marriage.[22]

Nonetheless, Father Candidori alerted Lilliana to the missing birth certificate. She had come to him, with her mother, to seek consolation and, if possible, obtain some practical advice on how to reconcile with her husband. On a return visit, she asked him more pointedly whether, if her husband sought an annulment, she would have the opportunity to tell her side of the story. Father Candidori reassured her that yes, she would, told her to leave her address, and sent her away with consolatory readings from the New Testament.

When she told her father about the missing certificate, he contacted his brother-in-law Milton in Rzeszów. They hadn't used birth certificates back then. What could be provided was the sworn and notarized testimonial on the part of the two aged temple keepers that they had assisted at the birth of Leonora Weinman, daughter of Isaak and Rose Ohlbaum Weinman, sometime in November 1899. Once this paper was filed, the Weinmans regarded the matter as closed.

Lilliana should get on with her life, Isaac wrote: she should be "happy as the day is long" to have rid herself of that man.[23]

Teruzzi did not press the issue because at the time, aside from the usual whirlwind of official business, he was racing to finish a memoir about his past governorship. *Cirenaica verde (Verdant Cyrenaica)* came out in January 1931 with Mondadori, Italy's foremost commercial press. Mussolini wrote the preface, ghoulishly titled "Cyrenaica, Green with Vegetation, Red with Blood," not, he said, because Teruzzi had any need to be introduced but because he was "his friend, a fascist of the first hour." More importantly, he wanted to credit Teruzzi for the "knockout blow against the Sanusi rebels."[24]

It was a big book, almost four hundred pages, dedicated to the memory all of the military who had perished under his command: "that the Roman Imperial Eagles would once more take flight." Pushed by the Fascist Militia, whose high command urged the rank and file to buy copies as a "gesture of appreciation for their commander," the book went through three editions within a year and was well and widely reviewed (even in English).[25]

The book, really a memoir and a plainly written report of things accomplished while he was governor, intended to deal with unfinished business. First and foremost, it aimed to reclaim Teruzzi's legacy. After his appointment as vice governor in March 1930, General Graziani had radically changed strategy. His predecessor's proposal of negotiation had not just failed—it had been always been wrongheaded, he argued. He showed as much by launching his campaign of annihilation of the Bedouin people of Cyrenaica, starting in early May, with "the total fusion" of civilian and military forces to deport the whole population of the Gebel, around 180,000 men, women, and children, to concentration camps in the Sirtic desert.

In January 1931, just as Mondadori was rushing Teruzzi's book out, Graziani's mighty camel, armored car, and airplane attack force, accompanied by massive publicity, was marching against the last bastion of Sanusi power, the Holy City of Kufra, to bomb and occupy the citadel. On February 20, 1931, the attack force executed the last scores of defenders, destroyed the treasure of books and manuscripts, and signaled the end of the Libyan resistance. By that time, Graziani had closed down all of the Sanusi's religious centers elsewhere, confiscated their property and lands, and cut off escape routes and the flow of food and material across the Egyptian border by building and garrisoning a twelve-foot-high concrete and barbed wire wall over the 270 miles from Jaghbub to Bardia. To isolate Umar al-Mukhtar's dwindling forces, he made civilian collusion with the rebels in any form a capital crime and set bands of mobile troops to chase down the few scores of remaining insurgents. A military court was flown to wherever colluders were arrested, to try them on the spot for capital crimes and to carry out the execution in front of their family and kin.

Teruzzi's Obeidats, the main tribe of the Marmarica region, has been the centerpiece of his argument about the virtue of a negotiated settlement. In mid-1931, the tribe had practically ceased to exist, at least in its place of origins. After 20,000 or so of the Obeidats had been relocated to camps near Tobruk, they were accused of plotting with Umar al-Mukhtar to breach the barbed wire to make a mass escape to Egypt. As punishment, they were then relocated 1,200 kilometers to the east in the concentration camp at Marsa al Brega. Of the 13,200 people transported—the men bringing 6,000 animals by a forced march of two months, the women, children, and invalids sent by boat—11,000 arrived. That September, Umar al-Mukhtar was chased down, captured, interrogated, and sentenced to death by the military tribunal. He was hanged in the presence

A concentration camp for six thousand inhabitants at Auaghir, outside
Benghazi, 1932. Photographed by Gaetano Nascia.

Archivio Storico MAECI

of 20,000 camp residents, sheiks trucked in from other places, and the
Arab notability of Benghazi.[26]

Teruzzi's book did more than vouch for his own efforts and tamp down the
niggling rumors fed out of Benghazi about his qualities as a soldier. With its
pacific images of urban renewal and native agriculture, the book was a good
distraction from the horrific accounts that were being circulated abroad
as news seeped out through Cairo and Tunis of Bedouin caravans being
strafed as they straggled toward the borders. Antifascist protestors had
taken to encircling Italian embassies abroad; in Geneva, delegates to the
League of Nations were calling for Italy to be sanctioned for war crimes.

"No single, infallible method [exists] for resolving colonial situations,"
Teruzzi reassured his readers: "What counted was constancy, and, maybe,
not enough attention was dedicated to pursuing negotiations." More than
the policy itself, it was the foreign press that was to be faulted for unfairly
exaggerating the "rigor of the methods taken" in disregard of Italy's "rights
and dignity," and of the Italian soldiers, who had "shed so much blood."[27]

Politics aside, his book paid significant cultural dividends. It put him in
the company of other fascists of stature, all of whom had published articles,
memoirs, and plays, no matter how bad. It earned him his first royalty

checks, put him in the company of Mondadori's pantheon of world-famous authors, made the local boy from the Genoa Gate an interlocutor of Milan's cultural establishment, and turned him into an expert on colonial questions.[28] In Milan, readers of the *Corriere della Sera*, miffed at the heavy expense of maintaining concentration camps, were reassured to hear that Teruzzi, too, had been skeptical about whether anything could ever put an end to the "nomadism" of the Arab people. Only a year after he criticized the "rigors" of Graziani's methods, Teruzzi reported he was "very favorably impressed" by the work of "militarizing and regimenting" going on, especially among the little boys, who in their uniforms had become "models of cleanliness and civility rare in colonial situations."[29]

Teruzzi's biggest satisfaction from the book was perhaps to have expunged his wife-consort, the vicereine, from both his story and the history of Cyrenaica. In 367 pages, there was not a mention of Lilliana and no photographs either: she had been cropped from the one family photograph he published, leaving him alone with his mother and sister.

Eventually, Lilliana received a copy that she kept all of her life. Lieutenant Iorio, her husband's onetime aide, gave it to her as a gift. In it, he had gallantly inscribed: "To one who has loved intensely. A happy-sad-very happy-memory."[30]

15

COMMANDING THE BLACKSHIRTS

[Hierarchy] has as its paramount need elites, true elites, not in
name alone, whose positions arise from their authority, as opposed to their authority arising from their position.

—JULIUS EVOLA, *Pagan Imperialism*, 1928

The summer before his book came out capped Teruzzi's second year of
service as commander of the Blackshirts. Not a week had gone by the
previous year that he hadn't reported to Mussolini at Palazzo Venezia,
gone out on military maneuvers with him, or accompanied him to one
political rally or another. Seeing the old trooper at the Duce's side in
front-page newspaper coverage or cinema newsreels, one could be forgiven for concluding that they were close comrades-in-arms, even close
friends. Teruzzi always had Mussolini's back. He glared at any distur-
bance, warmed up the crowd, and stepped back when Mussolini was ready
to speak. They would exchange approving glances at the high points. He
would bring the Duce out again if the crowd hadn't roared enough. Teruzzi once even spoke for him during an early experiment with sound recording when, one presumes, the Duce had momentarily lost his voice.[1] It
was a tribute to the bond between them that in September 1930, the
Fascist Grand Council endorsed the ten-year project to turn the National
Fascist Voluntary Militia (MVSN) into a fighting force, which, in combination with the armed forces, would represent "a formidable garrison on
which the nation can count in whatever emergency."[2]

The week-long summer maneuvers of the militia with the army at the
command of General Vaccari at Mentana had to be the culmination of
Teruzzi's deep wish—from the moment he had left the army—to remain
under arms and to serve both his new commander and his old general.
Teruzzi treasured the photo of the three of them together that appeared in

Illustrazione Italiana that summer, in coverage celebrating the maneuvers.[3] There was Mussolini, dressed in his uniform as first corporal of the nation, the rank he had during the war, alongside his general, the Hero of Montebello, a Gold Medal winner. Teruzzi still had a reverential regard for his general, whom he never addressed with the familiar *tu*, who had passed over his broken marriage though he had been the bride's witness at the wedding and had supported his every endeavor to give the militia a veneer of the respectability of the traditional army. Vaccari, too, had become a man of the establishment at his appointment to the Senate for life in 1929. Soon to retire, it made perfect sense for him to join the regime's flourishing military-industrial complex as president of Isotta Fraschini's board of directors. The luxury car maker had been bought out by Caproni, Italy's leading airplane manufacturer, after going bankrupt in the Depression, and with generous state subsidies, it was now being retooled to make bomber engines.[4]

Teruzzi's own rank in the military command was always problematic. At his appointment as governor of Cyrenaica in 1926, he had been promoted from major, his rank when he went into the reserves in 1920, to lieutenant colonel. Apparently, he didn't need a general's star to serve as the commander-in-chief of the colony's troops. He had regular army generals to command the troops in the field. In 1930, he was promoted to colonel. Apparently, that was as big a leap in rank as the army would countenance at the moment. It was a big enough concession in 1929 that he was decorated with the Grand Cross of Cavalier of the Military Order of Savoy. This was the highest award given by the king for feats of battle.[5]

Teruzzi was humble in his gratitude, and he looked very grand when he wore the three-tiered, green-enamled laurel topped by the crown of Sardinia on those ceremonial occasions that called for full dress uniform. Some regarded the decoration as a prostitution of the Savoyard military establishment. But such were the times. The gesture signaled a new, if uneasy, modus vivendi between the Fascist Militia and the King's army.

Teruzzi turned out to be at least as good as General De Bono and General Bazan, maybe even better, at sealing the bond. As a military man, he knew the protocols. And he had the advantage of having been a *squadrista*, so he knew the issues the men faced: their salary, benefits, and rank were to be as close to the army's as possible, short of offending the regular military. He had the deferential attitude toward rank and true respect for esprit de corps that was missing in most fascists, including Mussolini himself.

First Corporal of the Nation Mussolini, on maneuvers with Three-Star General Vaccari and Colonel Teruzzi, Lieutenant General and Chief-of-Staff of the Fascist Militia, Mentana, 1930

De Agostini Picture Library/Getty Images

Behind the facade of comity between militia and army, however, the situation was more complex. The militia was indispensable to the power and stability of the fascist regime. From 1930, as the Depression shook dictatorships elsewhere, notably in nearby Spain, where it had caused

217

General Primo de Ribera's regime to collapse in January and pitched liberal democratic countries into one political crisis after another, Mussolini's determination to rebuild fascism as a mass-based regime and to establish new organizations that would capture most of the population in one capacity or another in their activities helped carry him through the next decade. Teruzzi thus has multiple duties: to regulate the 350,000 and growing militia as a military corps, to recruit and train ever more widely, to provide military instruction to university students and youth eighteen years old and up, and to instill in them the regime's military values. Beyond this, he would have to prevent the armed forces from taking umbrage at the militia's privileges, costs, and overall amateurishness while—and this was Mussolini's real ambition—using the militia to force the military establishment's hand in foreign policy.

Unlike in Cyrenaica, Teruzzi never had to complain about a lack of money. Or rather, it sufficed for him to complain—once he had secured a direct budget line from the finance minister—and it was open sesame. He was ever the good quartermaster, cadging budgets, as he told Parliament, with "the voice of the faithful guard of the revolution."[6] From the Interior Minister's budget lines for the ordinary police, he secured funding for his political police. He similarly wrangled resources from the minister of war for training and maneuvers, from the minister of national economy for the forest militia, and from the minister of communications for the port and border, post office, and railroad militia. In the event of a call-up, to cover the volunteers pay while they were in service, the Fascist Party joined forces with the fascist trade unions to strong-arm employers to contribute two-thirds of their employees' daily wages to state coffers. The best part was that the commander of the MVSN did not have to account to any central authority.[7]

Like all of the top fascist hierarchs, Teruzzi availed himself of the spending on giant public works that Fascist Italy used to fight the economic depression. By 1933 his favorite architect, Cafiero, had drawn up plans for a giant new command headquarters. A full block long, on Via Slataper at the corner of Viale Romania, made out of austere brick and set off by a huge watchtower in rusticated stone, it looked like a Roman fortress. He had also brokered arrangements with the military establishment to train troops, use army matériel, conduct joint maneuvers, and find occasions to fraternize.

By the tenth anniversary of its founding, the MVSN had its own history office at Palazzo Viminale and its own prominent exhibit room at the immense exposition of the tenth anniversary of the revolution in Rome, together with its own newspaper and prime-time newsreel coverage for its rallies and commemorative ceremonies. There was a new service manual, written by Teruzzi himself with a seventeen-page 1935 addendum specifying the many varieties of uniforms for all subcategories of the militia.[8] Fascist Party *avanguardisti* matriculated at the annual ceremony of Fascist Enlistment Day, when they would be presented with their first rifle or a wooden facsimile or a plain pole, if nothing else was available. Militia maneuvers rattled somnolent, economically depressed towns with antiflak firing exercises against enemy aircraft, the sirens of emergency vehicles, and the shouts and shots from flanking operations to repel enemy landings. The MVSN's tenth anniversary celebration on February 1, 1933, had the militia brigade of war-mutilated and blind veterans as its centerpiece: they spoke in the intertitles of the newsreel to the nation: "You alone, Duce, can imagine what it means to take up arms again for men who had lost all hope of returning to the ranks."[9]

Teruzzi with MVSN volunteers at summer training camp, August 15, 1933

Archivio Istituto Luce

Though Mussolini had no concrete plans to use the militia outside of Italy, the volunteer citizens' army of Blackshirts—then 380,000 strong, half again as large as the regular army—was a disruptive force internationally as well as nationally. For the time being, it had no parallel in Europe—and would not until two years later, when the onetime lance corporal Adolf Hitler, bolstered by his two million Brownshirts (a force more than twenty times the size of the German army), would become chancellor of Germany. With the spectacle of its training maneuvers, parade routines, and sports and ceremonial functions, the Blackshirts gave the impression of being an invincible force, the loyal brainchild of a leader whose own military training was, at best, superficial. No fascist organization was more responsible for militarizing Italian society, and in the worst way possible: all of that sloppy training that made military life look easy, compatible with home life, and war a glad adventure; all of those men in their slovenly militia outfits, authorized to bully anybody who didn't look right, crowd the sidewalks, push passersby aside, and muscle their way to the head the line.[10]

Whether the militia could ever be good at making war was a big unknown. Some in Mussolini's circle were doubtful. In conversation, the quadrumvirs De Bono and De Vecchi could be heard ridiculing Mussolini's much touted *fiuto* (instinct) about every matter, including military matters, speaking of him as *un caporale di giornata* (a third-rate corporal): "What could he be expected to know about armaments, tactics, logistics," De Bono asked De Vecchi in an intercepted phone call.[11]

Marshal Enrico Caviglia, retired at the time and in self-exile, who had placed so much hope in the generation of young men coming out of the war, saw no way of overcoming Mussolini's innate handicaps. Most Italians had been ruled by kings with magnificent armies, whether Piedmontese, Lombards, or Neapolitans, he mused in his diary: "You take them, you dress them, organize them, and they know what to do." But Teruzzi and two of the quadrumvirs aside, the Grand Council had no real military expertise at all. And Mussolini was from the Romagna, a onetime papal state with no army of its own: "He has no clue about esprit de corps, military honor, authority, hierarchy based on rank achieved by long, loyal, and intelligent service," Marshal Caviglia concluded. "As far as he is concerned, any fool he names a general has authority because he has given it to him."[12]

Criticism only lulled the military into believing it was ultimately in command of making war. When Mussolini took back the War Ministry from General Gazzera in July 1934, he made General Baistrocchi his undersecretary. Federico Baistrocchi was a fine opportunist. He was a card-carrying fascist, but as an army man, he took it for granted that MVSN was a second-rate force. Once that had been acknowledged, cooperation with the militia was an act of noblesse oblige that would in no way sully the established army's professionalism.

Teruzzi's position as chief of staff of the MVSN made him formally second only to Mussolini in the fascist political hierarchy and of equal rank to the Fascist Party secretary. From the end of 1931, Achille Starace had held that position, and in the political choreography so important to Mussolini's public shows of authority, the two men always flanked him. Of course, this rank in itself tells us little about Teruzzi's political influence, social presence, or the personal qualities that made so many Italians come to identify him as a *gerarcone*, "a great hierarch," who was thought to exercise inordinate influence, his power derived less from the institution he ran than from his personal connection to the Duce. Teruzzi was present when the Duce cut ribbons to inaugurate monumental public works. In full dress uniform, he assisted at state occasions, and in somber black, head bared, he could be seen trooping in and out of Rome's basilicas after High Masses for the dead. He was the person to go to in order to get a recommendation for a son for a government post or to stand as a godparent at a child's baptism or witness at the wedding, which could add up to the same thing, or to push through the bureaucratic practice in Rome that could get your town a new school or hooked into the aqueduct or straighten out your war pension.

Hierarchy was the totalitarian state's chain of command, the means by which the Duce's orders were communicated from top to bottom. In principle, the Fascist Grand Council stood at the summit, the supreme organ of collective decision making, and just beneath it, reporting directly to Mussolini, came the chief of staff of the militia and Fascist Party secretary, the latter with his vice presidents, directory, and inspectors. At the provincial level, there were eighty or so *federali*, each with his own directorate, and at the town level, the secretary of the local *fascio*, with his own directorate as well. The numbers added up: at the mega-celebration held on October 28, 1932, for the tenth anniversary of the regime, 25,000 party hierarchs were summoned to Rome, not counting the big shots of other organizations, like the fascist trade unions, which had their own hierarchies.[13]

Hierarchy was also a social category. In theory, the hierarch would partake of the great leader's charisma and serve him as the warlord or priest of ancient times had served the godhead or king. With a bow to Nietzsche's idea of the Superman, the model hierarch dispensed with conventional morality to pursue a purer path based on the principles of loyalty, obedience, duty, and his unalloyed commitment to the cause. His ultimate aim was to refound the Italian state on a whole new moral basis. In the 1920s, with all the talk of modernizing capitalism, the model leader was a molder of men and things, captains of industry and glorified technocrats. By the 1930s, he was identified with the political boss-organizer, able to "reach out to the masses," incorporating them by the hundreds of thousands into trade unions, youth groups, women's associations, and after-work clubs.

By that time, fascists had pretty much stopped discussing the ideal hierarch in the abstract. As late as 1928, the fascist philosopher-ideologue, Julius Evola, who was then only a fringe figure, tried to reignite debate for fear that fascism would degenerate into just another system of cronyism. A true elite, he argued, acquired authority by virtue of its valor rather than by virtue of its position. Anything short of that was the "negation" of hierarchy and "a violent and artificial creation," producing "injustice, hence anarchy."[14] Nobody responded to his provocation. The common-sense definition inscribed in the PNF's political dictionary at the end of the decade was surprisingly individualistic and inegalitarian: hierarchy, as it was defined, harnessed "the power of individuals of greatly varying worth," only it did so "toward the goals of the fascist state" rather than in their own "egotistical interests."[15] That self-serving fluff went along with lots of claptrap about "making way for youth." In practice, once the regime was consolidated in the 1920s, youth got ahead in the time-honored bourgeois fashion: by means of family connections, coming from the right town, going to the right schools, getting the appropriate professional degree, and making a good marriage. Of course, they had to be good fascists, too. And what could attest to that better than the recommendation of a great hierarch?

By the same token, the great hierarch was deeply invested in protecting his own. In Teruzzi's case, that meant he dealt with the peccadillos of his own political retinue much as Mussolini dealt with his. Mostly it was by leniency, for all the reasons that leniency is shown to a favorite: because he is loyal to a fault, you know his weaknesses, and have trusted him with your dirty work; because the alternatives seem worse, and if you gave him up, your enemies would treat it as a sign of weakness.

Alessandro Tarabini, the *federale* of the province of Como down to 1929, was to Teruzzi what Teruzzi was to Mussolini. Fourteen years his junior, Tarabini still had to his credit that he had become one of Teruzzi's earliest acolytes and, as a licensed gymnastics instructor, brought his athletic skills to the sports-obsessed party. Going against him were his father, a municipal clerk alleged to have pilfered from the town treasury, and his younger brother, Cesare, who had recently been indicted and then released for the gang murder of the peasant laborer Brunati, a well-loved, much-decorated veteran who had insulted his honor.[16] Once Teruzzi became head of the MVSN, he promoted Tarabini to the rank of consul. He also arranged for him to be elected to parliament in the spring of 1929 to represent Como. Now that he was a national deputy, however, his mentor had to worry if he caused scandal. And that he did, more or less immediately, by racing his Lancia in the Mille Miglia event and striking and killing twenty-nine-year-old Ida Brunaschi as she returned from work at dawn, in Bologna. The prefect had already suspended his license for reckless driving under the influence of alcohol, which may have accounted for the three previous vehicular homicides imputed to him. When some brave soul stood up in the cinema and shouted, "When will these murders end?" scores of people joined in, forcing the prefect to revoke his license.[17]

When the local magistrate sought to lift Tarabini's parliamentary immunity to prosecute him, Teruzzi was forced to act. He would have to do so tactfully, for the Fascist Party had also launched a big investigation of the federation for skimming income from the fascist summer camps and illegal payoffs from local industrialists. First, he wrote to Como's prefect, asking him to take into account "General" Tarabini's situation as "a longstanding, faithful and honest Blackshirt." If the prefect had read the report of the Bologna prefect, which he included for good measure, he would find that the "Honorable Tarabini should not be faulted for an incident attributable to the imprudence of a girl who had not taken due precautions exiting the streetcar."[18]

By 1929, Mussolini was mostly leaving local party bosses to sort out affairs in their own bailiwicks. So he probably had paid little heed to the anonymous complaints coming in from Como, denouncing "the lurid clique," "the Teruzzi-Tarabini couple," the "wife, Teruzzi's mistress," his procurer for girls from the summer camps—all three of them shamelessly bound together by "unmentionable economic interests."[19] However, there had been a real hullabaloo surrounding the corruption charges, causing the Fascist Party to send in investigators. So Teruzzi made sure that Mussolini received a full report about the incident and was informed that his liege man had been exonerated, but not about his clever solution to address the protest: to promote Tarabini out of the province by making him commander of the militia for the new province of Alessandria. At that point, Tarabini moved to Milan, bought an apartment in a chic neighborhood, and had his first child (whose birth he announced to the world with an engraved card). In Milan, he joined Farinacci's clique, became notorious in the practice contemporaries described as "hierarch wheeling-dealing," and, in January 1943, during the last changing of the guard, became the National Fascist Party's vice secretary. Tarabini never looked back, though he did continue to visit his brother, who succeeded him as the province's *federale*.[20]

First Corporal Mussolini, if he wasn't on maneuvers and sleeping in the president's car, would go home every night to his large family at the princely Villa Torlonia on Via Nomentana. This was well known thanks to all of the propaganda being turned out on behalf of what we might call "fascism's family romance." The flip side of Mussolini the Duce (and, more recently, the first corporal of Italy) was Mussolini the Patriarch, a real family man. It was as if his propaganda served two different audiences. Alongside the militarism, there was always a more diffuse image of Mussolini living a bourgeois home life, whose fundamental conservatism was reinforced by the state's conciliation with the Church and the renewed sense of moral rectitude that ensued—not uncommon in the wake of great social upheavals.

This conservative family portrait was not lost on Teruzzi, who lived the regime's existential lies to the utmost. At the same time as it took people out of their core family unit to organize them into the militia, the party, the youth groups, women's associations, and leisure clubs, the regime celebrated the conventional mother-centered, women-at-home model of family life, with the view of rebuilding Italy's population size after the ravages of the war.[21]

While he didn't often go home, Teruzzi began to invest in his housing. Thanks to Lilliana's social ambition and business sense, in 1928 he had signed up for a unit in the handsome five-story apartment house being built on the Oppian Hill close by the Monti neighborhood, just overlooking the Coliseum.[22] It was a government-subsidized cooperative for military personnel, and he qualified, though, once he separated from his wife, not for the sizable unit he moved into on the building's first floor. The apartment was right next door to Italo Balbo, who was aeronautics minister at the time and who could later lay claim, by virtue of having a wife and three children, to the largest and best unit of all, the penthouse apartment. Over the next three years, Via Monte Oppio 5 would become an ever more central and prestigious address as the regime's vast urban renewal cleared out the surrounding medieval buildings and alleyways and completed the landscaping of the magnificent city park next door. By 1934, the upper floors had a bird's-eye view of the Coliseum, and Teruzzi, from his apartment on the first, had a stunning view from his windows of the Imperial Fora and the Via dell'Impero as it swept westward from Piazza Venezia to the Coliseum and turned sharply into the Via del Mare to go to the coast.[23]

Since ancient times, Rome's notables had established seaside or country residences in which to rusticate over the summer months. In 1930, Teruzzi pulled off a remarkable business coup by buying at auction a villa worthy of a real estate titan at Castiglioncello, twenty miles south of Livorno. Tucked between high hills terraced with olive trees and grape vines and a cypress-covered promontory cradling a tiny port, the town had long been a magnet for summer visitors. The Genoese baron Fausto Lazzaro Patrone, the newly ennobled "Guano King" (so crowned for the business that had made his fortune), had tried to colonize the town by building a gated community in the pine grove. But that enterprise had failed. By the turn of the century, Castiglioncello's image as an artistic and intellectual colony was consolidated by Italian impressionist painters who left a visual record of gauzy seascapes and rustics with flocks of sheep ruminating on distant vistas. Gabriele D'Annunzio, who rented a villa he called Godilonda ("enjoy the waves") and elegized the juniper groves "all abloom with violets, perfuming of resin and flowers," further embellished Castiglioncello's cultural pedigree. Luigi Pirandello holidayed there with Marta Abba at the Miramare Hotel, and Emilio Cecchi—the essayist and critic—was photographed strolling with the poet-novelist Massimo Bontempelli. By the 1920s, children who had summered together over the years intermarried and formed artistic and intellectual family dynasties.

Though not insensitive to that allure, Teruzzi knew Castiglioncello from his movement days, when, at the command of Costanzo Ciano, the naval hero and political boss of the whole coastline, he had been brought in to mediate factional fights among local *fascisti*. By the time he returned to the town in 1929, with his mother and sister in tow, Ciano had become minister of communications and fascist "railroad czar," famous for making the trains run on time. He also arranged for the trains to make more convenient stops. The new stop at Castiglioncello on the Rome-Genoa line put the seaside town within two hours of Rome and Florence.

It was at Castiglioncello that Teruzzi met Oreste Dal Fabro, also a self-made man, though his opposite in every other respect: from the small-town Italian south, trained as a lawyer; a cultivated, sensitive family man; politically liberal; and a top manager at the new steel mills at nearby Piombino. Dal Fabro had put his recently amassed wealth to use by buying the Kursaal, the local gentry's seaside club with its attached pine grove.. His hope was to contribute to the town's social luster by refurbishing the premises, while making a profit from building holiday villettes. Like many salaried men, his fortunes had collapsed in the economic bust after the war. This caused him to suffer a nervous breakdown. He was getting back on his feet psychologically when he met Teruzzi in 1929. Down to then, he'd also had a rough time with the local fascists, who had expropriated the villa on his property line belonging to a wealthy contessa for the new Fascist Party headquarters, together with most of the pine grove around the Kursaal. Consequently, he couldn't build the villettes as he had intended to remake his fortune. Facing bankruptcy, it couldn't hurt if he rented out rooms in his oversize, run-down villa to Teruzzi's sister and mother, and to Teruzzi himself whenever he could visit.[24]

Aside from being a patient and loving son to his difficult mother, Attilio Teruzzi turned out to be a gold mine of helpful ideas. He urged Dal Fabro, rather than selling the villa outright to pay off his debts, to put it up for auction. Teruzzi had contacts with Alfredo Bruchi, the general director of Monte dei Paschi of Siena, who had recently been elected to Parliament. He would borrow 140,000 lire in his own name, payable over thirty years, scoop up the heavily indebted property at auction, and then sign it over "clean" to Dal Fabro, who would place the property in his son-in-law and daughter's name and just pay him back. It was the least he could do to thank him for his hospitality. Dal Fabro basked in his kindliness. "Dead or alive," Teruzzi repeated, he would make the deal work.[25]

Once the auction had taken place, Teruzzi's friends said he would be a fool not to keep the villa for his own family's needs. While he mulled the question over, Dal Fabro obsessed over where he had gone, enraging Teruzzi with the implication that he had absconded. Mussolini had forbidden his men to act as covers for business deals, and Dal Fabro was smearing his good name. It heartened Teruzzi to hear from his Milanese friend, the big-time lawyer Angelo Fortunato Danesi, that this irritant was a nobody, with neither the income, connections, nor imagination to do right by the property, and he, Fortunato Danesi, intended to let Dal Fabro know he had insulted an important person who prided himself on his reputation.

When Dal Fabro went around denouncing Teruzzi for the injustice he had done him, he was told he was lucky that Teruzzi hadn't cashed the checks he sent him and kept the money. When he stopped coming for holiday after Teruzzi threatened him, and he went around saying, "I am the most robbed man in Italy," nobody seemed to care.[26]

Fantasizing about how to renovate the clunky neo-rococo Kursaal, Teruzzi recalled the sober modernism that Guido Ferrazza had brought to the renovation of the governor's residence in Benghazi. In Rome, everybody recommended a younger architect, twenty-nine-year-old Vittorio Cafiero, best known at the time for his startlingly beautiful sets for *The Last Days of Pompeii*. It was the Depression and Cafiero was eager for commissions, especially from such a prestigious patron. Teruzzi wanted his castle to be simple and homey and to embrace the whole Mediterranean seascape: from the tiny fishing port framed by the promontory and the island of Elba to the magnificently modernist smokestacks and storage towers of the Solvay chemical works to the south at Rosignano.

Cafiero experimented. Using reinforced concrete to an unusual degree for a private home, he gave the whole structure an aggressive modernity, softened by the inset iron window casements, cerulean blue shutters, and graceful pillars framing the panoramic front terraces. Inside, he knocked down walls to create a spacious salon, library, and game room, a second floor of bedrooms with a veranda, and, the true mark of modernity, several marbled, mirrored, brightly lit bathrooms. Teruzzi cut a deal with the town council to re-annex the pine grove in return for donating to the completion of the town's aqueduct, and he obtained zoning waivers, who knows how, to build a boat pier, a mooring station for hydroplanes, and an annex so that the custodian and his family could live in a small house instead of in the basement.[27]

Paying for it all left Teruzzi scrambling. Fortunately, he had his double salary as a deputy and militia general. And his Milanese friend Mario Marigo—who after launching his fortunes as a contractor in Cyrenaica had settled in Rome, was reaping endless profits from his contracts for the barracks, command posts, and depots for the Fascist Militia—did the construction work. Cafiero's career was launched. A year later he won his first major public commission, to design the new national headquarters for the Fascist Militia on Viale Romania. A few years later, as the new minister of Italian Africa, Teruzzi would commission him to join Guido Ferrazza in designing the new regulatory plan for imperial Asmara.

By the summer of 1932, Teruzzi's castle, when viewed from the sea, presented an austere and pugnacious counterpoint to the robber baron Patrone's neo-Gothic megalith, Villa Pasquini, on the mountain above. To deflect criticism, the word was that all of his sacrifices to build this abode were for his mother's sake.[28] Her asthma had become worse since her return from Benghazi. The dry sea air offered her relief. To honor her, and with a nod to its marine-blue trim, he called his new home Villa Celestina.

That September, after all of the vacationers had left, La Mamma and Amelia would have sat down with Teruzzi in the quiet beauty of Villa Celestina. Her son had to think of his future now, find a good companion, and have children.

16

IN THE GRIP OF THE INQUISITION

The blackest of crimes
upon the lily fairness
of your brow is written.

—VERDI'S *Otello*, Act 3, Scene 1

L illiana could never have been far from Teruzzi's mind. In January 1931,
he had become so obsessed with understanding how she could have
tricked him into thinking she was chaste that he consulted two of Italy's
leading gynecologists. Medical science had demonstrated that it was possible, both men reassured him. Women could clinch their muscles hard
around the male member while simultaneously releasing capsules of red
dye to simulate bleeding, have coitus coincide with their menstrual cycle, or
surgically repair their broken hymens.[1]

But being tricked into believing that one's wife was a virgin only to discover that she was not could not in itself be cause for the Catholic Church
to invalidate the marriage. Yet times were changing. Maybe there was
more wiggle room in 1931 than in 1929, when the fascists had become so
furious with the Vatican about its pretension to organize Catholic youth
groups in the wake of the Concordat—and the Vatican with the fascists over
the *squadristi*'s acts of retaliation against the adult Catholic Action clubs—
that Pius XI had threatened the whole fascist regime with excommunica-
tion. Recently, relations had been reset, largely thanks to the suave diplomacy
of the Jesuit priest Pietro Tacchi Venturi, who had shuttled between the
Papal Palace and Palazzo Venezia in the August heat.

But nothing was a given. Pius XI was a canny political strategist, as well
as a masterful theologian. In the meantime, the Vatican had embarked on a
religious crusade that put the sanctity of marriage front and center. Concor-
dats with states were indispensable. But diplomacy couldn't prevent the
Church from being beset by spiritual enemies on all sides, nor from its own

haplessness in the face of great issues of the day: the economic crisis and rising nationalism, together with the extremist politics that fed off of both, dividing the world more and more into fascist and communist camps. The Church's only salvation lay in reviving the faith. Marriage was the key, as the pontiff spelled out in his encyclical on the "chastity of marriage." In *Casti connubii*, the message he delivered to the Church's tens of hundreds of bishops on December 31, 1930, Pius declared marriage as the most important of all of the holy sacraments. Marriage established the family. The family generated more and more of the faithful. The more and more numerous faithful, enriched by family values, would in turn be steeled in their belief that they—indeed all humans—were made in the image of godliness. Thus armed, they could combat two of the gravest dangers to the faith, namely, the materialist idea of conjugality that made marriage an act of self-interest and social convenience, and the compulsion on the part of contemporary governments to meddle with the human body, which was also God's body. Whence the logic behind Pius's condemnation of divorce, abortion, family planning, and eugenics in any form.

Of course, the Church welcomed the fact that conservative movements and governments supported its positions on these matters, even if it was for their own purposes. That said, the pontiff was unwavering about the Church's doctrinal premises: individuals were the embodiment of godliness, their bodies inviolable; marriage was sacrosanct, the family the rock of the faithful. Over the next seven years, Pius would formulate equally unequivocal condemnations of Hollywood, Bolshevism, and German-Nazi paganism. God forbid that the Italy's fascist government would ever touch the sacrament of marriage.[2]

Then again, that message was intended for the Catholic faithful writ large, and the Catholic Church had never been a single corpus. The Church had first put itself on record opposing divorce at the Council of Trent in 1563. Yet over the centuries, individuals, mostly wealthy or influential, had found all kinds of subterfuges, from the sublime to the ridiculous, to invalidate their Church marriages. Would anything change because the pope had issued a new proclamation on the matter? The gossip generated by the more notorious decisions in the 1920s—invalidating the marriage of Italy's most famous inventor, Guglielmo Marconi to the Irish peer's daughter, Beatrice O'Brien, in 1927, and that of Marina, the eldest daughter of Italy's richest man, Count Volpi, to Prince Carlo Ruspoli in 1929 after two years of marriage and a child—made it seem that annulments were still readily available to the rich and powerful on trumped-up grounds: Marconi's was granted because the marriage had not been properly registered in his home parish; Marina Volpi's because she had not freely consented to marry, as her father had coerced her. Both then went on to remarry—or more properly, to marry for the first time, as their previous unions had never existed.

As it was, Church trials had always been shrouded in secrecy. That made it practically impossible to know the odds at the time or that, over the previous decade, only about twenty marriages a year had been declared null, in the sense that the Church had determined they had never been valid in the first place.[3]

On the positive side, the reconciliation between Church and state had opened the way to reinforcing at the highest levels the complicity between the Church establishment and the fascist regime that contemporaries called *clerico-fascismo*. As hierarchs and high prelates began to make one another's acquaintance, by appearing on the dais with one another to bless the inauguration of one or another of the good works of the fascist regime, the former learned that the gray eminences of the Church were cultivated, urbane, and reasonable men, and the latter, that the anticlerical reputation of leading fascists had been greatly exaggerated. Even so, if Teruzzi did resort to the Church courts to invalidate his marriage, he would find himself in the unenviable position of being the first to test whether fascist hierarchs counted among the "rich and powerful" who could work Church law in their favor.

Whether Teruzzi would have steeled himself to enter that company had Lilliana not suddenly reappeared on the radar is hard to know. After two years of quiet while she was based in Milan, she had started to move around again. She had long wanted to go abroad. But she only had her Italian passport, and she might well find herself barred at the frontier from leaving or banned from coming back. For assurances that no harm would come to her, Isaac stretched his connections to hire a Washington lobbyist (a "southern" and "Democratic gentleman") to contact Senator Bingham of Connecticut, who they knew to be a friend of Foreign Minister Dino Grandi. Initially, Grandi had been gracious enough: "Nothing prevents Signora Teruzzi from travelling whenever and wherever she pleases, with all of the courtesies due to her." But when she balked at replacing her old diplomatic passport with a normal one, and Senator Bingham contacted him once more, Grandi became furious. "Act like forty-two million other

Italians, if you are one," he wrote her, "turn over your illegal passport, and stop maligning Italy abroad. If you do not, under the law you will be arrested."[4] Lilliana was mortified. And all of that got back to Teruzzi.

The worst was that Lilliana had come to the decision to embrace her life in Italy by moving back to Rome, where she could enjoy a real home in a city with friendly people and a pleasant climate. Sometime in the fall of 1932, she purchased the upper floor of an elegant dove-gray four-story townhouse in Parioli. It was located on Via Paisiello at the corner of Via Carissimo, down the block from the Borghese Gardens. She could boast that the well-known architect Clemente Busiri Vici had designed the building and lived there himself. With its high ceilings and ample floor space, her own apartment offered the perfect backdrop for the genteel living she intended to cultivate. She furnished the rooms with rococo antiques picked up on the cheap from the estate sales of the Ruspoli, Rospigliosi, and other cash-poor papal princes. Then, she filled the built-in closets, a modern touch, with her true love: couture fashion. Patou and Lavin, her current favorites, whose bias-cut, hand-painted silk ensembles with coordinated capelets, complete with the big hats she always favored, made her with her striking carriage, and tall, now very thin silhouette look like a gorgeous fashion plate.

By that time, Teruzzi seems to have given up on finding a cause to have her arrested and expelled. Informers had to be disappointed that her tastes in men now ran to permanent bachelors, aides to the court, or junior commissioned officers of the king's army who wooed her with the canonical lines of Catullus begging Lesbia for "a hundred kisses and a thousand more." All of them were old-fashioned gentlemen, for whom ardor was the kiss pressed on the back of the hand on a Sunday afternoon outing to Tivoli or Lake Bolsena, a gentle squeeze on the dance floor, or a caress at the end of a hand of bridge. Without speculating about the crimp her disastrous marriage had put on her urge for male companionship, Lillian had never courted sexual danger in the best of times; or, better, given the man she married, she was clueless about where it really lay. In any case, Scialoja had practically sworn her to chastity; any mail could be trusted to be opened, the phone tapped, a man planted in her bedroom to catch her in flagrante delicto—grounds for arrest for adultery, or perhaps expulsion from Italy as a "woman of dubious morality."

Still, just being her willful, exuberant self, Lilliana was an affront. Wherever she went, she acted the diva, magnifying her presence by expecting special treatment. When people addressed *Donna* Lilliana as *Contessa* Teruzzi, she never corrected them. When supplicants wrote her for favors in the belief she had the ear of her husband—just as they supplicated Mussolini's wife, Donna Rachele, and the wives and sometimes even the lovers of other hierarchs—she never disabused them. In the public eye, she could have been one of those "countesses of the Viminale," so-called after the louche lovers and co-conspirators of important men who were said to loiter around the antechambers of the palace housing the Interior Ministry and secret police, as Lilliana herself had done in 1926 while Teruzzi was undersecretary. General De Bono notoriously had his *contessa*. Farinacci had his, a Milanese industrialist's wife who was murdered under mysterious circumstances in 1926. Teruzzi, informers said, had several: "Levantine" types, passing themselves off as cousins or nieces, confidantes or paramours, who slipped into fancy parties to steal the silver spoons and fancy perfume atomizers, defrauded restaurants and hotels, and cashed in on their paramour's gifts at pawnshops. Made grotesque, they were in reality clever, ambitious women acting on the principle that a political system rife with corruption and so welcoming to male imposters could accommodate a few female poseurs as well.[5]

Lilliana had barely been settled a month in her new home when a certified letter arrived with a Church seal, dated December 10, 1932, announcing that her husband had filed for an annulment. After being lulled in the belief that no grounds existed to invalidate the marriage, she read: First, she had violated the two conditions he had set before they wed, namely, that she be of legitimate birth and a virgin. Second, she lacked the capacity to consent to the marriage by reason of insanity. Third, she refused to have children.[6]

Scialoja told her that she needed a canonical lawyer as her advocate. He didn't have the legal credentials and had approached Francesco Pacelli on her behalf. However, the dean of the lawyers of the Sacra Rota, also Pius XI's leading legal advisor, claimed a conflict of interest. His younger brother Eugenio—the future Pope Pius XII—was currently the Vatican's cardinal secretary of state whose superior, Pius XI, was also the bishop of Rome, under whose jurisdiction the trial would be held. Scialoja was relieved. That meant that Teruzzi couldn't hire him either.[7]

Then they realized the trial had been moved to Milan and was set to open on January 2, 1933. Normally, the trial would be held in the diocese where the marriage had been celebrated or where the defendant resided. If the defendant was not Catholic, it could take place in the so-called actor's diocese. To have it in Milan, Teruzzi had fiddled the police records to have his official residence changed. It seemed like a smart move. Milan was his home territory. There would be less gossip and no Monsignor Candidori, the Rome tribunal's president, to affirm that there were no grounds for annulment. His brazenly anticlerical best friend, Farinacci, would be right at hand. True, he had no expertise in canon law. But he was a well-known perjurer, and his law practice now extended to every area of legal endeavor that stood to benefit from vehemence and bullying. True, he hadn't yet had the opportunity to strong arm a Church process. But at Cremona, he had kicked around enough priests and ravaged enough Catholic associations to make a good faith effort. At the very least, he and their other friends would steel the pathetic Teruzzi to defend himself.

Not that the Church of Milan was a pushover. Fascism was a passing regime; the Church was forever. Since 1929, the giant palace of the archdiocese, where the tribunal was housed, had become Ildefonso, Cardinal Schuster's earthly domain. On his way to becoming cardinal, Schuster had been the first bishop to be ordained with the express approval of the king, as stipulated by the Lateran Accords. Building on his fame as the "Cardinal of the Reconciliation," the onetime Benedictine monk had taken the sixteenth-century Counterreformation archbishop of Milan, Saint Charles Borromeo, as his model. His hope was to transform Italy's largest diocese into the most socially active, culturally lively center of Catholicism in Italy, perhaps anywhere. At the same time, Schuster gave his full benediction to the fascist regime for all the good it was doing in the world: during the 1930s, Duomo Square often served as northern Italy's largest fascist parade ground.[8]

The archdiocesan tribunal was no exception to Cardinal Schuster's reforming zeal. Its president, his friend, the canon of the Basilica of Saint Ambrose, Paolo Castiglioni, tapped the best legal minds of the archdiocese. Once the promoter of justice, Vittore Maini, the Curia's solicitor general, universally known as "a man of great intelligence and notable organizational skills," accepted the case for trial, Monsignor Castiglioni would serve as president or chief judge. Primo Fumagalli, the chief curator of the Ambrosian Library, would act as defender of the bond, asking questions like a prosecutor, to represent the Church's interest in preserving

The Duce watching over the Duomo of Milan, 1935. Photocollage by Mario Crimella.

Cardinal Alfredo Ildefonso Schuster, flanked by Milanese Church officials, 1935. Photographed by F. Sangiorgi.

the sacrament of marriage. Francesco Longoni, the well-known theologian from Monza, would do the hard work as judge-instructor or courtroom prosecutor, interrogating the witnesses. It was he, in his capacity as judge, together with Castiglioni and a third judge, Giuseppe Gornati, the archdiocesan chancellor, who would draw up the verdict. Francesco Ciceri, the onetime bishop of Pavia, would serve as the court clerk.[9]

How curious a process that had five Catholic priests—none with any direct experience of married life—trying to establish the whole and true picture of a marriage accused of never having existed. They would proceed by a true inquisition. Both the plaintiff's advocates or lawyers and the defense's would provide a list of witnesses, and each of them would be summoned one by one for a secret interrogation. Each, in turn, would swear to God to tell the truth; no lawyers could be present to correct their lapses as they responded to the list of questions prepared by the promoter of the holy bond with advice from the attorneys. Once they had done a first round, they would convene to scrutinize the recorded testimony, set a time frame for the parties to provide more evidence, and outline further points of investigation or additional considerations. Everything had to be translated: any English into Italian; all of the testimony into Church Latin, the language of the trial. Then the promoter of justice would ask for final summations from the plaintiff and the defendant, collect all of the findings, and send them to each judge separately for him to study and draw his own decision, before they met to issue their verdict. None of them could be said to be vastly experienced at the process; there were few cases at the time, one or two a year at best, and none in recent memory concerning someone of Teruzzi's rank and notoriety.[10]

And that was just to start. They would only deliver the first verdict. Under canon law, the case then went to the appeals court for confirmation and, if it was overturned, to Rome, to the Church's supreme court, the Sacred Roman Rota for the final verdict.

Teruzzi's petition sounded as if it had been concocted locally. Roberto Farinacci surely had his hand in it. The thirteen pages took the form of a melodrama. It set up a battle of evil against good, punctuated by dribs and drabs of Church legalese. "Lilliana Weinmann" [sic], also called "the Signorina," a foreigner, the consummate trickster, had conspired with her family to pursue Attilio Teruzzi, a good Italian man in search of a bride to settle down with and have a family, who acquiesced at first, only to be convinced of their love, until his people learned the truth and exposed her perfidy. For good to triumph over evil, the plot pointed to a necessary and inevitable denouement. That was for the Church tribunal to invalidate the marriage and make everything right again.

The starting point was the holy marriage itself, which had taken place on June 24, 1926. On that day, he had wed one Leonora Weinman, also called Lilliana, whose "parentage is still not certain down to this day, nor her place of birth and who declares herself of the Israelite religion and daughter of Isaac and Rose Ohlbaum from Rzeszów (Poland)."[11] Then, moving back to 1922, "or perhaps it was 1923," the petition detailed how he had first seen his future wife around Milan ("she being the kind of woman who calls attention to herself") and how he had first been introduced to her, involuntarily, on the train to Rome at the hands of a Mr. Ciulla, maybe her pimp, and then repeatedly been importuned when he had run into the Signorina in the company of the woman who passed as her mother. The two of them had accidently crossed paths on holiday, and at Rapallo, one August, he had chanced to make the father's acquaintance. He had dined with them once or twice and chatted afterward, "as happens under those circumstances." In 1925 or thereabouts, the Signorina made clear her fondness for him, asked if he would marry her, and he, to put off answering, replied, "Would she be willing to give up the stage?" To which she replied, "She could not tell him then."[12]

When she finally agreed to renounce her career and moved to Rome to marry him, "he was even more certain of having found a person who in her purity, culture, fine education, and the virtues she held to admire and possess would indubitably have made his life happy."[13] True, he had to overcome the suspicions of his friends and was furious when she couldn't produce her birth certificate—only some official-looking piece of paper. Nevertheless, the wedding went ahead as planned. To call it off would have been unbecoming, given his high status in the government.

The complaint had to recognize that the couple had consummated the marriage on the first night of their honeymoon and stated that Teruzzi had believed she was a virgin at the time. He couldn't deny he had written to her mother in gratitude for "this flower of a child." Precisely because he had doubts about her innocence due to her forwardness at their first embrace, he had been elated at her apparent intactness. Yet from their first intimacies, he had been disturbed by certain physical and psychic abnormalities: the thick black hair covering her body, mood swings that brought her from tears to laughter and back in an instant, and her relentlessly nasty remarks about people right to their faces. If at first they had both agreed not to have a child right away, afterward she sought in every way to avoid conjugal relations. Once back in Rome, his investigations had brought him to Mr. Ferulli, her onetime manager, who confessed to having had sexual relations with her. The packet of love letters proved it. Because she could not have been a virgin, the copious blood on her nightgown and sheets on their wedding night had to be the "fruit of her menstrual period." That also explained why, when he had asked to postpone the marriage for three days, she had refused.

Devastated by her betrayal, he finally understood what his friends and family had been saying all along, namely, that she was a completely "amoral woman": she had repeatedly humiliated his mother, rifled through his office safe box to steal his private correspondence, and acted with an eccentricity inappropriate to her station as his consort. For all these reasons, but specifically because she had broken the conditions he had set for the marriage, in March 1929, he had ended the relationship.

We have to wonder how a modern Milanese man, the chief of staff of a giant military organization, could have subscribed to such a story. But then again, what else would one expect from a thug and a cheat? Recall the terrible lies about the "Reds"; Farinacci's libels about poor, murdered Achille Boldori in 1921 Cremona; and how Teruzzi had clumsily embellished on them. Consider, too, what weird ideas misogynists concoct about female sexuality generally, and remember that Fascist Italy was dense with crazy ideas, anachronisms, and Manichean thinking about enemies, about the Duce as godhead, about reliving Roman times.

Since we have no other cases to compare to Teruzzi's, we can only speculate why his petition was conceived in this gross way. Church law was key here. He had to present his petition in terms of the several conditions for making a valid marriage, before setting out the violations which made it invalid. And in Church law, though the Code of Law had been revised as recently as 1917, these were still framed in medieval terms. One so-called impediment to making a valid marriage was *error*: that the couple did not know one another's true identity and the betrothed was deceived, like Jacob in the Biblical account (Genesis 29:17), whose veiled bride was not Rachel but her sister, Leah. The other *conditio*: that they both understood the conditions they had stipulated of one another. Lilliana had violated the terms he had set for their marriage, that he know her real identity, that she be a virgin, that they have children, and so on.

Aside from that, the Church process always heavily weighed character and motives. So it was important to emphasize his and her character. Melodrama was a powerful way. Since the trial would be conducted in secrecy, Teruzzi had no fear of being sued for defamation of character. And unlike a civil court, there were no sanctions for lying under oath. It was understood that if annulment were the only way to end a bad marriage, witnesses would tailor their testimony to help the plaintiff—or the defendant. It was up to the judges to weigh their veracity. If people lied, they had their conscience, and God, to answer to; and, if they had one, their confessor. If they were cynics, they could misquote Saint Thomas Aquinas as saying all lies are not equally sinful, depending on their motivation. If they were old-guard fascists called in to testify on their comrade's behalf, if they were anti-clericals and held the Church in contempt, it was a golden opportunity to spew sexually loaded garbage straight into the priest-judge's face.

Nothing that Lilliana and her family had yet experienced could have been worse. It wasn't just the absurdity of the accusations: that Lilliana had been Ferulli's lover was as preposterous an idea now as when Teruzzi had written, "Ferulli's lover could not be Attilio Teruzzi's wife." They were good Jews to whom reputation meant everything; the libel besmirched their whole family. Isaac wanted to sue Teruzzi for defamation but was told he could not. The petition was not a public document and not therefore subject to civil litigation. To fight the libel, they had to fight the annulment. Lilliana was so stricken that she fell sick and took to her bed, postponing the opening of the trial for two months.[14]

The more she learned about the annulment process, the more she was determined to fight it with "all of her energy," as she later told the Church tribunal, out of the "moral duty to defend [herself] against incredibly iniquitous accusations . . . to reestablish the accurate truth."[15] At times, she fought to reveal the giant conspiracy concocted by Teruzzi's retinue to impugn her moral influence over him as his wife. At other moments she insisted her family didn't believe in divorce. She fought as a Jewish woman to protest the hocus pocus of a religious establishment that she did not believe in, and which her husband boasted "he had in his pocket." She fought the case because she had the wealth to do so and the intelligence and feisty temperament to make her a ferocious litigant. She fought because a verdict of nullity would have the preposterous legal effect of erasing not only the religious marriage at Santa Maria degli Angeli but also her civil wedding at the Campidoglio. She fought it because of the absurdity that if the marriage was annulled, Donna Lilliana Teruzzi had never existed. She had been a pretend wife, a fake vicereine, the opera diva who had given up the stage for nothing.

With the trial set to start in January and no lawyer willing to take her case, she prevailed upon the tribunal of Milan to find her an advocate. It was her right. The tribunal agreed and put her in contact with Filippo Meda. She thereby found herself with Catholic Italy's counterpart to secular Italy's Vittorio Scialoja. A Milanese through and through, Meda was a former cabinet minister and Italy's leading Catholic statesman until the Italian Popular Party broke up in 1924 and the remnants were outlawed two years later. Though he had mostly retired from his law practice, he accepted the case for some of the same reasons as Scialoja had: as a moral duty and to defend the integrity of the legal process. And like Scialoja, once smitten by this passionate, wronged American, he committed himself to her cause though he, too, regarded it as unwinnable. Meda would be assisted by his law partner, his thirty-three-year-old son Luigi, a well-known antifascist, who surely well knew Teruzzi's *squadrista* background. Teruzzi would still be represented by his Neapolitan lawyer Buonocore, with the assistance of Don Giovanni Zanchetta. A Franciscan zealot and onetime collaborator of Agostino Gemelli, rector of the Catholic University, he was currently professor of religion at the Royal Conservatory of Music Giuseppe Verdi, a man about town, and deeply knowledgeable about the inner workings of the archdiocese.[16]

Since Cardinal Schuster's Church prided itself on its modernity, the court expected to set a brisk tempo for the depositions, starting in April, 1933. Because the Church required a higher degree of certainty than a secular court, the time between conducting the inquiry and delivering the final verdict, beyond reasonable doubt, could take a year or two. The sentence in the first degree would then have to be affirmed by the appellate court, or, if overturned, referred for a final judgment to the Sacred Roman Rota, the Church's supreme court.

Teruzzi was deposed first, on April 7, leaving his retinue at the door. He spoke about the lack of the birth certificate, saying that when it didn't arrive, his fiancée had seemed "cloaked like a veil." His mother and sister had witnessed his anxiety, and Farinacci pressed him about whether he was "sure of Weinman's identity and virtue." Teruzzi was asked whether he made virginity a condition of the marriage. He conceded: "Certainly, I never said directly 'I won't marry you if you're not a virgin,' nor that 'I would never marry a woman who was not a virgin.'" But it had been "an essential consideration," dictated by his "moral conscience"; in the "supposition that she were not a virgin, I would have adjusted my thinking accordingly." When asked why he had thought she was a virgin, he had answered: "From her genitals and blood." But he had "to confess my ignorance on the matter"; he had not "previously had relations with a virgin because I'm a man of honor." Only upon learning she had had a lover did he "understand that [menstruation] was a link in the logical chain."[17]

Piazza del Duomo was lit with bright spring sunshine on May 26, 1933, when Lilliana sat for her interrogation in Father Longoni's dark chambers. She was precise with names, dates, and places, as she outlined how they had met and spoke eloquently about the great love that had led to their marriage. She emphatically denied that Teruzzi had ever said anything that had let her suspect that he harbored doubts as to her honesty, legitimacy, or her "ardent desire" to have children. Asked about the possibility of reconciliation, she said she wanted only to meet with him: "For four years, I have wracked my brains to understand what happened in those too few days between his confiding letter of March 1 and the letter of March 13, for Teruzzi to have attained such a total knowledge of my so-called guilt to totally ruin a family."[18]

From the late summer of 1933 through early January, the witnesses for Teruzzi were heard, thirteen altogether, starting with his mother and sister, followed by Ferulli, and then Teruzzi's entourage—his faithful subordinates, high-placed friends, trusted maids, and the comrade-in-arms who had left no stone unturned to find proof of her treachery. Convoked one by one to respond to the judge's questions in the privacy of his chambers, they reveled in denouncing the tricks Lilliana Weinman had devised with the complicity of her family to cover up her shameful past in order to woo and wed Attilio Teruzzi. The most eloquent of the testimonies resonated with the themes of grand opera, speaking to the virtues of fidelity and family, the vagaries of fate, hubris, and jealous love. The crudest indulged in the malevolent tropes of popular melodrama, clucking about false identity, broken maidenheads, hairy hags, and evil-doing foreign

Jewish tricksters. The bawdiest sounded like Boccaccio's tales, telling about the tricks to repair broken hymens and of ruses, like peering through hotel keyholes, to catch the lovers in flagrante delicto. The most self-serious witnesses on Teruzzi's behalf swore to strip away the "veils" so that, her "mask off," the liar would be revealed "in all of her repulsiveness."[19]

Ferulli, trapped by the escapade of his rascally younger brother, Vincenzo, who had furnished Teruzzi with the letters, played his part. He spoke of his anger at Isaac for having broken Lilliana's contract with him, the fear of Teruzzi that led him to flee Italy, and his embarrassment at realizing he would have to testify against his former protégé under oath. Forced by the line of questioning to give a coherent account, he lied more and more outlandishly. How did he know her? They had been lovers since they had met through another budding opera singer in 1919; she had seduced him right then and there and had not been a virgin even then. What was his relationship to the parents? Being a man of independent wealth, he had no need to work for them. He had signed a contract with her to hide the affair from his wife. And the parents probably were aware of the subterfuge.[20]

Vincenzo Ferulli was brought in from Bari to reinforce his brother's testimony. After identifying himself with his new Fascist Militia card, he redoubled the lies: Once, he testified, when he accompanied Lilliana to the train station to welcome his brother at his return from a trip to Switzerland, she confided to him her intention to wed Teruzzi and then to divorce him and marry Umberto.[21] He also authenticated the original packet of letters that Teruzzi's advocates had submitted as evidence in the translation Teruzzi had read. Neither Meda nor Lilliana had known of the existence of these letters until then. The judges asked for them to be retranslated.

The more prominent the witness on behalf of Teruzzi, the more the show of contempt for the woman and, perhaps, for the whole process as well. Eugenio Morelli, a leading world expert on tuberculosis, spoke in his role as Teruzzi's friend, family doctor, and political client. He called Lilliana "a simulating adventuress, who sought to create a social position for herself on the back of an honest man." She was a *veropatica* ("a pathological liar"), "her body, reflecting her character, painted like a barbarian's."[22] The anticlerical Morelli flung his creepy misogyny like a filthy rag at the reverend interrogator, less perhaps to protect his friend than to protest that his friend had to endure this morally pusillanimous inquiry to be free of his awful marriage.

At last, Celestina could unburden herself. "No, I never personally believed she was not the Weinmans' daughter," she said. And she was sure she was pure. Her complaint was Lilliana's flippancy about the marriage, the jealousy that had led her to say she would divorce him if he didn't behave, and her heartbreak that her son had "married a woman who, besides not being of our religion, was a Jew." Amelia, the protective older sister, ever the educator, reproved herself for not having spoken to him before the marriage about the difference of culture, about her theater background and American education. The worst that the self-abnegating Amelia could say about her erstwhile sister-in-law was that she "loved nobody but herself; even her love for her parents was a put-on and a love that was in any case self-interested and that went the same for the love shown her brother."[23] That sounded kindly compared to other assessments of her character: "The worst in the world, never a delicate thought for his mother, nor toward the poor," said Zamboni, only a "giant vanity." "An ultra-skilled imposter, a spy," said Turrinelli (Milan's leading automotive engineer, a childhood friend). "Her mask stripped away all the ugliness and repulsiveness of her character showed," said Malgeri. "She was capable of any deed," said Varenna.[24]

Teruzzi, by contrast, was a "model son," "trustworthy," "sometimes with fits of temper, but sincere and generous," according to Zamboni. He was a figure of "absolute reliability [who] doesn't know how to lie, his sincerity is such that sometimes it compromises him professionally," said Turrinelli. "I am hugely fond of Teruzzi in spite of his defects because he has a profoundly good and profoundly honest character, inclined to believe everybody," said Malgeri.[25]

The day before Christmas 1933, three months after she testified to the priests about her son's unfortunate marriage, Celestina died. She was at his house in Rome. She had been ailing. Teruzzi was inconsolable. Telegrams poured in. The king sent a cable; Mussolini, too, who "wanted to be close to him spiritually in this moment of grief." The funeral transport conducted the day after Christmas under a freezing rain saw a "vast plebiscite of sorrow," an "imposing crowd" at what photographers from the Luce Institute treated as an affair of state. Costanzo Ciano and Achille Starace offered themselves as pallbearers, and scores of friends, uniformed militia officers, and undersecretaries followed the giant horse-drawn hearse as it transported the bier from Teruzzi's house to the church.[26]

The popes had made a practice of publicly mourning the deaths of their mothers, and in 1930, on the twenty-fifth anniversary of the death of Mussolini's own mother, Rosa Maltoni, the regime had launched its cult of motherhood by commemorating her as a "great educator and glorious mother." Her modest grave at Predappio would serve as a site of pilgrimage for hierarchs over the coming years, and youth camps and kindergartens were named after her.

Teruzzi became the first hierarch to make such a public show of his personal grief. Later that year, at Sterminazza, a tiny border town of Julian Venetia, with his sister, he inaugurated one of the new nursery schools to Italianize the Slavic-speaking children of the zone; who knows at what level of the fascist bureaucracy it had been decided to name the school after his mother? Over the entire coming year, official photographs showed him always wearing a black mourning band, looking sad and distracted. He put on weight. His beard got long and frowzy.

Teruzzi's mourning for his mother coincided with the sudden, rapid forward march that Mussolini had ordered from the spring of 1934. His purpose was to test the militia as an instrument of Italy's foreign policy bravado and war preparedness as he reacted to the dramatic global developments coming out of the Great Depression. First, there was imperial Japan's invasion of Manchuria on September 18, 1931, which Mussolini rightly intuited set off a power race to redivide the colonial world. Then there was Adolf Hitler's appointment as chancellor of Germany on January 30, 1933. It was not just the appointment itself but the rapidity, ferocity, and finality with which Hitler moved to outlaw the opposition, take over the entire state apparatus, and openly advocate German rearmament. Upon President Hindenburg's death in August 1934, Hitler acquired a far more absolute grip on power in Germany in only twenty months than Mussolini had secured over twelve years of ruling Italy. And Germany was on any score a far better endowed nation. Faced with Hitler's intention to extend German power into Austria and the Balkans—spaces Mussolini regarded as squarely within Italy's sphere of interests—Mussolini began to present himself as the pro-peace leader of Europe. He invited the German chancellor to Venice June 14–16, 1934, and had left their meeting convinced that he had persuaded Hitler to respect Austrian sovereignty, only to see him back the right-wing coup that barely six weeks later led to the assassination of the pro-Italian Austrian federal chancellor, Engelbert Dollfuss.

Mussolini thereupon dispatched 75,000 troops to the Brenner Pass. As Hitler backed down, Mussolini spoke of establishing a "Pax Romana," bringing together Great Britain, France, and the so-called Little Entente countries of Eastern Europe to forestall German rearmament and any further attempt to annex Austria to Germany. At Bari, on September 6, he spoke of his "sovereign contempt" for "certain doctrines from beyond the Alps advanced by the progeny of peoples who didn't know how to write . . . while Rome had Caesar, Virgil, and Augustus." And at Lecce, on the next day before a throng of 30,000, with Teruzzi at his side, the Duce cried: "Are you ready to rush to the defense of our fatherland and the fascist revolution?" The query was "met with a roar of yeses."[27]

The Duce was in full swagger. Teruzzi, by contrast, in his black band of mourning, straggly bearded and slow moving in the propaganda films, looked depressed. The Duce had been alerted to the public implications of Teruzzi's annulment trial in the fall of 1933, when the police had reported that Lilliana, who had finally secured her passport on February 26, 1933, was holding court at the Hotel Crillon in Paris. She had left Italy as soon as she testified at Milan in late May and was engaged in "a hostile campaign against the regime." It was "diabolical," really "perfidious," the way she "denigrated the regime," with insider gossip about various hierarchs, the Duce, too, and his lovers. Her father was reportedly giving money to antifascists and talking about denouncing Teruzzi's abuse of power to the Hearst press if he further damaged his daughter.[28]

Like Teruzzi, Mussolini was a sexually insatiable cheat; until recently, he had also been inclined to attach himself to a succession of forceful women of strong intellect, not unlike his indomitable school-teacher mother. But Mussolini had imposed order in his own personal affairs, or enough to please his wife and public opinion. By 1929, when his family had settled in Rome and his fifth and last legitimate child, Anna Maria, was born, he had a routinized family existence that prevented him from anything but the occasional escapades and intermittently servicing what he called his "harem." By that he meant the handful of women who had come to depend on him or who gratified his notion that they depended on him either because he had illegitimate children by them or because they had had long-standing affairs and he felt sympathy for their apparently loveless relationship with their own men. All the same, unlike Teruzzi he had no love for brothel sex, male exhibitionism, underage girl prostitutes, or women of other nationalities. And he was revolted by the very idea of homosexuality, his regime having passed strict laws to punish it and his police compiling files on any number of alleged homosexuals to blackmail them, including the heir to the throne, Prince Umberto, and Vatican eminences.[29] Pederasty, meaning Greek sex, or the sexual relations between dominant older men and ephebes of the Mediterranean world, was another matter. If Mussolini knew of the intimations about Teruzzi's polymorphous colonial sexual life, he would not have changed his estimation of Teruzzi as a man's man and a prodigious womanizer, with similarly ecumenical tastes.

So Mussolini would have found nothing especially scandalous about spy reports that Teruzzi could be found out every night with "dodgy female types—notorious for being fun-loving, out-in-public artistes, starlets, torch singers—dancing incessantly, until two in the morning," though he might have deplored what the informer denounced as "the most infuriating part," namely, he was always in uniform.[30] Mussolini might have had a salacious interest but probably nothing more in the telephone wiretaps of the ongoing conversations between Andalù, his Askari adjutant, turned social secretary, and Mrs. Dora, a procurer, who made clear that she had "fished around" and made arrangements to send over two young women, with a combined age of thirty-seven, for "that evening's soiree with his Excellency," girls who were "really chic," "top quality goods."[31]

He would have taken note of Teruzzi's off-and-on affair with Olga Vittoria Gentilli, the stage actress, famous for performing Victor Hugo's *Marguerite Gauthier*. At the peak of her career, circa 1915, the Signora, as her fans in the theater world called her, to underscore she was a real lady, not just an actress, had entranced many brilliant, passionate men across the political spectrum, from D'Annunzio to Antonio Gramsci and Piero Gobetti, and Mussolini, too.[32] Nearing fifty in 1933, with her cascade of cyclamen-dyed hair and kohled tragedienne eyes, Gentilli was still a diva as she moved from stage triumphs to her first celluloid successes. Teruzzi was at loose ends, a vigorous lover for his age, and he could be very sweet and generous, aside from it being amusing and useful to have such a high-placed friend. The Hotel Roma was their trysting place.[33] In time, they were regular bridge partners, together with other younger, upcoming divas of a stature someday to be similar to hers, notably, Anna Magnani.

Mussolini had also received reports about Teruzzi's relations with a certain Mrs. Nappi, whose home in Rome he visited regularly and whose family were summer guests at Villa Celestina. Informers worried about his service car being parked outside of her residence at all hours of the night and called her a "levantine speculator." It was the usual police misogyny that made them incapable of understanding that Anais Nappi née Vuccino, born in Istanbul, came from one of the oldest and grandest of the Italian merchant families of Istanbul, who had been expelled from the Ottoman empire in 1911 in retaliation for Italy's invasion of Libya. She was a restless and beautiful woman, and Mussolini, after meeting her at some event or another at Teruzzi's invitation, took to calling her "the Turk" with a familiarity that suggested he understood that Attilio needed a family.[34]

The point here was that Teruzzi, in his loneliness, and the Nappi family, in their need for the kindnesses of a high-placed friend, formed an odd triangle—or maybe a family pentagon. For Anais had two vivacious teenage daughters, and her husband, the considerably older Settimio Aurelio Nappi, a turn-of-the-century infantry colonel-gentleman-littérateur desperate to keep up appearances on a miserable military pension, had gone quite mad. When he was in a bad spell, he would write to the Duce in various disguises, claiming compensation for having been present with Teruzzi at the founding congress of the *fascisti* at San Sepolcro, or for being the brains behind the March on Rome, or for coming from a noble Romagnuole family that had its entire worldly goods confiscated for its patriotism during the Risorgimento. But many otherwise normal people were besotted by the romance of fascism, and early on police informers decided he was harmless.[35] And why not believe that if Teruzzi loved Mussolini and they loved Teruzzi, in some way, they were all connected by a common, overarching passion? That was the sense of the letter the Nappi daughters painstakingly wrote Mussolini, "the President," as they addressed him, in their New Year's Day card, 1934, the "great daddy of all of us," telling him, as so many adolescent girls did, that they "adored" him, and they wanted him to know how much Teruzzi adored him too.[36]

The belief that Mussolini had a special place in his heart for his right-hand man and that he alone could persuade him to behave eventually led a succession of exasperated women, including Lilliana, to seek Mussolini's personal intervention. With that conviction, Teruzzi's cousin Bimby, an earlier love from his pre-Lilliana days, had screwed up her courage to approach Mussolini. She had hoped to confide in him in person in the company of her best girlfriend, a schoolteacher. But since his secretary insisted his duties of office would not allow that, and she was promised whatever she wrote would be held in strictest confidence, she finally set out the great wrong that had resulted to her from her cousin's soaring political good fortune. She was, she wrote Mussolini, from Teruzzi's "same stock, the same humble, hard-working background," and she had been given to believe that once his marriage was annulled, they could marry, only to hear now that there were other snags, namely, that his mother and sister and also the Duce wanted him to have a more socially acceptable family, meaning a well-to-do wife and children.

More than that, Bimby Teruzzi spelled out in the eight very confidential pages, in perhaps the most radical way anybody could, the conundrum the hierarch faced: that Attilio was deeply touched by her "simple life, one of work, of purity, of sacrifice," but "his soul was at war between the heart and the brain," that "their marriage could be the source of unpleasant comments in his circle and could also displease His Excellency." The "prejudices of a society" could destroy the promise of what could make up a "solid and normal" family, a "true family based on love, esteem and tenderness" and "reciprocal happiness." And "his rapid social ascent, favored by good fortune and Mussolini," had caused him to renounce her, when, instead, far from being "an obstacle," she could provide the "simple but affectionate peace of mind to restore his strength of spirit." She rebelled at the idea that he should "play with [her] heart as if the heart of the humble hadn't the same value as every other heart." She begged Mussolini to demonstrate his "marvelous empathy" to act "like a beacon of light to bring balance back to [Attilio's] heart and life, to restore to his life that direction he dreams up but is unable to confront."[37]

In reality, Mussolini was only interested at the moment to prevent him from being blackmailed and held up to public ridicule. Bimby Teruzzi's letter dated from May, 1934. The following November, Mussolini's office had to send an investigator from the security police to Turin to find and destroy a set of compromising letters exchanged between Teruzzi and a young woman, the daughter of a well-regarded professor of economy and commerce. The source turned out to be the professor's unscrupulous lawyer, who had handled the case for his separation from his wife on the grounds that the wife, by her neglect, had encouraged their daughter's promiscuous behavior.[38]

When questioned, the father wept inconsolably, revealing the whole family tragedy: his son had committed suicide on the eve of the final examination for his degree, and he was still bitter at Teruzzi, who had abused his hospitality to seduce his twenty-year-old daughter. But he was aghast that the letters had been used to threaten Teruzzi and was convinced by the police investigator to hand over the originals to a notable in Turin whom he trusted. By the time the investigator had finished, the father had confided that at Lecco, the same thing had happened to another family that had hosted "the Honorable Teruzzi." But there the girl's boyfriend had intervened, the family had found out, and the girl had taken her distance. The father had offered to look into the case, if "it interested" the police. Of course, he had been told no.[39] Seducing your host's daughter was disgraceful but not illegal. The point of the investigation was to cover up trouble, not to stir up more.

No wonder the Duce could manipulate Teruzzi. But forcing him to shave off his beard, that was a step too far. That October, Teruzzi had exited the Map Room, white as a ghost. When he was asked in the antechamber what had happened, he replied: "He wants me to shave off my beard." To the natural question of what he was going to do, he replied, "I am going to shave it off."[40] The gossip flew. He had been ordered to do so because it was out of sync with the ideal of "youth," because it was going gray (and to snickers in the *Corriere della Sera*'s Rome press room, because it didn't match his other body hair), and because Mussolini didn't like beards or any facial hair for that matter.[41]

The stringer for *Time* picked up on the story, leading the magazine to editorialize about the "servility" of "hirsute Fascist underlings," who, with the exception of Italo Balbo, had rushed to shave off beards and whiskers. Some weeks later, Luce photographers captured Teruzzi sans beard at the inauguration of the new town of Littoria, his chin stubbly, wincing at the camera.[42] Of course, beards grow back. He never again was seen beardless, not while he was hiding from partisans in 1945 nor, later, in prison, despite the rule that prisoners had to be clean-shaven. At another moment, talking with his young lover Clara Petacci, Mussolini recalled the incident as part of the give and take, really the latter, of a long relationship. Mussolini had tried to console Teruzzi when he hadn't left the house for four days, at Palazzo Venezia. "You look well," he had told him, "you look young again." But Teruzzi had looked at him in a way that the Duce understood. Teruzzi said, "Yes, I look good, but I can't sleep, something is missing." And Mussolini said, "If you feel that way about it, keep it." Beards grow back, but that story never went away.[43]

Teruzzi's worst worries at that moment should have been focused on his annulment trial. Starting the previous January 14, 1934, Meda had called a handful of witnesses on Lilliana's behalf: both her parents; Father Candidori; the eminent gynecologist Ernesto Pestalozza, who confirmed she had consulted him about getting pregnant; Mr. Larkin, the director of the Chase Bank of Paris, a Catholic and a Knight of the Order of Malta, who had known Lilliana since she was nineteen and hoped his own young daughter would grow up to have an equally strong character; and her father's cousin, Ida Jolles, who had heard Ferulli confess to having said bad things about Lilliana to get revenge. In October, when the Church tribunal presented all of the testimony to the plaintiff's advocates so they could begin to prepare the final summary, they had to be troubled. If the Church courts gave credence to any testimony, it was from mothers and priests. Father Candidori was a godsend. When asked whether Lilliana was a reliable witness, he understood the nuance. In effect, he said, yes, she was religious in a Jewish way, meaning that she believed profoundly in God and let her Catholic servants practice their own religion. When asked about her morality, he described her as an "honest and correct person" who lived a "quiet life, level-headed, of lofty sentiments." When asked about Teruzzi's trustworthiness, he didn't reply.[44]

In a highly irregular last move, Teruzzi's lawyers called two final witnesses. Both were Milanese business potentates. Their purpose was to drive home as rudely as possible that Lilliana had understood and violated their understanding that he had not only supposed she was a virgin and wanted her to be so but that her virginity was a sine qua non of the marriage. Enrico Maria Varenna, Farinacci's inseparable co-conspirator, said no matter how hard he tried to tell Teruzzi Lilliana was a con artist, his "friend was overwhelmed with passion." Once, when Teruzzi had insisted she was pure, he replied that "to repair her virginity, a shoemaker would need to sew her up with giant laces."[45] Federico Azzoni, the Milanese patents lawyer and entrepreneur, another Teruzzi friend, insisted Teruzzi had told him if she was not a virgin: "I'll can the whole thing; nobody is going to say they've scammed me."[46]

On October 26, the witnesses for the plaintiff and for the defendant having all been heard, the court gave Teruzzi's advocates three months to present their final arguments. From that moment, Teruzzi's friends mobilized for his "defense." The first move was to ferret out more arguments to vilify Lilliana. Farinacci handled that, with help from Father Zanchetta. The second was, through Rome, to obtain the best legal help in Italy. Francesco Pacelli, the dean of the Rotal Lawyers at the time, would provide that. As noted above, he had turned down Lilliana on the grounds of a conflict of interest, that his brother, Eugenio, was Vatican secretary of state. But that conflict, arguably, had been resolved when the trial was moved to Milan. Or so it seemed, since he now accepted Teruzzi's case. In any event, he had a big office with two voracious lawyer sons, and the process promised to pay well. It was an interesting case not just politically, given Teruzzi's prominence and the American Jewish spouse, but also legally: consent had become a more complicated notion in contemporary times, as his own father, Filippo, had determined in several important annulment cases he had represented before the Rota. And, assuming Francesco Pacelli won the case, his great prestige would silence critics.

December 24, 1934, the first anniversary of Celestina Rossi Teruzzi's death, was the occasion to apotheosize her as mother of heroes, like the Roman matron Cornelia, mother of the Gracchi, the scourge of the Optimates on behalf of the ungrateful plebs of Rome, or Adelaide, mother of the Cairoli brothers, martyred for the nation's sake in the Risorgimento. Condolence notes from King Vittorio Emanuele III, Mussolini, and Francesco Pacelli (who was quoted as sending the pope's very own) provided the epigraphs for the little book commemorating her death. The photograph showing mother and son in Benghazi had cropped out Lilliana, as if he had never had a wife. Farinacci recalled that Celestina had welcomed and fed them as the comrades waited for the counterattack during the coup against the city government at Palazzo Marino. The famous scientist Morelli, who had denounced Lilliana as an "international spy," concluded his reminiscence with a special flourish: "Attilio was always the baby to be protected, and he, the strong type, who knew how to command an army of Blackshirts, was always waiting for his mama's caress and approval."[47]

Fascism had thus performed a miracle of statecraft, exploiting Catholic sentimentality to transform a hard-bitten, imperfect man into a figure of Christlike piety. "No gesture by a Soldier could have been more virile or beautiful," Civinini wrote, as he observed him with his beard damp from tears, praying over his mother's body.[48]

17

IN WAR, FULLNESS

War alone brings all human energies to their highest tension, and sets a stamp of nobility on the peoples who have the courage to face it.

—BENITO MUSSOLINI, *Enciclopedia Italiana*, 1932

My tigress heart is wounded, the insult invites revenge.

—EBOLI, Verdi's *Don Carlos*, Act 2, Scene 3

In Fascist Italy, 1935 began with a bang. On January 3, Haile Selassie, the emperor of Ethiopia, appealed to the League of Nations to intervene and prevent Italy from using a border skirmish at Walwal the previous December as a pretext to declare war. His appeal proved to be in vain, for the clash between Italian-led Somali troops and Ethiopian forces at the border watering hole was exactly the casus belli Mussolini had been waiting for to launch Italy's first wholeheartedly fascist war.

The war would be "fascist" in all of the senses that Mussolini clarified in the memo he drew up for his top military advisers the night before New Year's Eve. Fascist meant flouting international arbitration to turn a "diplomatic problem" into "a problem of force" whose only means of resolution lay in "the force of arms."[1] Fascist meant exploiting his genius at timing to mobilize Italy's rising power in the world and grab the African continent's only remaining sovereign state. Finally, fascist meant ignoring the protests of the League of Nations and the fact that it recognized Ethiopia as free, equal, and subject to its protection. Fascist Italy would also prove its mettle in the imperial arena by doing what other white, Western powers had not yet done: by seizing control of Ethiopia—the only African country that had never been colonized—it would snuff out Africa's greatest symbol of anticolonial resistance.

The first fascist war would thus be a war not so much for economic gain—although Italy's armament industries would surely be enriched by it and unemployment lessened—as for moral and political prestige. To show off fascism's civilizing mission, they would build roads and colonize as they went—like the ancient Romans—and they would free slaves and overturn the feudal monarchy. It would be fought by a levée en masse, throwing in a half dozen Blackshirt divisions rather than relying on its African mercenaries. It would be commanded in the field by the fascist quadrumvir General De Bono rather than by the army commander-in-chief Marshal Badoglio. It would have the whole nation behind it whatever the costs, all the more so if the League of Nations imposed sanctions on Italy as it threatened. The invasion would be launched "Japanese style," Mussolini wrote in his memo of December 30, 1934: with no official declaration of war, as imperial Japan had done with its surprise invasion of Manchuria in 1931. Fascism would thus fulfill its historical destiny by turning the Kingdom of Italy into an empire.[2]

On January 24, Mussolini publicly announced Italy's preparations for war, and on February 5 he took command of the Colonial Ministry. General De Bono, named high commissioner of Eritrea and Italian Somaliland, ordered the first contingent of 35,000 troops to embark for the Horn of Africa before he himself left to prepare the terrain. This, finally, was the war the Fascist Revolution had been waiting for. This would be the hour of the Blackshirts.

The week of February 21, 1935, while Teruzzi sat at the Supreme Council for three days of meetings to assess war needs, the Ecclesiastical Court of Milan released his advocates' final summation of his case. It was only intended for the eyes of the court and of the defendant, but it bore the title "In defense of Attilio Teruzzi"—who was of course the plaintiff, not the defendant—and opened like a declaration of war.[3]

The court, it began, had before it the case of a man in search of justice: "the orphaned son" of his "venerable Genetrix," his "conscience wracked by remorse at not having listened to her admonitions," his determination steeled "to bring God's blessing back into his sad, empty home." He was a "sincere, generous man of moral and religious character," all of the witnesses concurred, who, "midway in the road of life," had the misfortune to meet "a miserable adventuress who knew how to disguise herself as a pure and good young woman."[4]

The arguments sparkled with legal sophistry. With abundant citations of precedents set by the most influential of early twentieth-century Rotal lawyers, Cardinal Gasparri and Francesco Pacelli's own father, Filippo Pacelli, it presented a fresh definition of "consent" as a convergence of interests and intents, a mutual understanding, as opposed to a sine qua non stated in the cold language of a contract.[5] In its statement of the facts, the lawyers shredded the credibility of the sorry Jewish temple-keepers at Rzeszów, too ragged and filthy to keep proper records, of Isaac with his arrogant attacks on the plaintiff, and of Rose who could never summon up the gall to confirm outright that Lilliana was their daughter. The advocates tried to impugn Monsignor Candidori's credibility by suggesting he had been gulled by Lilliana's show of religious piety. And, with a final flourish, they popped in one of those sublimely ridiculous doubts about the validity of the marriage that on other occasions lawyers for the rich and powerful had pulled out to good effect: to accuse Lilliana of having taken the oath to respect her husband's faith (needed in order to get the papal dispensation to wed) not at the vicariate where the document was registered but elsewhere.

In the end, the twenty-eight pages of legal fireworks and ad hominem attacks hinged on the summation given in the document's final three pages. These made the case for why this "miserable adventuress" had made this sincere, gullible Christian her victim. The self-evident answer was that she was a Jew, not just any Jew but a Galician Jew, one of a whole community that revered the Talmud, who studied it from age ten and lived their lives by its sacred rule. The Talmud taught them that the non-Jew, being lower than Jews, was not entitled to God's help; that Jews alone, because they descended from Adam, regarded all the other peoples in the world as beasts, good only for slaughter, to be treated with contempt and hatred. The Talmud had taught her that it was permissible for a Jew to lie, even while acting civilly toward the heathen, "to honor the *goyem*, and say 'I love you,' to swindle a *goy*, but do so in a way that nobody can discover." The Talmud itself explained "why Signora Lilliana had to trick, invent, lie, swear false testimony, to simulate at every moment to conceal her degeneracy." Teruzzi's mother alone had understood this when she had testified that Lilliana "knew how to conceal her true self" and when she had grieved at her son's marriage to a person who was "not just not of our religion, but a Jew kneeling at the altar next to my son."[6] All of this was documented with citations and chapter and verse numbers from the so-called original texts: Babylonian, Hebrew, and Sanskrit sources, all allegedly verified for the exactness of their citation and translation by the Reverend Professor Filippo Faicchio, provincial minister of the Franciscan Order of Naples.

The "holy court" now had to choose between the word of a Jew and that of "this perfect soldier, this valorous combatant of the Italo-Turkish War, of the Libyan campaigns, the occupation of the Fezzan, the World War, this wise and able Governor whose deeds led to the possession of vast previously unoccupied colonial territories, and with that, we have said enough." The "defense" was signed and submitted to the court in the name of Francesco Pacelli, Giuseppe Buonocore, and Giovanni Zanchetta.[7]

"This was like a bomb. Everybody was mixed-up," said Isaac Lewin, the rabbi and Polish-Zionist activist who, after fleeing to the United States from the Nazis in 1939, became a renowned Hebrew scholar and historian of the Jews.[8] How he had gotten involved in the case is hardly self-evident. Lilliana had become frantic as she struggled to understand how "a deduction that from a cause of action between two married people [had] degenerated into an attack of anti-Semitism and of the basest denigration of the teachings of our holiest writers and of the Hebrew race, children of Israel."[9] Her father, who was in Antwerp, where he was operating a new factory, sprang into action. They would rebut the libel as their community had always tried to do, by taking it to the religious authorities. He contacted the chief rabbi of his hometown, Rzeszów, Aaron Lewin, a Talmudic scholar of great distinction and the founder of Agudat Israel, the political arm of Ashkenazi orthodox Judaism, and Lewin turned the matter over to Isaac, his brilliant eldest son.

In 1930s Poland, anti-Semitic slurs were nothing new. Isaac Lewin, who was a member of the town council at Lodz at the time, regularly heard his Polish Nationalist Party colleagues threaten in full session to kill all the Jews. Yet the Catholic Church itself had long ago emphatically condemned the notion that the Talmud instructed the Jews to lie to Gentiles and that courts could not admit Jews as witnesses. Lewin couldn't imagine why the Vatican secretary of state's own brother would be circulating this nonsense. But for fear it foretold the spread of violent anti-Semitism to Italy, he resolved to use his only weapon. That was to reveal the truth. And to that end, he wrote a three-chapter exegesis on the text, demolishing its preposterous errors and arguments, not least the idea that girls of ten studied the Talmud, when in fact women were not permitted to study it at all.[10]

Meanwhile, Lilliana tortured herself, scribbling on the backs of used envelopes, hotel stationery, and old receipts to try to resolve her own self-doubt, to understand what or who was to blame. She had never made a "mystery of being a religious Jewess," she wrote in one note. "My ancestors all up to my father were and are great believers of the Torah, which does not mean bigotry, incomprehension or ignorance. My Talmud teaches me the Ten Commandments, which are the Credo of the lives of my parents and mine, which had taught charity, benevolence, truthfulness." She had studied religion with Dr. Wise-Bethlen and Dr. Kohut: Had "they taught me to perjure, give false testimony, and if our Talmud teaches us and commands us to falsify, also the more we study the Talmud the less Jews are to be believed?" She would write them to ask where the Talmud said "such outrageous things."[11]

At no time did she accuse her husband of being the perpetrator of these distortions and untruths. She had never known Teruzzi to be anti-Semitic, nor Farinacci, for that matter, not the Farinacci she knew, who had Jewish friends, who sent her his picture when she got engaged, wishing "her true happiness all of her life," and since the early 1920s had depended for the operation of his whole Milan office on Jole Foa, his forty-five-year-old secretary of Jewish origin, the staunchest of fascists. As far as she was concerned, Francesco Pacelli was to blame. He was at fault for the "incorrect and dishonest act" of having refused to take her case out of conflict of interest, only to turn around and represent her accuser. "Had Nazism contaminated the Vatican Secretary of State's own brother?" Lilliana asked herself. "Did he really want to unleash an anti-Semitic campaign like the one that had begun in Germany?"[12]

Lilliana's shock, Meda's bewilderment, and Lewin's surprise were understandable. Canonical lawyers, including the dean of the Rotal lawyers, had not only concocted a libel long condemned by the Church, but they had also exploited the secrecy of the Church tribunal to propound it. Furthermore, this libel had been produced in the name of the commander-in-chief of the Fascist Militia at a moment when Mussolini was publicly avowing his rejection of Germany's anti-Semitism. Though German anti-Semitism had become increasingly rife and vicious since Hitler had come to power in January 1933, the date of Teruzzi's lawyers' anti-Semitic libel was still nine months from September 15, 1935, when Hitler's infamous Nuremberg Laws forbidding marriage and extramarital intercourse between Jews and Germans were codified. In sum, the libel against Lilliana Weinman was exclusively a fabrication of fascist Italy.

At Filippo Meda's request, the Church tribunal gave them two months and then stretched to two more to consider and respond. Lilliana seized that time to access the Church's corridors of influence. Conceivably, it was Monsignor Candidori who, after Lilliana had him and his sister over to dine, introduced her to Cardinal Raffaele Rossi, the onetime Barefoot Carmelite friar, now the secretary of the Sacred Consistorial Congregation—the office of the Curia responsible for appointing bishops worldwide. Highly esteemed for his ascetic life, he could be counted upon to stand outside of Vatican—and fascist—influence mongering. Conceivably, Cardinal Rossi introduced her to Cardinal Camillo Caccia Dominioni, the pederast-protégé of Pius XI who had his own reasons for abhorring a regime whose operatives had stored up a pile of evidence to blackmail him.[13] Whatever exactly he did, she claimed he gave her his full backing. Perhaps it was Caccia Dominioni who got her the sought-after audience with the Vatican fixer, Father Tacchi Venturi, who had famously been the go-between for Mussolini and the pope since 1929. In any case, neither Caccia Dominioni nor Tacchi Venturi was likely to have explained to her that the argument that Jews obey only the Talmud (and Lilliana's testimony was therefore considered worthless) was balderdash. This infamous blood libel had long been condemned by the Church. It was a mystery how the lawyer-statesman Francesco Pacelli could have subscribed to it.

Indeed, it was unlikely that Pacelli had even read the final summation, much less signed it. The recurrence of his heart condition had left him mostly bedridden since December. On April 22, 1935, he would die at sixty-three, with his brother at his deathbed to administer last rites.

Who, then, was responsible? Buonocore was in Naples and seemed to have dropped out of the case. But Zanchetta was a Franciscan and had published with Agostino Gemelli, the rector of the Catholic University, of which Meda was a founder and major benefactor. If Meda spoke with Gemelli, also a Franciscan, he could have been told that Father Faicchio, who had allegedly vouched for the veracity of the libel, belonged to the Order of the Minor Franciscan Friars and was normally cloistered in his study with his 2,000-volume library at the Franciscan monastery in

Afragola outside of Naples. It was true that he had recently published a scholarly book, *Pawn Shops and Franciscan Preaching in the 15th Century*, which retread long-held anti-Semitic canards about how Jewish usurers exploited the poor and how mendicant friars steeled the latter to resist, and over the previous year or so, he had been teaching at Bergamo. Conceivably, he had been consulted. But he himself would never have instigated such a shabby action.[14]

By whatever means, Meda learned that the perpetrator was Giovanni Preziosi, Farinacci's acolyte: "a de-frocked Catholic priest," as Meda described him to the Church tribunal, and "a well-known anti-Semite, already notorious for specializing in such undertakings."[15] Most people regarded him as a loathsome zealot. He was a creep. He brought bad luck. They cringed at being in the same room with him. A sad-sack southern intellectual, born to a poor family in small-town Avellino, he had been trained as a cleric, served as a Catholic activist on behalf of Italian immigrants to the United States, and founded his own exceptionally long-lived, intermittently brilliant magazine *La Vita Italiana* in 1913. He had then abandoned the priesthood to marry his life-long collaborator, Valeria Bertarelli, a married woman with a child, who had obtained a divorce in Fiume. By that time, Preziosi had become obsessed by "the forces of the occult," by which he meant the usual suspects: international Free Masonic conspiracies, vampiric German Big Banks, and, in the wake of the World War, the Jews and their co-conspirators, Bolshevik revolutionaries, who were both in cahoots with the aforementioned. His reading of the *Protocols of the Elders of Zion* had confirmed his thinking on that score, and it was he who made it available to his compatriots by translating and publishing the first Italian-language edition in 1921.[16]

A recruit to fascism before the March on Rome, Preziosi found a close affinity with his fellow southerner Farinacci. Since June 1931, after exhausting his usefulness as Farinacci's ally in Neapolitan machine politics, he had moved to Milan, where, with Enrico Varenna's financial backing, he and Farinacci arranged a "love marriage" to obtain a national audience for Preziosi's *Vita Italiana* by publishing it at *Cremona Nuova*'s shiny new typographic plant.[17] Their aspiration was to develop a more learned, cosmopolitan Italian variety of political anti-Semitism. This spoke to international Zionism's alliance with Bolshevism, the Italian Jews' treachery as their conflicted loyalties had them choose their religion and race over their nation, and their excessive power in finance, government, and culture. Italianness was achieved by the purity and elevation of the culture rather than by racial selection. In Italy, racial selection by means of sterilization, euthanasia, or selective breeding was condemned as "negative" eugenics by the Catholic Church, and most Italian experts scoffed at it as a fraudulent "Nordic science" inapplicable to human beings. Italy's more refined brand of "civilizational" anti-Semitism, they hoped, would become the new European norm, as distinct from and far superior to the cloddy biological racism Hitler was spewing out of Nazi Germany.

It can't be proved that Farinacci put up Preziosi to write the libel, then framed it for the defense's purposes, though it bore all the hallmarks of Farinacci's modus operandi. The wild and wooly lie had always been his forte. He had perfected his own histrionic style both in his courtroom performances and, only recently, by writing and staging a truly awful theater melodrama. As for his anti-Semitism: he had always despised Margherita Sarfatti, just as he came to despise Lilliana. And once he gathered that the Duce was no longer looking out for her, he Jew-baited for her cosmopolitan view, calling her a member of the "Race of Shylock."[18] Lilliana was an even better target. "Calumniate, calumniate," Filippo Meda would later write, "something will stick."[19]

Political anti-Semitism was on the rise in Italy. Following the arrest of a group of students, several from prominent Turinese Jewish families, caught trying to smuggle antifascist newspapers and leaflets into Italy in March 1934, the press had begun to speak of "antifascist Jews." At the same time, Mussolini's speech at Bari, which denounced Hitler for his fixation on race, suggested that Mussolini still professed to be an agnostic on the question of anti-Semitism. And yet he shared Farinacci's reprehension for the alleged Zionism of the League of Nations, promoted by the British—and could be heard denouncing the Jewishness of Italian finance capital, identified in Milan with Giuseppe Toeplitz of the Commercial Bank. Taking his lead from Mussolini, Farinacci began to single out the Jewish community and then specific Jewish leaders, calling on them to avow publicly their loyalty to Italy and the regime.[20] In Milan, he understood that the Church of Saint Ambrose, Cardinal Schuster's domain, was profoundly disturbed about how to react to Nazi anti-Semitism. But almost immediately he would have a few nibbles and bites—and begin to reel them in. He had Zanchetta on the hook. Later, Agostino Gemelli would take the bait, and after 1938, so would many others.[21]

At the moment, however, Farinacci's dirty trick seemed to backfire. On May 31, when Lilliana returned to the palace of the archbishop, before answering further questions, she was permitted to give an opening statement. She used it not to accuse her husband but to reveal a plot and to expose the hatred that inspired it. She spoke as if she had the whole Vatican establishment behind her. Father Tacchi Venturi had granted her an audience. She had explained the whole affair, and he had urged her through two mutual women friends "to go after them with everything she has, no pardon, no truce."[22]

On July 27, 1935, just as the tribunal's tortoise-paced deliberations halted for the summer, Fascist Italy took the last, irrevocable step short of invading Ethiopia and called up its military forces. Over the previous ten months, the regime had entertained various overtures from the British and French to colonize Ethiopia with no war, only to reject them as insultingly modest. Attempts on the part of the League of Nations to arbitrate had failed. The threats—that if Italy went to war, the League of Nations would impose sanctions—were dismissed as a conspiracy of "plutocratic" great powers wanting to prevent "proletarian" Italy from fulfilling its civilizing mission.

There had, however, been one major change in how to fight the war fascistically. The army chief of staff, Marshal Badoglio, had returned from Cyrenaica in February 1934, only to see how far Mussolini had fallen prey to the amateurishness of his military advisors, with the quadrumvir De Bono in the lead. "Audacity" may have worked for the March on Rome, but De Bono's precipitous timing had the troops ready to invade as early as the end of the rainy season, in October 1934. Had Mussolini surrounded himself with more competent military advisers, he would have understood that De Bono's sense of timing and logistics was laughable. This was a major war, Badoglio argued, not a colonial incursion. Fascist Italy couldn't afford to get bogged down, as had happened in Libya, much less risk another Adwa. The terrain was forbidding. The Ethiopians had a giant, if primitively armed, force, but they employed Western military advisers, had international opinion on their side, and would obtain reinforcements from sympathetic Europeans. The victory had to be quick and convincing. To mount the full-fledged war Badoglio recommended called for a major investment in logistics, technically prepared troops, and Italy's overwhelming air superiority. All these preparations would take three years.[23]

Mussolini was convinced to give up on his most amateur plans. In turn, Badoglio accepted Mussolini's timing. The war would still open in October 1935 in order to win it before the onset of the next rainy season. But Teruzzi would not be secretly training three battalions of Blackshirts to fortify garrisons in Italian Eritrea, as had been proposed in August 1934; and they would not be "outfitted like simple soldiers" and shipped out on commercial vessels so as not to arouse suspicion.[24] Five divisions of militia would still be mobilized to fight, Badoglio agreed, but at the command of army generals. The one exception would be the Fifth Division, the February First, named in honor of the date of founding of the Fascist Militia. General Teruzzi, who, at Mussolini's behest, would be promoted to the rank of brigadier general on August 10, 1935, would command that, with a regular army man, Lieutenant Colonel Gioda, as his second-in-command.

From July 16, 1935, Teruzzi had at his orders a force of about 10,000, counting three Blackshirt legions from Vicenza, Vercelli, and Pavia, two armored regiments, a unit of army engineers, and a complement of military police. Issuing the call to arms, he spoke with the heartfelt rhetoric of an old army man: "I'm proud to be at your head," he proclaimed. "Our greatly beloved King and the Duce, our guide, inestimably rely on us. Our goal is to fight and win, but to win we need to be strictly trained, not just daring. Here's to getting to work. Here's to us."[25]

For the next three months, the division trained out of Caserta, the onetime summer establishment of the kings of Naples, which for Teruzzi's purposes was the perfect location: close enough to Naples for him to enjoy the nightlife, while accessible to the sun-scorched hilltops of Benevento where the troops conducted war maneuvers, to hold the heights above the city of Capua against the enemy assault across the Volturno River. On November 2, the first of the troops of the Fifth Division embarked from Naples for the port of Massawa. With their scores of pack mules and field kitchens, armored vehicles, and motorcycles, they were the best-equipped Italian forces to have ever embarked for a warfront. Clad in "full and perfect colonial gear," they had brand-new machine guns, fresh-pressed khaki uniforms, two-liter water canteens, and a green and yellow pith helmet "as big as God's mercy," topped off with glare-free sunglasses.[26]

This was Teruzzi's moment. Propaganda newsreels capture him not once but three times on the gangplank at the port of Naples: at the send-off for two of Mussolini's sons, Bruno and Vittorio; with the young Ciano

February 1st Division at Caserta, ready to deploy to Ethiopia, October 1935.
Photographed by Riccardo Carbone.

Author's Collection

and the royal princes; and at last, with his own contingent, the last convoy
to Massawa. The ship's portside was draped with the division's motto:
"Forward for the cause with heart and dagger." His Milanese comrade,
the artist Mario Sironi, produced the division's postcard—an unsheathed
dagger, jutting skyward. Mussolini's postcard arrived with Teruzzi's sly
note: "You can see, Excellency, I am not passé"—*passatista*, meaning over
the hill, which the old guard, still capable of enviably modernist erections,
was not.[27] Like all of her friends, like most Italians, even staunch antifascists, Lilliana was swept up by war fever. On the eve of Teruzzi's departure, she had telegraphed him at his hotel in Naples: "Accompanying you,
with best wishes for you and for Italy. Lilliana."[28]

By the time Teruzzi landed at Massawa on December 6, Mussolini had
replaced General De Bono with Marshal Badoglio. Not unexpectedly, the
old quadrumvir had produced neither the audacious attack that the fascists needed nor the painstaking logistical buildup required once the
troops and supplies had been unloaded and reached the high plains around
Adwa, to move them southwestward over the practically roadless Eritrean

262

highlands into Ethiopia. It was the lack of sound logistics, Badoglio insisted, that had caused the Italian defeat at Adwa in 1896. Roads meant all the difference between an orderly retreat, which was a normal part of warfare, and the falling back that in Italy's experience at Adwa, and elsewhere, had turned into a catastrophic rout.[29]

At Badoglio's orders, Teruzzi's division, from its assembly point on the highlands of Eritrea at Dekemhare, instead of going to Adi Cajeh, on the border with Ethiopia, was ordered southwest, to take up position on the rocky heights above the Obel and Mareb Rivers across from the towns of Axum and Adwa. The terrain was practically impassable by mules and men, much less motorized troops, rising to 3,000 or 4,000 feet, riven by gulches, and covered with thorny, insect-infested shrubs. The daytime temperature rose to 110 degrees Fahrenheit in the shade. All of the legionnaires had arrived with the notion that they would be engaged in mobile warfare, leaping onto troop trucks, dropping off, running in pursuit of and cutting down fleeing Ethiopians.[30]

Instead, the orders were to build roads. There were no hydraulic excavators, scrapers, or compacters. The labor force was exclusively white, exploiting some of the best-trained, most ideologically committed Blackshirts of Italy—storekeepers, professionals, craftsmen—to blast, clear, grade, and pave using dynamite, pickaxes, wheelbarrows, and manual graders and rollers. In a shocking reversal of racial hierarchies, the fighting forces were all indigenous troops, Askari recruited from Eritrea, who periodically would head off on horseback and foot, to reconnoiter, engage in a firefight at a distance, and return with a spy or a turncoat to torture for information. The only time the militia forces saw a racially mixed fighting unit was on March 6. That was when Achille Starace, at the head of his notoriously murder-minded East African Mobile Column, put himself under Teruzzi's command for five days. Disappointed after rooting around the area to try to engage the Ethiopian forces, he had brusquely broken camp to set off on a maneuver toward Lake Tana, where, under the cover of machine-gun fire, carpet-bombing, and poison gas provided by the Italian Royal Air Force, he hoped for a final showdown.[31]

To keep up morale at Chessad Cuare, the fortification where they were stalled until orders came to descend to the river plain, Teruzzi would chug up to the very top of the last rocky hillock mounted on a tiny white mule, bloody at its bit, to inspect the fortifications, showing his own impatience for the fight as he looked out to the mountains of Adi Abo, toward

Ethiopia and Lake Tana. Or he would arrive in a sidecar, like a *squadrista* of the old guard his sleeves rolled up an ivory-handled dagger at his waist, to give the men a pep talk and remind them that the day would come when—with all of the machine guns blazing, daggers and grenades in hand—they would show the world how Blackshirts fight. They heard from spies that the enemy called him "Ras Teehm," meaning "beard" in Amharic, and so the troops grew beards to look like him.[32] The propaganda machine worked overtime to make the home audiences understand the importance of logistical support: Teruzzi's men were the true protagonists of the *The Road of Heroes*, as the prize-winning propaganda film was titled.

Accumulating truisms, prejudices, and arrogance from what little of the land and people they saw as they advanced, Italian soldiers, by the end of their tour of duty, could speak of "the audacity of the flies and mosquitoes," and of the women and how their hairdos indicated their sexual availability (braids if married; shaved, if not; virgins, shaved but for a cupie curl; women—neither widows, virgins, nor married—full hair). They could speak of the peaks of the Tecazzé beyond the rock spires and towers standing "like mute giants," of the "banditry" of the prisoners who foolishly escaped from the Italian's "concentration camps," only to be shot while fleeing, and of the effrontery of the Abyssinians, who appeared on the horizon, only to break up at the sound of the aviation forces and "dissolve like snow in the sun."[33] On their return to Italy, volunteers of the 107th Legion would boast of how they had "looked for and tracked the Abyssinians in an epic march across new lands, entirely unknown, never even traversed by indigenous troops and considered downright impassable for soldiers of the white race."[34]

That Italy would triumph over the ill-equipped Ethiopians was a given. Yet political exigencies called for speeding up practically every step of the war to face international diplomacy and public opinion with a fait accompli. And that led to all kinds of improvisation that belied the military establishment's careful planning.

Worrying that the main thrust from the north would be inadequate to entrap the Ethiopian forces, the army opened up a second front out of Somaliland under the command of General Graziani. Given the pressure to move quickly, as the League of Nations embargoed trade with Italy for its aggression against another League member, the Italian forces pressed into battle all of the Askari troops they could muster. To rush even more equipment and supplies to the troops, they bought up matériel from all over the Mediterranean, incurring huge cost overruns. To pay off the war-

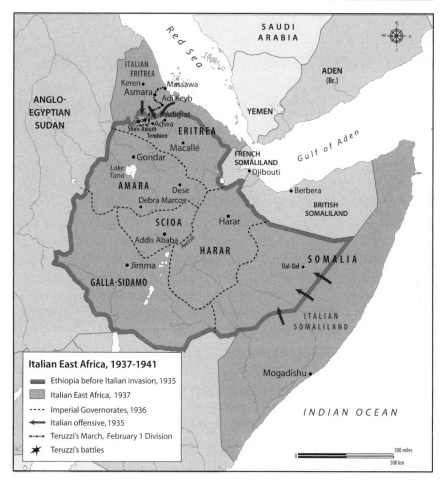

Italian East Africa, 1937-1941

- ▬▬ Ethiopia before Italian invasion, 1935
- ▨ Italian East Africa, 1937
- ---- Imperial Governorates, 1936
- ◄— Italian offensive, 1935
- ▬·▬· Teruzzi's March, February 1 Division
- ✴ Teruzzi's battles

© Victoria de Grazia

lords so that they would defect from Emperor Haile Selassie, the treasury minted money, triggering inflation. To speed up the conquest, Mussolini authorized the air force to bomb enemy troops with poison gas.[35]

On May 4, 1936, Marshal Badoglio had raced his troops to occupy the capital of Addis Ababa and declared victory. With no official declaration of war, there was no need for a signed surrender. On May 9, in Rome, broadcasting to the nation amid "oceanic" crowds, Mussolini announced Italy "finally has its Empire"—"the Fascist Empire," its "Empire of Peace," its "Empire of civility and humanity."[36] Plans called for immediate demobilization.

Everything was up in the air for Teruzzi's division. Villagers were surrendering as they passed. The troops were to complete the occupation of Ethiopia's mountainous Semien region by May 1. The rainy season was about to start, and Badoglio's last orders were that "everything had to be sacrificed for roads."[37] Faced with the choice to leave or stay on, Teruzzi, on May 10, 1936, handed over his command to Lieutenant General Vittorio Vernè. Marshal Badoglio welcomed him to board the first ship homeward bound together with a handful of other fascist notables turned warriors. Teruzzi had made an excellent impression on him for his—really, his troop's—self-abnegating service and his shared revulsion for the party secretary Starace's indiscipline at racing his troops to enter Addis Ababa ahead of Badoglio. Also, word had it that Teruzzi would make an excellent fourth at the bridge table on the return passage.[38]

The war had served its purpose on the home front: it had demonstrated that the militia was an invaluable force for overseas wars. It had also certified that even those of the old guard who had never before seen battle could become seasoned warriors. Before Teruzzi left for home, he visited Farinacci at the field hospital at Dessié, where he found him lying on a cot, his burned face bandaged, his right hand amputated. He had arrived in East Africa in early February 1936, after obtaining his pilot's license and receiving his commission from Mussolini. By April, he wrote Varenna, he was breathless, having flown 20,000 kilometers in just fifty-five days. In his only real battle feat, he had flown his Caproni bomber out of Maccalé with a squadron of fifty-five attack planes. Their target was Haile Selassie, who with his main army force was retreating across the Ascianghi Plain. Flying at altitudes as low as 30 feet, they struck with tons of high-explosive and gas bombs, inflicting thousands of casualties. It was only after the battle, relaxing by fishing with hand grenades in Lake Ascianghi, that he had blown off his hand.[39]

The war had helped join the young warriors of the regime to the old guard. Indro Montanelli, the future journalist and historian, then twenty-six and fresh out of university, had at his sole command a hundred native troops. Like Civinini and others before him, he fell for the war hero Teruzzi's rough charm. Montanelli listened to the aged, sun-creased veterans of the Libyan War, who—with their ancient watch fobs and sandaled pipe-thin legs—could have been a hundred years old, speak of Colonel Graziani and "Lieutenant Teruzzi," "who marched at the head of their Askari, their revolvers in the air." For Montanelli's cohort, "this war was like the long beautiful holidays that our great Daddy promised us as the prize for sitting still at school for thirteen years. And, we said amongst ourselves, it was about time."[40]

On March 5, as Teruzzi's division crossed the border from Eritrea into Ethiopia, Filippo Meda was in Milan summing up Lilliana's defense. His exposition was as calm, factual, and irreverent as Teruzzi's advocates had been choleric, melodramatic, and malicious. On the question of the law, he appealed to the precedent established in 1920 by the then Sacra Rota auditor, Cardinal-Bishop Luigi Sincero (who since 1934 had presided over the Pontifical Commission for the Authentic Interpretation of the Code of Canon Law). He had ruled that natural law, which is the basis of Church law, holds that consent is the basis of all marriage; and if this consent has not been given, the marriage is void. He had also specified that in canon law, consent means that the two spouses have the perpetual and exclusive right to each other's bodies for the generation of offspring. All of the other benefits the couple might bring to one another by contracting the marriage, like happiness, wealth, or delight in one another's beauty, physicality, or intelligence, were benefits above and beyond said contract. If they turned out to be lacking, the contract was no less valid.[41]

From that premise, Meda argued that to all appearances the marriage before the tribunal was completely solid. It had taken the plaintiff, Teruzzi, three years to come up with a case for annulment, and at the time he broke off the marriage, he himself had written to the defendant: "If you had made yourself loved by people I would probably have never learned what I know now." A "vendetta, a reprisal," Meda argued, had driven the break-up, and an animus drove the witnesses to testify against her. The virginity question was irrelevant, not that anything in the plaintiff's case had proven that the defendant was not a virgin. Her letters to Ferulli testified only to the "frivolity of usage" and "debasement of language" that had become universal in present-day times, not to any "carnal relationship." Moreover, the plaintiff's argument that the defendant could have manipulated the marriage date to coincide with her menstruation sounded straight out of Boccaccio's *Decameron*: Meda wasn't sure whether to call it "malicious or infantile." Either way, "it did no honor to the plaintiff." The testimony of Ferulli, a self-confessed adulterer, would never be valid under Roman law, Meda added, and in any case, "testis unus testis nullus" ("one witness equals no witness"). He wrapped up with a point of canon law, which is perhaps lambent in the Latin phrase he quoted but which read like a rebus in Italian, and sounds still odder in English, and nobody picked up on it at the time. In sum: a person cannot contract a true marriage if, in doubt about his spouse's purity, he intends to prove or disprove it by consummating the marriage and, on that basis, to decide whether the union is valid.[42]

Meda had much else to scoff at. On whether she was of legitimate birth: even if Lilliana lacked a proper birth certificate, she could not be proven illegitimate, given the preponderance of other evidence that she was her parents' daughter. On whether she was a mad woman: if "the tendency to exaggerate, arrogance and boastfulness" proved her "mental incapacity," then "our whole hemisphere would . . . have to be described as a madhouse."[43]

The judges hadn't yet started to deliberate by the time Teruzzi returned to Italy in late May. It is hard to imagine that since the previous July— when he had taken command of his division, much less over the period of the war, when he had been practically out of communication—he had followed the process with any attention. There was not much he could do following the submission of the final summary of his case in February 1935.

Lilliana, on the other hand, had been a busy bee. Senator Alfredo Felici, D'Annunzio's chief attorney and confidante, had become her latest and most prominent lay supporter. A wealthy, onetime radical republican Romagnuole, his wife, Olga, neé Schwartz, was Jewish, and he was a longtime friend of Margherita Sarfatti.[44] He was also a staunch fascist—but many staunch fascists found Teruzzi repulsive. And he may have become more willing to say so now that Teruzzi was no longer the head of the Blackshirts.

At taking up the generalship of his division in the summer of 1935, Teruzzi had resigned his position. In a hierarchy that prized multiple positions, he was still a deputy but no longer a member of the Fascist Grand Council. And at his return home, he was a general without a command, with no knowledge of when the War Ministry would assign him a new one. For the moment, Italy's first fascist war did not seem to have improved his fortunes. Marshal Graziani, who had been recently ennobled with the title of Marquis of Neghelli after the battle site that sealed his military success in Ethiopia, had been the war's true victor. On Badoglio's return to Italy on May 21, Graziani had been named the governor-general of Addis Ababa and viceroy of Ethiopia with the task of repressing the rebellion. Teruzzi himself had little desire to go back and would never have been high on Graziani's list, even if he had not had plenty of other generals to choose from.

Teruzzi's diminished stature showed on June 21, when Mussolini inaugurated the giant new Militia Command in Viale Romania in the presence of Luigi Russo, his successor as chief of staff. In choosing Russo, the Duce made it clear that he wanted a commander with practically no political profile whatsoever. A minute, beetle-browed onetime prefect and militia consul, Russo had a splendid war record and had left the service as a colonel, but he was a civilian, not a military man. And with two grown children, he was completely bourgeois in his family habits. Teruzzi was still center stage at the inauguration, decorated, uniformed, and positioned to catch the photographers' lens. But the official news agency, Stefani, had registered his declining fortunes and demoted him from the first official listed after the Duce to the eleventh. For the moment, he was only the "Honorable Deputy" to Parliament.[45]

By midsummer practically the only signs that Fascist Italy had been engaged in a war mobilizing a half million Italian men, draining the national treasury, and subjugating a whole people to Italian conquest were the scattered local ceremonies to welcome the troops home. It was time for a rest. For Attilio Teruzzi, that meant spending as much time as he could at Castiglioncello with Mrs. Nappi, her family, and his sister as house guests.

In mid-July, Lilliana was "having a very lovely time," playing lots of bridge with her friends, Norina, Sandra, Gugo, Arturo, and Margo, at Roman homes with beautiful terraces. Norina told her fortune—"and they said that is the greatest fortune they ever saw, it predicts a change of position in the most marvelous and glorious way with enormous money coming my way, and at least two new men in my life; and like Figaro in the Barber of Seville I said, 'Uno alla volta per carità ['One at a time, for goodness sake']."[46] She had become close to Father Candidori, who came by for lunch with his sister. She visited the Serafins, who were making plans for the wedding of their daughter Vittoria, to another musician's son, and couldn't settle on whether it should take place in Verona or Portofino. Mrs. Serafin, Lilliana wrote her parents, perhaps hoping for a big wedding present, mentioned in passing that she had heard from her dressmaker that Teruzzi had given the Nappis a silver tray service like the one they had received from the minister of the interior staff for their own wedding. That Saturday, she had gone to the Valadier for drinks and then on a car ride with friends out to the Appia Antica to see the full moon, returning at quarter to four in the morning. She was at the seaside at Maccarese when she heard that the Milan tribunal would deliver its verdict the following Friday, July 17.[47]

On Friday, "imagine my frame of mind," she wrote her parents, when after only twenty minutes she received a telegram from Meda. It just said, "Sentence pronounced which is favorable, Meda." Since he had always added kind regards, she was sure it was a fake. Then his express letter arrived: "The verdict is not only favorable, but completely favorable . . . 28 closely written pages of a very diligent study which I am certain you will read with the greatest satisfaction."[48]

And so she did. The court rejected out of hand the various accusations that Lilliana didn't want children, was illegitimate, and was a mad woman, and on that score they chastely paid tribute to her womanly poise and intelligence. They all but called Farinacci and company liars, and they spent page after page dissecting the discrepancies in Teruzzi's testimony, underscoring its bluster and silliness, all but concluding that his "patrons" had put words in his mouth. Whether she was a virgin or not was irrelevant, and not an issue they intended to take up. There was no mention whatsoever of the anti-Semitic libel: and that, surely, was exactly as Lilliana's backers in the Curia had intended.[49]

Lilliana's father, when she telegraphed him, cried with relief. Her mother was beside herself with pride: "Our Babele won one of those rare victories which few thought possible . . . She had Mussolini and the Catholic Church against her, and she could overcome them all, Thank God." Lilliana immediately told all of her friends, who congratulated her, as her mother put it, on "her success at beating the Devil."[50] Senator Felici told her to make three hundred copies of the verdict and distribute them "up and down" the country. Her longtime friend Gugo, a onetime military pilot, implored her "to revenge" herself, "now that [she has] the knife by the handle, as they say in Italian." When she urged him to be careful over the phone, he replied: "I wasn't afraid of him and his bullies when I was a simple pilot and he was *mezzo-padrone* of Italy, so you can about imagine how I feel today."[51]

When she went to the Valadier nightclub to celebrate, she caught sight of Malgeri, whom she wouldn't deign to acknowledge with a glance. ("He will surely die of a cancer of the throat," she told her parents.) He was with other fascist bigwigs, who knew she was Teruzzi's wife: "They watched me constantly and I danced every dance, each fellow handsomer than the last one."[52]

Lilliana conspired with Senator Felici about how best to inform Mussolini "about my situation." The gossip was that he already knew something about it; Teruzzi was out of favor—on his return from Africa, Mussolini had apparently told him he would have to return to his division in the Ethiopian backlands in August. He added that "leaving you killed him spiritually and politically." "There is a God," Lilliana gloated. "Everybody drank up Felici's words." Father Tacchi Venturi had recently become even more solicitous, eager to meet and sending his good wishes to her and her parents. She wanted him to "take the decision to Mussolini, he should see for himself the whole truth." But Felici scotched that. He drafted the letter in her name and told her to send it to Mussolini herself.[53]

Mussolini was on his holidays at Predappio when her letter with the package arrived. "Dear Mr. President," she wrote. "After three-and-a-half years, the verdict was completely favorable to me." She recalled his kindness at her *affiancement* and the homage she had written to him. She wanted the opportunity to clarify a few points. Before "departing from Italy forever, she hoped he would receive her," she wrote. "No!" he scribbled with his blue pencil, underscored twice, and added, "How [did this get] here?"[54]

The fascist regime was now in the fourteenth year of its existence. When Lilliana read the commendation that had accompanied Teruzzi's latest war decoration, she wrote her parents, "He should go into hiding." It read: "A bold general, self-assured, of strong character, generous and ardent, excellent organizer, worthy of every highest trust."[55] She may have been right that the gossip said the encomium was pathetic compared to that of other generals much his junior. But her belief that he was "finished" only showed how little she understood the fascist regime. A month earlier, on July 9, Teruzzi had been promoted to the rank of two-star general for his combat merits.

Meda told Lilliana to expect that the verdict would be sent to the archdiocese's appeals court. As she left, she wasn't sure she would return. Her parents wanted her help to put their business in Europe on a new footing. And she was ferocious at the prospect of booting the "cheating" relatives,

Marshall Pietro Badoglio, General Italo Balbo, and General Teruzzi wearing militia dagger on maneuvers in Italy, August 1936

Ullstein Bild Dtl./Getty Images

the *Mispuche,* out of the firm. First she took the baths at Bagnoles-de-l'Orne. Then, she went to Paris. She adored it, except, she joked to her mother, the service would surely suffer if the communists took over. She had seen it happen at Bagnoles. The *valet de chambre* was the communist floor delegate, and the chambermaid, his wife. They knew she was a "Fascista," and to convey their feelings about that, they slammed the door whenever they entered or exited her room.[56] When all was said and done, Fascist Italy was still her home.

Whether Teruzzi discussed his case with Farinacci, and how soon after the decision he might have done so, remains a matter of speculation. Following his return from Ethiopia and a series of operations, Farinacci was adjusting to the prosthetic hook the doctors had fitted to his right wrist. His convalescence was spent reading and taking comfort in the tens of hundreds of messages piling up on his desk to congratulate him on doing his patriotic duty.[57] And anyway, he couldn't be faulted for the outcome of Teruzzi's case. It had been a brave gambit. Cardinal Schuster's Church had decided to play hardball. Teruzzi needed a true divorce lawyer, a Prince of the Forum, to win.

While Mussolini was at war in Ethiopia, Hitler had rearmed and reoccupied the Rhineland, the demilitarized buffer between victorious France and defeated Germany and the linchpin of the Versailles treaty. The League of Nations, in its failure to curb Italy, had set a precedent. Now France and Britain had to face a militarized and belligerent Italy and Germany together, and Spain promised to be the new battlefield.

On July 17, 1936, General Francisco Franco, then at the head of Spain's colonial troops, mobilized all the nation's military forces and led a rebellion to overthrow the republic. Thirteen days later, after General Franco sought his help, Mussolini sent nine Italian military planes, their pilots dressed as Blackshirts, to provide Franco's forces air cover to cross from Spanish Morocco. The fascist old guard reckoned that Spain was the next place to take a stand. On August 14, Teruzzi turned in his division command and began the wait for a new assignment.

18

IN LOVE, TRIBULATIONS

Let thine heart be mine,
Let love enchain us,
Jew or Gentile, it doesn't matter,
Your fate shall be mine!

—LEOPOLD, Act 2, Scene 4, Halévy's *The Jewess*

On April 2, 1937, in the spring after the ruling on his annulment trial, Attilio Teruzzi arrived in Spain carrying a fake passport under his maternal grandfather's name, Cairati. Disguised as a Milanese businessman, he was on a secret mission with orders straight from the Duce.

Two weeks earlier, the 32,000 Blackshirts that Mussolini had clandestinely sent to Spain to back General Francisco Franco's coup had been routed at the town of Guadalajara, and the Spanish Republican forces, riding high on their first victory, were exhilarated. The antifascist press mocked Mussolini's vaunted military prowess: the lost battle was "Fascism's Caporetto," "the Duce's Skedaddle." Teruzzi's task, as "Inspector General and Supreme Commander of all of the functions of the Blackshirts," was to put things in order. Mussolini told the Italian commander in the field that he placed "full confidence" in his new envoy and was counting on him "for clear and decisive revenge, absolutely necessary from a military and moral point of view." This was bound to complicate the work of the twenty-odd Italian generals already in place.[1]

The Duce's high-handedness went with the territory. By the spring of 1937, it was an open secret that the Italian government had been supplying Generalissimo Franco, the self-declared head of state of Spain, with troops, tanks, airplanes, and weapons since the outset of the Spanish insurrection. This support had continued even after Italy signed a pact of nonintervention in November 1936, binding its twenty-eight signatories not to contribute to the widening of the civil war.

For this new, more aggressive, and more disruptive foreign undertaking, the young of the fascist regime bonded with the old guard. Galeazzo Ciano, Mussolini's thirty-three-year-old son-in-law, had been appointed minister of foreign affairs in June 1936, and he had made the intervention in Spain his first major foreign policy undertaking. Fascism's double-dealing was more aggressively on display than ever before.

As it fiercely denounced the USSR, France, and antifascist international volunteers for aiding the Spanish Republic and presented itself as working through traditional diplomatic channels on behalf of nonintervention, the fascist regime introduced the ferocity of Italy's own civil war of 1920–1922 into Spain's.

From August 1936, the first Italian volunteers arrived at Majorca under the command of the red-bearded and immense Arcnovaldo Bonaccorsi, one of the most brutal of the old guard *squadristi*. In the early fall, after Bonaccorsi's armed bands had conquered the Balearics, killing several thousand Spanish loyalists in the process, Mussolini followed up by sending three divisions of the Fascist Militia, the so-called Volunteer Troops Corps, or CTV, under the command of the regular army. Meanwhile, the foreign ministry's propaganda machine coordinated with Mussolini's office to champion the Spanish crusade as a mission against "Masonic-Bolshevism" on behalf of "Christian European civilization."[2]

Teruzzi's role in Spain had two dimensions. First, he was to work with the generals in the field to reorganize the CTV divisions, purge them of incompetent officers (he would send home a couple thousand), introduce better training, and deliver words of encouragement, decorations, and bonuses to raise morale; and second, to strategize the "revenge"—payback for the defeat at Guadalajara. What he saw upon reviewing the troops of the expeditionary force was the pathos of family men from Sicily and other regions of the Italian south: unemployed, landless, and drummed up by local party *federali* to fill quotas of volunteers. Most were unfit and untrained. Many were returning from service in Ethiopia and reenlisting to keep their pay—they didn't even understand they were headed to Spain.[3]

Teruzzi's second, self-appointed role was to advise the young Ciano. He mouthed what the Italian war correspondents said (but didn't dare write) about how poor a military leader Franco was, how astonishingly reactionary the Spanish rebels were, and how the "Reds" were doing a much better job at recruitment.[4] He suffered, he confessed to Ciano, at seeing

Franco deploy the Blackshirts without any real strategy. Worse still, the Italian army generals rebuffed his efforts to help! "My person counts less than zero," he wrote pathetically to Ciano. But if his authority was undermined, he would not be able to "galvanize" the Blackshirts' fighting spirit.[5]

By the summer of 1937, the Italian army command had succeeded in coordinating an attack strategy with Franco. In a great pincer movement, the combined Nationalist-Fascist forces would move northwest to attack the last important Republican strongholds on the Bay of Biscay. After the attack on Bilbao, which finally fell on June 19, the next bastion would be Santander, after which the troops would move south to reinforce the siege against Madrid.

The Battle of Santander went according to plan. From August, the Nationalist and CTV forces, with German and Italian air support, pummeled the Republic's Army of the North, forcing it to retreat westward along the coast. The final assault brought headquarters to the peak of Mount Maza behind the city, from where Teruzzi sent a self-flattering snapshot to Ciano that showed him looking unflappably heroic and Generalissimo Franco dwarflike and tentative.[6] As the two of them peered through their field binoculars, 60,000 Spanish foreign legionnaires, Moorish troops, and Italian "volunteers" moved down the fog-hung peaks under the cover of air and artillery bombardment to roust the city's 25,000 defenders. Fighting at first from ill-concealed machine-gun nests on the hillsides, protected by straggly lines of barbed wire, and ultimately waging hand-to-hand combat with rifles, dynamite, and hand grenades, the Republican troops fell back into the besieged town, where they were overwhelmed. Afterward, Teruzzi and his fellow general Bastico insisted that the 17,000 vanquished troops be rewarded for their gallant defense. Instead, Franco had thousands of them summarily executed.

Rome welcomed the victory as fascism's own: the front pages showed boisterous Italian troops hoisting Teruzzi and Bastico on their shoulders, and they all ran Franco's telegram to the Duce expressing "gratitude and pride at having Italian legionnaires under his command . . . in the name of Western civilization's struggle against Asiatic Barbarism." They also featured the Duce's reply, which gloried in "the "intimate brotherhood-in-arms that at the final victory will deliver Spain and the Mediterranean from all menaces against our common civilization." Teruzzi's telegram followed: "All the Blackshirts have completely and heroically fulfilled their duty. The Duce's orders have been carried out."[7]

Woe to anybody who suggested otherwise. Indro Montanelli, who had been captivated by Teruzzi's exploits in Ethiopia and was now an accredited war correspondent for *Il Messaggero*, had become thoroughly disenchanted. He was a keen observer of the fascist military road show mounted by Ciano, who had arranged for the insurgency to be covered by a raft of journalists, most of whom stayed well away from the heat of the fighting. The Battle of Santander had been a joke, Montanelli reported, sight unseen, a thirty-kilometer march without any resistance, with fake body counts and the "only enemy the heat." When Teruzzi and General Bastico complained, Montanelli was repatriated for "denigrating the armed forces" and, under pressure to make himself scarce, had the good sense to find work abroad for a couple of years.[8]

What Montanelli did not say at the time was that, by all appearances, Teruzzi was in good company with the other Italian generals. Dressed in swashbuckling uniforms topped with berets, they threw out pockets of coins to the crowd at their visits to the bullfights and traveled to and from the battlefields accompanied by lavish tent boudoirs. In this "swirl of activity," Montanelli recalled, "Teruzzi's harem was the most varied and active."[9]

In September, when Teruzzi went home on a ten-day furlough, nobody wanted him back: not Franco, who was furious at the Italians' grandstanding at Santander; not Ciano, who praised him for "his beautiful endeavor" and reiterated his personal affection for him but had been perplexed by Teruzzi's optimism on the war's progress; not the new commander in the field, General Berti, who had no use for this loose cannon "Inspector General."[10]

The only problem, Ciano hazarded, was how Mussolini could reward Teruzzi so that his dismissal wouldn't be "followed by the usual howls of criticism." It wasn't enough for them to meet in private, as they did on September 14, just the three of them, when the Duce, at hearing about the good progress of the war, had joked that "the British have their brains in the seat of their pants."[11] Ciano had married Mussolini's daughter Edda and always had ringside seats to the spectacle of his father-in-law's master stunts. On October 13, after accompanying Teruzzi to Mussolini's office and hearing Mussolini promise him a new position, he came away "glad that this faithful old soldier is to be rewarded—he did well in Africa and in Spain."[12] The next day, Mussolini's press office announced that the Duce had personally welcomed General Teruzzi back from his heroic exploits in Spain. It was the first time Mussolini publicly admitted that Fascist Italy had troops in Spain.

Since announcing the foundation of the Italian Empire in East Africa on May 9, 1936, Mussolini had been high-handed but inconclusive about how to rule Italy's colonial lands, now doubled in size. The Ministry of Italian Africa, as the old Colonial Ministry had been renamed the previous spring, was supposed to take charge. For that to happen, Mussolini would have to settle the situation of Marshal Graziani, who had been named the viceroy of Ethiopia practically at the moment of conquest. There was also the matter that, in reality, four-fifths of the country was still outside Italian control. Numerous Ethiopian notables had retreated into the backlands in order to continue the fight once Haile Selassie had fled abroad and Addis Ababa was under siege. Graziani's attempts to assert and retain control by using gas bombings and open grave executions—the very savageries he was known for—had only served to provoke an assassination attempt against him on February 19, 1937.

When the attempt failed, leaving Graziani gravely wounded, the Italians went on a weeklong murder rampage, killing thousands.[13] Further reprisals in a bid to crush the Ethiopian ruling class, including dragnets, executions, and internment camps, only whipped up more rebellion. And repression could only go so far as all of the existing camps filled up.[14] Throughout the spring, Graziani, fearful of being removed and constantly defending himself against malicious detractors, was behaving in an increasingly paranoid fashion. The drumbeat of crazy-sounding telegrams culminated in June, with the arrival through the diplomatic pouch of a packet of photographs of his naked body demonstrating that, though it had been pierced by a hundred bomb shards, it was all in one piece.[15]

Mussolini began to rethink his staffing choices. To signal that the land belonged to the Crown, he appointed Amedeo, the Duke of Aosta, to the position of viceroy. If his only goal had been to show the British (and any other European royal dynasty that might care) that the Kingdom of Italy had a monarchy equal in lineage to their own, the duke was a perfect choice. He was physiologically and psychologically as close to British royalty as the Italian nation could produce. The son of Emanuele Filiberto, the commander of the invincible Third Army, Amedeo had been schooled two years at Eton College (and two at the Royal Military School of Nunziatella in Naples), and his intelligence was reputed to be "as creaseless as Chinese silk." He had British hobbies and mannerisms as well, including a wry sense of humor. He was indeed "Your Highness," he joked, as he stood at six foot six inches tall. He had worked in East Africa on the Somali plantations of his uncle, the Duke of Abruzzi, and so he had some familiarity with the terrain. A distinguished military officer, he had piloted a bomber under Graziani's command in the campaign against Umar al-Mukhtar. And he had completed his law thesis with a deep genuflection to "the moral aspect of the colonial problem in modern states" by arguing that "states can morally justify their sovereignty over indigenous peoples only by improving the conditions of existence of the colonialized peoples."[16]

Since the duke would report to the minister of Italian Africa, out of respect for the duke's rank, Mussolini took the position himself on November 19, 1937. This was a good pretext to be rid of the current unpopular minister, Alessandro Lessona, and to appoint Teruzzi as his undersecretary. And so Teruzzi's rise within the fascist ranks resumed. Even Ciano, who was fond of him personally and paid reverence to men with more "guts" than "brains," was taken aback. Teruzzi was certainly one of fascism's meritorious, but he was, to his mind, not really more than "a loyal but mediocre executive—in fact more loyal than mediocre."[17]

That, apparently, was what Mussolini wanted for the position of undersecretary to the minister of Italian Africa. But who really understood what smart, much less good, government was under the fascist regime? In the next year or so, the Italian public would see the press celebrate Teruzzi as a "soldier in all of the fascist wars," as if his military experience made him a more credible government functionary. In May 1938, on the basis of his service in Spain, he was given a third star and promoted to the rank of lieutenant general.[18]

When Indro Montanelli had caricatured Teruzzi as a man awhirl at the center of "his harem," he hadn't known or cared that Teruzzi's private life had recently taken a remarkable turn. Teruzzi had become a much lonelier person on April 29, 1937, when his sister, Amelia, had died at only fifty-nine from "a fatal malady"—probably cancer. He had been truly close to this forbidding, doting older sister: "my most tender sister," as he wrote in her death announcement, whose "only joys in life" had been "drawn from her work" and who "gave her heart to the noblest of causes: Family-School-Fatherland." With the death of their mother, she had become the "repository of all of his family affections," Malgeri confided in *Il Messaggero*, which now had the biggest readership in Rome.[19] Teruzzi was in Spain at the time of her death, and Mussolini had immediately telegrammed his condolences: "In this hour of grief, I feel particularly close to you," he said. So did a myriad of other comrades, colleagues, and friends.[20]

Sometime in midwinter, Teruzzi had met Yvette Maria Blank. Physically, emotionally, and socially, she seemed to be what he needed. She was just twenty-seven, Lilliana's age when they had married, and had what contemporary Italians called a "Levantine" beauty, meaning that there was something racially exotic about her sweet, animated face, strong nose, intense eyes, and thick cap of dark, wavy hair. She was tall by Italian standards at five feet six inches and had the bosomy figure that Italy's Hollywood on the Tiber, Cinecittà, was popularizing as the cinematic ideal of female beauty. She was down-to-earth, told great stories, and liked to laugh, showing her big white teeth. From the trifles she left and hearsay, it appears that she was a passionate reader of Colette, Vicki Baum, and other contemporary women novelists. She also believed in palm readings, *nazar* amulets, and *hamsa* charms; loved dancing and the cinema; and may well have aspired to be an actress.[21]

Yvette was also an outsider. The misogynistic reports of the usual spies and informers that first give us a glimpse of her captured some of the basic facts: she was born in Cairo on September 6, 1909, to Alexis Herman Blank, the Romanian consul in Egypt, and Corinne Schmill, a housewife. The informers stumbled over her exact nationality: was she Turkish? Levantine? Egyptian? Some combination of the above? They then settled on the idea that she was Romanian, except that she didn't seem to speak Romanian. The one constant was her religion, which they identified as Coptic Christian, like her mother's, with the odd reasoning—who knows where they picked it up—that her father, though identified as Jewish, had converted at the time of their marriage.[22]

Was Teruzzi at all concerned that Yvette was Jewish? That her mother, Corinne Schmill, also called Corinne Jacob, was a Coptic Christian was implausible. The Romanians living in the big towns around the Eastern Mediterranean—Cairo, Alexandria, Istanbul, Salonika, and Beirut—were almost invariably Jews. Both before the Kingdom of Romania was founded

Yvette Blank, passport photo,
1937
Grimaldi Family

in 1881, but especially after the newly founded state revealed its anti-Semitic face, many of them had settled in the venerable commercial entrepôts of the region. Bucharest was known as the Paris of the East, and in Egypt, French had replaced Italian as the lingua franca. Not surprisingly, Yvette's first language was French. She spoke fluent Italian and, if the police are to be believed, no Romanian at all.

How had she ended up in Italy? The informers who reported that she had first arrived in 1928 were unable to say. Yvette herself left scarcely any records, except for a couple of cartons of old passports and identity cards, family photographs, and gee-gees. Nor did she pass on much by way of her childhood memories through her daughter or granddaughters. With some digging in Romanian sources, it came out that her father had been the honorary commercial consul in Cairo after World War I, filling the position while Romania worked out its complicated relations with the new Kingdom of Egypt. Maybe he was related to the so-called Romanian

Rothschilds—the banker-art patrons Maurice Blank and his son, Aristide. If so, he couldn't capitalize on their good fortune. There was some incident, and he was let go. A Reuters dispatch from 1924 in the *London Times* titled "Suicide of Romanian Consul" reports that Alexis H. Blank was found dead in the Nuzha Garden of Alexandria, with a note in his pocket saying he had killed himself for personal reasons.[23]

If Alexis Blank's granddaughter is right, Yvette's mother was subsequently killed in a car crash, and the orphaned girl went to Turin to live with an aunt, Madame Braunstein Gentille. Judging by Braunstein Gentille's home address, possession of a telephone (a rare commodity then), her apparent move to France in 1936, and the portrait photo of the elegant older woman among Yvette's things, she came from the same cosmopolitan Jewish world as her deceased sister and brother-in-law. Yvette was barely nineteen at the time she arrived and just twenty-six when her aunt left for France. Perhaps she decided that the *jeunesse dorée* of Turin's Jewish bourgeoisie didn't interest her or that there were few prospects in what was basically a gloomy factory town. Rome was the place to be.

When she arrived in Rome in late 1936, Yvette Blank was brave and vulnerable, the very incarnation of a New Woman in her eagerness to find her way. But job opportunities were limited. She needed a protector to find one. At some point, she befriended Anna Magnani, the up-and-coming theater and film actress who was her exact age. Maybe Teruzzi met her through Magnani, on whom he doted and who—though she herself preferred much younger men—was fond enough of him. In any case, the two women shared a physical resemblance, and they were both from Egypt. At least that was what Magnani let people believe. The truth was that it was her mother who lived in Egypt, after marrying an Italian who had settled in Alexandria and abandoning her daughter, born out of wedlock with another man, in her grandmother's care. The fact that both women were orphans tossed around by the melodramas of life made them kindred spirits.[24]

In Rome, spies overheard Yvette telling "big shots" that she was penniless and had debts everywhere, filling their ears with hard luck stories and threatening to kill herself. Italo Sulliotti, the well-known adventure storywriter and journalist and former director of the Paris-based *Italia nuova*—the party organ of Italian fascists abroad—asked her to become his traveling secretary. He was running a spy ring in Paris, and Yvette, attractive and mischievous, with impeccable French, would be the ideal operative.[25]

But that didn't work out, and an "important person," an informer reported, took her under his wing. This was none other than Teruzzi. He immediately found her a good position at the Società Italo-Francese del Sale, a public enterprise that could use her linguistic skills. But on April 1, 1937, the very day she was due to start, "His Excellency" left on a mysterious mission abroad, leaving orders to pay her 2,000 lire in severance, the equivalent of two months' salary. When Teruzzi invited Yvette to join him in Spain in July, she got a French visa on her Romanian passport, crossed the closed border at San Juan de Lutz by telling the guard that her presence was required to help a wounded person, and, after rendezvousing with Teruzzi, attached herself to his "harem."[26]

Yvette's relationship with Teruzzi continued after the two of them returned to Italy in September 1937. In January, she became pregnant. True, she had barely known him for fifteen months, and she loved her freedom. But practically nobody used contraception in Italy back then. Had she been wholly hostile to the prospect of bearing his child, she could have gotten an abortion, a risky move and expensive in Fascist Italy, where the liberal ban had been rewritten to make it a crime against the Italian state and abortionists were exposed to harsh penalties.

For Teruzzi, Iva, as he called her, was a handful: handsome and spirited, honest and loving, but also rebellious and needy. He was going on fifty-five and she was half his age. He was rich and powerful and had always wanted children. He couldn't marry her until he got his annulment, but she couldn't have cared less about conventions. In sum, Yvette Blank was a godsend.

As when he had courted and married Lilliana, Teruzzi's personal life choices were being made in perfect synchronicity with the historical moment. The second half of the 1930s in Fascist Italy was a hypersexually charged time. Demographically, Italians were young. The giant cohort born just after the close of World War I was just coming of age, and tens of thousands of teenage girls were growing up with new role models: doting fathers, who spoiled their independent-minded daughters; Hollywood divas with their equally attractive Cinecittà counterparts; and their Duce, a great father but also a passionate love-object.[27] The fascist slogan "make way for youth" was conceived to apply to the much-younger men who were due to move on up in the fascist hierarchy, but it appealed to the young women as well. Everything was designed to make the fifty-year-old hierarchs feel self-conscious about the passage of time, from the PNF secretary

Starace's gargantuan gymnastic rallies with their ridiculous shows of muscular prowess to show off the nation's physical fitness to their own dated look in the camera eye.

Fascism's theatrical approach to war-making—its propaganda rollouts, oceanic speeches before crowds numbering in the hundreds of thousands, the call-ups, send-offs, and returns home—created a reality split along gender lines. The men who fought abroad experienced war as excitement, as a rite of initiation. And sexually, in the mercenary hook-ups and rapes in Ethiopia, it often was. The women who stayed at home experienced the wartime as exasperation. And Mussolini could feel that he no longer captured their eros. "They placed me on high, they put me on a throne," he complained to his young lover, Clara Petacci. They made "a myth" of him. And then: "The empire! Women don't speak to an emperor. They ask for things, they talk about [my] greatness; physically, I mean nothing [to them]."[28]

Claretta (as she was known) was a New Woman, in the 1930s fascist style. The daughter of a Vatican doctor, she had first met Mussolini as one of thousands of adolescent girls who idolized him. That was in 1932 when her family's automobile had crossed paths with his by chance on the way to the seaside near Rome. After four or so years of feverish correspondence, she separated from her husband, a young air force pilot, and in 1936, with her family's backing, had become Mussolini's lover. She was just twenty-four at the time.[29] Their relationship began at the time of the Ethiopian war, and with the passage of months and then years, she campaigned to turn his admittedly polygamous proclivities into a jealously possessive monogamy, meticulously documenting her success—and ever less frequent setbacks—in her diaries. Mussolini felt hugely invigorated by his new love. Their relationship would last, with only a few brief interruptions, until April 28, 1945, when communist partisans executed her alongside him near the Swiss border.

It was unlikely that Mussolini confided in Teruzzi. But everybody knew about the relationship by 1938, and Teruzzi knew Clara well enough to stand as a best man at the wedding of her younger sister, Miriam di San Servolo, a rising actress, in 1941. The two men shared a sense of renewed virility. Clara saw them giggling and nudging one another on the rostrum, cracking jokes about fertility and wet nurses as they stood on the balcony of Palazzo Venezia to inspect the thousands of women on parade for the first annual review of the nation's fascist women. Mussolini caught her looking at him from the crowd. "Yes, I was happy, really," he later told her. "When I laugh and am in good spirits, the others are too."[30]

Certainly, if Teruzzi had not found Yvette, if he had not had the good fortune to have a child with her, his life would have become much harder. In 1937 the Duce discovered that Italians, left to their own devices, especially the thousands of veterans who had remained in Ethiopia after the war to work, were not at all inhibited about "race mixing." If there were no "white" brothels—and there never could be enough—they went with native prostitutes, and *madamismo,* meaning informal marriage, flourished as the luckiest settled in more permanent liaisons with local women. Historically, Italians, especially the lumpen Italians who emigrated, had settled in alongside whatever races they found. Beggars couldn't be choosers. But now the Third Reich's clamor about pure races, whether the true European "racial stock" was Aryan or Latin, had Mussolini more and more worried.

Because Mussolini was at bottom a crude social Darwinist who believed in the inevitable clash of peoples, and because he himself had a strong nativist streak, he was a sponge for the racial denigration of his own people. Who knows if this stemmed from his own discomfort at having been an Italian laborer in Switzerland, or the easy and widespread disdain for Italian indiscipline, or his own fears that Italians were unsuited for serious war making. In any case, from the second half of the 1930s, he dramatically changed his approach to shaping up his subjects. The mid-1920s had seen him exercising control over the bodies of Italians through the Fascist Party's giant panoply of organizations for children, university students, workers, party women, and housewives. And earlier, his *squadristi* had beaten, purged, exiled, and murdered those same bodies. Now he became increasingly obsessed with dictating his subjects' private habits, from the age at which they married to the number of children they should produce. It was as if he wanted to extend the control he exercised over the great arteries of the state, the military, and the administration into society's every vein, ever capillary—to command its very pores.[31]

. Throughout 1937 he obsessed about miscegenation, about whether harsher laws in East Africa or a better brothel system or both would discourage it. He fretted about declining Italian fertility rates, bringing forward new legislation to tax bachelors, and debating whether he should promote—and demote—high government functionaries according to their number of children. He even ordered his secretariat to count how many children each of the men on the Grand Council had, which, averaging around two, turned out to be well below the national standard. In his memoirs,

Federzoni recalled the lecherous whispers and snickering at the Grand Council meetings devoted to discussing these matters. "As usual," he wrote, there were "no proper ethical or legal guidelines." Mussolini acted purely according to his fixations, "beating about, proposing the wildest and most incongruous gimmicks, from obliging employees to marry to obtain a promotion, or even a bonus or an honorific, to threatening to confiscate the estates of the dead if these were beyond a certain size and the deceased hadn't left at least four living heirs."

Only a "real moral reform," the high-minded Federzoni concluded, would increase birth rates; "spurious incentives" would never do so, certainly not so long as the "fascist guides accompanying adolescent *avanguardisti* on their outings took the occasion of their comings and goings to initiate them into the mysteries of brothel sex."[32]

This was the backdrop against which Teruzzi learned that Yvette was pregnant. As she approached the date of delivery, September 1938, he was increasingly solicitous. She needed Italian citizenship; he did his best to have his cabinet secretary speed up the process. She needed a private maternity clinic; he made a reservation for the best, or maybe the most discreet, on Via Garigliano, in the fancy Salaria neighborhood.

Upon the birth of their daughter on September 8, 1938, he arranged for two city clerks to go to the clinic to fill out the baby's birth certificate. This gave Yvette as the mother, of course, but the father as "Unknown" since the baby was born out of wedlock. The baby was called Celeste, after his mother, followed by Adelia (perhaps after Yvette's aunt), then Lina (after his maid), and last, for good measure, Maria. The baby's surname was perforce Blank, and that would trigger no end of troubles in the coming years.[33]

When mother and daughter left the clinic, they went home to Teruzzi's apartment on Monte Oppio. In December, the baby was baptized at the Parish of Saint Joseph and listed on her mother's Romanian passport. A nanny was hired to help care for her. When Yvette began to accompany Teruzzi out into Roman society, dressed in a glamorous new wardrobe, her hair twisted up, in heels that made her tower over him, he proudly introduced her as "the mother of his child."[34]

Once his daughter was born, Teruzzi's annulment case took on a new urgency. From the moment the appeal was filed in late July 1936, there was no telling the outcome. The appeal was being heard in Pavia, just twenty-two miles due south from Milan. The diocese took inordinate pride in being the seat of the appellate court of the archdiocese, the only reminder of the 1,300 years of ecclesiastical autonomy it had enjoyed before Church modernizers had subjected it to the jurisdiction of Milan in 1817. Though it was home to some of Italy's oldest and best universities and theological seminaries, Pavia itself was a provincial town. But it had in its current bishop, Giovanni Battista Girardi, a vigorous reformer in the mold of Cardinal Schuster. He was a native son, *"eruditissimo"*—he taught biblical exegesis at Padua, and he had become something of a hero to Catholic student activists and young seminarians who, in their anxiety to know how their religion could salve the ills of the modern world, were up in arms about American divorce culture, immoral hierarchs, German racism, and the zealotry of party apparatchiks who meddled in religious affairs.[35]

This time Teruzzi left nothing to chance. The amateur Franciscan professor-lawyer Zanchetta was sent packing, the clownishly anticlerical Farinacci sidelined, and Buonocore returned to Naples to fulfill his innumerable obligations as professor, lawyer, and general fixer. The Pacelli brothers—really Carlo, the elder of the two—would anchor the case in Rome. The celebrated Milanese trial lawyer Angelo Fortunato Danesi would put his subtle strategizing, booming voice, and riveting verbosity to work locally. He happened to have known Mussolini from when they were both socialists; his younger brother Dino, an infantry lieutenant, had been his platoon leader, and the two had mourned like brothers when Dino had died on the Carso from a bullet to the spine.[36] Fortunato Danesi's legal versatility had been put to the test in the wake of Matteotti's murder, when he had been asked to finesse certain legal questions. He had also helped the hapless Teruzzi pull off his dirty house deal at Castiglioncello in 1931. He could, in short, be counted on, like the best divorce lawyers, to be resourceful and aggressive.

Fortunato Danesi got off to a roaring start on the morning of April 2, 1937, when the court at Pavia convened for the first time. The process should begin right away, he told the reverend judges, though he couldn't say when his client would show up. He broke the suspense on June 17, when Teruzzi was due to testify and did not appear: the general was "on a political mission abroad at this very moment, and—if it be legitimate for me to add—to command a military action against an international conspiracy of godless Bolsheviks, Freemasons, and Jews."[37]

By September 1937, when Teruzzi returned from "martyred Spain, full of Freemasons and Jews," the case had advanced nicely. Fortunato Danesi had asked the judge-interrogator to call back the louche Enrico Maria Varenna—but not the loudmouth Farinacci—to repeat that Teruzzi had made his future spouse's virginity a sine qua non of their marriage and, upon discovering that she was not a virgin, had "kicked her out and sent her running."[38] At Fortunato Danesi's request, Milan's onetime vice police commissioner was summoned to perjure himself by saying that the *Signora* was known to the police as a wanton liar, that the records showed her at it with her lover through the hotel keyhole, and so forth.[39]

When Teruzzi testified on September 27, 1937, coached by Fortunato Danesi's questions, he came across as sincere and truthful. He had loved his wife "and did everything to overcome the difficulty of living with a foreigner—I did my duty and I loved her." But nothing worked, which had made sense once he discovered that she had never been the woman he intended to marry.[40]

By early August 1938, with nothing more to add, Fortunato Danesi and Pacelli were strong-arming the court to wrap up the proceedings: the defendant, although summoned to testify early on, had not shown up, with the excuse that she was in New York. Upon learning she was at a safe distance, Fortunato Danesi proposed one last witness, Pietro David, Teruzzi's cabinet secretary at the Interior Ministry, who was coached to recall Lilliana's flippant talk about married life. She had said she would divorce her husband "if he ever stops being His Excellency," and, for that reason, he added, she refused to give up her American passport.[41]

When Lilliana did finally return to Italy, neither the defender of the holy bond nor the judge-promoter saw any reason to call her in to testify. That was just fine, so far as Teruzzi's lawyers were concerned. The honorable judges could only expect more excuses, delays, and lies from such a person, whereas in the figure of the honorable Teruzzi, they were dealing with "a person of political eminence" backed by "the consoling solidarity of important personages."[42]

On August 15, 1938, the judges adjourned to deliberate. Two weeks later they resurfaced with a decree, signed by all, stating that there was no basis on which to reconsider the matter.

Apparently, the case had begun to unravel even before it went to appeal when Cardinal Schuster, in his role as supreme head of the archdiocesan hierarchy, had caught a major flaw. His own judges had failed to address

Meda's most significant legal point: the court should never have accepted the case on behalf of a plaintiff who sought to invalidate his marriage on the ground that he had set out such and such a condition for marrying and then married with the intention of testing whether that condition had been met.

At some point in the early spring of 1938, when the appeal was well under way, the cardinal had reconfirmed his understanding of the law by obtaining a second opinion from the Sacred Congregation for the Discipline of the Sacraments in Rome. This was the office of the Catholic Church's Curia, or central government, responsible for overseeing that the seven holy sacraments of the Church were being properly administered. The congregation's legal scholars confirmed that Meda was right: Teruzzi could not make virginity a condition of marriage and then determine by means of intercourse—*a mezzo del coito*—whether this condition had been met.[43]

Lilliana hardly had a moment to savor her victory before Carlo Pacelli arranged for the inquiry about the case to be moved to another branch of the Curia, to the Supreme Sacred Congregation of the Holy Office. Since its establishment in 1542, at the height of the Counterreformation, when it was known as the Congregation of the Roman and Universal Inquisition, the Sant'Uffizio had been responsible for defending the unity of the faithful against heretics, schismatics, and apostates and from contamination by infidels, sects, and Freemasons. On occasion, the Holy Office also dealt with interfaith marriages. That, to Meda's "disgust," appeared to be the plan here. But to what end? He urged Lilliana to "use [her] connections" to find another lawyer, "capable of offsetting the influence and authority of your husband's patrons."[44]

Teruzzi versus Weinman had become mired in the fast-brewing conflict between Mussolini and Pius XI over the passage of the Fascist Race Laws. Over the course of 1938, beginning with a relentless barrage of anti-Semitic propaganda just before Hitler's visit to Italy in May and culminating in the promulgation of the so-called Race Manifesto of the Scientists in July, the Fascist Grand Council had approved a package of racial laws that, once passed by the Council of Ministers, was signed into law by the king on November 11, 1938.

Because Catholic Italy seemed set on its own more mild anti-Semitic trajectory, which the Church did not oppose, Cardinal Schuster had been as stunned as Pope Pius XI in midsummer 1938 at the publication of the Race Manifesto with Mussolini's whole-hearted approval. The manifesto was just short of blasphemous, affirming that human races exist; that they are purely biological; that there is such a thing as a pure Italian race, of Aryan origin; and that Jews do not belong to it. With the Church beset by so many modern-day evils—from divorce, birth control, and pornography to war mongering, Bolshevism, and Rotarians—the Jews were far from being the most significant problem. And even if, as some authoritative Catholic thinkers had argued, international Jewry had a hand in all of these plagues, that was not Pius XI's position. The manifesto stank of the paganism he had denounced in Nazi Germany. It would deal a big blow to Church doctrine and papal religious authority if Mussolini, in his "defense of the Italian race," took legal steps to exclude Jews and other non-Aryans from the body politic as Hitler had done.[45] Furthermore, if these unholy doctrines were made into law and the fascist regime successfully banned marriages between Italians and non-Italians, even if both of them were Catholics and had been wed before a priest, then Fascist Italy would be in violation of its treaties with the Vatican on marriage. Worse, such laws would violate God's law that made marriage the sacrosanct right of all humans as creatures of God. In sum, if Pius was intent on preserving the sanctity of marriage, he was bound to denounce anti-Semitism.

The Vatican communicated the pope's anguish to Mussolini through Father Tacchi-Venturi, who set once more to shuttling between Palazzo Venezia and the papal palace. But Mussolini was by now consumed by his own political demons, and the fascist government proceeded to issue a series of provisions to excise Jews from the social life of the nation. It did so through separate bills regulating the exclusion of foreign and Italian Jews from schools, academia, politics, business, the professions, the military, and public employment. Citing the defense of the race as a justification, the government deployed a task force to collect census data on all Jews residing in the Kingdom of Italy and advanced anti-Jewish legislation as punitive as any being passed in Europe at the time.

If, at first, Mussolini had been scornful of Hitler's ideological crudity, by 1936, his own racism had taken a biological turn. That was the year the fascists began to legislate in Italian Africa against sexual misconduct and social intercourse by separating whites from blacks according to racial criteria. As the world became ever more polarized over the course of the

Spanish Civil War, and Mussolini saw Judeo-Bolshevik forces arrayed on one side and Aryan Nazi-Fascists on the other, it was logical for him to align Italy with Germany not only diplomatically but also culturally and racially. The hierarchy of biology, behavior, and civilization being propagated by the Nazi establishment offered a new world order within which Fascist Italy could take its rightful place. To that end, fascist "race scientists," jurists, and policy makers rose to the Duce's challenge not to imitate Nazi Germany but to craft legislation suited to Italy's own high-minded racial ideals, the Kingdom of Italy's Roman law traditions, and fascism's intensely personalized style of despotic rule.[46]

But the decision to formulate the Race Laws in such a way as to directly challenge the Catholic Church was all Mussolini's. In 1929, his facile real politick, carelessness about religious interference in civil affairs, and shallow understanding of the moral basis of marriage had led him to agree to the Church becoming the arbiter of marriage and married life.[47] That decision had now come to haunt him. In a bid to reverse this capitulation, article 1 of Fascist Italy's new Racial Laws declared: "Matrimony between an Italian citizen of Aryan race and a person belonging to another race is forbidden. Matrimony celebrated in a way contrary to this decree is invalid." This may not have been substantially different from the first principle of the Nazi Nuremburg Laws, banning mixed-race marriages. But in Italy, it violated article 34 of the Catholic Church's concordat with the Italian state, which had conceded to the Church the right to manage matrimonial life.[48]

Pope Pius XI was now faced with the prospect of seeing Mussolini, the fallible Caesar, acting like the pagan Hitler, openly flouting Church law and morality. In the intimacy of his private life, that is exactly what he did. Confiding to Clara, sometimes in the presence of her sister, he ranted against Jews, blacks, miscegenation, and the tyrannical pretentions of the Church to decide on sexual and marital matters. "This Pope is a calamity with his campaign about this marriage thing," he grumbled on October 8, 1938. "The first thing is he will want an Italian to marry a Negro. Marriage with foreign whites is bad enough, in case of war, it breaks up the family; both husband and wife are dyed-in-the-wool patriots; it's in the blood. Let him give permission. I will never consent."[49] He felt that the pope was taking his stand, as he put it, "out of pity for the Jews." "Pig Jews, I would destroy the whole bunch," he told Clara three days later. The uncomprehending and at times openly hostile public reaction to the Race Laws made him furious. "Reptile Jews, slave Italians," he blustered. "If I put seventy thousand Arabs in concentration camps," he sputtered the next month, "I can do it to fifty thousand Jews. I'll find a big place and close them all up inside."[50] Talking about sex in Clara's coddling company only encouraged him to spew out his wrath. One week, from speaking about the "sexual question," and having had so many lovers he couldn't recall most of them physically, he passed to "the question of mixed marriages." "If the Vatican wants them, fine. However, we, the State won't recognize them, and they will be like lovers." The next week it was: "Vatican, miserable hypocrites. I prohibited mixed marriages, and the Pope asks me to let an Italian marry a Negro, just because she is a Catholic. Heck, no, before that, I'd smash in everybody's face."[51]

Perhaps some of Mussolini's rage was due to the realization that he had been trapped by the Church into making marriage indissoluble. After all, Catholic Hungary allowed divorce, and the Church had a concordat with Hungary. Clara records him as saying on November 15 that "there has to be some hope for people who have made a mistake. Here, too, we absolutely must modernize. Times have changed, we must adapt. It's logical, no?"[52]

Could he have been thinking of his relationship with Clara Petacci, who had married in 1934, had recently legally separated from her husband, and would one day get a divorce in Hungary? Or of his niece Rosina, who was separated from her impotent husband? Or was he musing on Teruzzi's plight? "There must be some way to liberate these people who are unhappy together to start on a new life if they want to," he told Clara. "It's not human or logical." Knowing that Pius XI was aged, often bedridden, and, Mussolini hoped, not long for this world, he added: "With the new pope I am going to impose at least five cases of divorce."[53]

Mussolini's challenge to the pope and the Fascist Race Laws' challenge to the Italian Church's right to regulate Catholic marriages made up the context in which Teruzzi's annulment proceedings were now playing out. And so it fell on Monsignor Emilio Ripa as the defender of the holy bond, the most senior, most experienced, and most gregarious of the priest-judges, to make sense of the case to bring it to judgment. In his youth, Monsignor Ripa had been the chamberlain of the venerated bishop, later cardinal, Riboldi (1839–1902) and at his side as the Dreyfus Affair dragged on for over a decade. One imagines he would, like his mentor, have championed the anti-Deyfusards, vilifying the French Jewish army captain as a German spy, in the cause célèbre of his day. Perhaps he would have agreed with Riboldi when he warned, quoting Milan's great archbishop Saint Charles Borromeo, that having too many Jews in high places was always a grave danger. He had some inkling of that world, as the master of the seminary's choir school, known, among other qualities, for the inventiveness of the sacred music medleys he arranged for the boy choristers.[54]

By that time, 1938, Lombard fascists, Farinacci in the lead, were championing a nativist anti-Semitism very much in the old-time Catholic spirit. In his newspaper articles, speeches, public lectures, and even a whole book, *The Church and Anti-Semitism* (1938), he wrote of the Holy Roman Catholic Church as the historic ally of princes and republics—endorsing ghettos, the wearing of Stars of David, and expulsions for Christ killers— whenever the Jews reverted to their habitually clannish and oppressive habits. Times had become truly bad once modern liberalism unleashed the Jews on society, and the modern Church succumbed to its flaccid notions of brotherly love. Farinacci sounded like the soul of Catholic piety when he avowed on behalf of Mussolini that it was only to safeguard Catholic faith that he had committed himself to the race campaign.[55]

"Throw your net on the right side of the boat and you will find some" (John 21:3–7). Farinacci was a resourceful fisherman. But Cardinal Schuster would never take the bait. He aligned himself with Pius XI against the rising anti-Semitism. But Agostino Gemelli, the rector of the Catholic University, did. If it was right for the Church to condemn the "un-Christian type" of anti-Semitism based on race, he argued, the Church should not be deterred from a "healthy evaluation of the dangers emanating from the Jews."[56]

In principle, the Church tribunal's defender of the bond was there to defend the sacrament, and the presumption was that he would side with whomever sought to preserve the marriage. But Father Ripa decided otherwise. The case was never about virginity or consent, he concluded, after studying all of the trial testimony. The problem, which, he noted, Teruzzi's mother had been the first to recognize, was that Lilliana was a Jew and she often talked about divorce. His sister, too, had warned her brother that Lilliana was from a different culture, one he couldn't understand. All of a sudden, the fact that she had kept her American passport became significant, in case she ever wanted a divorce. As a Jew, she could not believe in the sacramental nature of the marriage bond. But because she was Jewish *and* American, two cultures in which divorce was lawful and practiced, there was a good probability, given the "cunning" of the woman, that she had never believed in the indissolubility of marriage at all, whereas the "noble and sincere general" did.[57]

Even so, nothing proved with moral certainty that the woman believed in divorce. And so with regret, Father Ripa had to conclude that the marriage was valid. It must have flattered him to read the response from Teruzzi's lawyers. They disagreed, of course, with his refusal to consider the old consent question as sufficient to appeal the case, but they applauded him for his supposition that marriage was understood in a different way in Italy, and among Catholics, than in lands and among peoples that permitted divorce. In Rome, they added, it was becoming "prevailing theological theory."[58]

The battle lines were drawn, but with no victory in sight. The tribunal, following Cardinal Schuster's lead, still insisted that it had no cause to deliberate. When the Holy Office overruled it and instructed it to start the proceedings, the tribunal still wouldn't budge. It would still be insisting that it had no legitimate cause to proceed on February 3, 1939 after the Holy Office at the instigation of Carlo Pacelli, enjoined it once more to move on the case.[59]

It is surely an accident of history that at the very end of the following week, on Saturday, February 11, Pius XI, still at loggerheads with Mussolini over the Race Laws yet loath to break the Lateran Accords, had resolved to confront the issue by publishing another of his fulminating encyclicals. The pontiff would clarify once and for all that before God Almighty there were no races on God's earth, only different religious beliefs. Hence, laws barring Christians and non-Christians from marrying one another were an apostasy as well as a violation of the Vatican's treaty with Italy. Because he had been ailing, Pius intended to publish his encyclical to coincide with the celebration of the tenth anniversary of the Lateran Accords and the seventeenth of his coronation.[60]

The eighty-two-year-old pope died on February 10, the day before, and his unpublished encyclical was cleared from the agenda of urgent matters. Opinion immediately solidified that Cardinal Eugenio Pacelli, the Vatican secretary of state, should be his successor. Unlike Ratti, the often-prickly Milanese pope who had preceded him, the princely Roman Pacelli was suave and conciliatory. He would know how to deal with Germany and repair the now disastrous relations with Mussolini. On March 2, 1939, after only three rounds of balloting, the fastest conclave in three hundred years, the cardinals elected Pacelli, who was crowned Pius XII on March 12.

Three days after the papal coronation, Attilio Teruzzi, after meeting with Monsignor Alfredo Ottaviani at the palace of the Holy Office, sat down and wrote what Ottaviani, its assessor, needed to proceed. Teruzzi's letter expressed the urgency of his "quest for justice." After six years of litigation, he still had no final decision on the validity of his marriage: how could it be that the tribunal of the archdiocese of Milan, once it had delivered its own ruling, was still obstructing his hope "to reconstruct his family?"[61]

In April 1939, after the Pavia judges balked once more, the secretary of the Holy Office himself, Cardinal Francesco Marchetti Selvaggiani, turned up the pressure. In July 1939, when that had still produced no results, he sent them the precise legal formulation they should use to hear the appeal. It was Ripa's. The tribunal should still weigh the old counts that Lilliana Weinman had violated the terms of her husband's non-negotiable requirements for matrimony, namely, virginity and legitimacy. But in addition, they should consider whether she could have truly consented to marriage, if she did not believe that marriage was an indissoluble bond—views the groom did not share. At the same time, Teruzzi was instructed to avow in writing that he believed in the indissolubility of marriage and had wed Lilliana in the belief that she was of the same mind. He swore to that "in my condition as a Christian and on my word as a soldier."[62]

When the Church tribunal at Pavia issued its ruling on September 26, 1939, it began with two considerations. First, "Lillian [sic] was born in Poland into the Jewish religion, and divorce is permitted among Jews. Thus, the supposition that a woman of the Hebrew race and religion entering into matrimony does not intend to be bound in perpetuity is not without a serious foundation." Second, "Lillian was educated according to American custom, rather than as an Italian subject who would know from youth that the marriage bond is indissoluble. In America, not only are many citizens irreligious, but they are also adherents of various religions," and "according to the laws in effect there, divorce is admitted as an ordinary means of crossing over to new marriages, even for trivial reasons." The court then cherry-picked the testimony to demonstrate to "a moral certainty" that Lilliana Weinman had not contracted marriage with Attilio Teruzzi in order "to bind herself to him in perpetuity, but truly had the intention of divorcing if a new status and a change in condition of her bridegroom or other reason for divorce should persuade her otherwise."

Given that "marriage is never valid without [the conviction of] insepara-bility," the court declared the marriage null.[63]

In October 1939, Carlo Pacelli reassured Teruzzi that the case would now go to the Rota for the final decision.

It is hard to imagine Teruzzi finally preparing to settle down in September 1939, at the very moment Nazi Germany invaded Poland. But we have every reason to believe that he intended to marry Yvette once he secured the annulment. Photographs of her from that time on show her wearing a wedding band.[64]

Lilliana had long since left Italy by the time the court issued its judgment. In March 1939, six months from the date of the passage of the Racial Laws, her Italian passport would be invalidated like that of every other "foreign Jew" living on Italian soil. Well before then, she had taken her cue from the actions of other well-known Italian Jews. Margherita Sarfatti had found that her influence, wealth, and friends in high places had made no difference at all—nor did it matter that she was the mother of a Gold Medal martyr of the Great War or that she had converted to Catholicism in 1928. According to the Racial Laws, she was Jewish through and through. Mussolini wouldn't help her—except to leave the country. Nor would Cardinal Schuster, to whom she appealed. From Paris—where she moved in mid-November 1938, with plans to stay abroad indefinitely—she wrote of her plight to her American friend Nicolas Murray Butler, who was then president of Columbia University: "You know what happened to us! I am a Catholic, & so are both my children, both married to Catholics, & fathers & mothers of Catholic children." But, she explained, she and her husband, "being of Jewish descent," meant that "my son's glorious death, as a hero, at 17 years of age in the War, & my husband & mine own & my other son's fascist & Italian faith & works during all our lives, account to nothing. I am not permitted to print any articles in Italian papers or reviews & am not permitted to have even one single servant. . . . I do not know . . . what will happen to my moneys, houses, estates, etc. etc. being considered Jews."[65]

After returning to Italy in May 1938 so that she could be heard in Pavia—which never happened—Lilliana, too, decided to leave Italy for good. She sold her house and shipped her most valuable antiques to a warehouse in Rotterdam, leaving the rest of her stuff in storage, and returned to New York, where she was living in September 1939 when the war broke out in Europe. It would be a while before Lilliana would read the judgment

Yvette Blank with daughter, Mariceli, circa 1940

delivered that same month. The tribunal later said it had misplaced her address.

Lilliana never saw herself as a victim, in the company of an unknowable multitude of other Jewish people persecuted and chased from their homes. Once in New York, she threw herself into the family business: her great energy would be well spent getting the relatives, the gold diggers, out of her father's, mother's, and her affairs. By late summer, she had seen all of her old friends and made many new ones. She dined out most days and was planning to take up ballroom dancing, go on a September trip to Bermuda, and write a memoir. For the moment, she had dashed down some amusing anecdotes and reread her letters from 1926 to 1929. They sounded like "Alice in Wonderland," she told her parents: "I myself cannot believe them."[66]

19

IN EMPIRE, HOLLOW GLORY

In the history of colonialism, the case of Fascist Italy is absolutely new. . . . We have suddenly been confronted with this immense void, and given the peremptory order: "Fill it immediately."

—EUGENIO GIOVANNETTI, *Annali d'Africa*, 1938

To our misfortune, a void has been created in our lives that could easily hold a tower forty meters tall.

—VITALIANO BRANCATI, *The Lost Years*, 1936

On October 31, 1939—a little over a month after Teruzzi won his appeal—Mussolini announced the most significant changing of the guard in a decade. This brought in the so-called Ciano Cabinet, dominated by his son-in-law, which would last until early 1943. With little fanfare, he promoted Teruzzi, his undersecretary, to take his place as minister of Italian Africa.

Mussolini was angling to position Italy for the next war, whose "consequences," as he portentously told Clara Petacci, would be "incalculable." On September 1, 1939, after signing a non-aggression pact with the Soviet Union, Hitler had invaded Poland, triggering the pact's secret protocol to partition the country into a western sphere of influence under the Third Reich and an eastern sphere under the USSR. Mussolini, who had been completely blindsided by the deal, made his calculations. As expected, the French and the British, who had sworn to defend Poland, had declared war against Germany, only to hold back from attacking. That showed their weakness. At the same time, Hitler had made a misstep by provoking the United States to start to arm. He could be "content," Mussolini concluded, "they were all a little at each other's throats."[1] Meanwhile, he would shake everything up to signal Italy's readiness to engage.

In reality, the changing of the guard, though the most far-reaching in a decade, showed the old Mussolini, facing the ultimate test with the same repertoire of political tactics he had always used. On the one hand, there was the incitement to disorder: he would shake up the Fascist Party by replacing Achille Starace, who in his decade as the PNF's secretary had run it into the ground, with another younger, more vigorous *squadrista*, the war hero Ettore Muti—while Starace was reassigned to the Fascist Militia, to galvanize the junior officers with his pumped-up barracks routines. Mussolini made Marshal Graziani chief of staff to shake up the military's complacency and had one of Ciano's flacks, the amateur economist Raffaele Riccardi, replace the seasoned Felice Guarnieri as foreign trade minister. He then tightened his governing cabinet with a combination that had served him well in the past: his son-in-law remained foreign minister, while he held on to the Interior Ministry and all three of the armed services. He recycled fascism's best and brightest, notably, Dino Grandi, whom, having become persona non grata as ambassador to London, he appointed justice minister, and he kept Giuseppe Bottai as education minister. To some surprise, he had Teruzzi replace him as minister of Italian Africa.[2]

Rarely do we hear Mussolini reflecting candidly about his decisions. And without Clara Petacci's notes from their tryst the following weekend, we would have missed his musings on his top talent. It was Saturday, and he was grumping about the public's reaction to his actions. One "opinion," in particular, bothered him: the suggestion "that I am incapable of ridding myself of certain collaborators, that I've become so ancient that I no longer have the force of character, [that I've gotten] soft." The notably negative reaction to Teruzzi's promotion must have instigated these thoughts. Mussolini went on at some length about his merits, coming up with little beyond his own benevolence: "I've been particularly kind to him, by giving him my own ministry," he told Clara. Then again, "he has been plugging away for ten years . . . always doing very well."

The gist was that Teruzzi was no better or worse than the others: "It's true, he takes orders like everybody else, and I am always in charge. . . . He is a good man, a bit of a womanizer but he'll calm down. Then, who isn't a womanizer?" He then suggested that this hardworking time server was no different from any of his other "collaborators." They are all "good and energetic," he said with condescending self-satisfaction. They don't "do anything but execute orders, but I know how to motivate them."[3]

Teruzzi's new position made him second only to the Duce in the governing of colonial affairs. True, he had no real discretion on the main lines of fascist colonial policy, which had taken shape at the time of the conquest of Ethiopia and were broadly determined by the fact that Mussolini had no specific project for exploiting, much less controlling, a recently sovereign country whose land area was practically three times the size of continental Italy. The conquest had added 435,000 square miles of new territory to Italian colonial holdings, much of it unmapped, with practically no roads and no accurate population count—likely not five million, as originally estimated, but closer to twelve or maybe fifteen million.[4]

However policy was made, the job was huge. The former Colonial Ministry, now the Italian Africa Ministry, or MAI, had reorganized the entirety of the Italian Empire's holdings in the Horn of Africa (which they now called AOI, or Africa Orientale Italiana) by dividing them into six governorates. Each was ruled by a governor with his own military commander; each in turn was divided into multiple districts, each one of them administered by a district commissioner. An enlarged Eritrea and Somaliland comprised two governorates, and Ethiopia, three more. Addis Ababa, the Ethiopian capital, with the surrounding Scioa region, stood on its own, under the Duke of Aosta, who was also supreme commander of the AOI's armed forces and viceroy.

As the fascist empire sought to bring its new territories under its rule, it faced three problems. First, it had to deal with the native ruling class, whose support was indispensable. At the same time, Mussolini's idea was that imperial Italy's civilizing mission would never allow it to stoop to governing through the "old feudal hierarchy," even if exploiting their authority over the native peoples would greatly simplify matters.[5] The second problem was the huge cost in terms of men, matériel, and unrest that the project of decapitating the old elite would entail, assuming that repression would work—and from Graziani's murderous time as viceroy, there was little sign it would. The third problem was the social insecurity, compounded by the means brought to bear to end it, including military policing, segregated living, and laws against race mixing. Fascist Italy was still intending to settle AOI with hundreds of thousands, even "millions," of Italians, who, under laboratory conditions, would generate the true New Italians of fascism to improve the breed stock of the nation and defend the empire's perimeters. However, these pioneering "soldier-peasants" were no more likely to leave the small comforts of Asmara, Addis Ababa, Gondar, or Dire Dawa to brave the countryside than the timorous "metropolitans" of Teruzzi's Benghazi.

For all of these reasons, the fascist government allocated budget-breaking amounts of money to its African experiment. The first order of business after the settlement of the new administrative entities was to sort out, at least on paper, with laws and decrees and projects for urban planning and social engineering, just who would consort sexually with whom and who would live how and where within the new world of the empire. High colonial administrators would be at the top, of course, with their wives and families, for the very few who could afford to bring them. The new colonial administration would have to determine how all of the other distinctions could be sustained, the intimacy of contact between lonely and dependent settlers and resilient, opportunistic, and oftentimes gracious natives being practically unavoidable.[6]

Mussolini was struck by how quickly and completely Teruzzi, from the first moment of his appointment, had taken stock of the whole situation, or at least appeared to have done so. That was his great virtue: to bring to the task at hand the sum of his experiences in administration. This had increased vastly no doubt since his time as senior staff sergeant doling out supplies, World War I aide-de-camp, Fascist Party vice president, governor of Cyrenaica, and head of the MVSN. But his best suit was never administration, in the ordinary, more or less rule-minded, transparent, bureaucratic sense; it was to draw hither and yon on a seeming infinitude of civilian, political, and military connections, show them his rank and power and the resources to which he had access, and let them give and take according to theirs. To that roster, he had recently added a whole slew of Milanese capitalists eager to take advantage of the government boondoggles.

Teruzzi's major innovation, pioneered on his first tour of East Africa in March 1938, when he was still undersecretary, was to package all of his skills and passions in a grand tour he pretentiously called the "March." Part military inspection, part political junket, propaganda exercise, and victory parade, it mobilized a big press and publicity contingent as an integral part of his varied retinue, which reported back nonstop to the metropolis with telegrams, news dispatches, and vivid newsreels about his and Fascist Italy's imperial progress.

To placate the raised eyebrows of the old-time colonial establishment, Teruzzi dignified his organizational conceit with a British pedigree, saying that every imperial viceroy, upon his first appointment, undertook just that, to get a firm sense of the terrain.[7] First as undersecretary, in March 1938, then twice more once he had been promoted to minister, in December 1939 and again in January 1940, Teruzzi set off for four to six weeks with a retinue as large as fifty, crisscrossing the empire by plane and automobile, covering thousands of kilometers and creating a whirl of commotion at every stopover, like a "hurricane," as one foreign observer put it, or, as the British consul in Aden less generously suggested, some "wild brute."[8]

The first march was by far the most riotous. With the pretense of bringing to the frontiers of the empire all the civilities of Italy, "not for the exploitation of the subject populations but for their education and elevation by means of the discipline of labor," "open to all with the same humanity: indigenous and nationals," he filled the SS *Victoria* bound to Massawa with city planners, mapmakers, and geologists. They may or may not have been puzzled by his decision also to invite the comedian Totò's vaudeville troupe, including his best-known player, Anna Magnani, together with the recently pregnant Yvette, ill disguised as an aspiring soubrette.[9] He would have justified the decision like any general, that artists on tour were great for the troops' morale. Having also engaged a fleet of journalists, photographers, and film directors for this and future trips, he carefully crafted the official image he wanted the media to propagate. He was "a simple man who, whatever he may have accomplished in the past, never considers his work done," a man of "no hyperbole, a reformer, the master of a new style."[10] Every major newspaper in Italy covered the marches, sometimes day by day, and they generated a dozen propaganda films, passing themselves off as documentaries about the New Italian Empire. Mussolini, whose personal secretary Teruzzi instructed to brief him daily, reportedly followed his travels with "greatest interest" and had nothing but praise for his "indefatigable action."[11]

For the second march, on December 13, 1939, the SS *Colombo* bound for Massawa out of Trieste had unexpected cargo. It was filled with Jewish refugees from Austria en route to Egypt and from there to Teheran or Shanghai. Hitler had annexed Austria in March 1938, and they were the last to obtain exit visas. Teruzzi had been minister of Italian Africa for six weeks by then. The Italian Empire was now firmly allied with Hitler's Germany in the Pact of Steel, a promise of economic and military cooperation that their foreign ministers had signed the previous May. Teruzzi saw it as his mission to speed up the pace of empire building in the event of international conflict.[12]

To this end, he brought along architects and engineers to rebuild Asmara, Addis Ababa, and other smaller Eritrean, Somali, and Ethiopian towns, to accelerate road building—the goal was 20,000 kilometers—and to plan for whole new villages, hospitals, schools, and administrative buildings. By the third year, the empire had built a transportation system of upward of 10,000 kilometers of paved and unpaved tracks, and land surveyors were discovering the heretofore unexploited riches of the territory: not petroleum, as they had hoped, but high-quality coffee beans and bananas, hemp for textiles, wild animal stocks, and precious ores—gold, iron, and platinum—in addition to vast rivers and lakes, perfect for generating hydroelectric power.[13] He made a point, on the Duce's orders, to "insist on the race problem," by segregating the Italians as much as possible from the natives, forbidding sexual relations between them and expelling any Italian breaking the law from the empire.[14]

By the time of Teruzzi's last march, in February 1940, the start of the war in Europe had sent the local economy into a tailspin. Italians had stopped coming to AOI. Many wanted to go head home. And the truckers—increasingly beleaguered as commercial traffic shut down—protested his appearance, booing and shouting, "CITAO! CITAO!"—the name of the state transportation board he presided over, whose rate fixing and over-regulation they blamed for their bad plight.[15] To secure the backlands from guerilla attacks in the event of a war with Great Britain, the Italians sought to reinforce their truce with the most intractable of the former Emperor Heile Selassi's liege men, the ex-head of police of Addis Ababa, Ras Abebe Aregai. He had 20,000 warriors at his command. For months, the local military and political authorities had wooed him so that on arrival, Teruzzi could be present at his oath of allegiance. However, detachments of fascist Blackshirts at the command of militia general Arcnovaldo Bonaccorsi, who were hostile to any policy of reconciliation, sabotaged the endeavor by ambushing several of the ras's men. Instead of capturing the ras prostrating himself in front of the minister in a time-honored submission ceremony, cameras caught him galloping off with his men in a great cloud of dust. Mussolini's reaction, when telegraphed the news, was to telegraph back calling for immediate military action, "not excluding the use of gas."[16]

Nevertheless, Teruzzi was optimistic. In the preface to the forty type-written pages of his last and longest report to Mussolini, he judged that the near-total cessation of economic activity in Africa due to the war offered up an opportunity to draw up "a more total and far-reaching plan," which would show how the fascist empire would reshape the whole continent.[17] It was a "politically delicate moment," a "globally convulsive moment," he noted. The advantage was that they now had a "completeness of vision" that they had not previously enjoyed and "couldn't have had" in the past, when "everything was happening so rapidly" and there was "a lack of a clear method."[18]

For Teruzzi, East Africa was the Wild West. It had attracted lots of decent, ambitious, and gullible people eager for new starts. It also enticed his old comrade-in-arms, the "Butcher of the Balearics," Bonaccorsi, and some of the rottenest apples in the fascist barrel, including the onetime Italian Cheka members Dumini, Volpi, and Aldo Putato—all three prosecuted and found guilty of Matteotti's murder and subsequently released, paid off by Mussolini, and set adrift in the empire.[19] As sheriff and hanging judge in this lawless environment, Teruzzi acted without restraint once outside of Addis Ababa, where he had to try hard—and often failed—to abide by the niceties of rank and etiquette imposed by his unclear relationship to the Duke of Aosta.[20]

In the giant quantity of photographs and Luce propaganda films, with some slip-ups, he showed himself to be a benevolent custodian of the fascist empire, inaugurating electrical dams and launching boats on Lake Tana, gravely admiring ancient manuscripts at the Coptic monastery at Gondar, brooding at the gravesites of Italian soldier-martyrs. There was a mad-hatter quality to his schedule that hinted at the preposterousness of administering a territory of half a million square miles by means of month-long junkets. Ceremoniously welcomed at a back-country mission, he suddenly realized that the metal posts leading up to the church were shards from the poison gas canisters that the villagers had collected from the fields. Only the priest's irresponsibility or idiocy could have allowed them to be used to decorate the walkway. He ordered him to be expelled before speeding off with his convoy.[21] In the back country, it took days for the catering services to mobilize scarce pasta, meat, and wine and for the district commissioners to assemble the notables and bring out a halfway-decent crowd and for the propaganda services to mount the cameras to

Sanafè Elders, welcoming Teruzzi, Italian East Africa, July 1938
Archivio Istituto Luce

catch the cavalcade on arrival. When Teruzzi's caprices made them cut short his stay or change course, all of this painstaking expenditure of resources and goodwill was for naught.[22]

It was much discussed that he collected gifts at every major stopover. That was his booty, the homage due him as a ras. It was a currency Teruzzi would use at home to win over the ladies: ocelot gloves and leopard-skin hats, muffs, and booties that he was given were very much in fashion. The twenty leopard pelts he collected on his second trip should go straight to the usual Milanese tannery, according to his order to his cabinet secretary. For the men, he doled out hard-to-get packages of Sidamo, Harrar, and Djimma coffee beans. There were also the more conspicuous gifts: the water buffalo horns, elephant tusks, gold and silver amulets and necklaces, and carpets.[23] He had hoards in storage at Colle Oppio and the villa he rented at Sacrofano. The Duke of Aosta was so pained by this pagan tribute and by the complaints from local chieftains that he regularly provided monies to district commissioners to purchase facsimiles on the local market for the chieftains to pay their homage to the minister and his "caravan."[24]

Then there was his sexual conduct: Who could doubt that, given half an opportunity, he would revert to his rough, libidinous ways? At the end of the day, all the ceremonial events were tedious, especially the dinners organized by the district commissioners, who with their wives sought to maintain the civilities of Italian bourgeois living. As wives and mothers worried about how much familiarity to show the servants and wondered whether the indigenous men were being insolent or expressed concern about what their own family men thought as they gaped at native women, their breasts bared in pornographic poses in the tabloids, they also had to deal with their minister's brazen conduct. More or less openly, he would command prostitutes from the local brothel and cut short an interminable dinner to consort with them. He was notorious for having entertained bar girls while a guest at the Duke of Aosta's residence, Villa Italia, when the duke and duchess were away. The British liked to repeat the joke: "Why do gentlemen prefer blonds?" The answer: "Because Teruzzi prefers brunettes." Was it true that the inexhaustible fornicator was also a wanton pedophile? That on his tours, as one desperate letter writer communicated to the Duce, he recruited fourteen-year-old virgins, to the despair of their fathers?[25] Historians used to treating anonymous denunciations skeptically might now be less dismissive. For sure, Attilio Teruzzi would have responded to the scorn of *bien pensants* that he was being true to who he was, an old soldier, who had won the right to carouse. He would never have imagined that in a distant future, Italy's most distinguished military historian would dismiss him as "the Rutting Bull of the Empire."[26]

It is hard from any perspective, much less from the single vantage point of the actions of the minister of Italian Africa, to really know how, by 1940, the empire was getting on. By the fascists' own analysis, there were still huge problems to confront. Teruzzi often listed them himself, superficially, optimistically, almost fatalistically—as if to provide a laundry list to resolve them. Were one to consider only what the empire had accomplished in scarcely four years—in the numbers of roads, settlers, areas pacified, functionaries trained, and so on—the fascist regime could be proud. Were one, however, to consider the enormous budget-breaking investment, the payoffs might well appear patently unequal. For big business investors, it had been a win-win. The state monopolies were a cornucopia for the contractors and functionaries who legally, through their salaries, or illegally, by means of payoffs, took their skim from the conspicuous wealth generated by Mussolini's new Roman Empire.[27]

The honest colonial administrator generally broke even—the adventure and opportunity offsetting the physical hardships and the waning of ideals. For fascist functionaries of one kind or another, the party chiefs, militia consuls, and the like, the empire offered an opportunity not just to rule over other Italians but to preside over a racial hierarchy that put them at the top. At the bottom, they grouped all of the so-called inferior races, graded according to their beauty in the eyes of the Italians.

For working people like the truckers of CITAO who greeted Teruzzi sullenly at the time of his second march and were hooting and shouting by the third, life was probably no more miserable than it would have been in Italy, where few would ever have been able to accumulate the capital to purchase a truck. But so far from home, it was damnably lonely.[28] As for the indigenous people, the notables, who as in Libya were paid off if they complied, at least some of them rode around in fancy cars, even as they continued to rebel, infuriating the local fascists. Many others of them, the dirt poor, lived alongside dirt-poor Italians, fascinated by their incapacity to farm and that the so-called superior races were economically dependent on the families of their concubines, cuckolded by native men, and not even able to have their mixed-race offspring recognized as Italian.[29]

The Italian people in general, if they paid taxes, took a giant hit because of the colonies. Paying for the East African empire bankrupted the country.

And yet, a certain prestige did come from Mussolini's imperial project. This was in no small measure due to Teruzzi's marches and their coverage abroad, the elegance of the ministry's publications, and the refinement of its museums of colonialism and the expositions it mounted (concluding with the fabulous, if short-lived, Overseas Exposition inaugurated in May 1940 in Naples). By 1940, Fascist Italy claimed to stand as the progenitor of a new model of Western colonialism. The proof was in its brilliantly architected new towns, its leading-edge expertise in tropical disease, its archeological digs and erudite journals, its new imperial security force (the Polizia Africa Italiana or PAI), and its handsomely uniformed colonial women's auxiliaries. The country that had come to admire this colonial project the most at the end of the 1930s was none other than the world's most fearsome power, Nazi Germany.

Teruzzi wallowed in the admiration, and never more than when he welcomed to Italy General Franz Ritter von Epp, Hitler's colonial expert, infamous for his massacres of the Herero of German South West Africa from 1904 to 1908. Rather than drawing on its own colonial past, long buried after losing its late nineteenth-century colonial acquisitions to the war victors at Versailles, the Third Reich looked to the undertakings of Fascist Italy for inspiration. Hitler was planning the total overhaul of Slavic-Judaic Eastern Europe with his so-called General Plan East, once the Third Reich—following the takeover of Czechoslovakia in September 1938

Teruzzi inaugurating the Colonial Institute, Rome, 1940. Photographed by Adolfo Porry Pastorel.

Archivio Fotografico U. Cicconi-Vedo / Pastorel

and the invasion of Poland in September 1939—had completed its conquest of the Soviet Union. Racial hierarchies, apartheid on a continental scale, planned communities to breed the new Aryan Folk—Hitler would rush his plans, just as the Italians had done, learning from their experiments, once the soil had been cleansed of its alien and parasitical races.[30]

In Rome, the summer weekend starts on Friday, when ushers and porters skip out of work to idle in the sun and chauffeured cars line up at the ministries at two o'clock in the afternoon to drive the hierarchs to the seaside to join their families. On June 10, 1940, Italy declared that it would go to war on the side of Germany, so the early summer of 1940 became a *lieu de mémoire*. People later remembered that moment especially poignantly as the quiet before the catastrophe that would engulf the Italian peninsula in just a few months, causing the loss of empire in less than two years and resulting in Mussolini's ouster and execution in three. Some remembered it as the moment when they began their "long voyage across Fascism," as one erstwhile fascist, Renato Zangrandi, put it: they would experience the existential turbulence that so drastic a change of political compass entailed. A number of these would eventually join the armed resistance.

Teruzzi was one of the great hierarchs at the time. Perhaps he was the most conspicuous of them for his attraction to the *dolce vita* of Cinecittà, his glamorous parties and patronage of the young, and his many public appearances. For that reason, he figured in young peoples' musings about the existential void, that "emptiness" the Sicilian writer Vitaliano Brancati wrote about that "could easily contain a tower forty meters tall."[31]

For Elsa De Giorgi, the cinema star, Teruzzi was a familiar figure: there was the gossip; she saw him at celebrity events, and he was a good friend to her dear friend, Anna Magnani. She herself was from a patrician Umbrian-Florentine family and, by 1940, well-enough established as a film diva and theater actress that she could defend herself from the sexual pressures that starlets and walk-ons had to submit to in exchange for whatever favor this or that hierarch claimed to provide. That was the very subject of her beach conversation with Anna Magnani, she later recalled. It was June 9, the day before Italy went to war. They were at Fregene, with Dado, a young gay man from their circles. He was teasing them that they must have serviced some hierarch or another to get the fuel ration coupons for their cars. Magnani retorted that he was jealous because the hierarchs only liked to screw women—and she had just finished up saying:

"Well, up to now we've resisted these hierarchs, these senile fools." When she looked up: "Here comes one now. What an ass-face!"[32]

It was "Triton," as Elsa called him: his "fierce white beard, square cut, his face brightened by blue eyes of monkey-like vivacity." She paused to note "his affable, amused smile." "What are these lovely nymphs laughing about?" the Teruzzi she caricatured asked lasciviously. They giggled as he ogled Magnani's sumptuous bosom. "Tits of gold. Right, Your Excellency," she neighed with laughter, flashing her long white teeth. Elsa recalled the gossip: the time that Mussolini had ordered him to cut off his beard and he hadn't gone out of the house for three days; the child born late in life with an Eastern European Jewish woman, totally spoiled, screaming commands, who looked just like him, except for the beard; a wife he had married so long ago that everybody had forgotten; Mussolini's pressure to get him to remarry; his rants against the Vatican for its inaction.[33] But it was his fatalism that had struck her the most. When they pressed him to say something about the war, to denounce it, as they believed his old friend Balbo had done, he reacted with an anxious, irritable look but said nothing.[34]

At the time, young people hoped that Italo Balbo would save the day. He was well known to be against the war. Fascist Italy, he insisted, was not prepared: "Industrial warfare isn't made for *squadrismo*, and it's not made for individuals, no matter how excellent they are, but for organized masses."[35] But Balbo, too, was a "Sicilian Uncle," the proverbial father figure who forever betrays filial trust, who promises to pay the boat tickets to America and then doesn't show up at the quay, who promises to make Italy great and then absconds.[36] When the orders came to march, Balbo was at Tobruk, planning the invasion of Egypt, eager to demonstrate how airplanes could overwhelm British armored car defenses. Scarcely three weeks after the war started, on June 28, 1940, he was on a routine flight, a junket with his retinue of family and friends, when his plane was brought down by friendly fire, killing everyone on board.

How did Teruzzi face this loss, the old guard's first and only wartime fatality? Balbo was so spirited, such an intriguer, and catty. His jousts with Mussolini, which more recently had implicated Teruzzi, had been so unnerving. At the same time, nobody had been more openly a friend to Teruzzi. Balbo had been his neighbor for eight years on Colle Oppio. His visit to Cyrenaica in 1927 had brought Teruzzi such joy. He had been so thoughtful in bringing him to Odessa just after his break-up with Lilliana.

And his visit with Balbo to Libya the previous year—to see the colony flourishing in a way he could barely have imagined, with both men at the peak of their careers and at peace personally—was pure pleasure. Privately, he mourned with Balbo's widow and family. Publicly, he took his cue from the Duce, who didn't seem to mourn at all, having become more and more exasperated by Balbo's insolence, his flouting of the racial laws, and his opposition to joining the war alongside Hitler. With Balbo dead, Mussolini had immediately satisfied Graziani's longtime ambition by appointing him as his successor.

August brought Teruzzi to Castiglioncello as it had every year since 1932. The whole house had just been refurbished at the hands of Elena Fondra Asti, the interior decorator and artist whose work he had been introduced to in Asmara. The house had just been published in *Domus*, the Milanese architecture journal, as "a tasteful example of the vacation home of an important personage."[37] Castiglioncello was the place to be, and he was famous for his hospitality. The Cianos visited with their children from nearby Livorno. Ulisse Igliori, also a commander of the March on Rome, who had retired from politics to make millions in construction, was a regular. Arcnovaldo Bonaccorsi, on holiday from East Africa, played in the garden with his grandchildren. The house overlooked a good-sized dock, and young holidaymakers he knew from Rome came by to sunbathe. Had the regime not censored the tabloids, preventing them from publishing photographs of the hierarchs with their families, they might have captured Teruzzi with his two-year-old daughter, a robust blond-haired child at play with her dogs and Jolly, her pet goat, scratching around with her tin pail in the gravel with a little playmate while her young nanny stood nearby or walking across the pine grove hand-in-hand with her father to get an ice cream in Piazza della Vittoria.

And what of Yvette, her mother, the woman who could not be Teruzzi's wife? A regime that was so attuned to pageantry and propaganda, so focused on family and propagation, had little interest in documenting the hierarchs' home lives. So like many women, she remains only as a shadowy presence, all the more so because her status was so equivocal. The Pizzi family, Villa Celestina's longtime custodians, referred to Yvette with one of those Tuscan sobriquets. She was "the Spaniard," for the reason that she had first appeared on the scene after Teruzzi returned from Spain, looked Spanish (whatever that meant), and spoke with what could have been a Spanish accent. It never lodged in Pizzi family lore that the Spaniard was Mariceli's mother. The two or three photographs of her at Castiglioncello in the off season show a handsome, solitary figure, older than her years, one passionately hugging her child, the others all alone.[38]

Not only was she not the hostess, but there was no sign of her presence at the fancy parties, magnificent affairs in the eyes of the children who attended them from the sidelines—Benito Pizzi, the still-small son of Villa Celestina's custodian; his schoolmates, who lived to sneak a view inside the house; or Viviana Molinari, the teenage daughter of a down-at-heel family of local notables who regularly attended these affairs.[39] The whole town mobilized for days in anticipation; on the night of the party, the roadway would be lit up by hundreds of lanterns as the curious townspeople looked on. Andalù—Teruzzi's faithful Askari, with him since his time in Cyrenaica— stood at the gate, assisted by a troop of other onetime Askari, shouting, "Slow!" or "Stop!" as the cars rolled in through the pine grove: Luchino Visconti's white Bugatti, Alfa Romeos, a Lancia Dilambda, several Bianchis, a giant black and cream Hispano-Suiza, even some Rolls-Royces.[40] The stupefaction at the sight of the world's most luxurious automobiles in a nation of animal locomotion and just decent trains and buses was indelible.

Teruzzi would make his grand entrance once most of his guests had arrived, his Askaris behind him. He responded to the air kisses of the women he didn't know or who were only passing acquaintances with a sharp bow, a kiss on the hand, and a click of the heels; to his intimates he gave loud, wet smooches on the check. Everybody was there: cinema people, theater directors, famous writers, the international pseudo-aristocracy, a German noblewoman, an astoundingly beautiful young Greek heiress, the local notability—but nobody from the political world.

Teruzzi seemed to have settled down. He had missed his daughter so much on his last march in Africa that he called every day to hear "her little voice."[41]

When the summer ended and they all returned to Rome, Teruzzi would be completing the plans to build their new penthouse. Balbo's widow had wanted to downsize, and he had been happy to oblige her by exchanging his small seven rooms on the first floor for her immense twenty on the top. The city's zoning regulations had changed and now permitted elevations. He had his young Milanese architect friend Guglielmo Ulrich draw up plans for his "villa in the sky." This added a whole new floor, fronted by pillars and double glass, running the whole length of the building's facade. His new home had forty rooms. Its execution was

Teruzzi with daughter Mariceli, Rome, 1940. Photographed by Ghitta Carell.

perfect in every detail, from the recessed lighting of the giant salons, a fencing room, flower trellises, and reflecting pool to the furniture, which experimented with imperial materials—zebra fur, pear and cedar wood, mica, lacquered leather flooring, and one whole exuberant wall covered with elephant tusks. It would have done inestimable damage to the reputation of the minister of AOI if the public had even had an inkling of its sumptuousness. Still, the editors of *Architettura d'oggi*, the sleekest Italian architectural journal of the time, paid discreet homage to the architect of the grand project for having properly rendered the "revelrous refinement"— *aulicità gaudente*—of his patron.[42]

It must have cost at least a million lire, on top of the monthly fees he paid to the cooperative. None of the hierarchs or men of government could live on their stipend alone, unless they accumulated more than one position. Fortunately, Teruzzi had begun to collect his army pension in 1939. He received a monthly stipend of 50,000 lire for his service as president of the state monopoly on transport, the CITAO, and he could count once more on Mario Marigo to act as his contractor for the construction. By 1940, he had done so many people so many favors it would hardly be dishonorable or indecent to call on them for a little help. Marigo surely had no need to be asked: aside from his abiding friendship, he'd successfully bid on one contract after another to build roads and military garrisons in East Africa.[43]

Settling into his status as head of family had made Teruzzi reflect on his mortality. The good bourgeoisie of Milan had always commemorated their own in fine mausoleums at the Monumental Cemetery and now he commissioned Guglielmo Ulrich to design a funerary monument for Rome's equivalent, the Cemetery of Verano. Ulrich's design, a tall rectangle slab of white travertine sculpted in the neoclassical style, looked chaste and melancholy amid the baroque follies of the Romans. The remains of his older brother, Guido, were brought from Milan to join those of his mother and his sister, leaving two spaces for himself and another. Under the inscription "rest in peace," he carved his signature like a Roman senator, the bedrock of his family, as if ancestor care for all eternity were a duty but also perhaps a luxury that every top hierarch owed himself and his civilization.[44]

With Italy at war, the empire under attack, Yvette and Mariceli at the seaside, and the prospect of his Roman villa in the sky, the long summer of 1940 was possibly Teruzzi's happiest time ever, the happiest he could be.

IV

FALL

20

THE ROUT

Rout: contemporary usage: A disorderly retreat of defeated troops; "the retreat degenerated into a rout"; archaic: A disorderly or tumultuous crowd of people. "A rout of strangers ought not to be admitted"; rare: A packs of wolves. "A rout of wolves consumed the last of the carcass."

—*Oxford English Dictionary*

The beginning of the loss of faith; a painful, irrepressible phenomenon, its smirk an atrocious, unforgettable nightmare.

—Italian military officer, East Africa, 1942

It is impossible to say exactly when the happiest moment of Attilio Teruzzi's life came to an end, but things would never again be as simple as they were in the summer of 1940. Less than one year later, the Italian Empire in East Africa would cease to exist, the fascist regime would be reeling from defeats on all the war fronts, and Teruzzi's personal life would once more be in tatters. The irony was that the hierarch Teruzzi became increasingly visible as the public face of the empire exactly as it was unravelling, and his personal life fell apart along with it.

September had seen him drop off Mariceli and Yvette at Punta Ala, where they stayed with Balbo's widow and her three children while he went to Germany for ten days. In principle, it was a return invitation, but the international circumstances had changed dramatically. When General von Epp, the head of the Colonial Union, had visited Rome the previous May as the guest of the minister of Italian Africa, this hoary artifact of pre–World War I German colonialism had been treated to the fullness of Fascist Italy's imperial accomplishments at the just-inaugurated colossal Overseas Exposition in Naples. Since then, the Germans had invaded

France, Italy had joined the war on Hitler's side, and Britain was under assault. The Luftwaffe had spent the summer raining bombs on London, Britain was expected to capitulate at any moment, and Hitler was no longer sure what the Italians were bringing to the fight.

Consequently, Teruzzi was treated as a visitor of state, yes, but he brought back nothing. General von Epp accompanied him to Berlin, where he laid a giant wreath on the Tomb of the Unknown Soldier. From there, he had toured the western front fortifications with German field marshals to view France's capitulation firsthand, before returning to Berlin for the obligatory photograph opportunity with Hitler. In the image, we see the two men in intense conversation with one another. But Hitler always held his heart in his hand at these meetings one on one, and Teruzzi was captivated like a deer in headlights.[1]

Over the next few days, Teruzzi met with German experts to speak about the superiority of Italian methods of colonizing, especially when compared to British methods, underscoring that "the reorganization of

A night at the opera with Nazi colonial plenipotentiary General Franz Ritter von Epp, Rome, May, 1940. Photographed by Tito Farabola.

Archivio Farabola

Africa in a totalitarian way is fundamental to building the European New Order."[2] The SS treated him as a fascist plenipotentiary. Reinhard Heydrich, who as head of the Reich Security Central Office managed all of the security and secret police forces in the Third Reich, arranged for the SS's own budding colonial corps to train under Italy's relatively seasoned African police troops, the PAI, at their camp in Tivoli. Teruzzi then made his capstone appearance at Unter den Linden, where he stood in front of the Brandenburg Gate, braving frigid rain to review the Wehrmacht's Großdeutschland Regiment at its return from the conquest of France. It was an occasion to which he rose, literally, as he was wearing high-heeled boots, his arm outstretched in a passionately executed Nazi-Fascist salute. Both allies had an interest in showing off the heft and depth of their bond. General Teruzzi made Fascist Italy look like the handsome, powerful ally Hitler wanted. At the same time, he was eager to get home.

Hitler had been largely noncommittal. He said that the allies would discuss their mutual interests in Africa only after the British had been defeated and the war was over. From his own military's assessment of Italy's plodding

Teruzzi exiting Reich Chancellery with Reinhard Heydrich, right, and other Nazi officials, Berlin, September 1940

Ullstein Bild Dtl./Getty Images

Teruzzi reviewing the Großdeutschland Regiment, Berlin, September 1940

entry into the war, Hitler recognized that Germany would have to make a bigger commitment to the North African and Mediterranean fronts. To compensate, he intended to recalibrate the Reich's own geopolitical ambitions in the region. Hitler's future empire would reclaim its old African colonies—German East Africa, South West Africa, and Cameroon—and forge a more permanent alliance with the British dominion of South Africa. In sum, Italy would have to pay dearly for German help in the Mediterranean. Africa, recolonized by Axis Europe, would have to be shared.[3]

Teruzzi enjoyed his first taste of German power, especially as his proximity to it boosted his own prestige in Rome. On the trip home, at a stopover in Nuremberg, he picked out a present for Mariceli. It was the latest model German doll, with blond tresses and rosy porcelain cheeks. She cried, "Mutti," when squeezed, and, after being fed her water bottle, even wet her panties.

In the process of preparing for Italy's entry into the war over the course of the previous year, Mussolini had paid surprisingly little attention to the empire's Africa lobby. Italo Balbo and the Duke of Aosta were outspoken critics of joining Germany. Indeed, almost all the longtime colonial functionaries, as well as the king and key military leaders, notably Badoglio, were anti-German. Graziani was the usual odd man out, and for that reason Mussolini had promoted him to army chief of staff in 1939. All of the critics underscored the difficulties of defending the East African empire in the event of war. It had enormous, porous borders. It was not self-sufficient in any of the strategic matériel needed for modern warfare, like rubber or petroleum, and it depended on the Suez Canal for logistical support. Though Italy's army was far larger, the British forces were far more mechanized, even if they had not yet been readied for a far-flung global conflict. Nobody could speak with certainty about the loyalty of the indigenous people.

Far better, then, to stay out of the war and make Italy's non-belligerent status pay off. That was the near unanimous thinking down to May 1940—or, at the very least, to postpone any engagement until 1941 at the earliest. Britain might well arrange concessions from the French in the Western Mediterranean, Tunisia, or in the Horn of Africa—Djibouti perhaps. In the meantime, if Britain capitulated to Germany, as seemed possible after the speedy defeat of France in June 1940, Italy would finally acquire a corridor through the Sudan (then a British colony) to connect its Mediterranean and East African empire.

Given the fact that Teruzzi's entire geopolitical world view had originated in North Africa, it is a wonder that he could have deluded himself into believing that if Italy were to go to war on the side of Germany, Italian Africa would not be placed in serious jeopardy. And yet he did. Teruzzi's trip to Africa in January–February 1940 and the ten or so meetings he had with the Duce after his return—five alone in the month of May—likely played into Mussolini's decision to go to war on the side of Hitler.[4] Mussolini felt that war brought clarity, especially short, decisive wars, as the Germans' blitzkriegs promised to be. He had won all his domestic and foreign battles thanks to timing, by overturning expectations, violating the rules, quick comebacks, and resounding counterattacks. War, to his mind, was the great accelerator of change.[5]

At the same time, because he was vacillating about when, how, and against whom, Teruzzi could play his usual role, listening to Mussolini's gleeful blasts about the British having "their brains in their pants" or his bitterness about French "perfidy" and "meanness." By late April 1940, Teruzzi would have overheard him fume that "neutral Italy would lose its prestige for a century as a great power among the nations of the world and for eternity as a Fascist regime."[6]

"It is humiliating to remain with our hands folded while others were writing history. It matters little who wins. To make a people great it is necessary to send them to battle even if you have to kick them in the pants," he had told Ciano. To his son-in-law's perplexity, Mussolini "believe[d] blindly in German victory and in the word of Hitler as concerns our share of the booty."[7] No one—not Ciano, Grandi, or Bottai, just to name a few, nor the king—could influence him otherwise. He would not be swayed by the argument that Italy was unprepared for war nor, as Ciano pointedly put it, that Italy "unanimously detests the Germans."[8]

The notion that Italy might be unprepared was taken as a sign of weakness. There was no effective counterforce: neither an excoriating letter from Pope Pius XII would have worked, nor a stern warning from Roosevelt. Once Mussolini had made up his mind to go to war, on May 29 at eleven o'clock at night, the high command was formed, and "he realized his dream: that of becoming the military warrior-leader [*condottiere*] of the country at war." Ciano remarked that he had "rarely seen him so happy."[9]

A yes-man to Mussolini's worst instincts, Teruzzi brought to the table his steady optimism, awe at German military power, and disdain for the king and Badoglio. He affected his usual "good fella, little fella" look when General Armellini, Badoglio's chief of staff, went around to consult him about East Africa on June 4, as if to say, who are we to say what to do? In reality, he was always meddling in the military command's "natural hierarchies," Armellini observed.[10] Nobody could stop him from insisting on his own idée fixe about the battle tactic to pursue for the decisive win. He believed that if Germany declared war on France and Italy joined it, and both then declared war on Great Britain, Marshal Graziani should attack the British at once through Cyrenaica while the Italian forces attacked from Ethiopia through the Sudan. Then the British would be beaten in Africa as well as Europe. Teruzzi would repeat many times—practically to the eve of his death—that he had handed the military "the keys to victory," but nobody would listen.[11]

On June 10, as Italy entered the war in tandem with the German occupation of France, it engaged the British in North Africa. If, for a moment, the British were caught off guard by the Italian offensive, it soon became evident that Italy would fall far short of bringing to the Axis alliance the diplomatic heft or the firepower that it had promised. Militarily, Italy appeared unfit to pursue its grandiose two-front strategy of putting pressure on Britain both in the and in North and East Africa. Economically, it was faltering, as industry failed to make armament quotas, and shortages cut back on civilian consumption. Diplomatically, it added nothing to German efforts to bring Spain into the war. The fact that Franco was determined to stay neutral gave Britain access to the Mediterranean through the Strait of Gibraltar.

The Italian war in East Africa proved unconscionably short. On June 10, 1940, the Duke of Aosta became the commander of the Italian forces in what became known as the East African Campaign. He oversaw the initial Italian advances into the Sudan and Kenya, incursions into French Djibouti, and, in August, the invasion of British Somaliland. The thinking was that if Graziani was successful in reaching Suez at the same time, the British would be cornered, at least for a moment, until they were resupplied. By early December 1940, Mussolini's desert blitzkrieg, with troops mobilized like *squadristi* with armored trucks and aircover, had collapsed. Graziani, faced for the first time in his African career with overwhelming military firepower and Western troops refused to budge until the Germans had launched the Battle of Britain. For the first time, Mussolini grasped where Italy really stood: Teruzzi, his sounding board, spun his state of mind to the general staff, to show the Duce recognized mistakes had been made, but "nobody should say political faults." If there was political fault, he quoted Mussolini to whomever would listen, it was "impreparation," "the lack of sufficient forces and means," "not to have weighed the whole question, and [to have] impetuously play[ed] only a single card, Germany's rapid victory."[12] In other words, everybody else was responsible. As Mussolini mused along these lines, the British were poised on the Egyptian-Libyan border to counterattack.

In January 1941, the British army in East Africa forced the Italians to go on the defensive. In a matter of days, it demonstrated the vast superiority of its weaponry and gained the backing of the rebel Ethiopian ras, who had waited to see the likely winner before pitching in. The Italian forces, already low on supplies, were cut off from reinforcements from Italy once the British closed the Suez Canal to enemy traffic, and from reinforcements from Japan once the US fleet, as a neutral power, began to patrol the Indian Ocean to interdict war-related shipping.

The Italians mounted a strong defense at Cheren, but there, too, they were defeated opening the way to the British occupation of Eritrea. The Duke of Aosta—valiant though hardly a strong strategist—holed up with his troops at the mountain fortress of Amba Alagi. It was there, after being surrounded by 9,000 British and Commonwealth troops and more than 20,000 Ethiopian irregulars, that he was forced to surrender on May 18, 1941. Two weeks earlier, on May 5, 1941, a fine spring day scarcely eleven months after Fascist Italy entered the war, British troops entered Addis Ababa, choosing that date to make their arrival coincide with the moment, five years earlier, that Marshal Badoglio's triumphantly occupied Ethiopia's capital city.

The North African front, by contrast, turned into a three-year-long drama. In August 1940, Marshal Graziani received Mussolini's order to invade Egypt, and for the first time since his combat days in World War I, he was faced with a full-fledged European army. He held back his attack, waiting for the Germans to invade England to take the pressure off his forces. Threatened with demotion in September, Graziani ultimately followed orders, only to confront a British counterattack in November. The retreat was so ignominious that Graziani resigned his commission.

One wonders whether the fate of Benghazi had any special meaning to Teruzzi. When he had seen the city last in 1939, while visiting Balbo, it was the jewel he had envisaged with the architect Ferrazza in 1928: the cathedral cupola visible from the sea, rising above the minarets, the port finally finished, the metropolitan population redoubled and prospering, the city Arabs subdued, the Gebel tamed by Italian settlers, the Bedouins sparser and more ragged.[13] Since the start of the war, Benghazi had been hit by some 2,000 British air raids and had changed hands five times. At the time of their arrival on February 5, 1941, the British forces had sacked the city, and when they were driven out fifty days later, it was a pile of ruins. The Italians rounded up the many collaborators when they returned— Arabs, Levantines, and Jews—and incited Arab pogroms against the native Jews.[14]

In the aftermath of such destruction, local functionaries in Cyrenaica wanted to prepare for a rational "retreat of forces" toward Tripoli should the British break through again, so there would be no more Caporettos— or Adwas—in the Italian Empire.[15] But the best-laid plans for evacuation came to naught. On December 24, 1941, as the British forces occupied the city once again, the army command lost contact with the troops, and units disbanded so that all that remained of Italy's African Corps were a few truck columns and a horde of unarmed soldiers in full flight, outstripped in the speed of their retreat by state and party functionaries who, fleeing Benghazi for the safety of Tripoli, left everyone else in the lurch.

The plan of action had been sent to Teruzzi's attention, as minister of Italian Africa, but the sole surviving office copy bears no trace of ever having been opened. Maybe he saw another version. In any case, executing the plan wasn't his responsibility. Nobody—not the minister, not the military, not the Duce, nor the monarchy—took responsibility for the rout. Instead, they all blamed one another. Benghazi changed hands yet another time, on January 29, 1942, when the German field marshal Rommel's Afrika Corps invaded on his push toward Egypt.

Maybe Teruzzi couldn't really accept that the city he knew was doomed. On September 5, 1942, he officiated at the gala premiere of the cinema extravaganza *Benghazi*, which his ministry, together with the Popular Culture Ministry, had lavishly subsidized. Set in the late winter of 1941–42, during the fifty-six days of British occupation, the film ends as the city is recaptured by the Italian army (with the German army offscreen) as crowds brandish Italian and Nazi banners. Its director, Augusto Genina, specialized in the well-worn plot of the heroic Italian male, wrecked by his wrong-headed love affairs, who finds wholeness in colonial life doing battle—against the odds, in the desert, and defeating the enemy.[16] There was something of Teruzzi in him. This, Genina's most extravagant film, had his hero engage not only the British, with their barbarous troops, but also the machinations of riffraff Levantines and greedy Jews, as well the Bedouins's stealthy determination to reclaim their lost lands. In November 1942, the British retook the city.

From 1939 on, Teruzzi had put more and more pressure on Yvette to grant him custody of their child. In April of that year, by her account, he forced her to have the baby stay with him: "If I allowed it, then Mariceli would have everything, including his name," Yvette would later write to Mussolini. "If I didn't, not only would he not provide for me anymore, it would be as though I were dead to him. Threats he repeated other times in moments of fury to anybody who would listen. For the sake of the little one's happiness, I accepted the situation forced upon on me."[17]

In August 1941, he forced Yvette to write a letter to the Children's Court to make him Mariceli's legal guardian.

We can only surmise at the turn of events that had made Teruzzi, the doting father, so possessive of his child that he would jeopardize her happiness by threatening her mother. To understand the elements in play, we must return to an issue that previously had seemed quite irrelevant to their relationship: Yvette was Jewish. When the two first met in Rome in 1936, police informers had so little of what would soon be called "racial awareness" that they worried on any number of other counts—was she a prostitute, a spy, or a blackmailer? Was she taking jobs from Italian men? They never once mentioned that she was a foreign Jew.

Teruzzi hadn't made much of that likelihood either. Or maybe he didn't care to know. Yvette let herself be called a Coptic Christian, and he must have known little of her parents. He was familiar with Benghazi Jews, who had emigrated from Tripoli, and the Darnah Jews, who had come from Tunis. There were the Sephardim of the Levant and the Italian Jews of Istanbul, whom he knew of through Mrs. Nappi's family's connections. He had also learned of the Falashas, the 50,000 to 60,000 Jews living amid the Amhara of Ethiopia, who didn't read the Talmud but were thought to descend from some long-lost tribe of Israelites.[18] But none of these bore any obvious resemblance to the self-superior, Talmud-reading Ashkenazi from the shtetls of Eastern Europe, who, after emigrating to the United States, fortified by its repellant mixed-race culture, had produced the likes of the trickster Lilliana Weinman.

The fact is that from the fall of 1938, as the Fascist Race Laws went into effect, Yvette Blank became more and more Jewish, more of a foreigner, and increasingly vulnerable to persecution. Mariceli's status, as a result, became more uncertain too. The Fascist Race Laws held that a child would be considered Jewish if she had one Jewish parent—but not if the other parent was pure Aryan and the child had been baptized before October 1, 1938. Mariceli had been baptized on December 13 of that year in the parish near her birth father's home, bore her mother's name, and was on her mother's passport. Meanwhile, Teruzzi himself was under increasing pressure to show his own anti-Semitism.

Had Yvette become an Italian citizen in 1938, matters might have been settled very differently. But Teruzzi's attempt to get her citizenship in the late summer of 1938 had failed. At the time, there was some dickering about whether she needed a baptismal certificate. For the first time, information appeared in her file that her father was Jewish, her mother Coptic, and she, the informer tells us, was Catholic from birth.[19] Conceivably, she could not produce the certificate. Feet dragged, whether out of animosity toward Teruzzi or anxiety about the drastic changes in the laws of citizenship. Fortunately, Yvette had her Romanian passport with a valid residence permit, which she renewed in August 1938 and once more in 1939.

If he couldn't marry Mariceli's mother, he could at least eliminate the supposition that his daughter was an infidel foreigner by giving her his name. But again the law failed him. When he checked in 1939, there was no provision for a father to adopt a child born out of wedlock.

Given that the fascist regime had inherited its family laws from the liberal state, which had in turn derived its legislation from the legal codes established by Napoleon, the founding father of bourgeois patriarchy, one might expect that fascist law might have gone a step further to turn the father figure into a real despot. By the late 1930s, regime propagandists did indeed speak of fascism as having a "totalitarian family policy." And it was true that fascist regime did consider the family as the fundamental pillar of a well-ordered authoritarian state. However, it had no interest in the individual father, unless he was the head of a legitimate family and the children were his offspring with his legal wife. And so, Italian family law recognized Teruzzi as Mariceli's natural father, but he had no rights over her. The best he could do, for the moment, was to arrange to be the baby's guardian, with no obligation to provide for her.[20]

These problems might have been resolved had Teruzzi procured his annulment in a timely way. Our presumption, from the portrait-photograph of the couple with their daughter from 1941, is that they would have married had they been able to. The intent to be portrayed as a loving bourgeois family could not be more visible. Their little idol is their bond. Both are aglow at the sight of her. Yvette's ring finger shows her wedding band. It is just a bit awkward that the couple only connects to one another by clutching at Mariceli's stuffed bear.[21]

But Attilio was still legally married to Lilliana. True, in early 1940, the machinery of the Rota had budged. The Judge Promoter Enrico Quattroccoli heard testimony from a few more witnesses on Teruzzi's behalf, at the same time as he rejected yet another request from Carlo Pacelli to reintroduce the virginity question as the basis for annulment. He still had to get Lilliana's response. Filippo Meda had died on December 31, 1939, and she was in New York. Between one thing and another, it was not until late 1941 that Quattroccoli sent the whole package, seven years of proceedings, to the printer. The three auditor judges of the Rota

Teruzzi-Blank family portrait, Rome, 1941

Grimaldi Family

would study the documents as soon as they were selected.[22] At the moment, the docket was full. The plaintiff could count on being heard sometime the following year.

As Mariceli approached her third birthday, she reached the legal age at which Teruzzi, as her protector, could petition to become her legal guardian. The law regarded this status as useful for fathers of a family who may have wanted to attach a male apprentice or girl servant to the household.

It wasn't supposed to be used to legitimate the offspring of adulterous rela-
tionships, though it often was. For that step, he needed the mother to sign
on. And Yvette, under duress, had agreed to that.[23]

But he also needed Lilliana's signature. At this point, so far as he knew,
she didn't even know he had a child, and knowing her, he must have realized she would never agree to sign off on the matter. When the judge
hesitated, Teruzzi invited him to his office at the ministry to explain the
circumstances. Because of his "unfortunate marriage," he had had no
other family since the death of his mother. The woman in question "had
long abandoned Italy." Italy and the United States were at war; she was
"Jewish and American and thus an enemy twice over."[24]

Upon the court's favorable decision on August 10, 1941, Mariceli took
the surname Blank-Teruzzi. Meanwhile, the couple's relationship had deteriorated. Teruzzi had behaved generously and gallantly toward Yvette
while Mariceli was an infant, introducing her to his friends and associates
as the mother of his daughter. But this had not stopped his inveterate phi-
landering, and he became cold and officious whenever he was called out.
In better times, Yvette had put a good face on it. When he showed up late,
she would finish dressing, put on her lipstick, smile brightly, and head out
with him for the evening.[25] But at times, she couldn't bear him anymore
and moved into a hotel. He told her to get lost and then decided that the
baby needed her mother and summoned her back. Maybe he wanted her
back, too. He threatened her if she didn't stay, saying he would cut them
both off and refuse to see the child ever again. Mariceli was wildly attached to her father, and he adored her. What would Yvette do with the
child on her own? And so it went.[26]

The spread of anti-Semitism across Europe aggravated her situation. In
1940, after Marshal Antonescu, backed by Romania's fascists, the Iron
Guard, took over the government, Romanian Jews were deprived of their
right of citizenship. Consequently, Yvette had not been able to renew her
passport. In June 1940, as soon as Italy entered the war, the fascist government ordered all foreign Jews to be interned. That had the effect, upon
the expiration of her passport in 1941, of making her stateless, though not
necessarily Jewish—except that she was in Italy without proper identity
papers, like tens of hundreds of other foreign Jews who had found temporary refuge in Italy. It was probably at Teruzzi's behest that Carlo Pacelli,
who had become the chief administrative officer of Vatican City, had her
issued a Vatican identity card. This described Yvette Blank as a Romanian

citizen, with the profession of housewife, domiciled on Viale delle Medaglie d'Oro. In the early 1940s, that address would have been in a beautiful but desolate tract of countryside to the north of Rome, so that if she actually lived there, say, in a rustic villa or convent, or in some aristocrat's hunting lodge, it was as if she were in exile.[27]

Once Teruzzi officially became Mariceli's legal guardian, he wanted the child to drop her double name, Celeste Maria Blank-Teruzzi, and bear only his instead. There was a good reason for that. Blank was a foreign name, and foreign names had been outlawed, if not for people, for places and things. Yvette balked at that, and Teruzzi became furious. Sometime in December 1941, he barred her from having any further communication with their daughter.

Then, on February 20, 1942, he had Yvette sent to an internment camp on the island of Lipari. The record of her arrest filed at the archive of the Interior Ministery went missing. So the official pretext is not known. Conceivably, it would never have been known had it not been for her pluck and for her skill at crafting eloquent pleas for help and communicating them to people in high places. Sometime in early May 1943, fifteen months after she was interned, Mussolini received a long letter from Lipari, dated May 3. Here was yet another woman entangled with Teruzzi, supplicating Mussolini, as his friend and superior, for help. As it was, few women were more gifted than Yvette at crafting what Natalie Davis, the historian of early modern human relations, calls a "transactional" narrative. Yvette, who was less than a nobody in Italy, had to position herself as an honest woman, a good mother, Catholic, and willing worker if she was to gain his benevolence.[28]

She addressed Mussolini not as "Head of Government," she wrote, but as "a just and good man, generous especially toward the humblest." She trusted that "in his feelings of affection toward Attilio Teruzzi," he would deal with her case "confidentially." She had turned to him to be free "to remake her life, with dignity, to have news from her daughter, to see her, and to have custody at least six months a year." She pleaded for "proper identity papers so she could find a job to be able to live in an honest and decorous way and rebuild her life," separate from Teruzzi's. She wrote as "a mother in despair," certain that the Duce's "generous heart as a father" would grant her wishes for her daughter. She signed off: "I confide my very life to you."[29] There is no sign Mussolini answered.

How to explain this latest outrage? We must first consider the timing. Teruzzi had her sent to Lipari on February 20, 1942. From the perspective of Teruzzi's sense of power and vulnerability, that winter was a horrible time. To start, there was growing pressure from the Germans, who, with Italy's loss of the Horn of Africa, were having to send more and more troops to North Africa to confront the British. In those very weeks of January 1942, when Teruzzi made his decision to exile and intern Yvette, Reichsminister Goering was visiting Rome and had all the generals fawning over him. It was well known that the Germans deplored the fact that the Italians refused to take the racial issue seriously. Once the German and Italian leadership had issued their joint war communiqué insisting on their common battle against the "Jewish plutocracy," nobody high up wanted to be accused of being soft on Jews.[30]

Mussolini himself had always been susceptible to German criticisms, especially on that score. As early as June 1938, following Hitler's visit and still months before the Race Laws were passed, he had peremptorily told Farinacci to "get rid of" his longtime Jewish office manager, Jole Foa, saying that if "it [her existence] was known in Germany, it would make a terrible impression."[31] Farinacci had balked on the spurious grounds first, that he would have to pay her a hefty severance, given her seniority; second, that she was only a typist; and third, that he hadn't known she was Jewish until recently, when he had read her name on the lists of Israelites in Italy. It was also a question of principles: Mussolini knew that like him, he, Farinacci, was "completely for exterminating all of the Jews, but before getting to the humble and innocuous, let's start with the people of influence, especially those still occupying sensitive positions."[32]

In fact, Jole Foa had been at his beck and call for twelve years and had anchored his Milan office, affectionately signing herself off as his "Jewess" while he was off in Ethiopia. When Mussolini offered him 50,000 lire to cover the severance pay, Farinacci changed tack: Foa was an orphan, a spinster with no friends and the sole supporter of her sister, he wrote, none of which was true. Her coreligionists hated her and would never help her because she worked for him, which maybe was true. Moreover, people would think he was "a rogue toward a poor woman." Finally, he caved. Really, it was only a question of the timing: he said he'd have to wait until the summer holidays to fire her, so people wouldn't notice and think him a cad.[33]

It is plausible that Mussolini told Teruzzi to get rid of Yvette, though it is unclear whether that was because she was Jewish, because they were not married, or because she was a troublemaker. What is certain is that the more Fascist Italy showed in battle its inferiority to Nazi Germany, the more the Italians slipped down the racial hierarchy Hitler had ordained for Europe.

Over the winter of 1942, Mussolini was holding Teruzzi to a higher standard of conduct, and he felt the pressure. He had to do penance for the loss of East Africa. Gut-wrenching reports were arriving as Italy's famous fleet of ocean liners, refitted as rescue ships, returned thousands of survivors to the metropole. The rudest and most vehement condemnation of all came from his erstwhile friend, Arcnovaldo Bonaccorsi, who, after his infamous command of the dreaded volunteer Death Dragoons in Spain, with Teruzzi's help, had been promoted to consul general of the militia at Addis Ababa. Bonaccorsi had written a long letter to the Duke of Aosta in April 1940 after Teruzzi's visit to say that the empire was rotten and Teruzzi responsible. But this was no news, and the duke had simply filed it away.

Bonaccorsi had then written a full-fledged denunciation from Asmara in January 1942. Since 1941, he had been a British prisoner of war, after conducting one last do-or-die mission to strike the British from behind their lines that had ended badly—he nearly died of thirst when a rival fighting unit stole his commando's water and supplies. In this second denunciation, titled "Letter from AOI," he called Teruzzi "the Vampire of the Empire," the man entirely responsible for its "moral collapse," due to his arrogance, corruption, and blundering—and so, by extension, was Mussolini, who, knowing how incompetent Teruzzi was, had not fired him. This time, Bonaccorsi had his denunciation typeset, printed, illustrated, and published: the frontispiece, a photograph, showed Teruzzi dancing, in uniform, with a soubrette tight in his embrace.[34]

When the British occupied Addis Ababa in May 1941, they discovered the first letter, translated it for local propaganda purposes, and published excerpts in the *Times* of London. As they began to evacuate their prisoner-of-war camps in the spring of 1942 and to send captured soldiers to camps in Kenya and India, one of the rare Italian officers who escaped retrieved a water-stained, dog-eared copy of the 1942 denunciation and, on his return to Rome, filed it with the general staff. If anyone read it, they would have seen that Bonaccorsi started his letter to Mussolini by quoting the

Duce's own words: "I prize citizens who tell me the truth, even when it hurts."[35]

Whichever version Mussolini read, he was beside himself. In an attempt to placate him, Teruzzi spent the early winter of 1942 crafting an overly long, overly detailed assessment of who was responsible for the fall of Italian East Africa, putting most of the blame on the lack of preparedness of the colonial service and poor generalship.[36] Meanwhile, as racial purity was becoming a major issue in the relations between Germany and Italy, he scrambled to rearrange his private life. By early winter 1942, Hitler had embarked on his "Final Solution to the Jewish Problem," and he expected his allies, with Italy in the lead, to implement it in the lands they jointly occupied.

Teruzzi had also twisted and turned over how to address the problem of the Jews in the empire. On that score, he had come a long way since 1938, when, upon hearing the news of the Race Laws, he had asked for leniency in individual cases. On his travels through Liguria in early September 1938, he had heard of one Ilda Brunhild, a German Jew who had resided in Italy for seventeen years and recently become an Italian citizen. If forced to leave, she would be deprived of her only child, her daughter, "her everything, the sole comfort of her old age." Teruzzi had immediately brought the case to Mussolini's attention, and, as often happened when the Duce received these pleas for mercy, his office reassured the old lady of his "benevolent attention," telling her "to rest easy."[37]

Libya's Jews presented a conundrum. Balbo had resisted introducing the Race Laws, which would have been applied only to Italian Jewish citizens who lived in Libya, not to the several thousand native Jews, and in 1939, he had established a new category of second-class people, the so-called Italian citizens of Libya, but that only covered Italy's Muslim subjects. It was to clarify the status of the metropolitan Jews that on October 9, 1942, Teruzzi declared: "There should be no interpretative doubt, that all and every one of the limitations enacted in the Kingdom should be extended also to the Italian Libyan citizens of the Jewish race."[38] By that time, Cyrenaica had been occupied by the British, and Tripolitania would be overrun the following February. So all his ruling could do was to legalize ex post facto a policy that had already been in effect, confining tens of hundreds of Libyan Jews in desert concentration camps on suspicion that they would collaborate with the enemy.

While all of this was happening, Yvette found herself alone, with no work or income of her own, no passport, no ambassador to protect her, and no relatives to give her refuge or comfort. When her father had committed suicide in the public garden of Alexandria in 1924, he had written a letter to explain his reasons. She was staying at Castiglioncello, likely on her own. It was early February and the seaside village was empty and cold when "La Spagnuola" wrote a long letter, addressed to the Duce, and confided it to Signora Pizzi, the custodian's wife, whom she swore to get it to Mussolini. Then she tried to kill herself. That is the story gleaned from Pizzi family lore. Signora Pizzi had destroyed the letter immediately, which didn't prevent the whole family from being interrogated by the police for a month about its whereabouts.[39]

That was the last straw. A woman desperate enough to try to kill herself and to write to the Duce was capable of any scandal. Roman emperors had known how to deal with obstreperous wives, unruly concubines, or distraught lovers: they exiled them to the islands just off the western Italian coast. Mussolini had given a more modern twist to this age-old desire to eliminate bothersome women when he had had Ida Dalzer, his unrecognized first wife, permanently confined to a mental hospital for her relentless insistence that he recognize their son, Benito Jr. On several occasions, he obtained a police ban or *foglio di via* to dispatch one troublesome female or another to her hometown for "inciting scandal." The growing use of the category of "women of dubious morality" made dealing with refractory females simpler. They could be prostitutes, black marketers, Roma women, and, once Italy was at war, foreign wives of Italian nationals suspected of being spies, rumor mongers, or currency traffickers. By 1941, in a bid to keep detention conditions orderly and proper, the Interior Ministry had begun to set up all-women camps.[40]

And so we return to the matter of Yvette's confinement. The island of Lipari was practically a foolproof place to quarantine a willful, scandalous partner. It was off the northeastern coast of Sicily, two days from Rome by train and ferry, and impossible to escape from without a power launch. In the 1920s, it had been designated as the ideal place for high-profile political prisoners, including Carlo Rosselli, F. S. Nitti, and Emilio Lussu, who in 1929 had engineered a dramatic escape. In the 1930s, it had been converted into a detention center mainly for common prisoners. In 1941, once it was transformed into a full-fledged concentration camp, it prepared to receive a more cosmopolitan population of inmates. The first large contingent to arrive, three hundred to start, some with spouses, were Jews from Slovenia and Croatia. That was thanks to the courage of Italian military officers, who, after the Italian army occupied Yugoslavia in 1942, had bucked German pressure to dispatch them to Auschwitz.[41] Yvette must have been happy to welcome them. With the 1,200 lire a month that Teruzzi provided, she had been installed in a private lodging where she suffered from tedium, round the clock police surveillance, and curfews, but especially at the absence of news about her daughter.

Mussolini knew of Yvette's exile. Conceivably, he may even have ordered it. On February 19, the day before Yvette was arrested, Mussolini's appointment register shows Teruzzi as having met with him. Six months into her exile, on July 27, 1942, Teruzzi obtained the royal decree that was necessary to change Celeste Adelia Maria Lina Blank's given name to Maria Celeste Teruzzi. At the time, Yvette thought he had wielded his immense power to adopt the child outright. In reality, the courts kept to the sense of the law and had only granted the change to relieve the child from the stigma of having a foreign last name.[42]

21

COMEUPPANCE

Our duty has placed us at a crossroads: Nation or party, Italy or regime, King or Leader. It's a decision that lacerates, torments, devastates. That's what duty is about.

—GIUSEPPE BOTTAI, *Diary*, 1943

Teruzzi was at a loss as to how he would ever unbind his inconvenient marriage. Over the spring of 1942, the Rota had initiated the proceedings, only to be stymied when Lilliana refused to respond to its solicitation that she select a Rotal lawyer to represent her—her previous experience, as she later explained, "not being a happy one."[1] By the time she responded at the end of June, she had read the Pavia decision and was fully armed with annulment know-how acquired from what seems to have been intense and frequent communication with the Curia of New York, and perhaps even with the archbishop of New York himself.

The soon-to-be cardinal Francis Spellman was, at thirty-seven, an ambitious former Vatican bureaucrat. A great admirer of Pius XII, he was eager to act as a conduit for President Roosevelt, who, in the interests of the anti-Axis alliance, had recently reestablished the diplomatic links with the Holy See, which had been severed in 1867.[2] In 1942 Spellman had his ear cocked to news about the fate of the Jews in Eastern Europe. This arrived mainly through Polish Catholic diplomatic channels in the hope that the Catholic archdiocese would forward it to the Vatican, urging it to take a stronger stance on behalf of European Jewry. Spellman registered it, also to mollify rising American-Jewish outrage at the papacy's silence on the matter. Whether he passed it on to Rome is another question.

Isaac Lewin, who had helped Lilliana counter Farinacci's anti-Semitic libel in 1935, was among the most vigorous of the US-based activists and perhaps the most desperate. He had been living in New York City since fleeing Poland in 1939, just ahead of the Nazi occupation of Lodz, and had helped rescue a good number of Orthodox and Hasidic rabbis. But he had lost contact with his aged father, Aaron—once Lilliana's parents' rabbi—just as the German forces entered the city. After all other efforts had failed, Isaac Lewin had sought to bring the matter to the attention of the Vatican, which, with its apostolic missions, was the only organization that had the contacts to find and rescue his father. When he flagged Lilliana's case in New York City's Yiddish daily *Der Tog* on May 2, 1942, he was trying to ingratiate himself with Pius XII or with whoever might be in a position to reach him.

He happened to be doing library research in Italy, he wrote, when he was asked to intervene in a divorce case: an Italian lawyer (Francesco Pacelli) had used a claim of blood libel to help a fascist general (Teruzzi) in a civil suit against a Polish Jewish woman (Lilliana). And it was he, Isaac Lewin, who had alerted the lawyer's own brother, then Cardinal of State Pacelli, now Pius XII, asking him to overrule his own brother and do justice to the Jews. This account was a total fabrication; he was not in Italy at the time, and he had not been asked to intervene in the case, and it was not a civil suit. But any means could be justified to locate his father, who, unbeknownst to him, had been murdered the moment the Germans occupied Lodz.[3]

Likely, Lilliana was mortified by the publicity given to her case. Only close family knew. Fortunately, Lewin's article had been published in Yiddish, like the rest of *Der Tog*, giving her room to do some reputational damage control. She arranged a tabloid interview with the *New York World-Telegram*, and spun her story in a way that utterly dissociated herself from the "Polish Jewish woman" who had married a fascist general. Far from being some long-suffering Jewish ex-wife of a Blackshirt, she styled herself as a celebrity of sorts: she was "the only wife of any high ranking enemy official in this country."

For the reader of this puff piece, she was "an American 1st," an earnest, elegant New Yorker, "dressed dramatically" with black hair fashionably upswept, black mascara rimming her blue eyes, and wearing enormous gold cuff bracelets, "the gift of a rebel Libyan chief." She had put her knowledge of five European languages to use as a volunteer censor at the post office on behalf of the war effort. Perhaps there was some truth in her expressions of ambivalence: she was legally separated from her husband, "opposed to Fascist principles," and had no regrets that the "days of glory were gone." Yet, "sitting day after day listening to the radio with conflicting emotions for news of the man whom she once loved," she could not be "indifferent about his fate."[4]

With the New York Curia behind her and the United States gearing up for victory in the war in Europe, Lilliana had become boundlessly confident. She intended to launch her own suit before the Rota—a *querela nullitatis*—to overturn the Pavia decision, on the grounds that the tribunal had violated her "natural rights" by not calling her to testify and that its decision, in any case, was "preposterous." How did the court come to conclude that he intended to contract an "indissoluble bond before God" whereas she, as an American and a Jew, did not? It was "Mr. Teruzzi, who by listing at least five conditions for entering into the marriage," had "gratuitously passed his bad intent onto her." How had it come to the conclusion that the "Italian people have a monopoly on the sacrament of marriage?" "There are literally millions of American people, and not all of the Catholic faith, who respect the validity of their marital contracts and live and abide nobly by the terms of such solemn contracts." It wasn't out of "opportunism," she insisted, that she had maintained the marriage. Quite the contrary, "the name of Teruzzi is a very definite hindrance to my peaceful and happy existence . . . at the present time in view of the international situation."[5]

Why didn't she just let it go, then? To believe her, it was a matter of principle: "there has never been any divorce in my family, as far as any of us can remember, and please God, there will not be any now."[6] But her words ring hollow. Anyway, it wasn't quite true: her parents' marriage was impeccable, but at least one cousin had recently divorced, and nobody was overly scandalized. If she had really wanted a divorce, she could have gone to Reno, like the people in the movies. Chances were, if she wanted to marry again, it wouldn't be with a Catholic or with an Italian. But her marriage had long become an intractable political battle and so complicated and contorted that it would take a book to figure out why. Scialoja had seen that in his way; Meda, too, but in another way, and sooner or later, so did everybody who threw themselves into it, on her side or on his. At this particular moment, Lilliana saw no paradox at all in an American Jew fighting the Catholic Church to defend her right to preserve her marriage with a cad and a fascist, a declared anti-Semite, and an enemy of her country.

Since the Sacred Roman Rota was the Church's Supreme Court, the auditors were ever mindful of adhering to process, for example, to make sure defendants had proper counsel or adequate notice to appear in court. With the war tearing at family bonds and eugenicist states exploiting mental and physical disabilities to prevent or void marriages, the Rota leaned toward even greater caution. Over the summer of 1941, as the auditors remarked on the "sprouting" annulment mentality, Pius XII instructed them to exercise particular caution, holding up whatever arguments were advanced to "the highest judicial standards available to mankind." In other words, the Rota had to adjudicate the cases that came before it not just with an eye to the law—which, in those turbulent times, could no longer be trusted to serve as a sufficient lodestar—but to hold up their judgments to the standard of "moral certainty."[7]

All of these considerations—the uncooperativeness of Lilliana, advice from the Curia of New York, and the sensitivity of the case—must have contributed, on June 29, 1942, to the Rota's decision to postpone action sine die, maybe until after the war ended, whenever that might be.

By 1942, Mussolini's involvement in colonial affairs had dropped so steeply that Teruzzi had become the public face of Fascist Italy's collapsing empire. For that reason, when Teruzzi took center stage at La Scala to conduct the national celebration on Empire Day, May 9, 1943, his last major appearance, the party and press mobilized as if it were a major event. The day had been celebrated every year since 1936, when Mussolini had announced the founding of Italy's empire in East Africa. This year, there was no empire to celebrate. Flags fluttered from public buildings. Churches held masses for the war dead. The king handed out medals to their relatives, to soldiers on home leaves, and to dignitaries of cities that had recently been bombed in Allied air raids. But the ceremony was meaningless, all the more so since the nation was under siege.

With the fall of Tunis and Bizerte—the Axis's last military outposts in North Africa—just the day before, the Straits of Sicily were now open to the Allied armies to cross to the European mainland. Indeed, at the very moment of Teruzzi's speech, 140 American Flying Fortresses, escorted by 160 fighter planes, were approaching the port and city center of Palermo. Around one o'clock, just as Radio Roma had begun to transmit Teruzzi's speech and several thousand people were amassed in Piazza Balbo to listen, the bombers flew over, dropping their loads, striking terror and killing and wounding hundreds.[8] The last shard of Italy's African empire had turned into the launch pad for the invasion of Italy.

That Teruzzi was still minister of Italian Africa when Italy had lost practically all its colonies was of a piece with Mussolini's final cruel political
bluff. Four months earlier, on February 5, 1943, he had conducted what
turned out to be his last changing of the guard. All but one of the cabinet
members who had served him in the four years since he led Italy into the
war were ousted. These included Galeazzo Ciano, his own son-in-law
and minister of foreign affairs for seven years, and his longtime favorite
Giuseppe Bottai, a peerless legislator who had recently concluded the reform of the national educational system he began at the outset of the 1938
school year by expelling Jewish students and teachers from Italy's public
school system. Mussolini also replaced Dino Grandi, his onetime rival
(and soon-to-be nemesis) who in his current post as minister of justice had
just put the final touches on codifying the new Italian legal system.

The minister of Italian Africa was the lone survivor. "Do you know why
I only kept Teruzzi?" Mussolini asked the head of the secret police, Senise.
It's "because we've lost the colonies." Senise interpreted this as meaning:
"I don't trust anybody anymore, so I'll keep on someone who has no role
any longer, and thus no means to thwart me."[9]

Self-esteem required that Teruzzi treat his reconfirmation as a vote of
confidence. "At last, we are among gentlemen," he was heard to confide to
Umberto Albini, the new undersecretary of the interior, once a fascist
rabble-rouser, now matured into a respectably competent career prefect.[10]
The new cabinet, composed of inconspicuous technicians and yes-men,
revealed nothing about how the Duce would steer the nation as it faced
one air bombardment after another, stricter and stricter rationing, the
breakdown of services, labor strikes in the war factories, and steadily bad
news from the battlefront. Everybody was absorbed in gossiping about
what to make of it all, Bottai observed. That suited Mussolini's purposes
fine, Bottai concluded: "to distract people with two-bit tabloid speculation
from posing the truly important questions of the moment," that was
equally a way "to demonstrate his power over men."[11]

As the nuts and bolts of the colonial empire mattered less and less, and
the Duce ceased to issue marching orders altogether—except to declare,
"We shall return!"—Teruzzi was left to officiate over the truncated functions of his ministry. He chose the high road as the perfect hierarch carrying
out his duties and wrested another year of budget from the legislature.[12]

Perhaps it was horror vacui, his own terror at the emptiness of existence
if there was no grand gesture, no orders to march, that kept him going.

Over the spring of 1943, he rekindled the scientific prestige of Italy's civilizing mission by inaugurating the Center for the Study of the Mediterranean, whose goal was to foster "a more intense consciousness of the Mediterranean among the Italian people." He showcased his ministry's benevolent face by joining Maria José, Crown Prince Umberto's wife, and the king and the queen at various port cities to welcome home the so-called White Ships. Once the pride of Italy's maritime fleet, the four luxury ocean liners designed for the Durban, New York City, and Buenos Aires lines, had been refitted and their hulls painted white with giant red crosses, to repatriate the several thousand women, children, and men ineligible for the draft, who had been detained by the British in East Africa. He gave countless speeches, extemporizing, perfecting his oratory, doting on his anaphora, unwinding his thoughts and emotions over an hour or more. There was no authority higher than him, no Count Costanzo Ciano, who in Parliament would shout out: "Teruzzi, stop the bombardiering." As a token of his soaring self-esteem, he self-published—through the ministry's journal—his three favorite speeches under the title "Three Re-evocations."[13]

His "passionate and fiery" oration at La Scala was the last of these.[14] He had taken his watchwords, "We shall return," from Mussolini's May 5, 1943, address to the Blackshirts of Rome, which, apart from perhaps being the Duce's shortest ever speech, turned out to be his last as the Kingdom of Italy's prime minister. "The great undertaking hasn't ended," Mussolini had begun, referring to the Blackshirts' triumphal entry into Addis Ababa. "It has only been interrupted." He said he felt for "the indefinable suffering of millions and millions of Italians caused by 'nostalgia for Africa.'" He was emphatic: "The only cure that is known is to return." It was an article of faith: "And we will return!" For the rest, obedience: "the categorical imperatives at this moment" were to dispense "honor for the men who fight, scorn for cowards, bullets for traitors of whatever rank and race."[15]

Unlike the Duce, who spoke in his usual apodictic style, Teruzzi flailed about. His premise: "Fascism is by its nature imperial; therefore, it had lost nothing." His claim: "Against the enemy's barbaric superiority in matériel, we have given up some ground, but the battle continues."[16]

The lost lands, he went on to say, were no more lost than the North Italian plains that had to be abandoned in the retreat from Caporetto in 1917, only to be reclaimed a year later at the victory of Vittorio Veneto. The lands of the empire could never be truly lost, having been "vivified by our blood and toil." Once Italians grasped that Italy's battle was one with Europe's salvation, they would never give up. Italy, with its allies Germany and Japan, stood for "good and justice." The United States and Great Britain stood on the side of "the evil and unquenchable taste for conquest that Judaism and Bolshevism push beyond any measure." The Americans' "presence in the Mediterranean threatens Europe with suffocation and is intolerable"; "England's domination of the Mediterranean is intolerable and odious." Could there be any thought of abandoning the empire? "Never: from every man and from every woman in this divine land the cry, 'We shall return,' breaks forth. I repeat: 'We shall return.'"[17]

The British war propaganda apparatus, fed by government intelligence reports from East Africa, had long identified Teruzzi as a good target. The next evening, Italian listeners tuned into the BBC's clandestine Radio Londra would have heard Teruzzi's speech, intercepted by Great Britain's Ministry of Information, broadcast in snippets to highlight its absurdities and larded with antifascist propaganda and personal insults. "Tut-tut Teruzzi," the British press teased.[18]

The landing of the Allied forces in Sicily on June 10, 1943, set the stage for Mussolini's ouster two weeks later. In a ten-hour meeting at Palazzo Venezia that ran overnight from July 24 into the twenty-fifth, the Fascist Grand Council voted 19 to 8, with one abstention, in favor of deposing the Duce. The motion, proposed by Dino Grandi, returned the supreme command of the war effort to the king. When Mussolini went to Villa Savoia to hand in his resignation, the king had him arrested. The Grand Council majority, which included Ciano, Grandi, Federzoni, De Bono, and Bottai, had hoped the king would appoint Field Marshal Caviglia as prime minister. Instead, he named Pietro Badoglio, who ordered the continuation of the war alongside Germany, only to initiate secret negotiations with the Allies, which would lead Italy to capitulate on September 8, 1943.

Teruzzi was not on the Grand Council, which had not met since 1939, and whose roster of members had not been updated to include the minister of Italian Africa. Therefore, we have to speculate as to how he might have voted, whether for the king and the nation, as the Grandi proposal framed itself, or for fascism with (or better without) the Duce, as Farinacci proposed. We know that Teruzzi was present at all the important meetings leading up to Mussolini's decision, under huge pressure, to convene what would be his last Grand Council meeting.

On July 20, while Mussolini was at Feltre, just south of the Dolomites, meeting with Hitler, the Fascist Party Directory had been frantically called by the Fascist Party secretary, Muti, to meet and discuss what to do. Teruzzi had been a conspicuous presence in his colonial white linens, "perfumed like an old roué," railing against "the psychosis of defeat." When the party vice president, Tarabini, his onetime protégé who had just returned from Sicily, dangled the commander in the field Guzzoni's pocket watch, reporting that amid the chaos the general was prepared to die at his post and had asked him to bring it to his wife, Teruzzi made a flippant gesture—bull's horns, to ward off the evil eye. Farinacci kept shouting that the Duce had to be removed; in the end they all agreed with Teruzzi that they should show their loyalty to both the Duce and fascism by insisting he call a meeting of the Grand Council.[19]

When a more substantial group of the old guard met on July 22, and Mussolini at first rebelled and was then forced to acquiesce, Teruzzi felt some measure of sorrow and shock at the inexorability of the outcome. As they all left, he made what Bottai described as a "pathetic comment," remonstrating with the others that "given how wrecked he seemed, we shouldn't be adding to his grief."[20] Teruzzi would have had no doubts: behind the machinations of Grandi, Ciano, Federzoni, Bottai, and the rest, the plodding king was conspiring with his scheming courtiers, the Vatican, and the Piedmontese military in the figure of Marshal Badoglio to mount a coup. Farinacci, always the intransigent, put forward a minority proposal, namely, to put Italy's war machine under the command of the Wehrmacht. With German military might behind them, the fascists would call the people to arms to repulse the Judeo-Bolshevik-American invasion of the national territory, reigniting the revolution. If Mussolini did not go along, he would be replaced, presumably by Farinacci himself. This proposition made sense to Enzo Galbiati, the current head of the Fascist Militia, as well as to Renato Ricci, the onetime commander of the fascist youth groups, who was simple and violent, not unlike Teruzzi, and since 1939 had held the position of minister of corporations. Had Teruzzi been in a position to vote, chances are he would have backed that motion as well.

Meanwhile, Teruzzi had been confronted once more with the problem of what to do with Yvette. On June 20, as Sicily was about to be invaded, a midlevel Interior Ministry functionary had contacted him with a message from Alfredo Geraci, the concentration camp director at Lipari: Allied planes had bombed the ferry lines, cutting off the supply of water and food. Faced with curtailing rations once more, the growing insubordination of the prisoners, and the threat that if the tiny island was overrun by the enemy, there would be a mass breakaway, Geraci planned to disperse the two thousand or so prisoners to various places of detention on the mainland.[21] From the dossier, it looks like Teruzzi dragged his feet for a month before replying. Only on July 19 was it settled that Yvette would be interned in the special camp for "women of dubious morality" at Pollenza, near the central Italian town of Macerata. The interior minister's cautions on how to move her made that destination sound right: Blank was described as a "past lover of Teruzzi, who has a child by her, but who had broken off relations and under no circumstances wanted contact." She was to be escorted to her new place of detention by a double, experienced guard to prevent her from escaping. If she did, the Rome police were to be notified immediately. At her new camp, the director was instructed to make sure she had made no contact with one Gino Pizzi—the caretaker's son at Castiglioncello—presumably to keep her from entering into contact with her daughter.[22]

Yvette was still in detention at Lipari on July 25 when Mussolini's regime was toppled. The week after that, on August 2, the Badoglio government issued a directive to free everybody who had been imprisoned or exiled by the fascist dictatorship on political grounds. All of the internees, including Yvette, would have left the island right away. But the Allied invasion of Sicily was under way, and they were stuck there until the battle was over.

On the day Yvette was released, Teruzzi had been in jail for a week. Marshal Badoglio had hardly been in office for forty-eight hours when, amid chaotic rumors of counter-coups intended to reinstate Mussolini, the forces of order—the police, the SIM, and the army high command—began haphazardly identifying this suspect and that as they vied with one another for power. Badoglio ordered scores of arrests over the next ten days on various pretexts, from plotting with the Germans to return Mussolini to power to war profiteering. Teruzzi was at the top of the list, together with Bottai, Starace, Varenna, and Ricci.[23]

Nobody who read the list could figure out its logic, but, given his loyalty to Mussolini and strong ties with the Fascist Militia, Teruzzi's name came as no surprise. Not that the MVSN could be counted on anymore to save the Duce: on the orders of its current commander, Enzo Galbiati, the militia had affirmed its loyalty to the true commander-in-chief of the nation—the king—and hadn't budged from its barracks. Margaret De Wyss, a Swiss journalist and one of the tiny handful of foreign correspondents still left in Rome, overheard that Teruzzi was with three women, "in a somewhat awkward position"—possibly it was only his famous regular bridge party partners—when the police arrived on July 27 to arrest him. He stood up and blustered: "I was expecting this."[24]

The Regina Coeli jail was in chaos, according to the testimony of Teruzzi's Castiglioncello neighbor Silvio D'Amico, who'd been arrested at the same time, but as an antifascist. The only comfort D'Amico found was that the big hierarchs were being put in the same grim cells. True, the guards treated them more laxly than the antifascist political prisoners, uncertain whether they would come back to power and take revenge. If they had the money and somebody to give them a hand, they could upgrade to a paying cell. Teruzzi got the best. His friend Mario Marigo made sure of that, and he could purchase coffee and cigarettes from the prison guards. But short of having a wife or mother or sister who took it on herself to prepare food packages to substitute for the jail's revolting fare, he had to settle for the scraps of rabbit in ratatouille or other equally nauseating concoctions, sometimes supplemented by a glass of wine, a hunk of bread, rancid cheese, and a salted anchovy.[25]

Teruzzi had been at Regina Coeli for three weeks when he received his first family visitor. It was Yvette Blank. She had last been seen on August 17, when, in the final action of the Allied campaign to occupy Sicily, three PT boats with OSS officers aboard had drawn up to the cement pier at Lipari, raised a white flag, and accepted the island's surrender from the low-level officer in command of the port. As they hopped from their launches to the cheers of a small crowd, the OSS mission chief, Nate De Angelis, remembered being greeted by Felice Chilanti, a prominent fascist dissident who at Lipari had been converted to communism; Chilanti's wife; and a striking young woman whom they described as a "Slav, the ex-friend of the hierarch Teruzzi, who had ended up exiled for who knows what reason."[26]

Assuming Blank was treated like the other ex-prisoners, she would have been interrogated and then moved to the mainland to fend for herself. Since the coastal roads were rutted and bombed out, and she made it back to Rome in only three days, she may have hitched a ride with one of the

German convoys pulling back toward the north. On the morning of August 21, she went by the offices of the Interior Ministry to obtain a visitor's pass for Regina Coeli, which the functionary granted: her motive was "to talk with the General, her child's natural father, about making arrangements for the *bambina*." Mario Marigo, who "was known to have a positive influence" on Teruzzi and may have been taking care of Mariceli, was given permission to accompany her.[27]

At the sight of the father of her child penned up, wan and ragged, and surely breaking out in sobs at the sight of her, Yvette Blank forgave him. Early that September, when a reporter for the newly uncensored press gloried at the return of freedom by remarking that jailed fascists were now being treated just like ordinary inmates, his evidence was the "ex-Minister Teruzzi's wife." She was now "a regular" at the prison, lining up outside of the gates with the rest of the women to bribe the guards to deliver their food packages to their men.[28]

Teruzzi was still at Regina Coeli on September 8, 1943—Mariceli's fifth birthday—when Marshal Badoglio signed the armistice with the Allies to take Italy out of the war, only to be faced with the fury of its erstwhile German ally, whose armed forces proceeded to occupy the country. In principle, Italy was no longer a belligerent. But for the Germans, the Italians were traitors. To save himself from being captured by the Germans, Badoglio fled to the south of Italy, together with the royal family, abandoning Rome and the whole country to its fate. The Italian military forces, with no one in command, dissolved. Soldiers, not knowing whether to capitulate to the Germans or resist them, threw down their arms, stripped off their uniforms, put on civilian clothes, and rushed to the trains to return home.

The Italian commanders in Rome, fearing that the Germans would bombard the city before occupying it, as they had threatened to do, ordered their troops to pull back from the center toward the sea. As the armored car at the head of the retreating columns reached the Coliseum, where the Via dell'Impero passes below Colle Oppio and picks up the Via del Mare, they heard the sound of gunfire. Upon speculation that it was coming from Teruzzi's top-floor apartment on Via Monte Oppio, the gunners in one of the armored vehicles turned their gun turret toward the roof line and fired several rounds, sending plate glass, tiles, and cement from the penthouse cascading five stories down into the street. There were no snipers, according to later reports. Neighborhood people had spread the rumor, either out of fear or to take revenge or both.[29]

The day the German army occupied Rome, Hitler gave orders to rescue Mussolini, together with his top hierarchs, and bring them to Germany, where, under his protection, they could plan their return to power. On September 13, as German special forces flew to the Gran Sasso Plateau, where Mussolini had been sequestered, German armored vehicles rescued the various political and military leaders arrested by Badoglio from Regina Coeli and Fort Boccea and drove them to Villa Wolonsky, the German embassy on the southeast edge of Rome, now the headquarters of the German occupation.

Villa Wolonsky looked like the backdrop for a Greek tragedy. It was an unusually muggy mid-September day when the German military trucks unloaded the ex-bosses of the nation—generals, cabinet ministers, political bosses—ragged and unshaven, outside the colonnaded entrance way. With nowhere to go, the men huddled at the base of the stair ramps, feeding one another's fears at the pop-pop of machine guns and grenade explosions nearby that they had been rescued from their prison cells only to be executed.

That, in any case, was Field Marshal Enrico Caviglia's impression upon his arrival that afternoon. The kingdom's most senior military officer, now eighty-one and long retired, had rushed from his home in Genoa on the day of the armistice, September 8, to offer his services to the king, only to find that the king and Badoglio had fled. He was at the villa out of duty, as Italy's caretaker, to meet the German ambassador Rudolf Rahn, in the hope of identifying an Italian military commander who could work with the Germans to restore order as well as to seal the truce that Marshal Kesselring insisted on. If the Italians didn't end their defense of Rome, abandon their weapons, and retreat from the city center, the German commander-in-chief had said he would carpet-bomb the city—antiquities be damned, and he didn't care how many civilians died.

Caviglia was especially struck by the sight of Teruzzi in shirt sleeves, pants ripped, sweaty, and agitated. He had been an officer in his chain of command in the First World War. For Teruzzi, in turn, Caviglia had been his general, Gold Medal recipient, and the Hero of Montello, and at present the highest ranking in the military hierarchy. When their eyes met, Caviglia tells us, Teruzzi cried out, "passionately, grief-stricken, his chest palpitating: 'Marshal Caviglia, imagine an old soldier like me, who served Italy faithfully for forty-seven years, to jail him like a criminal, for no wrongdoing. Forty days of prison.'" More words tumbled out: "You, Marshal, you've saved Italy once again."[30]

As they entered the vestibule together, Caviglia urged him to stay calm, sit down, and wait, like the others, only to see him leap up and leave the room: "I have to see the Minister," he said, and returned several minutes later to report: "I told Minister Rahn that you are pure, crystalline, never factious, totally to be trusted in the holy cause of restoring order to Rome and Italy. I said that you are a real soldier, a real general, the only one, my own general." At that, he wanted to hug Caviglia; then he added: "To-morrow I leave by plane to go to Vienna to be with Mussolini, and I will tell him what you have done these days." Caviglia then told him: "Dear Teruzzi, tell Mussolini to get his friend Hitler to save Italy from the German troops, order them to pull back onto the Carnic Alps and position themselves to fight against Russia."[31]

Later Caviglia observed: "Teruzzi alone was worrying about Italy. The others were only thinking of getting home." He recalled Teruzzi's days as garrison postmaster at Massawa. "Poor Teruzzi, he has a lot of heart, and as much as he was corrupted by the regime, he was [acting] in good faith."[32]

This was yet another way of saying that fascism had promoted him beyond his merits and given him a bad commander in Mussolini. It was also a way for Caviglia to reiterate the choices that he himself had made to hold his peace, not "to create embarrassment" for the head of government, who had been chosen by the king.[33] Caviglia compared Teruzzi to Mussolini's other generals, like Ubaldo Soddu and Ugo Cavallero, also at Villa Wolonsky and desperate to get home to their wives. The Germans were pressing Cavallero to take command, and for reasons that are still unclear, whether by his own hand or at the hands of the Germans later that night, he died in the villa gardens from a shot with his own revolver.[34] Above all, when Caviglia spoke of Teruzzi's faith in the nation, he was denouncing Badoglio, who had fled and whom he always thought of as "a barnyard dog looking for treats." All of these men—who, unlike Teruzzi, had been promoted to the highest ranks for their military merits—had betrayed the nation. In Caviglia's mind, this made them worse than Teruzzi.[35]

That evening, Teruzzi and the others who were willing to rejoin Mussolini were all moved to Frosinone, where German planes picked them up and flew them to Bavaria. The Germans' intention, with Mussolini's weak assent, was to patch together a stop-gap government in northern Italy staffed by as many old guard loyalists as could be mustered. On September 27, after a brief visit to the Duce and his family, who were being held in luxury accommodations at the Hirschberg Castle fifty miles south of Munich, Teruzzi and the others were flown to Verona.

Upon landing in Verona, Teruzzi's main concern was to get back to Rome to see his daughter and check on his property. By then Rome had ceased being the capital of the Kingdom of Italy, and the Badoglio government had set up its administrative base at Brindisi. Henceforth, with the appellation of the "Kingdom of the South," it would act as a puppet of the Allied armies, which, after crossing from Sicily to the mainland in September 1943 and then landing twice again, at Salerno that same month and then at Anzio in January 1944, moved by fits and starts up the peninsula. Mussolini wanted to reinstate Rome as his capital, but in deference to the pope and to international opinion, deeply troubled over the possibility that the Holy City would be bombed, both sides agreed to move all military matériel out of Rome and to declare it an open city.

Rome, upon Teruzzi's return, with no government to speak of, was living under the terror of the first weeks of German occupation. As German troops pillaged shops and stole from passersby, the SS and security police were hunting down resisters, draft dodgers, and soldiers from the disbanded national army. The Fascist Party headquarters at Palazzo Braschi, after being closed down, had reopened so that diehards and opportunists could plot punitive expeditions against suspected antifascists and collaborators with the king. The jails had been broken open, and bands of common criminals were roaming the streets.[36]

Teruzzi's first concern was to size up his own losses. There was the penthouse on Colle Oppio. The shells lobbed at his home on September 9 as the Italian army retreated toward the port at San Paolo had collapsed the roof and shattered the glass facade. Then, on September 27, a group of nine fascist legionnaires dressed in militia outfits, armed with machine guns and claiming that they had been sent by the Fascist Federation of the Urbe to punish a traitor, had broken in and ransacked the place. When the police arrived, they found a man and woman drunk, asleep in a bed, liquor bottles littering the street; people from the neighborhood, disinhibited by two weeks of mayhem and glad to wreak revenge on the gerarcone's property, were making off with the porcelain dolls, bedding, toys, and other loot. Since the line between political reprisals and banditry was perilously thin, and the federation denied it had authorized any such attack, Teruzzi preferred to believe that he had been a victim of bandits rather than consider that he might have been a victim of men who believed he was a traitor to Italy.[37]

Meanwhile, he discovered that the previous August, while he had been locked up in Regina Coeli, the *carabinieri* had raided his homes with a warrant from the Badoglio government and confiscated all of his valuables. The government was trying to earn public trust when it ordered the first crackdowns against wartime profiteering, illegal imports, and currency violations. For that purpose it had installed a Commission for the Devolution to the State of Patrimonies of Illegitimate Provenance at the Palace of Justice, and the finance inspector, police commissioner, army, and *carabinieri* commands had vied with one another to draw up warrants. By the end of the first week of September, they had seized the "entire wealth" of Farinacci, Bottai, Starace, and others and were about to seize Ciano's.[38] On August 7 and 14, the military police unit at the command of Lieutenant Ezio Taddei, after raiding Teruzzi's residences at Colle Oppio and Sacrofano, had hauled in a sizable treasure, including thirty-three oriental carpets, East African trinkets, gold objects, and silver plates.

A telephone call to Antonino Tringali-Casanova, the former head of the Special Tribunal for the Defense of the State and now the minister of justice, secured Teruzzi the name of the chief prosecutor, Gabriele Viola, who had signed the receipt for the loot. Whatever he said when Teruzzi phoned him, Teruzzi became so furious that he rushed over to the Palace of Justice. He charged past the downstairs guards and pushed his way into Viola's chambers, with Luigi Licci, his onetime factotum and longtime neighbor, now a colonel in the carabinieri, in tow and also a handsome young legionnaire, Lieutenant Bianchi, just back from the Russian front.

Court proceedings would later give a blow-by-blow account of Teruzzi's outrage.[39] It lasted an hour. He threatened to blow Viola up with a hand grenade if his property, which had been illegally confiscated, was not immediately returned. He kept shouting that that "*porco*" Badoglio had set him up. Upon the arrival of the assistant prosecutor, Donato Bianchi, Teruzzi assaulted him, saying, "Get in here, and no yack." And his lieutenant "threatened he had his name, and he'd better get out of town, they'd be looking for him tonight." When Teruzzi asked him whether he was a fascist, and he replied that he had served in two world wars, Teruzzi smirked: "If everybody fought the war the way you did, no wonder Italy lost."

At the sight of Queen Elena's portrait, which had replaced the Duce's alongside the king over the prosecutor's desk, Teruzzi called her a whore. When Viola tried to calm him down, he threatened to pull the grenade pin and call the SS. At that point, Viola signed the release order. As soon as Teruzzi left, the prosecutor had an arrest warrant drawn up on charges of insulting a public official and aggravated assault on an officer acting in the line of duty. Both were serious charges under any law-abiding regime.

Once he had calmed down, the detail-minded, calculating Teruzzi took over. He was in real danger and eager to get back to the north of Italy. One assumes that his daughter, reunited with her mother, was safe at Castiglioncello or that both were now being harbored by the Marigos. He contacted a woman friend, the journalist Giulia d'Arienzo, and asked her to go by his house and destroy any incriminating documents. Then he commandeered three municipal fire trucks to move his stuff to Lake Garda, where he would regroup.[40]

22

LAST MAN STANDING

The human being should come to himself!
. . . But: how does a human being come to his self?
. . . Insofar as the human being does not choose and instead
creates a substitute for choosing, he sees his self
1. through reflection in the usual sense;
2. through dialogue with the thou;
3. through meditation on the situation;
4. through some idolatry.

—MARTIN HEIDEGGER, *Black Notebooks*, 1932

On a map of northern Italy, Lake Garda looks like a skinny triangle, its upper tip wedged like an arrow into the Tyrolean Alps as if to warn the German peoples to stay back, its base the enticing shoreline midway between Milan and Venice. Since the end of World War I, when Italy's frontier with Austria was pushed north to the Brenner Pass and previous generations of German-speaking residents were expelled from their lakeside villas, new visitors had arrived from the German lands, mostly vacationers— then, after 1933, refugees, mostly Jews, fleeing Nazi persecution. Desenzano, the lakefront's biggest town, should be called "Senzano-am-See," the locals joked, referring to the bronzed Teutons strolling on their bougainvillea-draped streets and the smells of schnitzel and fries wafting from the hotels.

That was before the middle of September 1943, when the German military occupation forces settled around Lake Garda as outright conquerors. The previous July, after the Allies invaded Sicily, the Third Reich had mobilized to block their advance up the peninsula. First, it had annexed outright the whole region to the south of the Alps, including the Trentino, South Tyrol, and the northern end of the lake. Then it had moved its central military command for Italy thirty miles due east of Lake Garda to Verona.

By the time the Führer had Mussolini rescued from the new Italian government's captivity on September 12, 1943, it had become evident that Rome was too exposed militarily to remain the capital of German-dominated Italy. Consequently, as Hitler prepared to deliver the Duce back to Italy, German army and SS men began requisitioning the lakeshore towns' large stock of hotels, sumptuous villas, and clinics to provide suitable accommodations for the ministers and functionaries who were to move from Rome.

From early October, Mussolini's offices at Palazzo Venezia were relocated to Palazzo Bettoni at Bogliaco and his household from Villa Torlonia to Villa Feltrinelli at Gargnano. The command of what remained of Italy's armed forces was established at Desenzano and the Interior Ministry at Maderno, while the German plenipotentiary, Ambassador Rahn, and Field Marshal Kesselring, the commander of the German forces in Italy, moved into two splendid villas overlooking Fasano. And so the beautiful shoreline around Lake Garda became the operational headquarters for Hitler's rule over four-fifths of the Italian peninsula, bringing all the major cities, from Naples, Rome, Bologna, and Florence to Genoa, Milan, Turin, and Venice under German occupation by the autumn of 1943.

The fascists called their new state the Italian Social Republic, or RSI, though it would become sinisterly familiar as the Republic of Salò, after the lakeside town from which the Popular Culture Ministry issued the communiqués for the new regime. Salò was also the seat from which the Foreign Affairs Ministry sought diplomatic recognition for the RSI abroad, never succeeding except among its Axis allies. In effect, all that was left of Mussolini's once grand Mediterranean empire was another puppet regime subject to Hitler's Fortress Europe. For the next six hundred or so days, the republic's existence would run parallel to that of the other Italy, the so-called Kingdom of the South, with its capital first at Brindisi and then, from June 1944, in Rome, which the "Repubblichini" denounced as a puppet regime of the Allies.[1]

Mussolini's condition of thralldom left him with no good options. He promised to carry on. But his fighting instincts had been dulled by age, depression, and family squabbles, mainly over his lover, Clara Petacci, who had taken up residence in the vicinity with her family. They had been dulled, too, by the loss of virtually all the men with whom he had risen to power. He had treated them all as being expendable. And yet his decision-making processes, his famous instinct, had depended on hearing of their clashes, listening to their gossip, studying their reactions. The very best minds, including Luigi Federzoni, Dino Grandi, and Giuseppe Bottai, and the most experienced organizers, notably Edmondo Rossoni, were no longer available. These were the men who had turned against him at the final meeting of the Grand Council and who were now in hiding or had fled abroad. His son-in-law had betrayed him as well. What remained at Salò was just the penumbra of that past.

Once he had recovered from the shock of his overthrow, from his unwanted rescue at the hands of Hitler's special forces, and from having been constrained by Hitler to take the reins of this last redoubt of his old empire, the Duce began to see the future once more in terms of the merciless class conflict he had thrived on from his time as a socialist. The desperate military combat, enemy bombardments, and shortages of every sort had once more turned the home front into a social battlefield, as in World War I. Everywhere there was talk of the American New Deal, England's Beveridge Plan, communist collectivism, and other types of welfare provision intended to give the laboring people their due. Of course, Fascist Italy had always maintained that its corporatist philosophy was at the forefront of the world critique of the brutal worker-capitalist relations of industrial society. It claimed to have realized its ideology of class harmony by establishing corporatist bodies bringing together workers and employers to negotiate their demands in the higher interest of the nation. The trouble was that the fascist regime had always been anti-worker, so that fascist labor reforms really only ever represented the interests of big capital. This time, Mussolini told himself, he would get it right, unsullied by compromises with the king, the Church, the army, the old elites, and the recalcitrant clay that was the Italian people—all of whom he blamed for his previous failures and his present predicament.

The Italian Social Republic would make its last stand under the banner of "socialization." Though it was not said outright, the fascism of the Italian Social Republic would thereby place itself at the forefront of the radical national socialist program that Hitler had forsaken by brutally exploiting all of the European territories subjugated by his armies. The social struggle would reinvigorate the Axis war effort on the continent as it became clear that Great Britain and the United States were willing to sacrifice Europe to the barbarous Judeo-Bolshevism of the Soviet Union.

That, together with the unleashing of Hitler's secret weapon, imagined as a superballistic missile capable of blowing the British Isles to smithereens, would bring the belligerents to negotiate an end to the war. Thereupon, Italy would arrive at the peace table with the Italian masses, meaning the workers and peasants of Italy, mobilized behind the Duce and fascism, its honor intact rather than by way of the ignominious capitulation that the conspirators of July 25, 1943 had perpetrated with the connivance of the traitor generals and the traitor-king Victor Emmanuel. In the end, the Duce's new state would regain the legitimacy it once had as the progenitor of the world fascist revolution. That vision—a chimera, of course—was his last and best hope.

In October, with the goal of "returning fascism to its origins," Mussolini established a new Council of Ministers and designated a new secretary to head the political formation that now went under the name of the Fascist Republican Party. On November 14, the party convened its founding congress in Verona to set out the basic principles of Mussolini's social republic, attracting to its support ideological oddballs as varied as those who had gathered around him at the Piazza San Sepolcro in 1919. Marshal Graziani, the only commander of high rank to commit to the new republic, was named minister of defense. He would form up four new army divisions from the thousands of Italian men the Germans had imprisoned in concentration camps upon the Kingdom of Italy's capitulation to the Allies on September 8, 1943.

With the expectation that the RSI was still under Mussolini's firm command, that it was merely working in collaboration with the German forces, and that its chief aim would be to preserve law and order, the new republic began to collect support. This came not only from die-hard fascists but also from leading industrialists, sympathetic churchmen, journalists, and the usual barefaced opportunists from across bourgeois society who saw no other good alternative.

In principle, Attilio Teruzzi was being offered a second chance. How would he redefine his responsibilities—to his office, his Duce, the principles of fascism, the nation, and his family—now that the original regime had been overthrown? On September 25, he had been returned to Verona by the Nazi leadership. By that time, it must have understood that it had deeply misjudged the forces he could bring to reinstating Mussolini's rule.

As soon as he could, Teruzzi had left for Rome, only to find his house in ruins and to learn that Mussolini's new republic intended to move its capital to the north.

On the last day of September, in Verona, Teruzzi swore allegiance to the new regime. Whether he wanted to occupy a new position is unclear. It was hard to see how the new regime could have engaged him. Or he it, for that matter. The "two indissoluble faces of totalitarianism," to use Italian historian Claudio Pavone's expression, were once again coming to clash under the RSI, with an extremism and violence hitherto unwitnessed on Italian soil.[2] On the one hand, there was the rigid hierarchal order of the absolutist state at the Duce's command, which his new regime was trying to impose once more on the whole society. On the other, there was the chaos arising from the fragmenting of every legal principle, including those formulated by the fascists, ever more subordinated to the Nazi war machine's effort to strip Italy of its resources on behalf of the ongoing conflict and to exterminate however many thousands of Jews fell under its power.

Teruzzi could conceivably have been enlisted to rebuild the militia. Imposing order on *squadristi* violence had once been his forte. But the new militia being shaped up to defend the republic from the growing resistance called for more zealous and bloody-minded energies. Other men had these qualities in abundance, and two notably so. Renato Ricci, the fifty-year-old onetime organizer of the Fascist Balilla youth groups, who though he was part of the old guard and, like Teruzzi, "had a beautiful fascist face," to recall Ciano's compliment, still resembled the giant, black-shirted, shaven-headed bruiser of a man he had been when he had led his squads against the Massa-Carrara marble workers in 1921. At the birth of the new regime, Ricci had set out at once to form an armed militia from the numerous young people who had rushed to join the last-ditch defense of their nation against the enemy.[3] The other was the intellectually refined Florentine political commissar Alessandro Pavolini, the former minister of popular culture. Appointed secretary of the new Fascist Republican Party—the sole legal political formation in the RSI—he revealed a taste for terroristic factionalism, a time-honored Florentine political practice that earned him his sobriquet as the "Saint-Just of Fascism." Come summer of 1944, Pavolini's Black Brigades were conducting raids, reprisals, and torture against antifascist partisans, who from the spring of 1944 were fighting both against the so-called Repubblichini and the German occupation forces.[4] The result was a bedlam of Dantesque ferocity as the brigades drew in armed irregulars, clueless teenage boys, and marauders in search of booty, revenge, and adventure.

In sum, the RSI was no country for old men. It was not for the loyal and mediocre, much less for those who had climbed the hierarchy tilting this way and that to satisfy Mussolini's appetite for divide and rule, accruing decorations, influence, and wealth. The new regime was being established as an antidote to the so-called *Geracume* or hierarch-scums, the whole "stinking bunch." Many of them had taken to the woods or simply disappeared, lying low in convents, monasteries, and friends' country houses or fleeing to Spain, Portugal, or Latin America. A few has-beens had dutifully made their appearance, like Achille Starace, who offered himself up for a new position, only to be waved away by the Duce, who, unmoved by his loyalty, regarded him as an embarrassing anachronism whose slavishness he could no longer tolerate. And then there was Farinacci, who had nothing to offer politically now that true and younger zealots had taken command of the party but could not be prevented, so long as he based himself at Cremona, from rabble-rousing and scheming to become the next Duce.

Teruzzi was tolerated, but barely. Whatever critics said about his vanity, mediocrity, and corruption, he had conducted himself loyally, suffered at the hands of Badoglio, and sworn allegiance to the new republic, and he still had access to the Duce. No rump Ministry for Italian Africa was established under the RSI. That allowed him to keep the honorific "His Excellency," and he retained his official position as division general, retired, which may have been his fondest aspiration anyway. Surely, not having a uniform to wear to show off his rank and service record must have been a form of defeat. Yet Teruzzi was a pragmatic man, a true soldier, who knew how to take the hard knocks. With no position forthcoming, his chief concern, not having received a salary check since July 1943, was to start the process to draw on his military pension.

How exactly Teruzzi operated in the coming months, what he did as he was tossed and turned about by the makeshift order of a new totalitarian statelet trying to establish itself amid an unfolding civil war, is not easy to know. Once he ceased to be a public man, the archival traces, scarce in the best of times, drop off dramatically; transcripts from his logorrheic, occasionally revealing speeches cease to exist, and he was no longer photographed, except for a handful of times, presumably by Yvette, in the company of his daughter.

We need instead to rely on the occasional sightings, the long periods of silence, and our familiarity with the man's small but strikingly visible stock of maneuvers to conjecture about his allegiances as Mussolini and fascism were put to their final test. Teruzzi had never been a fanatic. So one wouldn't expect him to be writhing about the political, much less moral, coherence of his past conduct. Yet one does wonder whether he reflected on the costs mounting to Italy as a nation and a people as Mussolini made his ruinous last stand.

That he ended up at Lake Garda at all testifies both to his deep belief in the Duce and to his profound lack of imagination as to life's alternatives. Or maybe he saw trusting the Duce as the only hope. He surely recognized now, as they all did, that Mussolini was fallible. Even so, for Teruzzi, as well as for other stalwarts, he was still their indispensable leader, the "One." The Duce alone, Hitler had made clear, was Italy's legitimate ruler. Hitler needed him to remain so, however little he took him into consideration in his policies toward Italy. He needed Mussolini to convince the Third Reich's other, smaller satellites that just as he showed respect for Mussolini, his most senior ally, he was willing to show respect for them too—Germany's ignoble brutality toward them notwithstanding. Nazi Germany also needed the RSI to administer these comparatively rich lands, far and away the most prosperous under Nazi occupation outside of France, if their labor and resources were to be exploited effectively. By the same token, Mussolini insisted that his person alone and the friendship Hitler bore him stood between Italy being treated like an ally, more or less, and Italy being treated like occupied Poland, ravaged by the Reich.

It is hard to imagine that Teruzzi embraced the RSI's new political program. He would have agreed with its republican character, for he had always distrusted the monarchy, and after the king's betrayal of Mussolini, he despised it. A true patriot, he believed in the goal of maintaining Italy's independence and territorial integrity. In principle, he had never ceased to be an "intransigent" who detested the affectations of the old elites—not even when he had become a full-fledged oligarch himself, with a keen taste for the comforts of the good life. But these views had little to do with the pugnacious and empty slogans now bandied about on behalf of "National Socialism."

In spite of his loyalty to the regime, he was far too much of a cynic to believe that fascism could recoup its purity by making gestures to nationalize private firms or set up committees to involve workers in shop floor management. He had never believed in these notions himself. They were too distant from his experience or sympathies. And the means proposed were risible. To the shock of the Germans—who had not experienced such an occurrence elsewhere—strikes broke out in Turin and Milan in the winter of 1943–1944. Workers were outraged over the shortages, the forced requisition of laborers for Germany, and the deaths of factory workers during the bombing raids, when the Germans had blocked management from letting them leave the shop floors to find sanctuary.

It is also unlikely that Teruzzi would have embraced the Repubblichini's terroristic plan for starting over. He had never been one for purges— he was with Mussolini on that score. Others, like Pavolini, thought that the new regime's foundational act should be to "confront Italy with the biggest betrayal in historical memory," by making an example of the nineteen Grand Council members who had deposed Mussolini. To that end, a special tribunal had been established at the Congress of Verona. But the kangaroo court that opened on January 7, 1944, and was in session for three days, had nothing noble or inspired about it. There were no Robespierres, no Dantons, no new Duces to give revolutionary legitimacy to the prosecution. All of the traitors, the six on the dock and the thirteen being tried in absentia, were accused of "aiding the enemy, betraying the ideals of fascism, attempting to jeopardize the operations of the country's armed forces and the country's resistance and independence." Their conviction was a foregone conclusion.[5]

All but one—Tullio Cianetti, the former head of the Fascist Trade Unions, who, on July 26, the day after the vote, had confessed his confusion to Mussolini and withdrawn his "yes" vote—were condemned to death. Cianetti was given a thirty-year sentence, and for everyone tried, there was no appeal. The executions of the other five were carried out by firing squad early on the morning of January 11.

Three of the accused had been especially close to Teruzzi in one way or another. Giovanni Marinelli, a gray figure, who had become administrative secretary of the party in 1921, at the same that Teruzzi had been named vice president, was never more than a pusillanimous time server and didn't generate much compassion. But to tie him straddled to a chair facing the wall and shoot him in the back? And to do the same to the aged quadrumvir De Bono—who'd been in the service of fascism since the March on Rome, a marshal in the king's army whom, as late as May 1943, Teruzzi himself had hailed as the greatest general of fascist Africa, and who, in his ingenuous testimony before the special tribunal, confessed that he understood little of politics and what was at stake during the Grand Council vote—made no sense. Nobody could impugn his patriotism or fail to recognize that at seventy-eight he had become addled with age or maybe only more foolish and lachrymose.

Finally, there was Galeazzo Ciano, Mussolini's son-in-law. Teruzzi had a deep personal tie to his father, Costanzo. He owed to him his mission to Spain, which had been the stepping stone to his post as minister of Italian Africa. He knew the Duce's daughter, Edda, had left no stone unturned to save him. Mussolini, too, would have blocked his execution had not Hitler, with his penchant for revenge, sworn him not to, through his plenipotentiary Rahn.[6] Teruzzi had seen so many deaths by then. Since the Great War, he had been in perpetual and often indiscriminate mourning for fallen comrades: fascist martyrs, the dead under his command in Cyrenaica, his own family members, the Duke of Aosta, and the other gallant soldiers sacrificed to defend Italian East Africa. If he could be philosophical and offer the Duce any solace, he might have told him that he had acted in the line of duty; fate had deprived him of both the power to judge Ciano and the power to save him. If only his daughter, Edda, and her children could comprehend his sacrifice.

Though his political life was in shambles, Teruzzi had been reunited sometime in October 1943 with Mariceli, now five, and Yvette. In the rosy version, out of harm's away, removed from his official duties—with life's lessons learned and his actions accounted for in some way by the forces of circumstance—he could finally be at peace with his family. And, in the handful of family photographs showing an amused-looking older gentleman in a wool coat and scarf playing with a laughing child splayed in the deep snow of the winter of 1943–1944, that moment seems to have arrived.[7] Then again, neither the logistical nor psychological conditions could have been easy. The couple had on their hands a precocious, temperamental child cocooned in privilege, who, from the tender age of three, had seen her mother banned from her life, and then her father taken off to prison, and had lost her home, neighborhood, nannies, playmates, pets, and dolls.

True, their temporary home at Villa Beltrami, located on the Riviera degli Olivi on the lake's eastern shore and close to the town of Garda, was peaceful and lovely, as well as relatively isolated from the headquarters of

Teruzzi with Mariceli, Lake Garda, winter 1944

the RSI. Yet for Mariceli to find herself alone with two parents who, as a couple, surely had lots to mend must have been as painful as it was joyous. As much as she loved her mother, she must have been puzzled by how to share her with her father and vice versa. Yvette may have forgiven Teruzzi for having exiled her, but she must have chafed at having to depend on him again for survival. During his imprisonment at Regina Coeli, he had had to rely on Yvette's cleverness and affection; he would have wanted to be on his best behavior, quiet and resolute. Faced with his stunning fall, his child and companion now totally dependent on his precarious situation, could he have mended his old habits?

At some level all the psychological baggage paled before the existential issue the family faced: Yvette was a Jew and her daughter was of "mixed race" in a land that had become subject to the same roundups, deportations, and annihilation that the Third Reich had been carrying out since it launched the Final Solution in the spring of 1942. Article 7 of the eighteen points of government issued by the RSI at Verona on November 14, 1943, had affirmed that "members of the Jewish race are foreign aliens; during this war they belong to an enemy nationality."[8] On November 30, the head of police of the RSI had issued Order No. 5 providing for the arrest and detention of all Jews on Italian soil and for the immediate confiscation of all of their belongings. Specifically, it ordered that whatever their status or nationality, their goods were to be confiscated in the name of the RSI and earmarked to benefit the victims of enemy air incursions. It also ordered that offspring of mixed marriages who had been recognized by the Race Laws as belonging to the Aryan race were subject to special vigilance by the police and that pending the establishment of the appropriate concentration camps, all the Jews arrested should be detained in local facilities.

From December 1943, the whole structure of persecution that the fascists had started to build in 1938 and had operated in a haphazard way through 1942—with the ostensible goal of segregation and expulsion—was mobilized for the goal of extermination. All the personnel of the appropriate ministries were to contribute in their various ways: the prefects, police commissioners, public security police, *carabinieri*, and miscellaneous state, municipal, and party functionaries. They based their operations on the very complete lists of Jewish families residing in Italy, cataloging their composition, sex, age, profession, which had been drawn up province by province starting in August 1938 and updated periodically. And they operated under a renewed barrage of anti-Semitic propaganda to incite denunciations.

By February, 1944, the detention camp originally built on a vacant piece of agricultural land at Fossoli to hold British prisoners of war had been converted into a full-fledged concentration camp. Located near Carpi, a rail junction in the province of Modena on the main Bologna–Verona trunk line going to the Brenner Pass, the camp facilitated the transportation of Jews previously detained in local jails, detention centers, or large prisons like Milan's San Vittore. The first convoy under the supervision of the Nazis' top specialist in such matters, Frederic Bosshammer, left for Auschwitz on February 22 carrying 650 people, only 124 of whom survived, included Primo Levi, the chemist and writer. In May, the security police combed through hospitals, asylums, old people's homes, and convents looking for Jews. By July, they were seizing even those with neutral country nationality. As the Allies were advancing and the Germans wanted to dismantle the camp and reestablish a new center on the border at Bolzano, the action was stepped up. When the last transport left on August 2, 1944, the train cars had two different destinations: those packed with so-called mixed-race people went to Bergen-Belsen, whereas so-called full Jews, including children of mixed marriages, were routed to Auschwitz.[9]

No objective measures could weigh the risks Yvette faced, starting in November 1943, and especially in those crucial seven months from February to August 1944, when the Italians and the Germans collaborated to eliminate the Jews from the territory under the control of the Italian Social Republic. Between native Italians and foreigners, of the roughly 30,000 to 35,000 Jews trapped in north-central Italy at the outset of the German occupation, 20 percent were arrested and deported. Of the 7,600 arrested after September 8, 1943, 6,806 were deported to German-operated concentration camps, mainly to Auschwitz, and almost all died. Among the dead, there were more foreign Jews than Italians, roughly 4,000 compared to 2,500, more old people than young, and more men, by a few, than women.[10]

The most important point here is that all of the Jews in the German-occupied territories of Italy were eventually the target of a persecution of cyclonic ferocity.[11] By far the biggest danger was to fall for the meanest ruse of all: that German totalitarianism was an implacable bureaucratic monster, admitting of no exceptions in its pursuit of the Jews, whereas Italian totalitarianism—whether because Italians were good fellows (*brava gente*), because the Church offered havens, or because fascist despotism always admitted exceptions—was a more humane and lenient totalitarianism. In Italy, even if the line between benevolence and brutality was narrowing, one could always hope for an escape route, by a bribe to a person of influence, through the work of a good Samaritan, or from some stroke of luck. Use your head and connections. Otherwise, you had yourself to blame. That was the story often told.

Did it help Yvette then that Attilio Teruzzi was a hierarch? Not in any obvious way. Quite the contrary: this was a time of settling scores, and it was widely rumored that Teruzzi had a Jewish wife—presumably alluding to Lilliana—and that he had had to forge documents for his Romanian Jew, that certainly referred to Yvette. The most extreme of the Italian anti-Semites, Giovanni Preziosi, was largely responsible for spreading this information. He knew a great deal about Lilliana Teruzzi's Jewishness from when he and Farinacci had concocted the anti-Semitic libel Teruzzi had unsuccessfully used in his annulment case in 1935. But that was another historical moment, when he had been a voice in the wilderness, inspiring only disgust. Since the establishment of the RSI, his fortunes had soared. With Hitler at Rastenburg, together with Farinacci, he helped the Führer understand why to his astonishment fascism in Italy had "dissipated like snow at springtime" and why the Duce, as Goebbels phrased it, "couldn't revive it." It was that "the Duce was still surrounded by traitors, former Freemasons and Jew-lovers who consistently give him wrong advice."[12]

The Germans in Italy despised Preziosi as an authentic psychopath, and the Italian authorities no less so. But the high patronage of Goebbels and Hitler propelled him forward, forcing Mussolini to read his letters about the necessity and urgency of "a complete solution to the Jewish question." The task at hand was "the total elimination of the Jew." By this he meant "to exclude from all the ganglia of our national life, from the military, from the courts, from teaching, from the central and peripheral hierarchies of the Party, the half-castes, those intermarried with Jews, and those with a drop of Jewish blood."[13]

The only serious way to do this was by using the same kind of genealogical tables the Germans used. On several occasions from January on, Mussolini received Preziosi at Villa Feltrinelli, and at Mussolini's proposal on February 12, 1944, the Council of Ministers of the RSI instituted the so-called General Inspectorate for Race, with Preziosi at its head. From March 13, 1944, Preziosi moved with his family to Desenzano to operate it full-time. Whether Mussolini intended thereby to endorse his work or to circumscribe it seems like a pointless debate, given that, under German surveillance, his intentions mattered less and less.

Not that Mussolini could not be trusted to be totally discreet on the matter of Yvette. The Duce is recorded as having seen her on at least one occasion, when he visited the hospital at Gargnano to see an old friend. The facility had been requisitioned by the SS to rehabilitate military officers gravely wounded on the Russian front, and it was the best in Italy. There were only two Italians there. Yvette had been admitted to it as the wife of a high personage after breaking her leg badly in an automobile accident. The Duce paid her his "cordial regards," according to his aide; it was no longer for him to mind who was with whom.[14] Whether Teruzzi could trust Mussolini for help if Yvette was picked up was a different matter.

When the Race Laws were first implemented in 1938, Teruzzi and other potentates of the regime, including the arch anti-Semite Farinacci, had sometimes gone out of their way to show their benevolence. Recall the case, from August 1938, when, at Mussolini's express command, Farinacci fired Jole Foa. He did it with the understanding that his fixer-friend Varenna would find a solution, given all of his connections, and Jole Foa had been found a position at the Milanese office of the SAMAO steel company. She was still working there on December 1, 1943, when the RSI's Order No. 5 to arrest and concentrate all Jews came out. Pressed by her friends, perhaps with Farinacci's help, she arranged to expatriate clandestinely to Switzerland. She got as far as Lanzo d'Intelvi, an Alpine ski village, where she was to cross, only to get cold feet—she was leaving everybody. Instead of going to meet the smuggler at the pickup point at the edge of the forest, she dawdled at the town inn. In a matter of days, she was arrested as a spy, jailed at Como, and then sent to San Vittore, where she was detained as a Jewish spy. During the two months of detention at Milan, her sister, Rinalda, said they supplicated Farinacci for help. But he did nothing. Jole believed that Farinacci was "too pure" to make the necessary compromises—with whom it is not clear. At the time, Farinacci was known to be helping other Jews, family men who had to have a certain wealth to pay all of the fees and bribes involved. Money aside, it called for too much explaining to help a reckless fifty-five-year-old spinster who should have left Italy in December 1943, when she had had the chance. Rinalda blamed his inaction on his "evil twin," Varenna. The upshot was that in April, Jole was transferred from San Vittore to Carpi. From there on May 4, 1944, she was boarded onto the tenth transport to Auschwitz, where, her sister eventually learned, she had been a "real champion" at finding food, surviving down to the very end, January 1945, when the Germans broke up the camp and she disappeared.[15]

It may have been in Yvette's favor that she had never been identified as Jewish on any public record, that she held a Vatican City resident identity card, if not a full set of false papers, and that her daughter was called Teruzzi. At Salò, the biggest risks arose from the chaos of illegalities. Suffice some incident at an open-air market, an incursion onto private property to search, say, for draft dodgers or partisans, or some mishap like a stalled engine at a checkpoint. Some busybody functionary could snatch the opportunity to pore over identity papers, start telephoning to check the records, and consign the suspect to the no-man's-land of detention. At Salò, zealous bungling and meanness, yet another dimension of bureaucratic incompetence, introduced an especially hideous happenstance to the now joint Nazi-Fascist war against the Jews.

Just to be safe, in February Teruzzi moved his family thirty-five miles up the winding lakeside road to Malcesine, where Lake Garda becomes pinched like a fjord and the houses cling to the rocky spurs of Mount Balbo. The village was guarded by the ancient castle of the Scaligeri, the Venetian warlords, and boasted a splendid Mediterranean microclimate that had once made the village a holiday idyll for Virgil, Catullus, and other well-known Roman vacationers. Teruzzi had located a treasure of a house for their stay. It was a rustic villa secluded on an embankment overlooking Viale Roma, near the town's center, with a back garden planted with a lemon grove, olive trees, and some palms and a splendid view of Lake Garda, which, when whipped up by the late afternoon storms, looked like the open sea.

The best guarantee for his family's security was that five months earlier, on September 13, 1943, the Germans had expropriated the house from Felix Heimann, a prominent Berlin Jewish businessman, privy councilor, and widower who, in 1934, had bought the house to keep company with his daughter, Elli, a painter, who had a cottage nearby. No physical harm had been done to him when the German soldiers had rousted him from his home. But he had suffered a stroke a few days later. That was all to the good, his beloved friend, the widow Frau Doctor Wiesa Jassé, wrote friends of his to tell his daughter who had moved to California and had tried to get him to come. He didn't suffer and had been prevented from dwelling on the "developments in his neighborhood" yet still had time to say his good-byes to his many friends before dying on October 13.[16]

Of course, Teruzzi wouldn't have known these details when he moved his things into the house, didn't pay the rent, and left Felix Heimann's heirs to pay the heavy tax that the RSI imposed on Jewish properties even after they had been expropriated. Rumor had it that Teruzzi had cajoled authorities to rule the property off-limits to searches. He also obtained a permit from the German authorities to carry a pistol and automatic rifle.[17]

By early summer, bands of antifascist partisans had begun to hazard their way down Mount Balbo to the village. Low-flying Allied warplanes were regularly bombing the lakesides, and the zone around Malcesine was being policed by the militia band named after the former Fascist Party head, Ettore Muti, who had been murdered in August 1943 at the hands of Badoglio's police. They were mere boys, poorly armed, often hungry, and Teruzzi had no trouble managing them with some encouraging words, food, and even a loan of a few hundred lire. When he ran into them later, he insisted that the money was only a loan, and they, as militia men on duty, should have had the discipline and honesty to pay it back.[18]

The real problem was the intentions of the Wehrmacht. The German armed forces had begun to pull back their lines of defense to the Brenner Pass and to pack the tunnels going north with dynamite in order to blow them up in the event that the Allies reached Lake Garda. They had also started to requisition houses. Teruzzi tried to get the Italian authorities to intercede with the German embassy so that he could remain at Felix Heimann's. But his effort failed when the hardworking, idealistic young functionary who had been asked to handle the request—as if Italy were still the playground of fascist hierarchs—refused point blank, adding that he wouldn't lift a finger for that "so-called gentleman" and wished "someone would put him out of his misery."[19]

By late August 1944, the Teruzzi family's worries about where to go next was a shared experience. More and more families of fascists and their collaborators arrived in the area seeking refuge as the Allies advanced north, liberating towns formerly under the grip of the Germans and fascists, and exposing them to retaliation. From August, the heads of the RSI had begun to think about finding refuge abroad for their families, if not for themselves. Many had moved to the border towns of Cadenabbia and Lenno fronting on Lake Como after the military front line reached Rimini and it looked like the Allies' invasion of the lower Po valley was imminent.

Some foresaw the next step: if the German forces retreated, they would join a government in exile across the Alps in Germany.

As it was, the only other escape route passed through Switzerland. If they could not find asylum there, they could nevertheless obtain papers to reach Spain, which was neutral, and via Spain or Portugal, they could move on to Latin America. However, Switzerland had been overwhelmed with refugees, and the Swiss government was refusing to grant prominent fascists safe passage, not even if they promised to move on to other countries right away, not even if the RSI upped the bribe of a hundred tons of rice monthly it had been paying the Swiss government since September 1944 to facilitate the escape from Italy.[20]

The German high command preferred that the high functionaries of the party and government—indeed, all fascists of a certain notoriety, which would have included Teruzzi—move to Germany in case of retreat. After the incident at Lenno—when antifascist partisans tried to kidnap and hold as hostage the family of the RSI minister of the interior Buffarini-Guidi—Plenipotentiary Rahn and SS general Wolf urged families to go to Zürs, one of the areas that, together with the shores of Lake Constance, had been designated for their welcome. The Alpine resort was reputed by the prewar European aristocracy, especially the British, to have the best skiing in the world.

Since the Arlberg Pass was closed from November to May by snowdrifts, they arrived by sleds, leaving from the train station at Langen, guided by drivers who before the war had used horses, tugging on their bridles to get up through the fresh snow, and now, due to the shortage of animals, were using Russian and Yugoslav prisoners of war. Zürs itself had little except for ten fine old hotels, the post office, and the tiny church at Lech. Fortunately, the Nazi Gauleiter of Innsbruck, together with Baron von Reichter, did the honors. They set up group tutoring for the children and entertained the bored suntanned wives, who were joined by their husbands at Christmastime. By December, almost all the families of government members had transferred there. Other prominent fascists, like Farinacci, who visited with his wife and two children, came as well. The ambassador, Giovanni Capasso Torre di Caprera, the RSI Foreign Ministry's liaison to the diplomatic corps, characterized it as "an elegant concentration camp for the top dogs."[21]

Zürs was no place for the hierarch once famous for his Roman penthouse and seaside fancy dress parties and infamous for his African orgies, even if he hadn't had to present himself with his Jewish companion. Teruzzi had judged, once they had to leave the villa at Malcesine, which may have been as early as July 1944, that the safest place was Gargnano itself, the little town on Lake Garda's southwestern shore where Mussolini had been installed with his family and entourage. The search for Jews had practically ceased by then, and the Nazis' Final Solution specialist Bosshammer had left Italy to serve elsewhere. SS and Italian special forces were on hand to protect Mussolini and his family, and the town was secure from partisan attacks. The school year was opening regularly in September, so Mariceli, who was now going on six, could start first grade.

Life had become stop gap now. Conceivably, Teruzzi thought about making a sneak visit to his beloved Castiglioncello. The town had been spared so far from being targeted by the Americans. But gasoline was rationed. It would be foolhardy to travel 350 or so kilometers over shellpocked and bombed-out roads. And for what? The Pizzi family had secured the most valuable furnishings in an underground storage area, sealing it up with a cement wall.

This thought had been foreclosed once and for all in mid-October 1944, when the US Fifth Army's Forty-Seventh Bombardment Group out of Fresno, California, after supporting the Allied landing at Salerno in September 1943 and flying raids over France, occupied the nearby military airfield at Rosignano. For the next several months, they bivouacked at Villa Celestina. Snapshots by the operations officer, Captain Charles F. Klauber, show his boys taking good care of the place in the intervals between bombing runs up and down the Po valley, leaning back on the modernist sofas with their long legs stretched out on the patterned marble floors.[22]

23

A BEARDED CORPSE

Lonely upon the earth, at war with cruel fate.

—MANRICO, in Verdi's *Il Trovatore*, Act 1, Scene 1

Once Rome was liberated by the Allied troops in June 1944, the stage was set for purging Italy of the fascist regime and punishing the people who had collaborated with it. The final reckoning would have to wait until the liberation of northern Italy. With the Allies' advance stalled before the German defense along the Gothic Line, stretching between Pisa and Rimini, that would only come about in the spring of 1945, when the Allies retook the offensive to break through, cross the Po River, and reach Milan.

In the meantime, the antifascist resistance and the Allied armies joined forces to channel the inevitable desire to settle scores into legal processes. It is true that this was an uneasy coalition. For many antifascists, the struggle against totalitarianism called for a total effort of political and moral reconstruction: wholesale purges, together with armed uprisings and a revolution. Getting rid of the fascist ruling class root and branch, which included the monarchy, big business, and the high military, was indispensable to building the new Italy. For the Allied armies, on the other hand, along with moderate and conservative forces and the established elites, the goal was to install as conservative a liberal-constitutional government as possible, one capable of forestalling the threat of a communist revolution. That called for limiting the purges to the most egregious personnel of the past regime and keeping the realms of finance, industry, and government administration substantially intact.

It was the push for total reconstruction that had carried the day when Rome was liberated from the Germans in June 1944. With the backing of the Socialists, the Communists, the Action Party, and others, Ivanoe

Bonomi, Badoglio's successor, resolved to initiate a deep purge. On July 27, the government issued Decree Law 159 establishing the Italian High Commission for Sanctions against Fascism. This created the government machinery to investigate and prosecute "members of the fascist government and the hierarchs guilty of having brought about the suppression of constitutional guarantees, destroyed popular liberties, created the fascist regime, compromised and betrayed the destiny of the nation and brought it to the current catastrophe," and to punish them with "life imprisonment and, in cases of graver responsibility, with death."[1]

On December 18, 1944, the commissioner designated for the "prosecution of fascist crimes," the Sardinian jurist Mario Berlinguer, issued a warrant for Teruzzi's arrest under article 2, which prosecuted "salient acts" to keep the regime in power, as vice secretary of the National Fascist Party, undersecretary at the Interior Ministry, commander in chief of the Blackshirts, and undersecretary and minister of Italian Africa. Teruzzi was also wanted under article 3, which prosecuted the overthrow of constitutional guarantees, as organizer of the fascist squads carrying out acts of violence and devastation, for promoting and directing the insurrection of October 28, 1922, and for the coup d'état of January 3, 1925.

Though the scope of the charges seemed large, their range made sense. The high commissioner, who was made equal in rank to the country's top magistrates, had a subcommission with a wide mandate to prosecute the whole range of crimes, from political crimes to illegal profiteering. For the moment, the goal, according to High Commissioner Carlo Sforza, was to "hit high and forgive low."[2]

The warrant for Teruzzi's arrest came with an addendum stating that he had specifically contributed to the "imperialist politics [that had] brought the country to the present catastrophe." Since his present position was unknown, for the moment he would not be charged under article 5 for the current, most heinous crime, treason, for collaborating with the "pseudo government of the Social Republic and relations with the German invader."[3]

On August 29, 1944, the police commissioner of Rome provided the high commissioner with a report on Teruzzi that characterized him as "the typical embodiment of fascist violence" and "the hierarch, perhaps more than every other, who symbolizes violence, criminality and fascist greed." It went on: since 1920, he had been "instinctively attracted" to the fascist movement; "his natural tendency to intimidation and bullying, in

which he excelled, showed once he took command of Milanese squads,"
in his "human insensibility," his "callousness and ferocious demeanor."
For this reason, Mussolini had promoted him to higher and higher positions, to make him one of the leading people responsible for the Fascist
Revolution. For the whole period of fascist domination, he had remained
in the foremost ranks, "never overlooking any occasion to take personal
advantage of every economic opportunity, succeeding thereby in accumulating truly fabulous wealth."[4]

The motivations of Pietro Morazzini, the police commissioner and author of this hyperbole, have to be suspect. He himself was an unsavory
character, who, as police commissioner for the Royal House, had been
responsible for arresting Mussolini outside of the king's villa before
going to work for Prime Minister Badoglio. As the Allies occupied Rome
in June 1944, many onetime collaborators changed their stripes. Settling
scores, if that was what it was, couldn't wait. Teruzzi thus stood accused of
being among the most abhorrent criminals of the fascist regime—even
before December 11, 1944, when he was tried in absentia through the regular criminal court system for his assault on Judge Viola.

The trial opened in Rome, not surprisingly, to a courtroom jammed
with spectators and reporters. It was, as it turned out, the very first trial of
a major fascist hierarch on a felony charge. The crowd packed in not only
to hear accounts of the truckloads of treasure Teruzzi had allegedly
brought back from his colonial trip—which must have accounted for his
1.4 kilograms of gold and 160 of silver—but also "his disgusting behavior."
He had burst into the magistrate's office "like a hooligan" with three ac-
complices at his side. He had blamed Badoglio for arranging the theft to
justify taking the law into his hands. He had shouted, "Cut the chitchat, I
have a grenade here, let's call the SS!" And his onetime flunky, friend,
and neighbor, Liccio, who had turned state's witness, volunteered that he
had been ready to use it, had not Judge Viola acted with such calm. After
the prosecutor had signed a release and the gang had tramped out, Teruzzi
had been overhead saying, "See, Bianchi, this is the way to get things
done, like in 1920."[5] This last line was perhaps too perfect to be true.

Weighing the verdict, the judge absolved Teruzzi for any crimes arising
from the property that had been confiscated from him: no proof had been
gathered that it had been illegally acquired. Weighing the sentence, he
considered the crimes in themselves, but especially the aggravating circumstances. Teruzzi had taken advantage of the breakdown of law and

order, and of his power as an ex-hierarch to hatch the plan. In other words, he had committed a criminal act that was conceived as an expression of the fascist order, even though that order had legally ceased to exist, and the judge wanted to reflect these considerations by meting out a harsh sentence. For the first crime, Teruzzi was condemned to serve four years and two months; for the second, two years and one month. Six years and three months altogether: there would be no amnesty.[6]

Around the time of the trial in December 1944, Teruzzi had become a regular visitor to Milan. He took a room at the Hotel Plaza near his old haunts, such as they still existed.[7] Over the previous year, air bombardments had shattered the glass-and-iron arcade of the Galleria, exposing La Scala's stage to the open sky, and knocked off the Duomo's spires, scattering the cathedral square with the heads and hands of bomb-mutilated saints, roof tiles, and marble shards. The Cova had taken a direct hit, and all the other cafés—Savini's, Biffi's, Milani's—were closed. The important venues in the neighborhood had been taken over by the Germans. The Hotel Regina-Rebecchino where Lilliana had once resided had become the Gestapo headquarters, and the Hotel Principe di Savoia, the German consulate.

Milan had now emerged as the most prosperous city in the whole Nazi-Fascist new order: its war industries were churning out matériel and arms for the Reich's war effort and textiles and other consumer goods for German civilians. The city's diligent *federale* Vincenzo Costa regularly sent convoys of municipal trucks as far away as Forlì, in the Po delta, to haul back meat, grain, and vegetables to feed the city's residents. The black market prospered, thanks to Milan's proximity to the long border with Switzerland, the readily bribable competing security forces, and the large number of people with lots of currency who saw no point to saving it. With money or barter, everything was available, from Scotch whisky and champagne, fine wines and imported liquors, American cigarettes and French perfumes to luxury cars whose original owners couldn't afford the bribes to obtain gasoline coupons, and every kind of sex. Northern European cities were starving that winter, but Rudolf Rahn, Hitler's plenipotentiary to Italy, prided himself on the fact that the bomb-scarred, refugee-filled land under his watch was the "paradise of Europe."[8]

Attilio Teruzzi had business to do in Milan. He had come up north with 400,000 lire in his bank account, plus the 100,000 lire in savings his sister had bequeathed to his daughter. He had no regular salary anymore, as he complained whenever he went by the office of Francesco Maria Barracu, the undersecretary at the Council of Ministers, the only official who knew what was happening. He hadn't been paid the last installment of his salary as president of CITAO, and nobody would tell him when he would get his military pension or what it would be worth, as the lira continued to devalue.[9] For Teruzzi, like the petty bourgeois of Italy during every war, ruinous inflation was just around the corner.

True, he had retrieved from the prosecutor's office in Rome the seemingly rich property the police had confiscated from him in August 1943. But what really did it add up to—the eight boxes containing precious objects for a total weight of 352 pounds of silver and a measly 3.09 pounds of gold? "Teruzzi's treasure," I've concluded, was largely made up of the roomful of dowry gifts from his wedding. At Lilliana's decision, after she had taken a few items of sentimental value, they had never been properly divided. He had kept them all that time, dutifully.

The only sensible thing to be done now was to have Maestro Serafin's silver goblets melted down or to sell the monstrous tea samovar for its metal content—the one Lilliana believed was 22-karat gold. He could also sell the set of gaudy silver trays from his staff at the interior ministry and the scores of other bibelots that Lilliana had estimated in June 1926 to be worth $100,000. There was no longer room to be sentimental about D'Annunzio's rose-enameled box, or Mussolini's coffer with the flag in ruby, diamond, and emerald chips, or Toscanini's silver gewgaw. Like everyone else, Teruzzi was looking for not just liquidity but portability: jewelry and gold watches, the small cache of gold doubloons Yvette's family had left her, Swiss francs. Some of his possessions, like the Ottoman carpets, he could offer as barter, though the market must have been glutted with such items. Automobiles had become cheap because there was no fuel. He was able to purchase a Lancia and had the connections he needed to get gas rations.

As for the rest, he still had his reputation as a fixer and still had many friends and contacts. They were useful when he needed to pawn his stuff, not that the gold plate, silver, or jewels extracted from the dowry bibelots got him very much. They were useful to give a hand to his second cousins, the Sozzi family, to obtain licenses to sell their men's socks, and to help his longtime crony, Mario Marigo, evade restrictions on fuel to keep his contracting business flourishing. They were useful when he passed by Gestapo headquarters, not as a spy or informer to be sure, but to keep his hand in play, to meet new lady friends, learn who was around, and find out what sort of information interested the Germans.

His contacts were especially useful when it came to making the acquaintance of the thirty-three-year-old German cultural consul, the cultivated, soigné, chatty Hans-Otto Meissner. The son of the former president of the Reich's Chancellor's Office, formerly the Reich's cultural consul in Tokyo, Meissner was the perfect Nazi for the Milanese elite—and for Teruzzi, too, who had at one time aspired to be part of it.

Through Meissner, Teruzzi made a new friend, a "real English gentleman," as Clara Petacci, an Anglophile, described him after he visited Gargnano to meet the Duce: John Amery, "Milord," as the Italians called him, Churchill's secretary of state for India, Leo Amery's renegade son. His Jewish father's worst nightmare, the adolescent, whom the Harrow headmaster had declared "the most difficult student ever," he had left London at twenty-three to volunteer on the Falangists' side in the Spanish Civil War and, after a fling with French fascists, had presented himself at Berlin to do radio propaganda against the British. Amery had so appalled his German keepers with his pregnant French girlfriend, lapdog (Polly), and weird behavior that they had foisted him off on the cultural consul Meissner and the Italians. When Teruzzi met Amery, he was being employed to transmit radio broadcasts to English speakers and make propaganda speeches to worker assemblies inside the big factories around Milan. His stock speech was earnestly populist: "Churchill and his clique" in no way represented the unanimity of opinion in Great Britain—only look at the 100,000-plus dissenters in British prisons. What bound together the so-called champions of democracy, Churchill and Roosevelt with "the Czar of Russia" and his "bestial Asiatic theory of communism"? It was "obvious: all of them hoped to exploit the labor and laborers of Europe."[10]

For Teruzzi, this made sense. And the young Amery appears to have found in him a trustworthy adult who shared his heartfelt views of the British—their avarice, cruelty to colonial subjects, and duplicity. Teruzzi may also have nurtured the hopeless thought that Amery, through his family connections in London, could be of service to the Duce to arrange favorable terms of surrender.

In December 1944, Mussolini made a surprise visit to Milan, the city that had once again, begrudgingly, become the capital of Italian fascism. What euphoria he excited as he addressed the huge crowd packed into the

Lyric Theater! After speaking and passing in review of the republican guards, fascist women's auxiliaries, and so on, he made a grand tour around the city by motorcade, cheered by ecstatic throngs.

In his speech, Mussolini spoke of the new weapons that, once deployed, would reestablish the balance of power between the Allies and the Axis, after which Hitler would seize the military initiative. The Germans had just recently bombed London with the first V1 and V2 rockets, and the sense that Hitler would prevail had been reinforced two days later with news of the German breakthrough in the Ardennes forest, blocking the Allied advance through Belgium. Local journalists turned into amateur nuclear physicists to write authoritatively about heavy water and bombarding atoms with uranium while the deranged fascist priest Father Eusebio welcomed Hitler's nuclear apocalypse from the pulpit. He had Hitler's word, the Duce confided to visitors: Germany would never capitulate. God might not pardon Hitler, but the last five minutes of the war would be decisive.[11] By early April, true believers had ample new material to nurture new delusions.

Teruzzi later admitted that he had believed in Hitler's secret weapon. He had also started to admire the military valor of well-known partisan chiefs.[12] Like other loyalists of the final hour, he was waiting for the Duce to make some kind of serious decision in the event of a defeat, to set up a government in exile, to select men capable of carrying on the cause if everything collapsed, to save himself.

But Mussolini always changed the topic. When the head of police proposed a project, meticulously studied in detail, to have him escape by submarine to Patagonia or Japan, he listened and then murmured, "[Jules] Verne." When he heard about generals in exile, he muttered, "Garibaldi." His only passion was for last stands, to turn Milan into an Alcatraz, like in the films, to fight to the death from cell to cell, or like Stalingrad, from house to house, until the whole city was an inferno. In time, the favorite plot was to retreat to the Valtellina in the Alpine mountains behind Como to continue war alongside the Germans, who would have withdrawn to Bavaria, with eventual relief coming from the secret weapon and from the inevitable conflict that would arise between the Anglo-Americans and the Russians once the two armies came into contact in Berlin.[13]

Mussolini wanted to live—that was for sure—to defend his record of two decades, to demonstrate the treachery of the Germans, even if he still had to profess his faith in them. He wanted to be introduced to the partisan forces, to know whether there was any way to reach an agreement, to join forces, anything not to turn his Italy over to the monarchy and Badoglio. Teruzzi, too, started to appreciate their military feats.

At the end of March, as the Allied forces prepared to cross the Po River, Marshal Graziani called for a general mobilization, and Teruzzi, who had been in the army reserves since 1938, stepped up to go back on active duty. Not that Marshal Graziani needed any more generals. He had barely mustered four divisions among the Italians in Germany, and many of them, as soon as they had been trained and brought back to Italy, deserted. But Teruzzi had been told by cabinet undersecretary Barracu, the last time he had inquired about his pension, that if he went back on active duty, it would start to be paid out.[14]

First things first: he had to go to the Unione Militare in Milan to be fitted for a new uniform. In the meantime, the Republican army had redesigned all the uniforms, styling them with wider lapels, high stiff collars, and vermilion general stars, to distance them from the king's army and bring them closer to the Wehrmacht's. Not even the leather gun belt of his uniform had been delivered by the time the Allies, after breaking through the German defenses, were pushing toward Milan. He hadn't shirked active duty; it was simply too late to report.

By the third week of April 1945, the waiting was over. The Soviets had entered Vienna. On April 16, Mussolini's Council of Ministers held its last meeting in Gargnano, and by April 19, he had overridden the Germans and installed himself at the Palace of the Prefecture of Milan at Via Monforte, under the eye of his SS guard. Although time was of the essence, Mussolini still had not made a decision about what to do. Republican loyalists were flowing into the city from all over Italy, many from the zones liberated by the swelling resistance movement; 12,000 troops stood at the ready, and 3,600 Germans were at the command of the Wehrmacht, alongside perhaps 10,000 Black Brigades, squads, irregular forces, and auxiliaries. Teruzzi arrived in Milan along with all the others. And, unlike Mussolini, who had sent his family ahead of him to Como, he had his family, Yvette and Mariceli, with him.

The choice had now come down to basically two alternatives. One was to break out, head for Como and, from there, go either northeast to the Valtellina for the last showdown, backed by party secretary Pavolini's force of 10,000, or northwest to the Alps to find a way to flee into Switzerland. The other choice was to surrender to the Allies, which had begun to look more and more improbable. The National Committee of Liberation of Northern Italy (CLNAI), which united the Italian antifascist forces fighting the German occupation in Lombardy and elsewhere, had ordered the insurrection to begin on April 25, signaled by a general strike. Their goal was to present the Allies as they entered Milan with the fait accompli: Italy, or at least this part of it, had overthrown Nazi-Fascism, driven out the Germans, and liberated itself.

On April 25, as the hours passed, Mussolini was presented with one last opportunity to negotiate a surrender. Cardinal Schuster, like a great medieval pope, offered to mediate. He had his black limousine pick up Mussolini and, with an escort of tanks and armored cars, bring him to the chancellery. After offering him a glass of rose petal liqueur and cookies, he counseled him "to expect a life of expiation in prison or in exile" and asked him whether he knew the story of Saint Benedict, who, upon receiving Totila, king of the Ostrogoths, at the Abbey of Montecassino, had called him to mend his cruel ways and urged on him a book of his to "bring him comfort in the sad days that stood on the horizon."[15]

Whether the cardinal could have brokered Mussolini's surrender is unclear. Upon hearing from an observer at the meeting that the German forces on Italian soil had arranged to surrender, Mussolini flew into a rage at their betrayal and rushed back to the prefecture. The walls were closing in. The CLNAI leadership had signed the decree sentencing "members of the fascist government and the hierarchs of fascism who had contributed to the suppression of constitutional guarantees, destroyed the people's liberties, created the fascist regime, compromised and betrayed the fortunes of the nation and conducted it to the present catastrophe" to be punished with the death penalty or, in less grave cases, by life in prison.

That evening, as the partisans occupied the center of the city, Mussolini and the top leadership fled north to Como in an armed convoy of fascist militia, intermixed with German troops. At Como, the fascist command decided the best chance of saving the Duce was to disguise him in the uniform of a German soldier in a German army convoy retreating toward the Swiss border. Near the village of Dongo, partisans stopped the convoy, recognized who he was, arrested him and brought him as a prisoner at a nearby farmhouse, where he was joined by Clara Petacci. On April 28, executioners under orders from the CLNAI arrived and shot them both. And so the purge began: over the next weeks, hundreds, maybe thousands, of fascists of all ranks were killed in skirmishes, reprisals, and summary executions.

The first announcement of Mussolini's death came on Sunday, April 29, when Radio Milan, updating listeners about the progress of the liberation, announced that Mussolini and eighteen others had been captured and summarily executed at the command of the CLNAI at Dongo. Their bodies had been trucked to Milan, where they had been dumped in a pile in the middle of Piazzale Loreto.

Since August 10 of the previous year, the square had become a ghastly reminder of the brutality of Nazi-Fascist rule. In retaliation for a partisan attack after they had taken command of the city, the Italians, obeying German commands, had randomly picked out fifteen inmates from the San Vittore prison, trucked them over the square, unloaded them, told them to run, and shot them as they scattered. Afterward, they had piled up the bodies and left them to rot by the Esso gas station. Piazzale Loreto was a major transport hub, and thousands of Milanese had witnessed the ghastly spectacle on their way to work or to shop, or when they came by to pay their respects.

By midday that Sunday, a huge crowd had gathered in the square to get a glimpse of the grotesquely swollen, blood-splotched corpses. When the security forces tried to press back the crowd by ordering the fire brigades to attach water hoses to the hydrants, somebody took the initiative to hoist the corpses up onto the rafters over the gas pumps—the best-known ones, anyway: Mussolini, Claretta Petacci, and then Pavolini.

This activity paused as shouts to move aside caused the crowd to pull back and an armored car arrived, its siren ringing, to drop off a group of partisans with a pale, unshaven prisoner in a sweat suit. It was Achille Starace. After fierce debates among the execution squad about whether he should be shot in the back or face, he shouted, "Get it over with!" He was shoved face up against the wall, shot down, his clothing stripped off, and his body slung up alongside the others. They then proceeded to hoist up two other bodies: One belonged to Paolo Zerbino, who was not a household name and nobody really recognized. But when they saw the other one, the corpse with the beard, the crowd started to shout, "Teruzzi, Teruzzi!" As the body was tied in place, somebody clambered up on top of the beam to scribble his name in grease paint, with a slash through the double ZZ to make it look like a swastika. Toward noon, Cardinal Schuster appealed to the National Committee of Liberation to put an end to the awful scene. Around quarter to two, after the bodies were taken down and removed to the city morgue, the crowd dispersed.[16]

By seven thirty the next morning, city coroners, surrounded by a crowd of journalists, Allied officials, and political authorities, undertook the autopsies, starting with the body of Mussolini. At the end of the day, only one body remained unidentified. The corpse with the famous beard was not in fact Teruzzi's. Some said the body belonged to Quinto Navarra, Mussolini's valet; others, to the German translator in Mussolini's convoy. An "innocent jeweler," a watchmaker, was another hypothesis; somebody told me it was his high school Latin teacher, and still others believed it was a well-known antifascist who had gotten caught up in the fury of the mob and been lynched.

Sometimes there was only one lynching. Other times three or four, or as many as seven "Teruzzis" were lynched at the time of the liberation. People spoke of them to denounce the barbarity of the crowd incited by communists, the foolishness of wearing a big beard in the midst of mayhem, and the strange hand of fate, which had innocents delivered to death and the guilty reprieved. They were mentioned to evoke the terror of exacting vengeance from the masked fascist bugaboo or the horrible denouement of a two-decades-long melodrama.

Teruzzi had turned into a bearded corpse, and he wasn't even dead. At the end of May, the unnamed body was just one of hundreds lying at the morgue waiting to be identified, collected, and buried.[17]

24

I SUFFER AND I WAIT

My conscience is my best defense.

—ATTILIO TERUZZI, May 1945

W hat, then, had happened to the real Attilio Teruzzi? His decision to
leave Milan was as rushed as Mussolini's. But he hadn't left with
the Duce's convoy, fortunately. He had used his old battle savvy and connections to muster his own convoy, with guard troops from the Muti Brigade. Militia men were mounted in armored trucks; Teruzzi was in his
Lancia with his driver, Yvette, and Mariceli; and John Amery—dressed in
his Falangist uniform—and his wife were in another car, also a Lancia,
with a Fiat M 13/40 tank leading the way.

Moving out on to the autostrada toward Como, Teruzzi was in his own
territory. He had come this way countless times, as his father's homeland,
the Brianza, lay to the right, and his mother's to the left. The socialist
towns he had terrorized in 1921 were just a few kilometers away. His onetime parliamentary district, Como-Lecco, at this pace, lay scarcely an
hour north. The whole area had now fallen under the control of the partisans, who, twenty-four hours into the insurrection, had begun to mount
roadblocks on all the highways and secondary roads to close off the escape
routes to Switzerland. The trick was to fly a white flag from the tank, as if
the convoy had surrendered in effect and was retreating north, and, if that
didn't work, get ready for a shootout. The convoy had barely gone fifteen
miles from Milan when they saw partisans standing on the highway over-
pass between Uboldo and Saronno preparing an ambush.

To everybody's surprise, the partisans held their fire. They represented
two different brigades, headquartered at the nearby Isotta Fraschini machine works. The larger of the two groups, maybe ten men, was composed
of communists belonging to the 183rd Garibaldi Brigade. They were eager

to carry out the orders to try and execute high-placed Nazi-Fascists on the spot, whereas the socialists of the 208th Matteotti Brigade, numbering maybe six or seven, wanted to wait and see on the matter of executions. Both were badly armed. Some had never used their guns except to hunt. Others later said that the sight of the woman at the front of the convoy waving a white flag tricked them into holding their fire.

All that changed when, at the sight of the militia men popping out from the trucks, they realized they had caught a big shot—a German general or a high fascist hierarch, maybe the Duce himself. As partisans shouted about what to do, one of the fascists accidentally exploded a grenade, tearing the treads off the tank and causing it to stall in the middle of the road, blocking the convoy as it tried to move out. The partisans frantically motioned to one another to start shooting, only to hold their fire as Father Benetti, the archpriest of Saronno, pulled up alongside the convoy.

His arrival became the pretext for a high-stakes shouting match. Whether the priest appealed to Christian pieties or plain common sense, telling the partisans that in the firefight they were just as likely to be killed as to kill, he managed to arrange a truce. The partisans would hold their fire, so the convoy could maneuver around the tank and proceed northward. The fascists applauded and one "big shot"—probably Teruzzi—effusively congratulated the priest. Not that anybody was converted: as it moved out, somebody in the convoy reportedly shouted: "It's you priests' fault that you don't know how to keep calm among the people." And Father Benetti shouted back, "Well, if you couldn't do it by force of arms . . ." As the convoy picked up speed, the partisans ran along the fields to overtake it. Once the roadway rose several yards above the ground, and the fascist militia had the partisans in their sights, they opened fire with machine guns and automatic weapons, killing several.[1]

Taking no more chances, Teruzzi had his driver exit at the next turnoff. They were now on the old road to Varese, the one he had always taken to Solbiate Comasco, his mother's village. Only a local could know that this road, with its various twists and turns, might eventually get him to the Swiss border. Later, he said he was looking for a hideaway in the countryside, where he could wait until he found a way to surrender to Allied troops who would treat him like a prisoner of war. As they reached the village of Cislago, a couple of miles along the Varese road, five partisans under the command of a local man, Santino Villa, waved the lone automobile to a halt.

Nobody recognized the elderly gray-bearded gentleman with the frightened woman and stony-faced child. It was not until they checked Yvette's handbag and found it full of jewelry, rings, cigarette cases, and what not that they, too, decided he was a big shot. It was late in the day by the time they brought him to the local liberation committee headquarters at Saronno and identified him. Directives were arriving to mitigate the CLNAI order to execute the hierarchs on the spot, and the carabinieri had arrived from the local command post to conduct the arrest. On April 29, the communist partisan commander Oliva had the satisfaction of taking Teruzzi into custody, escorting him to Milan, and confining him at the San Vittore prison to await trial.

The special assize tribunals set up in newly liberated upper Italy to prosecute the crimes of the regime hoped to work as briskly and with the same finality as the British—or the American—system of justice. Notwithstanding the crowds gathering around the prisons screaming, "Death to the fascists!" and the fistfights that broke out as partisans were released from San Vittore and the cells filled up with fascists, enough of a judicial structure had been set in place by May 1, 1945, for a magistrate appointed by the CLNAI to interrogate Teruzzi in his cell at 7:40 A.M. He read him the charges: that he had collaborated with the German enemy, organized the coup against the liberal state, and occupied positions of major significance to sustain the fascist regime in power. Not only did Teruzzi deny these charges, as a military man he expressed "a very strong wish to be considered a prisoner of war and be handed over to the Allies rather than to be held and tried by the CLNAI."[2] When the journalist from the socialist newspaper Avanti! interviewed him a few days later, he found Teruzzi in a spick-and-span cell, a peacock in well-pressed gabardine pants, a white summer-weight shirt, his upper cheeks smooth-shaven, his beard impeccably groomed.[3]

Yvette had done her best. Upon Teruzzi's capture, she had been driven back to Milan with her daughter, and they had found their way to the giant Catholic poorhouse-asylum founded by Father Orione at Cottolengo. Originally established as a home for the insane, since 1943, it had offered asylum to Jews and antifascists. With the liberation, it had opened its doors to a new clientele, the families of fascists—Mussolini's sister Edvige and her children had also found refuge there.

Mariceli spent her days observing the antics of the inmates; one, she told her granddaughters, chased her around the table with a knife in his hand. Yvette filled her time outside trying to contact Teruzzi's friends, who, unsurprisingly, had made themselves scarce. She collected information about his rights as a prisoner and sought to access the various bankbooks, each holding small amounts of savings, that she needed for them to survive.

Her evenings were spent composing cogent appeals to the highest authorities, which went unanswered. The one sent on May 5 was addressed to Cardinal Schuster himself. She pleaded with him to intervene so that Teruzzi would be treated as a prisoner of war under the terms of the Hague Conventions, just as Marshal Graziani had been after he was picked up by the American military at Como (and General Ruggero Bonomi as well). Teruzzi was a three-star general, she reminded the cardinal, who had fought in five wars and been decorated thirteen times. "I pray you, do it, as he is an honest man, he has done the right thing whenever he could, for the sake of the child." Failing that, given that he was suffering from asthma, cardiac problems, and a fractured arm, he needed to be placed in the prison infirmary.[4] Meanwhile, she made sure he was provided with fresh clothes, food packages, and a regular barber.

The journalists who interviewed him found him in fine shape psychologically as well as physically. Ever the hardened fascist, when asked how he was doing, he responded with barracks jargon: "Subisco e aspetto" ("I suffer and I wait"). He spoke volubly, whether ingenuously or disingenuously they couldn't quite tell. Yes, he had been a Repubblichino, but he had held no government positions. "My conscience is my best defense," he said. "If they want to prove I am an accomplice in twenty-five years of the regime, they will have to convict lots of other Italians as well. In effect, I am only responsible for a military action [the March on Rome] and as for Africa, I did everything to raise its level. I have always been far from the corridors [of power]." He played with his beard and repeated, "My conscience is at rest."[5]

The journalists scoffed at his lies. But Teruzzi appeared to believe what he was saying.

Before the liberation, there had been endless speculation about the criminal acts for which Attilio Teruzzi should be held accountable. Only one of these was clear: his attack on the Roman magistrate Gabriele Viola, in September 1943. That was one of the rare cases, if not the only one, of a big fascist caught, in flagrante, acting like a fascist and being tried and convicted accordingly. For the rest, there was a great gap, widened by the moral and legal chaos of the regime itself, between the legal and institutional means of bringing him to justice and the calls for vengeance that soon fixated on Teruzzi as one of the regime's three or four worst malefactors.[6]

This fixation was less a reflection of specific misdeeds than of Teruzzi's exceptional conspicuousness as minister of Italian Africa and his ubiquity in all twenty years of Mussolini's dictatorship. His carefully groomed public image as the great hierarch doing his duty to the Duce and the nation now appeared to conceal a cesspool of nefariousness that denunciation alone would never flush clean. This inchoate revulsion fed itself, it seemed, off the same Manichean passions that the fascist movement had played on since its inception, personalizing and dividing the world between good and evil, saviors and enemies.

Short of being channeled into a clear-eyed project, such revulsion could lead normally sober citizens to scream, "Teruzzi! Teruzzi!" at the sight of a suspicious-looking bearded man and lynch him, as happened in Milan in April 1945. These same people, not indifferent to the Church's plea to turn the other cheek or to their own feelings of complicity with a world that had been theirs for twenty years, sometimes said: "Let bygones be bygones." Or, as in the hardnosed Neapolitan axiom, "Chi ha avuto ha avuto, chi ha dato ha dato, scurdammece o passato," which we might translate as: "Who got, got, who gave, gave—the past is past, let's forget about it."

This dense moral fog began to lift on April 22, 1945, when the Bonomi government set up special assize courts to try collaborators province by province. The German forces had barely capitulated on April 29 before the CLNAI appointed the prosecutors and presiding judges for Milan. It also provided for the selection of popular jurors, by lottery, from lists drawn up from among "honorable men" (since women had not yet been granted the right to perform civic duties). These four-man juries would be sworn in to "examine with diligence and serenity, evidence and reasoning, prosecution and defense, form their own judgments with rectitude and impartiality, without animus or favor, to yield the judgment society awaits, a sincere and true affirmation of truth and popular justice."[7]

By May 15, the Milanese tribunal had set up its docket: Teruzzi would be the first great hierarch to be brought to trial. Given the alternative at the time, which was summary execution, the lot of thousands of people from late April into the summer months—or, conceivably, lynching the fascists, as the crowds milling around San Vittore kept threatening to do— this outcome seemed very good luck indeed.[8]

Luigi Marantonio was the presiding judge. Roman-born, in service since 1933—meaning he had made his career under the fascist regime— Marantonio was highly esteemed and known for his decorum and legal acumen. His courtroom was the largest of the fifty in the architect Piacen- tini's immense, recently completed Palace of Justice. Equivalent in size to Piazza Duomo, the building was late fascism's supreme accomplishment. He had taken his place at the bench, a walnut throne under the giant mo- saic of Lady Justice shown with her scales and blindfold—the fasci and lictors had only recently been gouged out of the wall. The prisoners' dock was a veranda closed by rosewood slats rather than the usual iron-barred tiger's cage. Teruzzi was only the fifth defendant before the newly consti- tuted court, which would try another 368 cases before the end of the year.[9]

On May 24, after only one day, the court was already a half day behind schedule. After rushing through the small fry—a woman spy; a national militia member; a collaborator with the Wehrmacht who had conducted reprisals, arrested Jews, and ratted on partisans; and a militia guard bully— the court tried the first well-known figure of the regime. This defendant, the so-called Socrates of the Social Republic, was eighty-six-year-old Vit- torio Rolandi Ricci, the renowned Ligurian jurist, former liberal party senator, and onetime ambassador to Washington. He had been indicted for "ideological collaboration" with the German invader for offering him- self to Mussolini to draw up a model constitution for the Republic of Salò. However much the judge admonished him to cut short his self-justifications and repartee, and his lawyer to curb his eloquence, the vivacious old man, the father of two sons killed during the war, kept on talking, even after being sentenced to a fifteen-year term, at which point he thanked the judge "for wishing me a long life."[10]

"Two rogues at the dock": that was L'Unità, the Italian Communist Party paper's description of Rolandi Ricci and Teruzzi as they stood side by side that morning. In reality, Rolandi Ricci looked like the stately liberal dip- lomat he had once been, and Teruzzi, frosty-haired and well turned out in his dark green jacket, khaki-colored gabardine pants, and tieless white shirt, could easily have passed as a well-off Milanese pensioner at a Sunday get-together—except when his blue eyes bugged out at the shouts of "Death! death! death!" coming from the public gallery.

Of the three counts against him, the prosecution focused on the last and gravest and least incontrovertible charge, namely, the betrayal of the nation by collaborating with the German invader. Not only had Teruzzi sworn allegiance to the RSI, to which he admitted, he could be presumed to have exercised influence, based on his reputation, and he had been called up as a general at the orders of Marshal Graziani. For the first two charges—making the coup and sustaining the regime in power—there was enough documentation that he had played a meaningful role, simply given the number and range of positions he had occupied in the party, militia, and government and the fact that he had been a leading figure during the March on Rome. But, in truth, nobody could specify exactly how power had been apportioned and wielded under the fascist regime.

Teruzzi had met his court-appointed lawyer, Edy Mugnoz, only long enough to register that he was from old Milanese stock—a reformer, now a socialist committed to preventing the spectacle of crowd justice wherever a death sentence was a foregone conclusion. Nobody would admit it publicly, but lots of Milanese had benefitted from Teruzzi's friendship and connections. Though the process stipulated that people could provide written accusations of criminal activities, the court had received only one. The note was vivid in its offer to help the court and, while the signature was illegible, sounded like it was from someone who knew the prosecutor; it urged him to interrogate Teruzzi about whether he knew a woman spy that he had introduced to the Gestapo and Repubblichini security forces and about his dealings with his relatives, the Sozzis, menswear merchants whose stocking factory, with Teruzzi's help, had made a sizeable fortune the last year of the war by flouting the regulations on pricing and rationing.[11]

Teruzzi helped himself by keeping his responses short, simple, and consistent with what he had told his interrogator at San Vittore. Until September 8, 1943, when Italy had surrendered to the Allies, he had always done his duty as a soldier of Italy, he said. For his loyalty to the nation, Italy, the traitor Badoglio had persecuted him; he had lost his homes to war and confiscation and gone north. He returned under arms in March 1945 to secure his pension. He hadn't even had time to get his new uniform, "not even to purchase a gun belt," he added, to the howls of amusement—and disbelief—of the crowd. When asked whether he had been at Marshall Graziani's orders after returning under arms he answered, "I don't believe so, since I never saw him."[12]

As for the other charges—that he had participated in the coup d'état or the March on Rome, as vice president of the PNF—in his interrogation, he had already told them he had followed orders and that he had commanded legions from Lombardy and Emilia Romagna but had not been undersecretary at the Interior Ministry at the time of the coups, either the first one in 1922 or the second in January 1925. And yes, he had been in contact with Mussolini. But as he had told his interrogators, Mussolini was "a centralizer, who decided as he wanted."[13] That was true enough.

The prosecutor asked for thirty years, only to hear the public shout out, "Too little! A *morte, a morte!*" in so unruly a way that the judge suspended proceedings for ten minutes, only to ask the defendant, when he resumed, whether he had any final comments. Teruzzi pressed his face through the slats to be seen and shouted: "I insist: after the 8th of September, I had no position of command of any sort."[14]

That simple statement helped. The jury, after deliberating for seventy minutes, found him guilty on all counts. The judge, following the advice of the prosecutor, unsure of whether Teruzzi had had "grave responsibilities" under the German occupation—and unable to identify and call to testify the eyewitnesses who had allegedly seen him in Milan in 1920–1922 with his "fascist Janissaries marching around the city beating up passersby"— sentenced him to twenty years for the first count, collaboration, fifteen years for second, the coup d'état, and fifteen years for the third, his important role in sustaining the regime.

As if one, the courtroom public screamed, "Give him death, give him death!" in disbelief that the sentence had spared "one of the principal men responsible for Italy's moral and material ruin."[15] His sentence— thirty years altogether (the second and third terms to run consecutively, the first added in)—was to run concurrently with the six years and three months he had received in Rome in December 1944. The appeals court, noticing that the lower court had overlooked it, also ordered the confiscation of all of his property.

Teruzzi had barely started to serve his sentence at San Vittore—which, made to hold 1,500, was now jammed with 3,700 prisoners—when Rome's court of assize flexed its judicial muscle to determine whether he had been properly tried on counts 2 and 3, in that he had "only" been given fifteen years for each. Simply by looking over how many bills he had presented to Parliament, how much space his wordy interventions occupied in the legislative record, and how many different positions he had held, moving between the party and the militia, civilian and military affairs, Rome and the colonies, the court found him to be a far more salient figure than portrayed at his Milan trial.

By the time Teruzzi had been flown to Rome in July, where he was imprisoned once again at Regina Coeli, and interrogated twice more, he had learned the self-exculpatory legal rhetoric of the thriving law business set up on behalf of fascist criminals. Accordingly, he had only been *a* commander at the March on Rome once the quadrumvirate was set up, not *the* commander; he didn't deny being a Milanese *squadrista*, "but he had never taken part in destruction or violence." He had been head of the Milanese action squads "but only for a few days, for once I showed I intended to give the squads the discipline they were wholly lacking, I was removed. When I was leader, not only did I not ever order violence or destruction, I tried to break the criminal impulses of my followers." His election to the position of deputy in April 1924 was in a national vote ratified before Parliament. He had always conducted himself with "a high sense of civic responsibility." If he "could have ever imagined that subsequently, retroactive laws made it illegal, I would have never been involved in politics." He had not engaged in making "imperialistic war," as all the fascist wars had been legal; and if the new justice system intended to hold people responsible for those wars, they would have to indict the king as well. In sum, he told his interrogator, "Every act of mine in government was directed entirely to the well-being of the people and the nation."[16] With no new evidence to the contrary, the prosecutors reaffirmed that the Milan court had done its work.[17]

Thirty years was tantamount to a life sentence for a sixty-three-year-old man. By then, the so-called Wind from the North demanding that revolutionary justice purge the fascist ruling class had begun to flag. After all was said and done, leaving aside the many summary executions and handful of capital verdicts for collaborating with the Germans, only one leading hierarch, Guido Buffarini-Guidi, who had been the interior minister at Salò, had been executed for his crimes after a regular trial, and that was because he had been tried in the incandescent atmosphere of

Milan in June 1945. And there was the incontrovertible proof that for the entire six hundred days of Salò, Buffarini-Guidi had collaborated with the German invaders.

How disappointing to contemporaries who, in their quest for true justice, would have wanted a full-scale accounting! And to the historian, as well, who hopes to weigh the particular nature of the wrongdoing and corruption that the fascist dictatorship facilitated, encouraged, or tolerated over the two decades it ruled Italy. Mindful of how difficult this full accounting would have been under any circumstance in 1945, much less later, it is worth pausing for a quick overview of Teruzzi's violations of existing laws.

To start with, at the time of the rise of fascism, we can count the shootouts at Seregno and Vigentino, destruction of *Avanti!*, and devastation of other socialist property. Then, there was his criminal trespassing during the coup against the city of Milan—for which he was actually indicted—the illegal requisitioning of military matériel, hijacking of trains, and occupation of public buildings during the March on Rome. True, all of these crimes, if he had been indicted, would have been amnestied under the Oviglio law just after the fascists seized power. We can add to that the electoral fraud during his campaign as deputy in 1924, the conspiracy to cover up the Matteotti murder, his responsibility as commander of troops in Cyrenaica for ordering the use of chemical weapons in violation of international law, his abuse of power in harassing Lilliana and her family, obstruction of justice in the Tarabini case, and illegal campaign contributions and payoffs at Lecco on the basis of evidence collected from a Fascist Party inquiry. Yet, still, we could include the use of public office—telephone, mails, telegrams, cars, adjutant Askaris, airplanes, ships—for personal profit, the illegal appropriation of gifts of office (elephant tusks, waterbuck horns, silver jewelry, leopard skins), zoning violations during his home renovations, conflicts of interest in the assignment of contracts, and his abuses of power in constraining the children's court judge to sign off on his illegal adoption of Mariceli and in the arrest and detention of Yvette at Lipari.

An analysis of his violations would also need to include his employment of underage prostitutes. It would necessarily raise questions of whether his application of the Race Laws to the empire was a violation of human rights and therefore covered by international law. Finally, during his last stand at Saronno, Teruzzi was accomplice to manslaughter, if not graver charges, for the shootout that killed several partisans.

As much as I sleuthed through the sources available, it was impossible to achieve a complete picture of his wrongdoing, much less find the evidence that would satisfy a court of law, much less in the face of repeated amnesties. It was second nature to Teruzzi, the impeccable quartermaster, to cover his tracks. And to obsess about his criminality, as his most acrimonious fascist accusers did, is to lose sight of the system that abetted him—and frankly, our own reaction that might judge him worse because he was a sexual libertine and a gangster in his treatment of women than because he was a mainstay of the fascist regime. In any case, people who commit the illegalities sanctioned by their times are practically impossible to be held accountable, if they are prosecuted only by their own judiciary. That is the impossible dilemma of what we now call transitional justice, formulated ad hoc as despotic regimes give way to democratic ones.

25

PENANCE

After the storm of hatred and blood, the rainbow of peace
shines on the world.

—PIUS XII, 1945

The sixteenth-century castle fortress of D'Avalos looms over the island
of Procida, massed on the sheer cliffs of the promontory 300 feet
above the water. In the past, the Bourbon kings of Naples had used this
stronghold to immure political opponents, bandits, and the criminally insane. "A center of horror encircled by beauty," as an illustrious political
prisoner-littérateur once described it.[1] In the 1880s, the Kingdom of Italy
had refurbished the fortress to serve as a modern maximum-security penitentiary. That was Attilio Teruzzi's destination at daybreak on November 19,
1945, when the police launch unloaded him in shackles, together with ten
other prisoners, at the island's lower marina.[2]

His arrival marked the end of a four-month judicial odyssey that had
started in Milan on May 24, 1945, when he had been found guilty for his
crimes under the purge laws and sentenced to thirty years in prison. Since
then, he had been transferred to the Regina Coeli prison, only to be
moved to Procida for fear, on the part of the minister of grace and justice,
that in the pandemonium of the overpacked prison, Teruzzi and other
fascist inmates would either be murdered at the hands of common criminals or, worse, be helped to escape.

For the remaining five years of his life, Teruzzi would live on the island
of Procida, spending all but the last three weeks in one cell or another inside the penitentiary. He had been brought back under the rule of law and
was now restrained by prison life. Who would this man become now that
he no longer had the props of the fascist state and his leader was dead?

394

Alessandro Sardi, the onetime undersecretary of public works, was on hand on November 19, together with the warden and prison chaplain, when Teruzzi's group trudged through the prison gates after the long trek up the mule path to Terra Murata. The baron of Rivisondoli, who had been jailed since 1944 but not yet tried, was jotting down notes for a prison memoir, his model the Risorgimento patriot Silvio Pellico's *My Prisons*—his testament of eight years of hard labor at Spielberg, the Hapsburg's dungeon fortress. As often happened, Teruzzi's body language invited comment. "Limping, hesitant, moving arduously," Sardi described him as another of the fallen heroes of the times: "the renowned beard, so long his pride and joy," no longer the "red ruff with which the good lion courted lovely damsels and wise older ladies," looked like the "wispy beard of a pensioned-off billy goat." Then the weary prisoner expressed who he really was, a coarse old soldier who had no use for his pitying glance. "His bunions hurt him," he grumbled.[3]

For Don Luigi Fasanaro, the sight of these "illustrious prisoners filing in front of him, bent over, their eyes glassy and impassive, their faces contracted," was a shock. An assistant chaplain at the time, his saintly predecessor's recent death would soon see him appointed chaplain, making him the most powerful religious figure on the island. For the first time, he saw men "who had once borne the destiny of the nation, prostrate at the feet of the Divine Prisoner of Love." Later he would reflect that "all of them had believed blindly in an ideal; for some, it took the form of the Duce, for others political ideology, for others making war. Their open despair, anguish, feeling of disorientation and alienation, [and] unrelenting despondency arose from a terrible disillusionment." This was the moment, Don Luigi said, when he rededicated his vocation to the redemption of his "brother inmates, the spiritually sick."[4]

His first act was to tap the compassion of the common prisoners for their "illustrious" brothers by having them help settle the newcomers into their barrack cells. They would be lodged on the upper floor, six to a room, near the chaplain's office, where they would make up their iron-coil cots with the wool bedding and arrange their few belongings in rusty bedside lockers. In a day or so, the new arrivals would learn the routines: the guards coming around three times a day, banging on the bars; the work in the prison gardens, workshops, and facilities. They would learn the hours of the prison library and daily Mass at the prison chapel at the

Abbey of Saint Michael Archangel. It was peaceful compared to Regina Coeli, and most political prisoners eventually adjusted to the embarrassment of having to use the toilet pot at the corner of the cell.

By the time Teruzzi's group arrived, the population of political prisoners far outstripped common criminals.[5] The four hundred political prisoners confined at Procida that winter represented an extraordinary hodgepodge, as we would expect from a regime that had been two decades in power and had seen every form of collaboration. Renato Ricci, the onetime leader of the fascist youth groups, who had headed the militia at Salò, had arrived with Teruzzi. So had two generals, Francesco Sacco and Giuseppe Conticelli. There was Guido Leto, the former chief of the secret police, and two prominent journalists, Ezio Maria Gray, the propagandist-littérateur, famous as the best orator in Italy, second only to the Duce, and Gaetano Polverelli, Mussolini's last minister of popular culture. Aldo Vidussoni, who was, at forty-one, the youngest of the group, had been the second-to-last (and shortest-tenured) secretary of the Fascist Party. Dino Gardini, former economic adviser to the Fascist Party and vice secretary, had morphed into a technocrat as president of the Minerals and Metals Institute. The group must have felt tainted by the presence of Amerigo Dumini, Matteotti's murderer: after drifting around Italian Africa for fifteen years, living off of payments for his silence, he had been captured by the Allies, only to escape and return to Florence, where, after committing more atrocities under the RSI, he had been captured once more. At Procida, he was waiting to be retried for Matteotti's murder. The twists and turns of life that had landed others there were harder to explain. And none perhaps so arduous as the path Giovanni Ansaldo, a onetime liberal socialist, had followed. In 1925, after launching the "Manifesto of Anti-Fascist Intellectuals" and being exiled to Lipari for a year, Ansaldo had reingratiated himself with Mussolini with his brilliant critical, but not overly critical, journalism and been co-opted by the minister of popular culture to run its radio broadcasting. In 1943, he had joined the Resistance and been arrested and held by the Germans in a concentration camp. When he was released and returned to Italy upon Germany's defeat, he was treated as a collaborator, tried, and sentenced to the ten years that he had just begun to serve.[6]

It was futile to talk politics, either past or present, as there was no news: no radios or newspapers, only tabloid magazines. The most illustrious prisoners by Don Fasanaro's reckoning—those of high rank who also contributed to the good of the community—followed their passions as they settled into the prison regime. Ansaldo conducted readings of the *Count of Monte Cristo*, and Marquis Francesco Jacomoni, the former viceroy of Albania, held classes for illiterates. The ex-minister of agriculture Acerbo planted the barren courtyard with eucalyptus and acacia trees. Teruzzi attached himself to Don Luigi to lay out the altar before the Mass and keep order in the abbey's magnificent library. His preferred company, aside from Ricci, who shared his cell, was not the military top brass or the intellectuals. It would be the most criminally compromised of the political prisoners, the twenty-two Italian soldiers who had been captured during the Allied campaign and had then been tried and sentenced by the Allied courts for criminal acts against British and US prisoners of war, several to the death sentence. At the finalization of the peace treaty in early 1947, they had been handed over to the Italians on condition—which to most Italians seemed absurd, especially after the new republic abolished the death sentence—that their sentences be enforced to the letter.

The whole dynamic of prison life changed upon the arrival of Rodolfo Graziani, marshal of Italy, on February 24, 1946, bringing back, if only momentarily, the lost solidarity created under the regime. At the time of the liberation of Milan ten months earlier, he had followed what he later insisted was the only honorable course of action: after fleeing with Mussolini to Como on April 26, 1945, rather than trying to reach Switzerland (as the reckless Mussolini had tried to do), he had surrendered to the enemy in his own homeland. By the enemy, he didn't mean the national resistance movement, which would have executed him immediately, but rather the Americans, who, precisely to avoid that end, had rushed one of their most experienced officers to Italy to spirit him into hiding and then transfer him to Algeria, where he was held in a British prisoner-of-war camp until arrangements could be made for him to stand trial in Italy for his crimes committed under the fascist regime.[7]

The whole penitentiary turned out to welcome Graziani: warden and chaplain, turnkeys, guards, and orderlies, political prisoners and common inmates. And, over the period of his stay, the prison higher-ups bent all of their discretionary power to accommodate his needs. Rather than a barrack cell shared with five others, he had a cell of his own, where he could stay in peace and quiet, lying on the two-meter plus iron bedstead the chaplain's father (at Signora Ines, his wife's request) had built to accommodate his huge height. Once Graziani had organized the microfilms of documents he said he had hidden under his uniform from the British—who, had they read them, would have sent him to Nuremberg to be tried for war crimes—Don Luigi provided him not with the treasured two sheets of writing paper allotted weekly to everybody else but with as much as he needed. As he wrote his account of events, he had a few good conversations with Teruzzi, to clarify his memory of the betrayals he had experienced at the hand of the Duce and especially to comprehend the events following Italy's betrayal by Badoglio that had led the Germans to occupy the country.[8]

Teruzzi had hardly been at Procida six months when the prison was swept by rumors that Palmiro Togliatti, the communist minister of grace and justice, was preparing an "act of clemency and of reconciliation." The government had set the referendum on the monarchy for June 2, 1946. And assuming that the "no" votes would win, the Italians would rid themselves of their fascist king and his heir, the House of Savoy's bland but potentially equally deleterious Prince Umberto. Following this, the nation, now a republic, would, as it had at other turning points in its past, follow with an act of benevolence. Many believed this should be the occasion for a general amnesty of crimes related to fascism, the war, and the liberation—all folded into one.

Quite apart from Pope Pius XII, who had been advocating forgiveness since the liberation, jurists protested that Italy's sophisticated tradition of Roman law would never have permitted punishment on the basis of laws that were not in existence when the alleged crimes were committed. They also objected that the antifascist laws, as they were administered, didn't distinguish between hierarchs acting toward political ends and civil servants just doing their duty. Other critics underscored that elites—in the monarchy, military, and business, not to mention the Church—were equally culpable for upholding the status quo. Some of the most clear-sighted among them recognized that large sectors of the lower classes had embraced fascism as a way of protesting the old elites.

Although politics grew ever more polarized as the Cold War gripped Italy too, the leading parties in the governing coalition agreed on an amnesty. The Christian Democrats did so for the sake of moving on in a conservative, anticommunist way; the Communists' leader, Palmiro Togliatti, did so for more complicated reasons. So many partisans had been jailed and would remain so as long as there was no amnesty, and the Left did not have the political clout to administer a more radical purge in the name of the people. Togliatti wanted to demonstrate the Italian Communist Party's good faith, to show that it was being steered by national interests, not by Moscow, and that it recognized that many Italians had collaborated with the fascist regime to protect their families. In sum, transitional justice had to take a whole new course.[9]

In the last week of June 1946, the prisoners learned by word of mouth that the amnesty bill had been approved. The courts would pardon all those who had sentences under five years and commute death sentences to life imprisonment and life imprisonment to thirty years. All other sentences would be reduced by two-thirds, and all financial penalties would be canceled.

Alessandro Sardi, who had not even been sentenced, was the first to be notified that he should pack his bags. Over the following few weeks, scores of others were released, including all of the men Teruzzi had arrived with, except for Dumini, who would be handed over for trial at the special court of assize and, on January 1, 1947, condemned to life imprisonment for the premeditated assassination of Matteotti.

By August 1947, Graziani, too, had left—not because he had been amnestied, for he, too, hadn't yet been tried, but because his appendix had burst and he had been transferred to a clinic in Rome. By the time *I Defended the Nation* was published that fall, the vox populi had turned in his favor: "poor soul," concluded many of the readers for its nineteen editions; he had only tried to defend his country. Only the communist press still referred to him as a "criminal dog" and a "traitor." He would not be brought up for trial until late 1947. By then, he had assembled a legal team so powerful that even the experienced Luigi Marantonio—the judge who, since presiding over Teruzzi's trial, had conducted dozens more—was bolloxed by Graziani's lawyers' legal subterfuges and delays. After two years, Marantonio turned the civil court trial over to a military tribunal that could be expected to be more lenient.

But Teruzzi remained. The amnesty had lifted his twenty-year sentence for collaboration and also the fifteen years for "significant acts" to keep the regime in power, but the court left standing the fifteen-year sentence for insurrection, as well as the six years and three months for his felonious assault on a prosecutor. An appeal filed on July 10, 1946, caused the fifteen-year sentence to be commuted to ten. But short of the success of another appeal, which his lawyer launched in March 1947, he would remain in prison until April 25, 1955, when he would be seventy-three years old.[10]

In January 1947, Lilliana returned to Rome for the first time since 1938. She was now forty-seven years old and a full partner in the family firm. A wealthy American woman, she was exquisitely dressed, wearing beautiful jewelry and in tip-top psychological form. She still had her furniture to get out of storage. The appeal to the Rota was due to start up again, and upon learning that her husband had not been amnestied, she intended to file for a legal separation on the grounds that he was a long-term convict. That would enable her to secure whatever property had survived and bring to a close that whole episode of her life.

Yet this goal was not going to be simple for a woman of her hypersensitivity about reputation. The moment she crossed into Italy from France, when she gave her name to the border guard, he burst out: "Egad, what a sinister name you have, dear lady, I hope it never gets to you."[11] As she settled in, she began to see lots more not to like about her once-adopted country. The year 1947 promised to be a firecracker of a year. On June 2 of the previous year, the country had voted out the Savoy monarchy and elected representatives to a national assembly to draw up the Italian Republic's founding constitution. But the broad-based political coalition that had governed the country coming out of the war was falling apart, with the Christian Democrats increasingly aligned with the United States, while the Left was vociferously anti-American, with the Communists closely aligned with the Soviet Union.

Lilliana wrote to her parents that she felt "tremendous undercurrents of hatred, antipathy and envy being studiously directed against America, and one feels it constantly."[12] The aristocracy she had once admired had all gone into the fashion business, she said, creating for themselves a "new virginity if communists win: they will show they aren't parasites."[13] She was stunned by the store windows in central Milan and Rome: "The luxury goods make Paris and Brussels look like Woolworths, not to mention Britain, where if you go to a restaurant you have to bring your own bread." In February, for Mardi Gras, there was "an orgy of masked balls, hemorrhaging money."[14]

Herbert Hoover passed through Rome on his mission of aid to Greece and decided to pour more money into, as Lilliana put it, "poor starving Italy." "It won't stop the communists, they don't need it," she wrote home, her sharp tongue intact. "Nobody is grateful, they should send it to Palestine."[15] She found herself speaking out against fascism everywhere she went: "Well, I am not getting nearly as many dinner invitations," she wrote. As far as she could see in Rome, "all that remains of fascism is the Church," which had become the biggest protector of the ex-fascists: "They would dig them out of the cemeteries if they could."[16]

From old acquaintances, she learned the fates of her friends and enemies. Maestro Serafin was back at La Scala, and both the opera board and his selfish daughter were giving him all kinds of trouble. Federzoni and his wife, Gina, had been banished: "I am here, they are in exile."[17] Malgeri had fled to Brazil. The pope's nephew, Pacelli, had arranged for Teruzzi's former chief of cabinet, Macciotta, to become an inspector general at the Vatican after he was purged. Varenna, who was in Milan, learned "his daughter [had run] off with a Communist to Switzerland, got pregnant, [and so was] in despair."[18] (Worse, she would commit suicide the following year.) Her music impresario friend Minolfi "died in a lunatic asylum after his nerves cracked up from bombings." Bice of Savoia, now widowed with two children, claimed that the fascists had brought them luck: after Teruzzi had Alberto exiled to Codogno, he had fallen off his horse while on duty, convalesced for three years at full pay, and used the income to make real estate deals that had left his family well off.[19]

All everybody really wanted to talk about was all of the illicit love affairs that had become public knowledge and all of the marriages that had broken up since the war, so Lilliana had an avid and sympathetic audience for her travails. In February, 1947 the Constitutional Assembly had started to debate whether Italian marriage law should finally become modern. Across the political spectrum, secularists and Catholics could agree that the solidity of the family was a considerable good in a nation torn apart by the war. But whether marriage should be indissoluble was another question entirely.

The jurist Piero Calamandrei argued that the Lateran Accords, by granting the Church sole discretion over marriage, should be counted among the fascist dictatorship's greatest crimes, as it had reinforced the Church's religious absolutism and swerved Italy away from its secularizing path. Did no one care that the number of married couples who separated annually had roughly doubled from 1932 to 1947?[20] But the Church had no intention of reversing its position; the salvation of religion depended on the sanctity of the family, and that, in turn, depended on the indissolubility of marriage. The Christian Democratic Party supported this position, and the Communists capitulated, fearful that if they offended the Church, they risked losing support of Italian women, who had just been given the vote. With no divorce, not even the "little divorce" that reformers sought, Italy's so-called marriage outlaws numbered upward of four million. Teruzzi, together with Yvette and Mariceli, would be counted among them. And Lilliana, as well.[21]

In February, Lilliana had a sudden change of heart about the separation. While reviewing files on her husband pulled from the state archives to prepare her case, she discovered the "whore's appeal" to Cardinal Schuster as the mother of "Attilio's bastard" and learned that he had legally adopted the child by "swearing that [she, Lilliana,] consented or some other corruption." All of a sudden, rather than worrying about "getting anything of his patrimony," she had to worry about "protecting my own." Her fighting spirit returned. "This is a joke I had not bargained for," she wrote spicily.[22]

It was all to the good. Rather than filing for separation on the basis of Teruzzi's conviction—that was "kicking a man when he was down (though nobody deserves it more)"—she would sue him for adultery. That was not going to be easy either.[23] First, the law didn't pursue men for adultery but only for "concubinage," which meant that the adulterer had introduced the lover into the family home. To get him on that, she would have had to denounce the affair within three months of its occurrence. Or she would have to demonstrate that this concubinage was ongoing notwithstanding the fact that he was incarcerated in a maximum-security penitentiary. Since that wasn't going to be possible, she had her lawyer file to disaffiliate "his bastard." She made herself miserable thinking about him. "What a pity," she wrote, "I have wasted my life for such scum."[24]

Those were the moments that made her obsess about getting back her long-lost elephant pin. Andalù, Teruzzi's old Askari, who had come by her hotel to look her up, recalled to her how hard she had tried to get it back. It probably wasn't true, as he told her, that Mussolini had told Teruzzi he had to give it back, or that he had seen the pin as late as 1943, just as Teruzzi was heading north, or that he might have given it to "the Nappi girls." His service to Teruzzi had ended around 1942, when Teruzzi, after finding him drunk, had gone into a rage and kicked him out, literally, all the way down the stairs and out onto the street. Since then, he had made do. At times, he worked as an extra at Cinecittà: if Hollywood on the Tiber was going to keep doing colonial films, they always needed black faces. Lilliana gave him 10,000 lire for the information and admitted that she was unlikely ever to retrieve the pin. Andalù would go on to become a television personality, as the African Stepin Fetchit on the long-running prime-time show *Friend of the Animals*; his task, at the command of the impresario Angelo Lombardi, "Take it away, Andalù," was to pick up the exotic animal, a cute lion cub or scary alligator, and carry it off screen.[25]

In Rome, Lilliana discovered, Teruzzi seemed to "have more friends than ever before." She met his old interior decorator and "learned a million things." She went out for dinner with the interior decorator's friend, the gay American actor Gar Moore, the handsome Fred in Roberto Rossellini's *Paisan*, and they ended up at a restaurant with Anna Magnani, who spooked her with her long, hard stare. "Somebody started to sing from the musical *Carousel*, 'If I Loved You,'" and Lilliana joined in "*voce pianissima*," and "everybody crowded around." She heard they were going to Ischia for the weekend. Procida was nearby. She hoped they would go "see Attilio, make him green with envy at the time they had."[26] She went to the warehouse where her lost furniture had ended up. It was close by Colle Oppio. The woman who lived in Teruzzi's old apartment showed her around, just enough for her to imagine how it had been, with its 360-degree view of Rome, rooftop pool, fencing room, and elephant tusk wall, like in a "thousand and one nights."[27]

When she wasn't with her lawyer working on her case, she was at the Rota archive working on her own. She had become an expert, she said—at least as good as her consultant, a senior judge on the Supreme Court—"on fine technical points of law, regarding canonical law, civil law, and the Concordat."[28] She proposed to defend herself, so "the distinction of trying (and winning) my own case, would be inscribed in Sacra Rota history." But Monsignore Borgia and Father Candidori firmly advised against it. They recommended an excellent churchman, and very cheap, at 30,000 lire (about $85) to handle the whole process.[29]

In April, Lilliana had just about settled all of her Italian affairs and had gone to Paris when she was blind-sided by another libel.[30] This one was public, proof of the return of the free press, sexist as ever, prurient, and not at all anti-Semitic. The *Europeo*, icon of Italy's new journalism, in its issue of May 11, 1947, published a whopper of an article, entitled "A Falangist Wife after the Fascist Wife." This featured an aged Teruzzi, shown white-bearded in a newspaper photograph from his trial, who from "his convent hideaway in central Italy," "as he worried about dying, wondered when he would finally be able to marry his companion of many years and give his name to his child."[31]

His case for annulment was coming up before the Rota, the piece went on. His wife, a Canadian Red Cross nurse who had come to Italy during World War I, had long been out of the picture. She had been a prostitute by profession. All of the other hierarchs knew that, except for the foolish Teruzzi who married her, only to separate after a few years, after which he had fiddled around with ballerinas and Contesse del Viminale and won decorations for military valor. While an inspector of the militia in Spain, he had met a Spanish Jewish girl, a Falangist, whom he had brought back to Italy, and intended to honor as his wife while raising their child with all of the perquisites of his status as a great hierarch. Teruzzi had gotten into furious arguments about her with Mussolini, who finally had promised to let Teruzzi marry the Jewish girl as soon as he got his annulment.

The lies were as mischievous as any that Farinacci had ever concocted, and Lilliana was sure that Varenna had planted the article. But its author, Nicola Adelfi (the pseudonym for Nicola De Feo), was a well-regarded in-vestigative reporter, and the editors intended to pass it as a serious piece of reporting rather than tabloid fodder, if they placed it on the same page with another piece of investigative journalism—on the revival of the Jewish theater in Eastern Europe. The tone was sympathetic, not melo-dramatic, the archetypes presented with a certain charm: to think of the repentant old fascist hidden in a convent in Tuscany, like a figure in Man-zoni's *The Betrothed*; or the opportunistic Canadian Red Cross woman, both a Protestant and a prostitute, straight out of lurid war novels; or the Falangist Jewish girl, like Micaela in *Carmen*. Even in a democracy, mi-sogyny could make foreign women appear extravagant.

Why should the Church alone have the power to annul a marriage? And if it did, shouldn't it use its own tricks to bring a happy ending to this sad story? The thrust of the article was to endorse the annulment not on the grounds Carlo Pacelli had advanced, that Lilliana was not a virgin, but rather on the legitimate ground that she didn't believe in the sanctity of marriage. In annulment law, it turned out, there was a precedent for annulling marriages on religious grounds. Carlo Pacelli's own grand-father, Filippo, had used exactly that argument in 1913 during an appeal in the notorious Castellane-Gould case to annul the French Catholic noble-man's marriage to the fabulously rich American socialite. The grounds were that as a Protestant, she didn't believe in the indissolubility of marriage.[32]

"I keep asking myself over and over, what I ever did to merit such a jour-nalist campaign against me," Lilliana wrote to her parents. "May God strike them dead, and may everything they love wither, Amen!" She was going to have to sue the publishers for libel if she didn't want to be "be-smirched."[33] The source, according to rumors, was "military circles"—maybe even General Graziani himself, embellished by his acolyte Carlo De Biase, a journalist turned historian. If she wanted to prove her case, her lawyer advised her, she would have to produce her bank statements from the 1920s to demonstrate that she had been supported by her father rather than by her wages as a prostitute or ask for testimony from Teruzzi's entourage, who would surely vouch that he was not responsible for making up such preposterous lies.[34]

By the time she headed home in October 1947, her romance with Italy was well behind her. With respect to all of her "experiences," she said as she left, she had "absolutely no regrets. I will go back for long visits as it is a fascinating charming country, delightful climate, and for these times, in comparison with other places very cheap." She felt "de-poeticized," she wrote her parents: "I am really pleased that I am completely disillusioned."[35]

Around the time Lilliana returned to the United States, Teruzzi reached the nadir of despair. On May 9, 1947, his March appeal to the court of ap-peals in Rome was redirected to Milan, which on October 16, after a de-tailed review, ruled that he had indeed been a major protagonist in the March on Rome—and was the only major figure still alive. The court would not amnesty his crimes but only commute his sentence another five years. He would be released on April 25, 1951. It also reconfirmed the confiscation of all his property. Add to that Lilliana's suit to annul his daughter's affiliation, and the Rota case was coming up again—the only good news now was that since he was penniless and propertyless, he wouldn't have to pay court costs.

Late that October, Francesco Argenta, the well-known investigative journalist, conducting an inquiry into Italian prisons for *La Stampa*, as he toured the prison with the warden, caught sight of Teruzzi busying himself in the prison library. Argenta was struck by the fact that Teruzzi was wearing an orange lounge coat over his prison uniform and had sashed it with a rainbow-colored scarf. It reminded him of the past, when Teruzzi had been the best turned out of the fascist hierarchs, changing his uniforms several times a day, depending on whether he was at a militia function, a military event, or going to a Grand Council meeting. It was a nice conceit. Teruzzi was a Milanese, after all, and he had always been a good dresser. He was at heart his old quartermaster self: "docile and meek, prompt and precise, dusting off the library furniture, ordering the books on the shelves, registering the volumes that were being checked out and controlling those being returned to make sure that his comrades hadn't scribbled in them." He was smoking hand-rolled cigarettes, as perfectly shaped as the top brands, and with the warden's entrance, since it was an infraction of the rules, he bucked to attention to conceal it.

Later, when Argenta met him along with Francesco Giunta and Renato Ricci in their shared cell, they talked about the amnesty. "Why us, why not

Teruzzi, prison librarian, D'Avalos Penitentiary, Procida, spring 1950

Archivio Farabola

the others?" Giunta asked. Ricci complained that there should have been "shared responsibility," whereas Giunta, with an eye to his appeal, said that he believed in the fairness of the process. Teruzzi said little, other than to obsess about the confiscation of his property, "about his daughter, his woman (wife or friend, whatever) whom he will never be able to re-embrace, and who from solid well-being had been plunged into poverty and hardship."[36]

Yvette and Mariceli had in fact moved to Procida in September 1946, having left Milan for Rome when Teruzzi was transferred to Regina Coeli. In Rome, they had been sheltered by the Ursuline nuns on Viale Brenta. With nothing to live on except some small savings and money from Teruzzi's friends, Yvette tried every means to tap into what remained of his wealth. She had gone to Castiglioncello to get stuff from the house to sell it, only to have the receiver turn her away and to discover, after staying the night at the custodians' house, that burglars had broken into the walled chamber and stolen the best items. She tried to have the stuff that had been confiscated at Teruzzi's capture returned, but Lilliana's lawyer had filed that she had first rights to it. She pleaded with the receivers that she, too, had been a victim of the Nazis, as a prisoner at Lipari, to obtain the 50,000 lire subsidy monthly, around $50, deducted from the income from renting Villa Celestina, which Mariceli had the legal right to as Teruzzi's dependent. But her status or non-status, as Teruzzi's child's mother, failed to open any doors.

Over the summer, she had a nervous breakdown. In the end she decided that if the two of them were to go to Procida, Mariceli could see her father, and the island itself was so impoverished they could live on the small sums Teruzzi's friends had given them, which was all they had. They found dignified enough rooms in the former fascist mayor's large, half-empty villa, built from his life savings as a tugboat pilot on the Suez Canal. It was grim to live under the shadow of a giant penitentiary. But what was the alternative?

Father Luigi spoke of Teruzzi as being "like the man in the New Testament who had built his castle on sand, and despaired as it crumbled." It was the minister of God's duty, observing this "inner struggle," to revive in him "that sense of self-respect which is the inalienable property of every human creature."[37] In Don Fasanaro's mind, his project to uplift Teruzzi spiritually was of a piece with the Holy See's project of moral redemption. He agreed with the prominent Catholic legal scholars who denounced the confinement of so many fallen fascists as a "crime against humanity." He welcomed to the penitentiary members of the Franciscan and Capuchin orders, as well as the Jesuits of the Marian Crusade, and made sure all the prisoners understood the blessed provenance of the mule loads of food that arrived at Christmas and Easter from the archdiocese of Naples. As he urged Teruzzi to confide in God, he also encouraged him to overcome his pride and confide his need for practical help to Princess Maria Pignatelli, whose husband, Prince Valerio, had been jailed at Procida after leading an insurrection against the Kingdom of the South. After backing an armed women's crusade to the Holy Land to rescue Jerusalem from Jews and communists, with Vatican support, the princess had founded the Italian Women's Movement on October 28, 1946, the thirty-fourth anniversary of the March on Rome.[38] Through her network of high-born women friends, she could secure legal aid for beleaguered families. It was not for himself that Teruzzi wrote, when he reached out to Don Luigi's Vatican contact, Don Silverio Mattei, asking him to put him in touch with the princess. It was on behalf of his daughter and her "heroic Mom, who have become the sole things that keep me anchored to earthly life."[39]

New Year 1948 marked the tenth year of the reign of Pius XII. It was also the peak of the Cold War romance of the Vatican with the United States. In 1946 the pope, under American pressure, had named several new cardinals from the Anglophone world, among them Archbishop Francis Spellman. On January 1, 1948, as the new constitution of the Italian Republic came into effect, the president set the first elections for Sunday, April 18. As soon as that happened, the CIA and the Vatican began collaborating to distribute millions of dollars to Catholic civic committees to defeat the Left.[40]

The auditors of the Rota had always represented the most international corps of prelates at the Roman Curia, and the three judges whose turn it was to preside over Attilio Teruzzi's long-postponed annulment appeal were Swiss German, Milanese, and Scots British—with three-quarters of a century of experience among them. The point of departure for the auditors was the judgment from Pavia in 1939 that determined with "moral certitude" that, as "a result of her race, religion, education, and especially her acquired disposition," Lillian Weinman had contracted marriage, with no intention "unbeknownst to Attilio Teruzzi" of binding herself to him in perpetuity.

To start, the court wanted to clarify the law bearing on these matters once and for all. The problem was *not* that the Catholic Church did not recognize as a sacrament the marriage contract between a Catholic, a person of the faith, and an infidel, or an unbaptized person. In doctrinal terms, the former, being of the faith, partook of the sacrament, while the latter, not being baptized, could not. Therefore, their wedding could never be a sacrament, even if the couple had been dispensed from the impediment created by the disparity of cult. A sacrament was a sacrament. However, the capacity to take the sacraments was irrelevant to the positive law that held, quoting Pius XI's affirmation from his encyclical *Casti Connubii* (1930), that "every true marriage is indissoluble," "*all* without exception."

A Church court could determine that the marriage was invalid if the goals of one or both of the contracting parties was "merely a sort of unstable and transitory union," as opposed to a "perfect and indissoluble marriage." In such a case, the judges argued, "it had to set the highest bar of proof." The court of Pavia had not done that. Its case was "ambiguous and weak." It had never accounted for the fact that "the couple had been cohabiting peacefully, the person who had ended the cohabitation was the petitioner, and the person opposing the annulment of the marriage had never professed to wanting a divorce."[41]

Beyond that, the auditors continued, there was the quality of the testimony of the witnesses brought in on Teruzzi's behalf, all of whom were joined to "Attiliius [sic]" by a strong bond of service and friendship. By then, Attilio Teruzzi was infamous: "a man having great power with public authority, and one of those who act on their first decision. From the moment that he terminated their conjugal cohabitation, he did not cease to persecute Lillian and her mother with implacable hatred." By contrast, "even now," after "so great a ruin of things," Lilliana remained "faithful to him as a legitimate wife, spurning divorce, which she could easily obtain from her own American courts and tenaciously defending the validity of her marriage."

Therefore, the court concluded, "having only God before our eyes, and, moreover, having invoked the name of Christ, we pronounce, declare, and definitively issue our decision: THE NULLITY OF THE MARRIAGE IN QUESTION HAS NOT BEEN PROVED."[42]

Father Luigi would never have second-guessed the Rota. It is possible that Teruzzi never confided to him his rage at the Church. Not that Father Luigi didn't have sympathy for his plight. His understanding of events was that Teruzzi's wife was "the daughter of a rich American industrialist, who had left him at the end of the war."[43] That put the fault on her, though his relationship with Yvette was still adulterous. It was Yvette, his "partner" (*convivente*), as Don Luigi called her, who, by her steadfastness, added to Teruzzi's worthiness in his eyes. It never occurred to him that she was a Jew. And she wasn't, not under Italian law nor in the religion she professed and raised her daughter, which was Catholic.

In the latter half of 1948, having recovered her health at Procida and with loans scraped together from all over, Yvette had opened a small hotel at Pizzaco, the village sculpted around the base of the penitentiary. She called it the Caravella. It was set between the citrus trees and cactus plants on the path down to the beach. At night, lanterns lit up the terrace, and the gramophone played jazz records. For the first time, relatives visiting the political prisoners—and the very few tourists—could stay in a lodging with an indoor toilet. "For sure, life offers so many unforeseen twists and turns," Yvette confided to Princess Pignatelli: "I never thought I would finish life as an innkeeper," she said, switching to French to say: "But there are no stupid professions, only stupid people."[44]

In 1948, Teruzzi lodged another appeal of his sentence. The only new element was that his lawyer thought that a letter from his daughter, now ten, might help. She was her father's daughter, and she pleaded to the "Signor Presidente" of the Council of Ministers, the prime minister, to commute her father's sentence: "Dear Mr. President, they all say that you are so good, and that you love your own grandchildren, so I have decided to write you. . . . Would you like to make me happy? Let my father return home. He has been imprisoned for over three years here at Procida, and when I want to see him, I have to go into the prison."[45]

Once more, he was turned down. Aside from dismissing "the child's ingenuousness" ("she denies that her daddy was a traitor, that he didn't love Italy, or do anything bad, because when she was little she always saw him dressed like a soldier wearing many decorations"), the court advised that any pardon at that moment would have a "deplorable effect on public opinion, by exciting approval from the moderate right and fury from the extremist left."[46]

By the time Teruzzi's various appeals were exhausted in 1948, he had nothing—not his home nor his pension nor his famous treasure—except his mausoleum at the cemetery at Verano and that only for as long as the rent on the plot beneath it was paid to the landlord, the city of Rome. As for his pension, the one he had so incessantly struggled to collect during the Republic of Salò, his condemnation had stripped him of the right to that as well.

As late as 1948, Teruzzi described himself as a fascist and as a general. That made sense: he had been loyal both to the idea or cause, as his fellow inmates called it, and to his service oath and rank. One wonders what he now felt for Mussolini. In July 1948, his fellow prisoner, Ricci, observed in the memoirs that he was writing, that "in politics, as in love, it is not a good idea to concede oneself body and soul to anybody. But the heart . . ."[47]

To renounce that passion was difficult, even for far more intelligent and emotionally resourceful people. One thinks of Giuseppe Bottai, who, following Mussolini's decision to go to war on the side of Hitler, was wracked with anguish over his disillusionment. "Our generation is one with Mussolini," he wrote. "It is not a question of taking his measure as distinct from us; but inside of us, and us inside of him." Bottai had been forced to recognize, as the war progressed, that Mussolini had become "more and more cynical and exploitative"; the people were a "pawn in his game," and "we [the hierarchs] the objects of his latest dictatorial experimentation."[48]

It is not at all clear that Teruzzi had to stop loving the Duce to get his priorities straight. He put his family first, which, he said, "anchored him to this earth," and never stopped trying to do his duty by his soldiers. He was the most senior officer at the penitentiary, when on June 7, 1949, his men, the twenty-two war criminals in cellblock 3, went on a hunger strike to force the government to release them. In a couple of days, it became a national cause. Don Luigi petitioned the king of England to pardon them. Police, reporters, and the Red Cross, with Principessa Pignatelli at the head, flocked to the island, waving the national flag. The news media echoed the nationalist right in their insistence that the government act on behalf of its veterans against the arrogance of the victor nations.

On the fourth day, as the fasting men were lying on the cell floor in a daze, "General" Teruzzi had slipped into the cellblock area, reached through the bars to hug the face of the one soldier still on his feet, handed him an award on parchment (decorated with the Italian red, white, and green) and two little plastic medals of honor, and then left without a word.

From the political prisoners in Cell 1: Dearest 22, you are in our hearts at every moment. The hour of your victory approaches, and it will be the greatest and most famous any group of Italians could conquer under the present circumstances. Have faith in

God and in your conscience. Draw . . . on the moral force upholding your honor and hope. Raise your hearts high. Long live
the crusaders of the Terra Murata.[49]

Whether Teruzzi wrote this or not, it perfectly expressed his thoughts:
crusaders, hearts, faith, conscience, victory, priest talk, patriotic cant, but
no violence, no Duce. These were new times. The government newsreel
of June 27 concluded with a sequence entitled, "The Hope for Liberty,"
showing the men at Terra Murata marching out of the penitentiary to
the Red Cross hostel where they would stay until their releases were
processed.

On March 29, 1950, Attilio Teruzzi's latest appeal, this time to obtain amnesty for his felony, the attack on Viola, was granted, and on Saturday,
April 1, he was set free. It was tabloid news. As he exited the prison gates, a
photo reporter from *Oggi* captured the elderly man in a natty wool suit,
handkerchief tucked in the vest pocket, giving a wolfish grin as his
daughter, a young lady in bobby socks and a pin-up sweater, threw herself
into his outstretched arms. He had 3,200 lire in his pockets, honestly
earned from his work at the library, his life savings. He wept as he stumbled down the cobbled path to the Caravella, clutching his daughter's
arm. Asked about his plans, he said he would stay on Procida, help his
wife with the bed and breakfast, and maybe, at a later time, once his political rights were restored, he would go back into local politics. If he
proved popular, who knows, he might even run for the town council.[50]
    Back at Yvette's hotel, Teruzzi was his joyful, cynical self, ordering
people around, talking about the past, and holding forth at the head of
table, his daughter on his lap. He had constant company in the promenade of local notables (the doctor, the priest, the mayor), journalists from
the Continent, and the prisoners on informal furlough from the Red
Cross hostel, who brought along their fiancées from the island. Yvette
could be seen running back and forth overseeing everything, helping to
feed the visitors and sending out for cigarettes. Vittorio Gorresio, *La Stampa*'s correspondent, described Teruzzi as garrulous and unregenerate.
    It was all a mistake, he insisted—he had told Mussolini to attack the
British in the Sudan in June 1940 while Graziani attacked Cyrenaica.
England, cut out from the Suez Canal, would have sued for peace.[51]
Gorresio's insinuation was probably right: this was the old fascist way,

Leaving prison, into Mariceli's arms, Procida, April 1, 1950
Author's Collection

second-guessing the generals, pulling hope out of the belief that Italy had a special rendezvous with history, playing the blame game, suffusing the culture of the state with the know-it-all of a master sergeant.

Within a few days of his release, after his wheezing and coughing got worse, the specialist called in from Naples diagnosed Teruzzi with congestive heart failure. He showed his usual bravado: "I've already been dead three times and even a hanged man." And then, with a look at the oxygen cylinder, he concluded: "That's my fourth firing squad, that one; but I have thick skin and I believe that when people give you up for dead, it lengthens your life."[52]

But this was a rendezvous Attilio Teruzzi could not avoid by dint of quick wits and physical courage. On the evening of April 26, the priest gave him last rites, and he died at dawn.

Years later, when I had the opportunity to talk with Don Luigi, he told me that Teruzzi had "died of joy." The priest was then close to ninety, still hearty, but depressed at his mortality as he reclined in his room in the abbey, looking out toward Capri, attended by a gorgeous, white-uniformed Russian nurse straight out of a James Bond movie. Joy, he meant, at being at home, joy at holding his eleven-year-old on his lap; at making love with his companion, a good woman, though not his lawful wife; and joy in the Lord. Italian Catholicism heartily approved of a man enjoying all three, in the presence of God.

The women composed the body on the bed for viewing. His decorations, but only from Italy's good wars—the Libyan War and World War I—were pinned on his pillow, which was covered with the Italian tricolor flag. Candles were lit on the bed stands. In the next twenty-four hours, the front room of the Caravella was crowded with villagers, inmates from the prison, and the first of a crowd of onetime comrades arriving from nearby Naples and Rome, together with a sizable contingent of neofascists from the Italian Social Movement.

Don Luigi conducted the funeral. The sun was still bright at five-thirty when they closed the casket and the procession headed out of the Caravella to go the Church of Saint Anthony Abbot. Don Luigi held the crucifix in the lead, surrounded by altar boys, and the bier was borne by the war criminal prisoners. Yvette and Mariceli were shrouded in black, followed by a chorus of orphan girls from the local convent, the lay nuns of Graziella carrying flowers, and more mourners than anybody remembered in those parts.

The funeral made an indelible impression on the children watching from the windows: flags and banners, lots of them, with words they couldn't decipher; all the men in uniform with their decorations, some carrying big wreaths—one man particularly memorable, though nobody knew who exactly he was, with his gray goatee and black shirt covered with medals and green-khaki pants over a wooden leg that thumped as he struggled up the cobbled path—the look on his face both angry and aggrieved. Many women came from outside, their faces pale, dressed in black, with black veils. Scores of telegrams of condolence poured in expressing "profound distress" at the "irreparable loss," "shared grief," and "fraternal participation."[53]

Graziani, too, though he was in jail at that moment, telegrammed his condolences. After eluding justice in the regular criminal courts, he had been tried by his peers in the special military tribunal, which found him guilty on only one count: collaborating with the Germans. He was condemned to nineteen years, one year less than Teruzzi had received, and four months later, between one amnesty and another, he would be freed on May 2, 1950, the week after Teruzzi's death.

Naples had become the moral capital of neofascism when the Italian Social Movement, the successor to the outlawed Fascist Party, was founded in November 1946. Under the watchwords "Neither renege nor restore," it grouped together a scattering of the old guard (all well known to Teruzzi), some survivors of Salò, and a few political neophytes who drew strength from allying themselves with the monarchists and the local populist machine. In Naples's first postwar elections, they had backed Teruzzi's one-time lawyer Giuseppe Buonocore, the head of the Catholic monarchists, to elect him mayor. But by 1950, Naples had become an important American military base. The new political establishment in Rome was embarrassed by the MSI's nostalgia for fascism and disturbed by its anti-American sentiments. Eager to keep the funeral from becoming a pretext for a neofascist demonstration, the prefect of Naples had a military reconnaissance plane circle overhead and the city police commissioner at the ready.

Later, Don Luigi protested at the suggestion that Teruzzi's funeral, which he had held only at the request of the family, had been "an apology for fascism." "Nothing could be more false," he insisted. Having come to know the deceased "intimately for five years," he had learned to "appreciate a man of undeniable qualities and rare sensitivity behind the rough and elemental appearance. My thoughts, then, were for Attilio Teruzzi, the man, friend, and brother."[54]

Movizzo, the ex-mayor, offered his family's crypt to house Teruzzi's remains while his friends raised contributions to place an appropriate commemorative marker at Verano. When Lilliana Teruzzi heard of her husband's death, she told her lawyer to have the US consulate in Naples send somebody to read the inscription at the cemetery—there was none—and to send her newspaper clippings about the funeral. Seeing the photographs of the aged man laid out on his deathbed, with a crucifix on his breast, and of the bereft daughter and her mother, whom most of the obituaries called his wife, must have given her some kind of closure.[55]

But why should Lilliana be made to subscribe to Catholic pieties or to a feel-good finale? She had the copyright on being called Teruzzi's wife, and when she read the *Manchester Guardian*'s jokey obituary, "A Fascist to the Beard," she sued it for libel: "Mrs. Attilio Teruzzi, his wife, did not live on Procida and had never run a boarding house."[56] And she won.

EPILOGUE

Died in Libya: in military jargon, (said of) a person or a thing that has been lost, forgotten, relegated to the past, that nobody knows anything about, or thinks about any more.

—ADRIANO MONACO, *Morti in Libia*, 1930

*D*e *mortuis nil nisi bonum.* Speak no ill of the dead. Teruzzi's obituarists drew on the tabloid pieties of the time and kept to the spirit of the old Latin saying. His death was a "pathetic closing" to "an adventurous life," one opined. Another suggested that one of the "most visible and important fascist hierarchs" had found religion after his near execution in northern Italy, having seen several men killed in his stead and having completed more prison time than any other. A couple thought that fate's "cruelest trick" was to strike him down so soon after he had been freed. For a journalist who attended the funeral, the "outpouring of feeling" showed that "human grief and pity know nothing of politics, with its hatred and rancor."[1]

Nobody at the time had the stomach to delve deeper. For the resurgent democratic press, the hierarchs were relics of the past, buffoons, stick figures. Teruzzi was conjured up in his fanciful uniform and chestful of decorations as an icon of "fidelity" and "impulsive mediocrity." "Mussolini had loved him for all of that" but above all for "his ingratiating optimism, predicting great victories on every front—in Libya, in Spain, in Africa." His friends believed he was committed to "the idea," his faith driven by a "generous impetus," but in truth he was a clown and a thug, driven by violence pure and simple.[2]

The editor in chief of *Il Mattino*, Giovanni Ansaldo, wrote the most measured assessment of him at the time. He had known Teruzzi up close, having been a fellow prisoner at Procida. For this reason, he surprised himself at taking so long to get his thoughts straight. Teruzzi was the "sergeant who went far," his obituary was subtitled. The gist was that after an "entirely honorable military career," it was probably "a mistake" for a man of Teruzzi's "great vitality, brusque temper, habit of command, knowing that his military career was at a dead end," to have turned to "politics." As often happened during "tumultuous waves of change," he had risen too high and been charged with positions of too great responsibility: "Even critics said he didn't do badly in Cyrenaica," Ansaldo mused, "even friends that he didn't do well as Minister of Africa." He was never on the take in the usual sense, despite his outsized real estate acquisitions. He had accepted his punishment with "a kind of moral nobility," and faith had taught him to curb "his impetuous outbursts of temper."[3]

Though it was not Ansaldo's intention to use Teruzzi's death to write a postmortem of fascism, he did so implicitly. And he let the regime off much too lightly, as if Teruzzi had started his fascist career in "politics" tout court, as if the fascist seizure of power was nothing but a "tumultuous wave" and Mussolini all but irrelevant. Then again, Ansaldo was still processing his own seesaw experience of the dictatorship at the time. Recruited by Galeazzo Ciano, he had become one of the premier journalists of the regime and had played a role for which he had been punished and ostracized and was still considered suspect by antifascists. When he had accepted the position at Il Mattino, Italy's conservative political establishment expected him to return the newspaper to its preeminence as the voice of anti-leftist Italian liberalism, and to thereby recover the legacy of his father and grandfather before him, both leading exponents of Italy's moderate liberal ruling class. He in turn had stipulated that he would neither be an "apologist," conducting "ideological executions," nor "a scourge of the past," by promoting the new antifascist canon.[4] Teruzzi, he concluded, had received the punishment he deserved.

That said, his family had been dealt a bad hand, and Ansaldo made a mental note to help them. Yvette and Mariceli had stayed on at Procida to mind the Caravella. But no amount of cheerful advertising could offset the fact that the little pensione stood under the shadow of a maximum-security penitentiary. With beautiful Capri and charming Ischia lying just across the bay, Procida was a place to avoid long before 1957, when the publication of Elsa Morante's prize-winning Arturo's Island made it a metaphor for terminal melancholy.

By 1953, Yvette had fallen so far behind on the rent that Ansaldo interceded with the prefect of Naples to obtain a one-time grant to promote tourism from the Office of the Prime Minister. Those 200,000 lire barely covered the arrears.[5] That year, with Mariceli now going on fifteen, the two women abandoned Procida for Naples. They found an apartment on a high floor in the rundown Palazzo Arpinio, likely with help from Ansaldo, who lived catty-corner on Via Chiaia in the giant Palazzo Cellamare. The frescoes in the entryway were flaking off, the stuccowork stained with leaks and mold, the coat of arms over the door chipped, and the ancient marble pavement furrowed by wheel ruts. But the building was a onetime residence of the noble Caracciolo family, just a short walk to the Riviera di Chiaia with its sunshine, sea air, and palm-shaded gardens, and the building custodian always greeted them as fallen nobility. Teruzzi would have approved.

Perhaps Ansaldo (or perhaps it was Paolo Laurino di Caracciolo, the building's owner, also a friend of Teruzzi from his Cinecittà connections) found Yvette a job as coat-check girl at the Opera of San Carlo, a fifteen-minute walk from the house. Laurino was an assistant film director at Cinecittà at the time. And in 1954, when Roberto Rossellini used his palace as the set for a scene in *Voyage to Italy*, with Ingrid Bergman and George Sanders, he employed Mariceli as a script girl. She would have stayed in Rome, enveloped by the affection of Anna Magnani and her father's many other friends, had her mother had the money to pay for her room and board.[6]

Around that time, Yvette made contact for the first and only time with "Mme. Attilio Teruzzi." She desperately needed her attention, and Lilliana hadn't responded to previous requests. Having heard from others that she was kind and understanding, Yvette wrote, she was asking her for an "act of goodness and generosity." Respecting Lilliana's rights as a wife—she herself, Yvette noted, had only briefly known Teruzzi before terrible times befell them—and certain she would want to help her deceased husband's child, Yvette explained that she and her daughter were destitute. She wanted to end the lease on the family mausoleum at Verano Cemetery and get back the two-million-lire deposit, which would then be divided between Teruzzi's two heirs under the law, two-thirds for his child and one-third for his legal wife. For that purpose she needed Lilliana's signature, which, we presume, Lilliana's lawyer sent.[7] Presumably it was Yvette, then, who had the family remains removed to a loculus in one of those anonymous high-rise cement crypts from the 1950s, where, when I visited Verano, it could be found on the top tier of five or six, with no marker at all, except for the family name scribbled in the wet cement at the time of the re-internment and a faded purple and green plastic nosegay that must have been tossed up there by some passerby.

It mattered terribly to me to know how Yvette's story ended. Scraping around, I had found one last archival trace of her life with Mariceli in Naples, a letter and a note from her to Giuseppe Bottai, in the digitized inventory of his papers, dated 1958. She was penniless, she wrote, her daughter very ill, and she was pleading for a recommendation from him for a position at the newly established Cassa del Mezzogiorno, postwar Italy's "New Deal" development project for the Italian South.[8] With no record of a reply, I used my historian's detective skills to check census data, housing records, and phone books for some trace of them. I even spoke to the building custodian at Palazzo Arpinio, who after forty years of service was to retire the very next day. He remembered them, he said, but they had left long ago. Had Yvette perhaps emigrated to Saõ Paulo or Montevideo, where onetime fascists went to rusticate? Could she have found another mate and be going under a new name? Maybe she had died or committed suicide like her father?

Later, at the ingenious suggestion of an enterprising local historian, a former student, I wrote an insert for *Il Mattino* asking for help: "What happened to Mariceli Teruzzi?" I asked, "The beloved daughter of Attilio Teruzzi, high official in the Fascist Militia and Minister of the Colonies?"[9]

That generated more in response than I dared hope for. I discovered that mother and daughter had survived, thanks in part to Giuseppe Bottai's recommendation on Yvette's behalf to the Cassa del Mezzogiorno. Many contemporaries and historians regard Bottai as a model fascist: a man with a conscience, sharp mind, and fine education; a family man, utterly honest in his personal dealings; the great hierarch who had done brilliant policy work reforming the educational system at the turn of the 1940s. He had come through for Yvette as a matter of civility and fairness to the family of a onetime comrade in arms. This was not inconsistent with his deep belief in acting not just within the word but within the spirit of the law. As minister of education at the time of the passage of the 1938 Race Laws, which he believed were for the good of the nation, he insisted that the directives applying to the school system be issued in September, before the school year started, so that the Jewish students and professors, who under the terms of the law were to be excluded, would not be expelled during the term, causing them humiliation, which was not the law's aim.

One time coworkers recalled Yvette as a ray of sunshine. She had grown heavy, one woman told me, but from her smooth pale skin and striking dark eyes, and judging by her daughter, she must have been a real beauty when she was young. She was so good-hearted that they had appealed to the director of their department to keep her beyond the retirement age, to let her complete the twenty years she needed to collect the minimum pension, and he had agreed. She had arthritic knees, so they set her up with a work stool. As she stapled together documents for filing, she told amazing stories about how she had lost track of Attilio, as she always called him, after he was freed by the Germans and had gone north; a gypsy woman who read her palm could see where he was—Garda—and she had been right.

Another woman, as she shared memories of Yvette, volunteered a story of her own. At four or so, she recalled thinking her older sisters' fiancés were too old for her; she herself was desperately in love with the Duce and had even hoped to marry him. She was always talking to her family about her wedding dress. When she had heard the shouts and firecrackers as her neighbors had celebrated the Duce's ouster, the other children had teased her that she would never marry him now, and she had cried for days.[10] She laughed at the foolishness of her misplaced passion. But Mussolini had been her first great love, and his overthrow, her first great heartbreak.

Bourgeois Naples is a small world. From the gossip about Mariceli, it sounded as if she had been left deeply scarred. After a brief, inauspicious marriage to a local playboy, which they had annulled—annulment law having become more flexible in the 1950s, under the influence of American Catholicism—she had married a much older man with whom she had long been besotted. He was a gentleman lawyer, who resembled her father in his athleticism and seeming power, but he was an infinitely patient and kind man, from the best Naples nautical club, and he was utterly devoted to his depressed, often-difficult wife. They had two beautiful girls, hardworking, adventuresome, and unmarried, both very close to their grandmother Yvette, who lived with them until her death in August 1989. His only failing was to die young and unexpectedly, with his office affairs not quite in order and a scoundrel for a partner. Mariceli was plunged once more into genteel poverty, together with her mother and two daughters.[11]

Fiammetta, the younger of the two, knew practically nothing about her grandfather, for her mother, who died in 2013, refused to talk about him. She keeps a framed photograph of him on a living room shelf, one that belonged to her mother and to Yvette before that. Dressed in his colonial whites, Teruzzi looks like the affable captain of a large Mediterranean cruise ship. Later, when Fiammetta shows me around Naples, if acquaintances ask how she knows me—an outgoing, messily coiffed professor from New York City—she trills: "She's writing a book about my grandfather." And when asked who he was, she says simply: "A famous fascist general." What more is there to say? He left them nothing: no property, no memories, no moral compass.

How incongruous Lilliana Weinman Teruzzi would seem in that world. She may be a problematic figure by any reading: the talented, headstrong, young Jewish American woman who shared all of the 1920s enthusiasm for fascism. Then again, with her exuberant personality and firm notion of her rights, she could never have been a committed fascist for long. It was her rectitude and perseverance that had exposed the injustice done to her and persuaded Vittorio Scialoja to defend her before the law and Filippo Meda to defend the integrity of Church procedures by taking up her defense and, ultimately, to pressure the high prelates to uphold Catholic justice against Caesar's wiles. And without the court record of the highs and lows of her marriage, we would not have her story.

Then again, what to make of *l'americana*, with all of her money, connections, business interests, and legal know-how, who never understood Fascist Italy? Why would she dedicate all of her resources for fifteen years to obstruct the only process that could set her free? In fiction, her actions would be the perfect payback against a thug. But for her to try to annul the adoption of his daughter?

If this were fiction, we would want Lilliana to walk away from the heady days when she had almost arrived in "Mussolini's inner circle." We would want her to return from the darkness of Fascist Europe to the fertile soil of American democracy, much as Henry James or Edith Wharton might have had her come home once her Atlantic mésalliance with the shady continental fascist was over. With their turn-of-the-century grasp of how easy it was for idealistic America to capitulate to the Eros of immoral Europe, they would have had her—bruised and uncomprehending of what had happened—lick her wounds, recoup, and bounce back into American society.

We could take the fascist spies' reports from the Hotel Crillon in Paris, who overheard her denigrating the regime with her insider information about the corrupt behavior of fascist men and encouraging other female malcontents to do likewise, to mount a narrative that made her out to be a precocious feminist antifascist. But that wasn't Lilliana. She never saw the man she married as a warmongering anti-Semite. She always clung to the memory of her "fascist wedding." Perhaps the spectacle had been too perfectly choreographed. It had been her best performance, and she was not prepared to let go of that triumph.

To want to fit her into the mold of an antifascist is to miss that what she identified as "totalitarian" was the claque around Teruzzi who destroyed her marriage and then ganged up with the Catholic Church to annul it. And it was to fighting them that she devoted fifteen years of her life, which she did very effectively.

And so her life went on. Her mother, Rose, passed away on August 25, 1948; her father, Isaac, on February 26, 1951. She lived in New York City at the Mayfair on Park Avenue until her death in 1987. In 1953, around the time she posed with friends at the Trevi Fountain on her last visit to Italy, her onetime infatuation for Italy gave way to a passionate Anglophilia, and she found a new satisfaction in traveling to and from the British Isles on the great ships. She retired from running the family business and lived off invested wealth. She stingily but ostentatiously patronized respectable causes, establishing an opera prize that remains to this day for debuting singers at the Metropolitan Opera, and contributing to and being a member of the board the Metropolitan Museum of Art, whose collections were eventually the beneficiary of her Parisian couture dresses, bags, and purses and Italian rococo furniture. She exploited her 1970s New York moment of fame when she fell victim to a celebrity robber at the Imperial Ball. For the record, she was "Countess Attilio Teruzzi," "the widow of one of Mussolini's most dashing generals," and the stolen jewels were worth $345,000.

At family events, she was a garrulous, exotic cousin, holding forth on life in Mussolini's inner circle. The women sometimes asked themselves why a Jewish woman, any woman, would marry a fascist and with a beard and so much older. The men questioned whether any of what she said was true. Nobody doubted that the marriage must have ended because of anti-Semitism. Yet she left her boxes of photographs, letters, and clippings, as if she wanted somebody to set the record straight. When I had just made a dent, a family member, her distant cousin by marriage, Jim Yaffe, a writer and an upstanding man, mused: "Lilliana liked the red carpet, she didn't like to look under it."

To write the history of fascism from the perspective of a broken marriage is a singular endeavor. Yet in the conundrum that was Fascist Italy, a conservative society wracked by the war and yearning to be modern, then seized by a movement that presented itself as at once revolutionary and reactionary, marriage remained foundational. Teruzzi and Lilliana's marriage, which sat at the intersection of the tussles between Church and state, between the establishment and fascist upstarts, between swaggering masculinity and the obstinacy of an American diva, plumbs the intricacies of public and private morality during this time of profound social upheaval.

A straightforward analytical history, seeking to impose the rigor of causality, to outline power structures and define key concepts, would grasp at these same threads, without managing to weave them together. The way I've written this story is perhaps more akin to the way human society really works. Mussolini's rule, with its pretentions to total power, could never have individuated it. Fascist Italy was in fact a much wider, more complex, and more diverse world than we take it to be and the regime was repeatedly confronted by the limits of its powers and capacities, a predicament palpably illustrated by Attilio Teruzzi's inability to dissolve his "fascist marriage."

Mussolini was likewise forced to contend with limits. That said, that his totalitarian aspirations could be rebuffed, that political life was a constant wrangle, that civil society played hide and seek made his rule no less, perhaps more, despotic.

Giovanni Ansaldo's most damning judgment was that Teruzzi had an "impetuous character" and a "weak notion of the law." This was a judgment that Marshal Caviglia shared. The consensus was that the onetime quartermaster-postman at Massawa had been promoted too high, that the tumultuous changes of the time had thrust him into positions where he could act with impunity.

What more does this irresistible ascent tell us about fascist rule? In 1947, as the Florentine jurist Piero Calamandrei reflected on the past regime, after having helped author the Italian Republic's new constitution, he spoke of those "miserable minor tyrants," who were key to understanding the "totalizing corruption" endemic to "fascism's system." He would surely have identified Teruzzi among them. It was this "pyramid of complicity" that undergirded the hierarchy, this "intermediary despotism," as every one of Mussolini's functionaries was compromised by his "violent deeds, abuses of office, and cynical maneuvering." These men supplied the personnel, built the patronage systems, performed the ceremonials, and offered the rationale for collusion with the regime.[12]

But to view fascism as "a pyramid" of complicity doesn't really acknowledge what the figure of Teruzzi does best in this history. He is in some respects a perfect exemplar of what the historian Claudio Pavone, picking up on Calamandrei's condemnation of fascism's systemic "duplicity," as a "regime of lies," called the "two indissoluble faces of totalitarianism."[13] The one face was its violence: the laws and legal principles it broke in its efforts to sustain itself; the other its moral and political claim to reimpose law and order in the name of the greatness of the nation by usurping the power of the state. Once the fascists had seized power, this second claim perpetuated itself in the greatly aggrandized sphere of government power at Mussolini's command.

From Pavone's perspective, Teruzzi came as close to being a perfect fascist as one could imagine: a "political blanksheet," as Massimo Rocca described him in 1921, he learned to politick under fascism.[14] A party intransigent, a parliamentary deputy, a statesman, commander of the militia, and division general, Teruzzi became a prolific legislator and learned the rhetoric that went with the territory, such that some regarded him as a fine orator. To overcome his lowly social origins, he studied and adhered to the proper protocol for a perfect hierarch, including finding what appeared to be the perfect wife. He maneuvered to acquire bon ton, sought to gain intellectual recognition by writing a book, cared for his political entourage with payoffs and cover-ups, and shed his antimonarchical and anticlerical values to show proper deference to the king and Church, while demonstrating his ongoing loyalty to the Duce—whose favor made him a player.

From the moment he entered Mussolini's camp, he acted as the interface between the Blackshirt violence against institutions and the military-like discipline constantly being exercised to restore them. He was the *squadrista* electoral campaigner, the heckler deputy in parliament at the time of Giacomo Matteotti's murder, the Interior Ministry undersecretary responsible for cracking down on *squadrista* violence. As governor to Cyrenaica, he showcased Fascist Italy's civilizing mission, rebuilding Benghazi while destroying the indigenous culture. As commander of the

Blackshirts, he created a disciplined force to give impetus to Mussolini's project of overthrowing the British-dominated international order. As minister of Italian Africa, he promoted the Italian Empire at the same time as he acquiesced to subordinating Fascist Italy to Nazi Germany in the hierarchy of nations.

The biggest quandary that Italian society presented to the jurist Piero Calamandrei and to the many militant antifascists who understood that the overthrow of Mussolini's dictatorship was not synonymous with the elimination of fascism was the question of how to undertake a comprehensive reform of civil society that might root out fascism for the long term. How could one reestablish a new and stronger sense of social solidarity to replace fascism's intense, seemingly inexhaustible organization of enthusiasm? How would people relearn how to act as if liberty were more than the freedom to look out only for one's own interests? How could one foster a rigorous and scrupulous understanding of what lay behind the law? This was no simple project. To eradicate fascism called for surpassing its pseudo-solidarities, by building an inexhaustible fund of democratic civic values. To do so, Calamandrei concluded, was "a perpetual political-ethical duty."[15]

One way for the historian to respond to that inspired imperative is to imagine alternative ways to reframe the past: to get at how, in one of the great turning points, the intuitive political genius of a Mussolini—with his bold claims, big lies, opportunism, tactical swerves, and immense political inventiveness—could acquire so much traction. What would it have taken for the honest little Italy of 1911 to have reestablished itself as a free trade nation after the war rather than warmongering because that was what it meant to be a great power? How could a renewed political democracy have neutralized the toxic paramilitary culture of the postwar years, to prevent it from turning class conflict and intensely polarized political passions into outright warfare?

What would it have taken for Teruzzi to return from the First World War with enough capital from his experience to grant him respect for his service and rank and a pension to secure his middling status? I wager that the reformist center would have seized back the political initiative and the economy would have recovered, and he could have settled back into society as a Milanese man on the make, ever the war-hero and well-connected through his Freemasonic brothers, military service, and local knowledge. He would have married soon enough, a woman of strong character, a school teacher, perhaps, like his sister. He had the know-how and networks to go into the import-export trade, flourishing under the setting sun of the Pax Britannica. He would have worked very hard and might have earned well, acquired property, settled into a family apartment in Milan with a seaside place in Liguria and an Alpine lodge in the Valtellina, had three children, been discreet about his circuit of lovers, voted conservative, exploited his bonhomie to become a player in Milanese affairs, and involved himself in the politics of Milan. He would perhaps have risen to become a manager at the Milan Fair, and maybe even run for the city council.

Maybe he would have resembled the Teruzzi released from prison in 1950, cocooned by the restoration of the rule of law, the succor of the Catholic Church, and a strong sense of duty now redirected toward his family. Instead, fate and character—really, the forces of history and the force of things—had sent him into Mussolini's camp, inflicting incalculable harm on his nation, his family, and himself.

It is not a concession to the ideology of letting bygones be bygones; we are not, as Italians say, "putting a stone on the past," if we remember Attilio Teruzzi, Mussolini's New Man, the perfect fascist, as an antihero for dark times and his Jewish American wife, Lilliana Weinman Teruzzi, as the heroine manquée.

ABBREVIATIONS FOR NOTES

Persons

AT   Attilio Teruzzi
IW   Isaac Weinman
LW   Lilliana Weinman
LWT   Lilliana Weinman Teruzzi
RW   Rose Weinman

Archives

F   Collection (Fondo)
gab   (gabinetto)
a   (armadio)
b   box (busta)
f   file (fascicolo)
sf   subfile (sottofascicolo)

ACS   Archivio Centrale dello Stato, Rome
       MF   Ministero della Finanza
             DG APR   Direzione Generale, Avvocazione dei profitti di regime
                         ES   Entrate Speciale, Serie fascicoli personali (1928–1970), b. 38
                                 AT   Attilio Teruzzi, f. 2
       MGG   Ministero di Grazia e Giustizia
             DG AP   Direzione Generale, Affari Penali
                         UG   Ufficio Grazie (1948), b. 28
                                   AT   Teruzzi, Attilio: Collaborazione ed altro, f. 1635

        MI   Ministero dell'Interno

             Gab. 1948   Gabinetto 1948, b. 8, f. 253

               DG PS   Direzione Generale, Pubblica Sicurezza
                     Affari generali e riservati,

                         AT   A1, 1943, b. 79, f. Teruzzi
                              Attilio

             PP FP   Polizia Politica, Fascicoli Personali

                 RW   Weinmann Rosa, b. 1450

                 YB   Blank Ivette, b. 146

          MRF   Mostra della Rivoluzione Fascista

RF   Roberto Farinacci, b. 35

AT   Teruzzi Attilio, f. 29

        SPD   Segreteria Particolare del Duce

             CR   Carteggio Riservato

                 AT   Teruzzi Attilio, b. 95

                 AF   sf. Fassoni, Amelia

                 LW   sf. Weimann [Weinman], Lilliana

                 SF   sf. Ferazzi, Silvia

                 YB   sf. Blank, Yvette

                 FM   Malgeri Francesco, b. 87

                 IB   Brunhild, Ilda, b. 141

                 IF   Fua [Iole Foa], b. 44

             RSI   Repubblica Sociale Italiana

                 SOI   Situation in Occupied Italy, b. 14,
                         f. 10, sf. 65

               Tarabini   Tarabini, Alessandro, b. 36, f. 471

             CO   Carteggio Ordinario

                 AT   Attilio Teruzzi, b. 699, f. 209567

                 SAN   Settimio Aurelio Nappi, b. 1189,
                       f. 509611

ADSP   Archivio Diocesano Storico di Pavia, Pavia

          NM, T-W   F. Cause Matrimoniali, 1939, b. Nullitatis Matrimoni,
                Teruzzi-Weinmann

AUSMAE Archivio Ufficio Storico del Ministero degli Affari Esteri, Rome

          GMSG   Gabinetto del Ministro e della Segreteria Generale
                (1923–1943)

            MAI   Ministero dell'Africa Italiana

                AS   Archivio Segreto

AUSSME Archivio Ufficio Storico Stato Maggiore Esercito, Rome Fondo biografico

         AT, Mil. Rec.   Terruzzi, Attilio b. 62, Military Record f. 13

AME	Archivio Arnoldo Mondadori Editore, Milan	
	AT f. Attilio Teruzzi	
	Bottai f. Giuseppe Bottai	
LWTP	Lilliana Weinman Teruzzi Papers	
	AR b. Annulment Records	
	CPM (1933–1936)	f. Court Proceedings Milan (1933–1936)
	sf. 2	Proceedings, Sessions 1–22 (Jan. 11, 1933–July 3, 1934)
	sf. 3	Proceedings, Sessions 23–28 (July 10–Sept. 29, 1934)
	sf. 4	Supplementary Proceedings (Oct. 26, 1934–July 6, 1935)
	sf. 5	Supplementary Proceedings
	sf. 7	Sentence
	sf. 8	DN LWT Defense Notes (1934–1936)
	CPP (1937–1939)	f. Court Proceedings Pavia (1937–1939)
	CPSR (1940–1948)	f. Court Proceedings, Sacra Rota (1940–1948)
	sf. 1 1947	Trial Preparation Documents Clippings
		b. Clippings, Miscellaneous, Memorabilia
	Correspondence	b. Correspondence
		f. Telegrams
	Diaries	b. Diaries
		f. Notebook-Reminiscences, 1938
	Family Documents	b. Family Documents
	Family Photographs	b. Family Photographs
	Family Records	b. Family Records
TNA	The National Archives, United Kingdom	
	FO Foreign Office	
	371	Political Departments, General Correspondence 1906–1966
		12394 Cyrenaica
		12396 Egyptian

NOTES

Prologue

1. LWT, Notebook-Reminiscences, n.d. [1938], in Diaries, LWTP.
2. Hannah Arendt, *Origins of Totalitarianism*, new ed. (New York: Harcourt Brace Jovanovich, 1973), 473–474.
3. Benito Mussolini, "L' azione e la dottrina fascista dinanzi alle necessità storiche della nazione" (Discorso a Udine) September 20, 1922 in *Opera Omnia*, ed. Edoardo e Duilio Susmel (Florence: La Fenice, 1956) vol. 18, 411.
4. Galeazzo Ciano, *Diary, 1937–1938*, trans. and ed. Andreas Mayer, with an introduction by Malcolm Muggeridge (London: Methuen, 1952), 35.

1. The Soldier

1. R. L., "La morte e i funerali di un ascaro valoroso ferito a Bir-el-Turki," *Corriere della Sera*, March 15, 1912, 4; C. S., "Le vicende della guerra," *Corriere della Sera*, March 7, 1912, 3.
2. Massimo Zaccaria, *Anch'io per la tua bandiera: il V Battaglione Askari in missione sul fronte libico, 1912* (Ravenna: Giorgio Pozzi, 2012). Dechasa Abebe, "Ethiopian and Eritrean Askaris in Libya (1911–1932)," *Ethiopian Journal of the Social Sciences and Humanities* 13, no. 2 (December 2017): 28–52, speaks to the Italians' unusual dependency on local forces compared to other European imperialists of the time. On Libya at the time of the Italian conquest: Claudio G. Segrè, *Fourth Shore: The Italian Colonization of Libya* (Chicago: University of Chicago Press, 1975); and the most recent Italian works: Nicola Labanca, *La guerra italiana per la Libia, 1911–1931* (Bologna: Il Mulino, 2012); and Federico Cresti, *Non desiderate la terra d'altri: La colonizzazione italiana in Libia* (Rome: Carocci, 2011). On Italian soldiery: Vanda Wilcox, "Italian Morale and the Soldiers' Experience in Libya, 1911–1912," in *The Wars before the Great War: Conflict and International Politics before the Outbreak of the First World War*, eds. Dominik Geppert, William Mulligan, and Andreas Rose (Cambridge: Cambridge University Press, 2015), 41–57.
3. R. L., "La morte e i funerali di un ascaro valoroso ferito a Bir-el-Turki," *Corriere della Sera*, March 15, 1912, 4.

4. First photo: Mario Corsi, *Illustrazione Italiana* 34, no. 25 (June 23, 1912), 613.
   Second photo: Gualtiero Castellini, *Illustrazione Italiana* 2, no. 24 (June 16,
   1912), 587.

5. Filippo Tommaso Marinetti, *La grande Milano tradizionale e futurista: Una
   sensibilità italiana nata in Egitto*, ed. Luciano De Maria (Milan: Mondadori,
   1969), 5.

6. Emilio Settimelli, *Gli odi e gli amori* (Rome: Casa Editrice Pinciana, 1928), 125.

7. Photograph: "Ritratto in uniforme: Attilio Teruzzi (1913)," in Fondo Fotografico
   Emilio Sommariva, SOM. ST. E. c. 4, Biblioteca Nazionale Braidense, Milan.
   On Sommariva: G. Ginex, ed., *Divine. Emilio Sommariva fotografo. Opere
   scelte 1910–1930* (Busto Arsizio: Nomos, 2004).

8. What Liberal Italy's imperfect democracy and deep social inequalities
   contributed to the rise of fascism has been much debated. Nick Carter,
   "Rethinking the Liberal State," *Bulletin of Italian Politics* 3, no. 2 (2011), is a
   handy assessment of conflicting views. British historians provide judicious
   overviews: Adrian Lyttelton, ed., *Liberal and Fascist Italy, 1900–1945* (Oxford:
   Oxford University Press, 2002); and John A. Davis, ed., *Italy in the Nineteenth
   Century* (Oxford: Oxford University Press, 2001).

9. Cited in John Woodhouse, *Gabriele D'Annunzio, Defiant Archangel* (Oxford:
   Oxford University Press, 1998), 26–27. For background: Axel Körner, *Politics of
   Culture in Liberal Italy: From Unification to Fascism* (New York: Routledge,
   2008).

10. Information on Celestina Rossi Teruzzi comes from the Parish Record Office,
    Comune di Solbiate Comasco (Province of Como). See also Julia Rossi Viande,
    Celestina Teruzzi, 1854–1933-XII (Rome: Novissima, 1934); and Giorgio Casti-
    glioni, *Solbiate: Storia di un paese e dei suoi abitanti* (Solbiate: Comune di
    Solbiate, 2008).

11. "Documento per Fermo Cristofaro Teruzzi," January 14, 1877, in Como and
    Lecco, *Registri di stato civile, 1866–1936*, Archivio di Stato, Lombardy.

12. Birth Register, 1882, in Archivio di Stato Civile, Milan. Baptism date in Baptismal
    Registry for S. Ambrogio, 1882, Archivio della Curia, Archdiocese of Milan,
    Milan; *Ruolo generale delle famiglie*, Archivio Storico Civico e Biblioteca
    Trivulziana, Castello Sforzesco, Milan. On late 19th century Milan, see: Maria
    Pia Belski, *Milano cresce, 1860–1918* (Florence: Firenze Libri, 1995); *Guida di
    Milano* (Milano: Tipografia Bernardoni di C. Rebeschini, 1882–1889); Luca
    Gambi and Maria Cristina Gozzoli, *Le città nella storia d'Italia: Milano*
    (Rome: Laterza, 1982), 295–306. On the changing character of Corso Genova
    and Porta Genova in the late nineteenth century, see Gaetano Savallo, *Nuova
    Guida della Città di Milano e Sobborgi pel 1881* (Milan: Agenzia Savallo,
    1881), and its successive editions, *passim*.

13. Viande, *Celestina Teruzzi*.

14. Henry James, *Italian Hours* (Boston: Houghton Mifflin, 1909), 125.

15. On melodrama in Milanese popular culture, see Bruno Barilli, *Il paese del melodramma* (Milan: Adelphi, 2000); Aldo Nicastro, *Il melodramma e gli Italiani* (Milan: Rusconi, 1982); Stefano Scardovi, *L' opera dei bassifondi: il melodramma "plebeo" nel verismo musicale italiano* (Lucca: Libreria Musicale Italiana, 1994).

16. "Guido Teruzzi," *Corriere della Sera*, August 12, 1930, 7. LWT, handwritten note, n.d. [but Spring 1934], in AR, CPM (1933–1936), sf. 8 DN, LWTP.

17. Alfredo Canavero, *Il '98 a Milano: fatti, personaggi, immagini* (Milan: Società Umanitaria, 1998); Louise Tilly, *Politics and Class in Milan, 1881–1901* (New York: Oxford University Press, 1992). Jonathan Morris, *The Political Economy of Shopkeeping in Milan, 1886–1922* (Cambridge: Cambridge University Press, 2002) shows that, like elsewhere, the daunting economic situation turned many small shopkeepers into political conservatives.

18. John Gooch, *Army, State, and Society in Italy, 1870–1915* (New York: St. Martin's Press, 1989), offers a good introduction in English. Beyond that, see Nicola Labanca, *L'istituzione militare in Italia: politica e società* (Milan: UNICOPLI, 2002); Giorgio Rochat, *Ufficiali e soldati: l'esercito italiano dalla prima alla seconda guerra mondiale* (Udine: P. Gaspari, 2000); and Lucio Ceva, *Storia della società italiana dall'unità a oggi*, vol. 11: *Le forze armate* (Turin: UTET, 1981), 15; as well as the work of General and Fascist Quadrumvir, Emilio De Bono, *Nell'esercito nostro prima della guerra* (Milan: A. Mondadori, 1931).

19. Military record and typed biography, n.d., 6 pp., both in Fondo Biografico, AT, Mil. Rec., AUSSME.

20. Giovanni Canevazzi, *La scuola militare di Modena, 1756–1914* (Modena: Giovanni Ferraguti, 1914–1921); this period piece has to be read together with Gian Luca Balestra's authoritative *La formazione degli ufficiali nell'Accademia Militare di Modena, 1895–1939* (Roma: Ufficio storico Stato Maggiore Esercito, 2000).

21. Antonio Sema, "La cultura dell'esercito," in *Cultura e società negli anni del fascismo*, ed. Gabriele Turi et al., 91–116 (Milan: Cordani, 1987); Eugenio De Rossi, *La vita di un ufficiale italiano sino alla guerra* (Milan: Mondadori, 1927). The best introduction to twentieth-century military life generally is by the University of Chicago sociologist Morris Janovitz, *The Professional Soldier: A Social and Political Portrait* (Glencoe, IL: Free Press, 1960); and Alfred Vagts, *History of Militarism*, rev. ed. (New York: Free Press, 1967).

22. On military wives: Antonella Buono, "Il matrimonio degli ufficiali nella legislazione italiana dall'Unità al 1971," *Rivista militare* 7–8 (1973): 999–1025, 1145–1168.

23. Alessandro Cova, *Graziani: un generale per il regime* (Milan: Newton Compton, 1987), 66.

24. Ottorino Mezzetti, *Guerra in Libia: Esperienze e ricordi* (Rome: Paolo Cremonese Editore, 1933), 141–142; Cova, *Graziani*,194.

25. On the diplomatic background of the Italian-Turkish War: Mark Choate, "New Dynamics and New Imperial Powers, 1876–1905," in *The Routledge History of Western Empires* (Oxford: Routledge, 2014), 118–134; Mark Choate, "From Territorial to Ethnographic Colonies and Back Again: The Politics of Italian Expansion, 1890–1912," *Modern Italy* 8, no. 1 (2003): 65–75; Nicola Labanca, *La guerra italiana per la Libia 1911–1931* (Bologna: Il Mulino, 2012), 27–120; T. W. Childs, *Italo-Turkish Diplomacy and the War over Libya 1911–1912* (Leiden: Brill, 1990); Angelo Del Boca, *Gli italiani in Libia: Tripoli bel suol d'amore* (Rome: Laterza, 1986), 3–202.

26. Giovanni Pascoli, "La grande proletaria s'è mossa," in *Limpido rivo* (Bologna: N. Zanichelli, 1924), 80–82; Giuseppe Finaldi, "Dreaming in the Desert: Libya as Italy's Promised Land, 1911–1970," in *Imperial Expectations and Realities: El Dorados, Utopias and Dystopias*, ed. Andrekos Varnava (Manchester: Manchester University Press, 2015), 193. On Marinetti: Antonio Schiavulli, *La guerra lirica: Il dibattito dei letterati italiani sull'impresa di Libia, 1911–1912* (Ravenna: Giorgio Pozzi Editore, 2009), 10 n9; also Gabriele Proglio, *Libia 1911–1912: Immaginari coloniali e Italianità* (Florence: Le Monnier, 2016).

27. Guelfo Civinini, "Panorama di vita di un vecchio fascista," *Corriere della Sera*, January 4, 1939, 3. For other Milanese war correspondents, see Isabella Nardi and Sandro Gentili, eds., *La grande illusione: opinione pubblica e mass media al tempo della guerra di Libia* (Perugia: Morlacchi, 2009).

28. In f. "Sintesi Diario 5th Battaglione eritreo, 1914," F. L-8, 92, f. 1, AUSMAE, "Come fu conquistata la Fezzan dalle truppe della colonna Miani," *Illustrazione Italiana*, 41, no. 7 (February 15, 1913), 159; Guido Fornari, *Gli italiani nel sud libico: la colonna Miani, 1913–1915* (Rome: Ministero dell'Africa italiana, Ufficio studi e propaganda, 1941), 104, 100–125; Angelo Del Boca, *La disfatta di Gasr Bu Hàdi: 1915: Il colonnello Miani e il più grande disastro dell'Italia coloniale* (Milan: Mondadori, 2004).

2. The Great War

1. John Keegan, *The First World War* (New York: A. Knopf, 1999), 349. Mark Thompson, *The White War: Life and Death on the Italian Front, 1915–1919* (New York: Basic Books, 2009) regards the Italian command as the harshest in the war, second only to the Russian in its treatment of the troops. For the effects on soldiers' morale: Vanda Wilcox, *Morale and the Italian Army during the First World War* (New York: Cambridge University Press, 2016).

2. "Brigata Barletta," in Ministero della guerra, Stato maggiore centrale, Ufficio storico, *Brigate di fanteria: riassunti storici dei corpi e comandi nella guerra 1915–1918*, vol. 5, 327–353 (Rome: Libreria dello Stato, 1927).

3. Orders in Attachments (Allegati), June 19–June 20, 1916 in "Diario dal 1 giugno 1916 al 30 giugno, 1916," 137° Reggimento Fanteria, in Fondo N-1/11, armadio 136/D, vol. 1163f, AUSSME.

4. AT, Mil. Rec., AUSSME. Emilio Lussu's fictionalized memoir from his time as officer in the Sardinian Brigade, takes place on the same slopes at the same time. Emilio Lussu, *A Soldier on the Southern Front*, trans. Gregory Conti (New York: Rizzoli Ex Libris, 2014). See also Giorgio Seccia, *Monte Zebio: dalla Strafexpedition alla vittoria finale 1916–1918* (Chiari [Brescia]: Nordpress, 2007), 200.

5. Vincenzo Ponzi: *Giuseppe Vaccari: Medaglia d'Oro* (Vicenza: Officina Tipografica Vicentina, 1931) in Fondo Vaccari, Correspondence, Generale Giuseppe Vaccari (b. 23), Museo del Risorgimento e della Resistenza, Vicenza; Gianni Pieropan, *Il Generale Giuseppe Vaccari (1866–1837)*, *Cronache*, ed. Amelio Maggio (Montebello Vicentino: Comune, 1987), 30–31, 84–97; Giuseppe Vaccari, Fascicolo personale, Senato della Repubblica, https://notes9.senato.it/web/senregno.nsf/6e64fa6139dfoba6c125711400382712/d91ed56b3ao1eee6412564 6foo61481c?OpenDocument.

6. Sandro Gerbi, *Raffaele Mattioli e il filosofo domato: Storia di un'amicizia* (Milan: Ulrico Hoepli Editore, 2017), 13–14. Giovanni Malagodi, *Profilo di Raffaele Mattioli* (Milan: Ricciardi, 1984), 16.

7. Thompson, *White War*, 258, 240.

8. Shiferaw Bekele, Uoldeul Chelati Dirar, Alessandro Volterra, and Massimo Zaccaria, eds., *The First World War from Tripoli to Addis Ababa, 1911–1924* (Addis Ababa: Centre français des études éthiopiennes, 2018); Angelo Del Boca, *La disfatta di Gasr Bu Hàdi: 1915 : Il colonnello Miani e il più grande disastro dell'Italia coloniale* (Milan: Mondadori, 2004).

3. Mutilated Victory

1. LWT, handwritten note, Spring 1934, in AR, CPM (1933–1936), sf. 8 DN, LWTP.

2. From Gabriele D'Annunzio's "La preghiera di Sernaglia," *Corriere della Sera*, October 24, 1918, 1. To understand the blood-and-guts imagery in D'Annunzio's own rhetoric: Barbara Spackman, "Il verbo (è) sangue: Gabriele D'Annunzio and the Ritualization of Violence," *Quaderni d'italianistica* 4, no. 2 (1983): 218–229. On the political usage see: Brian R. Sullivan, "Vittoria Mutilata," in *1914–1918-online: International Encyclopedia of the First World War*, ed. Ute Daniel, Peter Gatrell, Oliver Janz, Heather Jones, Jennifer Keene,

Alan Kramer, and Bill Nasson (Berlin: Freie Universität Berlin, July 21, 2017), https://encyclopedia.1914-1918-online.net/article/vittoria_mutilata; Vanda Wilcox, "From Heroic Defeat to Mutilated Victory: The Myth of Caporetto in Fascist Italy," in *Defeat and Memory: Cultural Histories of Military Defeat in the Modern Era*, ed. Jenny Macleod (London: Palgrave Macmillan, 2008), 46–61.

3. On the ludic-political dimensions of D'Annunzio's feats: Lucy Hughes-Hallett, *Gabriele d'Annunzio: Poet, Seducer, and Preacher of War* (New York: Knopf, 2013); Claudia Salaris, *Alla festa della rivoluzione: Artisti e libertari con D'Annunzio a Fiume* (Bologna: Il Mulino, 2002). On the Fiume occupation's significance to postwar Italian politics, the most incisive source is still Paolo Alatri, *Nitti, D'Annunzio e la questione adriatica, 1919–1920* (Milan: Feltrinelli, 1959).

4. Attilio Teruzzi's file at D'Annunzio's Archivio at Riviera di Gardone makes no mention of his actual presence at Fiume, although several of the dozen pieces of correspondence speak of the intimate comraderie between the two, as if Teruzzi had been there. More importantly, Teruzzi does not appear on the list D'Annunzio kept of the legionnaires who served him at Fiume. Folder Teruzzi, Attilio, Archivio Generale, Vittoriale degli Italiani.

5. Stefano Pivato, *Il nome e la storia: Onomastica e religioni politiche nell'Italia contemporanea* (Bologna: Il Mulino, 1999), 211–218.

6. Emilio Canevari, *La guerra italiana*, vol. 1 (Rome: Tosi Editore, 1948), 245–246. On Italian war veterans, see Angelo Ventrone, *La seduzione totalitaria: Guerra, modernità, violenza politica, 1914–1918* (Rome: Donzelli, 2003), 3–48; Giovanni Sabbatucci, *I combattenti* (Bari: Laterza, 1974). For a comparative perspective, see Angel Alcalde, *War Veterans and Fascism in Interwar Europe* (New York: Cambridge University Press, 2017).

7. Giorgio Rochat, *L'esercito italiano da Vittorio Veneto a Mussolini, 1919–1925*, new ed. (Rome: Laterza, 2006), 90.

8. Guelfo Civinini, "Panorama di vita di un vecchio fascista," *Corriere della Sera*, January 4, 1939, 3.

4. Enter the Diva

1. IW (NYC) to Secretary of State (Washington, DC), February 16, 1920, in Correspondence, LWTP; passport applications, 1921, in Family Documents, LWTP.

2. Roberto Moranzoni (NYC) to Carlo Clausetti (Milan), March 8, 1920, in Correspondence, LWTP.

3. LW (Milan) to IW (NYC), September 30, 1920; like all the other letters hers, her father's (IW), and her mother's (RW) are in Correspondence, LWTP.

4. Wacław Wierzbieniec, "Rzeszów," trans. Anna Grojec, in *YIVO Encyclopedia of Jews in Eastern Europe*, YIVO Institute, New York, November 23, 2010, http://www.yivoencyclopedia.org/article.aspx/Rzeszow; N. M. Gelber, "The History of the Jews of Rzeszów," in *Rzeszów* [Poland] *Community Memorial*, ed. M. Yari-Wold, 55–64, https://www.jewishgen.org/yizkor/rzeszow/rzeszow.html.

5. New York, NY, 13th Census of the United States of America, 1910; and New York, NY, 14th Census, 1920; both in Correspondence, LWTP. Passport applications, 1921, in Family Documents, LWTP. "Nathan Olbe Letter 1996," in The Oelbaums's website, http://www.oelbaums.com/oelbaums/nathan_olbe_letter.html.

6. On Kohut, see Karla Goldman, "Rebekah Bettelheim Kohut 1864–1951," in *The Encyclopedia of Jewish Women*, Jewish Women's Archive, Brookline, MA, https://jwa.org/encyclopedia/article/kohut-rebecca. On Lilliana's progressive home and school environment, see Joyce Antler, *The Journey Home: How Jewish Women Shaped Modern America*, rev. ed. (Boston: Schocken Books, 1999).

7. LW, *Diary, 1914–1915*, n.d. [likely June 1914], in Diaries, LWTP.

8. On the unique place of opera in bridging New York City's high-low, art-entertainment, and ethnic spectrum, see Mike Wallace, *Greater Gotham* (New York: Oxford, 2017), ch. 12, "Acropolis," esp. 382–388. On the Jewish elites see Stephen Birmingham, *"Our Crowd": The Great Jewish Families of New York* (New York: Harper Row, 1967), 330–340; Mary Jane Phillips-Matz, *The Many Lives of Otto Kahn* (Hillsdale, NY: Pendragon Press, 1984), 58. On the turn-of-the-century NYC opera world, see Elise Kuhl Kirk, *American Opera* (Urbana: University of Illinois Press, 2005); Irving Kolodin, *Story of the Metropolitan: A Candid History* (New York: Knopf, 1953), 314; and see also Charles Affron and Mirella Jona Affron, *Grand Opera: The Story of the Met* (Berkeley: University of California Press, 2014).

9. Kirk, *American Opera*, 87.

10. LW, *Diary, 1914–1915*, entry for May 13, 1915, in Diaries, LWTP.

11. Lazar S. Samoiloff, *The Singer's Handbook* (Philadelphia: Theodore Pesser, 1942), 118–119; "Three Samoiloff Artist-Pupils Debut," *Musical Courier*, March 9, 1916, 5; and a second engagement, "A Samoiloff Concert, February 22," *Musical Courier*, February 1, 1917, 39.

12. LW, *Diary, 1914–1915*, May 15, 1914, in Diaries, LWTP.

13. Sophie Braslau, "Making a Career in America," in *Vocal Mastery: Talks with Master Singers and Teachers*, ed. Harriette Brower (New York: Frederick A. Stokes, 1920), 187.

14. Giulio Gatti-Casazza, *Memories of the Opera* (New York: C. Scribner's Sons, 1941), 178; John Dizikes, *Opera in America: A Cultural History* (New Haven: Yale University Press, 1993), 370; Pierre Van Rensselaer Key, *Enrico Caruso: A Biography* (Boston: Little, Brown, 1922), 285.
15. Braslau, "Making a Career in America," 187.
16. Guglielmo Barblan, *Toscanini e la Scala; Testimonianze e confessioni a cura di Eugenio Gara*, ed. Eugenio Gara (Milan: Edizioni della Scala, 1972).
17. LW (Milan) to IW (NYC), February 3, 1921, in Correspondence, LWTP.
18. On Umberto Ferulli: Giuseppe Umberto Ferulli, in New York, Naturalization Records, 1882–1944, January 18, 1933, National Archives and Records Administration, Washington, DC; and Petitions for Naturalization from the US District Court for the Southern District of New York, 1897–1944, Series M1972, Roll 1025. See also LWT, "Note: Umberto Ferulli," n.d. [but 1934], in AR, CPM (1933–1936), sf. 8 DN, LWTP.
19. LW (Varese) to IW (London), December 15, 1920, in Correspondence, LWTP.
20. RW (Milan) to IW (NYC), November 9, 1920, in Correspondence, LWTP.
21. LW (Milan) to IW (NYC), November 9, 1920, in Correspondence. LWTP.
22. LWT, "Deposition," Session 5, May 20, 1933, in AR, CPM (1933–1936), sf. 2 LWTP.
23. On the "patriotic courtesan," see Giuseppe Antonio Borgese, *Goliath: The March of Fascism* (New York: Viking Press, 1938), 75.
24. LW (Milan) to IW (NYC), November 9, 1920 in Correspondence, LWTP.

5. In Mussolini's Camp

1. Guelfo Civinini, "Panorama di vita di un vecchio fascista," *Corriere della Sera*, January 4, 1939, 3.
2. "Service Record," Attilio Teruzzi, in Fondo Biografico, AT, Mil. Rec., AUSSME.
3. Benito Mussolini, "Dopo due anni," *Il Popolo d'Italia*, March 23, 1921. On fascism of the first hour, start with the classics, first and foremost, Angelo Tasca, trans. Peter Wait and Dorothy Wait, *The Rise of Italian Fascism, 1918–1922* (New York: H. Fertig, 1966), first published in 1938 while he was in exile in France under his pseudonym A. Rossi. See also Adrian Lyttelton, *The Seizure of Power* (New York: Scribner, 1973), 1–76; Salvatore Lupo, *Il fascismo: la politica di un regime totalitario* (Rome: Donzelli, 2000), 1–97; Emilio Gentile, *Storia del partito fascista, 1919–1922: movimento e milizia* (Rome: Laterza, 1989); Renzo De Felice, *Mussolini il rivoluzionario, 1883–1920* (Turin: Einaudi, 1963).
4. Gentile, *Storia del partito fascista*, 54–59.
5. Giorgio Rochat, *L'esercito italiano da Vittorio Veneto a Mussolini, 1919–1925* (Bari: Laterza, 2006) is still fundamental here, especially on the attempted coup of 1919. See, also, Marco Mondini, *La politica delle armi: il ruolo*

dell'esercito dell'avvento del fascismo (Rome: Laterza, 2006), 83–113; Marco Mondini, "Between Subversion and Coup d'état: Military Power and Politics after the Great War (1919–1922)," *Journal of Modern Italian Studies* 11 no. 4 (2006): 445–464; Gianni Pieropan, *Il Generale Giuseppe Vaccari (1866–1937), Cronache e ricordi*, ed. Amelio Maggio (Montebello Vicentino: Comune, 1989), 143–144.

6. Brian R. Sullivan, "Italian Naval Power and the Washington Disarmament Conference of 1921–22," *Diplomacy and Statecraft* 4, no. 3 (1993): 220–248.

7. Emilio De Bono, *La guerra: come e dove l'ho vista e combattuta io* (Milan: A. Mondadori, 1935), cited in Elvira Valleri Scaffei, "Emilio E. De Bono," *Dizionario Biografico degli Italiani*, vol. 33 (1987).

8. De Bono, *La guerra*.

9. Mondini, *La politica delle armi*, 60–64.

10. Paolo Spriano, *The Occupation of the Factories, 1920* (London: Pluto Press, 1975).

11. Mondini, *La politica delle armi*, 71–79.

12. Angelo Tasca, *The Rise of Italian Fascism*, 97–99; Gaetano Salvemini, *The Fascist Dictatorship in Italy* (New York: Henry Holt, 1927), 78.

13. Lawrence Squeri, "The Italian Local Elections of 1920 and the Outbreak of Fascism," *Historian* 45, no. 3 (May 1983): 324–336.

14. Tasca, *The Rise of Italian Fascism*, esp ch. 7, "The Posthumous and Preventive Counterrevolution," 81–130. In addition, see the social histories of north-central Italian provinces from the 1970s and 1980s, notably Paul Corner, *Fascism in Ferrara, 1915–1925* (New York: Oxford University Press, 1975); Anthony L. Cardoza, *Agrarian Elites and Italian Fascism: Province of Bologna, 1901–1926* (Princeton, NJ: Princeton University Press, 1983); Frank Snowden, *The Fascist Revolution in Tuscany, 1919–1922* (Cambridge: Cambridge University Press, 1989); Victoria de Grazia, *The Culture of Consent: Mass Organization of Leisure in Fascist Italy* (Cambridge: Cambridge University Press, 1981), esp. ch. 1.

15. For the best account of the incident's political and historical significance, see Matteo Di Figlia, "The Shifting Evocations of Squadrismo: Remembering the Massacre of Palazzo d'Accursio in Fascist Bologna," *Journal of Modern Italian Studies* 21, no. 4 (2016): 84–102. On squadrismo's role in fascism's rise to power, see Matteo Millan, "The Institutionalization of Squadrismo: Disciplining Paramilitary Violence in the Italian Fascist Dictatorship," *Contemporary European History* 22, no. 4 (November 2013): 551–573; as well as Matteo Millan, *Squadrismo e squadristi nella dittatura fascista* (Rome: Viella, 2014). See also Sven Reichardt, *Camicie nere, camicie brune: milizie fasciste in Italia e in Germania* (Bologna: Il Mulino, 2009).

16. MacGregor Knox, *To the Threshold of Power 1922–33*, vol. 1: *Origins and Dynamics of the Fascist and National Socialist Dictatorships* (Cambridge: Cambridge University Press, 2007), 323.

17. De Felice, *Mussolini il rivoluzionario*, is foundational here to capturing the mix of family background, sectarian politics, and personal furies that shaped the maximalist-socialist Mussolini. The best, most readily available English-language biography is Richard R. B. Bosworth, *Mussolini*, new ed. (London: Bloomsbury, 2010), chs. 2–6. On the impact of the war on Mussolini see Paul O'Brien, *Mussolini in the First World War: The Journalist, the Soldier, the Fascist* (Oxford: Berg, 2004); also Antonio Sema, "1914–1934: guerra e politica militare secondo Mussolini," in *Marte in orbace: guerra, esercito e milizia nella concezione fascista della Nazione*, ed. Virgilio Ilari and Antonio Sema, 15–49 (Ancona: Nuove Ricerche, 1988).

18. Cesare Rossi, *Trentatre vicende mussoliniane* (Milan: Ceschina, 1958), 28. On this key figure see Mauro Canali, *Cesare Rossi: da sindacalista rivoluzionario a eminenza grigia del fascismo* (Bologna: Il Mulino, 1991).

6. On the March

1. Cesare Rossi, *Trentatre vicende mussoliniane* (Milan: Ceschina, 1958), 32.

2. Vincenzo Mantovani, *Mazurka blu: la strage del Diana* (Milan: Rusconi, 1979).

3. LW (Milan) to IW (NYC), March 27, 1921, in Correspondence, LWTP.

4. "Il popolo di Milano in un impeto di pietà," *La Stampa*, March 29, 1921, 1.

5. *L'Ordine Nuovo*, March 24, 1921, cited in "La strage al Diana era nei piani di Mosca?" *Il Popolo d'Italia*, March 26, 1921, 1.

6. "I comunisti si dichiarano solidali con gli assassini," *Il Popolo d'Italia*, March 27, 1921, 1; also "Benito Mussolini, 'Accettiamo la sfida!'" *Il Popolo d'Italia*, March 28, 1921, 1.

7. "Il popolo di Milano in un impeto di pietà," *La Stampa*, March 29, 1921, 1; Mantovani, *Mazurka blu*, 488–496.

8. "Milano racccolta in atto di austera pietà attorno alle vittime," *Il Popolo d'Italia*, March 29, 1921, 1; "Il solenne pietoso omaggio di Milano alle vittime dell'attentato," *Corriere della Sera*, March 29, 1921, 3.

9. "Non Dimenticare il teatro Diana, per l'amore e la salvezza della Patria votate lista dei fascisti di combattimento," cited in Mantovani, *Mazurka blu*, 480, 518, 516.

10. Gaetano Polverelli, "Il risveglio della conscienza nazionale," *Il Popolo d'Italia*, May 4, 1921, 1.

11. B. Mussolini, "Per continuare," *Il Popolo d'Italia*, May 4, 1921, 1.

12. "Gli incidenti al comizio di Seregno," *Corriere della Sera*, May 11, 1921, 3; "Cose a posto: Un morto e un ferito grave a Seregno," *Avanti!* May 8, 1921, 2;

"Incidenti e feriti a Seregno," *Corriere della Sera*, May 6, 1921, 5; "Ultime di cronaca: La propaganda in provincia," *Corriere della Sera*, May 9, 1921, 3; "Revolverate e feriti a Seregno," *Il Popolo d'Italia*, May 6, 1921, 4.

13. "Agguati e conflitti fra fascisti e sovversivi: Mezz'ora di fuoco a Vigentino," *Corriere della Sera*, May 12, 1921, 3; "Battaglia e revolverate a Vigentino," *Il Popolo d'Italia*, May 12, 1921, 3.

14. Alexander De Grand, *The Hunchback's Tailor: Giovanni Giolitti and Liberal Italy from the Challenge of Mass Politics to the Rise of Fascism, 1882–1922* (Westport, CT: Praeger, 2001).

15. Adrian Lyttelton, ed., *Liberal and Fascist Italy, 1900–1945* (Oxford: Oxford University Press, 2002), 60–61.

16. Massimo Rocca, *Come il fascismo divenne una dittatura. Storia interna del fascismo dal 1914 al 1925* (Milan: Librarie Italiane, 1952), 149, claims credit for the term.

17. Salvatore Lupo, *Il fascismo: La politica di un regime totalitario* (Rome: Donzelli, 2000), 29.

18. Benito Mussolini, "Discorso al Teatro Augusteo di Roma," November 6, 1921 in *Opera Omnia*, 17. 211–212.

19. Rocca, *Come il fascismo*, 107.

20. Rocca, *Come il fascismo*, 99, 104, 137.

21. Antonino Repaci, *La marcia su Roma: mito e realtà*, 2 vols. (Roma: Canesi, 1963), 93; Balbo, *Diario*,1922 (Milan: Mondadori, 1932), 40.

22. Pietro Alberghi, *Modena nel periodo fascista 1919–1943* (Modena: Mucchi e Sias, 1998), 22, 25, 27.

23. AT, b. 38, f. 113.433: Carteggio Politico, Partito Nazionale Fascista, MRF, ACS

24. "Miscellaneous telegrams, letters, reports, July 22–25, 1922," in b. 32, f. 113, sf. 254 "fascio di Livorno," Carteggio Politico, Partito Nazionale Fascista, MRF, ACS; Rocca, *Come il fascismo*, 162.

25. On Balbo: Claudio Segrè, *Italo Balbo: A Fascist Life* (Berkeley: University of California Press), esp. 57–126; Giorgio Rochat, *Italo Balbo* (Turin: Unione Tipografico-Editrice Torinese, 1986); Giordano Bruno Guerri, *Italo Balbo* (Milan: Mondadori, 1998).

26. Balbo, *Diario*, 30.

27. Balbo, *Diario*, 30.

28. "Come fu ucciso a Cremona il presidente della deputazione provinciale: orribili particolari," *La Stampa*, December 13, 1921, 5; "Il funerale di Boldori domani," *Corriere della Sera*, December 14, 1921, 3.

29. "Rumoroso eco alla camera," *Corriere della Sera*, December 13, 1921, 3; also "La seduta di ieri alla camera," *Il Popolo d'Italia*, December 13, 1921, 1.

30. Rocca, *Come il fascismo*, 183–184. No single Italian fascist, except for Mussolini, has generated as many biographies, nor been so hard to pin down. To start: Francis J. Demers, *L'origine del fascismo a Cremona* (Bari: Laterza, 1979); Harry Fornari, *Mussolini's Gadfly* (Nashville, TN: Vanderbilt University Press, 1971); and Matteo di Figlia, *Farinacci: Il radicalismo fascista al potere* (Rome: Donzelli, 2007).

31. "Nefanda mistificazione social-pussista . . . ," *Il Popolo d'Italia*, December 14, 1921, 1; Attilio Teruzzi, "I primi risultati della inchiesta," *Il Popolo d'Italia*, December 14, 1921, 1; Bruno Gatta, *Gli uomini del Duce* (Milan: Rusconi, 1986), 107–108; "Un'inchiesta fascista," *Corriere della Sera*, December 14, 1921, 3.

32. Adolf Hitler, *Mein Kampf*, quoted in Martin Jay, *The Virtues of Mendacity: On Lying in Politics*, Richard Lectures (Charlottesville: University of Virginia Press, 2010), 2–3, 181.

33. "Un'inchiesta fascista," *Corriere della Sera*, December 14, 1921, 3; "La fine dello sciopero nel Cremonese," *Corriere della Sera*, December 14, 1921, 5.

34. Balbo, *Diario*. 33.

35. Balbo, *Diario*, 102, 109. On these events: Repaci, *La Marcia su Roma*, 1:39–49; Renzo De Felice, "*Mussolini il fascista. Vol. I: la conquista del potere, 1921–1925* (Turin: Einaudi, 1966), 270–271; and Sven Reichardt, "Propaganda and Violence: Fascist Demonstration Marches in Italy and Germany," in *The Street as Stage: Protest Marches and Public Rallies since the Nineteenth Century*, ed. Matthias Reiss, 169–191 (New York: Oxford University Press, 2007).

36. Angelo Tasca, *The Rise of Italian Fascism*, trans. Peter Wait and Dorothy Wait (New York: H. Fertig, 1966), 220.

37. "Spontanea, vigorosa reazione ai tentativi di paralizzare la vita cittadina con lo sciopero," *Corriere della Sera*, August 3, 1922, 4.

38. Giulio Goria, "I giorni della solitudine," *Paese Sera*, October 21, 1972, 3. On Mattioli, see Sandro Gerbi, *Raffaele Mattioli o il filosofo domato: storia di un'amicizia*, new ed. (Milan: Hoepli, 2017).

39. Goria, "I giorni della solitudine," 3.

40. Goria, "I giorni della solitudine," 4.

41. De Felice, *Mussolini il fascista*, 1:277; "Un colloquio di Gabriele D'Annunzio con i fascisti milanesi," *Il Popolo d'Italia*, August 3, 1922, 4; "L'assalto al palazzo Marino," *Il Popolo d'Italia*, August 4, 1922, 2; Umberto Foscanelli, *Processo a D'Annunzio (parla la difesa)* (Florence: Il Fauno, 1963), 85.

42. "Il discorso di Gabriele D'Annunzio dal balcone del municipio di Milano," *Corriere della Sera*, August 5, 1922, 3. Republished with variations in Gabriele D'Annunzio, *Il libro ascetico della giovane Italia* (Milan: L'Olivetana, 1926), 203–212.

43. "Tumultuoso epilogo dello sciopero generale in Italia," *Corriere della Sera*, August 5, 1922; De Felice, *Mussolini il fascista*, 272–281; "I baroni rossi cacciati

dal palazzo del comune," *Il Popolo d'Italia*, August 4, 1922; Repaci, *La Marcia su Roma*, 2: 35–44; Pietro Nenni, *Vent'anni di fascismo* (Milan: Avanti! 1964), 226.

44. Photograph: Palazzo Marino, with Teruzzi and Forni in foreground, August 4, 1922, FM A 415 / 2, in Raccolte Grafiche e Fotografiche del Castello Sforzesco, Civico Archivio Fotografico, Milan.

45. Repaci, *La Marcia su Roma*, 2: 47–49. Photograph: D'Annunzio at Hotel Cavour salutes Fascist columns, August 2, 1922, FM A415 / 1, in Raccolte Grafiche e Fotografiche del Castello Sforzesco, Civico Archivio Fotografico, Milan.

46. De Felice, *Mussolini il fascista*, 1: 279–280, 279 fn3.

47. Balbo, *Diario*, 141; Segrè, *Italo Balbo*, 96. On De Vecchi, see Enzo Santarelli, *Dizionario Biografico degli Italiani*, vol. 39 (1991). For background, emphasizing the illegal coup, as opposed to the legal maneuvering, in addition to older works, notably, Repaci, *Marcia su Roma*, see Giulia Albanese, *The March on Rome: Violence and the Rise of Italian Fascism*, trans. Sergio Knipe (London: Routledge, 2019); and Segrè, *Italo Balbo*, 105–113.

48. "Partito Nazionale Fascista: Comando Generale: Regolamento di disciplina per la milizia fascista," *Il Popolo d'Italia*, October 3, 1922, 2.

49. "Partito Nazionale Fascista: Comando Generale."

50. Balbo, *Diario*, 196–197.

51. Balbo, *Diario*, 201–202, 213.

7. Little Man, What Now?

1. Matteo di Figlia, *Farinacci: Il radicalismo fascista al potere* (Rome: Donzelli, 2007), 161.

2. Claudio Segrè, *Italo Balbo: A Fascist Life* (Berkeley: University of California Press, 1990), 115.

3. n.a. *Storia di Solbiate Comasco* (Solbiate Comasco: Tipografia Comune, 2007)

4. Attilio Teruzzi (Rome) to Gaetano Pirrone (Roccalumera, Messina), November 14, 1922, in b. 38, f. 113.433: Carteggio Politico, Partito Nazionale Fascista, MRF, ACS.

5. Photographic service: "Arrivo di una personalità, Palazzo Quirinale," November 4, 1923, in Fondo Pastorel, Archivio Storico Istituto Luce, Rome.

6. Massimo Rocca, *Come il fascismo divenne una dittatura* (Milan: Edizioni librarie italiane, 1952), 130.

7. Bimby Teruzzi (Milan) to Benito Mussolini (Rome), May 14, 1934, in SPD, CR, AT, ACS.

8. "Liliana Lorma all'Arena di Verona," in Scrapbook: "Reviews of performances," July 1922, in Clippings, LWTP. LW (Milan) to IW (NYC), December 5, 1922, in Correspondence, LWTP.

9. LW (Milan) to IW (NYC) December 5, 1922; LW (Milan) to IW (NYC), October 28, 1923, in Correspondence, LWTP.

10. Scrapbook: "Reviews of performances," October 1923, in Clippings, LWTP.
11. Rose Weinman, "Deposition" June 6, 1934, in AR, CPM (1933–1936), sf. 4, LWTP.
12. Rose Weinman, "Deposition," June 6, 1934.
13. Rose Weinman, "Deposition," June 6, 1934.
14. LW (Milan) to IW (NYC), December 27, 1923, in Correspondence, LWTP.
15. David Belasco, *Girl of the Golden West* (1905), novelized from the play (New York: Grossett, Dunlap, 1911), ch. 1.

8. Eros and Thanatos

1. On the 1924 elections: Alessandro Visani: *La conquista della maggioranza: Mussolini, il PNF e le elezioni del 1924* (Genoa: Fratelli Frilli, 1924).
2. Cesare Rossi, *Trentatre vicende mussoliniane* (Milan: Ceschina, 1958), 58.
3. "Il Partito fascista e i 'ludi cartaei,'" *La Stampa*, February 26, 1924, 1.
4. B. Mussolini, "Cinque anni dopo San Sepolcro," (March 24, 1924), *Opera Omnia*, ed. Edoardo and Duilio Susmel, vol. 10 (Florence: La Fenice, 1956), 216.
5. Mirko Riazzoli, *Cronologia di Lecco: dal 1815 ad oggi* (e-book 2017), 149–150; "I nostri candidati: Attilio Teruzzi," *Il Gagliardetto*, March 8, 1924, 3.
6. Mary Jane Phillips-Matz, *Puccini: A Biography* (Boston: Northeastern University Press, 2002), 286–288; Folco Portinari, *Pari siamo!: io la lingua, egli ha il pugnale: storia del melodrama ottocentesco attraverso i suoi libretti* (Milan: EDT, 1981), 210–215.
7. LW (Milan) to IW (Vienna), May 2, 1924, in Correspondence, LWTP.
8. LW (Milan) to IW (Vienna), May 2, 1924.
9. RW (Cairo) to IW(NYC), January 24, 1924, also January 16, 1924; RW (Cairo) to IW (NYC), February 28, 1924, all in Correspondence, LWTP/
10. RW (Cairo) to IW (Milan), March 6, 1924, in Correspondence, LWTP.
11. LW (Cairo) to IW (Milan), March 6. 1924, in Correspondence, LWTP.
12. LW (Milan) to IW (NYC), June 14, 1924, in Correspondence, LWTP.
13. RW (Varese) to IW (NYC), August 9, 1924, in Correspondence, LWTP.
14. RW (Varese) to IW (NYC), August 9, 1924.
15. RW (Varese) to IW (NYC), August 9, 1924. LW (Varese) to IW (NYC), August 9, 1924.
16. LW (Varese) to IW (NYC), August 9, 1924.
17. "Il comitato di maggioranza e la giunta delle elezioni," *La Stampa*, May 30, 1924, 1; "Le Commissioni parlamentari: L'On. Teruzzi nella giunta delle elezioni," *Il Gagliardetto*, June 7, 1924, 2.
18. Antonio Glauco Casanova, *Matteotti: Una vita per il socialismo* (Milano: Bompiani, 1974), 228–235.
19. The literature on the Matteotti affair is immense. For the most recent, grounded in the police and judiciary archives, see Mauro Canali, *Il delitto*

Matteotti: affarismo e politica nel primo governo Mussolini (Bologna: Il Mulino, 1997). For the most vivid account, by Mussolini's onetime oldest and dearest comrade, turned ex-comrade, as he was jailed and exiled by the regime for having been implicated in, and in turn, implicating Mussolini in the affair, see Cesare Rossi, *Il delitto Matteotti nei procedimenti giustiziari e nelle polemiche giornalistiche* (Milano: Ceschina, 1965).

20. Cited in "Tornata di venerdì, 30 maggio, 1924, Camera dei deputati, Atti parlamentari, https://storia.camera.it/regno/lavori/leg27/sed004.pdf, 58

21. "Tornata di venerdì, 30 maggio," 1924, 59, 60, 63.

22. Paolo Valera, *Mussolini* (1924; Genoa: Il Melangolo, 1995), 46.

23. Giuseppe Mayda, *Il pugnale di Mussolini: Storia di Amerigo Dumini* (Bologna: Il Mulino, 2004), 279, 295, 321; Canali, *Il delitto Matteotti*, 265, 518; Giorgio Cavallero, *Il custode del carteggio* (Milan: Piemme, 1997), 42, 281; Anon. [but Arnovaldo Bonaccorsi], *Lettera aperta dall'A.O.I* (Asmara: self-published, January 1942), 46.

24. Adrian Lyttelton, ed., *Liberal and Fascist Italy, 1900–1945* (Oxford: Oxford University Press, 2002), 237–268, provides the best background.

25. Paolo Cacace, *Quando Mussolini rischiò di morire: la malattia del Duce fra biografia e politica, 1924–1926* (Rome: Fazi Editore, 2007), 75–77.

26. "L' adunata fascista di Milano," *La Stampa*, July 15, 1924, 2.

27. Rose Weinman, "Deposition," June 6, 1934, in AR, CPM (1933–1936), sf. 4, LWTP.

28. Rose Weinman, "Deposition," June 6, 1934.

29. Franco Senestro, "Velia Matteotti, la donna che sfidò Mussolini," August 10, 2013, https://labottegadelciabattino.wordpress.com/2013/08/10/velia-matteotti-la-donna-che-sfido-mussolini/.

30. RW (Bergamo) to IW (NYC), September 7, 1924, in Correspondence, LWTP.

31. RW (Bergamo) to IW (NYC), September 7, 1924, in Correspondence, LWTP.

32. RW (Bergamo) to LW (NYC), September 7, 1925; and LW (Milan) to IW(NYC), December 1, 1924; LW (Genoa) to IW (NYC), January 1, 1925; all in Correspondence, LWTP.

33. "Bravo Teruzzi!" *Il Gagliardetto*, March 28, 1925, 3. On the assaults against the last communists, see Cesare Bermani, *Gramsci, gli intellettuali e la cultura proletaria* (Milano: Colibrì, 2007); "Il ritorno degli operai alla combattività," *L'Unità*, March 2, 1925, 2.

34. Mussolini, "Discorso del 3 gennaio alla Camera," January 3, 1925, *Opera Omnia* vol. 21, 240.

35. On the Interior Ministry's operations see Giovanna Tosatti, "Il prefetto e l'esercizio del potere durante il periodo fascista," *Studi Storici* 42, no. 4 (2001): 1021–1039.

36. For more on Federzoni, a central but insufficiently studied figure, see Silvana Casmirri, "Luigi Federzoni," in *Uomini e volti del fascismo*, ed. Ferdinando Cordova, (Rome: Bulzoni Editore, 1980), 243–301; Albertina Vittoria, "Luigi Federzoni," *Dizionario biografico degli italiani*, vol. 45, 1995. A work that is especially good on Federzoni's personality, based on studying his intense correspondence with Margherita Sarfatti in 1924–1926, is Paolo Cacace, *Quando Mussolini rischio di morire: La malattia del Duce fra biografia e politica, 1924–1926* (Rome: Fazi Editore, 2007), 46 ff.

37. Lyttelton, *Liberal and Fascist Italy*, 241.

38. "Il sottosegretario on. Teruzzi ricevuto dal re," *Corriere della Sera* May 19, 1924, 1.

39. "Le nomine di Teruzzi e Piccio," *Corriere della Sera*, May 14, 1924, 1. *Costruire: Rivista mensile fascista*, 1926, 28.

40. Anna Kuliscioff (Milan) to Filippo Turati (Rome), May 14, 1925, in Filippo Turati-Anna Kulisciioff, *Carteggio*, vol. 6: *1923–1925*, ed. Franco Pedone (Turin: Einaudi, 1977), 406. Insightful speculation about what the appointment meant is found in Lyttelton, *Liberal and Fascist Italy*, 279, 285–290. "Un 'nuovo passo della rivoluzione,'" *Corriere della Sera*, May 16, 1925, 2; "Inizio della 'rotazione' dei sottosegretari," *La Stampa*, May 14, 1925, 1.

41. Luigi Federzoni, *Italia di ieri: per la storia di domani* (Milan: Mondadori, 1967), 100.

42. "Banchetto in onore di S. E. Teruzzi," *Il Popolo d'Italia*, June 19, 1925; "Per il banchetto a S. E. Teruzzi," *Il Popolo d'Italia*, June 23, 1925, 4; "Per il banchetto di S. E. Teruzzi," *Il Popolo d'Italia*, June 24, 1925, 4; "Il grande banchetto di ieri sera in onore di S. E. Teruzzi," *Il Popolo d'Italia*, June 26, 1925, 8; "S. E. Teruzzi partito per Roma," *Il Popolo d'Italia*, June 27, 1925, 4.

43. Eugenio Castracane (Milan) to Benito Mussolini (Rome), March 23, 1925; telegram from B. Mussolini (Rome) to E. Castracane (Milan), June 16, 1925, in SPD, CR, AT, ACS.

9. *Conquering the Ice Princess*

1. LW (Milan) to IW and RW (NYC), May 19, 1925, in Correspondence, LWTP.

2. LW (Milan) to IW and RW (NYC), May 31, 1925, in Corrspondence, LWTP.

3. LW (Milan) to IW (NYC), September 27, 21, 28, October 10, 14, 1925, all in Correspondence, LWTP.

4. Report from Luigi Federzoni (Rome) to Osvaldo Sebastiani (Rome), November 9, 1927, in SPD, CR, AT, sf. AF, ACS; Luigi Federzoni, *1927: Diario di un ministro sul fascismo*, ed. Adriana Mocchi (Florence: Passigli, 1993), 169.

5. On the women's philanthropic circles and social debates of which Gina Federzoni was part, see Helga Dittrich-Johansen, "Per la Patria e per il Duce: Storie di fedeltà femminili nell'Italia fascista," *Genesis* 1, no. 1 (2002): 125–156, 136–137. More broadly, see Stefania Bartoloni, "Opera nazionale maternità e infanzia: cinquanta anni di vita, trenta anni di ricerche," *Italia contemporanea* 289 (April 2019): 147–165; and Stefania Bartoloni, "La ricerca della paternità: Responsabilità, diritti e affetti," *Genesis* 17, no. 1 (2018). In addition, see Victoria de Grazia, *How Fascism Ruled Women, 1922–1945* (Berkeley: University of California Press, 1996), 91, 98–99.

6. Adrian Lyttelton, ed., *Liberal and Fascist Italy, 1900–1945* (Oxford: Oxford University Press, 2002), 283–289.

7. LWT, handwritten notes, n.d. [but Spring 1934], in AR, CPM (1933–1936), sf. 8 DN, LWTP.

8. LWT, handwritten notes, n.d. [but Spring 1934], in AR, CPM (1933–1936), sf. 8 DN, LWTP.

9. Roberto Farinacci, *Un periodo aureo del Partito nazionale fascista: raccolta di discorsi e dichiarazioni*, ed. Renzo Bacchetta (Foligno: F. Campitelli, 1927), 44.

10. LWT, handwritten notes, n.d. [but Spring 1934], in AR, CPM (1933–1936), sf. 8 DN, LWTP.

11. Benito Mussolini, "October 28, 1925," in *Opera omnia*, vol. 21 (1956), 425.

12. Sindacato Istruzione Cinematografica, "III° anniversario della 'Marcia su Roma' solennemente celebrato a Milano," October 1925, code M011604, Archivio Storico Istituto Luce, Rome.

13. Photograph of Mussolini kissing LT's hand, photographer Argo di Strazza; photograph of "Mamma in the Box with Mussolini," both October 26, 1925; both in Family Photographs, LWTP.

14. RW (Milan) to IW (NYC), October 31, 1925; and LW (Milan) to IW (NYC), October 31, 1925; both in Correspondence, LWTP.

15. RW (Milan) to IW (NYC), October 31, 1925, in Corrrespondence, LWTP.

16. RW (Milan) to IW (NYC), October 31, 1925.

17. IW (NYC) to LW (Milan), November 16, 1925, in Corrrespondence, LWTP.

18. IW (NYC) to LW (Milan), November 16, 1925.

19. IW (NYC) to LW (Milan), November 16, 1925.

20. LW (Milan) to IW (NYC) April 1926, in Correspondence, LWTP.

21. LWT, handwritten notes, n.d. [but February–March 1934], in AR, CPM (1933–1936), sf. 8 DN, LWTP.

22. AT (Rome)- RF (Cremona) February 2, 1926 in Roberto Farinacci, b. 35, SPD, CR, ACS.

23. IW (NYC) to LW (Milan), November 3 and 13, 1925, in Correspondence, LWTP.

24. LWT, handwritten notes, n.d. [but 1935], in AR, CPM (1933–1936), sf. 8 DN, LWTP.

25. Mary Garden, cited in Susan Rutherford, "The Voice of Freedom: Images of the Prima Donna," in *The New Woman and Her Sisters: Feminism and Theater 1850–1914*, ed. Vivien Gardner and Susan Rutherford (Ann Arbor: University of Michigan Press, 1992), 107.

26. AT testimony, sf. Trial Transcript (Verbali), p. 24, in NM, T-W, ADSP.

10. A Fascist Wedding

1. IW (NYC) to LW (Milan) December 11, 1925, in Correspondence, LWTP.

2. LW (Milan) to IW (NYC), October 17, 1925, in Correspondence, LWTP.

3. LW (Milan) to IW (NYC), December 9, 1925, in Correspondence, LWTP.

4. IW (NYC) to LW (Milan), December 11 and 15, 1925, in Correspondence, LWTP.

5. Giuseppe Umberto Ferulli (Paris) to IW (NYC), October 14, 1925; LW(Milan) to IW (NYC), October 14, 1925; IW (NYC) to LW and RW (Milan), October 25, 1925; all in Correspondence, LWTP.

6. LWT, handwritten notes, n.d. [but 1935], in AR, CPM (1933–1936), sf. 8 DN, LWTP.

7. LW (Milan) to IW (NYC), September 10, 1925; LW (Milan) to IW (NYC), November 7, 1925; November 30, 1925; IW (NYC) to LW (Milan), December 15, 1925; IW (NYC) to LW (Milan), December 9, 1925; all in Correspondence, LWTP.

8. RW (Rome) to IW (NYC), n.d. [but likely December 23, 1926]; LW (Rome) to IW (NYC), n.d. [but likely December 26, 1926]; all in Correspondence, LWTP.

9. RW (Rome) to IW (NYC), December 23, 1926, in Correspondence, LWTP.

10. LW (Rome) to IW (NYC), December 23, 1926, Correspondence, LWTP.

11. LW (Rome) to IW (NYC), February 9, 1926, in Correspondence, LWTP.

12. LW to Benito Mussolini, March 12, 1926, in SPD, CR, AT, sf. LW, ACS.

13. "Girl Singer Leaves Stage to Wed Hero," *New York Evening Journal*, March 19, 1926; "Girl Singer Leaves Stage to Wed Hero," *New York American*, March 19, 1926; and later, "Fascists to Attend American Wedding," *Herald Tribune*, June 22, 1926: all in Clippings, LWTP.

14. IW (NYC) to LW (Rome), April 5, 1926, in Correspondence, LWTP.

15. LW (Milan) to IW (NYC), May 2, 1926, in Correspondence, LWTP.

16. LW (Milan) to IW (NYC), May 2, 1926.

17. LW (Milan) to IW (NYC), May 2, 1926.

18. "Wedding invitation, June 1926," in Family Documents, LWTP.

19. LW (Milan) to IW (NYC), December 1, 1925, in Correspondence, LWTP.

20. "Mons. Giuseppe Candidori, "Deposition," February 24, 1934, in AR, CPM (1933–1936), sf. 2, LWTP.

21. "Le imminenti nozze di S. E. Teruzzi," *Il Popolo d'Italia*, June 17, 1926, 2; "Le odierne nozze di S. E. Attilio Teruzzi," *Il Popolo d'Italia*, June 24, 1926, 3; "La celebrazione del matrimonio di S. E. Teruzzi," *Corriere della Sera*, June 25, 1926, 3; "Nozze Teruzzi-Weinmann: On. Mussolini testimone dello sposo," *Le Carnet Mondain*, June 30, 1926, 15, 571, 28–32; "Signor Mussolini Attends Italo-American Wedding," *The New York Herald*, June 29, 1926: all in Clippings, LWTP.

22. See Wedding Album in Family Photographs, LWTP; and LWT, handwritten notes, n.d. [but 1935], in AR, CPM (1933–1936), sf. 8 DN, LWTP.

23. "Picture Section," *New York Times*, July 11, 1926, 6.

24. RW, "Deposition," June 6, 1934, AR, CPM (1933–1936), sf.4 LWTP.

25. Anon. [but Alessandro Tarabini], "Voti ed auguri per le nozze di S. E. Teruzzi," *Il Gagliardetto*, June 23, 1926, 1; "Vicini nel dì del gaudìo come nel dì della lotta," *Il Gagliardetto*, June 26, 1926, 1.

26. LWT, "Deposition," May 26, 1934, in AR, CPM (1933–1936), sf. 2, LWTP.

27. LWT, "Deposition," May 6, 1934, in AR, CPM (1933–1936), sf. 2, LWTP; AT (Trieste) to RW (Rome), June 27, 1926, in AR, CPM (1933–1936) sf. 4. Attachments to Depositions of RW and IW, June 4, 1934.

28. Telegram from AT (Trieste) to General Giuseppe Vaccari (Rome), July 2, 1926, in Fondo Vaccari, Correspondence, Generale Giuseppe Vaccari (b.5), Museo del Risorgimento e della Resistenza, Vicenza.

29. "Donna Lilliana Weinman-Teruzzi dona tremila lire alle famiglie povere di Lecco," *Il Nuovo Prealpino*, July 26, 1926, in Clippings, LWTP.

30. "Smart Set Gathers at Lake Maggiore," *New York Herald*, October 5, 1926, in Clippings, LWTP. Gabriele D'Annunzio (Gardone) to AT (Rome), undated telegram [but late October 1926], in Folder Teruzzi, Attilio, Archivio Generale, Archivi del Vittoriale, Gardone; also Arnaldo Cortesi, "D'Annunzio Reportage: Seven Salutes for You and America Fired by D'Annunzio Birdmaker," *Herald Tribune*, October 24, 1926.

31. On the resurgent debate on fascist imperialism, promoted by *Gerarchia*, see Lorenzo Santoro, *Roberto Farinacci e il Partito Nazionale Fascista, 1923–1926* (Soveria Mannelli: Rubbettino, 2007), 297–323.

32. Margherita Sarfatti, *Guest Registries*, vol. 1: *March 15, 1926–July 14, 1938*. Copy courtesy of Emily Braun.

33. Tiziana Bertacci and Silvia Rubini, *Tra otium e negotium: le ville di Crespellano* (Crespellano: Comune, stampa 2002).

34. Emilio Settimelli, *Gli odi e gli amori* (Rome: Pinciana, 1928), 125–129.

35. Lyttelton, *Liberal and Fascist Italy*, 293–296.

36. LWT (Rome) to IW (NYC), October 2, 1926, in Correspondence, LWTP. For background see Lyttelton, *Liberal and Fascist Italy*, 292.
37. LWT (Rome) to IW (NYC), November 6 and November 12, 1926, in Correspondence, LWTP.
38. RW (Rome) to IW (NYC) November 12, 1926, LWTP.
39. "La partenza dell'on. Teruzzi per la Cirenaica," *Il Messaggero*, November 30, 1926, in Clippings, LWTP, 5. RW (Rome) to IW (NYC), November 30, 1926; and LWT (Syracuse) to RW (Rome), December 1, 1926, in Correspondence, LWTP.
40. RW (Rome) to IW (NYC), November 14, 1926, in Correspondence, LWTP.
41. LWT (Rome) to IW (NYC), November 20, 1926, in Correspondence, LWTP.
42. "New York City Girl is Vice-Queen of Cyrenaica: Elevation of her Husband to Italian Governorship follows real love Romance," with photograph under title "A Royal American," *New York American*, December 12, 1926, in SPD, CR, AT, sf. LW, ACS.

11. Mission to Benghazi

1. "L' arrivo del S. E. governatore," *Cirenaica Nuova*, December 2, 1926, 1.
2. "Il Governatore Teruzzi solennemente accolto a Bengàsi," *Il Messaggero*, December 3, 1926. See also Attilio Teruzzi, *Cirenaica verde* (Milan: Mondadori, 1930), 19.
3. LWT (Benghazi) to RW/IW (NYC), December 11, 1926, in Correspondence, LWTP.
4. *Cirenaica Nuova*, December 5, 1926, 1. Also the new column "Le giornate del governatore," starting on December 7, 1926. On *Cirenaica Nuova*, see Matteo Aguzzi, "Il quotidiano italiano di Benghazi al tempo della riconquista," unpublished manuscript, https://www.academia.edu/10395400/Il_quotidiano _italiano_di_Benghazi_al_tempo_della_riconquista.
5. Fascist imperialism picked up on liberal Italy's belated imperialist drive, drawing on pre-fascist Italian nationalists, notably Federzoni. On the continuities, but especially the ruptures with respect to the liberal past, in the 1920s, see Roberta Pergher, *Mussolini's Nation-Empire: Sovereignty and Settlement in Italy's Borderland, 1922–1943s* (Cambridge: Cambridge University Press, 2017); Aristotle A. Kallis, *Fascist Ideology: Territory and Expansionism in Italy and Germany, 1922–1945* (New York: Routledge, 2000). On Libya specifically see Claudio G. Segrè, *Fourth Shore: The Italian Colonization of Libya* (Chicago: University of Chicago Press, 1974). In Italian, to start, the classic Giorgio Rumi, "'Revisionismo' fascista ed espansione coloniale (1925–1935)," in *Il regime fascista*, ed. Alberto Aquarone and Maurizio Vernassa (Bologna: Il

Mulino, 1974), 37–73. See also Gian Paolo Calchi Novati, *L'Africa d'Italia: una storia coloniale e postcoloniale* (Rome: Carocci, 2011); Nicola Labanca, *Oltremare* (Bologna: Il Mulino, 2002); Giorgio Rochat, *Il colonialismo italiano* (Turin: Loescher, 1973).

6. On Libya, in addition to Segrè, *Fourth Shore*, see Ali Abdullatif Ahmida, *The Making of Modern Libya: State Formation, Colonization, and Resistance*, 2nd ed. (Albany: State University of New York Press, 2009); Anna Baldinetti, *The Origins of the Libyan Nation: Colonial Legacy, Exile and the Emergence of a New Nation-State* (London: Routledge, 2009); André Martel, *La Libye, 1835–1990: Essai de géopolitique historique* (Paris: Presses Universitaires de France, 1991); Angelo del Boca, *Gli Italiani in Libia*, 2 vols. (Rome: Laterza, 1986–1988).

7. Luigi Federzoni, *Venti mesi di azione coloniale*, ed. Ferdinando Nobili Massuero (Milan: Mondadori, 1926), 51. The argument is presented at its fullest in Luigi Federzoni, "Hegemony in the Mediterranean," *Foreign Affairs* 14, no. 1 (January 1935): 387–397. See also Alessandro Rosselli, "Appunti sul colonialismo fascista: *Venti mesi di azione coloniale* (1926) di Luigi Federzoni," unpublished ms, n.d., http://acta.bibl.u-szeged.hu/50006/1/mediterran_026 _089–098.pdf; Luigi Federzoni, *La rinascita dell'Africa romana* (Bologna: Zanichelli, 1929).

8. Pergher, *Mussolini's Nation-Empire*, 38.

9. On the concept of Eur-africa: Marco Antonsich, "Eurafrica, dottrina Monroe del fascismo," *Limes: Rivista italiana di geopolitica* 3 (1997): 261–262; and from the period, becoming more and more ambitious over time, Egidio Moleti di Sant'Andrea, *Mare Nostrum: Roma nella civiltà mediterraneana* (Lecco: Ed Tip. Soc., 1928), with preface by Attilio Teruzzi, rev. ed. (Milan: E.L.I.C.A., 1939). See also Paolo D'Agostino Orsini di Camerota, *L'Italia nella politica africana* (Bologna: Cappelli, 1926); and David Atkinson, "Geographical Knowledge and Scientific Survey in the Construction of Italian Libya," *Modern Italy* 8 (2003): 9–29.

10. For a vivid study of the lodges, see Knut S. Vikør, *Sufi and Scholar on the Desert Edge: Muhammad b.'Ali al-Sanūsī and His Brotherhood* (London: C. Hurst, 1995). British anthropologists, building on their championship of Sanusi nationalism after World War II, wrote the pioneering studies: Emyrs L. Peters, *The Bedouin of Cyrenaica*, ed. Jack Goody and Emanuel Marx (Cambridge: Cambridge University Press, 1990); and the postwar British classic, Edward Evans-Pritchard, *The Sanusi of Cyrenaica* (Oxford: Oxford University Press, 1949). Recent studies highlight the Italians' stumbling confrontation with the complex nationalist, religious, and tribal dimensions of local power structures: Eileen Ryan, *Religion as Resistance: Negotiating Authority in Italian Libya*

(New York: Oxford University Press, 2018); and Habib al-Hesnawi, "Note sulla politica coloniale italiana verso gli arabi libici (1911–1943)," in *Le guerre coloniale del fascismo*, ed. Angelo del Boca, 31–48 (Rome-Bari: Laterza, 1991).

11. Enzo Santarelli et al., *Omar al-Mukhtar: The Italian Reconquest of Libya*, trans. John Gilbert (London: Darf Publishing House, 1986).

12. *Sul bilancio delle colonie, discorso pronunciato alla camera dei deputati nella tornata del 21 maggio, 1928* (Rome: Tipografia della camera dei deputati, 1928–1929), 7. Luigi Federzoni, *1927: Diario di un ministro del fascismo*, ed. Adriana Mocchi (Florence: Passigli, 1993), entry for January 25, 1927 (p. 55).

13. Federzoni, *Venti mesi*, 55, 63–65.

14. LWT (Bengasi) to RW (Rome), December 18, 1927 (also November 6 and November 12, 1927), in Correspondence, LTWP.

15. Attilio Teruzzi, *Cirenaica verde* (Milan: Mondadori, 1930), 54.

16. LWT (Benghazi) to RW (Rome), December 11, 1926; and LW (Benghazi) to IW (NYC), January 7, 1927; both in Correspondence, LWTP.

17. Consul Stanhope Palmer to Secretary of State, May 12, 1927, FO 371/12396, TNA.

18. "Il vibrante discorso di saluto del Governatore," *Cirenaica Nuova*, January 13, 1929, 3.

19. On the influx of Milanese see "Fascisti milanesi a Bengasi," *Cirenaica Nuova*, March 16, 1928; "Il Circolo Meneghino," *Cirenaica Nuova*, January 10, 1929. On their welcome at the Governor's Mansion see LWT (Benghazi) to RW/IW (NYC), January 1927; and LWT (Benghazi) to RW/IW (NYC), April 1928; both in Correspondence, LWTP. On the high energy of the governor and the men around him see Stanhope Palmer (Benghazi) to Secretary of State, August 18, 1927, FO 371/12396, TNA.

20. As reported by RW (Salsomaggiore) to IW (NYC), September 18, 1927, in Correspondence, LWTP.

21. Samuel John Gurney Hoare, *Empire of the Air: The Advent of the Air Age, 1922–1929* (London: Collins, 1957), 139–140.

22. LWT (Rome) to IW (NYC), June 19, 1927, in Correspondence, LWTP. For the pomp and circumstance attending Balbo's visit, see "Sono venuto—ha detto Italo Balbo- con ali d'Italia,"*Cirenaica Nuova*, April 29, 1927; also "Il signorile ricevimento al Municipio in onore di S.E. Italo Balbo, ibid, 3.

23. Attilio Teruzzi, *Cirenaica verde*, 65–66, 291–292; Luigi Federzoni, *1927: Diario di un ministro del fascismo*, ed. Adriana Mocchi (Florence: Passigli, 1993), entries for February 17, 1927 (96); February 18, 1927 (98); February 22, 1927 (104); and February 24, 1927 (112).

24. "Cronaca di Bengasi," *Cirenaica nuova*, July 14, 1927, 5.

25. "Il vibrante discorso di saluto del Governatore," *Cirenaica Nuova*, January 13, 1929, 3.

26. Quote from Ulderico Tegani, *Bengàsi: studio coloniale* (Milan: Sonzogno, 1922), 125, who, more generally provides the most complete and vivid image of the evolution of the colonial city before the 1927–1928 makeover. See also Gaetano Nascia's photographic documentation in Francesco Prestopino, *Una città e il suo fotografo, La Bengasi coloniale, 1912–1941* (Milan: La Vita Felice, 2004); Teruzzi, *Cirenaica verde*, 300–304; and detailed reports by British consul Stanhope Palmer, who confessed himself "somewhat startled at the magnitude and costliness of the projects." Consul Palmer, reports, January 20, 1927; May 12, 1927; November 25, 1927; and December 12, 1927, FO 371/12396, TNA.

27. About Del Corno see LWT (Benghazi) to RW/IW (NYC), January 25, 1927, in Correspondence, LWTP; Teruzzi, *Cirenaica verde*, 299.

28. Guido Ferrazza et al., *Relazione sul piano regolatore della città di Benghazi* (Milan: Cromotipia Ettore Sormani, 1930), 3. On the fascinating Ferrazza: Marida Talamona, "Ferrazza Guido," *Dizionario Biografico degli Italiani* 46 (1996); also Francesca Zanella, *Alpago Novello, Cabiati e Ferrazza 1912–1935* (Milan: Electa, 2002). More generally see Vittoria Capresi, "Architectural Transfer, Italian Colonial Architecture in Libya: 'Libyan Rationalism' and the Concept of 'Mediterraneity,' 1926–1942," in *Colonial Architecture and Urbanism in Africa: Intertwined and Contested Histories*, ed. Fassil Demissie, 33–65 (Aldershot: Ashgate, 2012).

29. Ferrazza, *Relazione sul piano*, 5.

30. Mia Fuller, "Oases of Ambiguity: On How Italians Did Not Practice Urban Segregation in Tripoli," in *La Libia tra Mediterraneo e mondo islamico*, ed. Federico Cresti, 163–181 (Milan: Giuffrè, 2006); Sean Anderson, *Modern Architecture and its Representation in Colonial Eritrea* (New York: Routledge, 2015), 106–108, 117–121.

31. "Cronaca di Bengasi," *Cirenaica Nuova*, July 8, 1927, 5.

32. Teruzzi, *Cirenaica verde*, 50–52.

33. Teruzzi, *Cirenaica verde*, 50.

34. Teruzzi, *Cirenaica verde*, 52; "La giustizia in Cirenaica," *Cirenaica Nuova*, December 9, 1927 1. "La nuova legge di polizia," *Cirenaica Nuova*, December 11, 1927.

35. "La solenne inaugurazione dell'anno giudiziario," *Cirenaica Nuova*, January 19, 1927, 1. The arrests appeared in the crime docket in *Cirenaica Nuova*'s daily "Cronaca di Bengasi," from July to October 1927, 5.

36. Consul Stanhope Palmer to Secretary of State, December 12, 1927, also March 30, 1927, in FO 371/12396, TNA.

12. Insurgency and Betrayal

1. Mario Bassi, "Giornate bengàsiane," *La Stampa*, November 19, 1927, 5.
2. Bassi, "Giornate bengàsiane."
3. Attilio Teruzzi, "Account book, 1926–1927," in Family Records, LWTP.
4. Bassi, "Giornate bengàsiane."
5. Luigi Federzoni, *1927: Diario di un ministro del fascismo*, ed. Adriana Mocchi (Florence: Passigli, 1993), entry for February 26, 1927 (116).
6. Federzoni, *1927: Diario di un ministro*, entry for March 5, 1927 (125); Stanhope Palmer to Secretary of State, January 9, 1928, and October 29, 1928, in FO 371/12396, TNA.
7. Eric Armar Vully De Candole, *The Life and Times of King Idris of Libya* (Manchester: Mohamed Ben Ghalbon, 1989), 275.
8. De Candole, *Life and Times of King Idris*, 275.
9. Teruzzi, *Cirenaica verde*, 34–35; also Federzoni, *1927: Diario di un ministro*, entry for January 20, 1927 (48).
10. Teruzzi, *Cirenaica verde*, 35.
11. LWT, Notebook-Reminiscences, n.d. [but September 1938], in Diaries, LWTP.
12. Telegram: AT(Benghasi) to Luigi Federzoni(Rome) April 3, 1927, in F. L-8, 156, 1-3-5 AUSSME; Federzoni, *1927: Diario di un ministro*, entries for March 30, 1927 (p. 147); April 1, 1927 (149); April 2, 1927 (151); April 3, 1927 (152); April 4, 1927 (153); April 6, 1927 (158); April 8, 1927 (159); April 12, 1927 (162); April 14, 1927 (164).
13. "La Marcia della Colonna Ruggeri: Tre esecuzioni capitali a Cirene," *Cirenaica Nuova*, March 22, 1927. Stanhope Palmer, British Consulate, Benghazi, was the only one to underscore the connection, commenting on the incident and on the wholesale desertion of troops who were reputedly "loyal Arabs." Consul Stanhope Palmer to Secretary of State, "Report," April 4, 1927, in FO 371/12394, TNA.
14. Palmer, "Report," April 4, 1927, FO 371/12394, TNA.
15. Palmer, "Report," April 4, 1927, FO 371/12394, TNA.
16. Federzoni, *1927: Diario di un ministro*, entry for April 4, 1927 (p. 153).
17. Teruzzi, *Cirenaica verde*, 54–56. He dates the meeting to March 1927 rather than late July, possibly to underscore the extent of his relations to the Obeidat and, therefore, the reliability of his judgment about their trustworthiness.
18. LWT (Benghazi) to IW/RW (NYC), August 18, 1927, in Correspondence, LWTP.
19. "Discorso del Governatore," *Cirenaica Nuova*, August 13, 1927, 2.
20. "I particolari delle vittoriose giornate dell'11 e del 12 agosto: La relazione del Generale Mezzetti," *Cirenaica Nuova*, August 17, 1927, 1.
21. LWT (Rome) to IW (NYC), June 19, 1927, in Correspondence, LWTP.

22. LWT (Rome) to IW (NYC), June 8, 1927, in Correspondence, LWTP.

23. LWT (Rome) to IW (NYC), May 31, 1927; June 5, 1927; June 19, 1927; all in Correspondence, LWTP.

24. LWT, Notebook-Reminiscences, n.d. [but September 1938], in Diaries, LWTP.

25. RW (Salsomaggiore) to IW (NYC), September 18, 1927, in Correspondence, LWTP.

26. LWT (Milan) to AT (Benghazi), June 15, 1927, in Correspondence, LWTP.

27. As recorded in RW (Salsomaggiore) to IW (NYC), September 18, 1927, in Correspondence, LWTP.

28. LWT (Rome) to IW (NYC), September 24, 1927, in Correspondence, LWTP.

29. LWT/AT (Benghazi) to IW/RW (NYC), December 25, 1927, in Correspondence, LWTP.

30. Pietro Badoglio (Rome) to B. Mussolini, S. E. Il capo del governo (Rome), "Programma militare per le nostre colonie mediterranee," 4-page memorandum, November 9, 1927, in MAI, Libia 125/28, b. 150/4 Africa II, AUSMAE. On Badoglio: Piero Pieri and Giorgio Rochat, *Pietro Badoglio: Maresciallo d'Italia* (Turin: Union Tipografico-Editrice Torinese, 2002).

31. Graziani merits a new biography not just because he plays so incisive, emblematic, and continuous a role in Fascist Italy, and is so controversial, appalling anti-fascists and enthralling fascist apologists, but because the sources on him are so rich, including his several memoirs. Meanwhile, see Angelo del Boca, "Rodolfo Graziani," in *Dizionario biografico degli Italiani*, vol. 58, 829–834 (Rome: Treccani, 2002); Alessandro Cova, *Graziani: un generale per il regime* (Rome: Newton Compton, 1987), esp. 62–109, 194–195, 248–279, 192; Giuseppe Mayda, *Graziani l'Africano: Da Neghelli a Salò* (Florence: La Nuova Italia, 1992).

32. Teruzzi, *Cirenaica verde*, quote from 202–203, and the minute detailing of the negotiation from 186–212.

33. Federzoni, *Diario*, January 25, 1927, 55.

34. *Cirenaica Nuova*, November 4, 1927, 1.

35. Teruzzi, *Cirenaica verde*, 211–212.

36. Francesco Prestopino, *Una città e il suo fotografo: la Bengàsi coloniale (1912–1941)* (Milan: La Vita Felice, 1999), 130–131.

37. Abdellaziz el-Isaui (Sicily) to Governatore della Colonia (Benghazi), March 3, 1928, in Ministero Africa Italiana, 1925–1928, b. 150/4, Africa II, ACS.

38. "In un tripudio di sole . . . La risposta di S. E. il Governatore," *Cirenaica Nuova*, March 24, 1928, 2; Teruzzi, *Cirenaica verde*, 212; Mario Bassi, "La Senussia e la rivoluzione fascista; Dopo la sottomissione del Saied Reda," *La Stampa*, January 27, 1928, 2.

39. Memo from Luigi Federzoni to Attilio Teruzzi: Oggetto: riduzioni spese militari, October 7, 1928, S.E. Federzoni: colonie affari generali, f. 224R, SPD, CR, ACS

40. Telegram from AT (Benghazi) to Luigi Federzoni (Rome), February 19, 1928, Ministero Africa Italiana, b. 150/4, Africa II, 1925–1928, ACS.

41. "La Mamma di S. E. Teruzzi a Bengàsi," *Cirenaica Nuova*, July 15, 1927, 1.

42. LWT, Deposition, 1934, in AR, CPM (1933–1936), LWTP.

43. Pupy Torelli (Piacenza) to AT (Rome), December 5, 1925; Pupy Torelli (Piacenza) to AT (Rome), December 8, 1925; Pupy Torelli (Alassio) to AT (Rome), December 16, 1926; [name indecipherable] (Rome) to AT (Rome), November 24, 1926; all in Correspondence, LWTP.

44. On Zamboni see LWT, handwritten notes, n.d. [but 1934], in AR, CPM (1933–1936), sf. 8 DN, LWTP.

45. Tegani, *Bengàsi: studio coloniale*, 130–131.

46. Celestina Teruzzi, "Deposition," Session 8, August 30, 1933, in AR, CPM (1934–1936), sf. 2, LWTP.

47. Portrait photograph AT, with dedication, June 2, 1927, in Family Photographs, LWTP.

48. LWT, handwritten notes, n.d. [but 1934], in AR, CPM (1933–1936), sf. 8 DN, LWTP.

49. Telegram from Alessandro Chiavolini (Rome) to AT (Benghazi), November 2, 1928, in SPD, CR, AT, sf. LW, ACS.

50. LWT (Benghazi) to IW/RW (NYC) August 18, 1927, in Correspondence, LWTP.

51. LWT, scattered notes, n.d. [but 1928], in Diaries, LWTP.

52. LWT, Notebook-Reminiscences, September 1938, in Diaries, LWTP.

13. A Matter of Honor

1. AT (Benghazi) to LWT (NYC), December 29, 1929, in Correspondence, LWTP; telegrams from AT to LWT (NYC), December 19, December 20, and December 22, 1928, all in Correspondence, Telegrams, LWTP.

2. AT (Benghazi) to LWT, December 29, 1929, in Correspondence, LWTP.

3. Telegrams from AT (Benghazi) to LWT (NYC), December 27, 1928; January 2, 1929; January 8, 1929; all in Correspondence, Telegrams, LWTP. On the bad luck brought by the desecration of the Muslim cemetery, see British Consul to Benghazi R. W. Chafy to Secretary of State, "Report," February 14, 1930, in FO 371/12396, TNA.

4. "Il vibrante discorso di saluto del Governatore," *Cirenaica Nuova*, January 13, 1929, 1. On the two days of festivities beforehand see in passing: *Cirenaica Nuova*, January 10, 1929, 1; and *Cirenaica Nuova*, January 11, 1929, 1.

5. Telegram from AT (Benghazi) to LWT (NYC), January 12, 1929, in Correspondence, Telegrams, LWTP.

6. Telegrams from AT to LWT, January n.d., January 11, February 8, and March 1, 1929; all in Correspondence, Telegrams, LWTP.

7. Mary Jane Phillips-Matz, *Rosa Ponselle: American Diva* (Boston: Northeastern University Press, 1997), 226.

8. "East Side Girl Now Retired Opera Star, Visits Scenes of Childhood," *New York American*, January 7, 1929, in Clippings. LWTP.

9. "East Side Girl."

10. "East Side Girl."

11. Telegrams from AT (Rome) to LWT (NYC), February 24, February 28, and March 13, 1929; all in Correspondence, Telegrams, LWTP.

12. Telegram from AT (Rome) to LWT (NYC), March 23, 1929, in Correspondence, Telegrams, LWTP.

13. AT (Rome) to LWT (NYC), March 13, 1929, in Correspondence, LWTP.

14. "Notevole movimento nelle alte gerarchie del regime: Le gerarchie e il capo," *Il Popolo d'Italia*, December 19, 1928, 1.

15. Ugo Guspini, *L' orecchio del regime: Le intercettazioni telefoniche ai tempi del fascismo* (Milan: Mursia, 1973), 81.

16. Anonymous (n.p.) to Caro Amico [Benito Mussolini] (Rome), September 27, 1930, in SPD, CR, AT, ACS. See also "Mussolini assume il Ministero delle Colonie," *La Stampa*, December 19, 1928, 1.

17. Photograph "Teruzzi in conversation with black man (maybe Eritrean) in uniform," 3/7/1929, Limone Piemonte, photo no. A00008585, in Archivio Storico Istituto Luce, Rome.

18. Alberta Albertosi, "Deposition," January 2, 1934, in AR, CPM (1934–1936), sf. 2, LWTP.

19. LWT, "Note: Umberto Ferulli," n.d. [but February–March 1934], in AR, CPM (1933–1936), sf. 8 DN, LWTP.

20. Lilliana Weinman to Giuseppe Umberto Ferulli, thirteen letters dated Spring 1925 to November 1925, submitted to court, January 29, 1934, in AR, CPM (1933–1936), sf. 10, LWTP.

21. Alberta Albertosi, "Deposition," January 2, 1934; and Carolina Spertini, "Deposition," November 29, 1933; both in AR, CPM (1933–1936), sf. 2, LWTP.

22. AT (Rome) to LWT (NYC), March 13, 1929, in Correspondence, LWTP.

23. AT (Rome) to LWT (NYC), March 13, 1929.

24. Giuseppe Umberto Ferulli (Grumo Appula) to LW (Milan) July 11, July 21, August 2, August 7, and August 22, 1921; all in Correspondence, LWTP.

25. Giuseppe Umberto Ferulli, "Deposition," December 1, 1933; and Ida Jolles, "Deposition: Attachment 1," May 30, 1934; both in AR, CPM (1933–1936), sf. 2, LWTP.

26. LWT, "Deposition," May 26, 1934, in AR, CPM (1933–1936), sf. 2, LWTP; LWT, handwritten notes, n.d. [but February–March 1934], in AR, CPM (1933–1936), sf. 8 DN, LWTP.

27. RW, "Deposition," June 6, 1934, in AR, CPM (1933–1936), sf. 4, LWTP.

28. LWT, "Deposition," May 27,1934, in AR, CPM (1933–1936), sf. 2, LWTP.

29. Federico Azzoni (Rome) to IW (Rome), April 10, 1929, in Correspondence, LWTP.

14. To Kill a Marriage

1. Giorgio Agosti, ed., Diario, 1939–1945: Piero Calamandrei, vol. 1: 1939–1941 (Florence: La Nuova Italia, 1997), entry for November 11, 1941 (p. 398).

2. On Scialoja, in the absence of a proper biography, begin with Emanuele Stolfi, Dizionario biografico degli italiani, vol. 91 (2018), 91; and Ricordo delle onoranze a Vittorio Scialoja pel suo 25 anniversario d'insegnamento il 18 dicembre 1904 nella R. Università di Roma (Prato: Tip. Giachetti, Figlio, 1905).

3. Paolo Treves, Quello che ci ha fatto Mussolini (Turin: Einaudi, 1945), 268–269.

4. Cited in Ricordo delle onoranze, 12.

5. LWT, handwritten note, n.d. [but spring 1934], in AR, CPM (1933–1936), sf. 8 DN, LWTP. These were the same words Francesco Malgeri told Mussolini that Scialoja had used to deprecate the "men of the regime." Francesco Malgeri (Rome) to Benito Mussolini (Rome), May 22, 1929 in SPD, CR, FM, ACS.

6. Federico Azzoni (Rome) to Vittorio Scialoja (Rome), May 30, 1929, in Correspondence, LWTP; also Francesco Malgeri (Rome) to Benito Mussolini (Rome), May 22, 1929, in SPD, CR, FM, ACS. On this incident, see also Piero Calamandrei, Diario, 1939–1945, ed. Giorgio Agosti, vol. 1: 1939–1941 (Rome: Edizioni di Storia e Letteratura, 2015), 399.

7. Police orders: telegram from Arturo Bocchini (Rome) to Border Police, May 17, 1929; telegram from Dino Grandi (Rome) to Arturo Bocchini (Rome), May 22, 1929; and police reports of May 21 and May 24, 1929, in MI, PP, FP, RW, ACS. Adjutant-Commandant MVSN (Rome) to IW (Rome), April 12, 1929, submitted with Isaac Weinman and Rose Weinman typed depositions, June 6, 1934, in AR, CPM (1933–1936), sf. 4, LWTP.

8. LWT, "Deposition," May 27, 1933, in AR, CPM (193–1936), sf. 2. LWTP.

9. "Separation Agreement," June 2, 1929, in Family Documents, LWTP.

10. Federico Azzoni (Rome) to Vittorio Scialoja (Rome), May 30, 1929; and AT to LWT, June 3, 1929; both in Correspondence, LWTP.

11. Margherita Sarfatti, Guest Registries, vol. 1: n.p. but March 11, 1929. Source: Courtesy of Emily Braun. See also Emily D. Bilsi and Emily Braun, eds., "Margherita Sarfatti: The Antechamber of Power," in Jewish Women and Their

Salons: The Power of Conversation (New York: Jewish Museum; and New Haven, CT: Yale University Press, 2005), 99–112.

12. Giovanni Giuriati (Rome) to LWT (Rome), August 14, 1929, in Correspondence, LWTP.

13. Anselmo della Casa (Rome) to RW (Rome), November 25, 1929, in Correspondence, LWTP.

14. Bice Brusati (Rome) to LWT(Rome), n.d. [but April 1929], in Correspondence, LWTP.

15. LWT (Rome) to IW (NYC), March 17, 1947, in Correspondence, LWTP.

16. LWT, Notebook-Reminiscences, 1938, n.p., in Diaries, LWTP.

17. LWT, handwritten note, n.d. [but 1934], in AR, CPM (1933–1936), sf. 8 DN, LWTP.

18. Mark Seymour, *Debating Divorce in Italy: Marriage and the Making of Modern Italians, 1860–1974* (New York: Palgrave Macmillan, 2006), esp. chs. 6–7.

19. John F. Pollard, *The Vatican and Italian Fascism, 1929–32: A Study in Conflict* (Oxford: Oxford University Press, 1985), 66–70. A. C. Jemolo's 1949 history, *Church and State in Italy 1850–1950*, trans. David Moore (Oxford: Basil Blackwell, 1960) remains the most authoritative study of Church-State relations.

20. The historical-juridical study, John T. Noonan Jr., *The Power to Dissolve: Lawyers and Marriage in the Courts of the Roman Curia* (Cambridge, MA: Belknap Press of Harvard University Press, 1972) is unsurpassed, and likely unsurpassable, given his unimpugnable scholarship, legal brilliance, and the secret character of the Sacra Rota archive to which he had access. For practices and procedures during the interwar period see Gian Battista Nappi, *Annullamenti di matrimonio* (Milan: U. Hoepli, 1937); and Mauro Mellini: *Così annulla la Sacra Rota: Divorzio di classe nell'Italia clericale* (Roma: Samonà e Savelli, 1969).

21. Giuseppe Buonocore, *Il sacramento del matrimonio nel diritto canonico: dottrina e legislazione* (Rome: Pustet, 1929). Best known as the monarchist-Catholic first post-fascist mayor of Naples, this curious figure has no biography except the hagiographic Eugenio Cutolo, *Il travaglio politico di Giuseppe Buonocore* (Naples: L'idea, 1958).

22. Giuseppe Candidori, "Deposition," Session 19, February 24, 1934, in AR, CPM (1933–1936), sf. 2, LWTP.

23. IW (London) to LWT (Rome), November 19, 1929, in Correspondence, LWTP.

24. Teruzzi, *Cirenaica verde*, 43.

25. AT (Rome) to Arnaldo Mondadori (Milan), September 22, 1930; AT (Rome) to Mondadori (Milan), July 4, 1931, in AME, AT, FM.

26. Information on "Marsa al Brega," is found in *I campi fascisti dalle guerre d'Africa alla Repubblica di Salò*, http://campifascisti.it/scheda_campo.php?id

_campo=104; and details about the whole camp network in "Relazione sugli Accampamenti: Commissariato Regionale di Bengasi," July 28, 1932, in MAI, b. 5, f. 20, Materiale recuperato al Nord, vol. 5, AUSMAE. Nicola Labanca, "Italian Colonial Internment," in *Italian Colonialism*, ed. Ruth Ben-Ghiat and Mia Fuller, 27–36 (New York: Palgrave Macmillan, 2005) offers the most authoritative English-language account. Rodolfo Graziani had no qualms about publicizing his concentration system after World War II, once he was no longer in danger of being indicted for crimes against humanity: Rodolfo Graziani, *Cirenaica pacificata* (Milano: A. Mondadori, 1932), esp. 88–98, 262–278. Graziani shows side-by-side photographs of Bedouin encampments and concentration camp tents to demonstrate that the concentration camps represented significant improvement over the traditional standard of living. Rodolfo Graziani, *Libia redenta: storia di trent'anni di passione italiana in Africa* (Naples: Arti grafiche Torella, 1948).

27. Teruzzi, *Cirenaica verde*, 27.

28. On the book contract, leading to other contacts between Teruzzi and publisher Arnaldo Mondadori, who prized Teruzzi's alacrity at doing him small favors in Rome (such as obtaining a decoration for his brother, Bruno), see their several exchanges from September 22, 1930, to July 4, 1931, in AME, AT, FM.

29. Attilio Teruzzi, "Le risorse e l'avvenire della Libia nel giudizio del generale Teruzzi," *Corriere della Sera*, June 1, 1932, 2.

30. G-M Iorio's inscription, dated November 1932, is in LWT's copy, in Family Documents, LWTP.

15. Commanding the Blackshirts

1. "Il X annuale della Milizia a Roma," February 1, 1933, Giornale Luce B0207, Cinecittà Luce, Camera dei Deputati, http://camera.archivioluce.com/camera-storico/scheda/video/IL5000008616/2/Il-X-annuale-della-Milizia-a-Roma-.html. No source is better for studying the rough experiments choreographing rallies in the moment of passage from silent to sound than the Istituto Luce documentaries, 1930–1933. A keen-eyed account of Teruzzi at work is by an American journalist: David Darrah, *Hail Caesar!* (Boston: Hale, Cushman and Flint, 1936), 266–268.

2. "Fascisti to Create Formidable Army," *New York Times*, September 11, 1930.

3. *Illustrazione italiana*, vol. 57, no. 38, September 21, 1930, cover.

4. "Giuseppe Vaccari," in *Dizionario Enciclopedico italiano*, vol. 12 (1961), 587; Notizie statistiche sulle principali società italiane per azioni (Milan: Associazione fra le società italiane per azioni, 1934), 912. On Vaccari "the fascist" having to join but being unwilling to attend meetings of fascist senators, see

Fondo Vaccari, Correspondence, Generale Giuseppe Vaccari (b. 5), Museo del Risorgimento e della Resistenza, Vicenza.

5. "Cartella Militare," in Fondo Biograficio, AT, Mil. Rec., AUSSME. For the internal give and take around a nonunanimous decision, see Federzoni (Rome) to AT (Rome), December 18, 1928; Pietro Gazzera (Rome) to Committee on Ordine Militare Savoia (Florence), January 5, 1929; AT (Rome) to Pietro Gazzera (Rome), May 1, 1929; all in SPD, CO, AT, ACS.

6. Camera dei deputati: XVIII Legislature, "Proceedings," Session of May 31, 1929, p. 561.

7. Very little information is available on MVSN finances, but see Francesco Luigi Ferrari, *Il regime fascista italiano*, ed. Giuseppe Ignesti (Rome: Edizioni di storia e letteratura, 1983), 219 fn38. On the militia's relations with the army see Sergio Pelagalli, "Il generale Pietro Gazzera al ministero della guerra (1928–1933)," *Storia contemporanea* 20, no. 1 (1989): 138–144; Army General Quirino Armellini's sharp insights in *La crisi dell'esercito* (Rome: Casa Editrice "Priscilla:" Edizioni delle Catacombe, 1945), esp. 50–60; and, more generally, Virgilio Ilari and Antonio Sema, *Marte in orbace: Guerra, esercito e milizia nella concezione fascista della Nazione* (Ancona: Nuove Ricerche, 1988), 119–190, 270–320.

8. Attilio Teruzzi, *La milizia fascista e le sue specialità* (Milan: Mondadori, 1935).

9. "Il X Annuale della Milizia a Roma," February 1, 1933, Giornale Luce B0207, Cinecittà Luce.

10. Quintino Armellini, *La crisi dell'esercito*, 54–60.

11. Telephone intercept of conversation between Cesare De Vecchi (Rome) and Emilio De Bono (Rome), June 1930, cited in Ugo Guspini, *L'orecchio del regime: le intercettazioni telefoniche al tempo del fascismo* (Milan: Mursia, 1973), 96–97.

12. Enrico Caviglia, *I dittatori, le guerre e il piccolo re: diario 1925–1945*, ed. P. P. Cervone (Milan: Mursia, 2009), 335–356.

13. The best overview of the understudied relationship of fascist hierarchy to the ruling class, power elite, elites, establishment—all different concepts and all important given that the regime was twenty-one years in power—is Cesare Mozzarrelli, "Gerarchi/Gerarchia," *Dizionario del Fascismo*, vol. 1, ed. Victoria de Grazia and Sergio Luzzato (Torino: G. Einaudi, 2002), 583–587. See also Salvatore Lupo, *Il Fascismo: la politica in un regime totalitario* (Rome: Donzelli, 2000) for an astute analysis of fascist bureaucratic jockeying. On how Mussolini used his mythic status to manipulate political decision making, see Didier Museldiek, "Mussolini, Charisma and Decision-making," 1–18; and Goffredo Adinolfi, "Political Elite and Decision-making in Mussolini's Italy," 19–54; both in *Ruling Elites and Decision-making in Fascist-era Dictatorships*,

ed. Antonio Costa Pinto (Boulder: Social Science Monographs, 2009). Still useful are S. J. Woolf, "Il fascismo e i suoi gerarchi," in *Uomini e volti del fascismo*, ed. Fernando Cordova (Rome: Bulzoni, 1980), 547–561; and Mario Missori, *Gerarchie e statuti del PNF: Gran Consiglio, direttorio nazionale federazioni provinciali: Quadri e biografie* (Rome: Bonacci, 1986).

14. Julius Evola, *Imperialismo pagano, 1928* (Rome: Mediterranée, 2004), 209 and 208–211.

15. Lo Duca [*sic*], "Gerarchia," *Dizionario di Politica*, ed. Partito Nazionale Fascista, 4 vols. (Rome: Istituto della Enciclopedia italiana, 1940), vol. 1, 232.

16. Anonymous letter "Uccisione di un certo Brunati di Albese (Como)," September 18, 1929, in SPD, CR, RSI, Tarabini, ACS. On Como under fascism, see Vittorio Roncacci, "Oltre l'immagine: Como negli anni del fascismo," in Enrico Levrini, *Bagliori di giovinezza* (Varese: Macchione, 2003), 7–34, esp. 27–28.

17. Anonymous letter (Como), April 19, 1929; anonymous letter (Como), September 19, 1929; Informer's report, August 1929; all in SPD, CR, RSI, Tarabini, ACS.

18. Anonymous letter (Como), April 19, 1929; telegram from Prefect Rizzatti (Como) to Ministero Interno Gabinetto, June 9, 1929; Attilio Teruzzi (Castione della Presolana) to Alessandro Chiavolini (Rome), August 22, 1929, to forward to Mussolini, with copies of letter to Prefect (Como), August 23, 1929; and Report of Bologna's Prefect Trincea, on "girl's" death to Public Security Section, Ministry of the Interior, April 4, 1929, all in SPD, CR, RSI, Tarabini, ACS.

19. Informer's report, August 1929; also anonymous letter, n.d. [but Spring 1929], both in SPD, CR, RSI, Tarabini, ACS.

20. On Tarabini's subsequent rise to the top of the party hierarchy, see Informer's reports of October 6 and October 27, 1929; "Anonymous denunciation," December 5, 1929; and yet another entitled "Usque tandem?" January 16, 1930; Informer's report, January 6, 1943; all in SPD, CR, RSI, Tarabini, ACS.

21. Victoria de Grazia, *How Fascism Ruled Women, 1922–1945* (Berkeley: University of California Press, 1996), esp. chs. 3–4.

22. LWT (Rome) to RW/IW (NYC), June 17, 1927, in Correspondence, LWTP.

23. "Memorandum: Roma, Appartamento in via Monte Oppio, no. 5 assegnato ad Attilio Teruzzi, Cooperativa Edilizia Monte Oppio, 1947," in Presidenza Consiglio Ministri, 1948–1950, b. 49790, f. 7.2, ACS. On the changing cityscape see Piero Ostilio Rossi, *Roma: Guida all'architettura moderna, 1909–2000*, 2nd ed. (Bari: Laterza, 2003); and Italo Insolera, *Modern Rome: From Napoleon to the Twenty-First Century*, ed. Lucia Bozzola et al. (Cambridge: Cambridge Scholars Publishing, 2019).

24. "Ritratto di un amico, Odorico Dal Fabro," *Corriere Mercantile*, November 16, 1963, 3; Antonia Pizzi, *Castiglioncello: Villa Celestina alle origini ad oggi* (Castiglionello: Il Gabbiano, 2007), 33–37.

25. "Regio Tribunale di Livorno: Atto di citazione Odorico Dal Fabro (Livorno)," August 4, 1945, in MF, DG APR, ES, AT, ACS.

26. Sentence on Appeal: Avv. Odorico Dal Fabro vs. Intendant of Finance, etc." October 25, 1954, 3–4, Corte di cassazione: sezioni unite civili, in MF, DG APR, ES, AT, ACS.

27. Massimo Dringoli and Anna De Falco, *La Villa Celestina di Vittorio Cafiero a Castiglioncello dall'abbandono al recupero* (Trieste: EDITREG, 2005), 131–139; Pizzi, *Castiglioncello*, 37, 39.

28. "Eugenio Morelli," in *Celestina Teruzzi (1854–1933-XII)* (Rome: Novissima, 1934).

16. In the Grip of the Inquisition

1. His consultations are summarized in letters provided by Roberto Alessandri, chair professor of medicine at the Sapienza, and Rome's most prominent gynecologist from January 4, 1931, and Eugenio Pestalozza, the founding father of Italian gynecology and obstetrics, also a chaired professor at the University of Rome from January 31, 1931. These letters were later submitted to the Church Tribunal at Milan, and are now in AR, CPM (1933–1936), sf. 3, LWTP.

2. Lucia Pozzi, "The Encyclical *Casti connubii* (1930): The Origin of the XX Century Discourse of the Catholic Church on Family and Sexuality," in *La Sainte Famille: Sexualité, filiation et parentalité dans l'Eglise catholique*, ed. Cécile Vanderpelen-Diagre and Caroline Sägesser (Brussels: Les éditions de l'Université libre de Bruxelles, 2017), 41–54.

3. The most authoritative study of canon law procedures, based on his unique access to the Roman Rota archives is John T. Noonan Jr., *Power to Dissolve: Lawyers and Marriages in the Courts of the Roman Curia* (Cambridge, MA: Belknap Press of Harvard University Press, 1972). On numbers of annulments, more generally, and on the impact of celebrity annulments on attitudes toward the Church, divorce, and the elites who could obtain them, see George Seldes, *Vatican: Yesterday, Today, Tomorrow* (New York: Harper, 1934), 1–81, 115–124, 151–224; also Oliver Stewart's insightful *Divorce-Vatican Style* (London: Oliphants, 1971).

4. Dino Grandi (Rome) to LWT (Rome), May 18, 1932; Abel Gottheimer (NYC) to IW (London), n.d. [but May 1932]; Hiram Bingham (Washington, DC) to Dino Grandi (Rome), April 22, 1932; all in Correspondence, LWTP.

5. The figure first appears as a character in the US-based anarchist Carlo Tresca's New York-staged melodrama *L'attentato a Mussolini, ovvero Il segreto di*

Pulcinella (New York: Casa Editrice il Martello, 1925), set at the time of the Matteotti murder. The "Contessa" who is at the center of a plot to assassinate Mussolini is portrayed as the lover of both Cardinal Gasparri, the Vatican secretary of state, and PNF secretary Roberto Farinacci. Teruzzi appears to have been a notoriously gratifying target for these social climbers. See anonymous (Rome) to Eccellenza Benito Mussolini (Rome), August 20, 1939, in SPD, CR, AT, ACS, drawing a profile of the type: "Contessa" Ragnele, who flaunts herself as Teruzzi's "cousin," takes English lessons, fills her house with precious items; her daughter Fanne appears similarly presumptuous, talking about wanting to own a large villa, traveling abroad, and so on.

6. Introductory Petition ("Libello introduttivo"), December 11, 1932, in "Archidiocese Mediolanense, Teruzzi-Weinmann: Nullità di Matrimonio, In difesa di Attilio Teruzzi," January 11, 1935, in AR, CPM (1933–1936), sf. 5, LWTP.

7. LWT, handwritten notes, n.d. [but February–March 1935], in AR, CPM (1933–1936), sf. 8 DN, LWTP.

8. Paolo Quattrocchi, *Al di sopra dei gagliardetti: l'Arcivescovo Schuster: un'asceta benedettino nella Milano dell'èra fascista* (Milan: Marietti, 1985); Giorgio Rumi and Angelo Majo, *Il Cardinal Schuster e il suo tempo* (Milan: Massimo, 2007), 17–76.

9. Quattrocchi, 169; Angelo Majo, *Storia della Chiesa ambrosiana: dalle origini ai nostri giorni* (Milan: NED, 1995), 734; Federico Mandelli, *Profili di preti ambrosiani del Novecento* (Milan: NED, 1987, 116–126 Giorgio Vecchio: *Lombardia, 1940–1945: vescovi, preti e società alla prova della guerra* (Milan: Morcelliana, 2005), 26.

10. Monsignor Paolo Bianchi, Vicar of the Archdiocesan Tribunal, Archdiocese of Milan, interview with author, Milan, March 7, 2016.

11. Introductory Petition ("Libello introduttivo"), December 11, 1932.

12. Introductory Petition ("Libello introduttivo"), December 11, 1932, iv.

13. Introductory Petition ("Libello introduttivo"), December 11, 1932, v.

14. Dr. Alfredo Pratesi, "Letter to the Court," January 25, 1932, presented January 27, 1933, in AR, CPM (1933–1936), sf. 1. LWTP.

15. LWT, "Deposition," Session 6, May 26, 1933, in AR, CPM (1933–1936), sf. 2, LWTP.

16. Giovanni Zanchetta, *La regalità del Cristo*, (Milan: Soc. Ed. Vita e Pensiero, 1926 with preface by Franciscan Father Agostino Gemelli; also his *Il dogma* (Milan: Ufficio diocesano Cristiano, 1937); and *Il dominatore: comunismo o comunione?* (Milan: Soc. Ed. Pro Familia, 1938)

17. AT, "Deposition," Session 3, April 7, 1933, in AR, CPM (1933–1936), sf. 2, LWTP.

18. LWT, "Deposition," Session 6, May 26, 1933, AR, CPM (1933–1936), sf. 2, LWTP.

19. Eugenio Morelli, "Deposition," Session 12, November 1, 1933, in AR, CPM (1933–1936), sf. 2 LWTP.

20. Giuseppe Umberto Ferulli, "Deposition," Session 9, October 10, 1933, in AR, CPM (1933–1936), sf. 2, LWTP.

21. Vincenzo Ferulli, "Deposition," Session 15, December 1, 1933, in AR, CPM (1933–1936), sf. 2, LWTP.

22. Eugenio Morelli, "Deposition," Session 12, November 1, 1933, in AR, CPM (1933–1936), sf. 2, LWTP.

23. Celestina Rossi Teruzzi, "Deposition," Session 8, August 20, 1933; Amelia Teruzzi, "Deposition," Session 8, August 20, 1933, in AR, CPM (1933–1936), sf. 2, LWTP.

24. Antonio Zamboni, "Deposition," Session 10, October 27, 1933; Gino Turinelli, "Deposition," Session 10, October 27, 1933; Francesco Malgeri, "Deposition," Session 13, November 22, 1933; Enrico Maria Varenna, "Deposition," Session 24, July 24, 1934; all in AR, CPM (1933–1936), sf. 2, LWTP.

25. Antonio Zamboni, "Deposition," Session 10, October 27, 1933; Gino Turinelli, "Deposition," Session 10, October 27, 1933; Francesco Malgeri, "Deposition," Session 13, November 22, 1933; all in AR, CPM (1933–1936), sf. 2, LWTP.

26. "Gravissimo lutto della sua eccellenza Teruzzi," Il Messaggero, December 26, 1933; and telegram from B. Mussolini (Rome) to AT (Rome), December 25, 1933, in SPD, CR, AT, ACS. See also Foto attualità: "Funerali di donna Celestina Teruzzi, mamma di S. E. Teruzzi, capo di stato maggiore della M.V.S.N, December 13, 1933," photo no. A00052107–A0005214A, Archivio Storico Istituto Luce, Rome.

27. Benito Mussolini, "Al popolo di Bari," Opera Omnia, September 6, 1934, 26, 318; "Al popolo di Lecce," Opera Omnia, September 7, 1934, 26, 319.

28. Informer's reports of November 15, 1933 (Paris), and October 2, 1934 (Paris), in SPD, CR, AT, sf. LW, ACS.

29. Benito Mussolini stands somewhere between Napoleon Bonaparte and Silvio Berlusconi in terms of the interest drawn to his sexual persona. Historians want to know what that intensely sexualized persona reveals about him as a man and leader, about how it contributed to his personality cult, and what it suggests about sexual politics under fascism. His two most significant lovers, Margherita Sarfatti and Clara Petacci, are helpful here. The best-selling propaganda-biography, Margherita Sarfatti, The Life of Benito Mussolini (New York: Frederick Stokes, 1925), generates the myth of the Duce as the embodiment of heterosexual virility, violent, opportunistic, and antifeminist, yet surrounded by influential women, while Clara Petacci, Verso il disastro, Mussolini in Guerra, Diari 1939–1940, ed. Mimmo Franzinelli (Milan: Rizzoli, 2011), portrays the aggressive, jealous male lover. On the representations of

Mussolini's sexuality in propaganda and public images, see Luisa Passerini, *Mussolini l'immaginario* (Bari: Laterza, 1991). On Mussolini as "Latin lover" and cheat, see Roberto Olla, *Il Duce and His Women*, trans. Stephen Parkin (London: Alma Books, 2011); and R. J. B. Bosworth, *Claretta: Mussolini's Last Lover* (New Haven: Yale University Press, 2017). On the Duce as instigator of repression of unconventional male sexuality in the name of heterosexual virility, see Lorenzo Benadusi, *The Enemy of the New Man: Homosexuality in Fascist Italy*, trans. Suzanne Dingee and Jennifer Pudney (Madison: University of Wisconsin Press, 2012).

30. Anonymous (Rome) to Eccellenza Benito Mussolini (Rome), July 18, 1933, in SPD, CR, AT, ACS.

31. Ugo Guspini, *L' orecchio del regime: Le intercettazioni telefoniche ai tempi del fascismo* (Milan: Mursia, 1973), 103–104.

32. Alfred Testoni and Paola Daniela Giovanelli, *La società teatrale in Italia fra otto e novecento* (Rome: Bulzoni, 1984), 1384.

33. As reported by Lilliana Teruzzi, based on running into the couple at a Rome hotel in 1933, in LWT, handwritten note, n.d. [but Spring 1934], in AR, CPM (1933–1936), sf. 8 DN, LWTP.

34. Anonymous (Rome) to Benito Mussolini (Rome), July 26, 1930; also unsigned letter (Rome) to "Caro Amico" [Benito Mussolini] (Rome), September 27, 1930; both in SPD, CR, AT, ACS; also Count [name illegible, but Settimio Aurelio Nappi] (Milan) to Benito Mussolini, March 3, 1930 in in SPD, CO, SAN, ACS.

35. Count [name illegible, but Settimio Aurelio Nappi] (Milan) to Benito Mussolini, March 3, 1930; Osvaldo Fraiseri (Rome) to Benito Mussolini (Rome), August 1, 1933; S. A Nappi (Rome) to Benito Mussolini (Rome), May 4, 1935; also S. A. Nappi (Rome) to B. Mussolini (Rome), March 13, 1936; "Promemoria," S. A. Nappi (Belluno) to B. Mussolini (Rome) August 11, 1941; police "promemoria" judging Nappi to be harmless, April 14, 1930; all in SPD, CO, SAN, ACS.

36. M. L. and L. Nappi (Rome) to B. Mussolini (Rome), January 1, 1934; also their earlier letter of April 29, 1932; both in SPD, CO, SAN, ACS.

37. Bimby Teruzzi (Milan) to Benito Mussolini (Rome), May 12, 1934, SPD, CR, AT, sf. 4, ACS. These are to be read, too, in light of the many letters women sent in confidence to Mussolini: Camilla Cederna, ed., *Caro Duce: Lettere di donne italiane a Mussolini, 1922–1943* (Milan: Rizzoli, 1989); Alberto Vacca, *Duce! Tu sei un dio!* (Milan: Baldini Castoldi, 2013).

38. Report of police investigator Francesco Morelli (Turin) to Osvaldo Sebastiani (Rome), December 3, 1934, 5 pp., in SPD, CR, AT, sf. SF, ACS.

39. Report of police investigator Morelli, 5.

40. Mino Caudana, *1922* (Milan: Edizioni del Borghese, 1972), 239.

41. Informer's report, "La barba di S. E. Teruzzi," October 25, 1934, in SPD, CR, AT, ACS.

42. "Whiskers," *Time*, November 19, 1934, 23; see photograph captioned "Starace, Teruzzi e Mussolini durante la cerimonia di consegna del Premio di Poesia alle massaie di Littoria," December 18, 1934, in *Foto Attualità*, Archivio Storico Istituto Luce, Rome.

43. Petacci, *Verso il disastro*, entry for November 2, 1939, 232.

44. Giuseppe Candidori, "Deposition," Session 19, February 24, 1934, in AR, CPM (1933–1936), sf. 2, LWTP.

45. Enrico Maria Varenna, "Deposition," Session 24, July 24, 1934, AR, CPM (1933–1936), sf. 2, LWTP.

46. Federico Azzoni, "Deposition," Session 26, July 26, 1934, in AR, CPM (1933–1936), sf. 2, LWTP.

47. "Eugenio Morelli," in [n.a.], *Celestina Teruzzi* (Rome: Tipografia Novissima, 1934), unpaginated.

48. "Guelfo Civinini," in *Celestina Teruzzi*.

17. In War, Fullness

1. "Promemoria: Mussolini to Badoglio, Rome, 30 dicembre, 1934," cited in Giorgio Rochat, *Militari e politici nella preparazione della campagna d'Etiopia: Studio e documenti 1932–1936* (Milan: FrancoAngeli Editore, 1971), 376.

2. The best English-language introduction to the Ethiopian War is Alberto Sbacchi, *Legacy of Bitterness: Ethiopia and Fascist Italy, 1935* (Lawrenceville, NJ: Red Sea Press, 1997). The point of departure for Italian language studies is Riccardo Bottoni, ed., *L'Impero fascista: Italia ed Etiopia, 1935–1941* (Bologna: Il Mulino, 2008); in this volume see especially Nicola Labanca, "L'impero del fascismo. Lo stato degli studi," 35–61. To understand the Ethiopian war in the framework of Fascist war-making see Enzo Collotti, *Fascismo e politica di potenza: Politica estera 1922–1929* (Florence: Nuova Italia, 2000); and Giorgio Rochat, *Guerre italiane 1936–1943* (Turin: Einaudi, 2005).

3. "Petitioner's Summation," Mediolanen Teruzzi-Weinmann: nullità di matrimonio: In difesa di Attilio Teruzzi, submitted January 18, 1935, circulated February 25, 1935, in AR, CPM (1933–1936), sf. 5, LWTP. Introductory Petition ("Libello introduttivo"), December 11, 1932, in "Archidiocese Mediolanense, Teruzzi-Weinmann: Nullità di Matrimonio, In difesa di Attilio Teruzzi," January 11, 1935, in AR, CPM (1933–1936), sf. 5, LWTP.

4. Introductory Petition ("Libello introduttivo"), in AR, CPM (1933–1936), sf. 5, LWTP.

5. On Pacelli's successful use of this argument, see: John T. Noonan Jr., *Power to Dissolve: Lawyers and Marriages in the Courts of the Roman Curia* (Cambridge:

Belknap Press of Harvard University Press, 1972) 83, 114, 248–250; 257–259; 260–262; 288–289; 287–288.

6. "Petitioner's Summation," 24–25.

7. "Petitioner's Summation," 26.

8. Isaac Lewin, "Der itstiger poypst pius der tvelfter hot mit etlekhe yohr tsurik aroysgegebeben a psak kegn antisemitishn bilbul af'n talmud." *Der Tog: The National Jewish Daily,* May 2, 1942, 1, in f. Clippings, LWTP.

9. LWT, handwritten notes, n.d. [but February–March 1935], in AR, CPM (1933–1936), sf. 8 DN, LWTP.

10. Isaac Lewin, *In Defense of Human Rights* (New York: Research Institute of Religious Jewry, 1992), 13.

11. LWT, handwritten notes, n.d. [but February–March 1935], in AR, CPM (1933–1936), sf. 8 DN, LWTP.

12. LWT, handwritten notes, n.d. [but February–March 1935], in AR, CPM (1933–1936), sf. 8 DN, LWTP.

13. David I. Kertzer: *The Pope and Mussolini: The Secret History of Pius XI and the Rise of Fascism in Europe,* (New York: Penguin, 2014), 94.

14. On Catholic Jewish stereotypes see Daniele Menozzi, *'Giudaica perfidia': Uno sterotipo anti-semita fra liturgia e storia* (Bologna: Il Mulino, 2014); David I. Kertzer, *The Pope against the Jews: The Vatican's Role in the Rise of Modern Anti-Semitism* (New York: Vintage, 2002); David Nirenberg, *Anti-Judaism: The Western Tradition* (New York: W. W. Norton, 2013).

15. Filippo Meda, "Defendant's Summation," June 25, 1935, in AR, CPM (1933–1936), sf. 2, LWTP.

16. On Preziosi, see Giorgio Fabre, "Giovanni Preziosi," *Dizionario biografico degli Italiani,* vol. 85 (2016); and Aldo A. Mola, "Giovanni Preziosi," in *Dizionario del fascismo,* ed. Victoria de Grazia and Sergio Luzzatto, vol. 2 (Torino: G. Einaudi, 2003), 422–423. See also the ever-solid work of Renzo De Felice, *The Jews in Fascist Italy,* trans. Robert L. Miller (New York: Enigma Books, 1991); and Luigi Parente, Fabio Gentile, and Rosa Maria Grillo, eds., *Giovanni Preziosi e la questione della razza in Italia* (Soveria Mannelli: Rubbettino Editore, 2005).

17. Giuseppe Preziosi and Roberto Farinacci, "Matrimonio d'amore," in *Vita italiana* 19 (July 1931), 1–2. See also Matteo di Figlia, *Farinacci: Il radicalismo fascista al potere* (Rome: Donzelli, 2007), 202–207; and Michele Sarfatti, *The Jews in Mussolini's Italy: From Equality to Persecution,* trans. John Tedeschi and Anne C. Tedeschi (Madison: University of Wisconsin Press, 2007), 105–109.

18. Farinacci's animus toward Margherita Sarfatti ran deep. See Philip V. Cannistraro and Brian R. Sullivan, *Il Duce's Other Woman* (New York: William Morrow, 1993), 379, 394, 630n73.

19. Filippo Meda, "Defendant's Summation, " June 25, 1935, in AR, CPM (1933–1936), sf. 6. LWTP.

20. Sarfatti, *Jews in Mussolini's Italy*, 68–72.

21. Aaron Gillette, *Racial Theories in Fascist Italy* (London: Routledge, 2003), 67–68.

22. LWT, "Deposition," May 31, 1935, in AR, CPM (1933–1936), sf. 4, LWTP. On Tacchi-Venturi see Robert Aleksander Maryks, *"Pouring Jewish Water into Fascist Wine": Untold Stories of (Catholic) Jews from the Archive of Mussolini's Jesuit Pietro Tacchi Venturi* (Leiden: Brill, 2012).

23. Rochat, *Militari e politici nella preparazione*, 162–163; John Gooch, *Army, State, and Society in Italy, 1870–1915* (New York: St. Martin's Press, 1989), 239–251, 296–310.

24. Rochat, *Militari e politici nella preparazione*, 356.

25. Comando Divisione CCNN, February First, Fifth Division's military diaries: Allegati al Diario storico militare, July 24–December 31, 1935, vol. 1. in f. 1, b. 157, Fondo L-8, AUSSME.

26. Leone Concato, *Il battaglione vicentino: cronache del 142° Battaglione di Camicie nere della Colonna celere Primo febbraio, in Etiopia: 1935-XIII–1937-XV* (Pavia: Luculano Anastatica, 1938), 22.

27. Postcard from AT (Naples) to Benito Mussolini (Rome), n.d. [but October 1935], in SPD, CO, AT, ACS. See also the propaganda news film: "3000 CCNN si imbarcano per AOI," September 9, 1935, Giornale Luce B/BO753; and "Commandante Teruzzi della Divisione 1 febbraio con 3000 legionari," November 13, 1935, Giornale Luce B/Bo781; both in Archivio Storico Istituto Luce, Rome.

28. Telegram from LWT (Rome) to AT (Naples), November 12, 1935, in Correspondence, LWTP.

29. Rochat, *Militari e politici nella preparazione*, 142.

30. Concato, *Il battaglione vicentino*, 93–94.

31. Concerning day-by-day orders attesting to the arduousness of the labor, the "very difficult" terrain: the Comando Divisione CCNN February First, Fifth Division's military diaries: *Allegati al Diario storico militare*, March 1–April 30, 1936, vol. 3, in f. 1, b. 157, Fondo L-8, AUSSME.

32. Concato, *Il battaglione vicentino*, 145.

33. Leone Concato (*Il battaglione vicentino*) was pioneering in this respect: well-educated, a militia volunteer only because he couldn't get his pilot license in time, he earned his first accolades as a journalist from his diary, a profession he would pursued until the 1950s, when he made a fortune as an aviation industrialist.

34. "La 107 Legione CC NN, in AO, della 5 Divisione CC NN," in *La 107 Legione CC NN in AO* (Pavia: Industria Gradica Pavese, 1936); *Gli annali dell'Africa italiana* (Milan: Mondadori, 1938), 69–70.

35. Sbacchi, *Legacy of Bitterness*, 56, 60, 73.
36. Benito Mussolini, "La proclamazione dell'Impero," May 9, 1936, in *Opera Omnia*, vol. 29, (Florence: La Fenice, 1959) 268–269.
37. Rochat, *Militari e politici nella preparazione*, 162
38. Quirino Armellini, *Con Badoglio in Etiopia* (Milan: A. Mondadori, 1937), 272, photograph on 275.
39. Renato Canosa, *Farinacci: il superfascista*, (Milan: Mondadori, 2010) 233.
40. For background on Montanelli, see Nicola Labanca, "Constructing Mussolini's New Man in Africa: Memories of the Fascist War on Ethiopia," *Italian Studies* 61, no. 2 (Autumn 2006): 225–232.
41. Filippo Meda, "Defense's Final Summation," 12, in AR, CPM (1933–1936), sf. 6, LWTP. On Sincero see Harris M. Lentz III, *Popes and Cardinals of the 20th Century: A Biographical Dictionary* (Jefferson, NC: McFarland, 2001), 177.
42. Meda, "Defense's Final Summation," 18.
43. Meda, "Defense's Final Summation, "19.
44. On Alfredo Felici see "Alfredo Felici," *I senatori d'Italia, III. Senatori dell'Italia fascista*, Archivio Storico del Senato della Repubblica. https://notes9.senato.it /web/senregno.nsf/e38f2b0082a26247c125711400382e85/9df80a2dc5529f5b412564 6f005ba046?OpenDocument. M. Sarfatti to L. Federzoni, January 4, 1926, in Fondo Luigi Federzoni, b. 1, f. 1 "Margherita Sarfatti," ACS; Paolo Alatri, *D'Annunzio negli anni del tramonto*, 1930–1938 (Padua: Marsilio, 1984), 94.
45. "Il Duce inaugura Roma la caserma Mussolini e la sede del commando generale della milizia," *Corriere della Sera*, June 22, 1936. Foto attualità: "Il Duce inaugura la nuova caserma della milizia," Rome, 21.06.1936, in Senato, Archivioluce. http://senato.archivioluce.it/senato-luce/scheda/foto/IL3000022205 /12/Mussolini-al-centro-di-una-folla-di-militi-e-autoritagrave-fasciste -durante-la-cerimonia-di-inaugurazione-della-Caserma-Mussolini-per-la -Milizia.html.
46. LWT (Rome) to RW (London), July 28, 1936, in Correspondence, LWTP.
47. LWT (Rome) to RW (London), July 12, 1936; July 14, 1936 in Correspondence, LWTP.
48. LWT (Rome) to RW (London), July 28, 1936, in Correspondence, LWTP.
49. "Sentence: *Nullatatis Matrimonii*," July 17, 1936, in AR, CPM (1933–1936), sf. 7, LWTP.
50. LWT (Maccarese) to RW (London), July 22, 1936; RW (London) to IW (NYC), July 21, 1936; both in Correspondence, LWTP.
51. LWT (Rome) to RW (London), July 28, 1936, in Correspondence, LWTP.
52. LWT (Rome) to RW (London), August 5, 1936, in Correspondence, LWTP.
53. LWT (Rome) to RW (London), July 28, 1936; A. Felici (Rome) to LWT (Rome), n.d. [but August 1936]; both in Correspondence, LWTP. On Lilliana's contacts

with Tacchi Venturi: LWT (Rome) to RW (London), July 8, 1936; LWT (Rome) to A. Felici (Rome), n.d. [but late July 1936]; both in Correspondence, LWTP.

54. Letter with attached Annulment Process, LWT (Rome) to B. Mussolini (Forlì), July 29, 1936, in SPD, CR, AT, sf. LW, ACS.

55. LWT (Rome) to IW (New York)/RW (London), July 28, 1936; "Cartella Militare," Fondo Biograficio, AT, Mil. Rec., AUSSME.

56. LWT (Paris) to RW and IW (NYC), September 28, 1936, in Correspondence, LWTP.

57. Roberto Festorazzi, *Farinacci: L' antiduce* (Rome: Il Minotauro, 2004), 120–122.

18. In Love, Tribulations

1. Telegram from Benito Mussolini (Rome) to Colli [General Ettore Bastico] (Spain), March 31, 1937, "G. Cairati's (His Excellency Teruzzi) Mission to Spain," in GMSG, b. 1, f. 1244, sf. 38, AUSMAE. On the battle itself, see John F. Coverdale, "The Battle of Guadalajara, 8–22 March 1937," *Journal of Contemporary History* 9, no. 1 (January 1974): 53–75. The most up-to-date general account is Paul Preston, *The Spanish Civil War: Reaction, Revolution and Revenge*, rev. ed. (London: Harper Perennial, 2006).

2. On Fascist Italy's indispensable role in sustaining the insurgency through its first year see Javier Rodrigo, *La guerra fascista en la Guerra Civil española, 1936–1939* (Madrid: Alianza, 2016), excerpted in Javier Rodrigo, "A Fascist Warfare? Italian Fascism and War Experience in the Spanish Civil War, 1936–1939," *War in History* 26, no. 1 (2017): 86–104, who brings new archives to reconfirm Morton Heiberg, "Mussolini, Franco and the Spanish Civil War: An Afterthought," in *International Fascism, 1919–1945*, ed. Robert Mallett and Gert Sørensen, 55–68 (London: Routledge, 2002); and, especially, the pioneering Brian Sullivan, "Fascist Italy's Involvement in the Spanish Civil War," *Journal of Military History* 59, no. 4 (1995): 697–727. On the Blackshirts's military culture see Pierluigi Romeo di Colloredo Mels, *Frecce Nere! Le camicie nere in Spagna 1936–1939* (Genoa: Associazione culturale Italia storica, 2012); and Massimiliano Griner, *I ragazzi del '36: L' avventura dei fascisti italiani nella guerra civile spagnola* (Milan: Rizzoli, 2006).

3. Leonardo Sciascia captures Teruzzi's discomfort at the plight of the troops in his *Sicilian Uncles*, trans. N. S. Thomson (New York: Granta Books, 2001), ch. 2.

4. "Teruzzi's Report to Ciano on the Spanish Situation, signed with pseudonym Dr. Cairati," May 13, 1937, in GMSG, b. 1, f. 1244, sf. 38, AUSMAE.

5. AT to G. Ciano, April 6, 1937 (stamped "have read" by Mussolini), in GMSG, b. 1, f. 1244, sf. 38, AUSMAE.

6. Teruzzi sent the photograph, showing him with general at the observation post on Mount Mazza, August 18, 1937, to Ciano, in GMSG, b. 1, f. 1244, AUSMAE.

7. "Mussolini and Franco: Messages Exchanged," *Manchester Guardian*, August 28, 1937, 13; "La gratitudine di Franco in un messaggio," *La Stampa*, August 27, 1937, 1; telegram from G. Ciano (Rome) to Teruzzi (Santander), August 26, 1937, in GMSG, b. 30, f. 1 (347), AUSMAE.

8. Sandro Gerbi and Raffaele Liucci, *Indro Montanelli: Una biografia, 1909–2001* (Milan: Ulrico Hoepli Editore, 2014), 54–61.

9. Indro Montanelli, *La mia eredità sono io*, ed. Paolo di Paolo (Milan: Rizzoli, 2008), 117–118, 120–123. The Giornale Luce propaganda film "La corrida organizzata della Falange," dated September 29, 1937, three weeks after Teruzzi's return home, seems designed to show Teruzzi as the serious professional soldier, and the bullfight the embodiment of the picturesque traditionalist Spain the fascists were fighting to preserve. "La corrida organizzata della Falange," code B117205, Archivio Storico Istituto Luce, Rome.

10. Galeazzo Ciano, *The Ciano Diaries, 1934–1943*, ed. Malcolm Muggeridge (New York: Doubleday, 1946), entries for October 6 and October 7, 1937 (both p. 18). For Teruzzi's request for a furlough: AT (Miranda de Ebro) to Galeazzo Ciano (Rome), September 1, 1937, in GMSG, b. 38, f. 1244, AUSMAE.

11. Ciano, *Diary*, entry for September 13, 1937 (12).

12. Ciano, *Diary*, entry for October 7, 1937 (18), September 14, 1937 (12), and October 13, 1937 (20).

13. Ian Campbell, *The Addis Ababa Massacre: Italy's National Shame* (Oxford: Oxford University Press, 2017) is now the most authoritative study.

14. Alberto Sbacchi, *Legacy of Bitterness: Ethiopia and Fascist Italy, 1935* (Lawrenceville, NJ: Red Sea Press, 1997), 87–234; Charles Schaefer, "Serendipitous Resistance in Fascist-Occupied Ethiopia, 1936–1941," *Northeast African Studies* 3, no. 1 (1996): 87–115.

15. Giuseppe Mayda, *Graziani l'Africano: Da Neghelli a Salò* (Florence: La Nuova Italia, 1992), 11–12.

16. For his biography: Edoardo Borra, *Amedeo di Savoia: terzo duca d'Aosta e viceré d'Etiopia* (Milan: Mursia, 1985). See also Alfio Berretta, *Amedeo d'Aosta: il prigioniero del Kenia* (Milan: Garzanti, 1952), 123–126; and Sbacchi, *Legacy of Bitterness*, 57–58.

17. Ciano, *Diaries*, November 19, 1937 (34).

18. "Attilio Teruzzi: Military Record," in Fondo Biografico, AT, Mil. Rec., AUSSME.

19. Attilio Teruzzi, "Funeral announcement for Amelia Teruzzi," n.d. [but received by Mussolini April 30, 1937], and Francesco Malgeri, "Gravissimo lutto del generale Attilio Teruzzi," *Il Messaggero*, April 30, 1937, both in SPD, CR, AT, ACS.

20. Telegram from Mussolini (Rome) to AT (Rome), May 1, 1937; telegram from Mussolini (Rome) to AT (Spain), May 1, 1937, in GMSG, b. 24, f. 1 (341), AUSMAE.

21. Fiammetta Grimaldi, interview with author, Naples, August 2, 2014; also in Family Memorabilia, Grimaldi Family Collection, Naples.

22. Informer's reports, May 13 and June 10, 1937; "Police memo," July 23, 1938; all in MI, PP, FP, YB, ACS. Police misogyny is analyzed in Jonathan Dunnage, "Policemen and 'Women of Ill Repute': A Study of Male Sexual Attitudes and Behaviour in Fascist Italy," *European History Quarterly* 46, no. 1 (2016): 72–91.

23. On the Romanian communities, see Gudrun Kramer, *The Jews in Modern Egypt, 1914–1952* (London: I. B. Tauris, 1989), 11, 18–19, 47; Constantin Botoran," "Short Survey of Romanian-Egyptian Relations in the Period between the World Wars (1919–1939)," *Revue roumaine d'études internationales* 6 (1972): 272; Anca-Steliana Mirea, "Considerations conçernant les relations diplomatiques entre la Roumanie et l'Egypte de l'entre deux-guerres," GIDNI, vol. 4 (2014): 350–357, 352. "Telegrams in Brief," *Times*, November 15, 1924, 9.

24. Patrizia Carrano, *La Magnani* (Milan: Rizzoli, 1986), 59, 75, 87; and Matilde Hockkofler, *Anna Magnani: La biografia* (Milan: Bompiani, 1981), 21.

25. Informer's report, May 13, 1937, in MI, PP, FP, YB.

26. "Visa-stamps: Rumanian Passport, released Rome, April 15, 1937," in Family Documents, Grimaldi Family Collection.

27. On the impact of cinema divismo on political divisimo, see sociologist Franco Rositi, "Personalità e divisimo in Italia durante il fascismo," *Ikon* 17, no. 62 (1967): 9–48; and Stephen Gundle, *Mussolini's Dream Factory: Film Stardom in Fascist Italy* (Oxford: Berghahn, 2013).

28. Clara Petacci, *Verso il disastro, Mussolini in guerra, Diari 1939–1940*, ed. Mimmo Franzinelli (Milano: Rizzoli, 2011), 160–161. On the female cult of the Duce see Maria Antonietta Macciocchi, *La donna "nera": 'consenso' femminile e fascismo* (Milan: Feltrinelli, 1976).

29. On Clara Petacci's family, its social climbing, and heavy investment in the affair see R. J. B. Bosworth, *Claretta: Mussolini's Last Lover* (New Haven: Yale University Press, 2017).

30. Petacci, *Verso il disastro*, 160.

31. The best overview of this surge of interest in "demography," "race," and "moral reform" is Francesco Cassata, *Building the New Man: Eugenics, Racial Science and Genetics in Twentieth-Century Italy*, trans. Erin O'Loughlin (Budapest:

Central European University Press, 2011). Renzo De Felice signals this shift of politics from institutions to bodies as the true moment of affirmation of Mussolini's notion of totalitarianism in: De Felice, *Mussolini il duce, Vol. 2, Lo Stato totalitario, 1936–1940* (Turin: Giulio Einaudi, 1981), 288–301.

32. Luigi Federzoni, *Italia di ieri, per la storia di domani* (Milan: Mondadori, 1967), 158.

33. "Birth Certificate: Celeste-Maria Blank," Ufficio Anagrafe: Comune di Roma, Archivio di Stato di Roma.

34. Yvette Blank (Lipari) to Benito Mussolini (Rome) May 3, 1943, in SPD, CR, AT, sf. YB, ACS.

35. For biographical information on Giovanni Battista Girardi, see http://www .catholic-hierarchy.org/bishop/bgirg.html; Luigi Mezzadri, Maurizio Taglia-ferri, and Elio Guerriero, *Le diocesi d'Italia* (Rome: San Paolo Edizioni, 2008), vol. 3, 922; Giorgio Rumi et al., eds., *Brescia e il suo territorio* (Brescia: Cariplo, 1996), 134.

36. Angelo Fortunato Danesi, *E giunta l'ora!* (Milan: Treves, 1935). Federico Adamoli, ed., *Lettere dal fronte: la Grande Guerra raccontata nelle pagine del Corriere Abruzzese*, (Teramo: [n.p.], 2013), 41; Mauro Canali, *Il delitto Mat-teotti: affarismo e politica nel primo governo Mussolini* (Bologna: Il Mulino, 1997), 440.

37. Angelo Fortunato Danesi, June 17, 1937, in Court Proceedings, NM, T-W, ADSP.

38. Enrico Maria Varenna, "Deposition," May 14, 1937, in Court Proceedings, NM, T-W, ADSP.

39. Giuseppe Villa, "Deposition," June 23, 1937, in Court Proceedings, NM, T-W, ADSP.

40. Attilio Teruzzi, "Deposition," September 27, 1937, in Court Proceedings, NM, T-W, ADSP.

41. Pietro David, "Deposition," January 18, 1938, in Court Proceedings, NM, T-W, ADSP.

42. Angelo Fortunato Danesi, "Memorandum," August 5, 1938, in AR, CPP (1937–1939), LTWP.

43. "Decree of the Tribunal of the Archdiocese of Pavia," August 30, 1938, in NM, T-W, ADSP.

44. Filippo Meda (Milan) to LWT (Rome), October 29, 1938, in Correspondence LWTP; also LWT, "Memorandum," October 1, 1942, in AR, CPSR (1940–1948), LWTP.

45. David I. Kertzer, *The Pope against the Jews: The Vatican's Role in the Rise of Modern Anti-Semitism* (New York: Vintage, 2002), 202.

46. Olindo de Napoli rightly emphasizes fascist jurists' pretentions to confront Roman Law and German jurisprudential traditions. Olindo de Napoli, *La*

prova della razza: cultura giuridica e razzismo in Italia negli anni Trenta (Milan: Mondadori, 2009). See also Michael Livingston, *The Fascist Race Laws* (Cambridge: Cambridge University Press, 2014).

47. Michele Sarfatti, "Legislazioni antiebraiche nell'Europa degli anni trenta e Chiesa Cattolica: la 'nuova' classificazione di ebreo e il divieto di matrimoni 'razzialmente misti,'" in *Les racines chrétiennes de l'antisémitisme politique (fin XIXe–XXe siécle)*, ed. Catherine Brice and Giovanni Miccoli (Rome: Publications de l'Ecole française de Rome, 2003), 273.

48. For a good introduction to the origins of fascist racial legislation as an autochthonous development, as opposed to being imposed from outside by Mussolini's alliance with Hitler, see Annalisa Capristo and Ernest Ialongo "On the 80th Anniversary of the Racial Laws: Articles Reflecting the Current Scholarship on Italian Fascist Anti-Semitism in Honor of Michele Sarfatti," *Journal of Modern Italian Studies* 24, no. 1 (2019): 1–13. Michele Sarfatti, *The Jews in Mussolini's Italy: From Equality to Persecution*, trans. John Tedeschi and Anne C. Tedeschi (Madison: University of Wisconsin Press, 2006) is key here; see also the revised Italian edition Michele Sarfatti, *Gli ebrei nell'Italia fascista: vicende, identità, persecuzione* (Turin: Einaudi, 2018).

49. Clara Petacci, *Mussolini segreto: diari 1932–1938*, ed. Mauro Suttora (Milan: Rizzoli, 2009), entry for August 28, 1938 (p. 401).

50. Petacci, *Mussolini segreto*, entries for October 8, 1938 (421), October 9, 1938 (422), and October 11, 1938 (423).

51. Petacci, *Mussolini segreto*, entries for November 8, 1938 (452) and November 16, 1938 (459).

52. Petacci, *Mussolini segreto*, entry for November 15, 1938 (457).

53. Petacci, *Mussolini segreto*, entry for November 15, 1938 (457).

54. Pietro Stella, "Filoebraismo cattolico in Piemonte e in Lombardia dalla rivoluzione francese al caso Dreyfus," *Rivista di storia della Chiesa in Italia* 58, no. 1 (2004): 104.

55. Roberto Farinacci, *La Chiesa e gli ebrei* (Rome: Tipografia Tevere, XV, 1937); Giovanni Sale, *Le leggi razziali in Italia e il Vaticano* (Milan: Rizzoli, 2010), 94–95, 212–213.

56. Cited in Hubert Wolf, *Pope and Devil: The Vatican's Archives and the Third Reich*, trans. Kenneth Kronenberg (Cambridge, MA: Belknap Press of Harvard University Press, 2012), 116–117.

57. Angelo Fortunato Danesi and Carlo Pacelli to Emilio Ripa (Pavia), "Risposta alle *Animadversiones* del difensore," Milan, July 10, 1938, p. 7, in NM, T-W, ADSP.

58. "Risposta alle *Animadversiones* del difensore."

59. Felice Magnini (Pavia) to Carlo Pacelli (Rome), February 3, 1939, in NM, T-W, ADSP.

60. Emma Fattorini, *Hitler, Mussolini and the Vatican: Pope Pius XI and the Speech That Was Never Made*, trans. Carl Ipsen (Cambridge, MA: Polity Press, 2011), 29.

61. Attilio Teruzzi (Rome) to Mons. Alfredo Ottaviani (Rome), regarding his "Ricorso Teruzzi a Suprema Sacra Congregazione, March 15, 1939," in NM, T-W, ADSP.

62. Francesco Marchetti-Selvaggiani (Rome) to Giovanni Battista Girardi (Pavia), June 10, 1939; Felice Magnini (Pavia) to Carlo Pacelli (Rome), June 23, 1939; Attilio Teruzzi (Rome) to Tribunale ecclesiastico (Pavia), July 1, 1939; all in NM, T-W, ADSP.

63. Sentenza Causa Matrimoniale Teruzzi-Weinman, September 26, 1939, AR, CPP (1937–1939), LWTP; Rev. Edoardo Casiroli, September 1, 1939, and Rev. Carlo Rossi, September 1, 1939, voted yes to the reasoning provided by Emilio Ripa, but provided no argumentation of their own. In NM, T-W, ADSP.

64. Photograph of Yvette Blank hugging her daughter, Mariceli Blank, n.d. [but fall 1941], in Family Photographs, Grimaldi Family Collection.

65. Philip V. Cannistraro and Brian R. Sullivan, *Il Duce's Other Woman* (New York: William Morrow, 1993), 511–522, quotation at 522.

66. LWT (NYC) to IW/RW (London), n.d. [but August 1939], in Correspondence, LWTP.

19. In Empire, Hollow Glory

1. Clara Petacci, *Verso il disastro, Mussolini in Guerra, Diari 1939–1940*, ed. Mimmo Franzinelli (Milan: Rizzoli, 2011), May 14, 1939 (p. 231)

2. "Reshuffle in Italy," *Times*, November 1, 1939, 8; "Mussolini Changes in Army and Cabinet," *Manchester Guardian*, November 1, 1939, 9.

3. Petacci, *Verso il disastro, Mussolini in Guerra, Diari 1939–1940*, May 14, 1939 (p. 232).

4. Roberto Almagia, et al., "Africa Orientale Italiana," *Enciclopedia Treccani*, 1, Appendice (Rome: n.p., 1938), http://www.treccani.it/enciclopedia/africa-orientale-italiana_%28Enciclopedia-Italiana%29/.

5. The official line is brazenly stated in Corrado Zoli, "The Organization of Italy's East African Empire," *Foreign Affairs* 16, no. 1 (October 1937): 80–90.

6. Haile Larebo, "Empire Building and Its Limitations: Ethiopia (1935–1941)," in *Italian Colonialism*, ed. Ruth Ben-Ghiat and Mia Fuller, 83–94 (New York: Palgrave Macmillan, 2002); Alberto Sbacchi, *Legacy of Bitterness: Ethiopia and Fascist Italy, 1935* (Lawrenceville, NJ: Red Sea Press, 1997), esp. chs. 5–8.

7. Eugenio Giovannetti, "Il Viaggio di S. E. Attilio Teruzzi in A.O.I.," *Gli Annali dell'Africa Italiana* 1, no. 2 (August 1938), 440.

8. Report from British Consulate, Harar, April 13, 1940, to Secretary of State" April 13, 1940, in India Office Records (IOR), Records of the Secretariat of the Colony in Aden (R/20/B/1451), file "General Teruzzi's visit to Italian East Africa" (f. C.25/9), British Library. (Hereafter IOR R/20/B/1451, f. C.25/9, British Library.)

9. Attilio Teruzzi, "Speech Addis Abeba, June 3, 1938," quoted in "Viaggio di Teruzzi dal 23 maggio 1938 al 30 giugno, 1938," in MAI, AS, b. 287, AUSMAE.

10. Quoted in Giovannetti, "Il Viaggio Teruzzi in A.O.I.," 439. See also "Viaggio di S. E. Teruzzi," in MAI, AS, b. 134, AUSMAE; as well as "Segnalazione della stampa, S. E. Teruzzi in A. O. I.," 29-5-1938, in MAI, gab. 2024, AUSMAE. The marches coopted up-and-coming filmmakers, like Arturo Gemmitti, as well as promising writers, notably Dino Buzzatti, in addition to the old guard, Guelfo Civinini. On filmmakers, see Gianmarco Mancuso, "L'impero visto da una cinepresa: Il Reparto 'Africa Orientale' dell'Istituto Luce," in *Quel che resta dell'impero: la cultura coloniale degli italiani*, ed. Valeria Deplano and Alesandro Pes (Milan: Mimesis, 2015), 259–278. On Buzzatti, see Marie-Hélène Caspar, *L'Africa di Buzzati: Libia, 1933; Etiopia, 1939–1940* (Paris: PUF, 1997). The domestic news barrage was echoed abroad by foreign correspondents. See, for example, "Italian Policy in East Africa: General Teruzzi on the Colour Line," *Times*, July 29, 1938, 8.

11. Telegram from Renzo Meregazzi, Chief of Cabinet of the Minister of Africa (Rome) to AT (SS Victoria), May 25, 1938; telegram from Benito Mussolini (Rome) to AT (Addis Abeba), June 23, 1938; both in MAI, AS, b. 28, AUSMAE.

12. "Programma della visita di S. E. Attilio Teruzzi, Jan 11–25, 1939," in (MAI, AS, b. 256, AUSMAE.

13. On road building see Angelo Piccioli, "Le opere stradali," *Annali dell'Africa italiana*, 2, no. 4 (1939), 320–360.

14. Telegram from AT (Macallè) to Benito Mussolini (Rome), May 5, 1938, in MAI, AS, b. 28, AUSMAE.

15. Report from the British Consul, Addis Ababa, to Foreign Secretary, March 1, 1940, 2 pp., in IOR R/20/B/1451, f. C.25/9, British Library.

16. Anthony Mockler, *Haile Selassie's War*, 2nd rev. ed. (New York: Signal Books, 2005), 202.

17. "Viaggio di S. E. Teruzzi in AOI del gennaio 1940," in MAI, AS, b. 256, AUSMAE.

18. AT, Report "Il Governo Generale dell'AOI, Addis Ababa, January 18, XVIII (1940)," in MAI, AS, b. 256, AUSMAE.

19. Giorgio Cavallero, *Il custode del carteggio* (Milan: Piemme, 1997), 47; Lino Calabrò, *Intermezzo africano: ricordi di un residente di governo in Etiopia*,

1937–1941 (Rome: Bonacci, 1988), 68, 89. See also P. M. Masotti, *Ricordi d'Etiopia di un funzionario coloniale* (Milan: Pan, 1981), 23; Massimo Borruso, *Il mito infranto: la fine del sogno africano negli appunti e nelle immagini di Massimo Borruso, funzionario coloniale in Etiopia, 1937–46* (Rome: Piero Lacaita, 1997).

20. Luigi Federzoni, *Italia di ieri per la storia di domani* (Milan: Mondadori, 1967), 148; British Consul, Harar, Report, March 4, 1940, reported by British Consul of Addis Ababa to Secretary of State, in IOR R/20/B/1451, f. C.25/9, British Library.

21. Angelo Del Boca, *Gli italiani in Africa orientale: Vol. 3. La caduta dell'Impero* (Bari: Laterza, 1982), 137.

22. British Consul, Harar, Report, April 24, 1940.

23. Telegrams from Aide-de-Camp Colonel Giovanni Osti (AOI) to Head of Office, Beniamino de Muro (Rome), January 17, 1939; Giovanni Osti to Beniamino de Muro, February 10, 1939; both in "S. E. Teruzzi, Viaggio in AOI dal 23/12/38 al 11/2/39," MAI, AS, b. 280, AUSMAE.

24. Calabrò, *Intermezzo africano*, 89; Masotti, *Ricordi d'Etiopia*, 3; Angelo Del Boca, *Gli italiani in Africa Orientale*, vol. 3: *La caduta dell'Impero* (Bari: Laterza, 1982), 131–140.

25. Letter with illegible signature (Rome) to "his Eccellenza," Il Duce, Capo dei Ministri [B. Mussolini](Rome), October 22, 1939, in SPD, CR, AT, ACS.

26. Giorgio Rochat, email exchange with author, September 14, 2007.

27. Alessio Gagliardi, "La mancata 'valorizzazione' dell'impero: Le colonie italiane in Africa orientale e l'economia dell'Italia fascista," *Storicamente* 12, no. 3 (2016): 1–32.

28. Nicola Gattari, *La strada per Addis Abeba: lettere di un camionista dall'Impero, 1936–41*, ed. Sergio Luzzatto (Turin: Paravia scriptorium, 2000); and Paul Corner, *The Fascist Party and Popular Opinion in Mussolini's Italy* (Oxford: Oxford University Press, 2002), 202.

29. Haile M. Larebo, *The Building of an Empire: Italian Land Policy and Practice in Ethiopia, 1935–1941* (Oxford: Clarendon Press, 1994); Giulia Barrera, "Mussolini's Colonial Race Laws and State-Settler Relations in Africa Orientale Italiana (1935–1941)," *Journal of Modern Italian Studies* 8, no. 203 (2003): 425–443. See also Giulia Barrera, "Sessualità e segregazione nelle terre dell'impero," in *L' Impero fascista: Italia ed Etiopia, 1935–1941*, ed. Riccardo Bottoni, 393–414 (Bologna: Il Mulino, 2008); Gian Luca Podestà, "Colonists and 'Demographic' Colonists: Family and Society in Italian Africa," *Annales de démographie historique* 122, no. 2 (2011): 205–232.

30. Patrick Bernhard, "Hitler's Africa in the East: Italian Colonialism as a Model for German Planning in Eastern Europe," *Journal of Contemporary History* 51, no. 1 (2016): 61–90; Patrick Bernhard, "Borrowing from Mussolini: Nazi

Germany's Colonial Aspirations in the Shadow of Italian Expansionism," *Journal of Imperial and Commonwealth History* 41, no. 4 (2013): 617–643.

31. Vitaliano Brancati, *Gli anni perduti*, 3rd ed. (Milan: Bompiani, 1945), 89.

32. Elsa de Giorgi, *I coetanei* (Turin: Einaudi, 1955), 8.

33. de Giorgi, *I coetanei*, 8–10.

34. de Giorgi, *I coetanei*, 11.

35. Claudio Segrè, *Italo Balbo: A Fascist Life* (Berkeley: University of California Press, 1987), 392–407.

36. Leonardo Sciascia, *Sicilian Uncles*, trans. N. S. Thomson (New York: Granta Books, 2001), ch. 2. First published in Italian in 1958.

37. Elena Fondra, "Villa Celestina a Castiglioncello," *Domus* 141 (1939): 7–21.

38. Photograph of Yvette Blank in bathing suit; photograph of Yvette Blank with Mariceli Blank, both in Family Photographs, Grimaldi Family Collection, Naples.

39. Gian Piero Celati and Leo Gattini, *La ciminiera dimezzata* (Pisa: Fabrizio Serra Editore, 1997), 55.

40. Viviana Molinari, *Bella marea* (Rome: Serarcangeli, 1989), 71–77, 84–89.

41. Postcard from Attilio Teruzzi to Yvette Blank n.d. [but February 1940], in Miscellaneous, Grimaldi Family Collection.

42. Luca Scacchetti, *Guglielmo Ulrich, 1904–1977* (Milan: 24 Ore Cultura, 2009), 58–59, 112.

43. *Annuario generale d'Italia e dell'Impero italiano* (Milan: n.p., 1938), 63; *Notizie statistiche per le società italiane per azioni* (Milan: Credito Italiano, 1940), 73.

44. Photograph album, "Cappella Funeraria Famiglia Teruzzi, Roma," in Fondo Archivistico Guglielmo Ulrich, Centro Studi e Archivio della Comunicazione, Parma.

20. The Rout

1. See photograph, "Adolf Hitler in conversation with the Italian Colonial Minister Attilio Teruzzi (left) in the Reich Chancellery with translator, September 17, 1940"; also "Hitler alone with Teruzzi," both by *Presse-Illustrationen* photographer Heinrich Hoffmann, Archive of Ullstein Bild / Ullstein Bild via Getty Images, https://www.gettyimages.com/photos/attilio-teruzzi.

2. Quoted in "'Teruzzi in Deutschland," *Afrika Nachrichten* [Leipzig], October 10, 1940, in digitized clippings, Hamburgisches Welt-Wirtschafts-Archiv, http://webopac.hwwa.de/Pressemappe20/PM20.cfm?T=P&qt=232251&CFID=15395396&CFTOKEN=68997503. On the visit itself, see "Corrispondenza relativa ai rapporti con la Germania, 1940"; and telegram from A. Zamboni (Berlin) to Minculpop (Rome), September 18, 1940, in "Viaggio in Germania

di S. E. Attilio Teruzzi (September 1940)," in f. 702, 385, AS, GM, MAI, 1923–1943, AUSMAE.

3. M. W. Graham, "The Diplomatic Struggle for Africa," in *Africa, the Near East and the War* (Berkeley: University of California Press, 1943) 198–201; Erik S. Roubinek, "A 'Fascist' Colonialism? German National Socialist and Italian Fascist Colonial Cooperation, 1936–1943," in *Nazi Germany and Southern Europe, 1933–45*, ed. F. Clara, C. Ninhos, and S. Grishin (London: Palgrave Macmillan, 2016), 183–197.

4. Teruzzi's audiences with Mussolini, May 1940, in *Mussolini's Appointment Calendar, 1923–1943*, curated by Amedeo Osti-Guerrazzi, German Historical Institute of Rome.

5. On Italy's war aims, see Davide Rodogno, *Fascism's European Empire: Italian Occupation during the Second World War* (Cambridge: Cambridge University Press, 2006). For the war's impact on the regime, see Philip Morgan, *The Fall of Mussolini: Italy, the Italians, and the Second World War* (New York: Oxford University Press, 2007).

6. Galeazzo Ciano, *The Ciano Diaries, 1934–1943: The Complete, Unabridged Diaries of Count Galeazzo Ciano, Italian Minister of Foreign Affairs, 1936–1943*, ed. Malcolm Muggeridge (New York: Doubleday, 1946), entry for April 1–2, 1938 (p. 236). On the British see entry for October 13, 1937 (15).

7. Ciano, *Diaries*, entry for April 11, 1940, (235–236).

8. Ciano, *Diaries*, entry for April 6, 1940, (232–233).

9. Ciano, *Diaries*, entry for May 29, 1940, (256–257).

10. Quirino Armellini, *Diario di guerra: nove mesi al commando supremo* (Milan: Garzanti, 1946), 19.

11. Giuseppe Bottai, *Diario, 1935–1944*, ed. Giordano Bruno Guerri (Milan: Rizzoli, 1982), 245, 284; Enrico Caviglia, *I dittatori, le guerre e il piccolo re: Diario, 1925–1945*, ed. Pier Paolo Cervone (Milan: Mursia, 2009), 345.

12. Armellini, *Diario di guerra*, 205.

13. "L'accesa economica della Libia nella documentata relazione al Duce di S. E. Teruzzi," *La Stampa*, November 29, 1939, 1.

14. On wartime Benghazi see Patrick Bernhard, "Behind the Battle Lines: Italian Atrocities and the Persecution of Arabs, Berbers, and Jews in North Africa during World War II," *Holocaust and Genocide Studies* 26, no. 3 (2012): 425–446.

15. Prefect report, "Relazione sul ripiegamento nella Cirenaica," December 1941, in MAI, AS, b. 252, AUSMAE.

16. Franco Mariotti, *Cinecittà tra cronaca e storia: 1937–1989* (Rome: Presidenza del Consiglio dei Ministri, Dipartimento per l'informazione e l'editoria, 1990), 124. On the film itself, see Ruth Ben-Ghiat, *Italian Fascism's Empire Cinema* (Bloomington: Indiana University Press, 2015), 243–295.

17. Yvette Blank (Lipari) to Benito Mussolini (Rome), May 3, 1943, in SPD, CR, AT, sf. YB, ACS.

18. Daniel Summerfield, *From Falashas to Ethiopian Jews: The External Influences for Change c. 1860–1960* (London: Routledge Curzon, 2003), 96–102, 188fn52–58.

19. Beniamino De Muto (Rome) to Michelangelo Di Stefano (Rome), "Practica cittadinanza," Yvette Blank, July 18, August 18, August 19, and August 28, 1938; also July 23, 1938; in MI, PP, FP, YB, ACS.

20. Martina Salvante, "'Less Than a Boot-Rag': Procreation, Paternity, and the Masculine Ideal in Fascist Italy," in *Masculinities and the Nation in the Modern World*, ed. Pablo Dominquez Anderson and Simon Wendt, 93–112 (London: Palgrave, 2015).

21. "Family Photograph with AT," in Family Photographs, Grimaldi Family Collection, Naples.

22. Sacra Romana Rota, *Mediolanen. Nullitatis Matrimonii (Teruzzi-Weinman) Summarium* (Vatican City: Typic Polyglottis Vaticanis, 1942).

23. Yvette Blank (Lipari) to Benito Mussolini (Rome), May 3, 1943, in SPD, CR, AT, ACS.

24. "Affiliation affidavit," August 10, 1941, in AR, CPSR (1940–1948), sf. Miscellaneous attachments, LWTP.

25. Fiammetta Grimaldi, interview with author, Naples, August 2, 2014.

26. Yvette Blank (Lipari) to Benito Mussolini (Rome), May 3, 1943, in SPD, CR, AT, sf. YB, ACS.

27. "Identity card, Vatican City," in Family Documents, Grimaldi Family Collection.

28. Natalie Zemon Davis, *Fictions in the Archives: Pardon Tales and Their Tellers in Sixteenth-Century France*, 2nd rev. ed. (Stanford: Stanford University Press, 1987), 3–6, 148fn7.

29. Yvette Blank (Lipari) to Benito Mussolini (Rome), May 3, 1943, in SPD, CR, AT, sf. YB, ACS.

30. Bottai, *Diario (1935–1944)*, entry for March 1, 1943 (p. 363).

31. Letter Roberto Farinacci (Cremona) to Benito Mussolini (Rome), June 6, 1938; Memo from Benito Mussolini about Iole Foa, Forlì, June 9, 1938, with addendum, June 16, 1938, Riccione, authorizing payout; both in SPD, CR, IF, ACS.

32. Roberto Farinacci to Benito Mussolini, June 9, 1938, in SPD, CR, IF, ACS.

33. Roberto Farinacci to Benito Mussolini, June 9, 1938, in SPD, CR, IF, ACS.

34. Arcnovaldo Bonaccorsi, "Lettera aperta dall'AOI, Asmara, January 1942," frontispiece, in Fondo N-8, b. 1522, f. 10, AUSSME.

35. Translated and published as "Black Shirt General's Report on Ethiopia: Severe Criticisms of Fascist Regime," *Ethiopia Star* [Addis Ababa], November 30,

1941, 4; "Criticism of Contractors and Monopolies," December 7, 1941, 3; December 14, 1941, "Bread and the Whip for Ethiopians," 4. The original letter is partially reproduced in Richard Pankhurst, "La fine dell'Etiopia italiana nel libello di Arconovaldo Bonaccorsi," *Studi Piacentini* 11 (1972): 65–82.

36. Report, "H. E. Teruzzi for Mussolini," July–August 1942, in Fondo N-8, b. 1522, f. 10, AUSSME.

37. Ilda Brunhild to Benito Mussolini, n.d. [but September 1938]; AT (Rome) to Mussolini's secretary, Osvaldo Sebastiani (Rome), September 12, 1938; Osvaldo Sebastiani (Rome) to Ilda Brunhild (Pieve Ligure), September 12, 1938; in SPD, CR, IB, ACS. Alexander Stille, *Benevolence and Betrayal: Five Italian Jewish Families under Fascism* (1991; reprint New York: Picador, 2003).

38. Giuseppe Acerbi, *Le leggi anti-ebraiche e razziali italiane ed il ceto dei giuristi* (Milano: Giuffrè, 2014), 86fn96.

39. Antonella Pizzi, interview with author, Castiglioncello, August 9, 2016.

40. Annalisa Cegna, "'Di dubbia condotta morale e politica': L'internamento femminile in Italia durante la seconda guerra mondiale," *DEP (Deportate, esuli, profughi, Rivista telematica di studi sulla memoria femminile)* 21 (2013): 1–27.

41. On the transformation of the Penal Colony of Lipari into what the Italians designated as a "Concentration Camp," see Carlo Spartaco Capogreco, *I campi del Duce: l'internamento civile nell'Italia fascista, 1940–1943* (Turin: Einaudi, 2004); and the essays in Costantino di Sante, ed., *I campi di concentramento in Italia* (Milan: FrancoAngeli, 2001).

42. Letter Blank to Mussolini, May 3, 1943; Public Notice, October 27, 1941, in *Gazzetta Ufficiale del Regno d'Italia*, October 28, 1941, 447, changed Mariceli's name from Celeste Blank Teruzzi to Maria Celeste Blank Teruzzi, "The Announcement of Decree, April 18, 1942," in the *Gazzetta*, April 22, 1942, 2382, announced the "suppression of the foreign last name Blank."

21. Comeuppance

1. Typescript from LWT to Tribunal Neo-Eboracense, October 1, 1942, for forwarding to Sacred Roman Rota, in AR, CPSR (1940–1948), LWTP.

2. Luca Castagna, *A Bridge across the Ocean: The United States and the Holy See between the Two World Wars* (Washington DC: Catholic University of America Press, 2014), 136–150, 154–158.

3. Isaac Lewin, "Der itstiger poypst pius der tvelfter hot mit etlekhe yohr tsurik aroysgegebeben a psak kegn antisemitishn bilbul af'n talmud." *Der Tog: The National Jewish Daily*, May 2, 1942, 1, in Clippings, LWTP; reprised at greater length as Lewin's first "human rights case," in Isaac Lewin, *In Defense of Human Rights* (New York: Research Institute of Religious Jewry, 1992), 11–24.

4. Helen Worden, "Wife of Fascist General Acts as Voluntary Censor Here," *New York World-Telegram*, June 1, 1942, 1.

5. LWT to Tribunal Neo-Eboracense, typescript, October 1, 1942, in AR, CPSR (1940–1948), LWTP.

6. LWT to Tribunal Neo-Eboracense.

7. Pius XII, "Allocuzione alla Sacra Rota Romana," October 3, 1941, in *Acta Apostolicae Sedis*, vol. 33 (1941), 421–426; also October 1, 1942, n. 1, in *Acta Apostolicae Sedis*. vol. 34 (1942), 339; both cited in Antonio S. Sánchez-Gil, *La presunzione di validità dell'atto giuridico nel diritto canonico* (Milan: Giuffrè, 2006), 54fn63–64.

8. Alessandro Bellomo and Clara Picciotti, "Maggio 1943: una pioggia di fuoco si abatte sulla città," in *Bombe su Palermo: Cronaca degli attacchi aerei 1940–1943* (Genoa: Associazione culturale Italia, 2008) 121–130.

9. Paolo Monelli, *Mussolini piccolo borghese*, 6th ed. (Milan: Garzanti, 1965), 310.

10. Bottai, *Diario (1935–1944)*, entry for February 12, 1943 (p. 362).

11. Bottai, *Diario (1935–1944)*, entry for March 1, 1943 (363).

12. "Commissioni legislative riunite del bilancio e dell'Africa italiana," Camera dei fasci e delle corporazioni, XXX Legislatura, 1, *Resconto dell'adunanza*: May 5, 1942, 915–913, 920–928.

13. Attilio Teruzzi, "Tre rievocazioni," *L'Azione coloniale*, no. 5 (May 1943), 358.

14. "Per i caduti, per i combattenti," *Popolo d'Italia*, May 9, 1943, 1.

15. Benito Mussolini, *Opera Omnia*, ed. Edoardo Susmel and Duilio Susmel, 44 vols. (Florence: La Fenice, 1951–1980), vol. 31, 178.

16. Italian text is published in "Rievocazione," *L'Azione coloniale*, no. 5 (May 1943), 358; and it was partially translated in "Italian Empire Day: 'We Have Lost Nothing,'" *Scotsman*, May 10, 1943, 1; "Teruzzi-Tut Tut! Italy Has Lost Nothing," *Western Daily Press and Bristol Mirror*, May 10, 1943, 1.

17. "Rievocazione," *L'Azione coloniale*, no. 5 (May 1943), 358.

18. "Teruzzi-Tut Tut! Italy Has Lost Nothing"; "We Have Lost Nothing," *Courier and Advertiser*, May 10, 1943.

19. Bottai, *Diario*, July 16, 1943, 393. De Bono, cited in Domenico Mayer, *La verità sul processo di Verona* (Milan: A. Mondadori, 1945), 33; Federzoni, *Italia di ieri, per l'Italia di domani,'* 192–194.

20. Bottai, *Diario (1935–1944)*, entry for June 27, 1943 (p. 385). Gianfranco Bianchi, *25 luglio: crollo di un regime* (Milan: Mursia, 1963), 442–443.

21. Telegram from Camp Director Geraci to Police Inspector Livoti, Messina, June 19, 1943, in Confinati, Affari per provincia, 1940–1942, Direzione Polizia Giudiziara, b. 12, DG PS, MI, ACS.

22. Communication from Head of Police to Prefect of Macerata, July 17, 1943, in Questura gabinetto, b. 17, f. Blank Ivette, Archivio di Stato di Macerata.

23. Attilio Tamaro, *Due anni di storia, 1943–1945* (Rome: Tosi, 1948), 279.

24. Margaret de Wyss, *Rome under the Terror* (London: Hale, 1945), 64; Amedeo Strazzera-Perniciani, *Umanità ed eroisimo nella vita segreta di Regina Coeli* (Rome: Azienda libraria Amato, 1946), 14.

25. Silvio D'Amico, *Regina Coeli* (Palermo: Sellerio, 1994); Strazzera-Perniciani, *Umanità ed eroismo*, 12, 14.

26. Sandro Attanasio, *Sicilia senza Italia, luglio-agosto 1943* (Milan: Mursia, 1976), 204–205.

27. Memo, Director for Prison Relations (Direttore Sezione Carceri) August 21, 1943, in f. Teruzzi Attilio b. 79, MI, DG, PS, A1, ACS.

28. "Come si comportano 'i gerarchi in gabbia,'" *La Stampa*, September 3, 1943, 1.

29. "Memo: Cooperative Apartment Monte Oppio 5," October 6, 1949, in f. 49790, 7–2, PCM, Gab. 1948–1950, ACS.

30. Enrico Caviglia, *I dittatori, le guerre e il piccolo re: Diario, 1925–1945*, ed. Pier Paolo Cervone (Milan: Mursia, 2009), 480–481. Pier Paolo Cervone, *Enrico Caviglia, l'anti-Badoglio* (Milan: Mursia, 1992), 257.

31. Caviglia, *Diario*, 481.

32. Caviglia, *Diario*, 481.

33. Cited in Giorgio Rochat, "Caviglia, Enrico," *Dizionario biografico degli italiani*, vol. 23 (1979).

34. Ugo Cavallero, *Comando Supremo, Diario, 1940–1943 del Capo di S.M.G.* (Bologna: Cappelli, 1948), xviii–xix.

35. Giacomo Carboni, *L'Italia tradita dall'armistizio alla pace* (Rome: E.D.A., 1947), 55.

36. Anthony Majanlahti and Amedeo Osti Guerrazzi, *Roma occupata 1943–1944: itinerari, storie, immagini* (Milan: Il Saggiatore, 2010), p. 61–80.

37. "Denunciation of Criminal Act," Questura of Rome to Military War Tribune and Command of Rome, Open City, September 28, 1943; Tribunale Militare Territoriale di Guerra. Roma, May 25, 1944; Rome July 9, 1947; October 10, 1948. "Viene sentito Teruzzi, detenuto a Procida," in "Sentencing: Court of Assize, January 31, 1950," in Corte d'Appello–Corte d'Assise, b. 995, f. 2342, Archivio di Stato di Roma.

38. "L'Indagine sugli illeciti arricchimenti: alte personalità del regime fascista fermate per aver accumulato ingenti fortune," *La Stampa*, September 3, 1943, 1.

39. *Bollettino*: N. 37, A/E, December 12, 1944; also Court Sentencing: December 14, 1944 in f. 3505, b. 68, Tribunale penale di Roma: anno 1944. Archivio di Stato, Rome.

40. Mauro Canali, *Le spie del regime* (Bologna: Il Mulino, 2004), 78, 716fn220.

22. *Last Man Standing*

1. The Italian Social Republic has recently generated a disputatious, more archivally based, and richer historiography than in the past. For an up-to-date introduction, see James Burgwyn with Amedeo Osti Guerrazzi, *Mussolini and the Salò Republic, 1943–1945: The Failure of a Puppet Regime* (New York: Palgrave Macmillan, 2018). Within the framework of the Nazi New Order, see Enzo Collotti, "'Salò' nel Nuovo Ordine Europeo," in *La Repubblica sociale italiana 1943–1945*, ed. Pier Piaggio Poggio (Brescia: Fondazione Luigi Micheletti, 1986). Framed as a reprise of the civil war in the wake of World War I, with all of the nuance owed to grasping the moral as well as political-ideological stakes, see Claudio Pavone, *A Civil War: A History of the Italian Resistance*, trans. Peter Levy and David Broder (London: Verso, 2013).

2. Pavone, *A Civil War*, 285.

3. Sandro Setta, *Renato Ricci: dallo squadrismo alla Repubblica Sociale* (Bologna: Il Mulino, 1986), 237–266.

4. H. James Burgwyn, with Amedeo Osti Guerazzi, *Mussolini and the Salò Republic, 1943–1945*, 31–57.

5. Renzo Montagna, *Mussolini e il processo di Verona* (Milan: Omnia, 1946), 147–150.

6. Dominic O. Mayer, *La verità sul processo di Verona* (Milan: Mondadori, 1945), 32–33.

7. Photograph of "Attilio Teruzzi and daughter, Mariceli in snow, winter, 1944," in Family Photographs, Grimaldi Family Collection, Naples.

8. Matteo Stefanori, *Ordinaria amministrazione: gli ebrei e la Repubblica sociale italiana* (Bari: Laterza, 2017).

9. Stefanori, *Ordinaria amministrazione*, 45.

10. Stefanori, *Ordinaria amministrazione*, 127–129.

11. Carlo Gentile and Lutz Klinkhammer, "L'apparato centrale della Sicherheitspolizei in Italia: struttura, uomini e competenze," in *I signori del terrore: polizia nazista e persecuzione antiebraica in Italia, 1943–1945*, ed. Sara Berger. 37–68 (Sommacampagna, Verona: Cierre edizioni: Istituto veronese per la storia della Resistenza e dell'età contemporanea, 2015).

12. Michele Sarfatti, ed., *La Repubblica sociale italiana a Desenzano: Giovanni Preziosi e l'Ispettorato generale per la razza* (Florence: Giuntina, 2008).

13. Sarfatti, *Repubblica sociale italiana*, 7, 89.

14. Antonio Bonino, *Mussolini mi ha detto: memorie del vicesegretario del partito fascista repubblicano 1944/45*, ed. Marino Vigano (Rome: Settimo Sigillo, 1995), 51.

15. "Persecution of Foa, Jole," in f. 16/11/1890, Centro Documentazione Ebraica Contemporanea, Milan; Renata Broggini, *Frontier of Hope: Jews*

from Italy Seek Refuge in Switzerland, 1943–1945 (Milan: Mondadori, 1998), 451–517.

16. Postcard from Frau Dr. Wiesa Jassé (Malcesine) to Hans Schaeffer (Jönköping), October 20, 1943; Hans Schaeffer (Jönköping) to Elli Heimann (Pasadena), April 4, 1944; Elli Heimann (Pasadena) to Hans Schaeffer (Jönköping), March–April 1947, f. 9, b. 3, in the Hans Schaeffer Papers, AR 7177, Leo Baeck Institute, New York, NY; Martha Heimann-Roger, February 14, 1947, to Direzione Generale della Pubblica Sicurezza, in SB. 13, SI, PS, MI, ACS.

17. "Authorization card," 1944, in Family Documents, Grimaldi Family Collection.

18. Carlo Rivolta and Pierangelo Pavesi, *Erano fatti così* (Copiano, Pavia: MARO, 2005), 119–120.

19. Luigi Bolla, *Perché a Salò*, ed. Giordano Bruno Guerri (Milan: Bompiani, 1982), 202.

20. Martin Kuder, *Italia e Svizzera nella seconda guerra mondiale* (Florence: Carocci, 2002), 152; see also Marino Viganò, "Mussolini, i gerarchi e la 'fuga' in Svizzera (1944–45)," *Nuova Storia Contemporanea*, n. 3 (2001), 47–108.

21. Ermanno Amicucci, *I 600 giorni di Mussolini: dal Gran Sasso a Dongo* (Rome: Faro 1948), 205–209, 212.

22. Photographs of Villa Celestina posted by Captain Charles F. Klauber, DFC Operations Officer, Website, 47th Bomber Group, http://www.47thbombgroup.org/pictures/klauber/4.html.

23. A Bearded Corpse

1. On the purges, there is a rich yet still incomplete literature. The conceptual problem of how to analyze transitional justice in legal as well as political and cultural terms has still not been addressed with respect to the immense number and variety of trials of the period from 1944 to 1947. To start, see Roy Palmer Domenico, *Italian Fascists on Trial, 1942–1948* (Chapel Hill: University of North Carolina Press, 1991); Lamberto Mercuri, *L'epurazione in Italia, 1943–1948* (Cuneo: L'Arciere, 1988); Hans Woller, *I conti con il fascismo: l'epurazione in Italia 1943–1948* (Bologna: Il Mulino, 1997); Romano Canosa, *Storia dell'epurazione in Italia* (Rome: Baldini e Castoldi, 1999); Cecilia Nubola, "Collaborazioniste: Processi e provvedimenti di clemenza nell'Italia del secondo dopoguerra," in *Nei tribunali: Figure della clemenza fra tardo medioevo ed età contemporanea*, ed. Giovanni Focardi and Cecilia Nubola: 221–270 (Bologna: Il Mulino, 2011).

2. Domenico, *Italian Fascists on Trial*, 79.

3. "Teruzzi Attilio: Arrest Warrant: High Commissioner Sanctions against Fascism," signed Mario Berlinguer, December 18, 1944; Report: Commissiario

di polizia, nucleo polizia giudiziaria to L'alto commissario aggiunto per la punizione dei delitti del fascismo, December 19, 1944; both in f. Teruzzi, Attilio, Corte di Assise Straordinaria di Milano, Trial folders (Fasci Processuali) 1945, Archivio di Stato di Milano.

4. "Confidential information collected by LWT's lawyers on Attilio Teruzzi, March 1947, including Memo: Royal Questor of Rome: High Commission for the Punishment of Fascist Crimes," August 8, 1944, AR, CPSR (1940–1948), sf. 1, 1947 Trial Preparation Documents, LWTP.

5. "Rome Questor's Criminal Denunciation to Military War Tribunal and Command of Rome, Open City, September 28, 1943," in Corte d'Appello–Corte d'Assise, b. 995, f. 2342, Archivio di Stato di Roma.

6. Court Sentence, December 1, 1944, f. 2342, b. 995, CC, ASR.

7. Informer's report, December 1944, f. 6719, Teruzzi, Attilio, Div. 1, Gabinetto, F. Questura di Milano, ASM.

8. Quoted in Victor Barthelemy, *Du communisme au fascisme, histoire d'un engagement politique* (Paris: Éditions Albin Michel, 1978), 447. On Costa, see Luigi Ganapini, *Una città, la guerra: lotte di classe, ideologie e forze politiche a Milano 1939–1951* (Milan: FrancoAngeli, 1988).

9. AT (Procida) to Silverio Mattei (Rome), November 7, 1947, with "Promemoria sulla vicenda giudiziaria del Generale Attilio Teruzzi" and "Promemoria sulla situazione finanziaria," in Fondo Movimento Italiano Femminile, "Teruzzi Attilio, November 1947–February 1950," b. 72, f. 3030, Archivio di Stato di Cosenza. Corte di assise straordinaria di Milano (1944–1948), Archivi giudiziari, ASM.

10. Romain Rainero, *Propaganda e ordini all stampa: da Badoglio alla Repubblica sociale italiana* (Milano: FrancoAngeli, 2007), 299–302; "John Amery: The Anti-Semitism of the 'Perfect English Gentleman,'" *Patterns of Prejudice* 36, no. 2 (2002): 14–27; Rebecca West, "The Crown vs. John Amery," *The New Yorker*, December 15, 1945, 67–81.

11. Ermanno Amicucci, *I 600 giorni di Mussolini: dal Gran Sasso a Dongo* (Rome: Faro, 1948), 210–211.

12. Nazzareno Nicotra, "Una bella prigione, piena di fascisti," *L'Unità*, May 13, 1945, 1.

13. Ermanno Amicucci, *I 600 giorni di Mussolini*, 231.

14. "La mano della giustizia sui crimini fascista," *Avanti!*, May 25, 1945, 3.

15. Pier Giuseppe Murgia, *Il vento del Nord: storia e cronaca del fascismo dopo la Resistenza, 1945–50* (Milan: Kaos, 2004), 24.

16. Mirco Dondi, "Piazzale Loreto 29 aprile: aspetti di una pubblica esposizione," *Rivista di storia contemporanea* 19, no. 2 (1990): 219–248.

17. Piero Saporiti, *Empty Balcony* (London: V. Gollancz, 1947), 104; Luigi de Vincentis, *Io son te . . .* (Milan: Cebes, 1946); Raffaele De Capria, *Ferito a*

morte (Milan: Bompiani, 1962), 125; Carlo Borsani, Jr., *Carlo Borsani: una vita per un sogno, 1917–1945* (Milan: Mursia, 1995), 27. Luciano Garibaldi and Pietro Carradori, *Vita col duce: l'attendente di Mussolini, Pietro Carradori, racconta* (Milan: Effedieffe, 2001), 166; Italo De Feo, *Diario politico, 1943–1948* (Milan: Rusconi, 1973), 189; Giovanni Ansaldo, *Anni freddi: diari, 1946–1950* (Bologna: Il Mulino, 2003), 80–81.

24. I Suffer and I Wait

1. Pier Angelo Gianni, "26 Aprile 1945, Mussolini passa da Gerenzano?" *Geranzano Forum*, October 17, 2004. http://lnx.gerenzanoforum.it/index.php?option=com_content&view=article&id=228:26-aprile-1945-mussolini-passa-da-gerenzano&catid=82&Itemid=611. Daniele Premoli, "Più efficace della parola è l'opera," in *Cattolicesimo a Saronno durante l'episcopato del card. Schuster, 1929–1954* (Tricasi: Youcanprint Self Publishing, 2017), 84–86; Giovanni Nigro, *Fuori dall'officina: la resistenza nel Saronnese* (Saronno: ANPI, Grafiche Trotti, 2005), 77. Interview of Luigi Damiazzi in Pierluigi Galli, "Antifascisti, partigiani e popolazione a Saronno, 1943–1945," in *La resistenza in provincia di Varese: il 1945*, ed. Luigi Ambrosoli (Varese: Istituto varesino per la storia della Resistenza e dell'Italia contemporanea, 1986), 191–202, esp. 197, 200–202; Luigi Borgomaneri, *Due inverni, un'estate e la rossa primavera: le Brigate Garibaldi a Milano e provincia, 1943–1945* (Milan: FrancoAngeli, 1985), 116–211; Massimiliano Griner, *La pupilla del duce: la Legione autonoma mobile Ettore Muti* (Roma: Bollati Boringhieri, 2004), 196.
2. "Verbale dell'ufficio di polizia," May 1, 1945 in f. Teruzzi, Attilio, Corte di assise straordinaria di Milano, 1944–1948, Archivi giudiziari, Archivio di Stato di Milano.
3. "I gerarchi nel 'covo' di San Vittore," *Avanti!* May 22, 1945 [Roman edition], 1.
4. Amnistia, 1947, F. Teruzzi, Supplemento letter: Yvette Blank (Milan) to Cardinal Schuster (Milan), May 3, 1945, in Fondo Corte d'Assise di Appello, Archivio di Stato di Milano.
5. "I gerarchi nel 'covo' di San Vittore," *Avanti!*, May 22, 1945 [Roman edition], 1; Nazzareno Nicotra, "Una bella prigione, piena di fascisti," *L'Unità*, May 13, 1945, 1.
6. Anon., *Come rubarono: Starace, Farinacci, Teruzzi, Pavolini* (Rome: Edizione A.M.M., 1945).
7. Giovanni Pesce, *Quando cessarono gli spari: 23 aprile–6 maggio 1945: la liberazione di Milano* (Milan: Feltrinelli, 1977), 184.
8. On postwar violence see Mirco Dondi, *La lunga liberazione: giustizia e violenza nel dopoguerra italiano* (Rome: Riuniti, 1999); Gianni Oliva, *La resa*

dei conti. aprile-maggio 1945: foibe, piazzale Loreto e giustizia partigiana (Milan: Mondadori, 1999).

9. Elenco Sentenze Anno 1945, in Archivi Giudiziari, F. Corte d'Assise straordinario di Milano (1944–1948), Sezione Speciale di Milano 1945, f. 1, 100, Archivio di Stato di Milano.

10. Luigi Ganapini, *La repubblica delle camicie nere* (Milan: Garzanti, 2010), 165.

11. Assise straordinario, Archivi Giudiziari, F. Corte d'Assise straordinario di Milano (1944–1948), Archivio di Stato di Milano.

12. "La mano della giustizia sui crimini fascisti," *Avanti!* May 25, 1945.

13. "Trent' anni ad Attilio Teruzzi," *Corriere dell'Informazione*, May 25, 1945. 1

14. "Trent' anni ad Attilio Teruzzi."

15. "Anche Teruzzi se la cava," *L'Unità*, May 25, 1945, 1.

16. Rome: Processo verbale di interrogatorio dell'imputato, September 19, October 11. Signed: Dr. Antonio Jannacone, in Corte di Cassazione, Summer–October, 1947, Archivio di Stato di Milano.

17. "Sul capo di Teruzzi pende ancora la pena di morte," *Corriere dell'Informazione*, May 26, 1945, 1.

25. Penance

1. Giovanni Ansaldo, *Illustrazione italiana*, "La rocca di Procida," March 15, 1951, 57.

2. Memo: Transport of political prisoners, November 24, 1945, to Police Commissioner, in MI, Gab. 1948, ACS.

3. Alessandro Sardi, *Ma non s'imprigiona la storia* (Rome: Centro editoriale nazionale, 1962), 355.

4. Sardi, *Ma non s'imprigiona la storia*, 52, 28.

5. Memo: Penitentiary Procida, External Surveillance, May 5, 1946, in MI, Gab. 1948, ACS.

6. "Gerarchi fascisti in galera," *Secolo Nuovo: Gazzetta di Milano*, April 4–6, 1946; Giovanni Ansaldo, "La rocca di Procida," *Illustrazione Italiana*, 1951, 57–62; Pier Giuseppe Murgia, *Il vento del nord* (Milan: Kaos, 2004), 137–140.

7. Murgia, *Il vento del nord*, 141–143; Monsignor Luigi Fasanaro, *Chi li ricorda? Memorie di un Cappellano e dei suoi carcerati politici e comuni* (Torre del Greco: A.C.M. SpA, 2005), 39–45. Sardi, *Ma non s'imprigiona la storia*, 540–542.

8. Rodolfo Graziani, *Ho difesa la patria* (Milan: Garzanti, 1948), 365.

9. Domenico Peretti-Griva, "Il fallimento dell'epurazione," *Il Ponte* 3, no. 11–12 (1947): 1075–1081. The most influential history places the onus for the amnesty on the Communist Party, especially Togliatti: Mimmo Franzinelli, *L' amnistia Togliatti: 22 giugno 1946: colpo di spugna sui crimini fascisti* (Milano: Mondadori,

2006). Legal scholars who weighed in at the time bring an important perspective to the amnesty as a response to the accumulation of legal as well as political issues related to the purges, the political transitions, and the administration of justice under an administrative and legal system that were themselves legacies of fascist rule.

10. "Specchietto per la grazia sorrana," October 11, 1948, in MGG, DG, AP, UG, AT, ACS.
11. LWT (Milan) to IW and RW (NYC), January 1, 1947, in Correspondence, LWTP.
12. LWT (Milan) to IW and RW (NYC), January 1, 1947.
13. LWT (Rome) to IW and RW (NYC), February 8, 1947, in Correspondence, LWTP.
14. LWT (Rome) to IW and RW (NYC), January 6, 1947, in Correspondence, LWTP.
15. LWT (Rome) to IW and RW (NYC), February 8, 1947, in Correspondence, LWTP.
16. LWT (Rome) to IW and RW (NYC), February 1, 1947, in Correspondence, LWTP.
17. LWT (Rome) to IW and RW (NYC), February 8, 1947, in Correspondence, LWTP.
18. LWT (Rome) to IW and RW (NYC), February 8, 1947, in Correspondence, LWTP.
19. LWT (Milan) to IW and RW (NYC), January 1, 1947, in Correspondence, LWTP.
20. Atti: 4 marzo 1947–15 aprile 1947, Afternoon session, Friday, April 18, 1947, 3000, Italy, Constituent Assembly (1946–1948).
21. Mark Seymour, *Debating Divorce in Italy: Marriage and the Making of Modern Italians, 1860–1974* (New York: Palgrave Macmillan, 2006), esp. ch. 3, "Divorce, Italian Style." See also Marzio Barbagli, *Provando e riprovando: matrimonio, famiglia e divorzio in Italia e in altri paesi occidentali* (Bologna: Il Mulino, 1990), 270.
22. LWT (Rome) to RW and IW (NYC), February 20, 1947, in Correspondence, LWTP.
23. LWT (Rome) to RW and IW (NYC), February 1, 1947, in Correspondence, LWTP.
24. RW (NYC) to LWT (Rome), February 21, February 10, and February 8, 1947; LWT (Paris) to RW (NYC), April 11, 1947; all in Correspondence, LWTP.
25. LWT (Paris) to RW (NYC), April 11, 1947, in Correspondence, LWTP.
26. LWT (Rome) to RW (London) and IW (NYC), February 14, 1947, in Correspondence, LWTP.
27. LWT (Rome) to RW (London) and IW (NYC), February 14, 1947.
28. LWT (Rome) to RW and IW (NYC), March 1, 1934, in Correspondence, LWTP.
29. LWT (Rome) to IW and RW (NYC), March 6, 1947, in Correspondence, LWTP.

30. LWT (Rome) to IW and RW (London), August 14, 1947, in Correspondence, LWTP.

31. Nicola Adelfi, "Una moglie falangista dopo la moglie fascista," *L'Europeo*, May 11, 1947, 7.

32. John Thomas Noonan, Jr., *Power to Dissolve: Lawyers and Marriages in the Courts of the Roman Curia* (Cambridge, MA: Belknap Press of Harvard University Press, 1972), 291–301.

33. LWT (Paris) to IW and RW (NYC), April 11, 1947, in Correspondence, LWTP.

34. Emanuel Cammarata, LWT's lawyer (Milan) to LWT (NYC), October 7, 1953, in Correspondence, LWTP.

35. LWT (Paris) to IW and RW (NYC), January 1, 1947; LWT (Paris) to RW (NYC); also April 11, 1947, in Correspondence, LWTP.

36. Francesco Argenta, "Inchiesta sulle carceri, perche noi soli?" *La Stampa*, October 30, 1947, 3.

37. Fasanaro, *Chi li ricorda?* 53.

38. Federica Bertagna, "Un'organizzazione neofascista nell'Italia postbellica: il movimento italiano femminile 'Fede e famiglia' di Maria Pignatelli di Cerchiara," *Rivista Calabrese di Storia del '900* 1 (2013): 5–32.

39. AT (Procida) to Silverio Mattei (Rome), November 7, 1947, with "Promemoria sulla vicenda giudiziaria del Generale Attilio Teruzzi," and "Promemoria sulla situazione finanziaria," in Fondo Movimento Italiano Femminile, "Teruzzi Attilio, November 1947–February 1950," b. 72, f. 3030, Archivio di Stato di Cosenza.

40. Luca Castagna, *A Bridge across the Ocean: The United States and the Holy See between the World Wars* (Washington, DC: Catholic University of America Press, 2014), chs. 5–6.

41. "The Sacred Roman Rota, A Definitive Sentence in the cause of the Nullitatis Teruzzi-Weinman (February 7, 1948)," English translation, 12 pp., March 1948, in AR, CPSR (1940–1948), LWTP

42. "Definitive Sentence," 12.

43. Fasanaro, *Chi li ricorda?* 50.

44. Yvette Blanc [sic] (Procida) to M. Pignatelli (Naples), n.d. [but February 1948], in Fondo Movimento Italiano Femminile, "Teruzzi Attilio, November 1947–February 1950," b. 72, f. 3030, Archivio di Stato di Cosenza.

45. Letter Maria-Celeste Teruzzi (Procida) to President of Council of Ministers (Rome), August 4, 1948, in MGG, DG, AP, UG, AT, ACS.

46. "Specchietto per Grazia Sovrana a favore di Attilio Teruzzi," October 11, 1948, in MGG, DG, AP, UG, AT, ACS.

47. Sandro Setta, *Renato Ricci: dallo squadrismo alla Repubblica sociale italiana* (Bologna: Il Mulino, 1986), 306.

48. Giuseppe Bottai, *Diario, 1935–1944*, ed. Giordano Bruno Guerri (Milan: Rizzoli, 1982), entries for April 17, 1940 (177), January 17, 1941 (202), and January 20, 1941 (203).
49. Fasanaro, *Chi li ricorda?* 178.
50. *Oggi*, April 13, 1950, back cover. "Teruzzi liberato dal penitenziario farà l'albergatore a Procida," *Corriere della sera*, March 31, 1950, 2.
51. Vittorio Gorresio, "È morto a Procida, l'ex-gerarca fascista Teruzzi," *La Stampa*, April 28, 1950; Antonio Savignano, "La breve libertà di Attilio Teruzzi," *Il Roma*, April 28, 1; n.a. [but G. Ansaldo], "Teruzzi ha chiuso a Procida la sua vita avventurosa," *Il Mattino*, April 27, 1950, 1.
52. n.a. [Ansaldo], "Teruzzi ha chiuso."
53. Giacomo Retaggio, *A Procida non caddero bombe* (Naples: Arti Grafiche P. Dragotti, 2000), 158–159. "Teruzzi ha chiuso a Procida la sua vita avventurosa," *Il Mattino*, April 27, 1950; "Stamattina all'alba si è spento Attilio Teruzzi," *Il Roma*, April 27, 1945; Antonio Savignano, "La breve libertà di Attilio Teruzzi," *Il Roma*, April 28, 1950. "I funerali di Teruzzi," *Il Mattino*, April 28, 1950, in Clippings, LWTP.
54. Fasanaro, *Chi li ricorda?* 51.
55. I funerali di Teruzzi," *Il Mattino*, April 28, 1950, in Clippings, LWTP.
56. "A Fascist to the Beard," *Manchester Guardian*, April 28, 1948. "Madame Teruzzi: A Correction," *Manchester Guardian*, February 10, 1951.

Epilogue

1. Antonio Savignano, "La breve libertà di Attilio Teruzzi," *Il Roma*, April 28, 1950. "Teruzzi ha chiuso a Procida la sua vita avventurosa," *Il Mattino*, April 27, 1950; also "Teruzzi si spegne," *Il Mattino*, April 25, 1950; "I funerali di Teruzzi," *Il Mattino*, April 28, 1950, in Clippings, LWTP.
2. Vittorio Goresio, "E morto a Procida l'ex-gerarca Teruzzi," *La Stampa*, April 28, 1950, 1; also "E morto Teruzzi all'Isola di Procida: Poco dopo la scarcerazione," *Corriere della Sera*, April 26–27, 1950, 1; whereas the socialist and communist press ignored the event.
3. Giovanni Ansaldo, "Teruzzi ha chiuso a Procida la sua vita avventurosa," *Il Mattino*, April 27, 1950; and Giovanni Ansaldo, *Anni freddi: Diari, 1946–1950* (Bologna: Il Mulino 2003), entry for April 26–27, 1950 (p. 95). On the re-emerging conservative-moderate apologetics on behalf of the regime see Cristina Baldassini, *L'ombra di Mussolini: L'Italia moderata e la memoria del fascismo, 1945–1960* (Soveria Mannelli: Rubbettino, 2008).
4. Ansaldo, "Teruzzi ha chiuso a Procida."
5. Memo: Francesco Diana, prefect (Naples) to Francesco Bartolotta, Capo Gabinetto Presidenza Consiglio Ministri, March 1953; Yvette Blank (Procida)

to Prefect of Naples, March 11, 1953; both in f. Ivette Blank, Ved. Teruzzi, Pensione "Caravella" Procida, 1953, f. 2.3.3, n. 49320 PCM, ACS.

6. Fiammetta Grimaldi, interview with author, Naples, July 24, 2014. Photograph of Mariceli Grimaldi with Anna Magnani, Rome, 1954, in Family Photographs, Grimaldi Family Collection, Naples.

7. Giulio Galeazzi (Rome) to Lilliana Weinman (NYC), June 21, 1956; Yvette Blank (Naples) to LWT (NYC), October 8, 1956; both in Correspondence, LWTP.

8. Yvette Blank (Naples) to Giuseppe Bottai (Rome), January 21 and October 13, 1958, in Bottai, Correspondence Blank Teruzzi, Yvette, 1958, b. 19, f. 349, item 354, FM.

9. "Chi ha visto Mariceli Teruzzi, "*Il Mattino,* June 9, 2008, 3.

10. Prof. Maria d'Anna, Pieve Ligure, telephone interview with author, June 14, 2008.

11. Alfonso Maffettone, "Storica USA scrive a Il Mattino," *Italia Estera,* June 10, 2008. Fiammetta Grimaldi, interview with author, Naples, June 20, 2008.

12. Piero Calamandrei, "Recensione di Stefano de La Boetie, Il Contro'uno" (1947), in Piero Calamandrei, *L'oro di noi poveri e altri scritti letterari,* ed. Claudia Forti (Florence: Ponte alle Grazie, 1994), 259–261, motifs of analysis that are picked up in Piero Calamandrei, *Il fascismo come regime della menzogna* (Rome: Editori Laterza, 2014).

13. Claudio Pavone, *A Civil War: A History of the Italian Resistance,* trans. Peter Levy and David Broder (London: Verso, 2013), 285.

14. Massimo Rocca, *Come il fascismo divenne una dittatura: Storia interna del fascismo dal 1914 al 1925* (Milan: Librarie Italiane, 1952), 99, 104.

15. Piero Calamandrei, in *Il Ponte,* 1, 2 (1945) 103. See also Calamandrei, *Il fascismo come regime della menzogna,* 17; Pavone, *A Civil War,* 622.

ACKNOWLEDGMENTS

This history is the outcome of a long road trip, one that took twelve years, led me to places I had never imagined, brought me good luck, and made me dear friends. Along the way, I also accumulated many debts to many people. Let me start in New York City, where the project was conceived, by thanking the redoubtable Elaine Yaffe, who was the first to glimpse the historical value of Lilliana Teruzzi's papers. She and her late husband, Jim, spoke wryly of cousin Lilliana's Italian adventures, leaving me keen to learn more. Barbara Landau, Elaine's sister, was instrumental for having conserved the papers after Lilliana's death, as was her late husband, W. Loeber Landau, who generously granted me permission to use them. Thanks to their daughter, Donna Landau Hardiman, president of the Isak and Rose Weinman Foundation, Lilliana's little archive will now find a permanent home at YIVO Institute of Jewish Research in New York City.

In Italy, the lively interest of the Sitia-Calissano family—especially Cino and Anna, who had many questions about the Big Fascist and his American wife—encouraged me to explore the high roads (the archives) as well as the byroads of unfamiliar neighborhoods in Milan and Rome, tiny towns in Como Province, and the lakeside villages around Garda. In Naples, thanks to Marcello Anselmo, I located Fiammetta Grimaldi, Attilio Teruzzi's granddaughter, whose recall of her grandmother, Yvette, set me on a whole new course. It was another one of Naples's miracles that, while browsing through the used book stalls at Piazza Dante, I met the storied typographer Mario Raffone, who happened to be from Procida. He introduced me to Teruzzi's onetime confessor, Don Luigi Fasanaro, and made me at home under the shadow of the D'Avalos Prison. Through the Most Reverend Paolo Bianchi, vicar of the Ecclesiastical Tribunal of the Archdiocese of Milan, I was introduced to Professor W. L. Daniel of George Washington University, who gave me my first proper, and properly severe, introduction to the intricacies of canon law. Through the architect Antonella Pizzi, the granddaughter of Villa Celestina's caretakers, I was introduced to the little world of Castiglioncello, where our protagonist spent his happiest times. And through Claudio Castiglioni, an ex-partisan and the archivist of the antifascist resistance at Saronno, I met the town's historian, Beppe Nigro, who walked me over the terrain where Teruzzi made his last stand.

My thanks go to Muhammad T. Jerary, director of the Libyan Studies Center, and to Leonardo Paggi, president of the Associazione per le Memorie della Repubblica, the co-organizers of the Libyan Arab Jamahiriya's first conference (Tripoli, 2006) on European concentration camps. They gave me my first indelible glimpse of the ruin Fascist Italy brought to its North African colonies.

Time and again, I had help from fellow researchers, traveling the same or adjacent routes, starting with the late Alessandro Visani, my earliest guide through the National Archives in Rome. My thanks go to Stephen Madsen, Matteo Dominioni, Erika Diemoz, Simone Ubertino Rosso, Mario De Prospo, Eleonora Landini, Michela Ponzani, Annalisa Cegna, and Matteo Stefanori and to several former students who are now fellow historians: Roy Domenico, Marcello Anselmo, Jan Lambertz, Martina Salvante, Dominique Reill, Giuliana Chamedes, Michael Ebert, and Eileen Ryan. When I was on unfamiliar terrain, I received generous advice from Giorgio Rochat, Mauro Canali, Mauro Passerin, Amedeo Osti Guerrazzi, Marida Talamona, Paul Arpaia, Emily Braun, Mia Fuller, and Beth Sanders. I am ever grateful to have been able to talk through ideas with my friends Mariuccia Salvati, Michele de Giorgio, Paolo Macry, Gabriele Pedullà, Patricia Gaborik, Temma Kaplan, Carmen Boullosa, and Mike Wallace. I am deeply thankful, too, to my dear colleague friends in the Jean Howard Reading Group at Columbia University; to my department colleagues, Michael Stanislawski and Rebecca Kobrin, for their advice on the Jewish communities of New York City and Galicia; and to Robert Paxton, who as a teacher and colleague has been a longtime interlocutor on these terrible matters. Discussions with Robert Corban and Noelle Turtur helped me clarify next moves, as did the comments on my work in progress by colleagues at the University of Pennsylvania, at Columbia, and in Konstanz and Naples. I am especially indebted to Sergio Luzzatto, Ilaria Pavan, Jonathan Beard, and the scrupulous Harvard University Press readers for calling attention to errors of fact and interpretation.

What a joy it was to stay at the American Academy in Rome for two precious periods of research and writing in fall 2007 and spring 2013: I can't thank enough my gracious hosts, the AAR's then president, Adele Chatfield-Taylor, and two successive directors, Carmela Vircillo Franklin and Christopher Celenza. And how I treasured, in May and June 2017 and 2018, my sunlit study overlooking the Rhine at the Institute for Advanced Study at the University of Konstanz. There, with thanks to my dear host Sven Reichardt, I rethought the story of Teruzzi, with his two Jewish wives, and began to see it through the larger framework of the rise and fall of Nazi-Fascist rule in Europe. I am also grateful to the German Historical Institute of Rome and its director, Martin Baumeister, for their hospitality and research assistance.

As the book took shape, my agent, Sydelle Kramer, urged me to tell the story—though it was ugly. Rebecca Chaplan gave me courage to flex my narrative skills, and David Lobenstein helped me learn to do it better. Joyce Seltzer, my editor at Harvard, took the manuscript firmly in hand before yielding it at her retirement to Joy de Menil. It was blissful to see Joy at work and to work with her to give this story its proper human, as well as political, sense. Harvard's seasoned editorial staff, notably, Joy Deng, Anne McGuire, and Simon Waxman, redoubled her effort. So did my own formidably skilled helpmates, notably Martha Shulman, Margaret Scarborough, and Akua Banful. I am also grateful to Isabelle Lewis, who crafted the maps, Francesca Croce and Vanessa Kowalski, who compiled the photographs, and Angela Piliouras who saw the book through production during the pandemic.

At the most daunting moments near the end, I could count on the constancy of my sisters, Catherine Vanderpool and Jessica de Grazia; the forbearance of my daughter, Livia Paggi; the enthusiasm of my son-in-law, David Sher; wild walks on Hampstead Heath with my cousin, Margreta; exhilarating but daunting glimpses of what a true novelist might do with the story from Anne-Marie de Grazia, my father's widow; and, ultimately, the joyful prospect that once this voyage was completed, there would be wonderful new opportunities for new adventures in the company of my two little granddaughters.

I would never have come so far if not for the spirited intellect and adventurousness of Nancy Goldring, my *compagna di strada* since college. And without the unalloyed affection, love, and unflagging assistance of James Periconi, my sweetheart, *compagno di vita*, I'd still be wandering in the desert.

INDEX

abortion, 179, 230, 283

Acerbo, Giacomo, 72, 95, 397

Acerbo Law, 95–98; also known as Trickster Law, 96

Achard, Giulia, 202

Adelfi, Nicola (Nicola De Feo), 404

Africa, 321; Britain in, 325–327, 334; colonies in, 146; Germany and, 322, 327; Italian wars in, 35, 153, 325–327, 334–335; Jews in, 303, 335; moral and political claims on, 149; Race Laws in, 291, 304, 335; World War II and, 323–327. *See also* Africa, Italian; Africa Orientale Italiana (AOI); colonialism, Italian; colonial ministry; colonies, Italian; empire, Italian; imperialism, fascist; *individual cities*; *individual colonies*; *individual countries*; Ministry for Italian Africa (MAI)

Africa, Italian: end of, 319; ports/harbors in, 158; under RSI, 359. *See also* Ministry for Italian Africa (MAI)

Africa Orientale Italiana (AOI), 301–309, 334–335, 341–343. *See also* Africa, Italian; colonialism, Italian; colonial ministry; colonies, Italian; empire, Italian; imperialism, fascist; Ministry for Italian Africa (MAI); *individual colonies*

Agnelli, Giovanni, 79

Air Force, Italian Royal, 149, 172, 263, 265. *See also* military, Italian

Albertosi Alberta, 192, 194–195

Albini, Umberto, 342

Americans: divorce and, 294, 295; Mussolini on, 1. *See also* United States

Amery, John, 377, 383

Amidei-Barbiellini, Bernardo, 104

Amisani, Giuseppe, 207

amnesty, for fascists, 398–399, 405, 406–407, 412

anarchists, 18, 38, 49, 56, 60, 63, 142, 465fn5

Anceschi, Antonio, 156

annulment: accusations against Lilliana, 188–189; after Race Laws, 292–296; anti-Semitism in, 258, 259–260; appeals, 286–289, 292–296, 400; as Catholic Church procedure for nullification of marriage, 42, 230–231, 233, 404–405; Celestina's testimony in, 243; Church law and, 238–239; Lilliana's defense, 267–268; Lilliana's reaction to, 256, 257; Lilliana's resistance in, 239, 338, 339–340; Lilliana's testimony, 241; Lilliana's witnesses, 250, 254; Pavia decision, 408, 409; public implications of, 245; publicity, 339; Rota and, 210, 233, 236, 240, 251, 267, 296, 330, 338, 340–341, 400, 403, 404, 405; Rota decision, 408–409; speed of, 329–330; Teruzzi's testimony/witnesses, 240–243, 250, 287–288, 409; verdicts, 270–271, 289, 299, 408–409

Ansaldo, Giovanni, 396, 397, 417–418, 424

antifascism, 96, 113, 202, 213, 240, 245, 259, 274–275, 344, 358, 370, 398, 497. *See also* National Committee of Liberation of Northern Italy (CLNAI); purge of fascists

anti-Semitism: in annulment trial, 254–260, 367; Church and, 293; citizenship and, 331; Farinacci and, 258, 259–260; in Galicia, 49; in Germany, 256; in Italy, 289; Mussolini's, 135, 259; Nuremberg Laws, 257, 291; in Poland, 255; political, 259;

anti-Semitism (*continued*)
in press, 258–259; in Romania, 281; spread of, 193, 331. *See also* Jews; Race Laws
Antongini, Tom, 156
AOI (Africa Orientale Italiana), 301–309, 334–335, 341–343
Aosta, Duke of (Amedeo of Savoy), 278–279, 301, 307, 323, 325, 326
Aosta, Duke of (Emanuel Philibert of Savoy), 28, 33, 54, 132
Aquinas, Thomas, 239
Arabs: in Benghazi, 161; at Darnah, 35; resistance in Italian colonies, 13, 151, 160–162, 165–170, 172–176, 212–213; view of imperialism, 160. *See also* Islam; Muslims
Architecture Today, 315
Aregai, Abebe, 304
Arendt, Hannah, 6
Argenta, Francesco, 405–406
Arpinati, Leandro, 59
Askari, 13, 30, 157, 168, 188, 246, 263, 264, 266, 392, 433fn2
assassination attempts, on Mussolini, 133, 142
Asti, Elena Fondra, 312
Avanti! (newspaper), 78, 385, 392
Aventine secession, 110–111
Azzoni, Federico, 197, 250

Badoglio, Pietro, 54, 81, 181, 260; Arab resistance and, 174, 175; in colonies, 166; Ethiopia and, 261, 262–263, 265, 266; Fezzan campaign, 172; as governor of Libya, 182, 189; Italy's capitulation in World War II and, 344, 348, 398; as prime minister, 345, 346; Teruzzi's relations with, 261, 263, 266, 272, 324, 346, 350, 352, 359
Baistrocchi, Federico, 221
Balbo, Italo, 70, 72, 249; after coup d'état, 84–85; background of, 71; in Benghazi, 157; coup de main and, 73–74; death of, 311–312; governor of Libya, 312, 335; march on Ravenna, 73, 74–75; in March on Rome, 80, 81, 82; opposition to World War II, 323; Race Laws and, 335; as rival to Mussolini, 59; in Royal Air Force, 149; in *squadristi*, 62; as Teruzzi's neighbor, 225, 313; Teruzzi's relations with, 190, 311–312, 319; in United States, 181
Barco, Antonio, 31

Barletta Brigade, 28, 30–32, 33, 139, 192, 437fn2
Baronicini, Gino, 81
Barracu, Francesco Maria, 376, 379
Basilica of Santa Maria degli Angeli, 136, 138, 192, 210
Bassi, Mario, 163–164
Bastianini, Giuseppe, 69
Bastico, Ettore, 276, 277
battles: of Adwa, 24, 167, 260, 263, 326; Bir El-Turki, 13; Caporetto, 28–29, 30, 167, 274, 326, 343; Dogali, 114; El-Raheiba, 167; Gsar bu Hadi, 34; Guadalajara, 274; Isonzo, 19, 29, 30, 34; Maharuga, 26; Montello, 28, 36, 349; Santander, 226–227; Shara al-Shatt, 14
Bava Beccaris, Fiorenzo, 21, 22
Bazan, Enrico, 190
beards, 23, 62, 106, 249, 264, 311, 395
Benetti, Antonio, 384
Benghazi: Arabs in, 161; budget for, 164–165, 166–167; governor's residence, 159; Italian population of, 163; Lilliana in, 157; Teruzzi in, 142–144, 154–162, 173; Teruzzi's departure from, 183–185; Teruzzi's projects in, 158–160; transformation of, 163–164; urban renewal plan for, 159–160; in World War II, 326–327. *See also* colonialism, Italian; colonies, Italian; empire, Italian; imperialism, fascist; Libya
Berlinguer, Mario, 373
Berti, Mario, 277
Bianchi, Donato, 352
Bianchi, Michele, 69, 76, 80, 82, 181
Bigi, Bernardino, 157, 177
Bissolati, Leonida, 72
Black Brigades, 358, 379
blackmail, vulnerability to, 116, 246, 248, 257
Blackshirts, 4, 253. *See also* militia; MVSN (Voluntary Militia for National Security); *squadristi*
Blank, Alexis Herman, 280, 282
Blank, Aristide, 282
Blank, Celeste Adelia Maria Lina. *See* Teruzzi, Maria Celeste (Mariceli)
Blank, Maurice, 282
Blank, Yvette Maria: in Africa, 303; after Teruzzi's capture, 385–386; after Teruzzi's death, 418–422; background of, 280–283; and Caravella hotel, 410, 412, 414, 418; citizenship

Hoover, Herbert, 401
housing: Castiglioncello, 225–228, 287, 312–313, 346, 371, 407; Lilliana's in Rome, 242; in Malcesine, 368–369; on Monte Oppio, 313, 315, 348–349, 351–352; Teruzzi's, 224–228; Villa Beltrami, 362
Hungary, 292

Igliori, Ulisse, 104, 312
imperialism, fascist, 141, 341–344; Arab view of, 160. *See also* Africa, Italian; Africa Orientale Italiana (AOI); colonialism, Italian; colonial ministry; colonies, Italian; empire, Italian; Ministry for Italian Africa (MAI); *individual colonies*
imprisonment, Teruzzi's, 346–350, 405–408; appeals, 410–412; release, 412. *See also* amnesty; sentence, Teruzzi's
inflation, 265, 376
Interior Ministry: Federzoni in, 112, 142; Mussolini's control of, 142; oversight of *squadristi*, 139–140; Teruzzi appointed to, 111–114
internment camps, 331, 332, 337; Blank in, 327, 332–333, 336–337, 407; at Fossoli, 365; Lipari, 332, 333, 336–337, 345–346, 347; release of political prisoners, 346; for women, 336, 346
intransigents (fascist faction), 70, 74, 103, 112, 113, 140, 142, 345, 360
Iorio, G. M., 214
el-Isaui ez Zintani, Abd el Aziz, 173, 174
Islam: resistance to colonialism, 151–154. *See also* Muslims
Italian Africa, administration of. *See* Ministry for Italian Africa (MAI)
Italian Cultural and Educational Cinema Institute (LUCE), 120, 243, 249
Italian High Commission for Sanctions against Fascism, 373–375. *See also* purge of fascists
Italian Popular Party (PPI), 37, 53, 240
Italian Republic, 398, 400, 408
Italian Social Movement (MSI), 414, 415
Italian Social Republic (RSI), 355–360, 388; Jews under, 364, 365, 366–371; leaders' attempts to escape, 369–370; Teruzzi and,

357, 359–360, 361, 389. *See also* Republichini; Republic of Salò
Italy: after World War I, 36–37; alliance with Germany, 303; centralized state of, 57; debt, 125; early years, 16, 18; economic development of, 16, 18; internal problems, 36–37; Lilliana's departure from, 296, 298; relation with Germany, 309, 322, 333, 334; relation with United States, 125; Triple Alliance, 16; women in, 125–126

Jacomoni, Francesco, 397
James, Henry, 19
Jews: Blank's Jewishness, 280–281; characterization of, 254–259 (*see also* anti-Semitism); in colonies, 303, 335; from Croatia, 337; divorce and, 294, 295; Dreyfus Affair, 292–293; in Eastern Europe, 338–339; expelled from education system, 342, 420–421; Final Solution and, 5, 335, 364–371; in Galicia, 42, 254; Gina Federzoni, 141; internment of, 331, 332, 337; Jole Foa, 256, 333, 367; in Lipari, 337; marriage and, 293–294; mixed marriages, 135, 210, 289, 292, 408–409; Mussolini and, 333–337; persecution of, 364–371; Race Laws and, 290–292, 296, 328, 335, 364; reputation of, 239; from Slovenia, 337; Talmud, 254–256, 257, 328; Teruzzi's treatment of, 335; under RSI, 364, 365, 366–371; Vatican's stance on, 338–339. *See also* anti-Semitism; Blank, Yvette Maria; Race Laws; religion; Sarfatti, Margherita
Jolles, Ida, 250
Judaism, reformed, 43
Jung, Aldo, 165

Kahn, Otto, 43
el Kekhia, Omar Pasha, 161
Kesselring, Albert, 349, 355
king, Italian. *See* monarchy, Italian; Umberto I (king of Italy); Victor Emmanuel III (king of Italy)
Kingdom of the South, 355
Kingdom of the Three Venices, 54
Klauber, Charles F., 371
Kohut, Rebekah, 43
Kuliscioff, Anna, 113

statesmen, 202, 240; and the Resistance, 372, 390; shifts in, 9, 30, 65, 80, 86, 111, 114, 155, 222, 253, 274, 279, 286, 334; and Teruzzi's redemption through religion, 407–408, 418; under fascist rule, 5, 6, 387, 424; violence and, 7, 106–107, 111, 274, 425
Morante, Elsa, 418
Morazzini, Pietro, 374
Morelli, Eugenio, 242, 251
mothers: of heroes, 251; mourning deaths of, 244
Mount Zebio, 31
Mugnoz, Edy, 389
al-Mukhtar, Umar, 153–154, 167, 212–213
Muslims: in Libya, 13–14. *See also* Arabs; Islam; religion; Sanusi
Mussolini, Alessandro, 60
Mussolini, Arnaldo, 105
Mussolini, Benito: after Matteotti's murder, 107–108; on American women, 1; approval of Lilliana, 126, 131; control of Teruzzi, 120; coup de main to appoint as prime minister, 73–79; death of, 380–381; German rescue of, 349, 350–351, 355; invited to form government, 81; Jews and, 333–337; mother of, 244; need for party, 69; ouster of, 344–345, 346, 355–356 (*see also* Italian Social Republic [RSI]); political genius of, 426; qualities as leader, 51; rivals of, 59–60; start of World War II and, 299–300; Teruzzi introduced to, 50, 51; as Teruzzi's commander, 131; Teruzzi's feelings toward, 411; Teruzzi's loyalty to, 142–143; Teruzzi's relation with, 215–216; as Teruzzi's superior, 116–119; women and, 336 (*see also* Mussolini, Rachele; Petacci, Clara; Sarfatti, Margherita); in World War I, 27
Mussolini, Rachele, 108, 126, 233
Muti, Ettore, 300, 369
mutilated victory, 36, 437
MVSN (Volunteer Militia for National Security), 85, 189, 190, 215; budgets for, 218; criticisms of, 220–221; effects of, 220; Mussolini's plans for, 218, 220; relation with army, 86, 216–218; Teruzzi and, 86, 183, 216–219, 268–269. *See also* Blackshirts; militia; *squadristi*; War Ministry

Naples, neofascism in, 415
Nappi, Anais, 246–247, 269
Nappi, Settimio Aurelio, 247
National Bloc, 64–65
National Committee of Liberation of Northern Italy (CLNAI), 380–381, 382, 385, 386–391
National Fascist Party (PNF): establishment of, 68; executives, 69; founding of, 52; records of, 52; Teruzzi in, 53, 69–75; violence of, 70. *See also* fascism; fascists
Nazi-Fascist New Order, 9, 321, 375, 426
Nazis. *See* Germany; Hitler, Adolf; World War II
neofascism, 414, 415
Nerone (Boito), 99
New Men, 5, 7, 87, 114, 467fn29; postwar vision for, 32–33
newspapers. *See* press; *individual newspapers*
New Women, 125–126, 131
New York City: conditions in, 185; Lilliana's return to, 185–187, 298; Metropolitan Opera, 41, 43–44. *See also* United States
New York Times, on Teruzzi-Weinman wedding, 4
Nietzsche, Friedrich, 7, 155, 222
Nitti, Francesco Saverio, 37, 54, 56
Nobili Massuero, Ferdinando, 156, 184
normalization, of fascism, 3–4
Nuremberg Laws, 257, 291

Obeidats, 166, 168, 212
O'Brien, Beatrice, 230
officers, 22–24; after World War I, 38–40, 48, 55–56
Ohlbaum, Reisla. *See* Weinman, Rose
opera: after World War I, 45; during World War I, 43–44; in New York City, 43–44; in Rome, 130 (*see also* Carelli, Emma; Costanzi Theater). *See also* La Scala
Origins of Totalitarianism, The (Arendt), 6
Otello (Verdi), 88
Ottaviani, Alfredo, 295
Oviglio Law, 85, 392

Pacelli, Carlo, 287, 288, 289, 294, 296, 329, 331, 404
Pacelli, Eugenio (Pius XII), 251, 294–295, 339, 341, 398